GREAT POWER DIPLOMACY

SINCE 1914

Norman Rich
Professor of History, Emeritus
Brown University

Boston   Burr Ridge, IL   Dubuque, IA   Madison, WI   New York
San Francisco   St. Louis   Bangkok   Bogotá   Caracas   Kuala Lumpur
Lisbon   London   Madrid   Mexico City   Milan   Montreal   New Delhi
Santiago   Seoul   Singapore   Sydney   Taipei   Toronto

McGraw-Hill Higher Education ✈

A Division of The **McGraw-Hill** *Companies*

GREAT POWER DIPLOMACY: SINCE 1914

Published by McGraw-Hill, a business unit of The McGraw-Hill Companies, Inc. 1221 Avenue of the Americas, New York, NY, 10020. Copyright © 2003 by The McGraw-Hill Companies, Inc. All rights reserved. No part of this publication may be reproduced or distributed in any form or by any means, or stored in a database or retrieval system, without the prior written consent of The McGraw-Hill Companies, Inc., including, but not limited to, in any network or other electronic storage or transmission, or broadcast for distance learning. Some ancillaries, including electronic and print components, may not be available to customers outside the United States.

This book is printed on acid-free paper.

2 3 4 5 6 7 8 9   BKM BKM   0 9 8 7 6 5

ISBN 0-07-052266-9

Publisher: *Lyn Uhl*
Sponsoring editor: *Monica Eckman*
Lead project manager: *Susan Trentacosti*
Production supervisor: *Susanne Riedell*
Freelance design coordinator: *Gino Cieslik*
Supplement producer: *Kate Boylan*
Cover design: *Ryan Brown*
Typeface: *10/12 Garamond Book*
Compositor: *G&S Typesetters*

Cover images: © CORBIS

Library of Congress Control Number: 91038951

www.mhhe.com

◻

About the Author

Norman Rich is Professor of History, Emeritus, at Brown University. After receiving his Ph.D. in history from the University of California, Berkeley, in 1949, he served for five years on the Board of Editors of the captured German Foreign Office documents, a project sponsored by the U.S. Department of State, the British Foreign Office, and the French Foreign Ministry. He has taught history at Bryn Mawr College, Michigan State University, and Brown University, where he helped direct the program in International Relations. He has been awarded research fellowships at the Center of International Studies, Princeton, and St. Antony's College, Oxford, and in addition has been awarded Guggenheim and Fulbright fellowships for research in England and in Germany.

His publications include *Friedrich von Holstein: Politics and Diplomacy in the Era of Bismarck and Wilhelm II,* 2 vols. (1965); *The Age of Nationalism and Reform* (1970, 2nd edition 1977); *Hitler's War Aims,* vol. I, *Ideology, the Nazi State, and the Course of Expansion;* vol. II, *The Establishment of the New Order* (1973-74); and *Why the Crimean War? A Cautionary Tale* (1985, paperback edition, 1990). He is a co-editor of *Documents on German Foreign Policy,* in many volumes, (1949 ff.) and, with M. H. Fisher, of *The Holstein Papers. Memoirs, Diaries, Correspondence,* 4 vols. (1954-61). He has contributed numerous articles and book reviews to American, Canadian, and European journals.

For Ning

Contents

TEN   *The Manchurian Crisis*   122

The Japanese Interest 122   The Japanese Takeover 125   The Chinese and Soviet Reaction 126   The Western Response 128   The Response of the League of Nations and the Stimson Doctrine 129   The Establishment of the Puppet State of Manchukuo 130   The Lytton Commission 130   The Japanese Takeover of Jehol and the Truce of Tangku 131

ELEVEN   *East Asia: From the Manchurian Crisis*   133
                     to the Sino-Japanese War

The Japanese Government and its Policies 133   China after the Manchurian Crisis 136   The Marco Polo Bridge Affair: The Beginning of World War II in Asia 137   International Reaction 141   Changes in the Japanese Government 142

TWELVE   *Western Europe: From Versailles to Hitler*   143

The French Search for Security 143   The Weapon of Reparations 144   The Russo-German Rapallo Treaty 145   The Franco-Belgian Occupation of the Ruhr; the German Inflation 146   The End of Inflation; The Dawes Plan 147   The Locarno Treaties 148   Briand and Stresemann 149   The Disarmament Problem 152   The Kellogg-Briand Pact 153   The Failure of Disarmament Negotiations 154   Reparations, the Young Plan, and the Evacuation of the Rhineland 155   The Maginot Line 156   Briand's European Federation Plan 157   The Coming of the Great Depression 158   The Impact of the Great Depression on Germany 159   The Austro-German Customs Union 160   The End of Reparations 162   The End of German Democracy 162

THIRTEEN   *Western Europe: Mussolini and Hitler*   164
                  to the Spanish Civil War

Postwar Italy 164   Mussolini 165   Italian Fascism 168   Mussolini's Imperialism 168   Hitler 170   Nazi Ideology 172   Germany's International Position in 1933 173   The Ethiopian Crisis 175   The German Diversion: Saar Plebiscite and German Rearmament 176   The Stresa Front and the Franco-Russian Alliance 176   The Anglo-German Naval Agreement 177   The Italo–Ethiopian War and World Reaction 178   The Remilitarization of the Rhineland 179   The End of Ethiopia 181

FOURTEEN   *The Spanish Civil War*   183

The Political Background 183   The Plot against the Republic 184   The Role of Foreign Intervention 185   Francisco Franco 186   The Falange 187   The International Dimensions of Foreign Intervention 188   French and British Nonintervention 191   German Frustration 193

FIFTEEN   *From the Spanish Civil War*   195
          to the Eve of World War II in Europe

Italy, Germany, and the Problem of Austria 195   The Policy of Appeasement 197   Hitler's Annexation of Austria 198   The Selling Out of Czechoslovakia: Sudeten Crisis and Munich Agreement 200   Kristallnacht and Hitler's Violation of the Munich

SIXTEEN

World War II in Europe: From the German Attack on Poland to the Russian Campaign

208

SEVENTEEN

World War II in Asia: From the China Quagmire to Pearl Harbor

233

EIGHTEEN

Hitler's Declaration of War on the United States, the War in the Pacific, and the Turn of the Tide

249

NINETEEN   **The Grand Alliance: To the Fall of Mussolini**

258

TWENTY   **Laying the Foundations of the Postwar World**

276

THIRTY-NINE   *The Disintegration of Yugoslavia*   552

List of Maps

Preface

With the breakup of the Soviet empire and the end of the Cold War, many Americans believed they could look forward to a new world order, an end to the arms race, and the reward of a peace dividend. Communist China and "rogue states" still loomed as potential threats to American security, but on the whole Americans thought they were free to pursue their own interests and ignore appeals for international cooperation in dealing with global problems.

Americans were jolted out of this complacency on September 11, 2001, when terrorists on a suicide mission, using hijacked commercial aircraft as their weapons, destroyed the World Trade Center in New York, a prime symbol of the modern global economy, and attacked the Pentagon, the nerve center of the American military establishment. The events of September 11 revealed that the United States, and the Western world generally, had a new and perhaps even more dangerous enemy than the Soviet Union and Communism—namely, fanatics who, inspired by religious fervor and hatred for Western cultural values, used the weapon of terrorism to attack and destroy Western societies.

The events of September 11 have been described in apocalyptic terms as the end of the world as we know it. But there was nothing new about terrorism, which for centuries has been employed throughout the world as an instrument of protest or intimidation. Nor was terrorism new to the United States. What made September 11 so different was the magnitude of the catastrophe, terrorism on so great a scale that the most complacent Americans were shocked into recognizing a fact that should have been obvious all along: the vulnerability of the United States and indeed of all modern industrial societies, with their nuclear reactors and gasoline refineries, dams and pipelines, bridges and tunnels, and the high-rise buildings of their cities that can be rendered uninhabitable simply by cutting off their supplies of power and water.

The reaction in Washington has been an abrupt about-face in the conduct of American foreign policy. Gone—at least for the moment—was the arrogant assumption that America was free to pursue policies in line with its own interests, whatever their effect on the rest of the world; gone the opposition to any foreign intervention unless American interests were directly threatened; gone the call for the withdrawal of American troops from international peacekeeping missions. In place of its former unilateralism, Washington now trumpeted the need for international cooperation in battling terrorism. America's leaders did more than preach. Calling upon the world for support, they went to war in Afghanistan to root out the terrorists whom they accused of having been responsible for the disasters of September 11.

Altogether, the events of September 11 have stimulated a renewed awareness, dimmed in recent years by Americans' preoccupation with their own well-being, of the need for the active involvement of the United States in dealing with global crises. At the same time, as America assumes greater international responsibilities, there is a greater need than ever for American leaders and American public opinion to be well-informed about international affairs and to be able to view crisis situations in historical perspective.

There is a much-quoted saying that those who do not learn from the mistakes of history are doomed to repeat them. But one should beware of such simplistic formulations. One can find "lessons" of history to back up virtually any argument, and what they teach depends entirely on which lessons are chosen and how they are interpreted. The experience of the past can never provide a blueprint (model, paradigm) that can be applied automatically in confronting crisis situations, for every crisis is unique and must be dealt with on its own terms, in its own temporal and geographic setting, with special attention to the character of the personalities involved, their ideologies, fears, and ambitions, and the nature of their power and control. What history *can* provide, however, is the background for understanding crisis situations, for such situations cannot be appraised with any degree of authority without a sound knowledge of their origin and development.

The present study is essentially a record of that background, a straightforward chronicle of international diplomacy that takes the story from World War I to the dissolution of the Soviet Union, the last of the great European empires, and the breakup of Yugoslavia. Apart from brief references to more recent events, I have not taken the story further because we do not yet have reliable evidence on which to base an informed discussion. Like my earlier volume covering the years 1814 to 1914, the present work concentrates on the diplomacy of the *great* powers because the policies of those powers not only determined the fate of their own citizens but affected, often critically, the destinies of people throughout much of the rest of the world.

In 1914 the world's great powers were still the great powers of Europe—Austria-Hungary, Britain, France, Germany, and Russia—but already by the end of the nineteenth century international politics had become global in scope. The United States and Japan had joined the ranks of the great powers, and they all had indulged in a final splurge of imperialism (often called the New Imperialism, though there was nothing new about it) which had brought the greater part of the world under their formal or indirect control. The two World Wars accelerated the pace of globalization, but even in the era of the Cold War, when the world seemed divided into rival camps, that rivalry was played out in a global arena, and regional crises in Africa, Southeast Asia, or the Middle East became focal points of international attention.

In discussing international crises in this age of globalization, I have made a particular effort to demonstrate their global interrelationship, to show how the Japanese takeover of Manchuria affected events in Europe, or how Germany's early victories in World War II influenced policy decisions in Tokyo. At the same time I have endeavored to see global politics from the point of view of the major players in the game, to understand the making of policy decisions in Tokyo and Moscow as well as in Berlin, London, or Washington. This in turn has required an attempt to understand the makers of those policy decisions—their personal, political, and ideological motivations; their differing and often conflicting opinions; and the infighting among them to determine the ultimate control over their countries' policies.

In recent years there has been a trend among historians to dismiss political history as old-fashioned and to condemn its concern with a country's leadership and high-level decision making as elitist. In place of political history, they have called for the study of long-term developments—what French historians have called the *longue durée*—and for the stories of ordinary men and women who make up the vast majority of the world's population.

One can only welcome the further study of long-term developments and fresh research into the lives and customs of "the people," but I consider the neglect of the study of politics and political leadership to be as regrettable as it is mistaken. The policies of Stalin and Hitler, of Mao Tse-tung and Pol Pot, have had an immediate as well as long-term impact on the societies and peoples they governed, or misgoverned, and for the millions of their victims there has been no *longue durée*. Moreover, there might have been no *longue durée* for any of us had it not been for the political restraint of Kennedy and Khrushchev during the Cuban missile crisis, though we should bear in mind that the policies of these same men created the conditions for that crisis.

Distasteful though it may be, we must face the fact that we live in a political world, that the lives of all people, elite or otherwise, are inevitably affected by politics, and that politics are made by political leaders, whatever their color, gender, or social status. In an essay of 1854, written before he set forth his own laws of history, Karl Marx wrote: "Men make their own history, but they do not make it under circumstances of their own choosing but under circumstances already established, given and transmitted from the past." With this volume, I have attempted to describe what I consider the most significant of those transmitted circumstances insofar as they relate to international affairs.

I have no bold new interpretations to offer, no ends of history or fresh inversions of Marxist or Freudian theory. But all along, my overriding concern has been the problem of the preservation of peace. In the early nineteenth century, with the grueling experiences of the French Revolution and the Napoleonic wars behind him, the Austrian statesman Prince Metternich declared that the preservation of peace was the supreme duty of a civilized man. Today, in our age of nuclear, chemical, and biological weaponry, the preservation of peace between states armed with weapons of mass destruction has become more than a civilized duty; it has become a condition for the survival of life on earth.

My thanks to Donald Lamm, the former president of W. W. Norton and Co., for permission to use material from my book *Hitler's War Aims*. Sergei Khrushchev provided

□

The Usage and Spelling of Names and Dates

The political and social upheavals that have taken place in the nineteenth and twentieth centuries have been accompanied by a large-scale alteration of the names of persons and places, with the result that both usage and spelling have become controversial and even emotional issues.

In dealing with place names I have used the English name when this is common practice: Munich, not München. Otherwise I have used the name most commonly employed at the time of the events under discussion: Danzig, not Gdansk, in the years before 1945. However, when name changes reflect important political change, I have adopted those changes. After the Communist revolution, Russia became the Soviet Union and St. Petersburg, which has been given the more Russian name of Petrograd at the start of World War I, became Leningrad—but is now once again St. Petersburg. In 1930, the intensely nationalist government of the Republic of Turkey replaced the old Byzantine place names with Turkish: Constantinople became Istanbul, Adrianople became Edirne, Smyrna became Izmir.

For the names of persons I have used the spelling most commonly employed by the bearers of those names or most commonly used at the time of the events under discussion. I have generally anglicized given names: William and Francis, not Wilhelm or Franz. For transliterations of both names and places I have used the most simple and literal form: Milosevich, not Milosevic.

China poses a particularly difficult problem. On January 1, 1979, the Chinese government officially changed the transliteration of Chinese names for international usage from the Wade-Giles (and other systems) to the Pinyin system. In Pinyin, the ancient capital of Sian became Xian, the province of Kwangtung became Guangdong. But certain commonly used transliterations accorded with neither system. The Wade-Giles spelling for Peking, for example, would have been Peiching, which is actually closer to Beijing, the Pinyin spelling now in use. I have retained the Wade-Giles system for the names of persons: Mao Tse-tung, not Mao Zedong; Chou En-lai, not Zhou Enlai. But for the names of persons I have retained commonly used spelling that does not accord with either system. Chiang Kai-shek, whose real name was Chiang Chung-cheng in Wade-Giles, becomes Jiang Jieshi in Pinyin and as such is barely recognizable. As most of the events recorded in this volume took place before the official adoption of the Pinyin system, I have retained the earlier transliterations that were used in the histories and documentary records compiled before 1979.

In quotations I have used the spelling and punctuation found in the documents from which they were taken, except of course of translations. All changes of my own are in square brackets. All dates have been standardized to accord with the calendar in use in Europe and the United States in our era. Thus the Bolshevik Revolution, called the October Revolution according to the Old Style Russian calendar, becomes the November Revolution in the Western calendar which was adopted by the Soviet government.

Introduction

In Europe, the years at the turn of the nineteenth century into the twentieth century were known as the *belle époque,* and the developments in science and technology encouraged the belief that the human race (or at least its European component) was embarked on a steady course of humanitarian and material progress. The British writer Norman Angell observed that the interlocking and interdependent nature of finance, trade, and industry had so profoundly altered the climate of international politics that political and military power had become meaningless. His book, *The Great Illusion,* became a best-seller in seventeen countries and its author won a Nobel prize. It was published in 1910.

The outbreak of war in 1914 destroyed these optimistic assumptions and ended a century of relative peace in Europe. During this period, peace had been preserved most effectively by statesmen who recognized, or who allowed themselves to be persuaded, that their interests and those of their country were best served by settling international differences through negotiation and compromise, and that wars, even if successful, would inevitably threaten the existing international and social order.

Fears about the revolutionary consequences of war were fully borne out in World War I and its aftermath. The governments of three of the great European imperial powers were swept away. Austria-Hungary was permanently eliminated from the ranks of the great powers, Germany became a republic and the German emperor fled into exile into Holland, Russia was engulfed in revolution and the tsar and his family were murdered by the Bolsheviks. The governments of victorious Britain and France survived, but the resources of both powers has been seriously eroded, with consequences that would become evident in the interwar years. The real victors in World War I were Japan and the United States, which had invested relatively little in the conflict and had taken over a large share of the markets of the world from their European competitors. Japan now stood poised to dominate the affairs of East Asia, while the United States, already dominant in the Western Hemisphere, loomed as the greatest of all the world's great powers.

A different kind of victor in World War I was the ideology of nationalism—the principle of national freedom and self-determination—which the Western Allies had trumpeted as a major war aim and which was enthusiastically endorsed by the American president, Woodrow Wilson. Nationalism, which held that every nationality had a right to its own national state governed by members of that nationality, had long been a powerful ideological force in Europe. It had provided the principal ideological thrust for the political unification of Italy and Germany, it had stoked the fires of the Balkan revolutions against the Ottoman empire, and it was the assassination of the heir-apparent to the multinational Habsburg empire by a Bosnian-Serb nationalist that lit the fuse setting off World War I.

With the triumph of the Western Allies in 1918, the principle of national self-determination became the alleged basis for all postwar treaty settlements. Germany and Russia were stripped of frontier territories, which were conferred on neighboring states on the grounds of nationality. Austria-Hungary was divided into a conglomerate of small, sovereign national states. And a Turkish nationalist government, which ousted the regime of the Ottoman sultan, gave up the greater part of what remained of the Ottoman empire's non-Turkish territory in Europe and the Middle East.

To those who accept the ideological premise that nationality is the sole legitimate basis for a state, the downfall of multinational empires and the establishment of states on the basis of the principle of national sovereignty and self-determination was a noble achievement. These principles were violated by the Allies in numerous instances, most glaringly in their arrangements for the Middle East, nor did it escape notice that the victorious powers did not apply these principles in their own colonial empires.

Yet those principles were to triumph in a large part of the world before the century was out. They provided a major source of inspiration and moral justification for revolutions against the colonial powers, while in the colonial powers themselves there was a swelling chorus among idealists condemning the evils of imperialism as well as a growing realization among the leaders of those powers that they lacked the resources to suppress what were widely perceived to be national liberation movements.

Unfortunately, even as idealists hailed the destruction of the world's empires and the liberation of their peoples from colonial rule, the national governments of many of the successor states engaged in suppressing the newly won freedoms of their own people and in some cases proved far more oppressive than the imperial governments they had displaced.

But there has been another and infinitely more sinister side to nationalism. The concept of *nation* has always been associated with ethnicity, a belief that members of a nation are also members of the same race, however race might be defined. As people grew more self-conscious of their ethnic-racial identity, pride in that identity was translated into claims of superiority over other nations and races. The bland assumption of racial superiority had been a prime ingredient in nineteenth-century European imperialism, which enabled Europeans to believe that they were not only entitled to rule over "the lesser breeds without the law" but that they were bringing the fruits of a superior civilization to the people subjected to their rule.

The ideology of nationalism, as well as its association with race and ethnicity, was to find eager acceptance in every part of the world. Japan's victory in 1905 over Russia, one of the greatest of the European great powers, had been an inspiration to the world's non-European peoples. But in Japan itself that victory evoked a very European sense of racial superiority, already nourished by Japan's easy victory over China a decade earlier, that was to be a potent ideological ingredient of Japanese imperialism after World War I.

It was in Europe itself, however, that racial-nationalism was to emerge in its most virulent and specific form, a development all the more shocking because it took place in Germany, a fountainhead of European culture. After World War II, as the scale and barbarity of Nazi racial policies were revealed, the cry went up of Never Again. Yet that cry went unheard in many parts of the world, including Europe, where various agencies have pursued fanatic policies of genocide in the name of religion, political ideology, or racial purification.

A second powerful ideological force that emerged in the twentieth century was Communism, which aspired to far more than national liberation and purported to be dedicated to the removal of the social and economic inequalities in human society. It was a noble ideal that continues to inspire men and women who seek to improve the human condition, and it is one of the major tragedies of our era that so attractive an ideal has been so grotesquely betrayed. For, on behalf of the creation of an egalitarian society and the destruction of capitalist imperialism, Communist governments have engaged in mass murder on a scale never before seen in history.

Communist leaders and their apologists have contended that, no matter how great the human suffering their policies entailed, those policies were essential to the creation of an ideal society and for its defense against the forces of counter-revolution. It may be, as many analysts of Communist governments have argued, that Communist rhetoric concealed the megalomania, power-hunger, and chilling inhumanity of Communist leaders. But, as we now know from Communist sources, some of the most prominent of those leaders believed in their rhetoric. During the Cuban missile crisis, Fidel Castro was prepared to accept the annihilation of his people if this could contribute to the destruction of the capitalist United States and advance the cause of Communism. And in China, Mao Tse-tung actually welcomed the prospect of a nuclear war, which would ensure the ultimate triumph of the Communist cause. As he calmly informed the Soviet leader, Nikita Khrushchev, China could afford to lose a third to one-half of its population, but in such a war the capitalist states would be wiped out.

The terrorist attacks on the United States on September 11, 2001, have reminded us that Communism has not been the sole breeding ground of anti-Western or anti-capitalist fanaticism. The cry has now gone up that the great threat to Western security and the Western way of life is terrorism inspired by religious fanaticism and a rejection of Western values, and that our security requires the elimination of terrorists and governments that support them. But, as noted earlier, there is nothing new about terrorism, whatever its sources of inspiration. And we should be aware of the awkward fact that to eliminate what we perceive as terrorist threats, we will have to resort to terrorism ourselves—as we did in the two World Wars of the last century and in our recent intervention in Afghanistan. The world is seething with a multitude of threats, however, and perhaps the most valuable service history can provide is a sense of perspective in dealing with them and a warning of the dangers of a simplistic approach to crisis situations.

ONE

□

World War I, Part 1

The overwhelming impression of horror that dominates our reflections about World War I tends to obscure the fact that, in its early stages at least, the war was greeted with enthusiasm by the vast majority of the populations in all the belligerent countries. The coming of war seemed to clear the air of frustrations and uncertainties, to offer clean, honorable, and clear-cut solutions to the complex problems of domestic and foreign politics. The general enthusiasm for war was a dramatic demonstration of the extent to which the spirit of nationalism had come to dominate the emotions and command the loyalties of the peoples of Europe in the years before 1914. Support for the war cut across class and professional lines, as socialists joined with liberals and conservatives in voting for war credits. It should also be remembered, however, that at this time war was still considered not only a legitimate but honorable course for the settlement of international disputes. War was glorious, a demonstration of a nation's virility in a world where, according to the widely accepted view of the social Darwinists, only the fittest would survive.

A spur to the general enthusiasm for war was the general certainty that this war would not only be glorious but short. For years European military leaders, presumably the most competent men produced by their country's military and naval academies, had been working on plans which could not fail to lead to certain and speedy victory. Economists, equipped with a wealth of theory and statistics, contributed to the belief that the next war would necessarily be short because no country's economy could support the staggering costs which a modern war would entail. The most respected experts everywhere predicted that the victor in the next war would be the country that struck first and most effectively against the forces of its enemies, a belief that does much to explain the emphasis on speed of mobilization and the seemingly irresponsible disregard of political and diplomatic considerations as the powers rushed into war in the summer of 1914.

As we now know, the predictions of Europe's most respected military and economic experts and the popular beliefs they helped to foster were wrong. The anticipated short war lasted more than four years, and its outcome was finally decided by a power that had hardly figured in the calculations of European leaders when the war began.

MAP 1 EUROPE ON THE EVE OF WORLD WAR I. ITALY ENTERED THE WAR IN 1915 ON THE SIDE OF THE ENTENTE POWERS

Triple Alliance
Triple Entente
NORTH SEA
ATLANTIC OCEAN
BAY OF BISCAY
BALTIC SEA
BLACK SEA
ADRIATIC SEA
MEDITERRANEAN SEA
AEGEAN SEA
English Channel
UNITED KINGDOM
Glasgow
Belfast
Dublin
Manchester
Birmingham
London
NORWAY
Christiania
SWEDEN
Stockholm
JUTLAND
DENMARK
Copenhagen
NETH.
Amsterdam
BELG.
Brussels
LUX.
ALSACE-LORRAINE
GERMANY
Hamburg
Danzig
Königsberg
Posen
Berlin
Leipzig
Cologne
Frankfurt
Munich
Oder R.
Elbe R.
Rhine R.
Vistula R.
FRANCE
Paris
Seine R.
Marne R.
Loire R.
Rhône R.
Lyons
Bordeaux
Marseille
SWITZ.
AUSTRIA-HUNGARY
Prague
Vienna
Budapest
Cracow
Lemburg
Trieste
Sarajevo
Save R.
Danube R.
RUSSIA
St. Petersburg
Reval
Riga
Vilna
Warsaw
Brest-Litovsk
Minsk
Smolensk
Moscow
Orel
Kursk
Karkov
Kiev
Odessa
Rostov
Kasan
Tiflis
Yalta
Crimea
Carpathians
Volga R.
Don R.
Dnieper R.
ITALY
Milan
Genoa
Venice
Florence
Rome
Naples
Sicily
Corsica
(France)
Sardinia
(Italy)
Malta
(Britain)
SPAIN
Madrid
Barcelona
Pyrenees
Ebro R.
Tagus R.
Balearic Islands
PORTUGAL
Vigo
Lisbon
Gibraltar (Britain)
Tangier
Melilla (Spain)
SP. ZONE
Casablanca
MOROCCO
(France)
Algiers
ALGERIA
(France)
Tunis
TUNIS
(France)
ROMANIA
Bucharest
BULGARIA
Sofia
SERBIA
Belgrade
MONTENEGRO
ALBANIA
Tirana
GREECE
Salonika
Athens
Crete
OTTOMAN EMPIRE
Constantinople
Bosporus
Dardanelles
Gallipoli
Angora
Rhodes
(Italy)
Cyprus
(Britain)

❑ *The War Plans of the Major Belligerents*

Despite the enormous intellectual and financial capital invested in military preparations, it is remarkable that the war plans of the major powers were so flawed and inflexible. It is even more remarkable that the powers made so little effort to coordinate those plans with their allies, either before or during the war. Germany and Austria-Hungary went to war without anything like a joint plan and without even adequate knowledge of the strength of each other's forces. British and French coordination was restricted to a prewar agreement to place a British expeditionary force on the left flank of the French, a plan that forfeited the flexibility provided by British naval superiority that enabled an expeditionary force to land at some point on the continent where it might seriously cripple the German war effort. French and Russian coordination was limited to agreements to launch simultaneous major offensives.

The French plan for war against Germany in 1914, Plan No. 17 in the succession of such preparations, reflected Napoleon's dictum that in evaluating the fighting effectiveness of a soldier, the moral outweighed the physical by three to one. To take full advantage of the superior élan of the French soldier, Plan 17 called for a massive offensive against the German lines in Alsace and Lorraine, where the initial French victories were expected to spark revolt among the indigenous population against their hated German oppressors and create chaos behind the German lines. But as was the case with so many war plans, the French plan was designed to fight earlier wars, in this case the Napoleonic wars in which the bayonet still played a decisive role. It took no account of the terrible effectiveness of the machine gun and modern artillery as defensive weapons, nor did it allow for a flexible response to any offensive the Germans were likely to mount.

The German war plan had been conceived by General Alfred von Schlieffen after the formation of the Franco-Russian alliance in the 1890s to cope with the problem of a two-front war. It called for concentrating most of the German army in the west, which was to sweep through the lowlands of Belgium and Holland (whose territory was deemed essential for so vast an offensive), encircle the French army, and drive it against the German frontier fortifications, where it would be annihilated or compelled to surrender. The entire operation was to be carried out according to a precise timetable calculated to knock France out of the war before the Russians, who were expected to mobilize more slowly, could mount an offensive of their own. With France defeated, German troops could be transferred to the east to fight the Russians in what would now be a one-front war.

Admirers of the Schlieffen Plan have blamed its failure on the incompetence or loss of nerve of the German generals of 1914 who had the task of carrying it out. Basically, however, the plan was fatally flawed not only from a military but above all from a political point of view. It was flawed militarily because it relied too heavily on perfect timing, making too little allowance for the inevitable accidents and errors in every military campaign. The German armies would be advancing through terrain intersected by networks of rivers and canals, where the bridges and railways would have been destroyed by retreating armies and the roads clogged by refugees. The French, on the other hand, operating on interior lines, their railways and highways intact, would be able to transport troops and supplies to any part of the fighting front. Even if the Germans could bring up artillery and supplies in time to support their troops, the troops themselves would be exhausted after their long marches and would be facing a relatively fresh adversary.

The truly disastrous features of the Schlieffen Plan, however, were political. The plan required violating the neutrality of three states, Belgium, Holland, and Luxembourg (though by 1914 the plan had been revised to exclude Holland), whose sovereignty and territorial integrity were guaranteed by international treaties signed by all the great powers, including Germany. Such treaty violations would destroy Germany's moral position at the very start of the war. They were also certain to bring Britain into the conflict, as the British had warned the Germans time and again. Schlieffen, however, did not think British intervention merited serious consideration—it was a military axiom that the British navy would be of no use in defending Paris—and, like so many military leaders, he failed to appreciate the full importance of the moral factor.

The flaw in the Schlieffen Plan that proved decisive in the crisis that set off the war was its inflexibility. The crisis had originated in the Balkans with the assassination of the Habsburg heir to the throne; the Austrians held Serbia responsible for this outrage, and the Russians began to mobilize to protect Serbia, thus throwing off the Schlieffen Plan's reliance on the slow pace of Russian mobilization. Failing to pressure the Russians into halting their mobilization, the Germans found their only plan for war against *Russia* in the east required that they they first go to war against *France* in the west.

❑ *The War in the West*

On August 4, 1914, the Germans crossed the frontier into Belgium, the first step in carrying out the Schlieffen Plan. This violation of Belgian neutrality brought Britain into the war against Germany. The French offensive, prescribed by Plan 17, was supposed to be coordinated with a major Russian offensive in the east. However, because they found the bulk of the German forces employed in an attack through Belgium, the French decided not to wait for the Russian steamroller but to put Plan 17 into operation immediately by attacking the thinly held German lines in Alsace and Lorraine.

In the ensuing Battle of the Frontiers, the French found that the bayonet, no matter how vibrant the spirit behind it, was no match for troops equipped with machine guns and artillery behind a network of fortifications. Between August 14 and August 25, the French lost the appalling total of 300,000 men, the flower of the French army and the greatest losses sustained in so brief a period by any army in the entire war.

The Schlieffen Plan also failed. Belgian resistance disrupted the German timetable for their sweep into France. Even so, the Germans pushed ahead with remarkable speed and by the first week in September they reached the Marne River. But by now their troops were exhausted, and already they were encountering serious supply problems. Their units advancing on foot outstripped their artillery and ammunition wagons, drawn by horse and mule and slowed down by the wholesale destruction of roads and bridges in the Low Countries. A further complication was the unexpectedly rapid arrival of the British Expeditionary Force, which first made contact with the Germans on August 23 and played a critical part in preventing the Germans from turning the French flank.

Meanwhile, the Russians, who had mobilized far more quickly than the Germans expected, were advancing into East Prussia. At this point the German high command made a move that some military historians believe to have been the fundamental reason for the failure of the Schlieffen Plan. Confronted with panicky appeals for reinforcements in East Prussia, the German high command violated Schlieffen's alleged deathbed admonition to "keep the right wing strong" and detached four divisions from their western armies for service in the east—a weakening of the right wing that is supposed to have doomed the Germans' western offensive. As it proved, the reinforcements from the west had not even been necessary, for the Russian offensive was stopped before the troops from the west arrived.

After a bitterly fought battle along the Marne River from September 5 to 12, the Germans were compelled to withdraw to defensive positions. Both sides now engaged in flanking maneuvers as the Germans, too late, tried to secure the channel ports to prevent the further landing of British troops and supplies. By the end of the year a front had been established in the west from Switzerland to the sea. Over the next four years some of the bloodiest battles in history were to be fought along this western front, but the front itself was to remain relatively stable. After the first Battle of the Marne, the war in the west was essentially a stalemate.

Efforts to break that stalemate revealed the intellectual poverty of the military leadership on both sides. Both used massive bombardment to soften up the enemy lines, thereby informing the enemy where an attack was about to take place. Thousands of men were then sent over the top, to be slaughtered by artillery and machine gun fire in the vain hope of effecting a decisive breakthrough. Yet both sides employed the same strategy, if strategy it can be called, in the expectation that their next attack would achieve the breakthrough that would win the war.

❑ *The War in the East*

In contrast to the west, the war in the east was a war of movement in which immense tracts of territory were won and lost, but here too the war eventually became a de facto stalemate. The Germans and Austrians won some spectacular victories (and suffered severe setbacks). But the crucial point about the war in the east was that Russia remained in the war until March 1918 and thereby prevented the Germans from concentrating their power in the west.

The Germans paid a high political price for their victories in the east. Those victories made national heroes of two generals, Paul von Hindenburg and Erich Ludendorff, who assumed credit for turning back the Russian 1914 offensive, although the victorious German strategy had actually been the work of a brilliant staff officer, Colonel (later General) Max Hoffmann. As the war dragged on, Hindenburg and Ludendorff exploited their popularity and prestige to transform the German government into a military dictatorship and organize the country for total war. By holding out for extravagant war aims, they snuffed out the initiatives of other German leaders to negotiate a compromise peace. By insisting on imposing punitive conditions on Russia in 1918, they delayed the transfer of Germany's eastern armies to the western front, thereby destroying Germany's last slim chance for victory. Far from accepting responsibility for Germany's military defeat, they blamed that defeat on the country's civilian leadership, claiming that the army had been stabbed in the back, a myth that fatefully undermined the authority of Germany's postwar democratic government, the Weimar Republic.

Ludendorff lost much of his prestige by joining in Hitler's effort to overthrow the Bavarian government in November 1923, the so-called Beer Hall Putsch. Hindenburg, however, went on to be elected president of the Weimar Republic, and it was Hindenburg who appointed Hitler chancellor in January 1933.

The brilliant Max Hoffmann, the brains behind the Hindenburg-Ludendorff team, did not share the public adulation of his superior officers. He considered Ludendorff to be arrogant and inflexible, blind to the political implications of his policies and limited by a vision that never transcended the use of brute force. As for Hindenburg, "this great military genius and idol of the people" was a man of straw. "No one in history ever became so famous at the cost of so little intellectual and physical exertion."

❏ The Gallipoli (Dardanelles) Campaign

There were military campaigns in other parts of Europe and the world, but most of these were correctly regarded as side-shows which could have no decisive bearing on the outcome of the war. An important exception was the Gallipoli campaign conceived by the first lord of the admiralty, Winston Churchill. The campaign was to be directed against the Ottoman empire (Turkey), which had joined the Central Powers in the first months of the war. The Allied objective was to gain control of the Turkish Straits, the narrow waterway between the Mediterranean and Black seas, and to seize the Turkish capital of Constantinople. If successful, the Allies would knock Turkey out of the war and open the most important transport route from Western Europe to Russia, facilitating the shipment of desperately needed military supplies to Russia. Control of the Straits would also enable the Allies to outflank the Austro-German position in the southeast, put pressure on the neutral Balkan states to enter the war on their side, and perhaps achieve the decisive breakthrough that eluded them in the west.

The Gallipoli campaign failed owing to inadequate support, woefully inadequate intelligence, and inept leadership. The Allies might have overrun the weak Turkish fortifications guarding the Straits if they had attacked with vigor and determination. Instead, after losing four naval vessels on March 16, 1915, in an attempt to force the Straits, they postponed a second attack for a month to bring up troops for a ground attack, giving the Turks ample time to strengthen their positions. When the Allies finally did attack, they did so without adequate information about the strength and disposition of the Turkish forces and even without maps of the terrain they were attacking. Although their troops fought with desperate valor, they never succeeded in breaking through the Turkish lines. The Turks meanwhile had received valuable advice from German staff officers for strengthening their fortifications, and in the campaign itself they were commanded by Mustafa Kemal, who proved to be one of the few genuinely imaginative and talented generals produced by any country during World War I. After the war Kemal was to demonstrate even greater talent as a political leader and diplomat and play a decisive role in the creation of the modern Turkish state.

❑ *The War at Sea*

As critical as any military front for the outcome of the war was the war at sea, where the British navy maintained its superiority and gradually built up a naval blockade around Germany that was to prevent Germany from importing critical raw materials, including food, from abroad. The proud German battle fleet, built at such cost materially and diplomatically, challenged Britain's naval supremacy in only one major engagement, the Battle of Jutland, May 31–June 1, 1916. Inflicting greater damage on the British fleet than they themselves sustained, the Germans claimed victory. But they failed to break the British blockade, the German merchant fleet was driven from the seas, and most of the German battle fleet spent the rest of the war in port, a potential but never effective threat to British naval supremacy.

The German submarine fleet posed a far more immediate and dangerous threat. Despised and virtually ignored before the war began, submarines quickly proved their worth in sinking Allied naval and merchant vessels. By 1916 they were sinking ships at such an alarming rate that it seemed possible they might subject Britain to an economic blockade even more effective than Britain's blockade of Germany. The British eventually countered the submarine threat by instituting a convoy system that provided merchant ships with a naval escort. British shipping losses remained high, but the rate of those losses declined sharply.

Because Britain was receiving substantial supplies shipped on vessels of neutral countries, most importantly from the United States, the German high command listened with increasing interest to the pleas of German naval commanders to engage in unrestricted submarine warfare and their confident prediction that the resulting stranglehold on the British economy would compel Britain's surrender within six months. Early in 1917, the kaiser and his military and naval experts overrode the objections of his civilian advisers and made the decision to launch unrestricted submarine warfare. They realized this step would almost certainly bring the United States into the war, but decided to gamble for an all-out victory, which at that time the submarine alone seemed able to provide. Within six months, they reasoned, the militarily unprepared Americans could do little to affect the outcome of the war, and by that time American intervention would be futile. For, with Britain out of the war, the German armies would be able to overrun France, close all the French ports, and thus cut off all enemy access to the continent.

The German experts proved to be wrong again. Britain was not defeated in six months. Unrestricted submarine warfare did indeed bring the United States into the war, and with American intervention every possibility for an all-out German victory was eliminated and an all-out German defeat assured.

❑ *Wartime Politics and Propaganda*

As the war dragged on, the governments of all the belligerent powers found it necessary to pay renewed attention to problems of politics and diplomacy they had ignored in their rush to battle. At home, they faced two major problems: organization and morale. They had to organize the human and natural resources of their respective countries for a long war. They had to maintain the loyalty of their people, sustain their willingness to fight, and bear the sacrifices which grew steadily greater as the war continued.

They dealt with the problem of organization by imposing ever stricter controls on every aspect of their countries' society and economy. The inevitable result was that all governments became increasingly authoritarian. Germany, for example, was transformed into a virtual military dictatorship as the home front, as well as the conduct of the war, was brought under the authority of the high command. Indeed, all the belligerents thought it necessary to resort to various forms of censorship and the curtailment of civil liberties.

Particularly vicious was the propaganda mounted by the belligerents to generate support for the war and boost civilian morale. As the need for sacrifices mounted and government controls became increasingly oppressive, propaganda campaigns became steadily more strident and simplistic. There was a monotonous similarity to all of them. The war was a defensive war brought on by the hatred, jealousy, and insatiable lust for conquest of an unscrupulous enemy. It was a just and moral war, a life-and-death struggle to safeguard the very existence of one's country, a war of civilization against barbarism, a war between the forces of good and evil. The enemy were inhuman monsters, guilty of the most horrifying crimes not only against soldiers in the field, but against innocent women and children.

These propagandistic appeals to fear and hate were intertwined with appeals to idealism and visions of a brave new world that would emerge once victory had been achieved. It would be a peaceful, just, and moral world, because the enemy alone was militaristic, unjust, and immoral. Because the enemy alone was responsible for the war, he must be rendered incapable of ever threatening their security again. His territories must be divided, his economic assets confiscated, while at the same time he should be required to pay for the total costs of the war. The victorious governments would not only be morally justified but were morally and politically obligated to secure territorial gains and reparations at the expense of the enemy so as to destroy once and for all his capacity for aggression and repay their own people for their valor and wartime sacrifices.

These simplistic conceptions and extravagant war aims were to contribute significantly to the failure of all wartime projects for a negotiated peace and do much to poison the atmosphere of the postwar world. They also fostered hopelessly unrealistic expectations that made the task of peacemaking more difficult and created a postwar intellectual climate of disillusionment and cynicism.

❑ *Wartime Diplomacy*

In the realm of diplomacy the belligerent powers faced three critical tasks: to retain the loyalty of their allies and sustain their determination to fight the war to a successful conclusion; to undercut the alliances of their opponents; and to win the neutral states to their side, or at least ensure their continued neutrality.

In their diplomacy as in their domestic politics, all belligerents employed propaganda on a massive scale to convince allies and neutrals of the justice and morality of their cause and the corresponding injustice and immorality of the enemy. But the crucial determinant, for major and minor powers alike, was self interest, which in the case of the United States included such long-term considerations as to whether victory by one side or another would critically jeopardize America's future political and economic security.

In persuading a state where its self-interest lay, the belligerent powers were to find that, whether dealing with allies or neutrals, their most effective instrument was outright bribery. To prevent an ally from being lured by enemy promises into making a separate peace or otherwise deserting the cause, that ally was promised far more lucrative spoils than anything the enemy could offer. And to win over neutrals or even persuade them to remain neutral, the belligerents sought to outbid each other with similar promises of territorial and financial gain. To confirm such promises, the belligerents made a succession of wartime secret treaties, many of them conflicting and contradictory, which, like the extravagant expectations aroused by wartime propaganda, were to pose serious problems in making peace. They also contributed significantly to poisoning the international atmosphere of the postwar world.

❑ *Japan's Entry into the War*

In the diplomatic struggle in which all the belligerents engaged after the outbreak of war in 1914, the first winners were the Allies. On August 23, 1914, Japan, the ally of Britain since 1902, declared war on Germany. Far from being a gesture of loyalty to Britain, the Japanese entered the war with the primary purpose of taking over Germany's colony on China's Shantung Peninsula and the German-held islands in the Pacific north of the equator. Once this purpose had been achieved, the Japanese limited their military cooperation to sending destroyers to the Mediterranean for convoy duty and stalking German raiders in the Pacific.

Fearful that the Japanese might take advantage of the war in Europe to encroach on British interests in the Pacific, the British concluded a secret treaty with Japan on February 16, 1917, recognizing Japanese claims to the territory they had conquered from the Germans, but in return they secured Japan's recognition of British claims to the German-held islands *south* of the equator.

Although Japan's contribution to the final Allied victory was negligible, Japan's entry into the war enabled the Japanese to take a place among the major powers at the postwar peace conferences, where their territorial claims were to lead to embarrassing complications.

❑ *The Entry of the Ottoman Empire*

The Germans scored a more significant diplomatic victory with the Ottoman empire's entry in the war on their side in November 1914.

The importance of the Ottoman empire lay in its geographic position. Linking Europe, Asia, and Africa, the empire stretched from Bulgaria to the Persian Gulf, from the Caucasus mountains to Egypt. The capital of the empire, Constantinople, dominated the Turkish Straits, the strategic waterway between the Mediterranean and Black Seas that provided Russia's only access to the open sea in southern Europe and its major ice-free access to the open sea anywhere. As we have seen, a primary purpose of the Allies' Gallipoli campaign had been to break through the Ottoman barrier so as to open the Turkish Straits and facilitate the large-scale shipment of military supplies to Russia. The Allied failure to do so meant that Russia's capacity to wage war, despite its immense manpower resources, remained severely restricted.

The Germans' success in securing the alliance with Turkey has been attributed to their economic influence in that country and to the presence of a German military mission recently entrusted with the reorganization of the Turkish army. But the Allies had even greater economic interests in Turkey; a British naval mission had been entrusted with the reorganization of the Turkish fleet; and a French mission had been brought in to reorganize the Turkish police. All European powers had spent large sums bribing Turkish officials and had influential partisans within the Turkish government.

The most obvious, and surely also the most important, reason Turkey sided with Germany was that Germany was at war with Russia, which since the days of Peter the Great had encroached steadily on the territories of the Ottoman empire. The Turks had long regarded Russia as a mortal threat to the very existence of their realm. They therefore had compelling reasons of self-interest to side with any power that seemed capable of defeating or seriously weakening the northern colossus.

Apart from their successful defense of the Straits, the Turks contributed little to the war effort of the Central Powers. They did almost nothing to coordinate their military strategy with their allies. Early in the war, they mounted an ill-conceived campaign against Russia in the Caucasus and lost an entire army in that futile endeavor. They failed to make a determined effort to capture the Suez Canal, which would have been a severe blow to the Allies, or to cut off their oil supplies from the Middle East. But the very possibility of a Turkish threat to their interests in the Middle East compelled the Allies to divert troops to this area and thereby set up a number of the war's so called sideshows.

A horrifying blot on the Turkish war effort was the Turkish government's use of the cover of wartime emergency to engage in a systematic slaughter of Turkey's Armenian population on the pretext that the Christian Armenians constituted a dangerous subversive force within the largely Muslim Ottoman empire. The Turkish program of genocide was as short-sighted as it was inhuman, for many of Turkey's best educated and skilled workers and technicians were Armenians. With their destruction, some of Turkey's most critical industrial and construction projects requiring professional expertise, including the building of the Bagdad railway, virtually came to a halt.

The Germans protested often but in vain (for practical as well as humanitarian reasons) against the Turkish treatment of the Armenians. The Germans were equally unsuccessful in most of their other endeavors in Turkey. German political and business leaders had hoped to exploit the Turks' constant need for money, equipment, and technical assistance to acquire a dominant and impregnable influence on the Turkish government and economy. The Turks, however, were shrewd bargainers, and while they asked for much they gave away little, with the result that they retained substantial control of their own affairs and were never reduced to the role of a German satellite.

❑ *Italy's Entry*

Since 1882 Italy had been allied with Germany and Austria in the so-called Triple Alliance, but in May 1915 Italy entered the war on the side of the Allies. The Germans and Austrians bitterly criticized what they regarded as Italy's betrayal of its alliance obligations by failing to enter the war on their side in 1914. But the Triple Alliance had been a defensive agreement, and Austria's ultimatum to Serbia and subsequent declaration of war, whether justified or not, was clearly an act of aggression. In October 1914 the Italian prime minister, Antonio Salandra, announced that his country was free from all preconceptions, prejudice, and sentiment: "We must have no other thought than exclusive and unlimited devotion to our country, to *sacro egoismo* for Italy."

With the failure of Germany to win a quick military victory in the summer of 1914, there could be little doubt that the Italians, if they entered the war at all, would come in on the side of the Allies. Italy's long and exposed coastline had always made that country extremely vulnerable to attack from the sea. From the beginning of the war the sea was controlled by the Allies, who were thus in a far better position than the Central Powers either to threaten or to protect Italy. Further, the Allies were able to offer the Italians far more in return for their entry into the war. By the Treaty of London of April 26, 1915, the Allies promised to give Italy all Austrian territory south of the Brenner Pass (the South Tyrol and the Trentino); all Austrian territory at the head of the Adriatic Sea, including Austria's major seaport, Trieste; a third of Austria's territory along the Dalmatian coast, including a number of the Dalmatian islands; and a virtual mandate over Albania, with outright possession of the seaport of Valona and the Bay of Saseno. They confirmed Italy's possession of the Dodecanese Islands and Libya (acquired in Italy's recent war with the Ottoman empire), while promising the Italians substantial territorial gains in Asia Minor and East Africa. Italy was granted an immediate loan of 50 million pounds and promised a substantial share of the war indemnity to be imposed on the Central Powers.

The Allies also agreed to support Italy in preventing the papacy from taking diplomatic steps to arrange a negotiated peace (which might prevent the Italians from getting everything they had been promised through the Treaty of London), and they engaged not to sign a separate peace with the Central Powers in their own right. As stipulated by the London treaty, which provided that Italy enter the war within one month after its signature, Italy declared war on Austria-Hungary on May 23, 1915. Germany severed diplomatic relations with Italy on the following day, but Italy did not declare war on Germany until August 28, 1916.

❑ *The Involvement of the Balkan States*

Bulgaria entered the war on the German side in September 1915, lured by the prospect of recouping its losses in the Balkan war of 1913. Early in October Bulgarian forces joined an Austro-German offensive against Serbia which finally broke that country's resistance. With the conquest of Serbia, the Central Powers controlled a continuous stretch of territory from the North and Baltic Seas through the Balkans to Constantinople, and from Constantinople through Anatolia to the Persian Gulf.

In August 1916, in return for lavish promises of Austro-Hungarian territory, the Romanians entered the war on the side of the Allies. The Central Powers responded with an invasion of Romania and within weeks they had occupied the greater part of the country. But a major objective of their Romanian campaign—the relief of their desperate oil shortage by gaining control of the Romanian oil fields at Ploesti, the most productive in Europe—was frustrated by British sabotage of the Romanian oil wells.

In October 1915 British and French troops began landing at the Greek harbor of Salonika after receiving assurances from the Greek prime minister, Eleutherios Venizelos, that they would encounter no opposition. The Allied plan was to advance up the Vardar valley to break the Central Powers' hold over the southern Balkans and sever communications between them. But, despite sending almost half a million men to Salonika, the Allies hesitated to advance through this difficult terrain and did not mount a campaign in the Balkans until the final weeks of the war.

The Greeks did not enter the war officially until July of 1917, despite generous territorial offers at the expense of their detested enemies, the Turks. This delay was due to a power struggle between Prime Minister Venizelos, who favored joining the Allies, and King Constantine, the brother-in-law of the German emperor, who opposed entry not so much out of family loyalty as because he resented his prime minister's usurpation of power. When Greece finally came in on the side of the Allies, that event was completely overshadowed by the revolution in Russia and the entry of the United States in the war.

❑ *The Wartime Secret Treaties among the Allies*

The Allied success in securing America's participation in the war on their side was far and away the most important diplomatic achievement during the war and decisive for its outcome. Long before that participation had been assured, however, the Allied powers had not only been engaged in negotiations to enlist the support of neutral states but had found it necessary to wage major diplomatic campaigns to ensure the loyalty of the allies they already had. For this purpose they concluded secret treaties with each other embodying promises of territorial and economic gain greater than anything the enemy might offer—so great indeed that in some cases they gave away territories and rights they had once considered vital to their own national security.

❑ *The Turkish Straits*

The Turkish Straits were a case in point. Throughout the past century the defense of the Straits against Russian encroachments had been a cardinal principle of British policy, and the Crimean War (1853–1856) had been fought to keep the Straits out of Russian hands. But by 1915 the British were prepared to abandon the Straits to Russia to secure Russia's approval and support of their Gallipoli campaign.

When that campaign was first mooted, the Russians, who had long coveted the Straits, had feared with good reason that if the British and French conquered the Straits and Constantinople, they would very likely choose to stay there. Before they would agree to the Gallipoli campaign, therefore, and before they would promise any kind of diversionary support by mounting a campaign of their own against the Turks, the Russians demanded "that the question of Constantinople and the Straits must be definitively solved according to the time-honored aspirations of Russia." These aspirations included the incorporation into the Russian empire of the city of Constantinople, the territory on both sides of the Turkish Straits, southern Thrace, the islands in the Sea of Marmara, plus the islands of Imbros and Tenedos, which guarded the entrance to the Dardanelles. In return for these immense concessions, the Russians assured London and Paris that "the special interests of France and Great Britain in the region designated above will be scrupulously respected."

The French, reluctant all along to divert troops to Gallipoli, had grave reservations about making such far-reaching concessions. The Russians, however, were adamant. The tsar impressed on the French ambassador to St. Petersburg that Russia's agreement to cooperate in the Dardanelles campaign hinged on the question of Constantinople, where Russian prestige and crucial strategic interests were at stake. In return for Constantinople, Russia was willing to agree to anything the French might desire at the expense of France's archenemy Germany. "Take the left bank of the Rhine," the tsar said. "Take Mainz, take Koblenz, go even farther if you see fit." But the French foreign minister, Théophile Delcassé, although considered so pro-Russian that he was often referred to as Delcasoff, continued to hesitate. He favored the internationalization of the Straits and suggested a noncommittal reply to the tsar's proposals.

The British were far more amenable to Russian demands. They believed that present military necessities were more important than past diplomatic principles, and they anticipated far greater military advantages from a successful Dardanelles campaign than did the French. Their decisive consideration, however, appears to have been their fear that Russia might make a separate peace with Germany in return for German promises to give Russia a free hand in East Asia and the Middle East at the expense of the British and of Germany's allies, the Turks. The Russians did their best to nourish this fear, and Sazonov, the Russian foreign minister, who posed as the most fervent advocate of a war to the finish against Germany, used a far from subtle form of

blackmail by threatening to resign in favor of ministers more receptive to German offers unless Russian demands respecting the Straits were met.

The British gave in almost at once, the French somewhat later. By notes of
March 12 (British) and April 12 (French), 1915, they yielded to all Russian demands,
their only conditions being that Constantinople be made a free port and that there
should be commercial freedom for merchant ships passing through the Straits.

❑ Conflicting Promises to the Arabs

The Anglo-French agreement with Russia over the Straits opened the way for negotiations over the rest of the Ottoman empire. These negotiations were to produce a succession of further agreements, many of them conflicting or contradictory, which gave
rise to misunderstandings, accusations of bad faith, and conflicts that have continued
to poison the international atmosphere in the Middle East to the present day.

Already in February 1914, half a year before the war began, Ibn Ali Hussein, the
grand sharif (governor) of Mecca, had sounded out the British government about supporting Arab efforts to secure their independence from the Turks. After Turkey entered the war on the side of Germany, the British Foreign Office empowered Sir Henry
McMahon, British high commissioner for Egypt, to negotiate with Hussein. The Arab
leader's demands were far from modest. He wanted British recognition of an independent Arab native land (whether he meant one state or several remained ambiguous)
which was to include all of Syria (with the Mersina and Alexandretta districts in the
north), the entire Arabian Peninsula (apart from Aden, which was already a British
protectorate), the entire Sinai Peninsula, all of Mesopotamia (Iraq), and the territories
later to be designated Palestine and Transjordan.

On October 24, 1915, McMahon addressed a letter to Hussein on behalf of the
British government promising British recognition and support for Arab independence throughout the region he had designated "wherein Great Britain is free to act
without detriment to the interests of her ally, France"—already an immense qualification. There followed a list of other qualifications, chiefly areas along the Mediterranean and Persian Gulf coasts where British interests "required special administrative
arrangements."

Two months later, in December 1915, the British concluded an agreement with
another Arab leader, Abdul Aziz ibn-Saud, the ruler of Nejd (a region in the east-
central part of the Arabian Peninsula), recognizing his authority over several areas
already promised to Hussein. The contradictions in this case were due to the fact
that the British negotiations with Hussein had been conducted by the Foreign Office
through the high commissioner in Egypt, whereas the negotiations with ibn-Saud had
been conducted by officials of the India Office.

❑ The Sykes-Picot Agreement

The promises to Hussein and ibn-Saud were soon to be contradicted by agreements
between the Allies themselves, the fruit of negotiations between Sir Mark Sykes, assistant secretary to the British War Cabinet, and François Georges-Picot, former French

consul general in Beirut. An agreement initialed on January 3, 1916, provided for the partition of the entire central and southern sectors of the Ottoman empire into British and French spheres of influence. The British sphere included Bagdad and Basra (the territory north of the Persian Gulf, key to the protection of British interests in Persia), and the ports of Haifa and Acre on the Mediterranean coast. The French were to have the coastal area of Syria and a large part of south-central Anatolia (Cilicia). In the rest of this region, although Britain and France were prepared "to recognize and uphold an independent Arab State or Confederation of Arab States," that area too was divided into British and French spheres. The French were conceded predominant influence in the territory to the south and east of Cilicia and the Syrian coast, while the British were to control the territory south of the French zone, from Egypt in the west to the regions surrounding the districts of Bagdad and Basra in the east.

The Sykes-Picot agreement included a provision for Palestine, which had never been a separate political or religious administrative district of the Ottoman empire but was a Judeo-Christian conception of what constituted the "Holy Land." As defined on the Sykes-Picot map, Palestine was a narrow coastal strip between Haifa in the north and Gaza in the south, bordered on the east by the Sea of Galilee, the Jordan River and the Dead Sea. This region, whose exact territorial delimitations are still the subject of passionate debate and bloody conflict, was to be under some form of international administration.

❏ *Agreements with Russia and Italy*

To secure the agreement of Russia to Sykes-Picot, Britain and France concluded a treaty with Russia conceding Russia the right to annex outright an enormous expanse of Ottoman territory along Russia's southern and eastern frontiers, altogether an area of some 60,000 square miles between the Black Sea and the Mosul-Urumia region to the south and east.

Informed of these concessions to Russia, the Italians promptly demanded their share of the spoils and were duly awarded control over the entire southern half of the Anatolian Peninsula, plus indirect control over a region extending as far north as the territories allotted to Russia.

Britain and France subsequently repudiated the agreement with Italy on the specious grounds that the Italians had failed to participate in the Allied military campaigns in the Middle East and that Russia's consent had not been obtained. This repudiation was bitterly resented by the Italians and was to make for yet another nasty altercation in drawing up the postwar peace treaties.

❏ *The Balfour Declaration*

On November 2, 1917, the British foreign secretary, Arthur Balfour, wrote to Lord Rothschild, president of the British Zionist Federation: "I have much pleasure in conveying to you, on behalf of His Majesty's Government, the following declaration of sympathy with Jewish Zionist aspirations which has been submitted to and approved by the Cabinet: His Majesty's Government view with favor the establishment in Palestine of a National Home for the Jewish People and will use its best endeavors to facilitate the achievement of this object, it being clearly understood that nothing shall be done which may prejudice the civil and religious rights of existing non-Jewish communities in Palestine, or the rights and political status enjoyed by Jews in any other country."

Balfour himself, as well as Prime Minister Lloyd George, were clearly motivated by sympathy for the Zionist movement and the centuries-long plight of stateless Jews. "Both the Prime Minister and myself," Balfour said shortly after issuing his Declaration, " have been influenced by a desire to give the Jews their rightful place in the world." Some time later, in defending his policy before the House of Lords, Balfour observed that the whole culture of Europe had from time to time "proved itself guilty of great crimes against this [Jewish] race." It was time "to give [the Jews] the opportunity of developing in peace and quietness, under British rule, those great gifts which hitherto they [could] only bring to fruition in countries which know not their language and belong not to their race. . . . That is the aim which lay at the root of the policy I am trying to defend; and though it is defensible on every ground, that is the ground that chiefly moves me."

The British government had more immediate objectives, in the first instance the need to head off a German pro-Zionist proclamation proposed in the spring of 1917 by Arthur Zimmermann, the head of the German foreign office. There was also the urgent question of whether the Declaration could be turned to account in Russia; whether Russian Jews would use their influence to keep Russia in the war; or, if it were too late for this, whether they would seek to obstruct German exploitation of Russian resources, especially in the Ukraine. "It was believed also," Lloyd George explained after the war, "that such a Declaration would have a potent influence upon world Jewry outside Russia and secure for the Entente the aid of Jewish financial interests." Such aid was seen as being especially valuable in America, for "the Allies had almost exhausted the gold and marketable securities available for American [arms] purchases."

There were more long-range political calculations. In making his case for a Jewish homeland in Palestine, the Zionist leader Chaim Weizmann had pointed out that Zionist settlers brought to Palestine under British auspices might provide valuable aid in countering the spread of French influence in the Middle East; it would be a distinct advantage for Britain to have a pro-British population in the territory east of the Suez Canal. Balfour wholeheartedly agreed. What was needed was a Jewish state in Palestine in which Jews would constitute a majority of the population. Only a large-scale settlement, built up under British auspices, would provide the strong and reliable ally the British needed to strengthen their position in this part of the world. "We are consciously seeking," Balfour told Louis Brandeis, the American Zionist leader in 1919, "to reconstitute a new community and definitely building for a numerical majority in the future."

Balfour's statements about British objectives in Palestine mirrored those of the Zionists, who aspired to the creation of a state in which they would at last be the masters of their fate and not have to rely on the forbearance of others. The aim of the Zionists, Weizmann told the Paris Peace Conference in 1919, was "to build up gradually a nationality which would be as Jewish as the French nation was French and the British nation British. Later on, when the Jews formed the large majority, they would be ripe to establish such a government as would answer to the state of the development of the country and to their own ideals."

❑ *The Anglo-French Arab Declaration*

On November 7, 1918, just a little over a year after the British issued the Balfour Declaration on behalf of the Jews, the British and French governments issued a similar declaration on behalf of the Arabs. Their objective in the war in the Middle East was "the complete and definite emancipation of the peoples so long oppressed by the Turks and the establishment of national governments and administrations deriving their authority from the initiative and free choice of the indigenous populations. In order to carry out these intentions, France and Great Britain are at one in encouraging and assisting the establishment of indigenous Governments and administrations in Syria and Mesopotamia . . . and in territories the liberation of which they are securing, and recognizing these as soon as they are established."

These were noble sentiments, but nowhere throughout the Arab world did the French and British see fit to honor their own statement of principle in spirit or in deed. In a memorandum of August 1919, Balfour himself noted the contradictions between the covenant promised the Arabs and the actual policies of the victorious Allies. He argued that in Syria the population had no choice but to accept a French-controlled administration, but he believed the contradictions to be even more flagrant in the case of the "independent nation" (the term is Balfour's) of Palestine. "For in Palestine we do not propose even to go through the form of consulting the wishes of the present inhabitants of the country. . . . The four Great Powers are committed to Zionism. And Zionism, be it right or wrong, good or bad, is rooted in age-long traditions, in present needs, in future hopes, of far profounder import than the desires and prejudices of the 700,000 Arabs who now inhabit that ancient land. . . . So far as Palestine is concerned, the Powers have made no statement of fact [to the Arabs] that is not admittedly wrong, and no declaration of policy which, at least in the letter, they have not always intended to violate."

❑ *The Franco-Russian Agreements over Germany*

While the Allied governments were negotiating over the future partition of the Ottoman empire, the French were seeking support for their war aims vis-à-vis Germany in Western Europe. Fearing that the British and particularly the Americans would not agree to peace terms with Germany sufficiently stringent to ensure the permanent security of France, the French government sent a diplomatic mission to Russia early in 1917 to secure Russian support for French war aims in Europe. The tsar, already beset by domestic problems that would shortly overthrow his government, agreed without reservation to all the French conditions: France was to regain Alsace and Lorraine with "at the very least" the frontiers of 1790, including the entire Saar region. The rest of Germany's territory on the left bank of the Rhine was to be divided into self-governing states, politically and economically independent of Germany, with no armed forces of their own. These states were to be occupied by the French until the terms of a final peace treaty with Germany had been completely fulfilled, a process that might require a generation. These terms were confirmed by a formal exchange of letters between the French and Russian governments on February 14, 1917.

The Russians now raised demands of their own. In return for their support of French war aims against Germany, they wanted French support for Russian territorial expansion in the east. This time it was the French who agreed unconditionally. For, whatever the disadvantages of such an extension of Russian influence, it would contribute to "the necessary enfeeblement of Germany." On March 10 the French sent the tsarist government a note formally recognizing Russia's "complete liberty to fix its western frontiers."

The letter exchange of February 14, like all other wartime treaties between Russia and the Western Allies, was to be repudiated by the Bolsheviks in the second stage of the Russian Revolution. That exchange, nevertheless, represents the most important official statement of the war aims of France and tsarist Russia in Western and Central Europe.

❑ The War Aims of the Central Powers

Germany

In the course of the war, the Germans were even more prolific than the Allies in defining their territorial and economic objectives. Unlike the Allies, however, who had embodied many of these objectives in actual treaties, the German war aims had for the most part been put forward in memoranda prepared by political and military officials and by representatives of every conceivable interest group. The Treaties of Brest-Litovsk (see pp. 27–28) were the first documents that set forth in official form the extent of German ambitions, and then only for Eastern Europe.

Because there were so many formulations of German war aims, the nature of those aims varied widely depending on who was drafting them, to whom they were addressed, and the shifting fortunes of war. At their most extravagant, they included demands for territorial and economic concessions that would have given Germany domination over Eastern as well as Western Europe, created a German colonial empire stretching from sea to sea in Central Africa, and required reparations that would pay off the entire German national debt.

As the war dragged on, the views of German individuals and organizations changed markedly. Matthias Erzberger, the leader of the powerful Catholic Center party, who had put forward one of the most extravagant formulations of war aims in September 1914, was a chief sponsor of the Reichstag's Peace Resolution, passed by an overwhelming margin in July 1917, calling for a peace of reconciliation, with no annexations or indemnities. Chancellor Bethmann-Hollweg's views underwent a similar shift. A memorandum drafted by his secretary in September 1914 listed conditions which he evidently believed the German government must demand to justify the already terrible costs of the war to the German people. These included territorial annexations at the expense of France and Belgium, the incorporation of Luxembourg into the German empire, a war indemnity that would make France economically dependent on Germany, and the enrollment of much of the rest of Europe in a German-dominated economic association.

By 1917, however, Bethmann too saw that Germany no longer had the power to hold out for extravagant war aims. He now seemed prepared not only to abandon all territorial and economic demands, but actually to make concessions to France in Alsace on behalf of peace. Although these views were never put forward officially, Bethmann's change of attitude was sufficiently conspicuous to arouse the ire of the German military leadership. On April 23, 1917, he was summoned to an imperial council in Kreuznach, where he was called upon to reach agreement with the high command on a common formulation of war aims, that is, to endorse the views of the high command. The Kreuznach program called for Germany's annexation of the greater part of the Baltic states; complete domination over an "independent" Poland; the incorporation of Luxembourg into the German empire; the annexation of the Belgian coast, with Belgium itself to become a vassal state; frontier "rectifications" at the expense of France; and the annexation of France's Longwy-Briey ore fields. Further questions relating to the Balkans, Asia Minor, and overseas colonies were to be referred to other departments for further discussion. Austria-Hungary was to be allowed to extend its dominion over Serbia, Montenegro, and Albania, which were to be attached to the empire in the form of a South Slav state. The Austrians were also to receive compensation in western Wallachia.

Bethmann duly endorsed these war aims, but pointed out that they could only be realized if Germany were in a position to dictate the peace, which he clearly believed was no longer possible. He added the further critical reservation that he did not consider himself bound to continue the war until these objectives had been achieved. The high command was not amused. In July 1917 Ludendorff secured Bethmann's dismissal and his replacement as chancellor by Georg Michaelis, a nonentity who would not presume to contest the army's authority.

Austria-Hungary

Austro-Hungarian war aims reflected the usual differences between the Austrians and the Hungarians. The Hungarians continued their prewar objections to bringing more Slavs into the empire because this would dilute their own influence. Officially, therefore, the Austrians went no further than asking to be allowed a free hand with Serbia, Montenegro, and Albania. The Austrians wanted frontier rectifications at the expense of Italy; the Hungarians, at the expense of Romania. In Eastern Europe, Austro-Hungarian interests clashed with those of Germany, and the Germans hardly bothered to conceal the fact that their weaker allies would have to be content with what Berlin was prepared to concede them.

Already the first months of the war had revealed the extent of the Habsburg empire's weakness. After that, many Austrian as well as Hungarian leaders appeared willing to settle for the preservation of their empire and the recovery of territories lost in the fighting. They deeply resented German demands that they cede imperial territory to Italy as the price for keeping Italy neutral, and they suspected that Germany would be prepared to sacrifice Austrian interests on behalf of making peace with Russia. It is little wonder, therefore, that the Austrians would later be willing to sell out their German allies to save what they could of their Habsburg heritage. (See p. 31.)

TWO

❑

The Russian Revolutions and the Treaties of Brest-Litovsk

Even as the French and Russian governments were negotiating their secret treaties dividing the postwar spoils, a revolution was taking place in Russia that was to alter the entire political and military situation in Europe and ultimately have worldwide repercussions.

❑ *The March Revolution*

Early in March 1917 an epidemic of strikes and demonstrations erupted in St. Petersburg (called Petrograd since the beginning of the war to give the city a more Russian-sounding name), which were followed by a mutiny of troops stationed in the capital. This began the first stage of the Russian revolution that was to overthrow the tsarist government and pave the way for a second revolution that established a Communist dictatorship in Russia. On March 11 the Russian parliament, the duma, refused to obey an imperial decree ordering its dissolution, and shortly afterwards it set up a provisional government made up of the duma's leading members. (Note: for Russian dates, I have used the Gregorian calendar throughout instead of the Old Style calendar, which is thirteen days earlier and was still in use in Russia until January 31, 1918. Thus the 1917 November revolution, Gregorian calendar, was the October revolution, Old Style.)

On March 15 Tsar Nicholas II, seemingly without support from any quarter, yielded to the urging of his advisers and abdicated on behalf of himself and his hemophiliac son in favor of his brother Michael. But Michael refused to accept the crown and called upon all citizens to rally round the provisional government, which was expected to rule the country until more permanent institutions could be established. Thus this first stage of the Russian revolution was not so much a revolution as a renunciation of power and responsibility on the part of the old regime, its confidence sapped by war, the breakdown of the economy, and a long succession of military defeats.

The policies of the new provisional government disappointed the leaders of the Central Powers, who had hoped that the turmoil of revolution would lead to Russia's withdrawal from the war. Instead, the new government proclaimed its determination to go on fighting, and the socialist leader Alexandr Kerensky, minister of justice in the original provisional government who became minister of war in mid-May and prime minister in June, launched a major Russian offensive in the early summer of 1917.

Kerensky's offensive, carried out by ill-equipped and war-weary troops, proved a dismal failure and did much to erode whatever popular support the provisional government possessed. For the Russian people as a whole were thoroughly tired of the war, and the new government, instead of embarking on a bold program of reform and famine relief to meet the demands and needs of urban workers and peasants, was calling for still more sacrifices.

❑ *The Bolshevik Revolution*

Desperate to encourage antiwar sentiment in Russia, the German government in April 1917 transported to Russia a group of radical Russian revolutionaries living in exile in Switzerland who were calling for the overthrow of the provisional "bourgeois" government and an immediate end to the war. These revolutionaries were leaders of the Bolshevik party, the most tightly organized of Russia's revolutionary movements. They arrived in Petrograd via Germany and neutral Sweden on April 16, 1917.

The Bolsheviks understood the mood of the country far better than did the leaders of the provisional government. Besides demanding an immediate end to the war, they called for the confiscation of all landed estates and the transfer of power to the proletariat and the poorer peasants—the most effective appeals that could have been made to the Russian masses at that time. The first Bolshevik attempt to overthrow the government was badly bungled and their leaders were jailed or once again fled into exile. But following the failure of Kerensky's offensive and his suppression of a military coup in the summer of 1917, Kerensky made the fatal mistake of looking to the Bolsheviks for support.

The Bolsheviks did not bungle again. On November 7, 1917, with the support of local councils (Soviets) of workers and revolutionary soldiers and sailors stationed in the capital, they seized the major government buildings and sources of power essential to the conduct of government and the economy—power stations, railroads, telegraph offices and other channels of communication, and the local military arsenals. Once in control of the major power centers, the Bolsheviks proceeded to act as the official government of Russia and to crush opposition forces, which were as yet weak and disorganized. They now faced the far more formidable tasks of consolidating their authority, extending their control over the rest of the former tsarist empire, and making peace with the Central Powers.

❑ *Lenin*

The leader and guiding spirit of the Bolshevik party was a short, bald, thickset man named Vladimir Ilich Ulianov, who had assumed the pseudonym Lenin in 1912 when publishing a pamphlet on revolutionary tactics.

There were no obvious features in Lenin's family background or childhood that would explain how he and all his siblings became passionate revolutionaries. He was born in 1870 in the provincial town of Simbirsk on the Volga. His father was a superintendent of schools who was subsequently ennobled; his mother was the daughter of a doctor and substantial landowner. Radical political theories were part of the intellectual climate of opinion of that era, however, and the execution in 1887 of Lenin's much-admired brother for taking part in a conspiracy to assassinate Tsar Alexander III undoubtedly reinforced whatever revolutionary inclinations he already had.

In the same year as his brother's execution, Lenin graduated from the Simbirsk secondary school. By a strangely ironic coincidence, the director of that school and author of Lenin's graduation report was Feodor Kerensky, the father of the socialist leader Alexander Kerensky, whose government Lenin was to overthrow in November 1917. The elder Kerensky described Ulianov as gifted, hard-working, and reliable, "first in all his classes, and awarded a gold medal upon graduation as the outstanding student in ability, development, and conduct." To secure Lenin's admission to Kazan University and allay suspicion stemming from the conduct of his brother, Kerensky noted that neither in nor out of school "has a single instance been observed when Ulianov, by word or deed, caused dissatisfaction to his teachers or the school authorities." His mental and moral instruction at home, too, had been beyond reproach. "Religion and discipline were the basis of his upbringing, whose fruits are apparent in Ulianov's exemplary conduct."

Kerensky's evaluation could hardly have been wider of the mark, for Lenin was soon to be expelled from Kazan University for engaging in revolutionary agitation and devoted himself to the study of revolutionary theorists, above all the works of Marx and Engels. Solicitous friends secured his admission to the University of St. Petersburg where he took a law degree in 1891, but he never practiced law and instead became a professional—and brutally tough-minded—revolutionary. During a famine on the lower Volga in the winter of 1891–1892, he derided humanitarian relief efforts as "sickly sweet sentimentality, so characteristic of our intelligentsia." Famines were a direct product of the existing social order, he said, and could only be abolished through the abolition of that order. As it was, they performed a useful function by undermining the faith of the peasants in the tsarist government and sowing the seeds of revolution.

A relatively mild prison sentence in 1895 was followed in 1897 by a three-year exile to Siberia, where he lived in a peasant's hut and was allowed a remarkable degree of freedom. He was able to correspond with friends in European Russia, and was given free access to books. Here he translated a work on trade unionism by the British social activists Sidney and Beatrice Webb, and wrote an impressive scholarly treatise of his own, *The Development of Capitalism in Russia*. One year into his exile he married a fellow revolutionary, Nadezhda Krupskaya, who was to be his lifelong helpmate. Hardly returned from exile in Siberia, he went into exile abroad, frequently in despair that he would not live to see the revolution he so fervently desired.

His hopes revived with the outbreak of war in 1914, which was placing an unprecedented strain on the social and economic fabric of all the belligerents, and he rejoiced in how it seemed to be preparing the soil for revolution. Unlike the many liberals and radicals who were calling for a restoration of peace, Lenin hoped the war would continue until it had completed the evisceration of the capitalist states. It would then be the task of revolutionaries to transform the present conflict into a civil war and launch the world revolution.

In his theoretical writings, Lenin described the war as an inevitable product of the capitalist system, which had outgrown the investment opportunities available within capitalist states and compelled them to engage in imperialism. Imperialism in turn had brought them into competition and eventually into mortal combat with each other, a struggle that would inevitably destroy them and with them the entire capitalist system. Imperialism thus represented the final stage of capitalism.

Lenin considered himself a Marxist and a dedicated exponent of Marxist theory. "Orthodox Marxism," he said, "requires no revision of any kind, either in its theories of philosophy, political economy, or historical development." He described Marxist theory as "the objective truth" which could not be changed in any way without deviating from that truth and falling into bourgeois reactionary falsehood. Yet Lenin's own interpretation of Marx was in many cases not only a deviation from but a transformation of Marxist ideas.

Lenin built on Marx's view of history as a succession of class struggles and his belief that the final struggle—between the governments of the capitalists and the proletariat—was at hand. With Marx, he believed in the inevitable triumph of the proletariat, which would be followed by a reorganization of society in accordance with scientific social laws, whereby the workers would control the means of production and share in the common ownership of property. With that, all reason for conflict would be removed, the class struggle would come to an end, and the state would gradually wither away.

Marx had recognized that the organization of society in accordance with scientific laws would require some sort of supervisory agency, and he assigned this supervisory role to the state in the period immediately following the revolution. On this point, too, Lenin agreed with Marx, but he put far more emphasis on the need for a supervisory agency and envisaged an indefinite period of dictatorship in the postrevolutionary era.

Central to Lenin's own political thought was the importance of power, which he saw as the essential instrument of revolution and which he believed had been the decisive weapon through which previous rulers had exercised oppression over the working classes. To overcome this oppression and overthrow the governments of the landlords and capitalists, the revolutionary movement must exercise power in a manner no less absolute or ruthless than had the prerevolutionary autocracies.

Although all his revolutionary activity was ostensibly dedicated to the workers, Lenin did not believe that the workers could be entrusted with power, much less the labor movement, which, if left to itself, would inevitably become petty bourgeois. A genuine revolutionary consciousness could only be instilled in the workers by a revolutionary intelligentsia, a socialist vanguard made up of full-time professionals "who will devote to the revolution not only their spare evenings but their lives." The leadership that would be required for this purpose was to be exercised in the first instance by the Bolshevik party, which Lenin did not conceive as a mass party with maximum enrollment, but as a small, tightly controlled and disciplined hierarchical organization, its members carefully chosen for their loyalty and obligated to carry out the tasks set by the party leadership. Thus with the triumph of the revolution, the dictatorship of the proletariat of Marxist theory would in fact be the dictatorship of the party—or rather of the leaders of that party. Lenin made no attempt to disguise that fact. "Classes are led by parties and parties are led by individuals who are called leaders," he said shortly after coming to power in 1918. "Soviet socialist democracy is not in the least incompatible with individual rule and dictatorship. . . . All slogans about equal rights are nonsense."

Lenin paid lip-service to the idea of national self-determination when he found it expedient to do so—expediency explains the many contradictions in his policies and political pronouncements—but he saw clearly that nationalism could never be reconciled with his own ideal of international communism, and further, that national revolutions threatened the very existence of the multinational state of which he was now the leader. "There is not a single Marxist," he declared, "who, while adhering to the foundations of Marxism and Socialism, would not say that the interests of Socialism are above the rights of nations to self-determination."

Although Marxism-Leninism (i.e., Marxism as interpreted by Lenin) was to become a catechism for Communists in every part of the world, Lenin's stature as a major historical figure does not derive from his theories about revolution and leadership, but from his astounding success as a revolutionary leader.

Lenin possessed all the obvious attributes of a successful leader: intelligence, energy, willpower, and the ability to inspire fanatical devotion among his followers. Journalist, pamphleteer, orator, coiner of slogans and phrases, he was a masterful propagandist, acutely attuned to the aspirations and prejudices of his audience. But his less obvious qualities may have been an even more important factor in his success: his fanaticism, his total dedication to his cause, and his dogmatic certainty as to the correctness of that cause and its inevitable victory. Yet he was anything but dogmatic in his actual conduct of politics, for he was prepared to abandon principles he had once held sacred in the interests of expediency, and to adopt policies he had condemned as heresy when advocated by others but which he called tactical diversions when practiced by himself.

By his friends Lenin has been described as a lover of children, animals, and nature, a delightful companion, always bubbling with humor and enjoyment of life, the instigator of practical jokes and inventive diversions, a never-failing source of happiness and laughter. All the bleaker does this attractive facade make the political Lenin, this terrifyingly ruthless and pitiless leader, who derided mercy and compassion as bourgeois qualities while condemning thousands to imprisonment and death. He once confessed to the writer Maxim Gorky that he was reluctant to listen to music because it made him want to stroke the heads of people who could create such beauty "while living in this vile hell." If you succumbed to stroking them, however, you might get your hand bitten off. "You have to hit them on the head without mercy."

Lenin was the prototype of statesmen who believed that the ends justified the means. The first step was the seizure of power; the second, to retain it. These goals could only be achieved through dictatorial government, the suppression of all civil liberties, and mass terror. Lenin expressed confidence that the ultimate goal, a classless society, would be achieved some day, but he devoted comparatively little speculation over how this proletarian paradise would function, a reticence typical of utopian theoreticians. Meanwhile he showed no concern for the welfare of the Russian people, regarding the enormous sacrifices he demanded of them as unavoidable and inconsequential.

❑ Lenin's Peace Initiative

Just one day after the Bolshevik seizure of power, Lenin made a dramatic gesture to fulfill the Bolshevik pledge to make peace immediately. In what he called a Declaration of Peace, issued November 8, 1917, he appealed to all the peoples and governments involved in the present war to begin negotiations at once which should lead to a "just and democratic peace" without annexations or indemnities. All secret treaties were to be abrogated, and in future all international negotiations were to be conducted openly, in full view of the public. As a first step in the abrogation of secret treaties, the Bolshevik government intended to publish the Allies' wartime treaties "concluded by the governments of landlords and capitalists" in order to expose to the peoples of the world the immoral nature of those regimes, the sordid motives for which they were fighting, and the hypocrisy of their claims to be waging war on behalf of freedom and self-determination. To cleanse the world of such corruption, Lenin called upon the class-conscious workers of the world, particularly those of such "advanced" nations as Britain, France, and Germany, to liberate humanity from the horrors of war and to free "the toiling and exploited masses from all forms of exploitation and slavery." They should overthrow the governments of landlords and capitalists which were responsible for the present war and follow the example of the Bolsheviks in Russia, who proposed to initiate peace negotiations immediately.

Lenin's peace initiative was greeted enthusiastically by the leaders of the German government, for the withdrawal of Russia from the war would at last allow them to concentrate the bulk of their military might on the Western front and greatly increase their chances for final victory in that sector. With the surrender of Russia in sight, however, the Germans yeilded to the temptation to realize their extravagant war aims in the east. Taking advantage of Russia's weakness, they advanced farther into Russia to gain control of still more territory. They thereby delayed the conclusion of a final peace treaty with Russia and the wholesale shift of their forces to the west.

❑ The Disintegration of the Russian Empire

To gain the support of the indigenous populations in the Russian territories they occupied and to contribute further to the disruption of Russia, the Germans made use of one of the most effective propaganda devices employed by the Allies. Taking up the slogan of national freedom and self-determination, they encouraged uprisings among the non-Russian nationalities within the old Russian empire and supported their efforts to form independent national governments.

The non-Russian nationalities did not require much encouragement. As early as November 28, 1917, the Estonians proclaimed their independence from Russia. Their example was followed in December by the Finns and Moldavians, and early in 1918 by the Poles, Lithuanians, Latvians, White Russians (Belorussians), Ukrainians, Don Cossacks, Georgians, Armenians, and other nationalities of the Caucasus area. The Bolshevik peace initiative thus led in the first instance not to peace but to the disintegration of the tsarist empire.

On December 15, 1917, the Bolsheviks arranged a formal armistice with the Central Powers and asked for a peace treaty based on the principle of no annexations or indemnities. The Germans agreed to this request on condition that the Western Allies agree to conclude a peace treaty with the Central Powers on the same terms. When the Western Allies failed to respond to Russia's plea for such a treaty, the Germans reaffirmed their willingness to abjure annexations and indemnities. But they also felt obliged to adhere to their promise to support the aspirations of the Poles and other non-Russian nationalities for freedom and self-determination. The Bolsheviks, protesting that the Germans were using the slogan of self-determination to disguise their own imperialist ambitions, refused to conclude a treaty on these terms, and on February 10 they broke off negotiations with the declaration that, treaty or no treaty, the state of war between Russia and the Central Powers was now at an end.

This second Bolshevik declaration of peace did nothing to change the situation. The Germans resumed their advance into Russia, and the disintegration of the Russian empire continued. Lenin himself had consistently argued that the government had no alternative but to accept the German terms. Those terms were admittedly rotten, but if war were continued, the Bolshevik government would be overthrown and peace would then be made by some other government. To his colleagues' call for a revolutionary war, Lenin contemptuously replied that they should "stop playing with revolutionary phrases." "To wage a war an army is needed, and we don't have one." The coming of world revolution and the final triumph of socialism were scientific certainties, but the Bolshevik government could not afford to base its policy on the expectation of an imminent revolution in Germany because it was impossible to predict when that revolution would take place, and the present situation called for an immediate decision. The fundamental task of the Bolshevik government was to remain in power and consolidate its position. For this purpose it needed peace and it needed time. The necessary time could be bought by giving up territory, which would be recovered in any case with the overthrow of the capitalist-imperialist governments. Lenin's clinching argument was that the Germans had not presented the one demand the Bolsheviks could not accept, namely, their abdication of power. "All other demands can and should be met."

Faced with a German ultimatum and Lenin's threat to resign if they continued to procrastinate, a majority of his colleagues at last voted for peace.

❏ *The Treaties of Brest-Litovsk*

Early in 1918 the Central Powers concluded two peace treaties in the town of Brest-Litovsk in what was still Russian Poland. The first of those treaties, signed February 9, was with the newly independent Ukrainian People's Republic. It provided for the restoration of the prewar frontiers between Austria-Hungary and the Ukraine. Farther north, however, the frontier was to be determined by a multinational commission "according to ethnographic conditions" and "after taking the wishes of the inhabitants into consideration," another bow to the principle of self-determination. The contracting parties renounced all indemnities, they agreed to enter into economic relations with each other without delay and to abolish all tariff and transport restrictions so as to speed the development of trade. The Germans and Austrians hoped the Ukraine would provide them with desperately needed supplies of grain and other raw materials. That hope was never fulfilled because of the chaos prevailing in every part of Eastern Europe at this time and because of Germany's failure to speed the restoration of peace.

The terms of the Central Powers' treaty of Brest-Litovsk with Russia signed March 3, were considerably harsher. Russia was compelled to renounce all those areas of Western Russia where non-Russian nationalities had declared their independence and set up governments of their own. Russia was to refrain from all interference with the internal affairs of these territories, whose future status was to be determined by Germany and Austria-Hungary "in agreement with their populations." As soon as a general peace had been concluded and Russia had demobilized completely, the Germans would withdraw their own armies from the territories of these newly formed states.

Russia was to recognize the independence of Finland and the Aaland Islands, of Estonia, Livonia, and the Ukraine (whose boundaries with Russia were precisely defined). All Russian troops, official and unofficial (i.e., Communist party militias and guerrillas), were to be removed from their territories. Estonia and Livonia were to be occupied by German police forces until proper national institutions had been established there and public order secured. All contracting parties were to respect the political and economic independence of Persia (Iran) and Afghanistan.

The Russians were to evacuate all Ottoman territory occupied during the war and restore to Turkey the districts of Ardahan, Kars, and Batum, the fruits of Russia's victory over Turkey in 1877-1878. The Germans did not turn the evacuated territories over to Turkey, however, but insisted on provisions that would enable the non-Turkish nationalities of these territories to declare their independence and set up their own governments. In making this further gesture on behalf of the principle of self-determination, the Germans appear to have been genuinely concerned to prevent further Turkish massacres of the Armenians. But the Turks suspected, with ample justification, that the Germans' principal motive was to extend their own influence over this area. By the summer of 1918, however, the Germans were no longer in a position to intervene effectively in the Caucasus region or anywhere else, for they were now committing the bulk of their remaining resources to their final, unsuccessful, offensive in the west.

❑ *The Treaty of Bucharest*

On May 7, 1918, the Central Powers recorded their final triumph in World War I with the surrender of Romania and the conclusion of the Treaty of Bucharest. Romania was treated comparatively leniently. Austria demanded a few small strategic frontier posts in the passes of the Carpathian Mountains; Bulgaria received an extension of territory in the Dobruja region along the coast of the Black Sea south of the Danube; and Germany obtained a ninety nine-year lease of the Romanian oil fields, which meant the transfer of those oil fields from a British to a German-controlled consortium.

❏ *German War Aims in the Light of Brest-Litovsk*

In the course of the war, the Germans had been as prolific as the Allies in defining their territorial and economic goals, but as noted earlier, German war aims had never been set forth in international treaties. The Treaty of Brest-Litovsk is therefore of particular importance as being the first public document that revealed the extent of German ambitions in Eastern Europe. Because this treaty was abrogated after Germany's defeat in the west, the British historian John W. Wheeler-Bennett has called it the "forgotten peace," and in his book on the subject he sought to remind the Germans and all others who thought Germany had been subjected to an excessively harsh peace by the Allies of the kind of peace Germany had imposed on Russia.

The Treaty of Brest-Litovsk was undeniably harsh, but instead of comparing it to Versailles, it would be more pertinent to compare it to the secret treaties concluded by the Allies in the course of the war, when any means seemed justified to achieve victory. The Treaty of Brest-Litovsk was drawn up while Germany was still at war and while the British blockade still throttled German commerce. Its primary objective was to destroy Russia's ability to wage war in the east and enable Germany to transfer its forces to the west before the power of the United States (which had declared war on Germany on April 6, 1917) could be brought to bear in Europe. Its primary economic objective was to give Germany access to desperately needed supplies of food and raw materials. The Treaty of Versailles, on the other hand, was drawn up after the war had been won; many of its provisions violated Wilson's Fourteen Points, which the Allies had accepted with reservations (see p. 38) as the basis for that treaty. Most importantly, Versailles was imposed on a German democratic government which had been created in response to the demands of the Allies and which they had every interest in supporting. By contrast, Brest-Litovsk was imposed on a Communist regime which the imperial German government had every interest in discrediting and ultimately destroying.

The evidence we now have of German wartime ambitions leaves no doubt that the Germans would not have granted the Russians a more lenient peace no matter what their form of government, and that if they had triumphed in the west, they would have demanded major territorial and economic gains in Western as well as Eastern Europe and overseas. Their lip-service recognition of the principle of self-determination was as great a sham as the Allies' promises to the Arabs, for the new national states carved out of the old Russian empire would have been little more than vehicles for the extension of German political and economic influence. An all-out German victory would thus have meant the establishment of German dominion over Europe and the destruction of the European balance of power, just as many American interventionists had feared.

But in this connection several questions remain open. Was Germany still capable of achieving an all-out victory in 1918? If the United States had not intervened, would the European belligerents have found themselves obliged to conclude a negotiated peace? And would a negotiated peace have been more successful in preserving peace in the long run than were the treaties actually drafted by the victorious Allies? These, like so many questions in history, cannot be answered. It is nevertheless noteworthy that the only peace the Allies were obliged to *negotiate* with a member of the Central Powers (the Treaty of Lausanne with Turkey, see p. 87–88) was the only treaty that survived the interwar years.

◻

THREE

World War I, Part 2

◻ Peace Moves

War weariness had increased substantially among the peoples of all the belligerent powers as the war entered its third year, a sentiment that gave rise to increasingly insistent calls for a negotiated peace, a peace of compromise and reconciliation.

The first determined and practical bid for peace among the belligerents came from Austria-Hungary. In November 1916 Francis Joseph, emperor of Austria and king of Hungary since 1848, died at the age of eighty six. The death of the venerable Habsburg monarch marked the end of an era, but for many observers it seemed to symbolize the end of the Habsburg monarchy itself.

Francis Joseph was succeeded by his grand-nephew Charles, who from the time of his accession resolved to take his country out of the war on the most favorable terms he could arrange, if necessary at the expense of his German allies. The peace initiative of Charles was exactly the kind of move all belligerents had feared their allies might make and which they had tried to prevent through their wartime treaties. In their efforts to retain the loyalty of the Habsburg monarchy, the Germans had included substantial gains for Austria-Hungary in their war aims. But by the time Charles succeeded to the crown, he was advised by his ministers that the monarchy could not remain in the war much longer without risking total collapse and disintegration. Accordingly, in January 1917 he informed the Allies of Austria's willingness to make a separate peace. The Austrians offered to support France's claim to Alsace and Lorraine; the restoration of Belgium, which should receive compensation for all losses and damage suffered during the war; the restoration of Serbia and recognition of the Serb claim to an outlet to the sea by giving them northern Albania. The Austrians were also prepared to allow Russia to have Constantinople at the expense of their Turkish allies. The only Habsburg territory the Austrians themselves were willing to give up was the Trentino (the predominantly Italian sector of South Tyrol), which was to go to Italy, but only in return for adequate compensation.

The Austrian peace initiative foundered over the objections of the Italians, who refused to agree to any peace that did not give them everything promised in the Treaty of London. Owing largely to the refusal of the Italians to scale down their demands, Allied negotiations with Austria came to an end in June 1917.

The revolution in Russia in March 1917 and the possibility that Russia might withdraw from the war strengthened the hand of Germany's most influential military leaders who still sought a decisive military victory. But the situation in Russia also gave new weight to the arguments of proponents of a negotiated peace, because the Central Powers might never again be in so favorable a bargaining position. On July 19, 1917, the German Reichstag, by a vote of 212 to 126, approved a resolution for a peace of reconciliation with no annexations or indemnities.

The advocates of a negotiated peace in Germany, however, lacked the power to implement their policies. Under pressure from his generals, the kaiser dismissed Chancellor Bethmann-Hollweg and appointed as his successor Georg Michaelis, a civilian figurehead for the military leadership dominated by the strong-willed and intransigent General Ludendorff. Michaelis agreed to endorse the Reichstag peace resolution "as I interpret it," but he made no serious move to negotiate with the Allies, and the German military leadership was determined to carry on the war to total victory.

In the Allied countries, too, the proponents of a negotiated peace were displaced or silenced by advocates of an all-out victory. In Britain, the government of Herbert Asquith, which included ministers who favored negotiation, gave way in December 1916 to a government under David Lloyd George, who called for total victory and the knockout blow. In France, the veteran statesman Georges Clemenceau, the most vehement advocate of victory *sans phrase,* became prime minister and minister of war in November 1917. Even in Russia, the dominant figure in the revolutionary government that had taken over power in March 1917 was the socialist leader Alexandr Kerensky, who launched an offensive in the summer of 1917 to achieve total victory in the east.

But already in April 1917, the military and diplomatic scene was decisively altered with the entry of the United States in the war on the side of the Allies.

❑   The Intervention of the United States

If the Germans had gained a quick and decisive victory over the Allies in 1914, as they had confidently expected, there would have been no American intervention in World War I. Even so, despite America's increasing involvement in international affairs in the years before 1914, it was not until almost three years after war had broken out in Europe that the United States entered the conflict. The traditions of American isolationism and avoidance of entangling alliances proved to be powerful forces of inertia, and Americans in general knew little about the issues at stake.

The longer the war lasted, however, the more likely it became that the United States would become involved, because from the beginning of the conflict the United States was caught in a dilemma which many Americans did not recognize. While Americans in general may have wanted to stay out of the war in Europe, they also refused to agree to any restriction of their freedom to trade with belligerents and bitterly resented any violation of their rights as a neutral state. By insisting on their right to continue to trade with belligerents after the British blockade effectively prevented shipments to Germany, the United States in effect ceased to be a neutral power because virtually all American shipments went to the Allies. The Germans attempted to restrict the flow of American goods to the Allies by the only means available to them—submarine warfare—which Americans regarded as a violation of their freedom of trade and neutral rights. The German submarine campaign was the major factor in influencing American public opinion against Germany and the decisive issue in bringing about American intervention.

There were, of course, a multitude of other reasons for American intervention. Prominent among these was the fact that many of America's most influential political and business leaders were sympathetic to the Allied cause. With some notable exceptions American journalists, too, tended to be pro-Ally and gave ample publicity to accounts of German atrocities, which contributed to the steady rise of anti-German sentiment in American public opinion. A fundamental consideration for American leaders who viewed the war in a long-term perspective was their belief that a German victory would upset the world balance of power, give Germany hegemony over Europe, and make Germany so powerful that it would pose a serious threat to the interests and security of the United States.

Yet, no matter how great the power and influence of American interventionists or how convincing their arguments, it is doubtful whether they could have propelled the United States into the conflict had not the Germans themselves forced the issue by resorting to policies that aroused the emotional indignation of the American people. Early in 1915 the Germans announced their intention to create a submarine blockade around Britain comparable to Britain's naval blockade around Germany, and on February 18 the German government issued a proclamation that henceforth all vessels bearing food and arms to Allied countries would be sunk without warning. Germany's submarine campaign struck the public imagination as a particularly sinister and unsportsmanlike method of waging war, which not only threatened America's commercial freedom but seemed to confirm Allied charges of German brutality and ruthlessness.

On May 7, 1915, Americans were stunned by the news that a German submarine had sunk the British luxury liner *Lusitania* with a loss of 1,198 lives, including more than 100 Americans (an estimated 1,503 had been lost on the *Titanic*). Before the *Lusitania* had sailed from New York, the Germans had published warnings in major American newspapers advising against sailing on her because she was carrying arms and ammunition and was therefore subject to attack. These warnings were largely ignored, however, and they were not considered or remembered in the general indignation aroused in America by this latest example of German barbarity. The American government issued two vigorous notes of protest, to which the German government responded that in future no passenger ships should be sunk without warning and that provision would be made for the safety of noncombatants on board. The Germans lived up to this promise for the rest of the year despite the restriction this imposed on their submarine warfare, and the intensity of the furor in America over the *Lusitania* gradually subsided.

In November 1916, Wilson was elected to a second term as president of the United States. The dominant mood of the American public still appeared to be opposed to intervention, for the slogan "He kept us out of war" proved to be one of the most effective and popular of his campaign. Wilson tried. In December 1916, he circulated a peace note to the belligerent powers asking them for a statement of acceptable peace terms. The response of the Germans seemed positive, but so vague and so filled with reservations as to render it meaningless. Indeed, the German reply appears to have been nothing more than an effort to deceive Wilson and gain time, for it was drawn up after the German government had made the decision to resume unrestricted submarine warfare and thus gamble for total victory.

The Allies' reply to Wilson was much more specific and the first public pronouncement about their war aims. These, they said, were based on the principles of national freedom and self-determination. They therefore demanded the liberation of the Italians, Slavs, Romanians, Czechs and Slovaks from foreign domination, and freedom for those populations subject to the "bloody tyranny of the Turks." Thus the Allies committed themselves officially to the dismemberment of the Habsburg and Ottoman empires. The Allies also demanded the restoration of Belgium, Serbia, Romania, Russia, and Northern France; the return of Alsace and Lorraine to France; the establishment of a united Polish state (under Russian control); and the payment of a war indemnity to reimburse those countries invaded by the Central Powers for the destruction they had caused.

Despite his sympathy for the Allies, Wilson was dismayed by the extent of their demands. In an attempt to scale them down and lay the groundwork for a negotiated peace, he delivered his famous "Peace without Victory" speech on January 22, 1917. A peace imposed by victors upon vanquished, he said, would be accepted in humiliation and bitterness and would be a peace founded on quicksand. Only a peace negotiated among equals could be expected to endure.

If the kaiser and his military leadership had possessed a minimal sense of realism or political common sense, they would have seized on Wilson's appeal for a negotiated peace. For here was a golden opportunity to secure Wilson's mediation while they were still in a favorable military position and to blame all failures of negotiation on Allied intransigence. Instead, the German leaders decided to achieve a total victory, which alone would enable them to realize the extravagant war aims they deemed essential to secure their country's future as one of the world's great powers and to compensate their people for the sacrifices of war. With their decision to achieve total victory, they ensured their country's total defeat.

On January 21, 1917, the Germans announced their intention of resuming unrestricted submarine warfare. Wilson reacted immediately, as he had threatened to do, by severing diplomatic relations with Germany. By taking this step he may have hoped that Germany would back down. But Germany did not back down, and soon the American press was filled with reports of the sinking of neutral vessels with the loss of their passengers and crews, including many Americans. Even the most skillful diplomacy could not have counteracted the effect of this news on American public opinion.

As if determined to make his own contribution to Germany's record of political bungling, the head of the German Foreign Office, Arthur Zimmermann, sent a telegram to the German diplomatic representative in Mexico on January 19, 1917, instructing him to persuade the Mexican government to enter the war on the German side if the United States went to war against Germany. With the bulk of the American army employed in Europe, Mexico would have a golden opportunity to reconquer Texas, New Mexico, and Arizona. The German representative was to suggest to the president of Mexico that he should invite Japan to adhere to the German-Mexican alliance. This telegram was intercepted by the British, who lost no time in passing it on to the Americans and releasing it to the press.

The Zimmermann telegram was simply one more log cast on the bonfire already blazing as a result of the submarine campaign, and another example of the Germans' incredible lack of realism and their failure to appreciate the effect of their actions on other countries. By resuming unrestricted submarine warfare, they had in effect thrown down the gauntlet to the United States, and Wilson responded accordingly. On April 2, 1917, he asked the American Congress for a declaration of war. "Our object is to vindicate the principles of peace and justice in the life of the world against selfish, autocratic power, and to set up amongst really free and self-governed peoples of the world such a concept of purpose and action as will henceforth ensure the observance of these principles." On April 6, the United States declared war on Germany and by the summer of 1918, far earlier than the Germans had anticipated, American soldiers were already playing a substantial role in stemming the final German offensive. Meanwhile, another calculation of German military and naval experts had gone awry. They had predicted that within six months after launching unrestricted submarine warfare, Britain would be obliged to sue for peace. After six months, however, the British did not sue for peace but were, on the contrary, more determined than ever to fight the war to a victorious conclusion.

❑ Wilson's Fourteen Points

Well before America's entry into the war, Wilson's efforts to bring about a negotiated peace and his idealistic pronouncements had evoked a warm response from the war-weary peoples of Europe and from those proponents of compromise and moderation who had been thrust aside in their respective countries by advocates of all-out victory. But Wilson was not the only statesman addressing European idealists and lovers of peace. In Russia, the Bolsheviks had long been demanding an immediate end to the war. On November 8, 1917, the day after the Bolshevik seizure of power, Lenin had issued his Declaration of Peace calling for an immediate peace without annexations or indemnities and for a revolution of the working classes against the governments of all the belligerent powers. (See p. 26.)

To counteract the Bolsheviks' call to revolution and their condemnation of the Allies' imperialist war aims (supported by their publication of the Allies' wartime secret treaties), Wilson presented the world with a new formulation of Allied objectives. In a speech before a joint session of Congress on January 8, 1918, he set forth his famous Fourteen Points. Wilson's speech was intended to serve notice that his government would not condone the imperialist peace envisaged by the Allies in their wartime treaties. It was also addressed (as Lenin's Declaration of Peace had been) to the peoples of the belligerent countries to secure their support against their governments if such support should be necessary. But above all it was addressed to the government and people of Russia.

At the very beginning of his Fourteen Points speech, Wilson mentioned the negotiations now going on at Brest-Litovsk and praised the principles expressed by the Bolshevik representatives, in particular their insistence, "very justly, very wisely, and in the true spirit of modern democracy," that their negotiations should be held in the open with the whole world as audience. The Russian people were now calling for definitions of principles on the part of the Western Allies in a voice "more thrilling and more compelling than any of the many moving voices with which the troubled air of the world is filled." They now seemed to be prostrate "before the grim power of Germany, which has hitherto known no relenting and no pity." Yet the Russians' soul was not subservient, they would not yield in principle or in action. Speaking of the Bolshevik negotiators at Brest-Litovsk, Wilson said: "Their conception of what is right, of what is humane and honorable for them to accept, has been stated with a frankness, a largeness of view, a generosity of spirit, and a universal human sympathy which must challenge the admiration of every friend of mankind." They had called upon the West to state its desires and in what, if anything, Western purposes differed from their own, and he believed the people of the United States would wish him to respond with utter simplicity and frankness. Wilson proceeded to do so. "Whether their present leaders believe it or not, it is our heartfelt desire and hope that some way may be opened whereby we may be privileged to assist the people of Russia to attain their utmost hope of liberty and ordered peace."

In the Fourteen Points themselves, Wilson began with a demand identical to that of Lenin in calling for the abolition of secret diplomacy and secret treaties and for "open covenants of peace, openly arrived at." Wilson went on to enunciate principles of his own, the most important of them hedged with critical reservations. In Point Two he called for absolute freedom of navigation upon the seas alike in peace and war, a principle especially dear to Americans and a major concern in the present conflict. To justify the British blockade, however, he was obliged to add "except as the seas may be closed in whole or in part by international action for the enforcement of international covenants." He advocated the removal of all economic barriers to international trade, but only "as far as possible"; the reduction of armaments "to the lowest point consistent with public safety"; the impartial adjustment of colonial claims "with the interests of the subject populations receiving *equal* [emphasis added] consideration with the governments seeking title."

Wilson's sixth point, and one of the most important in terms of diplomacy as well as propaganda, was a brief (and remarkably cumbersome) restatement of his appeal to the government and people of Russia, which included a plea to all other governments to receive Bolshevik Russia into the world community of nations. "The treatment accorded Russia by her sister nations in the months to come will be the acid test of their good will, of their comprehension of her needs as distinguished from their own interests, and of their intelligent and unselfish sympathy."

In Western Europe, Wilson called for the evacuation and restoration of Belgium and the invaded territories of France, and asked that "the wrong done to France by Prussia in 1871 in the matter of Alsace-Lorraine . . . should be righted." Italy's frontiers were to be readjusted along clearly recognizable lines of nationality. The principle of self-determination was also to be the basis of a new order in Eastern Europe and the Middle East, with provisions made for the autonomous development of the peoples of Austria-Hungary and the Ottoman empire. Serbia, Montenegro, and Romania were to be evacuated and restored, with Serbia accorded free access to the sea. The Turkish Straits were to be opened permanently to trade. An independent Polish state, including all territory indisputably inhabited by a Polish population, was to be established and guaranteed free and secure access to the sea. Finally, in Point Fourteen, Wilson called for the establishment of a general association of nations "for the purpose of affording mutual guarantees of political independence and territorial integrity to great and small nations alike."

With few exceptions, the Fourteen Points were remarkably vague and subject to wide differences of interpretations. Clemenceau scoffed that Wilson had put forth fourteen points, whereas the good Lord himself had been satisfied with only ten. The very vagueness of the Fourteen Points, however, contributed to their propaganda value, for by admitting broad differences of interpretation, they could mean all things to all people.

❑ Germany's Defeat

In the spring of 1918, with the failure of Germany's submarine campaign and the entry of the United States into the war, the German high command launched yet another offensive on the western front in the hope of effecting a decisive breakthrough before American military power could be brought to bear in Europe. The German offensive was surprisingly effective, but their cause was doomed. On August 8, 1918, the Allied armies, heavily reinforced by the Americans and supported by a large contingent of tanks, mounted a massive counteroffensive. For the first time in the war German troops recoiled, demoralized and in disorder, although they eventually succeeded in retiring to new defensive positions which they were able to hold until the end of the war.

Even the most optimistic German military leaders now realized that a final German victory was impossible. Germany's only hope lay in holding out on the western front and securing a compromise peace through the mediation of Woodrow Wilson, who had so often proclaimed his desire for a conciliatory settlement. The Germans were given little time to explore the possibilities of negotiation, however, for now the eastern front had begun to crack. In September 1918 the large Allied army which had been assembled at Salonika finally went into action against Bulgaria. By September 29 the Bulgarians asked for an armistice, thereby leaving the Balkans open to Allied invasion. At this point Ludendorff lost his nerve. After having rejected all appeals for a compromise peace and having denounced advocates of negotiation and compromise as defeatists and traitors, he now demanded that the German government arrange an immediate armistice.

On October 4, 1918, in response to Ludendorff's plea, the last in a succession of imperial chancellors, Prince Max von Baden, appealed to Wilson for an armistice based on the Fourteen Points. On November 5 the American government informed

elucidation

the Germans that Wilson had obtained the consent of the Allied governments to negotiate on this basis, but to obtain their consent he had agreed to two major reservations: a British demand that the Allies reserve to themselves all future decisions with respect to freedom of the seas, and a French demand for an "elucidation" of the somewhat vague Points Seven and Eight of the Fourteen Points calling for the restoration of Belgian and French territories invaded by the Germans. "The Allied Governments feel that no doubt ought to exist as to what this provision implies," the French amendment stated. "By it they understand that compensation will be made by Germany for all damage done to the civilian populations of the Allies and their property by the aggression of Germany by land, by sea and from the air." This "elucidation" was to be the basis for the Allies' subsequent demand for reparations, one of the most controversial items in the final peace treaty.

The most immediately significant addendum to the Fourteen Points was formulated by Wilson himself. He refused to negotiate an armistice with what he called "the military masters and monarchial autocrats" who had hitherto conducted German policy. In a note of October 23 to Prince Max von Baden, he declared: "The Government of the United States cannot deal with any but veritable representatives of the German people who have been assured of genuine constitutional standing as the real rulers of Germany." One may wonder whether Wilson himself was fully aware of the significance of this condition, for in refusing to negotiate with Germany's government of "military masters and monarchial autocrats" he was in effect demanding a German revolution.

Wilson's demand was also a terrible political blunder, as should have been obvious at the time. For it was Germany's military and autocratic government that had taken Germany into the war and lost it, and it was Ludendorff, by now Germany's de facto military dictator, who had demanded an immediate armistice. This military-autocratic government therefore should have been compelled to assume responsibility for the loss of the war, appeal for an armistice, and submit to the Allies' final conditions for peace. Instead, Wilson's demand shifted the terrible moral burden of defeat and submission to Allied conditions from those who should have borne it onto the "veritable representatives of the German people." He thereby created the opportunity for Germany's military masters and autocrats to concoct the myth that the German army (and thus the German military leadership) had not lost the war at all but had been stabbed in the back by a government of civilians who had sold out their country for their own nefarious political purposes. Because Germany had actually defeated Russia and the German army still held lines deep in Belgian and French territory at the time of Germany's surrender, this "stab in the back" thesis was widely accepted by German public opinion. The only stab in the back involved here, however, was the one Wilson unwittingly delivered against the veritable representatives of the German people, who were now obliged to assume the humiliation of surrender and defeat and whose government was thus hopelessly compromised from the start.

On the same day that Germany appealed for an armistice based on the Fourteen Points (October 4, 1918), the Austro-Hungarian government addressed a similar appeal to the American president. The Tenth of Wilson's Fourteen Points—"the peoples of Austria-Hungary, whose place among the nations we wish to see safeguarded and assured, should be accorded the freest opportunity of autonomous development"—was sufficiently ambiguous to allow the rulers of Austria to hope that the autonomous development of their peoples might take place within the old imperial framework. This hope was quickly shattered. Wilson demanded that Austria grant independence to its subject nationalities, which meant nothing less than the breakup of the Habsburg empire. It is not true, as some historians have contended, that that empire had already broken apart when Wilson posed this demand, although as the war dragged on there were increasing signs of disaffection throughout the Habsburg lands, including the German provinces. It was not until October 21, 1918, however, that the Czechs proclaimed their independence, and not until October 29 did a Yugoslav National Council proclaim the independence of the south Slav people within a Southern Slav national state. Moreover, several months were to go by before national governments were actually formed to take over the administration of these new states.

❑ *The Armistice, November 11, 1918*

Following his success in persuading the Allied governments to agree to a peace based on the Fourteen Points (with the significant reservations mentioned above), Wilson left it to the Allied military leaders to work out the actual terms of the armistice. As conceived by Marshal Ferdinand Foch, the French commander-in-chief of the Allied armies, these terms had to be so severe as to make it impossible for the Germans to resume the war if they balked at signing the final Allied peace treaty. In accordance with the Fourteen Points, the German armies were to evacuate all occupied French and Belgian territory as well as Alsace and Lorraine. In addition, German troops were to withdraw from all German territory on the left bank of the Rhine and from a broad zone on the right bank between the Dutch and Swiss frontiers. These Rhineland territories were to be occupied by Allied and American troops, who were to have absolute rights of requisition in these areas and whose costs were to be charged to the German government. This meant that the Germans had to give up all their present defensive positions and that the Allies would be given control of a substantial part of the heartland of Germany's industrial economy and be in a position to take over the entire Rhineland at a moment's notice.

In Eastern Europe, the treaties of Brest-Litovsk and Bucharest were to be annulled, and German troops were to retire behind the boundaries of August 1, 1914, but with the interesting reservation that German troops should only withdraw from Russia's prewar territories "as soon as the Allies shall think the moment suitable, having regard to the internal situation in these territories"—that is, German troops were to remain so long as they were needed to protect these territories from the Bolsheviks.

Germany was to give up the greater part of its heavy artillery, machine guns, mortars, aircraft and all other military equipment, all of its submarines and almost all other naval vessels, and the greater part of its rolling stock (railway engines and carriages). The existing naval blockade set up by the Allies was to remain in place, all German merchant ships found at sea were liable to seizure, and there was to be no transfer of German merchant shipping under a neutral flag. The initial armistice was to run for

36 days and was to be renewed periodically until a final peace treaty had been drawn up and signed.

On October 18, 1918, Foch received the German armistice delegation (headed by a civilian political leader, Matthias Erzberger) in his railway coach in the forest of Compiègne, where he presented them with the Allies' armistice terms.

Upon learning of these conditions, which would end Germany's capacity to wage war and leave the country at the mercy of the Allies, German military leaders once again called for a continuation of the war. But by now the German home front had begun to crumble. The German battle fleet, immobilized throughout the greater part of the war, received orders to undertake a last desperate sortie to challenge the Allies' naval supremacy. Understandably reluctant to go out on so ridiculous a suicide mission, the German sailors at the naval base of Kiel mutinied on October 28, an uprising that set off revolutionary disturbances in many other parts of the country—later cited as evidence supporting the stab in the back theory.

As noted earlier, by stipulating that he would only negotiate an armistice with the "veritable representatives of the German people," Wilson had in effect demanded a German political revolution, and the Germans now duly provided it. On November 9 the imperial chancellor, Prince Max von Baden, announced that the kaiser had abdicated (he had done nothing of the kind, but was subsequently persuaded to flee to Holland; he did not abdicate officially until November 28). Prince Max himself then resigned and turned the government over to the socialists, the majority party in the Reichstag. Later that same day, Philipp Scheidemann, a leader of the Social Democratic party, announced that Germany was now a republic. It was one of history's strangest revolutions.

On November 11, 1918, the Germans submitted to Allied terms and signed the armistice agreement. World War I was over.

FOUR

❑

Peacemaking, 1919

❑ *The Erosion of Idealism*

The Allied armistice with Germany of November 11, 1918, which brought an end to the fighting on the western front, was hailed with hysterical jubilation by the peoples of the victorious powers and by much of the rest of the world. Not only had the war been won, but it seemed to have achieved most of its major objectives, certainly those objectives dearest to the heart of Western idealists. German militarism was crushed, Germany's despotic government had been overthrown. The Habsburg and Ottoman empires, which had held so many nationalities in thrall for so many centuries, had collapsed and from their ruins were emerging independent national states. The autocratic government of Russia, too, had been swept away and replaced by a regime which seemed to promise a better way of life for the Russian people. Idealistic visitors to Russia from the West hailed the Communist regime as a "new civilization," and the famous American journalist and reformer Lincoln Steffens declared after a journey to the Soviet Union that "I have seen the future and it works." With the major autocratic governments of the world eliminated and the major liberal democracies victorious, there was widespread confidence that a new and better world would emerge from the ashes of the old, and that the "war to end all wars" had succeeded in doing just that.

In Germany, too, there was a spirit of restrained optimism. Germany, after all, had agreed to make peace on the basis of Wilson's Fourteen Points. Despite revolutionary turmoil and the efforts of Communist leaders to fulfill Lenin's prediction that a Communist regime would soon be established in Germany, moderate political leaders with the support of the army, police, and other forces of order prevailed. In the period after the armistice, democratic elections were held to select delegates to a constituent assembly which was to draw up a constitution for the new German republic, and on February 8, 1919, these delegates assembled in Weimar, the city of Goethe and Schiller, where they established the framework of what was to be known as the Weimar Republic.

Unfortunately, idealists had failed to take into account the difficulties which all governments would have to face after the war: the transition from war to peacetime economies, the economic dislocations caused by war and revolution, the breakdowns in the production and distribution of basic economic necessities in large parts of Central and Eastern Europe, the problem of dealing with millions of displaced persons, and the human frailties of the leading statesmen involved in the process of peacemaking.

Perhaps worst of all, the war was followed by a rapid erosion of idealism among the peoples of the world and the resurgence of feelings of hatred, revenge, and greed. When Wilson came to Europe in December 1918 he was greeted everywhere by enthusiastic crowds, his path was strewn with flowers, and throughout Western Europe boulevards, squares, and bridges were renamed in his honor. His values and programs for peace seemed to have evoked the latent idealism he believed to be the dominant quality in all people, and succumbing to this apparent adulation, he came to regard himself as the spokesman of the common man and men of goodwill everywhere.

Yet even as he made his triumphal progress through Europe, the common man was rejecting his programs through the democratic institutions he believed in and wished to see extended throughout the world. In the Congressional elections in the United States of November 1918, the supporters of Wilson's program for a just and equitable peace were soundly beaten by candidates who advocated a punitive peace to put an end once and for all to German militarism, which Allied propaganda had so long represented as the sole threat to world peace. With that threat removed, anti-Wilson candidates saw no need for the United States to be involved in entangling alliances, which George Washington had so eloquently advised his fellow-countrymen to avoid, or for joining a League of Nations, which would drag America into every kind of future international dispute.

The November debacle in the United States was followed by the so-called Khaki election in Britain in December 1918, as the British prime minister, David Lloyd George, at the head of a shaky coalition government, tried to exploit Britain's victory in the war to shore up his political position at home. Far more closely attuned to the real feelings of the public than Wilson, Lloyd George conducted a campaign appealing to the renewed spirit of hatred and revenge. Rejecting Wilsonian idealism, he called for a punitive peace, the punishment of German war criminals, and payment by Germany and its allies for the total cost of the war, demands which were converted into the popular slogans of "hang the kaiser" and "squeeze Germany till the pips squeak." In France, Prime Minister Clemenceau had consistently advocated a punitive peace that would eliminate the German menace and guarantee security for France. And Vittorio Orlando, the Italian prime minister, tenaciously demanded all that had been promised to Italy in the wartime Treaty of London, and more, plus a generous share of the war indemnity that would be imposed on the Central Powers.

❏ *The Blockade Problem*

Meanwhile, in Germany and throughout much of Central and Eastern Europe, the suffering endured by the civilian population resulting from the food shortages that had developed in the last years of the war had not been eased by the armistice, because after the signature of that document and throughout the peace negotiations in Paris the Allies had refused to lift their naval blockade around Germany. Instead, the Allies had actually extended the blockade to the Baltic Sea to cut off shipments from Scandinavia. Even the German fishing fleet had been forbidden to put to sea. The primary purpose of maintaining the blockade was to keep pressure on the Germans to ensure their signature of the final peace treaty drawn up by the Allies. Although the Germans signed that treaty on June 28, 1919, the blockade was not finally lifted until after the Reichstag's ratification of that document on July 12.

An international relief effort began to function early in 1919 to relieve starvation in Eastern Europe, but Germany was excluded from this relief program. It was not until mid-March that the French agreed to allow food shipments to Germany in return for the surrender of Germany's merchant fleet and payments in foreign securities, and it was not until the end of March, almost four months after the armistice, that food actually began arriving in Germany. As a result of the blockade and delay in food shipments, the Germans were subjected to more severe food shortages in the winter of 1918-19 than they had experienced in the previous war winters, terrible as those had been. At the same time a particularly severe worldwide influenza epidemic ravaged all of Europe, striking hardest at populations suffering from chronic malnutrition and cold. According to German estimates, approximately one million Germans died of malnutrition and influenza during that first postwar winter.

It would be impossible to exaggerate the German sense of bitterness over the blockade issue, which was second only to the Treaty of Versailles itself in the hierarchy of grievances the Germans leveled against the Allies in the postwar world. An appeal to his colleagues by Lloyd George early in March 1919 to allow shipments of food to the Germans proved to be fatefully prophetic. "The Allies are now on top," the British prime minister said, "but memories of starvation might one day turn against them. The Germans were being allowed to starve whilst at the same time hundreds of thousands of tons of food were lying at Rotterdam. . . . The Allies were sowing hatred for the future: they were piling up agony, not for the Germans, but for themselves."

❏ *The Paris Peace Conference*

The peace conference which was to work out terms for a final settlement to end World War I formally opened in Paris on January 18, 1919, a date deliberately chosen by the French because it was on this day that the German empire had been proclaimed in the Hall of Mirrors of the palace at Versailles in 1871. In his opening address to the conference Raymond Poincaré, president of the French republic, took note of this fact and that the German empire, "born in injustice" had now "ended in opprobrium."

Assembled were seventy delegates representing twenty seven of the allied states that had won the war, all of them accompanied by a large staff of experts. No delegates from the defeated countries or from the Bolshevik government of Russia were invited to attend. The fact that Paris was selected as the site of the conference proved to be significant, because throughout their deliberations the delegates were enveloped in the atmosphere of hatred for Germany that inflamed the population of the French capital.

In the beginning the great powers at Paris attempted to guide the deliberations of the conference through a Council of Ten consisting of two representatives from each of the five major powers—Britain, France, Italy, the United States, and Japan. The Japanese, however, only participated actively in dealing with matters affecting East Asia and the League of Nations, and the leaders of the other powers soon decided they could negotiate more efficiently without a second representative. So the Council of Ten in effect became a Council of Four—Clemenceau, Lloyd George, Orlando (the Italian prime minister), and Wilson. In late April 1919, when Orlando found that he was not going to be conceded the full extent of all Italian claims, he left the conference in protest and the guiding body at Paris was reduced to a Council of Three.

Despite the first principle enunciated in Wilson's Fourteen Points about the desirability of open covenants openly arrived at, the Big Three in Paris behaved very much like the traditional diplomats Wilson at least professed to despise. Their negotiations were conducted in secret, and they reserved to themselves the right to make all major decisions. In 1919, however, in contrast to the pan-European peace conference following the Napoleonic wars in 1814–1815, there was no Talleyrand—indeed there was no one—to speak for the defeated powers or for the Russians. And among the Big Three, remarkable as each of them was in their very different ways, there was no one who combined the breadth of vision, sense of perspective, restraint, and diplomatic skill of a Castlereagh or a Metternich.

❑ The Peacemakers of 1919: Clemenceau, Lloyd George, and Wilson

Clemenceau

It was said of Clemenceau, the French prime minister and head of his country's delegation at the peace conference, that he had one great illusion, France, and one great disillusion, mankind. Clemenceau's admiration for the glories of French civilization can hardly be called an illusion, however, and his cynicism about mankind was tempered by a passionate love of the arts. He was the friend and patron of Fauré and Debussy, and an enthusiastic champion of French impressionist painting. While other critics were still reviling the impressionists as incompetent botchers, he saw in their works fresh manifestations of the French genius.

In the tradition of three generations of his family, Clemenceau was trained as a medical doctor, but instead of practicing medicine he went to the United States in the turbulent era after the Civil War. Here he remained for four years, married the orphaned ward of a Protestant minister who bore him two daughters and a son. The marriage, evidently a disaster from the start, ended in separation after seven years.

Clemenceau returned to France in time to experience the humiliation of his country's defeat at the hands of Prussia in 1871, a catastrophe that instilled in him a passionate and life-long hatred for Germany and Germans. At the end of the war with Prussia, he entered politics and quickly established himself as a leader of the radical Left. An eloquent speaker, a master of sarcasm and invective, he earned the nickname of the Tiger for the unrelenting savagery of his attacks on his opponents. Political and social radical though he might be, Clemenceau's overriding concern throughout his long and checkered political career was the welfare and security of France. In 1917 Clemenceau took over the leadership of France during some of the darkest days of the war, and it was he who ultimately led his country to victory.

At the Paris conference, the very quality that made Clemenceau a great wartime leader—his single-minded devotion to France—proved to be a shortcoming when it came to considering the problems of Europe and the world as a whole. In his loathing for the Germans, he failed to appreciate that the future political stability and economic recovery of Europe required the reintegration of this populous and economically productive people into the European political and economic system. And in his obsessive concern for France, he failed to pay sufficient regard to the revolutionary developments in Eastern Europe, the ambitions of Japan in East Asia, or the problems arising from the dissolution of the Habsburg and Ottoman empires.

Lloyd George

Lloyd George was the counterpart of Clemenceau as the wartime leader who had thrust aside the advocates of a negotiated peace and rallied his country to an all-out victory. Like Clemenceau he was a staunch defender and promoter of his country's interests as he understood them. And, again like Clemenceau, he was a champion of political and social reform. Before the war he enjoyed his finest political hour as chancellor of the exchequer when in 1909 he brought in his so-called People's Budget, which aimed at shifting a far larger share of the tax burden onto the shoulders of the rich through income and inheritance taxes. With the veto of that budget by the House of Lords, Lloyd George played a leading role in the parliamentary battle that virtually eliminated that body's political power.

Besides sharing Clemenceau's patriotism and political radicalism, Lloyd George possessed a similar physical energy, ambition, love of power, and political ruthlessness that seem to be indispensable qualities for political success in a modern democracy. But in contrast to Clemenceau's brutally direct political style, Lloyd George was mercurial. Vivacious, amiable, witty, with a quick and incisive mind, he had an uncanny instinct for sensing the mood of a given political situation and a willingness to adjust his policies accordingly.

Yet it would be unfair to describe Lloyd George, as some critics have done, as little more than a masterful opportunist whose guiding principle was political expediency. His battles on behalf of political and social reform may have benefitted his political career, but they were fought on the basis of his belief in the principle of social justice. It would be more charitable as well as accurate to say that Lloyd George, in his frank disavowal of consistency, was more honest than most of his political counterparts in acknowledging that politics is the art of the possible, that policies have to be adjusted to achieve the possible, and that rigid adherence to principle may destroy the chance of accomplishing anything.

Wilson

Whereas Lloyd George has been criticized for his lack of principles, Woodrow Wilson has been seen as being rather too generously supplied with them. He was born in Virginia, the son of a Presbyterian minister, whose religious faith was to be the dominant ideological influence throughout his life, the moral foundation of his political thinking, beliefs, and values. His religion was also a principal source of his formidable moral strength, for Wilson never doubted that God controlled history and used men and nations in the unfolding of His plan according to His purposes.

After a brief stint as a lawyer, Wilson earned a doctorate in history and government, subjects he subsequently taught at Princeton before becoming president of that university in 1902. In 1910 he made a successful run for the governorship of New Jersey, and a bare two years later, as the candidate of the Democratic party, he was elected president of the United States, the beneficiary of a split in the Republican party between the supporters of William Howard Taft and Theodore Roosevelt.

Wilson's biographer Arthur Link notes that few men have come to the White House with a better knowledge of American politics and government. With the outbreak of World War I, however, much of Wilson's attention had to be devoted to foreign affairs, and here he was deficient both in knowledge and experience. He knew no modern foreign languages and, although trained as a historian, his ignorance of the history and civilization of the world beyond the frontiers of his own country was astonishing.

Perhaps it was his very ignorance of the complexities of international affairs that gave Wilson the confidence to assume primary and quasi-exclusive responsibility for the conduct of American foreign policy. As described by Professor Link, he took complete control of problems he considered critically important, by-passed the State Department, negotiated behind the backs of his secretaries of state, and "acted like a divine-right monarch in the general conduct of affairs." Link believes that two other aspects of his personality were to influence his conduct of foreign policy: his egotism, manifested in his conviction that he was an instrument of divine purpose, and his driving ambition, "fixed as much by a longing for personal distinction as by a desire to serve God and mankind."

Egotist though he might be, Wilson was willing to share the honor of being an instrument of the divine purpose with the American people, who, he said, had done more than all others to advance the cause of human welfare. Uniquely superior morally and spiritually, Americans were "custodians of the spirit of righteousness, of the spirit of equal-handed justice, of the spirit of hope which believes in the perfectibility of law and the perfectibility of human life itself."

It was with these views about his own and America's mission that Wilson arrived at the peace conference in Paris, preceded by his Fourteen Points, to which he had since added Four Principles, four additional points, and Five Particulars. One hesitates to imagine the reaction to Wilson's conception of America on the part of Clemenceau, who had seen something of American righteousness and even-handed justice while lynchings were taking place in Wilson's native Virginia and the politics of New York City were being conducted from Tammany Hall. In an effort to find a polite formula to describe Wilson's idealism, Clemenceau could do no better than speak of the president's *"noble candeur"* (naiveté, ingenuousness), which the official record tactfully changed to *"noble grandeur."*

Wilson's most bitter critics, however, were those who shared his ideals and had expected him to provide the leadership for the creation of a better world. Among the disillusioned was the distinguished economist John Maynard Keynes, a representative of the British treasury at the peace conference. "It was commonly believed at the commencement of the Paris Conference," he wrote, "that the President had thought out, with the aid of a large body of advisers, a comprehensive scheme not only for the League of Nations but for the embodiment of the Fourteen Points in an actual Treaty of Peace. But in fact the President had thought out nothing; when it came to practice, his ideas were nebulous and incomplete. He had no plan, no scheme, no constructive ideas whatever for clothing with the flesh of life the commandments which he had thundered from the White House." The kindest thing Keynes had to say about Wilson was that he was a "generously intentioned man," but otherwise he found him ill-informed, mentally slow, unadaptable, and totally insensitive to his surroundings—"a blind and deaf Don Quixote." His thought and temperament were essentially theological, not those of a student or scholar, and Keynes missed in him the cosmopolitan culture "that marked Clemenceau or Balfour [the British foreign secretary] as exquisitely cultivated men of their class and generation." Nor did Wilson make any consistent effort to fill in the gaps in his own knowledge by drawing on the collective wisdom of the large body of experts who had accompanied him to Paris.

On this point Keynes' evidence is misleading. Wilson in fact relied heavily on experts for matters of detail, but his exclusive assumption of the direction of the American side of the negotiations at Paris was to make for a far more dangerous situation than Keynes realized. The treaty Wilson was negotiating depended for its ratification on a two-thirds majority in the Senate, which was now controlled by the Republicans, many of them severely critical of Wilson's peace program. Yet Wilson had not seen fit to bring a single major Republican political figure with him to Paris, nor did he bother to consult regularly with Senate leaders about the course of his negotiations. In the end this incredible negligence and Wilson's subsequent refusal to modify the final treaty to meet the objections of its critics was to doom his treaty in the Senate, and therewith also America's participation in the League of Nations and the entire postwar treaty system.

❑ *The League of Nations*

In the last of his Fourteen Points, Wilson had called for "a general association of nations . . . formed under specific covenants for the purpose of affording mutual guarantees of political independence and territorial integrity to great and small states alike." On January 25, 1919, the delegates at the peace conference unanimously adopted a resolution for the creation of a League of Nations and proceeded to appoint a commission, with Wilson as its chairman, to draft a covenant for the League and define its functions.

As established by the covenant, the League was to consist initially of all states represented at the peace conference, but provision was made for the subsequent admission of other states upon the approval of two-thirds of the existing membership. All member states were to be represented in a General Assembly with one vote each, but the great powers ensured their control of League affairs by setting up a Council consisting of representatives of the five great powers (Britain, France, Italy, Japan, and the United States), and of the representatives of four other states to be chosen periodically by the Assembly. A permanent Secretariat located in Geneva was to serve as the League's bureaucracy. Member states were to afford each other mutual protection against aggression, meaning that the League would in effect be a large-scale defensive alliance.

To give the League power to curb arbitrary actions on the part of its members, Article 16 of the covenant provided that any nation resorting to war in defiance of the League "shall ipso facto be deemed to have committed an act of war against all other members of the League." An economic boycott was to be imposed immediately on the offending state, and the Council of the League was to decide on military action to be taken against that state.

The covenant also contained provisions for the peaceful alteration of the status quo. "The Assembly may from time to time advise the reconsideration by members of the League of treaties which have become inapplicable and the consideration of international conditions whose continuance might endanger the peace of the world."

Besides its functions as a defensive alliance and arbiter of international disputes, the League was to devote itself to problems of international disarmament, health, labor, and similar matters of international concern, and permanent bureaucracies such as the International Labor Organization and the International Health Organization were set up to deal with these problems.

❑ *The Fate of the Fourteen Points: Colonies, Shantung, and Racial Equality*

Apart from the League of Nations, Wilson's Fourteen Points fared badly at the peace conference. As noted earlier, the leaders of the great powers, including Wilson himself, did not even make a pretense of negotiating on the basis of his first point, which called for "open covenants of peace, openly arrived at." Point Two, dealing with freedom of the seas, had been set aside in the prearmistice agreement with Britain, and there was little meaningful support for Points Three and Four on the removal of international economic barriers and the reduction of armaments except for those of the enemy. Point Six had stated that the treatment of Russia would be the acid test of the goodwill, intelligence, and unselfish sympathy of her sister nations, but Russia had not been invited to send representatives to the Paris conference, German troops had been left on Russian soil to deal with the "internal situation" (i.e., the threat of Bolshevism), and the Allies had already begun to send their own troops into the country—the start of the long and confusing Allied intervention in the Russian civil war.

Point Five, calling for "a free, open-minded, and absolutely impartial adjustment of colonial claims," was given similar cavalier treatment. This adjustment was to be based on a strict observance of the principle that the interests of the populations concerned must have equal weight with that of the governments seeking title. But the Allies took it almost entirely upon themselves to determine the interest of the populations concerned and parcelled out all of Germany's former colonies among Belgium, Britain and its dominions (Australia, New Zealand, and South Africa), France, and Japan. To cover up this violation of Point Five, the conference declared that the assignment of most of these territories to the victor powers was to be temporary only and that they were to be held as mandates under the League of Nations.

The Allied distribution of their pounds of colonial flesh, which violated not only Point Five but the principle of self-determination, was not achieved without serious differences among the various claimants. One of the most awkward of these proved to be Japan's claim to the rights Germany had extorted from China in 1898 in China's Shantung Peninsula, which the Japanese had conquered in the first weeks of the war together with the German-held islands in the Pacific north of the equator. The Japanese claim to these territories was subsequently confirmed in treaties with the major Allied powers (Britain, France, and Italy) and with the government of China itself, at that time so weak and divided as to be unable to resist Japanese pressure. At the Paris conference, however, the Chinese representatives argued that China's entry into the war against Germany in 1917 had canceled out all Chinese treaty commitments to Japan and that the Japanese occupation of Shantung violated Chinese sovereignty as well as the principle of self-determination. So effectively did the Chinese present their case that they brought about a de facto stalemate over the Shantung question.

The next Japanese initiative presented the peace conference with an even more perplexing moral dilemma. They asked that the League covenant dealing with religious equality be amended to include a clause recognizing the principle of racial equality and guaranteeing alien nationals residing in the League's member states "equal and just treatment in every respect, making no distinction, either in law or fact, on account of their race or nationality." This Japanese proposal met with fierce opposition from Prime Minister William Hughes of Australia, who spared his British and American colleagues the need to take an immediate stand of their own on this thorny issue. The objections to a racial equality statement have been criticized as outright racism, but the Japanese amendment also raised legitimate legal concerns. It would have permitted—even required—League interference in the domestic affairs of its member states and, among other things, would have put an end to their right to restrict foreign immigration.

The Japanese were willing to change the wording of the clause, asking only that the covenant endorse of the principle of equality of *nations* and the just treatment of their *nationals*, therewith omitting the inflammatory term *race* altogether. But again the objection was raised that such a formula would encroach on the host country's sovereignty. The Japanese thereupon demanded that the issue be submitted to a vote by members of the League Commission. Of the seventeen members of the commission, eleven voted for the Japanese amendment, but Wilson, as chairman, ruled against its adoption on the grounds that decisions on questions of principle required a unanimous vote. Quite apart from Wilson's own ambivalent feelings about the racial question, he could hardly have acted otherwise, for the passions aroused by this issue threatened to undermine the entire peacemaking process.

Denied their racial/national equality amendment, the Japanese demanded an immediate and definite settlement of the Shantung question, threatening to walk out of the conference if their demands on this question were denied. Once again Wilson bowed to political expediency. The Japanese were duly granted former German rights to Shantung, with face-saving reservations that these rights were to be restored to China at some unspecified date. This face-saving failed to mollify the Chinese, who left the peace conference and subsequently refused to sign the Treaty of Versailles.

❑ *The South Tyrol and Fiume*

The Fourteen Points had called for a readjustment of Italy's frontiers "along clearly recognizable lines of nationality," the restoration of a Polish state "which should include the territories inhabited by indisputably Polish populations," and for the freest opportunity for autonomous development for the peoples of the Austro-Hungarian and Ottoman empires.

These were noble goals if one accepts the relatively modern belief that nationality is the sole legitimate basis of a state and thus the principal criterion for determining its territorial configuration. The great difficulty here is that there are few areas of the world inhabited by a single, well-defined ethnic group. On the contrary, in most parts of the world nationalities have been jumbled together over the centuries as a result of wars and migrations into a confused and disorderly multinational mosaic. But even states with a relatively large and cohesive ethnic population are generally faced with a mixture of nationalities along their frontiers.

Italy is a case in point. In the Treaty of London of April 26, 1915, which had brought Italy into the war, the Italians had been promised all they had claimed on the grounds of nationality—and a great deal more: the entire South Tyrol to the Brenner Pass, a large part of the Dalmatian coast, as well as territorial compensation in the Middle East and Africa. In Europe, these promises to Italy involved two violations of the nationality principle. A quarter million German-speaking Austrians (and only ten thousand Italians) lived in the northern part of the South Tyrol, and the population of Dalmatia was predominantly Slavic. Wilson, however, agreed to Italy's claim to the entire South Tyrol, presumably because the Italians had convinced him that the Brenner frontier was a strategic necessity, and he chose to ignore (or was not aware of) the ethnic problem involved. Harold Nicolson, a member of the British team of experts in Paris and heretofore an enthusiastic Wilsonian, had written that the moral effect of this violation of the nationality principle could hardly be exaggerated. "If Wilson could swallow the Brenner, he would swallow anything."

But not everything. Informed by his advisers that the Dalmatian people were predominantly Slavic, Wilson rejected the Italian claims to Dalmatia, promised them in the London treaty, and their additional claim, on ethnic grounds, to the Dalmatian port city of Fiume (Rijeka in Serbo-Croatian, population, 49,000). The Italian people responded with massive public demonstrations, and to protest Wilson's decision on Fiume the Italian delegates walked out of the peace conference. It was a futile gesture, and the Italians returned a few days later. But the stalemate over Fiume continued and was not resolved until after the adjournment of the peace conference, and then only temporarily.

Insignificant as the Fiume question seems in retrospect, it virtually dominated the peace conference in the spring of 1919, and it remained critically significant because Fiume became a symbol and focal point of Italian nationalist frustrations. In the belief that they had somehow been cheated and betrayed by their allies in Paris, Italian patriots now looked increasingly to nationalist demagogues who promised future glories to justify their wartime sacrifices. It was on the tide of this nationalist fervor that Benito Mussolini came to power in 1922.

❑ *The German Problem*

Far more difficult than fixing the frontiers of Italy, which was done entirely at the expense of the former Austro-Hungarian empire, was the establishment of the future frontiers of Germany. Having suffered two German invasions during the past fifty years and being fearfully aware of Germany's larger population and greater economic resources, the French were determined to impose peace terms on Germany that would eliminate for all time the German threat to French security.

The French had already taken important steps in that direction through the Allied armistice agreement with Germany. Germany was disarmed, deprived of its naval and air power. The French were assured of the recovery of Alsace and Lorraine, and Allied troops were to occupy the Rhineland at Germany's expense. In Eastern Europe, in accordance with the Fourteen Points, Germany was to be stripped of territory for the purpose of reestablishing an independent Polish state with a corridor giving Poland access to the sea. The French had also secured what they hoped might be a stranglehold over the German economy when Wilson agreed to their demand that Germany pay compensation for all damages to the Allies' civilian populations by land, sea, and air.

But the French thought they needed a great deal more. They wanted to annex the coal-rich Saar Valley, despite its predominantly German population, as compensation for the German destruction of French coal fields. In the Rhineland, they wanted the establishment of one or more independent republics linked to France through a customs union, their independence guaranteed through "permanent [Allied] military surveillance the length of the Rhine." In Eastern Europe, they wanted to make Poland as large as possible at Germany's expense and to make East Prussia independent. Finally, on the question of reparations, many French leaders were no longer satisfied that Germany pay compensation for damage to the Allies' civilian populations; they wanted Germany to pay for the entire cost of the war.

In a memorandum of March 25, 1919, Lloyd George appealed to the French for moderation in the interest of establishing a lasting peace and preventing the spread of Bolshevism, which had now triumphed in Hungary as well as Russia and threatened to engulf all of Eastern and Central Europe. If the French persisted in their demands over the Rhineland, the Saar, and Poland, Germany too might well "throw in her lot with Bolshevism, and place her resources, her brains, and her vast organizing power at the disposal of the revolutionary fanatics whose dream is to conquer the world for Bolshevism by force of arms."

Clemenceau was not impressed by the British prime minister's specter of the Bolshevik bogey, which he believed the Germans were deliberately inflating to escape punitive peace terms. In his reply to Lloyd George, he restated the French case with regard to the German boundaries. If the British leader were really anxious to build up barriers against Bolshevism, Clemenceau argued, he should give Poland and Czechoslovakia, as well as France itself, hard and fast military guarantees. Otherwise the new states in the east might indeed fall prey to Bolshevism, and the only existing barriers between Germany and Bolshevik Russia would be removed.

Because the reestablishment of a Polish state with access to the sea had been among Wilson's Fourteen Points, Clemenceau had little trouble securing agreement to a large proportion of Polish territorial claims, but elsewhere he was blocked by the principle of self-determination. After long and bitter argument, Clemenceau at last agreed to drop French demands for the Saar and a separate Rhineland in return for the promise of an Anglo-American guarantee of military support for France in the event of an unprovoked German attack. In making his concessions, however, he insisted on conditions that would leave open the possibility for France to gain its territorial objectives in the future. The Allies were to occupy the Rhineland and the Saar for fifteen years, with the significant qualification that this occupation might be extended if Germany failed to fulfill its treaty obligations. This meant that the future control of the Rhineland would require imposing treaty obligations on Germany that could not be fulfilled in the foreseeable future, if ever. Here the issue of reparations assumed decisive importance.

The reparations question was to make for some of the most complex problems of the postwar world, but the fundamental French purpose was eminently simple: France wanted reparations payments for their own sake, of course, as compensation for its wartime losses and to revive its own economy. But far more important, France wanted to use reparations as a political and economic weapon that would not only cripple the German economy but allow for Allied intervention in German domestic affairs in the event of nonpayment.

During Lloyd George's Khaki election campaign, the British electorate had given vociferous support to Clemenceau's demand that Germany pay for the total cost of the war, for Britain had suffered relatively little damage to its civilian population, and payment for total war costs would give Britain a substantially larger share of German reparations payments. Yielding to the objections of his economic advisers, Lloyd George did not support Clemenceau on this issue. He nevertheless made a bid for a greater share of reparations for Britain by proposing that pensions and separations allowance be included in the category of civilian damages. This proposal was enthusiastically endorsed by the French, who favored anything that would increase Germany's reparations burden. Strangely enough, it was also endorsed by Wilson despite the arguments of his legal advisers that the inclusion of pensions was contrary to all logic. Wilson is reported to have brushed aside this objection with some annoyance. "Logic! Logic! I don't give a damn for logic. I am going to include pensions." Pensions were therefore duly included.

In the end, however, a final settlement over reparations was postponed. Unable to agree on a reparations total that would satisfy public opinion in their respective countries and fearful of naming a sum that might provoke a genuine revolution in Germany, the Allies evaded a final decision on reparations. Instead, they turned the problem over to an Allied reparations commission, which was instructed to compute the reparations bill and to enforce its total payment without reference to a definite time limit. To allow for an even greater reparations total, the French left open the possibility of future German reparations to Russia, which was conceded the right to obtain restitution and reparations from Germany if at any time the Russian government should wish to avail itself of that privilege.

☐ *The Presentation of the Peace Terms*

On May 7, 1919, the final Allied draft of the peace treaty with Germany was presented to the German delegation at the Trianon Palace in Versailles. In handing over the treaty to the Germans, Clemenceau, the president of the conference (who addressed the representatives of the new German republic as plenipotentiaries of the German empire), spoke briefly and bitterly of the merciless war the Germans had imposed on the Allied and associated powers. "The time has now come for a heavy reckoning of accounts."

In making his formal reply to Clemenceau, Count Ulrich von Brockdorff-Rantzau, the German foreign minister and chief of the German delegation, shocked the conference by his tactlessness in remaining seated and by his scathing repudiation of the charge that Germany bore sole responsibility for the war and war crimes. In an emotionally charged bid to capture the moral initiative, he dilated on the Allies' refusal to lift their naval blockade after the armistice. "Crimes in time of war may be unpardonable," he said, "but they are committed in the heat of the conflict. The hundreds of thousands of non-combatants who have died of the blockade since the 11th of November were killed in cold blood after victory had been won. Think of that when you speak of crime and punishment." Brockdorff-Rantzau assured the conference that the Germans were well aware of the extent of their defeat and the hatred of their enemies, but, though impotent militarily, they were not defenseless for the Allies were bound to honor the principles which they themselves had put forward and accepted as the basis for peace. "The principles of President Wilson are binding on you as well as on us," he said, and he warned his listeners that a peace which could not be defended before the world as a just peace would not endure but would on the contrary perpetually stir up resistance against it.

Wilson was not edified by this German appeal to his own principles, and he was appalled by what he termed Brockdorff-Rantzau's "abominable manners." "The Germans are really a stupid people. They always do the wrong thing. . . . This is the most tactless speech I have ever heard. It will set the whole world against them." Wilson contended that the Germans—not just the ruling class, but the entire nation—deserved the peace they had been given. "I think it is profitable that a nation should learn once and for all what an unjust war means," he said.

The Germans received the Allied peace terms with amazement and consternation. For, apart from the League of Nations, which they perceived as little more than a disguised anti-German alliance, they saw little resemblance between the Allied terms and the Fourteen Points, which, according to their prearmistice agreement with the Allies and the United States, were to have been the basis of a final peace treaty. Further, in notable contrast to the treatment of France in 1814, the Germans had been denied the right to be represented or to plead their own cause at the peace conference. The only concession the Allies made on this score was to give the Germans fifteen days to submit their "observations" in writing on the terms of the treaty.

In response to the Germans' long and detailed observations, the Allies agreed to hold plebiscites in disputed areas assigned to Poland. Otherwise the Germans argued and pleaded in vain.

In late June the Allies resolved to put an end to German procrastinations and complaints and presented them with an ultimatum: sign, or the war would be resumed and Germany would be invaded by Allied troops. The socialist chancellor of the new German Republic, Philipp Scheidemann, resigned rather than sign the treaty, as did Foreign Minister Brockdorff-Rantzau, but a new German cabinet recognized that it had no choice but to submit. It announced that it was doing so under protest, however, and that its signature of the treaty did not mean that it was abandoning its condemnation of the "unheard-of injustice of the conditions of peace."

On June 28, 1919, the German delegates, all of them civilians, were conducted into the Hall of Mirrors in Louis XIV's palace at Versailles, where the German empire had been proclaimed in 1871 and where the defeat and collapse of that empire was now endorsed. After the signature ceremony Clemenceau announced tersely: "*La séance est levée*," and with that the Germans were led out "like prisoners from the dock," as one observer described the scene. Wilson's aide, Colonel House, expressed dismay at the total lack of chivalry on the part of the Allies. He believed the entire affair had been elaborately staged to make it as deliberately humiliating to the enemy as possible, and compared the signature ceremony to the ancient custom of dragging a defeated enemy behind the chariot of the victor.

FIVE

❑

The Peace Treaties

❑ *Peace with Germany: The Treaty of Versailles*

The Treaty of Versailles embodied the terms of the armistice agreement with Germany and the conditions worked out by the Allied negotiators at the Paris Peace Conference. By the standards of the nineteenth century, the terms of the treaty were harsh, though, as we know now from captured German documents, they were far less harsh than the terms the Germans would have imposed on their adversaries had they won the same clear-cut victory. They were also far less harsh than many Allied leaders and public opinion had desired and expected.

Alsace and Lorraine were to be returned to France, Belgium was to be restored as an independent state and given the tiny former German frontier territories of Eupen, Malmédy, and Moresnet. The French were to be given economic control of the coal-rich Saar Valley. The Saar, however, was not to be annexed outright to France but placed under the administration of the League. After fifteen years the inhabitants were to be allowed to decide by plebiscite whether they wished to remain under the League, be incorporated into France, or return to Germany. Allied forces were to occupy German territory on the left bank of the Rhine, the cost of the occupation to be paid by Germany. These forces were to be withdrawn in stages at the end of five, ten, and fifteen years—but with the significant qualification that this withdrawal was to take place only if Germany lived up to the terms of the treaty. To eliminate any advantage the Germans had had in the past for invading France and ensure that any future war between Germany and France would be fought on German soil, the treaty stipulated that all German territory on the left bank of the Rhine and all territory on the right bank to a depth of fifty kilometers be permanently demilitarized—a provision that gave the Allies their most potent weapon for enforcing the treaty, for it left Germany's industrial heartland open to Allied invasion and occupation.

In the north the principle of self-determination was to be served by holding plebiscites in Schleswig (as the Germans had promised but failed to do in 1866) to determine how much of that province should be turned over to Denmark. These resulted in the incorporation of northern Schleswig into Denmark in July 1920.

MAP 2   GERMANY AFTER THE TREATY OF VERSAILLES

Legend:
- Territory lost without plebiscite
- Territory lost after plebiscite
- Territory retained after plebiscite
- Demilitarized zone

Labels on map:
- LITHUANIA
- ALLENSTEIN, 1920
- MARIENWERDER, 1920
- EAST PRUSSIA
- POLAND
- Niemen R.
- Memel (Klaipeda)
- Königsberg
- Warsaw
- Vistula R.
- DANZIG FREE CITY
- Danzig
- POLISH CORRIDOR (POMORZE)
- Posen (Poznan)
- Breslau
- UPPER SILESIA, 1921
- CZECHOSLOVAKIA
- HUNGARY
- ROMANIA
- Budapest
- Bratislava
- Danube R.
- Vienna
- AUSTRIA
- Berchtesgaden
- Prague
- Pilsen
- Munich
- Ulm
- Nuremberg
- SWEDEN
- BALTIC SEA
- Copenhagen
- Stettin
- Berlin
- Oder R.
- Dresden
- SAXONY
- Leipzig
- Weimar
- Erfurt
- THURINGIA
- GERMANY
- Elbe R.
- Hamburg
- Lübeck
- Kiel Canal
- DENMARK
- Island of Heligoland
- SCHLESWIG, 1920
- Bremen
- Weser R.
- NORTH SEA
- NETHERLANDS
- The Hague
- Rotterdam
- Rhine R.
- Brussels
- Liège
- BELGIUM
- Lille
- Paris
- FRANCE
- Düsseldorf
- Essen
- Cologne
- Aachen
- Ruhr R.
- Koblenz
- Frankfurt
- Main R.
- Mainz
- RHINELAND
- LUX.
- MORESNET EUPEN MALMÉDY
- SAAR BASIN, 1935
- LORRAINE
- ALSACE
- Strasbourg
- Basel
- SWITZ.
- Moselle R.
- Danube R.

56

In the east, the new state of Poland was awarded the greater part of province of Posen (Poznan), a large part of West Prussia, and a strip of territory between Germany and East Prussia (the Polish Corridor) which was to give Poland access to the sea. The ancient Hanseatic city of Danzig, with a predominantly German population, was made a free city within the Polish customs union to serve as Poland's seaport. The important industrial region of Upper Silesia was also assigned to Poland, but in response to German protests the Allies allowed plebiscites to be held in this territory—the only significant concession to German "observations" on the terms of the treaty. Those plebiscites resulted in a three-to-two majority for the Germans. Refusing to accept these results, the Poles sent troops into the disputed territory. The problem was then referred to the League, which in October 1921 divided the region in accordance with local majorities whereby the principal mining and industrial districts were awarded to Poland.

Another Hanseatic seaport with a predominantly German population, the city of Memel, was placed under inter-Allied administration, but in January 1923 Memel was taken over by the new state of Lithuania. The Allies took no effective steps to reestablish their own control over the city.

Germany was obliged to surrender all its overseas colonies, which were declared to be mandates of the League and were divided between Belgium, Britain and its Dominions (Australia, New Zealand, and South Africa), France, and Japan.

All German fortifications were to be dismantled, all German rivers and the strategic Kiel Canal (between the North and Baltic seas) internationalized. Germany as a whole was to be disarmed, its army limited to 100,000 men who were to be recruited for long periods of service to prevent a repetition of the trick Prussia had practiced on Napoleon of giving brief intensive training to the soldiers permitted to them by treaty, and then training another group until a substantial army had been built up. The German navy was to be restricted to little more than a coast guard. Germany was not permitted to have submarines or an air force. The disarmament of Germany was supposed to be the prelude to a general world disarmament process, but no such disarmament took place in continental Europe or most other parts of the world, so that the Germans were later able to condemn this provision too as an example of Allied hypocrisy.

Much as the Germans might resent the territorial and disarmament provisions of the Versailles treaty, the terms they regarded as far and away the most onerous were those dealing with reparations. To begin with, there was Article 231, which the Allies inserted in the treaty to justify their claim to reparations. That article required that Germany and its allies accept full responsibility for causing the war; hence they should bear full responsibility for its costs. This article, which became known as the War Guilt Clause, aroused the passionate indignation of Germans of every political stripe and set off bitter historical controversy that simmers to the present day.

Then there was the problem of reparations themselves. As mentioned earlier, the Allies, unable to agree on a reparations figure at the peace conference, had left the problem to a Reparations Commission, which was to report to the Allied governments on May 1, 1921. Moderates among the Allies hoped that the passions of war would have died down by that time and that they might then have a better chance to secure

agreement on a realistic rather than punitive reparations total. The Germans, however, saw this postponement in an entirely different light. They believed they were to
be burdened with reparations so overwhelming that the Allies did not dare name a
final figure, and that they were being compelled to sign a blank check which would
keep their country in a permanent state of economic bondage.

The reparations the Germans were required to pay immediately (that is, before
the final Reparations Commission report due in May 1921) were in themselves very
substantial. Germany was to pay the equivalent of twenty billion gold marks (roughly
five billion dollars) to surrender all German-owned property abroad, all its merchant
vessels over 1600 tons, half of its smaller vessels, and a third of its fishing fleet. German shipyards were to build new merchant vessels for the Allies to help replace the
large number sunk by German submarines during the war. Part of Germany's initial
reparations payments were to be made in the form of shipments of raw materials,
primarily coal. In the event of any delay or default in reparations payments, the Allied governments were entitled to take any measures they saw fit to deal with the
situation.

The Treaty of Versailles also included provisions for a trial of the kaiser and other
major German war criminals, the only part of the treaty that was never put into effect.

❑ *Peace with Austria, Hungary and Bulgaria*

The Treaty of Versailles with Germany was the most important of the peace treaties
concluded after World War I, but the separate peace treaties concluded with the other
Central Powers were scarcely less significant, for they revolutionized the political and
economic situation throughout much of Central and Eastern Europe.

The territorial provisions of the Treaty of St. Germain with Austria, signed September 9, 1919, did little more than register the breakup of the Habsburg empire,
which had already taken place. Austria was obliged to recognize the independence of
Czechoslovakia, Yugoslavia, Poland, and Hungary. To Poland, Austria ceded the eastern portion of the province of Galicia, Austria's share of the eighteenth century partitions of Poland. To Italy, Austria ceded all territory south of the Brenner Pass (the Trentino and South Tyrol), Trieste (the major seaport of the Habsburg empire), the Istrian
Peninsula south of Trieste, and islands along the Dalmatian coast. The Austrian army
was limited to 30,000 men; Austria was not allowed an air force and, cut off from the
sea as it now was, it obviously could not maintain a navy. Additionally, Austria was
to assume its share of the reparations burden and of the debts of the former Austro-
Hungarian empire.

Perhaps the most significant provision of the Treaty of St. Germain was the actual
prohibition of the operation of the principle of self-determination so far as the Germans were concerned. The majority of the inhabitants of what was left of Austria
spoke German and regarded themselves as Germans, and on March 12, 1919, the Austrian parliament had voted for union with Germany. But by the terms of St. Germain,
Austria was forbidden to unite with Germany or conclude any kind of agreement
which might lead to closer relations between the two countries. That the Allies should

MAP 3   THE PEACE SETTLEMENT IN EASTERN EUROPE, 1919-1923

insist on such a provision was thoroughly understandable. They could not afford to allow Germany to emerge from defeat larger in terms of both territory and population than before the war; nor could they afford to allow the creation of a stronger Austria, which might be tempted to reassert its dominion over its lost territories. However, this undeniable violation of the principle of self-determination was to provide the Germans with yet another moral argument to denounce Allied peace terms and the hypocrisy of their principles.

A less glaring but nonetheless significant violation of the principle of self-determination was the inclusion of three million Germans (the so-called Sudeten Germans) in the new state of Czechoslovakia, who were to provide the moral leverage for Hitler's breakup of Czechoslovakia in 1938–1939. (See pp. 200–202.)

A final peace treaty with Hungary, Austria's partner in dominion over much of Central Europe, was delayed by a revolution in that country. In March 1919 a liberal-socialist government, which had taken over the administration of Hungary after the flight of the Habsburgs, was overthrown by the forces of a newly formed Hungarian Bolshevik party under the leadership of Béla Kun. There ensued a Red terror, a slaughter of leaders of the old order, and a takeover of industries and farm lands by workers and peasants that produced additional chaos in what was already a catastrophic situation.

The Bolshevik revolution in Hungary gave the Romanians an excuse to intervene, ostensibly to suppress the Bolsheviks but also to take revenge on the hated Magyars, who had kept a large Romanian population in bondage for so many years. The Romanian invasion inaugurated a second reign of terror, as Hungarian opponents of Béla Kun wreaked vengeance on the Bolsheviks while Romanian troops systematically plundered the countryside. The Romanians did not leave until November 14, 1919. The regime of Béla Kun was succeeded by a conservative government under the leadership of Miklós Horthy, a former admiral in the Austro-Hungarian navy, who took the title of regent and exercised authority in the name of the exiled Habsburgs.

By the terms of the Treaty of Trianon finally concluded between Hungary and the Allies and signed on June 4, 1920, Hungary lost over three-quarters of its territory and over two-thirds of its population. Slovakia and Ruthenia were ceded to Czechoslovakia, Croatia-Slavonia and part of the Banat (province) of Temesvar to Yugoslavia. The remainder of the Banat of Temesvar (about two-thirds), Transylvania, and part of the Hungarian plain were ceded to Romania. A small part of western Hungary (the Burgenland) went to Austria for reasons of nationality. The Hungarian army was restricted to 35,000 men. Like Austria, Hungary was to assume its share of the reparations debt as well as the debts of the former Austro-Hungarian empire.

Bulgaria, which had lost substantial blocs of territory following its defeat in the Second Balkan War of 1913, was obliged to give up even more territory as a result of its defeat in 1918. By the terms of the Treaty of Neuilly, signed November 27, 1919, Bulgaria ceded the entire Dobruja to Romania; all Bulgarian territory along the Aegean coast to Greece; and pockets of strategic territory in the mountains on Bulgaria's western frontier to Serbia, now Yugoslavia. The Bulgarian army was limited to 20,000 men, and the country was obliged to assume its share of the reparations burden.

❑ *Peace with the Ottoman Empire*

The great difficulty for the Allies in making peace with the Ottoman empire was their lack of agreement over the division of the spoils, a problem made even more difficult by Russia's withdrawal from the war and the ensuing conflicts over what was to be done with the Ottoman territory previously promised to Russia. British, French, Italians, Greeks, Armenians, Kurds, Arabs, and Jews were joined by bankers, oil men, and other business interests in putting forward a bewildering variety of claims based on wartime promises and treaties, reasons of strategic and economic necessity, and the principle of self-determination.

The Treaty of Sèvres of August 10, 1920, stripped the Ottoman empire of all its non-Turkish territories. The Ottoman government was required to renounce all claims over its former possessions in North Africa and over all non-Turkish territory in Asia Minor. It was to recognize Britain's annexation of the island of Cyprus (occupied by Britain since 1878), Italian sovereignty over the Dodecanese and Aegean islands already occupied by Italy, and Greek sovereignty over the Aegean islands already occupied by Greece. The empire was to cede to Greece the strategic islands of Tenedos and Imbros, lying just off the entrance to the Dardanelles, as well as the greater part of eastern Thrace, thus advancing the Greek frontier to within twenty miles of Constantinople.

In Anatolia, the heartland of the empire's Turkish population, the Allies were also generous with their territorial awards. The British claimed oil-rich Mosul and its surrounding territory for their mandate of Iraq, while the French took over Cilisia for their mandate of Syria. In Eastern Anatolia, the Allies paid tribute to the principle of self-determination by recognizing the full extent of the claims of the Armenians and Kurds. The principle was again invoked to sanction the Greek occupation in May 1919 of Smyrna (Izmir, in Turkish) in western Anatolia, which the Greeks claimed on ethnic grounds on the basis of their own statistics. Just one month earlier, however, that principle had been flagrantly violated when the Italians, without ethnic claims, occupied the province of Antalya (Adana) in southwestern Anatolia, promised them by their allies in their secret wartime treaties.

Within three years, however, virtually all the provisions of the Treaty of Sèvres affecting Anatolia were to be overturned by a Turkish nationalist revolution and the conclusion of a new peace treaty between the Allies and a Turkish nationalist government. (See Chapter 7.)

❑ *The Minority Treaties*

Finally, the Allies provided for the conclusion of a set of Minority Treaties, initiated in the first instance at the Paris Peace Conference by the Committee of Jewish Delegations, which was particularly concerned with the large Jewish minority in Poland. In the Treaty of Versailles, Poland assumed the obligation to embody in a treaty with the Allied powers "such provisions as may be deemed necessary . . . to protect the interests of the inhabitants of Poland who differ from the majority of the population in race, language, and religion." This Minority Treaty was signed on June 28, 1919, at the same time as the Treaty of Versailles.

Similar Minority Treaties were subsequently incorporated in all the postwar treaties to safeguard minorities in Czechoslovakia, Romania, Yugoslavia, and Greece, as well as in the defeated states of Austria, Hungary, Bulgaria, and Turkey.

❏ *The Problem of Ratification*

The signatures on the postwar treaties by the representatives of the belligerent powers were not the end of the peacemaking story, for those treaties still had to be ratified by the governments of the signatory states.

Among the leaders of the Big Three, Lloyd George encountered the least opposition. Only four members of Parliament voted against the Treaty of Versailles, three of them Irish members who demanded self-determination for Ireland.

Clemenceau had a far more difficult time in France, and from July to October the Chamber of Deputies was the scene of angry and bitter debates. The treaty with Germany was condemned as far too lenient, Clemenceau himself was denounced for his failure to secure the political breakup of Germany, the frontier of the Rhine, the annexation of the Saar. Celebrated at the time of the armistice as Père la Victoire (father of victory), he was now vilified as Perd la Victoire (loser of victory), who had sold out the interests and security of France to Lloyd George and Wilson.

The ratification debate was finally won by Clemenceau, his clinching argument being that Anglo-American military guarantees were indispensable to France's future security and that the concessions to Lloyd George and Wilson had been necessary to secure them. But Clemenceau also made a convincing appeal to the deputies' sense of political reality. He pointed out that it was impossible to draft a treaty that would provide a permanent solution to all problems. The provisions of the existing treaty gave France a variety of weapons to defend and promote French interests and hold Germany in check. But these would only be of value in so far as the French themselves remained alert and resolute in upholding and enforcing them. "The treaty will be what you make it."

Wilson met with even greater difficulties. Ratification of the treaty required a two-thirds majority in a Senate now controlled by the Republicans, some of them outright opponents of the treaty, others alienated by Wilson's failure to involve or consult with them in the negotiating process. He might nevertheless have secured the necessary majority had he been willing to agree to modifications and reservations in the text of the treaty which would have removed the most serious objections of its critics. But Wilson was in no mood for compromise. On June 25, 1919, he cabled from Paris that ratification with reservations would be the equivalent of rejection.

The subsequent political battle over ratification was not a simple struggle between internationalists and isolationists, as it has sometimes been described. Critics of the treaty had important and legitimate reasons for desiring reservations. At the heart of their objections were the articles in the League Covenant which impinged on American sovereignty and required that the United States assume seemingly limitless international obligations—for example, the need to provide military assistance against aggression at any time and place.

The modifications in the treaty desired by the so-called reservationists would have restricted the jurisdiction of the League. But they would not have destroyed it, as Wilson contended, and might even have brought the Covenant more into line with the realities of international politics. For, as experience was to show, the countries that became members of the League were as reluctant as the Americans to relinquish their sovereign powers to the League's jurisdiction or to allow the League to determine when and where they should take military action against aggressors.

Exhausted by a nationwide speaking tour to drum up support for a treaty without reservations, Wilson suffered a stroke in late September. His will, however, remained unshaken. When the treaty with reservations came up for a vote in the Senate, he ordered his supporters to vote against it, with the result that this treaty narrowly failed to win the necessary two-thirds majority. The treaty without reservations, which Wilson demanded, did not even win a simple majority but went down to defeat 53 to 38. Still, Wilson did not give in. When a second (and, as it proved, final) vote on the treaty with reservations was held in the Senate, he issued the same instructions to his supporters and reaped the same results. In demanding all, he lost all.

The United States eventually signed separate peace treaties with Germany, Austria, and Hungary in July and August 1921 which ensured for America all the privileges embodied in the treaties of Versailles, Saint-Germain, and Trianon, but eschewed all commitments for their defense.

❑ *Concluding Observations*

As with all major events in history, there have been many diverse and conflicting interpretations about the peace treaties following World War I. The debates over the treaties were most intense—and most politically significant—in the years between the two world wars, when questions about the justice of the treaties critically affected the policies of both victors and vanquished.

Defenders of the treaties have generally subscribed to the fundamental principles on which they were allegedly based, namely, national freedom and self-determination. They argued that the Treaty of Versailles, the most severely criticized of the postwar agreements, was far more reasonable than might have been expected given the pressures exerted on the peacemakers for harsher terms. In all the treaties the principle of self-determination was observed insofar as possible, and major injustices of the past were rectified. The new states of Eastern Europe, although far from perfect from an ethnic point of view, were the best one could do in this region of scrambled nationalities and certainly far preferable to the multinational empires that had preceded them. Ethnic principles had even been observed in dealing with Germany, despite the demands of many Allied leaders that Germany be deprived of far more territory and divided into smaller, and hence weaker, units. Even reparations, about which the Germans complained so vociferously and which critics condemned as the worst feature of the treaty, did not constitute an intolerable burden. As finally pared down by the

Allies, the annual payments amounted to a good deal less than Germany's expenditure on armaments after the advent of Hitler.

Defenders of the treaties have also generally taken a favorable view of the League of Nations, which they believed might have served as an effective instrument for the settlement of international disputes if it had been given adequate support. The postwar treaties and the League did not break down because of their inherent flaws, so their defenders contend, but because the Allies failed to defend them with sufficient vigor and determination and because the United States withdrew from the international system it had done so much to establish.

Critics of the postwar agreements have focused their attacks on the Treaty of Versailles, which has been seen as a disastrous compromise between a harsh and a soft peace. If the aim of the Allies had been to destroy Germany's capacity to commit aggression, they should not have allowed Germany to survive as a unit but should have stripped it of more territory and divided the rest into small and weak states, their future independence guaranteed by the victor powers. As it was, Germany, although wounded and temporarily shackled by punitive restrictions, had been left as the largest and most populous state in West-Central Europe. In time this Germany was bound to recover, throw off the restrictions imposed by the postwar treaties (for treaties are never permanent), and reemerge as the strongest state in Europe, a menace to international peace and security.

If on the other hand the Allies wanted to enroll Germany as a cooperative member of the international community, as the allies of 1815 had attempted to do with post-Napoleonic France, then the terms of Versailles were too harsh and the Allied treatment of Germany in general unnecessarily humiliating. The Allies also committed a disastrous political mistake in imposing Versailles on a German democratic government, which Wilson had demanded as a condition for peace with Germany and which the Allies had every interest in supporting. By saddling that government with the stigma of territorial losses, the burden of reparations, and Germany's responsibility for launching a war of aggression, the Allies undermined Germany's nascent democracy from the start and rendered it dangerously vulnerable to antidemocratic forces of the Left and Right.

Most severe were the criticisms directed against the economic provisions of Versailles. "The great crime is in the reparations clauses," Harold Nicolson wrote to his wife in late May 1919. "You see it gives them no hope whatever, either now or in the future." This absence of hope—a belief that the reparations demanded by the Allies never *could* be paid—meshed with the German conviction that they were as unjust as they were unreasonable and therefore never *should* be paid. This attitude, shared by virtually all Germans of all political persuasions, set off a vicious circle of German resistance and French retaliation. The result was chronic economic instability and resentment, eased only temporarily by a few years of relative prosperity fueled by massive borrowing from the United States, that created a socioeconomic breeding ground for political extremists.

Critics believed the treaties affecting Eastern Europe were similarly flawed. By breaking up this region into a multitude of weak sovereign states, the Allies had established conditions that made for political and economic anarchy. Each of these states strove for maximum political and economic autonomy, and each conducted its own foreign policy, erected its own tariff barriers, and sought support among the great powers as the Balkan states had done before 1914. The treaties made Eastern Europe a power vacuum that was certain to be filled sooner or later by one of the stronger European powers, whether by France or by a revived Germany or Russia.

The fundamental criticism with respect to Eastern Europe was directed against the assumption that the principle of self-determination should be considered the sole legitimate basis for a state. The Allies themselves had flagrantly violated that principle by forbidding rump Austria, now predominantly German, to unite with Germany, but they had been unable to avoid similar violations and ethnic incongruities in creating the new states of Eastern Europe which were to become breeding grounds for future conflict. Few of the new states showed signs of becoming viable democracies or of willingness to live at peace with one another, as advocates of national freedom and self-determination had confidently expected they would.

And what of the countries beyond Europe, in other words the greater part of the world? With all their talk about national freedom and self-determination, the British and French continued to retain their colonial empires, as did the Americans and all other Allied states. Instead of being given their freedom, the inhabitants of the former German colonies and much of the old Ottoman empire had been divided among the victor states under the hypocritical disguise of mandates of the League of Nations.

Critics also expressed reservations about the League itself. This organization was not an international parliament but an association of sovereign states whose members would not necessarily yield to decisions reached by majority vote. The League had no army capable of imposing its mandates on great or small states. It was therefore possible for a state to disregard an unfavorable League decision if it felt strong enough to do so. States working through the League would therefore be compelled to resort to force, as they had always done, if they were determined to impose the will of the League (and thus of themselves) on a recalcitrant government.

The debates over the peace treaties were no mere academic exercises but were to have profound political significance in the postwar world. The vast majority of Germans were convinced that they had been cheated and betrayed—a belief fostered not only by nationalist fanatics but by respected scholars at home and abroad. They therefore felt no moral obligation to live up to the terms of a treaty they had been compelled to sign and which they denounced as the *Diktat von Versailles*.

But among the Allies too, especially in Britain and the United States, there was a growing feeling after the war that the Germans had a case. The charge that the treaties violated the Allied armistice agreements, the barrage of criticism directed against their economic as well as political provisions, and the many obvious Allied violations of the principle of self-determination not only in Europe but in their colonial empires sapped the Allies' confidence in their own moral position and allowed the moral initiative to pass to Germany. The vacillations in the policies of Allied leaders in the postwar era, their failure to defend the provisions of Versailles when confronted with Hitler's violations of that treaty, and their adoption of a policy of appeasement stemmed at least in part from a guilty belief that the postwar treaties had indeed violated the principles on which they were supposed to have been based.

More significant in the long run was the growing doubt in Allied countries about the morality of their own colonial empires, a decline in confidence about their right to rule, and their adoption of policies of appeasement in response to the demands of the colonial peoples, whose rebellions in the name of national freedom and self-determination would ultimately bring about the disintegration of the world's major colonial empires.

❑ *The Great Powers in 1919*

After their triumph in World War I the two major victorious European powers, Britain and France, seemed to have emerged from the conflict more powerful than ever.

France had improved its strategic and economic position in Europe through the defeat of Germany, the recovery of Alsace-Lorraine, and the acquisition of control over the coal-rich Saar region. Outside Europe, France had extended its colonial empire and spheres of influence in Africa and the Middle East. Reparations from the Central Powers gave promise of an influx of capital for rebuilding French territories damaged by the war and the revitalization of the French economy. The French army of 1919 was one of the largest and best equipped in the world and was now the predominant military force in Europe.

Britain, too, seemed stronger than ever before. The German threat to Britain's naval supremacy and national security had been eliminated, and for the time being Britain no longer had to fear German economic rivalry. Britain had extended its empire and spheres of influence on an even greater scale than France. The British navy now reigned supreme in European waters. Britain was also to receive reparations that were expected to pay for the renewal of its antiquated industrial establishment, which had been seriously overtaxed by four years of wartime production.

Many British and French political leaders, as well as large segments of public opinion in both countries, believed they had actually gained renewed power and security through their victory in 1918. This confidence ignored the fact that already well before 1914 the strength of both countries had steadily declined in relation to that of other powers. They faced growing political and economic competition not only from Germany but from the United States and Japan. And within their colonial empires they were confronted with ever-increasing unrest among their subject peoples. This decline in their relative strength was enormously accelerated by their involvement for four years in the most destructive war in history.

Throughout the nineteenth century, the population of France had grown slowly in comparison to that of France's competitors and rivals. Similarly, France's economic productivity, especially its heavy industry, had not kept pace with the economic expansion of rival powers. Then came the losses of World War I in which France, with a smaller demographic and economic base to begin with, suffered comparatively greater losses than any other major power. More than half of all French males between the ages of 22 and 32 in 1914 were killed outright in the war, many more of all ages were incapacitated. One-tenth of the country, including some of its most productive industrial and agricultural areas, had been devastated.

France's international position after 1919 was also significantly weaker. In 1914 France had been allied with Britain and Russia and was on better terms with Italy than Italy's nominal allies, Germany and Austria. By 1919 France had not only lost its alliance with Russia, but was confronted with a hostile Bolshevik regime dedicated to world revolution and the overthrow of all "capitalist" governments, and thus also the government of France. Britain and the United States had concluded a treaty with France guaranteeing military aid against renewed German aggression, an agreement that seemed to compensate for the loss of Russia. But Britain's adherence to this treaty was dependent on its ratification by the United States, and when the American Senate rejected ratification, France lost its alliance with Britain as well. Italy, too, angered at not having received all it had been promised in return for its entry into the war, had been transformed from an ally into a hostile rival. Nor was French power enhanced by the extension of the French colonial empire and overseas spheres of influence. On the contrary, the growing unrest throughout the French colonial empire and France's effort to retain control of its overseas possessions was to prove a serious drain on French military and economic resources.

Like the French, the British had suffered grievous human and economic losses in the recent war. With Britain's wartime withdrawal from the markets of the world, the United States, Japan, and other competitors had moved in, and in most areas the British found it impossible to recoup their prewar economic position. Nor did the British benefit from the economic collapse of Germany. For, although Germany had been Britain's greatest prewar competitor, it had also been Britain's greatest customer. Further, to meet the costs of the war, the British had been obliged to sell a great part of their overseas securities and therewith lost a large proportion of the enormous profits previously derived from their so-called "invisible exports"—interest from investments, insurance premiums, banking, and shipping charges. The war had also prevented the modernization and renewal of Britain's industrial plant, which was already antiquated in comparison to that of Britain's major competitors in 1914, an obsolescence that was to prove a serious handicap as Britain sought to regain its prewar markets.

Britain's strategic position, too, had suffered a comparative decline. The German naval threat had been eliminated, to be sure, but the defeat of Germany did not mean that Britannia once again ruled the waves, for the United States and Japan now had substantial fleets capable of challenging British naval supremacy in almost every part of the world. More serious still, British strategic security on its tight little island could no longer be assured through sea power. The success of Germany's submarine campaign during the recent conflict had revealed the vulnerability of conventional warships, and military aircraft, which were certain to be developed into far more formidable weapons than the primitive machines used in the late war, threatened to eliminate altogether the strategic advantage of Britain's island position. To an even greater extent than France, because of the greater size of its empire, the British international position was weakened by unrest among its subject peoples. In important parts of the empire, notably Australia, New Zealand, and Canada, the white settlers who now formed a majority of the population generally remained loyal to Britain. But even these countries were seeking greater independence and frequently pursued policies at variance with those of London.

Among the victorious European powers, Italy alone did not come out of the war with enhanced prestige. The Italians had suffered serious military setbacks, and the war had exposed military and economic weaknesses that deflated—but by no means eliminated—Italian pretensions to great power status. Although Italy was awarded more territory at the expense of the Habsburg empire than could be justified on ethnic grounds, Italian leaders, with the enthusiastic support of patriotic public opinion, complained bitterly that they had not been conceded everything promised them in their wartime secret treaties and denounced the postwar treaties as *la vittoria mutilata*. Italy, instead of standing with France as a staunch defender of the postwar treaties, emerged from the war as a revisionist state determined to alter the postwar international system in Italy's favor.

Russia, which had withdrawn from the war following the Bolshevik revolution, had been seriously weakened by the war itself and was subsequently weakened further by civil war, Allied intervention, and widespread famine. When it became obvious that the revolution in Russia was not about to ignite a worldwide proletarian revolution, as Lenin and other Bolshevik leaders had confidently predicted, the Bolshevik government concentrated on the consolidation of Communist rule in Russia itself and promoted a program of industrialization to restore Russian economic and military power. Under the leadership of Moscow, Communist parties abroad continued their revolutionary agitation, but until the mid-1930s Moscow itself generally pursued a cautious and quasi-isolationist foreign policy. By its very existence, however, Bolshevik Russia was to exercise immense influence on the policies of Western leaders, whose fear of Communism, at home and abroad, was to blind them to the other dangers of anti-Communist political movements.

The Austro-Hungarian empire, broken up into a mosaic of small states by the postwar peace treaties, was the only prewar great power that was permanently eliminated as a major player in international politics.

Very different was the case of Germany. Stripped of valuable territories in the east and west, saddled with a reparations burden that seemed to deny all possibility of economic recovery, forbidden to maintain more than a token army or navy, Germany, too, seemed to have been eliminated from the ranks of the great powers. Germany itself had not been broken up, however, with the result that postwar Germany, despite its losses, remained the largest and most populous state in Western Europe and thus, potentially, the most powerful. Because of France's fearful awareness of that potential, French foreign policy in the postwar years was dedicated to preventing a revival of German power and building up France's own security through international treaties and guarantees.

The greatest beneficiaries of the civil war in Europe were the two non-European powers involved in that war, the United States and Japan. Neither had invested a significant proportion of its resources in the war, both had reaped immense profits from the sale of war materials and basic economic necessities to the European Allies, and both had used the temporary absence of the Europeans from the markets of the world to take up the slack and establish their own economic predominance in areas previously controlled by the Europeans. The Japanese had taken advantage of the war in Europe to establish a virtual protectorate over the government of China. And they had been rewarded for their participation on the side of the Allies by being conceded the former German rights over China's Shantung Peninsula and the German-held islands in the Pacific north of the equator. The war, in fact, had enabled Japan to make itself the dominant power in East Asia.

Unlike Japan, the United States did not exploit the war to extend its territorial possessions, but American business interests garnered even greater profits from the sale of arms and other goods to the Allied powers and from the opportunities to move into global markets abandoned by the European belligerents. As a result of this lucrative wartime trade the United States was no longer a debtor but a creditor nation. Already the world's greatest economic power, it was now also the world's greatest military power, and on the basis of that power the United States might have assumed a decisive leadership role in world affairs. But following the victory over Germany and the long and bitter wrangles over the peace treaties, there was a reaction in America against assuming further foreign commitments.

This was not a retreat into isolationism, as has frequently been alleged, because over the next decade the United States was to be deeply involved in international negotiations dealing with a broad range of political and economic problems. What the Americans refused to do, however, was assume the burden and responsibility of world leadership or provide guarantees of support for the international system they had done so much to create. American public opinion demanded the speedy demobilization of their manpower together with the scaling down of their military and naval establishments and the taxes required to support them. With the refusal of the American Senate to ratify the treaties negotiated by President Wilson, the United States rejected membership in the League of Nations, as well as all guarantees of support for the postwar peace treaties, an abandonment of global responsibilities that was to have disastrous consequences.

Throughout the postwar years, Americans never seemed to recognize the implications of their disarmament and failure to assume the burdens of international responsibility. Confident that they represented the world's greatest power, they thundered warnings to aggressors in the belief that these would be heeded to avoid incurring America's wrath. The aggressors, however, looked to the reality of American power, not to its potential, and believed they could disregard American warnings with impunity so long as the United States lacked the means, and seemingly also the will, to back them up.

As a result of the refusal of the United States to assume the burden of leadership in international affairs, this role was left by default to the European powers that had exercised it over the past century, in the first instance to Britain and France, then increasingly to Italy, Germany, and Russia. Thus, despite the relative decline in the strength of the European powers, the lineup of the world's great powers during the interwar years remained much the same as it had been in the century before 1914. Japan now exercised preponderant influence in East Asia, to be sure, but the major international decisions affecting much of the rest of the world, including Asia, were still being made in the capitals of the great powers of Europe.

❑

SIX

The Aftermath of Empire: Russia and Eastern Europe

The Allies' armistice agreements with the Central Powers and the postwar peace treaties did not bring peace to large parts of the former Russian, Austro-Hungarian, and Ottoman empires, or to many of the countries of Eastern Europe. Well before the end of the war and throughout the early postwar years, most of these territories were wracked by revolution, civil and foreign wars, and foreign intervention, the horrors of these conflicts frequently exceeded by the even grimmer horrors of mass political extermination, genocide, famine, and disease.

❑ Russia: The Bolshevik Consolidation of Power and the Civil War

In dealing with postwar Russia, we must recall that the Bolshevik revolution in November 1917 was followed almost immediately by a spate of revolutions carried out by the non-Russian nationalities of the tsarist empire seeking independence from Russian overlordship. (See pp. 26–27.) These nationalist independence movements were supported in the first instance by the Germans as a means of weakening both Russia and its Bolshevik government. Subsequently they became part of a massive and brutal civil war waged between the Bolsheviks and their opponents, a conflict complicated and rendered even more brutal by foreign intervention.

The Russian civil war began immediately after the Bolshevik seizure of power and was waged over the next two years largely in the frontier regions of the old tsarist empire, from the White Sea to the Caucasus and along a wide front in Siberia. Given the weakness of the Bolsheviks in 1918, the resources of their country drained by four years of war and revolution, faced with rebellion throughout their frontier provinces and with the intervention of major foreign powers on the side of their opponents, their survival and eventual victory in the civil war seem miraculous.

But, as we can see in retrospect, the Bolsheviks enjoyed many advantages not obvious to contemporary observers. Perhaps their greatest advantage was the lack of unity and the incompetence of their opponents. The Bolsheviks, and foreigners

MAP 4   *THE RUSSIAN CIVIL WAR AND ALLIED INTERVENTION. DOES NOT SHOW
JAPANESE-AMERICAN INTERVENTION IN ASIA.*

Russian losses by the Treaty of
Brest-Litovsk, March 1918

Former territory of the Russian Empire
occupied by German and Austrian
forces prior to November 1918

Occupied by British forces in March 1918,
Later joined by U.S. and other allied forces

Areas of Turkish incursions and
Occupation during 1918

Area gained by Turkey, 1921

Curzon Line

Russian-Polish and other Soviet
western border, 1922–early 1939

0   300   600 Miles

generally, referred to those opponents indiscriminately as the Whites, as though they were a unified body of monarchists intent on restoring the pre-1914 political, social, and economic system. In fact, these opponents were a heterogeneous jumble of peoples and parties that included socialists and liberals as well as monarchists, ethnic independence movements, military adventurers, and bands of marauders living off the land with little sense of political purpose.

The Bolsheviks, on the other hand, were united under the ruthless centralized leadership of Lenin; they had a clear sense of purpose and were imbued with a quasi-messianic ideological fervor. They were also masterful propagandists. They generated widespread popular support through their decrees redistributing the lands of the tsarist aristocracy to the peasants, and they skillfully exploited popular fears that victory for the Whites would mean the restoration of those lands to their former owners. They used the issue of foreign intervention to portray themselves as the true representatives of the Russian people, the defenders of the sacred soil of Russia against foreign imperialist invaders in league with the reactionary forces of landlords and capitalists.

But Lenin, never a sentimentalist, did not rely on popular support, ideological fervor, or personal loyalty in imposing and maintaining his control over the Bolshevik state and Communist party organizations. One of his first acts after coming to power was to revive one of the most reviled institutions of the tsarist regime, the secret police, which the Bolsheviks called the Commission to Combat Counter-Revolution, Speculation, and Sabotage (Cheka), frequently renamed and known later by the initials OGPU, GPU, NKVD, and MVD. This organization was used to root out and suppress all real and suspected opponents of the regime in areas under Bolshevik control. Savage and remorseless in its employment of terrorist tactics, the secret police carried out mass arrests and executions, maintaining a cadre of spies and informers which supervised all sectors of the party and government to ensure the loyalty and obedience of its members.

By far the most important prop of the Bolshevik government, however, was the Red Army, the creation of the Bolshevik commissar for war, Leon Trotsky (Lev Davidovich Bronstein), an organizer of genius, an inspiring and imaginative military leader, as tough, calculating, and cold-blooded as Lenin. Early in the civil war, Trotsky reintroduced compulsory military service, and within a year he had assembled an army of three million men, their training and combat operations entrusted to officers of the old imperial army, most of them dragooned into the service of the Bolsheviks by threats of imprisonment, execution, or the detention of their families as hostages. To ensure the loyalty of officers and conscripts alike, they were kept under the close supervision of Bolshevik "military commissars" and subjected to a steady barrage of revolutionary rhetoric reinforced by terror and intimidation. They were enjoined to give no quarter to the "lackeys of foreign imperialism and enemies of the people," but warned that the Soviet government would punish "its sluggish and criminal servants no less severely than its enemies." If they retreated without orders "the first to be shot will be the commissar, the second, the commanding officer."

In the sphere of military operations, the Bolsheviks had the advantage of controlling the interior lines, which allowed them to move troops from one theater to another more easily than their opponents. The armies of the Whites, on the other hand, operated on widely scattered fronts, their strategies were uncoordinated, and their leaders were divided by personal rivalries and political differences. The national independence movements seeking to throw off Russian control were similarly divided, jealous and suspicious of each other, and receptive to Bolshevik promises to recognize their right to self-determination and warnings that victory for the Whites would mean their renewed subjugation to Russian rule.

Also divided as to aims and purposes were the Allied governments supporting the Whites—Britain and its Dominions, France, Japan, and the United States. The French were primarily concerned with building up the newly established state of Poland, which they wished to make as large and strong as possible as a bulwark against Germany. In Asia, the Japanese sought greater security against Russia by extending their control over a large part of Siberia, an expansionist program that aroused the suspicions and hostility of the Americans and the British. But for the most part the Allied governments failed to pursue purposeful or consistent policies in Russia. Allied and American soldiers, weary of war and eager to go home, saw no reason for their presence in Russia, and their governments, hopelessly misinformed about what was going on in that country, never united behind any one faction of the Whites or coordinated their own military efforts. In the end they failed to achieve the one purpose that all ostensibly had in common: the defeat of the Bolsheviks.

Nevertheless, although Allied intervention failed to bring down the Bolsheviks, it played a significant and perhaps decisive role in preserving the independence of several of the frontier states that had declared their independence from the tsarist empire: Finland, the Baltic states (Estonia, Latvia, Lithuania), and Poland. Elsewhere, however, although the fortunes of war frequently shifted dramatically, the Bolsheviks triumphed all along the line. By the winter of 1920 they had succeeded in reestablishing Russian control over Belorussia (White Russia) and the Ukraine; early in the following year they regained control of Georgia, Armenia, and Azerbaijan; and by the winter of 1922 they regained all territory lost to the Japanese in East Asia. In December of that year the Moscow government proclaimed the formation of the Union of Soviet Socialist Republics, which brought together Russia, the Ukraine, Belorussia, Transcaucasia (Georgia, Armenia, and Azerbaijan), and the Far Eastern Republic (eastern Siberia.) The preamble to the constitution of this new union was a triumphant proclamation of the superiority of Bolshevism over capitalism. In the camp of capitalism: national enmity and inequality, colonial slavery and chauvinism, national oppression and pogroms, imperialist brutalities and wars; in the camp of socialism: mutual confidence and peace and the brotherly collaboration of peoples.

This proud pronouncement was tragically at variance with the actual situation in the Soviet Union, which was on the verge of economic collapse as a result of wartime economic dislocations, a severe drought, and centralizing policies designed to regulate every aspect of the economy. Confronted with economic catastrophe, Lenin demonstrated once again his ability to face reality. He did not hesitate to appeal to the despised capitalists for aid, who were lured into investing in Russia by prospects of gaining access to the raw materials and markets of that vast and populous country. At the same time Lenin began to relax government economic controls, inaugurating what he called the New Economic Policy (NEP), which opened up opportunities for private enterprise in every sector of the Russian economy. Under the New Economic Policy and fueled by substantial foreign investments, the Soviet economy gradually recovered.

In May 1922, Lenin suffered a stroke which completely incapacitated him. He died in January 1924. In the ensuing struggle for power, the victor was not the brilliant Trotsky but a stolid Georgian, Joseph Dzugashvili, better known by his pseudonym Stalin, the man of steel, who had gained control of the apparatus of the party, a position he used to make himself master of the state and eventually to eliminate all rivals for state and party leadership.

❑ *Bolshevik Ideology and Foreign Policy*

When the Bolsheviks seized power in November 1917, they had no foreign policy and saw no need for one. Confident that their revolution in Russia was but the prelude to world revolution, they believed that foreign relations would simply cease to be a problem. In his memoirs, Leon Trotsky, who became the first Bolshevik commissar for foreign affairs, recalled that upon taking office he assumed he would need do no more than "issue a few revolutionary proclamations to the peoples of the world and then close up shop."

Negotiations with the Germans at Brest-Litovsk taught the Bolsheviks that they not only needed a foreign policy but that their very survival depended on their ability to deal with foreign powers. As noted earlier, Lenin took the lead in facing the grim realities of international life. The world revolution might be inevitable, but it was impossible to predict when or where it would take place, and the Bolsheviks could not afford to stake their survival on revolutionary expectations. The immediate and essential task of the Bolshevik government was to survive and consolidate its power. Once socialism had been made unconquerable in Russia—but only then—could the Bolshevik government provide effective support for world revolutionary movements. The goal of world revolution remained the same, however, because socialism could never be secure until the world's capitalist-imperialist governments had been overthrown.

In March 1919 the Bolsheviks founded the Communist International (Comintern), which they conceived as the central organization of all the world's Communist parties. An executive committee with headquarters in Moscow was to exercise supreme authority over those parties, which were required to adhere to the policy line set by that committee and to renounce all loyalty to their own countries. Foreign Communist parties were assigned a dual role: to promote revolution in their respective countries and to render every possible assistance to the Soviet Union in its struggle against counterrevolution. They were given detailed instructions on how to build up their influence and prepare the way for revolution. They were to establish their own youth groups, trade unions, and comparable organizations, which would be subject to the same discipline as the Communist parties themselves. While building up their own organizations, Communists were to infiltrate non-Communist political parties and their affiliates with the aim of taking over their leadership and bringing them under Communist control. Further, Communists were to engage in undercover operations. "The general state of things in Europe and America imposes on Communists of the world the obligation to form illegal Communist organizations along with those existing legally," which at the decisive moment should do their duty to the party by assisting in the revolution in every possible way.

The Comintern addressed particular appeals to the colonial peoples of the world, the subjects and putative victims of the capitalist-imperialist powers. "The colonial question has been placed on the agenda to the fullest extent," the Comintern announced in its first manifesto of April 6, 1919. "Colonial slaves of Asia and Africa! The hours of the triumph of the proletarian dictatorship in Europe will also be the hour of your own liberation." In his "Theses on the National and Colonial Question," adopted by the second congress of the Comintern in August 1920, Lenin declared that the policy of the Comintern "must be to create a close alliance between Soviet Russia and all national and colonial liberation movements. . . . The Communist International has the task of liberating the working people of the entire world. The white, yellow, and black-skinned working peoples of the world are fraternally united in its ranks."

While urging Communists everywhere to use every possible stratagem to undermine capitalist governments, Lenin recommended that the Soviet Union itself should actively seek economic and political agreements with the capitalist powers to rehabilitate the Soviet economy and above all to prevent the formation of an anti-Soviet coalition. Meanwhile, Communists should never forget that accommodation with the capitalist world was only a temporary expedient and that war was inevitable. "As long as capitalism and socialism exist, we cannot live in peace."

The ideology of Soviet foreign policy did not change after Lenin's death in 1924. In the ensuing struggle for power between Leon Trotsky and Stalin, Trotsky held that the primary goal of Soviet policy should be the promotion of world revolution. But Stalin, the eventual victor in that struggle, agreed with Lenin that the consolidation of Communist power in Russia was the essential prerequisite for the triumph of world revolution. But for Stalin, too, world revolution remained the ultimate goal. Again like Lenin, Stalin acknowledged the need for changes in tactics to correspond with changes in the global political situation and with the ebb and flow of the revolutionary movement. It was the responsibility of the most politically advanced element (i.e., the Communist party) to gauge the direction and strength of the tide and then to devise tactics best suited to promote the overall objective of world revolution. Communists should therefore understand that policies described as "co-existence" or "peaceful competition" were merely tactical expedients for achieving that objective.

❏ *The New and Reconstituted States of Eastern Europe*

In the mid-nineteenth century, the Czech patriot and historian František Palacký had deplored German nationalism because it would inevitably undermine the Habsburg empire, "whose preservation . . . is, and must be, a great and important matter not only for my own nation, but also for the whole of Europe, indeed for humanity and civilization itself." Only through the Habsburg empire could the peoples of Eastern Europe be protected against Russian expansion and domination, "an infinite and inexpressible evil, a misfortune without measure or bound." Because none of the nationalities in this region was strong enough to stand by itself, their union in one state was essential. "If the Austrian state had not already existed, the interests of Europe and indeed of humanity would have required that we create it."

In 1918 the Austrian state was destroyed, and its territories, as well as the border provinces of the German and Russian empires, were broken into a mosaic of smaller states by the postwar peace treaties. The boundaries of these new states were supposed to have been established on the basis of the principle of self-determination, and idealists expressed the hope that the peoples of this region, released from the bondage of autocratic empires and endowed with the right of self-government, would make use of their political freedom to form governments on the model of the Western democracies.

This hope was not be be fulfilled. Instead of becoming democracies, all the states of Eastern Europe with the exception of Czechoslovakia, confronted with a multitude of political and economic problems, turned to some form of dictatorial government. The attempt to establish national boundaries on the basis of national self-determination was in itself a hopeless task, for the nationalities in this area were inextricably intermingled. Some of the newly formed or enlarged states were as multinational as the empires they had displaced; all of them contained ethnic minorities who resented the rule of the new national majority as much as previous minorities had resented their imperial overlords. Further, each of these states, whether newly created, enlarged, or diminished by the postwar treaties, was dissatisfied with its existing territorial status and laid claim to territories allotted to its neighbors. Ethnic and territorial grievances were reinforced by economic hardship, the result of the devastations of war, the postwar agricultural depression, currency instability, the dislocations caused by the redrawing of state boundaries, and the misguided attempts on the part of national leaders to build up the economies of their own states at the expense of their neighbors through tariffs and other impediments to international trade.

Viewed by outsiders, the squabbles among the peoples of Eastern Europe seem for the most part inconsequentially petty, but as in the century before 1914, their rivalries and hatreds made for constant political ferment in this region. The great importance of these quarrels in terms of international politics was the temptation they offered for exploitation by one or more of the great powers, with the result that seemingly minor parochial problems could be transformed into major international crises. The most famous case in point was the incident that set off World War I—the assassination of the Austrian heir to the throne by a Bosnian Serb nationalist in the Bosnian capital of Sarajevo. But problems in Eastern Europe were to play an equally dramatic and in many ways an even more decisive role in setting off World War II. The most significant of those crises took place in two of the newly independent states to emerge in Eastern Europe after World War I: the 1938 Sudeten crisis in Czechoslovakia, and the 1939 crisis with Poland over Danzig and the Polish Corridor (see pp. 200 and 208). But an explosive situation was also created in Serb-dominated Yugoslavia, whose full significance would only become apparent during World War II and its aftermath.

❑ *Poland*

When World War I began there was no state of Poland. The lands inhabited by Polish-speaking people were ruled by Austria, Germany, and Russia, which had participated in three partitions of the ancient kingdom of Poland in the late eighteenth century. Ever since that time, Polish patriots and foreigners sympathetic to their cause had sought the restoration of an independent Polish state. An opportunity to do so seemed to have arrived with the outbreak of war in 1914.

The French, traditionally sympathetic to the cause of Polish independence, had refrained from taking any initiative in the Polish question for fear of offending their Russian allies. The need for French restraint was removed following the March 1917 revolution in Russia and a proclamation by the Russian provisional government calling for the establishment of an independent Polish state that would include all territory in which Poles constituted a majority of the population. In December 1917 Stéphan Pichon, the French foreign minister, announced in the Chamber of Deputies that the French government desired the establishment of a "united, independent, and indivisible" Polish state. One month later Woodrow Wilson included the establishment of an independent Polish state with access to the sea in his Fourteen Points.

On November 3, 1918, eight days before the German armistice, Polish leaders proclaimed the establishment of an independent Polish Republic. The French promptly accorded official recognition to the new state, which was not only to be given access to the sea but was to be reconstituted within its "ancient boundaries." These were defined by the Poles as the boundaries of the kingdom of Poland in 1772, before the three partitions of the country, and would have meant the incorporation of large numbers of Ukrainians and other non-Polish nationalities. The Poles turned aside objections that the inclusion of these people would violate the principle of self-determination with the argument that historical claims transcended those of ethnicity. They abandoned the principle of self-determination once again in claiming Upper Silesia and much of East Prussia, with their predominantly German populations, this time on the grounds of economic and strategic necessity.

After bitter debate, the peacemakers at Paris had agreed that the fate of Upper Silesia and East Prussia should be decided by plebiscites. When these plebiscites resulted in victory for the Germans, however, the Poles refused to accept their verdict and Polish troops occupied Upper Silesia. The League of Nations then ruled that the disputed territory be divided on the basis of majorities in local plebiscites, whereby the most important industrial sector of Upper Silesia was awarded to Poland. The Germans would have resented the new state of Poland no matter where its boundaries had been established, but the League verdict over Upper Silesia added yet another item to the long list of Germany's postwar grievances.

The Poles once again resorted to military force to support their eastern frontier claims. Taking advantage of Red Army's involvement on other fronts, they invaded Bolshevik-held territory in April 1920. Within a fortnight Polish forces had reached the Dnieper River and by May 7 they had captured Kiev, the capital of the Ukraine. But the Poles had overreached themselves. The Bolsheviks rallied remarkably quickly and launched a counterattack that drove the Poles from the Ukraine and brought the Red Army to the outskirts of Warsaw by mid-August.

Now it was the Bolsheviks who overreached themselves. Confident that Polish workers and peasants would rise up against their bourgeois oppressors and join forces with their Russian comrades, Lenin ordered the Red Army's advance into what had recently been Russian Poland. As we now know from Soviet documents, Lenin grotesquely overestimated the revolutionary ardor of the European working classes. He confidently expected that the installation of a Bolshevik regime in Poland would be followed by a Communist revolution in Germany, which in turn would set off a revolution in England. That revolution was to be supported by a German Communist army operating in conjunction with the Red Army, which would also come to the support of revolutions unleashed by Communist parties in Czechoslovakia, Hungary, Romania, and Italy.

But Lenin was to find that Polish patriotism and hatred of the Russians surpassed by far Polish class hatred. The Poles fought as Poles, and with substantial aid from the French they turned back the Red Army. Defeated in Poland and faced with the advance of a White army in the south, the Bolsheviks agreed to an armistice on October 12, 1920. The Treaty of Riga of March 18, 1921, established a boundary between Russia and Poland that was to to endure until Germany and Russia engaged in a fourth partition of Poland at the outset of World War II. The Riga treaty did not give the Poles the frontiers of 1772, but it nevertheless incorporated large numbers of Ukrainians, Belorussians, and other non-Polish nationalities into Poland, where national and ethnic minorities now constituted over one-third of the country's total population.

The extension of Poland's frontiers in non-Polish territories that had once been part of the tsarist empire ensured that Russia as well as Germany would be an enemy of the new state. Besides their conflict with Russia, the Poles engaged in territorial disputes with their smaller neighbors: with Lithuania over the city of Vilna and its surrounding territory, which the Poles took over by military force after the League of Nations had awarded it to Lithuania; and with Czechoslovakia over the important coal-mining and railway center of Teschen, which, although eventually divided between the two countries, was to lead to lasting enmity with the new state of Czechoslovakia.

❑ *Czechoslovakia*

In the years before 1914 Czech nationalists for the most part had abandoned the theories of Palacký about the desirability of preserving the Habsburg empire and had become vigorous advocates of independence from Habsburg rule. With the outbreak of World War I, several of the most eminent Czech leaders sought refuge abroad, where they endeavored persistently and ultimately successfully to persuade the governments of the Allied powers to recognize their claims to national freedom. Like the Poles, they wanted their state established within their "historic borders," which in their case were those of the ancient Kingdom of Bohemia and included the provinces of Bohemia, Moravia, and Austrian Silesia, all of them located in the Austrian part of the Austro-Hungarian empire. From the beginning of their campaign for independence, however, the Czechs seemed to take for granted the inclusion of Slovakia in their new state, even though Slovakia had never been within their historic borders and had been part of the ancient kingdom of Hungary for over a thousand years.

At the beginning of World War I, the Czechs and Slovaks had not figured prominently in Allied calculations, and the breakup of the Austro-Hungarian empire had not originally been an Allied war aim. The awakening of Allied interest in the Czechs and Slovaks was due in large measure to the skillful lobbying efforts of Czech émigré leaders. In February 1916 they set up a Czechoslovak National Council in Paris presided over by the highly respected scholar and humanist Tomáš Masaryk and his able lieutenant Eduard Beneš, his primary adviser on foreign policy. Within a year this organization had won a firm commitment from the French, who informed Wilson in January 1917 that "the liberation of the Czechoslovaks from foreign domination" was one of France's war aims. The French subsequently sent the Czechs official assurances of support for their establishment of an independent state "within the historic borders of your provinces."

This recognition of their historic borders was of prime importance for the Czechs because the ancient kingdom of Bohemia included a ring of mountains surrounding the plains of Bohemia and Moravia that constituted a natural defensive barrier against Germany and Austria. Because the inhabitants of this frontier region were for the most part German, the assignment of this territory to the Czechs was another violation of the principle of self-determination, but the French agreed with the Czech argument that their need for this strategic frontier should override ethnic considerations.

On October 28, 1918, the Czechoslovak National Council, now recognized by all major Allied states as the government of Czechoslovakia, issued a formal declaration of independence. This was followed by a declaration of a Slovak National Council that the land of the Slovaks should form part of a Czechoslovak state and that there now existed a single Czechoslovak nation.

In establishing the frontier of Czechoslovakia, the Slovaks were encouraged by the French to extend their territorial claims in the Danube valley on the grounds that the possession of this Hungarian-speaking area was essential to the political and economic well-being of the new Czechoslovak state. Although these claims went beyond anything that could be justified on an ethnic or historic basis, the French insisted that on this question there could be no negotiation or compromise with the Hungarians. With French military support, Czech and Slovak troops moved into the Danube valley where they took over all former Hungarian territory north of the river plus a small enclave to the south. Included in these Danube lands was the city of Bratislava (in Hungarian, Pozsony; in German, Pressburg), for many years the capital of the ancient kingdom of Hungary, which now became the capital of Slovakia.

The Czechoslovaks made additional territorial gains at the expense of Hungary with the annexation of Ruthenia (the sub-Carpathian Ukraine). Although here, again, they had no historic or ethnic claim to this territory, they argued that the predominantly Slavic population people of this region wanted freedom from the non-Slavic Hungarians, and that, as in the case of the Slovaks, their freedom and future security could be guaranteed most effectively by their inclusion in the Czechoslovak union.

As finally constituted, Czechoslovakia, like Poland, was not a national but a multinational state. Besides the Slovaks, the new state included over three million Germans, three quarters of a million Hungarians, half a million Ruthenian-Ukrainians, some 200,000 Jews, 76,000 Poles, as well as smaller numbers of Romanians, Gypsies, and other ethnic minorities. The presence of these minorities proved to be a serious weakness. The Germans and Hungarians, who had occupied favored positions in the Austro-Hungarian empire, were especially resentful of their subordination to Czech rule, and both bitterly denounced the violations of the principle of self-determination in establishing the Czechoslovak state. But the Slovaks too were never happy in their partnership with the Czechs. With their largely agrarian and Roman Catholic population, the Slovaks found themselves at a disadvantage with the Czechs, who had enjoyed better educational and commercial opportunities under Austrian (as compared with Hungarian) rule and, in taking over the key positions in the government and bureaucracy, they treated the Slovaks as second-class citizens.

Despite its ethnic problems, Czechoslovakia was the most politically stable and economically prosperous state in Eastern Europe during the interwar years. Its treatment of its minorities was more fair and humane than that of any other Eastern European country, and it was the only state to retain a genuinely democratic government until its destruction by Hitler. A large part of the credit for this admirable record must be attributed to the leadership of Masaryk and Beneš, whose guidance of the new state through its first years of independence was an even greater achievement than their success in its creation.

❑ *Yugoslavia*

Two overlapping but contradictory ideals went into the forging of a union of south Slavs (Yugoslavia) after World War I: Serbian nationalism, which aspired to the creation of a Greater Serbia through the incorporation of the south Slavs within a Serb-dominated state; and a Yugoslav nationalism, a belief on the part of politically conscious south Slavs that, for all their religious and cultural differences, they were a closely related people who should be united in a single state for their mutual protection but should enjoy maximum autonomy and opportunity for independent development.

As finally constituted, the Kingdom of the Serbs, Croats and Slovenes (the state was not officially called Yugoslavia until 1929) included the prewar kingdoms of Serbia and Montenegro and the south Slav provinces of the old Habsburg empire, including Bosnia-Herzegovina, a former province of the Ottoman empire which the Habsburgs had formally annexed as recently as 1909. This accretion of territory created a state more than double the size of prewar Serbia that embraced virtually the entire south Slav population of Eastern Europe except for the Bulgarians. Yet throughout this territory, as elsewhere in Eastern Europe, there was a large admixture of peoples of other nationalities (Albanians, Vlachs, Germans, Hungarians, Bulgarians) and religions (Eastern Orthodox, Roman Catholics, Muslims, Jews.) And among these were people whose ethnic status was mixed or difficult to define. Such was the case of the Macedonians, who had been under Turkish rule as recently as 1912 and whose lands were now divided between Greece, Bulgaria, and Yugoslavia. Macedonian nationalists professed to be a separate nationality, but they were claimed as fellow nationals by the Greeks and Bulgarians as well as by the Serbs.

Among the south Slavs themselves there were also significant differences. The Slovenes and Croats, former subjects of the Habsburg empire, were for the most part Roman Catholics and used the Roman alphabet; the Serbs and Montenegrins were largely Eastern Orthodox and used the Cyrillic alphabet. During the long years of Turkish rule, many Slavs (and others) had converted to Islam, and some of them had profited handsomely by their conversion at the expense of their Christian brethren. Quite apart from differences in religion and written language, there were significant historical and cultural differences between the south Slavs of the former Habsburg empire and those who had lived for centuries under the rule of the Ottoman Turks.

Dangerous fresh differences arose over the question of setting up the government of the new state that reflected the contradictory ideals involved in its formation. Serbian nationalists, the advocates of a Greater Serbia, wanted a centralized administration that could be used as an instrument for the extension of Serbian power and influence. Yugoslav federalists, on the other hand, most of them former citizens of the Habsburg empire, wanted a political structure in which each of the south Slav peoples would be guaranteed maximum political, cultural, and religious autonomy.

In the end, the proponents of a Greater Serbia triumphed all along the line, thanks in large part to the Serbian army, which had fought with the Allies and remained in place after the war, whereas Croat and Slovenian forces, which had been enrolled in the armies of Austria-Hungary, were disbanded. In November 1918, a Yugoslav National Council, dominated by Serbs, invited Crown Prince Alexander of Serbia to become ruler of the south Slav union. Following the official establishment of the Kingdom of the Serbs, Croats, and Slovenes in December 1918, the Serbs made ruthless use of their power to install Serbs in the major posts in the government and bureaucracy, and the Serbian army was declared the country's military arm. When the Croatians boycotted a constituent assembly where they were certain to be outvoted, the Serbs were left with a free hand to draw up the Yugoslav constitution, which provided for a centralized administrative system for the entire country that gave official sanction to the dominant role of the Serbs.

The new constitution was a victory for the advocates of a Greater Serbia, but their dominion was achieved at the cost of intensifying the antagonism of the Croats and other national minorities. As ethnic tensions reached a climax in 1928 following the assassination of a major Croatian political figure, King Alexander imposed a royal dictatorship on the country with the avowed aim of inspiring a new south Slav patriotism that would transcend ethnic parochialism. It was in line with this program that the name of the country was changed to Yugoslavia. But the campaign to generate Yugoslav patriotism was a failure. A majority of Croatian leaders refused to cooperate with the royal dictatorship that denied them the autonomy they sought. The few who accepted office under the monarchy were denounced as traitors and lost whatever popular support they may have had. The king thus had no alternative but to leave the administration under Serbian control. Instead of transcending ethnic divisions, his regime became an even more obvious instrument of Greater Serbian centralists, while the country itself remained bitterly divided.

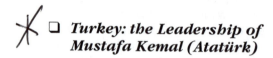

SEVEN

The Aftermath of Empire: the Middle East

❏ *Turkey: the Leadership of Mustafa Kemal (Atatürk)*

In Eastern Europe, the Allies made sincere efforts to reorganize the political configuration of the area on the basis of the principle of self-determination. They made no such effort in the Ottoman empire. The twelfth of Wilson's Fourteen Points had promised the Turks a "secure sovereignty" and the non-Turkish peoples of the empire "an unmolested opportunity for autonomous development." The Allies, who had never subscribed to this article, fulfilled neither promise. Far from conceding the Turks a secure sovereignty, they awarded large segments of the predominantly Turkish portions of the Ottoman empire (Anatolia and eastern Thrace) to the Armenians, Kurds, Greeks, and Italians, and to their mandates of Mesopotamia (Iraq) and Syria. Further, they imposed humiliating restrictions on the sovereignty of what they left to the Turks. All these territorial awards and restrictions were formally embodied in the Treaty of Sèvres of August 10, 1920, imposed by the Allies on the Ottoman government. (See p. 61.)

Well before the signature of the Treaty of Sèvres, the humiliations inflicted on the Turks and the depredations of foreign powers had given rise to a powerful Turkish nationalist movement under the leadership of Mustafa Kemal, Turkey's outstanding military commander in the recent war. Over the next decade, Mustafa was to carry out three separate but interlocking revolutions in the Turkish portions of the former Ottoman empire: a domestic revolution that overthrew the government of the sultan, an international revolution that overthrew the Treaty of Sèvres, and a social revolution designed to bring Turkey in line with the "progressive" states of Western Europe. In the course of these revolutions, Mustafa established the Turks' "secure sovereignty" over their country, he freed them from the last vestiges of foreign imperialism, and he inaugurated their liberation from centuries of traditional behavior that had heretofore stultified Turkey's modernization.

MAP 5   *THE PARTITION OF THE OTTOMAN EMPIRE. SEE ALSO MAPS 11 AND 15*

Born in 1881 to a lower middle class family in the seaport city of Salonika, at that time still part of the Ottoman empire, Mustafa chose a military career as the only one that offered opportunity for advancement to a man without wealth or social connections. As Mustafa himself tells the story, already in preparatory school he had demonstrated outstanding mathematical talent, for a teacher called him Kemal (Perfection), a name he was to use almost exclusively in later life. He served with distinction in the pre-1914 Italian and Balkan wars, but it was his role in the defense of Gallipoli during World War I that made him a national hero and earned him a reputation as a masterful organizer and strategist, a reputation subsequently reinforced on other fronts.

After the war, Kemal took over the leadership of the Turkish nationalist movement, its objective the recovery of the Turkish territories that the Allies had allocated to their various surrogates. Turkish nationalist activity was centered in eastern Anatolia, out of reach of hostile armies, where they established a government independent of Constantinople. As leader of the Turkish nationalist movement, Kemal demonstrated political and diplomatic skills quite as impressive as his qualities as a military commander. He imposed discipline and order on the heterogeneous political and religious factions within the nationalist camp. In dealing with the sultan, who was not only the legitimate political leader of the Ottoman government but also, as caliph, the religious leader of the world's Muslims, he took care to avoid offending the sensibilities of political and religious conservatives. And in dealing with foreign governments he set aside personal prejudices while assessing the possibilities for exploiting the differences between them.

Central to Kemal's political and diplomatic success was his clear conception of his objectives. These were embodied in a National Pact formulated in a succession of nationalist congresses under his leadership and adopted by a popularly elected Turkish parliament in January 1920. Unlike many Turkish nationalists, Kemal accepted the loss of the Ottoman empire's non-Turkish territories and was prepared to hold plebiscites in disputed border regions. But he insisted on maintaining the essentials of his political program: the establishment of a single Turkish sovereign state that should include all territory inhabited by a Turkish-Muslim majority, "united by religion, race [Kemal's term], and feelings of mutual respect and sacrifice."

Kemal and his nationalist government faced a formidable array of foes: the legitimate government of the sultan in Constantinople, backed by the armies and navies of the Allies; the British and French in southern Anatolia, supporting the territorial claims of their mandates of Mesopotamia and Syria; the Italians in Antalya; the Greeks in Smyrna; Armenian and Kurdish nationalist movements in eastern Anatolia, where the Armenians were backed by a British expeditionary force sent there originally to protect the area from the Germans and left there to defend it against the Bolsheviks.

Kemal's most immediate concern was the buildup of his own armies, a task facilitated by an influx of war veterans and younger men into his nationalist forces. He saw from the first, however, that he would never muster sufficient military strength to defeat his opponents, and that he could only overcome them by exploiting their differences. Skilful diplomacy, therefore, would be even more critical to his success than his military buildup.

❑ *The Armenian Question*

In May 1918 the Armenians, who inhabited the border regions of Russia, Turkey, and Iran, had set up an independent state in the Armenian provinces of Russia (the Republic of Erivan), and they were receiving Allied encouragement to incorporate the eastern provinces of Turkey, claimed by the Armenians on ethnic grounds.

In dealing with the Armenian question, Kemal set aside the centuries-old Turkish hostility to Russia and his personal dislike of Bolshevism to conclude a military alliance with Russia, whose interests were also threatened by the Armenian nationalist movement. Kemal's initial effort to cooperate with Russia over the Armenian question was a failure, for the Bolsheviks had their own Armenian agenda. Instead of supporting Turkey, they concluded an agreement with the Republic of Erivan recognizing Armenian claims in Turkey, confident that a Bolshevik-inspired revolution would soon restore Russian control over an Armenia enlarged at Turkey's expense. In October 1920, the Bolsheviks did in fact overthrow the government of the Republic of Erivan and made Armenia a republic of the newly formed Soviet Union.

Kemal now decided to act independently in dealing with the Armenians. Taking advantage of the Red Army's involvement in war with Poland, he demanded that the Armenians withdraw their forces from Turkish territory and agree to a plebiscite in the disputed areas. When the Armenians rejected these demands, he went to war with the Armenian Soviet and succeeded in regaining all former Turkish territory, including the districts of Batum, Kars, and Ardahan, lost by the Ottoman empire to Russia in 1878. In a peace treaty of December 2, 1920, he secured the Armenian Soviet's recognition of these Turkish conquests, and, to eliminate any future Armenian ethnic claims, he compelled them to acknowledge that there were no Armenian ethnic majorities in any province of Turkey.

By this time the Bolshevik government, still faced with civil war and foreign intervention on several fronts, decided to accept Kemal's offer to cooperate over Armenia. In November 1920 the Bolsheviks established official diplomatic relations with Kemal's nationalist government, and early in the following year they concluded a treaty of friendship with Kemal that settled their Armenian differences. In the Treaty of Moscow of March 16, 1921, Russia formally acknowledged the Armenian government's cession of Kars and Ardahan; in return, the Turks restored Batum to the newly created Soviet Republic of Georgia and thus, in effect, to Russia. A critical point in the Moscow treaty was the provision that the status of the Turkish Straits should henceforth be determined exclusively by states bordering the Black Sea, a provision designed to prevent further intervention on the part of Britain, France, and other Western powers in this strategic area.

❑ *Diplomatic Settlements with France and Italy*

With the Armenian question settled, Kemal turned his attention to southern Anatolia, where the French and Italians were having difficulty making good their territorial claims. Kemal took advantage of their predicament and growing Franco-Italian hostility to Britain over a variety of issues to arrange settlements with both countries in order to remove them from the ranks of his opponents. At almost the same time as the signing of his treaty of friendship with Moscow, he concluded treaties with France (on March 9) and Italy (on March 13). The French agreed to give up the Cilician district of southern Anatolia, which they had claimed for Syria, and to supply the Turkish nationalists with arms in return for Turkish recognition of their mandate over Syria. The Italians for their part agreed to give up their claims in Anatolia in return for economic concessions and Turkish recognition of their possession of the former Ottoman territories of Tripoli, the Dodecanese islands, and Rhodes, which the Italians had seized during their war with the Ottoman empire in 1912.

The treaties with France and Italy were major diplomatic achievements. They represented the de facto recognition by both countries of Kemal's nationalist government and, more importantly, they marked the breakdown of French and Italian cooperation with Britain, which was now left as the sole backer of the government of the Ottoman sultan and Greek interests in Anatolia.

❑ *The Expulsion of the Greeks, the Chanak Crisis, and the Abolition of the Sultanate*

Of all the humiliations inflicted on the Turks after World War I, the Allied cession of Smyrna to Greece was the most galling, for they had ruled over the Greeks for centuries and regarded them as a subject and inferior people. The Greeks made no attempt to soften the blow. After their takeover of Smyrna, they proceeded to settle ancient scores by a wholesale butchery of the Turkish population. A horrified British observer reported that the hatred between the Greeks and Turks was "as unreasoning as it is rabid" and "has to be seen to be believed."

Kemal had postponed dealing with the Greeks to concentrate on negotiations with more dangerous powers and the buildup of his own armies. Meanwhile, to avoid a fight before his diplomatic and military preparations were complete, he had conducted a strategic retreat that had enabled the Greeks to penetrate deeply into Anatolia. In August 1922, with his preparations completed, he launched a massive counteroffensive against the overextended Greek lines. Within a fortnight he had routed the Greek armies, in early September the Turks captured the city of Smyrna, and by the end of that month the last of the Greek forces had been driven from Anatolia.

The triumphant Turkish nationalists then turned north against the Ottoman capital of Constantinople, where the British, deserted by their French and Italian allies, remained as the sole defenders of the Sultanate and the shambles of the Treaty of Sèvres. As the Turks advanced toward Chanak, an outpost of the Ottoman territory defended by a small British force, Prime Minister Lloyd George appealed to the British Dominions for military support. New Zealand alone agreed to send a contingent. South Africa and Newfoundland promised only moral support, but both Australia and Canada responded with an outright refusal. In this, the so-called Chanak Crisis, Dominion status emerged for the first time as Dominion independence, a key moment in the devolution of the British empire.

Lloyd George, his Middle East policy in ruins, agreed to an armistice and the negotiation of a new peace treaty with Turkey. The British debacle in the Middle East, which coincided with political and diplomatic setbacks in other areas, brought down the Lloyd George government. He resigned on October 19, 1922, never to return to office.

To negotiate a new peace treaty with Turkey, the Allies issued invitations to both the government of the sultan and the Turkish nationalists. Realizing that this dualism would weaken Turkey's negotiating position and undermine the authority of his nationalist government, Kemal decided he could no longer postpone a decisive step in his domestic revolution: the Sultanate would have to go. Addressing his nationalist parliament, where feelings of loyalty to the sultan remained strong, Kemal pointed out that the constitution adopted by this parliament in January 1921 had vested sovereignty in the nation, not the sultan, and that parliament should now give practical expression to its own principles.

Kemal's arguments overcame the opposition of Turkish conservatives, and on November 1, 1922, the nationalist parliament voted to abolish the Sultanate. On November 17 Sultan Mehmed VI left his country on a British warship, ending the line of Ottoman rulers which had extended in unbroken male succession from the thirteenth century. The office of caliphate, which gave the sultan religious authority over the world's Muslims, was not abolished but was invested in another member of the House of Osman, its functions now strictly limited to religious affairs.

❑ *The Treaty of Lausanne*

A conference to negotiate a new peace treaty with Turkey convened on November 20, 1922, in the Swiss city of Lausanne. In these negotiations, Kemal once again demonstrated an impressive sense of realism and restraint. He made no effort to regain the non-Turkish territories of the Ottoman empire in North Africa, Asia Minor, and the Mediterranean. But he negotiated with stubborn tenacity to obtain what Wilson had defined as "secure sovereignty" over the Turkish portions of the empire. He made no concessions to the Armenians and Kurds in eastern Anatolia or to the Greeks in eastern Thrace, where he recovered all the empire's prewar territory as well as the islands of Imbros and Tenedos, lost to the Greeks in the Treaty of Sèvres. He compromised only over the boundaries of Mesopotamia and Syria, leaving Mosul (thought to be a potentially rich source of oil and claimed by the British on behalf of Mesopotamia) to future negotiation and confirming a previous treaty with France making Alexandretta a special administrative district of the French mandate of Syria.

Kemal's greatest success, achieved only after bitter negotiations that for a time threatened the breakup of the conference, was the complete abolition of the so-called Capitulations—treaties imposed on the Ottoman government giving foreigners special rights and privileges in the Ottoman empire. He therewith put an end to the last vestiges of foreign imperialism in Turkey. Alone among the defeated Central Powers, Turkey was not obliged to pay a war debt or reparations of any kind.

Kemal's diplomatic talents were nowhere displayed more impressively than in his negotiations over the Turkish Straits and his renewal of Turkey's nineteenth century partnership with Britain to block Russian ambitions in the Middle East. In his treaty with Russia of March 16, 1921, Turkey had agreed that the future status of the Straits should be determined exclusively by states bordering the Black Sea. In partnership with Britain, Kemal now negotiated a new Straits Convention, signed February 1, 1923, which provided for freedom of navigation and the creation of a demilitarized zone on the European and Asiatic shores of the Straits under the joint guarantee of Britain, France, Italy, and Japan. With that, Turkey in effect secured an international alliance to oppose possible future encroachments on the part of Russia. The terms of the Straits Convention were embodied in the final Treaty of Lausanne, signed by all the powers at the conference on July 24, 1923, but never ratified by the Soviet Union.

❏ *The Greco-Turkish Population Transfer*

To settle the problem of national minorities in Greece and Turkey, these countries concluded a separate agreement that required all Greeks in Turkey and all Turks in Greece to leave the cities and lands their forefathers had inhabited for centuries. The ensuing population transfer, in which a half million Turks and one and a half million Greeks were involved, proved to be a brutal operation that prompted the American historian Raymond Sontag to write in 1931: "No more terrible indictment of nationalism is conceivable." Professor Sontag spoke too soon. The world was to see infinitely more terrible indictments of nationalism as the century wore on. The Greco-Turkish population transfer has been defended as having "solved" this particular minority problem, whereas the problems of the Armenians, Kurds, and other minorities in Turkey continue to fester to the present day. This "solution" in itself, however, represents a fundamental indictment of nationalism, for it concedes that the political, ethnic, or religious differences fostered by nationalism are irreconcilable and can only be resolved through population transfers—or by genocide.

❏ *Kemal's Social Revolution*

Until his death in November 1938, Mustafa Kemal was consistently reelected president of the Turkish Republic and was conceded dictatorial powers, which he used to carry out the social revolution designed to transform Turkey into a modern Westernized state. To facilitate communication with the world's major political and commercial countries, the Arabic alphabet was replaced by the Latin, and the calendar was changed to conform to the Western Gregorian system. In 1928 the government was officially secularized, the article in the constitution declaring Islam to be the state religion was abolished, and Muslim religious orders were suppressed. Two years later, Byzantine geographic names were changed to Turkish: Constantinople became Istanbul; Angora (since 1923 the capital of Turkey) became Ankara; Adrianople, Edirne; Smyrna, Izmir. There followed a 1934 decree requiring all Turks to adopt surnames in the Western manner, at which time Mustafa Kemal was awarded the name of Atatürk, the father of the Turks.

❑ *The Non-Turkish Territories*

The ethnic minorities in Turkey and the inhabitants of the non-Turkish territories of the Ottoman empire were far less successful than the Turks in achieving political sovereignty and independence.

Point Twelve of Wilson's Fourteen Points assuring the non-Turkish peoples under Turkish rule "an absolutely unmolested opportunity for autonomous development" was evidently never meant to apply to the various countries of North Africa or the Mediterranean islands, which, although still under nominal Turkish suzerainty in 1914, were actually under the direct or indirect control of Britain, France, Italy, and Greece. Neither during nor after the war did these states make any serious move to relinquish their authority. (See Chapter 28.)

Even in the non-Turkish territories that had remained under Ottoman rule, the Allies signally failed to provide their inhabitants with an unmolested opportunity for autonomous development. In Anatolia, owing to the success of the Turkish nationalists, the Allies were unable to live up to their promises to the Armenians and Kurds. But the Allies also failed to honor their promises in regions where they had a comparatively free hand, notably those made to the Arabs who constituted a majority of the population in the empire's non-Turkish territories.

The Arabs had ample reason to expect more generous treatment. As we have seen, to secure Arab support against the Turks, the British had made conflicting and contradictory commitments to Arab leaders promising them independence and freedom from Ottoman rule—commitments that had ignited Arab uprisings against the Turks and set the stage for the legendary exploits of T. E. Lawrence. On November 7, 1918, the British and French issued their Arab declaration, cited earlier, stating that their objective in waging war in the Middle East had been the "complete and definite emancipation of the peoples so long oppressed by the Turks." Britain and France were "at one in encouraging and assisting the establishment of indigenous governments in Syria and Mesopotamia" as well as other territories still being liberated.

The Allies were soon to reveal that they never had any intention of honoring this declaration. Article 22 of the Covenant of the League of Nations, published in June 1919, provided that the subjects of former empires "not yet able to stand by themselves" should be placed under the tutelage of more advanced nations who would act as Mandatories on behalf of the League. Included in this category were "certain communities formerly belonging to the Turkish Empire," whose existence as independent nations could only be provisionally recognized "subject to the rendering of administrative advice and assistance by a Mandatory until such time as they are able to stand alone." The only concession to the hapless Muslim populations was that their wishes "must be a principal consideration in the selection of the Mandatory."

Arab leaders, their awareness of their ethnic identity aroused by their wartime experiences and by the ethnic-nationalist ideas emanating from Europe, were understandably infuriated by the mandate provision of the League Covenant. On July 2, 1919, a Syrian National Congress meeting in Damascus presented a resolution to an Allied commission investigating the problems of the Middle East denouncing the mandate provision and calling for the complete political independence of a Syrian state extending from the Taurus range in the north to the Gulf of Aqaba in the south and to the Euphrates and Khabur rivers in the east. The resolution rejected all French claims to Syria (assigned to France by Sykes-Picot) and it demanded an end to all French involvement in the country "under any circumstances and in any place." It also rejected the "pretensions of the Zionists to create a Jewish commonwealth in the southern part of Syria, known as Palestine" and called for an end to all Zionist migration "to any part of our country; for we do not acknowledge their title but consider them a great threat to our people from national, economic, and political points of view." Besides demanding independence for themselves, the Syrians called for the independence of an "emancipated Mesopotamia" and the removal of all economic barriers between Mesopotamia and Syria, presumably with a view to the eventual union of these two countries.

The Allies, preoccupied with the problems of Europe, ignored the resolution of the Syrian National Congress as they ignored their promises to the Arabs. In a memorandum of August 11, 1919 (see p. 17), Arthur Balfour, the British foreign secretary, acknowledged the contradictions in British policy, but Britain had conceded authority over Syria to France, and good relations with France were more important than keeping faith with the Arabs; therefore, the Syrians would have no choice but to accept a French-controlled administration. In Palestine, where the contradictions of British policy were even more glaring, the wishes of the Jews were to have priority, for their needs were of far greater import than the "desires and prejudices" of the region's Arab inhabitants. Moreover, if Zionism were to have an impact on world Jewry, Palestine must be made available to the largest possible number of Jewish immigrants and should extend into the lands lying east of the Jordan River.

A second Syrian National Congress meeting in Damascus in March 1920 restated Arab demands for the complete independence of Mesopotamia as well as Syria, but once again Arab wishes were ignored. In April, Allied leaders agreed on final peace terms to be imposed on the Ottoman empire and on the assignment of mandates in Asia Minor. As already decided in a long succession of earlier negotiations, Britain was assigned Mesopotamia, which was now officially named Iraq and would later include the oil-rich province of Mosul. Britain was also assigned Palestine, which was to include the lands on either side of the Jordan River and extend south to the Gulf of Aqaba. The Balfour Declaration was incorporated in the terms of the Palestine mandate, but with the very important proviso that its application could be postponed or withheld in the territory east of the Jordan (the future Transjordan). Syria, with Alexandretta, was assigned to France. All these arrangements were embodied in the Treaty of Sèvres, presented to the Ottoman government on June 10, 1920, and finally signed under protest on August 10. The provisions of the Sèvres treaty dealing with the empire's non-Turkish territories were not affected by the subsequent Treaty of Lausanne.

❑ *Saudi Arabia*

The dream of Arab nationalists to create a united Arabian state in the predominantly Arab territories of the former Ottoman empire had long since been shattered. Sharif Hussein of Mecca, the beneficiary of promises made in the name of the British Foreign Office (see p. 14), had proclaimed himself king of the Arab countries, but Britain and France recognized him only as King of the Hejaz, the region of the Arabian Peninsula skirting the east coast of the Red Sea. Here his authority was challenged by Ibn-Saud, the beneficiary of promises by Britain's India Office, who was the ruler of the Nejd territory in the peninsula's interior and leader of a fanatical Muslim sect known as the Wahabis. Following a succession of defeats by Ibn-Saud, Hussein abdicated as King of the Hejaz in October 1924, as did his son fifteen months later. In January 1926 Ibn-Saud had himself proclaimed King of the Hejaz and Sultan of Nejd, and thus ruler over a large part of the Arabian Peninsula. A year later the British recognized Hejaz and Nejd as an independent kingdom, which was renamed Saudi Arabia in September 1932.

The Arabs observed with some cynicism that the only predominantly Arab territories of the former Ottoman empire where the British and French refrained from exercising a direct tutorial role was Ibn-Saud's kingdom in the Arabian Peninsula, the most politically and culturally backward segment of the Arab world. Elsewhere, in blatant violation of their promises, they divided the Arab territories into spheres of influence between themselves and in doing so established five new political entities: Syria, Lebanon, Iraq, Palestine, and Transjordan.

❑ *Syria and Lebanon*

The Syria assigned as a mandate to France in April 1920 was far smaller than the country claimed by the Syrian National Congress in 1919, which extended south as far as the Sinai Peninsula and thus included the territory assigned to Britain as the mandate of Palestine. Syrian nationalists were thus infuriated from the start by this truncation of their territorial claims. But their most intense fury was directed against the mandate system as such and the imposition of French authority over what was left of Syria. They attempted to resist, but after a short but brutal struggle, the French defeated the ill-equipped and poorly organized Arab forces and entered Damascus on July 25, 1920. French rule was thus inaugurated in an atmosphere of violence and resentment, which continued to simmer throughout the years of the French mandate.

The one district of Syria with a predominantly Christian population was Lebanon, which the French greatly enlarged in the hope of securing Christian support for their rule in the Levant and making Lebanon itself a stronger pro-French base. By enlarging Lebanon, however, the French also enlarged Lebanon's Muslim population, thereby setting the stage for ugly political and religious confrontations.

On May 23, 1926, after a succession of religious crises, the French yielded to the appeals of Lebanese Christians to make Lebanon an independent republic, though under conditions that left France a large measure of authority. Lebanon did indeed become something of a pro-French base, but by making Lebanon independent, the

French intensified the animosity of Syrian nationalists, who have never abandoned their claim that Lebanon was an integral part of Syria.

❏ *Transjordan*

The British, too, created a new state in the Middle East. In March 1921 they used their superior military power in the region to claim a broad strip of Syrian desert east of the Jordan River on behalf of their mandate of Palestine. This was done to extend the boundaries of Palestine to the frontier of Iraq, an arrangement that gave them an over-land route for a rail or pipeline from Iraq to the sea through territory entirely under British control. As noted earlier, however, although, the Balfour Declaration had been incorporated in the terms of the British mandate, that Declaration did not apply to the territory east of the Jordan, where it could be postponed or withheld altogether. From the beginning, therefore, this region had a special status within the mandate. That special status was confirmed officially on May 26, 1923, when the area east of the Jordan was made an autonomous administrative district which became known as Transjordan.

The status of Transjordan was transformed from autonomy in 1926 to independence in 1928, but throughout the interwar years Britain continued to exercise predominant authority over the country. After World War II Britain recognized the independence of Transjordan, which in May 1946 was officially named the Kingdom of Transjordan and in June 1949 was renamed the Hashemite Kingdom of Jordan.

❏ *Mesopotamia (Iraq)*

In their mandate of Iraq, the British initially faced even more violent opposition than the French in Syria. To bring the country under control they were obliged to reinforce the 100,000-man army already stationed in Iraq (as compared to the 15,000 kept there by the Turks before 1914), and for a time it seemed that hatred for the British would transcend the traditional hostility between the country's various religious and ethnic factions. But the British adopted more conciliatory policies than the French in Syria. In October 1922, to make their rule more palatable to Arab nationalists, they transformed their mandate into an alliance. A decade later they granted the country complete independence, though with reservations that enabled them to preserve sufficient influence to protect British interests.

British control was facilitated by religious and ethnic differences among the native population and by the Iraqi government's need for British support to cope with religious and ethnic opposition. The Muslims were bitterly divided between the two major sects, the Sunnites and the Shiites. The Shiites, the more fundamentalist group, believe that doctrine must be based solely on the Koran and that the religious authority of a caliph derives exclusively from Muhammad and his direct descendants. They thus reject the authority of caliphs who cannot claim such direct descent. The Sunnites, on the other hand, besides using the Koran as a source of doctrine, accept traditional Muslim law based on the words and deeds of Muhammad (Sunna) and they recognize the authority of caliphs (spiritual leaders) who were not direct descendants of the prophet.

In Iraq the Sunnites, on the whole better educated and more prosperous, exercised predominant influence in the country, although they constituted a minority of the Muslim population. Their influence and policies were resented by the poorer and more conservative Shiites, who regularly obstructed programs they regarded as incompatible with the teachings of the Koran. Concentrated in the south and supported by their co-religionists in Iran (the stronghold of the Shiite sect, where the majority of the population was Persian, not Arab), the Shiites were a major obstacle to a unified Muslim stance against the British.

The Muslims were also divided along ethnic lines. The largest ethnic minority in Iraq were the Kurds, who were Sunnite Muslims but not Arabs. A seminomadic people, the Kurds inhabited the mountainous frontier districts of Iraq along the borders of Turkey and Iran, which also had substantial Kurdish minority populations. Inspired by ethnic-nationalist sentiment, the Kurds in all three countries have rebelled frequently against their governments with the objective of establishing an independent Kurdish state. Each time their revolutions have been suppressed with brutal ferocity.

In Iraq, as elsewhere in the Middle East, the problems of religious and ethnic schism remain unresolved.

❑ *Palestine: the Zionist-Palestinian Problem*

The most explosive religious and ethnic problem in the British mandate of Palestine was created by the Balfour Declaration—the provision of a national home for the Jews in Palestine without prejudicing "the civil and religious rights of the existing non-Jewish communities," who in 1917 made up 93 percent of the population of that region.

Until 1917 the region known as Palestine had been part of the Ottoman empire. It was not a separate political or administrative district with well-defined boundaries, but was a name conventionally used for the territory claimed as the heritage of the Jews, who had been expelled by the Romans in 135 A.D. following the last of a succession of rebellions against Roman rule. With the expulsion of the Jews, even Jewish place names had been changed, and the region was called Palestine after its earlier Philistine inhabitants—a name that continued to be used over the centuries to designate the territory encompassing the Holy Places sacred to Jews, Christians, and Muslims. In 1917, Palestine formed part of the Ottoman vilayet (administrative district) of Beirut and the Sanjak (province) of Jerusalem. Palestine became a separate political entity only in modern times when the region was made a mandate of Britain by the Allied Supreme Council on April 25, 1920. Since then its political status and its boundaries, as well as its name, have remained in dispute.

Despite the Balfour Declaration's acknowledgment of the rights of Palestine's non-Jewish communities, the terms of the mandate stated plainly that a prime task of the mandatory was to support Zionist aspirations in Palestine. The Balfour Declaration was incorporated in the preamble; Article 2 made the mandatory responsible for creating such "political, administrative, and economic conditions as will secure the establishment of a Jewish National Home"; and Article 6 required that the mandatory, "while ensuring that the rights and position of other sections of the population are not prejudiced," would facilitate Jewish immigration and settlement.

There were major differences among the Jews themselves over their plans and aspirations in Palestine. The Jewish Zionists, to whom the Balfour Declaration had been addressed, had called for the establishment of "a home in Palestine" for the Jewish people at the first meeting of a Zionist congress in 1897. At that same congress they had created a World Zionist Organization to secure international support for a Jewish state in Palestine, which they envisaged as a national state comparable to the national states of Europe. From the beginning, the Zionists insisted that a Jewish national home must be in Palestine, for Zionism could only exist in the ancient land of Zion.

Though there were numerous varieties of Zionism, the most influential Zionist leaders were practical politicians who saw the need to play a careful diplomatic game and cultivate support in the governments of the great powers. Splitting off from the main body of Zionists in 1935 was a more radical nationalist group, the New Zionist Organization, which demanded a Jewish national state that would include all of Palestine and Transjordan. Jewish Marxists, on the other hand, disdained Zionism as a reactionary-bourgeois-capitalist movement. Also rejecting Zionism were ultra-Orthodox Jews, who felt that political nationalism would undercut the religious basis of Judaism and believed that the return to Zion must come about through divine intervention, not through a political-temporal agency.

From the time of the establishment of the British mandate, however, the Zionists were the principal agents for Jewish interests in Palestine. The president of the World Zionist Organization was also the president of the Jewish Agency in Palestine, which in Article 4 of the British mandate was designated as the organization to cooperate with the mandatory power in the establishment a Jewish national home.

The Palestinian question is an example of a genuinely tragic situation in history: a problem not of right versus wrong, but of two profoundly held and contradictory conceptions of right. For a large majority of Jews, secular and religious, Palestine was their ancestral and spiritual home from which they had been driven by the Romans two thousand years ago and scattered throughout the countries of the world, where they had frequently been subjected to vilification and persecution.

For the Palestinian Arabs, the land of Palestine was not only their ancestral but their present home, where in 1917 they constituted a large majority of the population. The Syrian Arabs insisted that "the area known as Palestine" was an integral part of Syria, while Arabs in general were uncompromisingly opposed to the mere suggestion that any part of Palestine should be made a national home for the Jews. They feared the consequences of unlimited Jewish immigration, which in time might overwhelm the native Arab population. And they foresaw the possibility that Jews in Palestine, with the support of their co-religionists abroad, would have the money to acquire a major share of the land through purchases from the impoverished Arabs.

The Arabs had reason for concern. Between 1917 and 1931 the number of Jews in Palestine rose from about 60,000 to 175,000. After Hitler came to power in Germany, another quarter million Jews immigrated to Palestine, so that by 1939 they made up about 28 percent of the population. During this period, Jewish ownership of land more than doubled, from 150,000 to 384,000 acres.

Even before the inauguration of the British mandate, Palestine had become the scene of violent confrontations between Arabs and Jews, and during the mandate years those confrontations increased in scale and frequency. A British commission of enquiry sent to Palestine in 1936 concluded that the contradictions inherent in the terms of their Palestine mandate could never be resolved. It therefore recommended a partition of the mandate into three parts: a Jewish state along the coast; an Arab state united with Transjordan; and the territory around Jerusalem, a holy city to Jews and Muslims as well as to Christians, which was to remain a British mandate. Both Jews and Arabs, in agreement for once, bitterly denounced the partition scheme. The Jews complained that it violated the Balfour Declaration; the Arabs objected to partition on principle.

With the rejection of the partition plan, the British put forward a proposal to make Palestine independent within ten years and to form a government in which both Arabs and Jews would be represented in such a way as to safeguard the interests of each community. This plan, embodied in a so-called White Paper of 1939, was rejected by the Jews because it limited Jewish immigration to 75,000 over the next five years, after which it would cease altogether, and because it included further restrictions on the sale and transfer of land. They objected further that, under any genuinely representative administrative system, the Jews would always be outvoted by the Arab majority. But the Arabs too rejected the plan. They opposed all Jewish immigration and reaffirmed their demand for an independent Palestinian state, administered and controlled by its Arab majority population.

With the outbreak of war in 1939, the Jews proclaimed their solidarity with Britain. Although many Arabs sided secretly or openly with Germany, they never took advantage of the opportunities of the war to form the pan-Arab union envisaged by Arab nationalists, nor did any significant Arab group or faction join forces with Germany.

❑ *The Oil Factor: Persia (Iran)*

In the decade before 1914 and for almost a decade after World War I, the oil factor in the calculations of the great powers regarding the Middle East was based entirely on the speculation that oil actually existed in this region. Because up to this time the only oil produced in the Middle East had come from the nominally independent country of Persia, where a New Zealander named William Knox d'Arcy had paid lavish sums in bribes to secure a concession from the Iranian government for oil exploration. On May 26, 1908, d'Arcy finally struck oil, and in the following year the Anglo-Persian Oil Company was formed to raise the necessary funds to exploit the d'Arcy concession. That company built a 138-mile pipeline from the oil fields to the Persian Gulf and a refinery on the island of Abadan in the Shatt al-Arab estuary of the Tigris, Euphrates, and Karun Rivers.

The exploration for oil in Persia had been followed with intense interest in Britain by Winston Churchill, appointed first lord of the admiralty in October 1911, and John Fisher, the former first sea lord, who in 1912 had promoted the conversion of the British navy from coal to oil. Convinced that their naval rivalry with Germany would lead to war, they were seeking sources of fuel whose production and price could be controlled by Britain. To prevent Anglo-Persian's absorption by a foreign oil consortium and to preserve exclusive British control, Churchill and Fisher (now head of a Royal Commission on Fuel and Engines) persuaded their government to invest 2.2 million pounds in Anglo-Persian in return for 51 percent of the stock and the appointment of two directors to the company's board.

During World War I, the British successfully defended southwestern Persia, where the major oil fields and the Abadan refinery were located, and by 1916 Anglo-Persian was providing one-fifth of the oil needed by the British navy. After the war, with the breakup of the Ottoman empire, the British attempted to consolidate their position in Persia through a treaty of August 9, 1919, reaffirming that country's territorial integrity and offering military and financial support that would have made Persia a de facto British protectorate. "We possess in the southwest corner of Persia great assets in the shape of oil fields, which are worked for the British Navy and which give us a commanding interest in that part of the world," Lord Curzon, the British foreign secretary, noted in a memorandum to the cabinet in support of the treaty. The Persian government, however, already resentful of Britain's "commanding interest" and unwilling to subject their country to even greater British control, refused to ratify the August 9 treaty.

In February 1921 Reza Khan, an officer in Persia's Cossack Brigade (established under tsarist auspices but now independent of Russian control), carried out a coup d'état and established a new government with himself as minister of war and commander-in-chief of the army. Four years later, after inviting Sultan Ahmed Shah to take "an extended and prolonged tour" of Europe, Reza deposed Ahmed and elevated himself to the Peacock Throne as Reza Shah Pahlavi.

Because of the Persian government's dependence on oil revenues, Reza allowed Anglo-Persian to continue its operations in Persia, but from the beginning the company's relations with his government were strained. They seemed to break down altogether when on November 16, 1932, following the plunge in oil revenues during the world economic depression, Reza abruptly cancelled the concession granted to d'Arcy in 1901. After extensive and acrimonious negotiations, a new treaty was signed in May 1933 that extended the Anglo-Persian concession to 1993 but drastically reduced the concession area (from 500,000 square miles to 250,000, and, by 1938, to 100,000) and substantially increased Anglo-Persian's payments to the Persian government. A company executive complained that "we had been pretty well plucked," but Anglo-Persian remained in business. In 1935, when the shah changed the name of his country to Iran, Anglo-Persian became the Anglo-Iranian Oil Company.

❑ *Mesopotamia*

No oil had been discovered in the territories of the Ottoman empire before 1914, but speculation about the existence of oil had already led to a good deal of diplomatic and commercial maneuvering. Speculators were primarily interested in Mesopotamia, which geologists considered the most likely source of oil. So great was the confidence that oil would indeed be found there that in 1916, as the war drove home the importance of a secure oil supply, Maurice Hankey, the secretary of the British War Cabinet, thought the establishment of British control over Mesopotamia should be considered a primary British war aim. This view was shared by Arthur Balfour, the British foreign secretary, who ensured that Britain should remain the "guiding spirit" in Mesopotamia after the war.

To supply the necessary spirit, British troops remained in Mesopotamia after the 1918 armistice with Turkey, and in 1920 the British were assigned the mandate for Mesopotamia, which was now officially named Iraq. Six years later, after long and acrimonious negotiations, Britain managed to secure the greater part of oil-rich Mosul for their Iraqi mandate.

As early as 1912, a canny Armenian-American named Calouste Gulbenkian had put together an organization, the Turkish Petroleum Company, which merged the interests of the major players in the game at that time: Germany's Deutsche Bank, Royal Dutch/Shell Oil, and the British-controlled Turkish National Bank, in which Gulbenkian himself was the silent holder of 30 percent of the shares. After the war the French were given the German 25 percent interest in the Turkish Petroleum Company, though with the proviso that "the said company shall be under permanent British control." When Mesopotamia became the British mandate of Iraq, "said company" was awarded a monopoly concession for oil exploitation in the country. Under heavy American pressure, the British subsequently agreed to make half their holdings available for purchase by American oil interests.

All this time no commercially viable source of oil had yet been discovered in Iraq, but the speculation about the existence of oil proved justified, for in June 1927 Turkish Petroleum struck oil near Kirkuk in the Mosul province. The discovery of oil spurred the conclusion on July 21, 1928, of a final agreement among the competing interests within Turkish Petroleum. Roughly equal shares went to Royal Dutch/Shell, Anglo-Persian, to the French, and to a Near East Development Company (created to hold the interests of the American companies involved), while five percent went to Gulbenkian, the founder of Turkish Petroleum who had continued to play a leading role in negotiations among rival interests.

With the coming of the great depression, the Iraqi government followed the example of Iran in seeking greater revenues from Turkish Petroleum, which in 1929 was renamed the Iraq Petroleum Company. Iraq Petroleum managed to make a far better bargain than Anglo-Iranian, securing an extension of its concession rights which gave the company a virtual monopoly over oil production in Iraq. In return, the company pledged to build pipelines to Haifa and Tripoli on the Mediterranean coast and to begin annual payments of 400,000 pounds to the Iraqi government. The pipeline to Tripoli, completed two years ahead of schedule, began delivering oil in July 1934; that to Haifa, in January of the following year.

❑ *Bahrain and Saudi Arabia*

The greatest oil fields in the Middle East were found in the 1930s in Saudi Arabia, which geologists had written off earlier. Interest in the possibilities in Saudi Arabia was stimulated by the discovery in 1932 of oil in the Bahrain Islands off the southeastern coast of Saudi Arabia, where Frank Holmes, another New Zealander, was granted an oil concession by the Sheik of Bahrain in 1925 as a reward for his success in drilling for water. So convinced were experts that there was no oil in this region that Holmes was long regarded as a nuisance in his search for financial backing. He finally aroused the interest of the Standard Oil Company of California (Socal). To overcome the objections of the British to this intrusion of foreign influence on the Gulf coast, Socal set up a Canadian subsidiary, the Bahrain Petroleum Company, to hold the concession, and provided guarantees to ensure Britain's political and strategic primacy in the area. Drilling began in October 1931, and seven months later Bahrain Petroleum struck oil, thereby revealing that there might also be oil on the Saudi mainland.

In Saudi Arabia itself, King Ibn-Saud, like the Sheik of Bahrain, was originally more interested in drilling for water than for oil, and his relations with foreign business interests were constrained by the hostility of his puritanical Muslim subjects to all modern/foreign innovations. But he too felt the cold economic blasts of the great depression in the 1930s, which brought about a sharp decline in the number of pilgrims to Mecca, his kingdom's major source of revenue. With the discovery of oil in Bahrain, several foreign companies now sought concessions in Saudi Arabia, which held out the promise of unprecedented financial opportunities.

The king and his agents bargained shrewdly. On May 29, 1933, the Saudi government sold an oil concession to Standard Oil of California for modest initial loans and advance royalty payments, but the concession also provided that upon the discovery of oil the government was to receive a loan of 100,000 pounds and a royalty of four gold shillings per ton of oil thereafter. The concession was to cover 360,000 square miles and was to run for sixty years. When the Texas Company joined Standard of California's operations in Saudi Arabia, the enterprise was renamed the Arabian-American Oil Company (Aramco), which struck oil in March 1938. Saudi Arabia and Aramco were on their way to riches.

◻

EIGHT

East Asia: Japan and China, to the Washington Conference

◻ *The Pre-1914 Background*

Among the countries of East Asia, Japan alone had managed to evade European imperialist domination in the years before 1914. This achievement was due in large measure to the timely recognition on the part of a remarkable group of Japanese statesmen that they could only maintain their country's political independence by yielding to European cultural imperialism and adopting European administrative, economic, and military systems. So successful were they in readjusting their country's institutions along European lines that Japan not only retained its independence but by the early twentieth century had become one of the world's great powers in its own right. In 1895 Japan had surprised the world by defeating the far larger and more populous Chinese empire; ten years later it scored an even more surprising victory by defeating Russia, the greatest (in terms of size) of the European great powers.

China had not been so fortunate. By 1914 a large part of the vast Chinese empire had been divided into spheres of interest among the European powers and Japan, a situation which the American-sponsored Open Door notes (that China should be open to the trade of all countries on an equal basis) did not effectively alter or disguise. Rivalry among the powers had nevertheless prevented the outright partition of China, so that China survived as a sovereign state, recognized as such by foreign powers, even though the empire suffered severe territorial losses, notably to Russia in the north.

In 1911 a revolution in China resulted in the ouster of the Manchu (Ching) dynasty, which had ruled China since the mid-seventeenth century, and the establishment of a republican government under the provisional presidency of a medical doctor turned professional revolutionary named Sun Yat-sen. In February 1912 the last of the Manchus, the three-year old Hsuang-tung emperor, abdicated; he was to reappear on the stage of history as Henry Pu-yi, the puppet ruler of Manchuria after the Japanese seized control of that region in 1931.

Following the abdication of the emperor, Sun resigned as provisional president and was succeeded by a former imperial prime minister, Yuan Shih-kai, who was widely regarded as the only man with sufficient political experience and military support to lead the new republican regime and avoid civil war. Early in 1914 Yuan abolished the trappings of republican government, suspended parliament and all provincial assemblies, and established himself as dictator.

In the last years of the empire and even under the strong hand of Yuan, the central government of China had not been able to assert its authority over the country's outer provinces. Shortly after the 1911 revolution two provinces, Outer Mongolia and Tibet, broke away from China altogether and proclaimed their independence. Yuan died in June 1916, and with his death the authority of the central government disintegrated still further as local military leaders (the so-called warlords) established their rule over large parts of the country and waged war against each other to extend their own spheres of authority.

❑ Japan, China, and World War I: The Twenty-One Demands

It was in this period of growing anarchy in China that the Japanese moved to extend their dominion over that country. Japanese ambitions on the Asian mainland had been powerfully stimulated by their victories over China and Russia, but in both cases the Japanese had been deprived of the full fruits of victory by the intervention of the European powers and the United States. Upon the outbreak of war in Europe in 1914, and with American attention also focused on Europe, Japanese expansionists saw they now had a magnificent opportunity to realize their ambitions in East Asia without the interference of rival powers.

In 1902 Britain had concluded an alliance with Japan (renewed in 1905 and 1911), largely as a means to block Russian and German expansionist ambitions in Asia. In 1914, this alliance with Britain gave the Japanese a convenient pretext to enter the war on the side of the Allies and to take over the interests of Germany in East Asia— China's Shantung Peninsula and all German-held islands in the Pacific north of the equator.

The Japanese now proceeded to apply European imperialist techniques in dealing with China itself, using the familiar pretext that their sole concern was to help the Chinese government restore law and order and protect the lives and property of foreigners. On January 18, 1915, they presented the government of Yuan Shih-kai with their notorious Twenty-one Demands. These included China's agreement to transfer to Japan all German rights in the Shantung Peninsula; an extension to ninety-nine years of Japanese leases to the harbors of Port Arthur and Dairen on China's Liaotung Peninsula (the so-called Kwantung Lease Territory, acquired by Japan after its victory over Russia in 1905); control of the major Manchurian railways and other special economic privileges in Manchuria; the transfer to Japan of a substantial interest in the major industries, arsenals, railways, and harbors of China proper; and a promise by China to reject all future demands on the part of any other country for territory along the Chinese coast. In a final set of demands, which the Japanese designated "desirable items," Japan called upon the Chinese government to agree to the appointment of Japanese advisers to supervise China's political, economic, and military affairs—"items" that would have reduced China to the status of a Japanese protectorate.

Yuan immediately leaked the Japanese demands to the foreign press in the hope of receiving foreign, especially American, support in rejecting them, and the Japanese were sufficiently alarmed by this possibility to agree to a postponement of a discussion of these "desirable items." No effective foreign support was forthcoming, however, and after five months of procrastination Yuan finally yielded to Japanese ultimatum. He agreed to virtually all their claims apart from the "desirable items," which the Japanese may have intended to impose at a later date.

The American president Woodrow Wilson attempted, but failed, to rally international support for China because the attention of all major powers was concentrated on the war in Europe. In fact, the British, eager to secure Japanese naval support in the Mediterranean (and safeguard their own interests in the Pacific), made concessions of their own to Japan at China's expense. On February 16, 1917, they concluded a secret treaty with Japan promising to support Japanese claims to Shantung and the German-held Pacific islands north of the equator. In return, the Japanese promised to provide naval support in the Mediterranean and to recognize British claims to the German-held Pacific islands south of the equator. This bargain was subsequently endorsed by Russia, France, and Italy in secret treaties of their own with Japan.

The Europeans and Americans did not abandon China altogether. To save China from Japan, as well as defend their own interests there, they urged the Chinese government to join Japan in declaring war on Germany (which it did in August 1917), so that China might be represented at a postwar peace conference. At such a gathering, the European powers and the United States might be able to support China in countering Japanese demands and repudiating treaties imposed on China during the war. As we have seen, this stratagem failed at the 1919 Paris Peace Conference, but it was to prove successful at a conference held in Washington three years later. (See pp. 105–106.) In yet another diplomatic move to support China, the United States concluded an agreement with Japan in November 1917 recognizing Japan's "special interests" in China in return for pledges of Japanese good faith in maintaining China's territorial integrity, independence, and the Open Door policy.

❑ *Japanese and Allied Intervention in Siberia*

Japan's ambitions on the Asian mainland were not restricted to China. With Russia weakened by the war against Germany, revolution, and civil war, Japanese imperialists saw a splendid opportunity to extend their authority over large tracts of Asiatic Russia, much of which the Russians had acquired from China as recently as the mid-nineteenth century. To give some semblance of legitimacy to their own activity in this region, the Japanese concluded a succession of agreements with the Chinese government, or what they chose to recognize as the Chinese government, providing for joint military operations in Siberia "if the general peace and tranquility in East Asia were menaced."

The plans of Japanese imperialists for intervention in Siberia revived a debate within the Japanese government over a basic question of foreign policy: should Japan give priority to maintaining close diplomatic and commercial ties with the West, which would leave Japanese security and prosperity heavily dependent on the West, or should Japan acquire an empire on the Asian mainland that would enable the Japanese to become independent of the West but might involve them in dangerous international complications? The arguments of the expansionists had prevailed during World War I, but Japanese moderates, who since 1914 had expressed misgivings about their country's aggressive China policy, now warned even more strongly against intervention in Russia. They pointed out that intervention would be disastrous for Japan's postwar relations with Russia, which would inevitably recover its status as a great power sooner or later, and that Japanese expansionist policies were certain to provoke dangerous hostile reactions on the part of the American and other European governments.

The policies of the European Allies played into the hands of the Japanese imperialists. The Japanese had not responded to Allied appeals to send a large expeditionary force to the continent to support the Russian war effort—the Japanese could only welcome the weakening of Russia, their major threat to Japanese interests on the Asian mainland. But after the Bolshevik revolution and Russia's surrender to the Central Powers, the renewed Allied appeal for Japanese intervention in Russia opened out many promising possibilities.

The Allies argued that Japanese intervention was essential to prevent a German takeover of Russia, aided by their one and a half million prisoners of war in that country, and they feared the German seizure of the vast stores of military equipment they had shipped to Russia, which was now lying in the northern ports of Murmansk and Archangel and the Pacific harbor of Vladivostok, The Japanese had reason to question the seriousness of a German threat to Vladivostok, and they suspected that what the Allies really wanted was the overthrow of the Bolsheviks.

The Japanese played a cautious and devious game. In response to Anglo-French pressure, they protested that they could not afford to arouse the suspicion and hostility of the United States and that they could only consider taking action in Siberia if assured of American approval and support. This argument may have reflected the views of Japanese moderates, for Japanese military leaders, supported by the imperialist faction in the imperial government, had long since made detailed plans for intervention in Siberia. But Japanese imperialists, too, could only welcome assurances of American approval.

Wilson refused to provide the desired assurances. He saw no possibility of re-establishing a viable Eastern front via Siberia and insisted that the war could only be won in Europe. Moreover, with a view to postwar problems, he opposed any action on the part of the Allies that might impinge on Russia's political sovereignty or territorial integrity or that might be interpreted by the present Russian government as a hostile act.

His European allies seethed with frustration. On March 18, 1918, Arthur Balfour, the British foreign secretary, appealed to Wilson in the name of the Allied governments to give the Japanese the assurances they requested to enable them to intervene in Siberia, because Japan was the only state that could prevent Russia from being ravished by the Central Powers. As Wilson persisted in his refusal, the Allies shifted to an argument that addressed the concerns Wilson himself had expressed: Given the present anarchic conditions in Russia, the Japanese would feel obliged to intervene to defend their present and future interests; only through an agreement with Japan could the Allies secure Japanese guarantees to respect Russian sovereignty and territorial integrity.

Wilson remained unmoved and the Japanese remained cautious. Early in April 1918, the Japanese landed a small contingent of marines in Vladivostok in response to an alleged Bolshevik attack on the lives and property of foreigners in that city. But farther than that they would not go. When the Allies asked whether the Japanese would participate in an *inter-Allied* campaign in Siberia, they still insisted that they would do so only with American approval. The Allies appealed again to Washington: would the *United States* participate in an inter-Allied Siberian campaign? After some hesitation Wilson at last decided in favor of participation, a decision that inaugurated the fateful and futile American intervention in Russia that was to cloud Russo-American relations for years to come.

Wilson appears to have been won over by the argument that some kind of inter-Allied cooperation was necessary to control the Japanese. But the officially announced reason for American intervention in Siberia was a Czech appeal to the Allies to come to the aid of the Czechoslovak legion in Russia. That legion, about 60,000 strong in 1918, was made up of Czech and Slovak deserters and prisoners of war from the Austro-Hungarian army who had volunteered to fight on the side of Russia and who, now that Russia had withdrawn from the war, were trying to make their way back to Western Europe by way of Siberia and the harbor of Vladivostok.

Having at last agreed to intervene in Siberia, Wilson ignored his European allies and acted unilaterally in dealing with the Japanese. On June 7 the American secretary of state informed the Japanese that the United States would like to invite Japan to join on an equal basis in an immediate program to rescue the Czechoslovak legion. If such action was agreeable to Japan, the United States hoped Japan would join in a declaration to the effect that the purpose of sending troops was to aid Czechoslovaks against German and Austrian prisoners of war (Wilson had received totally false reports that these prisoners were blocking the Czech exodus), that they had no intention of interfering with the internal affairs of Russia, and that "they guaranteed not to impair the political or territorial integrity of Russia."

The wording of Wilson's invitation suggests that, although he was undoubtedly sincere about his concern for the Czechoslovaks, the primary purpose of American intervention was in fact to restrain the Japanese. Soviet scholars and their Western acolytes have long argued that American and Allied intervention was a capitalist-imperialist plot designed to destroy Bolshevism and the Soviet state. So far as Wilson is concerned, this interpretation is contradicted by all available evidence. As noted earlier, Wilson had originally opposed intervention altogether, and when he finally agreed he demanded that Japan join America in a pledge to respect Russia's political and territorial integrity. Further, he ordered that American troops sent to Russia avoid all involvement in Russian domestic affairs. This proved impossible once Americans arrived in the country, but the fact that Wilson issued such an order seems to confirm his intention to honor that pledge.

What Wilson could not have known was the effect that his decision to intervene would have on the Japanese government, where Wilson's invitation to join in an expedition to Siberia ensured victory for the imperialist party. That invitation, with its many restrictions, was not at all what Japanese interventionists had in mind, but they urged its immediate acceptance: once intervention had taken place, the conditions under which it was carried out could be modified to suit their own purposes.

In their reply to Wilson's invitation, the Japanese agreed to almost all of the president's conditions, but from the first they hedged about the size of their military commitment and reserved the right to send additional troops if circumstances required. And from the first, Japanese military leaders blandly ignored their government's pledges and proceeded to implement their own long-prepared plans for expansion on the Asian mainland. Instead of the seven thousand troops proposed by Wilson, they sent well over ten times that number to Siberia. By December 1918 Japanese forces had gained control over an area extending as far as Lake Baikal in the west and had taken over the Trans-Siberian railway, while another 10,000-man division moved into the zone of the Russian-controlled Chinese Eastern railway that cut across northern Manchuria to Vladivostok.

It was soon obvious to the American and Allied governments that they would be unable to restrain the Japanese without a far larger investment of their own troops in East Asia, but this was a commitment they were unable to make. Now that Germany had been defeated, they were under powerful domestic pressures to bring their troops home. Nor were Allied and American leaders necessarily opposed to Japanese involvement in Russia and Manchuria, although they took care not to make such sentiments public. The Japanese thrust into these areas diverted them from Western spheres of interest in East Asia, and their intervention in Russia might have the salutary effect of overthrowing the Bolsheviks or creating an effective barrier against the Bolshevik menace. When the Americans and their European allies prepared to withdraw their forces from Russia in January 1920, they made no objection to a Japanese proposal to send an additional five to six thousand troops to reinforce their garrisons in Siberia. Nor did they voice any significant opposition to the Japanese takeover on July 3, 1920, of Russia's half of the island of Sakhalin, allegedly as compensation for the massacre of Japanese soldiers in the Siberian city of Nikolaevsk in the previous May.

Meanwhile, virtually nothing was done to evacuate the Czechoslovaks, whose rescue had been the ostensible reason for American and Allied intervention in Siberia. Nor did the Czechoslovaks seem in any hurry to be evacuated, for by this time many of them had become deeply involved in the Russian civil war. By January of 1919, however, a Bolshevik offensive compelled the Czechoslovaks to withdraw from the Volga front, but the last of them did not reach Vladivostok until May of the following year. There they sat for another fifteen months because of Allied delays in providing for their evacuation, and it was not until September 1921 that the last members of the Czechoslovak legion finally left Russia.

With the departure of the Czechs, the Japanese seemed to have been left in an ideal position to regulate affairs in Siberia as they saw fit. But in Russia, as later in China, they were to find that it was easier to occupy a country than to bring its territory and population under effective control. As the Bolsheviks gained in strength and the native populations grew more restive, the Japanese found their occupation of Siberia was becoming ever more costly. In Japan itself, meanwhile, the moderates within the Japanese government, who had never abandoned their criticism of their country's imperialist ventures, demanded the abandonment of what by now seemed futile and endless military adventures that were sapping the country's strength while at the same time exposing it to international opprobrium. After lengthy and heated domestic debate and subjected to intense international pressure, the Japanese government at last agreed to accept an American invitation to participate in an international conference in Washington.

❑ *The Washington Conference,*
November 12, 1921 to February 6, 1922

With the Japanese installed in many parts of China and Siberia, the Europeans and Americans faced the problem of how to restore their influence and safeguard their interests in East Asia. For this purpose they resorted to that most familiar of diplomatic stratagems: an international conference, where the Japanese would be confronted with diplomatically phrased demands to honor their pledges to respect the sovereignty and territorial integrity of both China and Russia. As was tacitly understood by all the conference participants, these demands were backed by the threat of war or other retaliatory measures in case the Japanese resisted diplomatic pressure for concessions and compromise. It was a stratagem that had been used successfully against Russia to cut down Russian gains after the Russo-Turkish war of 1877, and against Japan itself after the Sino-Japanese war of 1895.

Upon securing the approval and support of London, the United States issued invitations to all states with interests in East Asia to attend a conference in Washington to discuss the problems of the Pacific and the question of international disarmament. Of the nine countries invited to attend, only two were actually East Asian states: China and Japan. Apart from the United States, all the others were European: Belgium, Britain, France, Italy, the Netherlands, and Portugal. The most glaring omission was Bolshevik Russia, whose government was not recognized by the United States. Before the conference even convened, the Russian government announced that it would not recognize any of its decisions, a nonrecognition that proved to be curiously ironic, for Russia was to be a major beneficiary of those decisions.

The first concrete result of the negotiations at Washington was a Four-Power Treaty, signed December 13 by the representatives of Britain, France, Japan, and the United States, whereby the signatories agreed to respect their mutual rights "in relation to their insular possessions and insular dominions in the region of the Pacific Ocean." This treaty achieved one of Britain's objectives at the conference: the termination of the Anglo-Japanese dual alliance, with its provisions for mutual military support in the event of international controversy. That alliance was now absorbed in the new Four-Power Treaty, which was essentially no more than a consultative pact. With that step the British eliminated the danger that they might be drawn into a conflict with the United States in the event of an American war with Japan, which was already regarded as a distinct possibility.

In communicating the provisions of this treaty to the conference, the American senator Henry Cabot Lodge, who had opposed the Treaty of Versailles and the League of Nations, announced with some pride that, unlike Versailles and the Covenant of the League, the present treaty imposed no binding commitments on its signatories. "There is no provision for the use of force to carry out any of the terms of the agreement, and no military or naval sanction lurks anywhere in the background or under cover of these plain and direct clauses." Critics of the treaty, at that time and since, have regarded this very lack of enforcement provisions as a fatal weakness. As is the case with all treaties, however, their effectiveness depends less on enforcement provisions than on the recognition on the part of the signatory governments that their own interests are best served by honoring their treaty obligations.

A Nine-Power Treaty, signed by representatives of all the participating states on February 6, 1922, provided that the signatories "respect the sovereignty, the independence, and the territorial and administrative integrity of China." The signatories promised further to provide the fullest opportunity for China to develop an effective and stable government, to maintain the principle of equal opportunity for the commerce and industry of all nations throughout the territory of China, to refrain from taking advantage of conditions in China to seek rights and privileges that would impinge on the interests of friendly states, and to refuse to countenance actions inimical to the security of friendly states. In a second Nine-Power Treaty of February 6, the signatories agreed in principle to grant China tariff autonomy and empower the Chinese government to increase its customs dues.

As was the case with the Four-Power Treaty, the two Nine-Power Treaties contained no enforcement provisions. An even more serious omission, however, was the lack of any definition of what constituted "China." The Chinese government, weak and wracked by domestic controversy, lacked the power to exercise effective authority over many parts of what had once been the Chinese empire, especially over the warlords of the outlying provinces and the warring factions in the three provinces of Manchuria. In the international crises that were soon to develop over Manchuria, the Japanese were to insist that they had long ceased to regard Manchuria as part of China and that their agreements to respect Chinese political and territorial integrity had therefore never applied to Manchuria.

These problems lay in the future. At the Washington conference the Japanese behaved with exemplary restraint. Two days before the signature of the Nine-Power Treaties, the Japanese, in a dramatic reversal, relinquished their claim to former German rights in China's Shantung Peninsula, which they had extorted at the cost of so much ill-will at the Paris Peace Conference. The Japanese also reversed their policy toward Russia. In a declaration of January 23, 1922, the Japanese promised to respect the territorial integrity of Russia, and shortly after the Washington conference adjourned they promised that the evacuation of Siberia would be completed by October 1922, a promise they honored. Finally, through a convention of January 20, 1925, the Japanese established diplomatic relations with the Soviet Union and promised to withdraw their troops from northern Sakhalin in return for extensive economic privileges.

The available Japanese documents throw little light on Japan's motives for making these concessions. The Japanese were under heavy international diplomatic pressure, and, as observed earlier, the occupation of Shantung and Siberia were proving to be increasingly difficult and expensive. But the reason these concessions could be made at all was that the Japanese government had come under the temporary control of moderates, who favored maintaining good relations with the West and fostering Japanese interests through trade and industry.

❑ *The Agreement on Naval Disarmament*

Besides dealing with the problems of the Pacific, the Washington conference had been convened to negotiate a treaty for the limitation of international armaments as called for by the Treaty of Versailles, which stipulated that the disarmament of Germany was to be followed by a gradual reduction in the armaments of all countries. Even when governments sincerely desire an arms limitation treaty, however, negotiations on this subject are inherently difficult because each country has its special needs, and each fears that its security will be threatened or its prestige tarnished if it makes meaningful concessions. The negotiations in Washington dealt only with naval armaments, but even here the participants could agree only on limiting the construction and maintenance of capital ships (vessels over 10,000 tons).

The Five-Power Treaty on capital warships, signed February 6, 1922, provided that no new ships of this class should be built over the next ten years and established a ratio for those that might be retained by the signatory powers. Britain, with its naval commitments in every part of the world, and the United States, with its need for a two-ocean navy, were both granted a ratio of five. Japan, whose interests were confined almost exclusively to the western Pacific, received a ratio of three. France and Italy were allotted the same ratio of 1.67, a provision that infuriated the French, who resented being placed on a par with Italy and who claimed that they too needed the equivalent of a two-ocean navy, one for the Mediterranean and another for the Atlantic. As a result of France's anger over the capital ship ratio and the inability of other powers to agree on further disarmament formulae, no limitation was imposed on the building and maintenance of warships below the capital ship class, including submarines.

The acceptance by their delegates of a ratio lower than that of Britain and the United States also infuriated Japanese patriots. Yet, though the head of the Japanese delegation found it necessary to explain to his government his reasons for agreeing to a seemingly unfavorable capital ship ratio, it was Japan that stood to gain most from the Washington agreement on naval armaments. Capital ships, with their greater cruising range, were far more necessary to Britain and the United States in carrying out naval operations in East Asian waters than to Japan, whose geographical position enabled it to make more effective use of smaller vessels. With no restrictions at all on the construction or possession of warships below 10,000 tons, the Japanese could build up preponderant naval power in the western Pacific despite their lower capital ship ratio.

The Washington treaty gave the Japanese another and perhaps even greater advantage in this respect: it stipulated that Britain and the United States should not build or maintain any new naval bases east of Singapore, north of Australia, or west of Hawaii, a provision that vastly enhanced the significance of Japan's geographical position because no limits were imposed on the construction of new naval bases on the islands of Japan.

In America and throughout much of the world, the Five-Power Treaty on naval disarmament was hailed as a first step towards a more comprehensive disarmament agreement and thus a major contribution to world peace. Even at the time, however, it should have been obvious that such optimism was sadly misplaced, for the Washington Conference had demonstrated the enormous difficulties standing in the way of meaningful arms control.

The French, who had played a leading role in preventing the limitation of naval vessels below the capital ship class, had also blocked the negotiation of a treaty for the overall reduction of international armaments. The French government expressed its willingness, indeed its desire, to escape the costs and sacrifices which the maintenance of a large and well-equipped modern army entailed. But if France were to disarm, it must first receive guarantees in the form of binding defensive treaties from its former allies and the United States, guarantees which these countries had promised but had so far refused to provide. So long as France was left to stand alone and forced to bear the major responsibility for defending the postwar international order in Europe, France would be obliged to maintain an army large enough to fulfill its obligations and was entitled to take any measures to ensure its own safety. Confronted by this renewed French request for an "entangling alliance," the American delegates promptly abandoned their disarmament proposals, and no other power represented at the conference was prepared to press the issue at this time.

NINE

❑

East Asia:
From the Washington Conference
to the Manchurian Crisis

❑ *China: Nationalism, Marxism,*
and the Bolshevik Interest

The Washington Conference, with its renewed international recognition of the sovereignty and territorial integrity of China, did nothing to stem the tide of rising nationalist sentiment in that country, where resentment of foreign interference in Chinese affairs had risen to new heights during World War I. On May 4, 1919, Chinese nationalists in Peking staged major demonstrations to protest foreign encroachments, in particular the award to Japan of China's Shantung Peninsula at the Paris Peace Conference. In retrospect, this May Fourth Movement can be seen as a landmark in the emergence of nationalism as a dominant force in Chinese politics.

The growth of nationalist sentiment in China, as in many other parts of the world, was accompanied by a growing interest among intellectuals in Marxist political and economic theories. Their "scientific" certainty about the ultimate triumph of the proletariat and call to revolution against the exploiting classes provided an intellectual stimulus as well as a political action program. Throughout China study groups were set up to study and propagate the theories of Marx. One of these groups was led by a student from Hunan named Mao Tse-tung.

The Chinese interest in Marxism was soon to be matched by the interest in China on the part of the Russian Bolsheviks, who saw the immense possibilities opening out to them in this vast and populous land. Although Marx had predicted that the first great proletarian revolutions would take place in capitalist-industrialized societies, the first major successful Communist revolution had occurred in Russia, still a largely agrarian country. Lenin therefore foresaw the possibility of similar revolutions in the countries of Asia, which housed the majority of the world's population. "It is precisely this majority," he said, "that with unexpected rapidity has been drawn into the fight for its own freedom in recent years." From this phenomenon he concluded that "the final victory of socialism is fully and unconditionally guaranteed."

To win the favor of the Chinese, the Bolsheviks issued a series of dramatic proclamations denouncing the unequal treaties imposed on China by Russia's tsarist government, which the Bolsheviks declared to be null and void. On September 27, 1920, in one of the most sweeping of these proclamations, the Bolshevik government announced that it "restores to China, without compensation and forever, all that has been predatorily seized from her by the tsar's government and the Russian bourgeoisie." These generous proclamations, issued while the Bolsheviks were still confronting civil war and international intervention, had the desired effect of inspiring friendly feelings for the Bolshevik government among politically conscious Chinese, many of them already attracted to Marxism and thus particularly susceptible to the overtures of a Marxist regime.

Over the next decade, however, as the Bolsheviks consolidated their own power, they abandoned this program of self-denial and reverted to a policy of outright imperialism in areas of greatest importance to Russia—the territories directly on the Russian border: Manchuria, Outer Mongolia, and Sinkiang (Chinese Turkestan).

❑ *The Chinese Political Situation; Sun Yat-sen*

In dealing with China in the years after World War I, a major difficulty for the Soviet Union, and indeed for all foreign governments, was the chaotic Chinese political situation. Even under the relatively strong hand of Yuan Shih-kai, the Chinese government had been unable to assert its authority over the country's outer provinces. After his death the authority of the central government had disintegrated still further. Most foreign states recognized the government in Peking as the "official" government of China, although Peking itself was ruled by a bewildering succession of warlords who exercised no real authority beyond the area controlled by the warlord of the moment. Manchuria, which included the three eastern provinces of Heilungkiang, Kirin, and Liaoning (Fengtien), was ruled by a warlord named Chang Tso-lin, who since 1924 was also in control in Peking and was supported by the Japanese so long as he was seen as a guardian of Japanese interests. Elsewhere in China, power was exercised by rival warlords who sought foreign recognition and support through concessions to foreign interests and who engaged in chronic civil war to extend their power base.

Prominent among the contenders for leadership in China was Sun Yat-sen, the first president of the Chinese Republic, who had been supplanted almost immediately by Yuan Shih-kai. (See p. 99.) Even before Yuan's assumption of dictatorial powers, Sun, fearing for his life, had fled to Japan. After Yuan's death in 1916 he returned to China and in July 1917 was elected head of a military government in the southern city of Canton. He was largely a figurehead leader, however, for the real power in the Canton government was exercised by a succession of warlords, and even their authority was limited to the region immediately around the city of Canton.

Sun was a useful figurehead. A man of great personal charm and magnetism, he was one of the most popular and admired Chinese revolutionary leaders, and his name conferred a certain prestige on any regime with which he was associated. Even more important, Sun was well-known abroad and had a large number of foreign contacts through which he could raise money and political support.

Born in 1866 into a peasant family in Kwangtung province, Sun at the age of thirteen joined an elder brother in Honolulu, where he went to a Church of England school and was converted to Christianity. He subsequently obtained a medical degree in Hong Kong, but he never practiced medicine. Instead, he devoted himself to the cause of revolution and traveled widely throughout Asia, Europe, and North America to raise money and secure support for his revolutionary enterprises. While in London in 1896, he was kidnapped at the orders of the imperial Chinese government which regarded him as a dangerous subversive. He was saved from extradition and certain execution by the intervention of a former medical professor, who aroused British public opinion on his behalf and in the process made Sun internationally famous.

Besides his foreign fame and contacts, Sun had a political asset that in the beginning seemed pathetically meager. This was his leadership of a political party, the Kuomintang (National People's Party), founded during the first months of the presidency of Yuan Shih-kai to defend parliamentary government. Yuan ordered the party dissolved in November 1913 and arranged for the assassination of the party's leader. After Yuan's death the party was reorganized under the leadership of Sun Yat-sen, but it remained scarcely more than an association of political intellectuals with little popular support until it received an infusion of new energy and ideas from the Bolsheviks.

❑ *The Kuomintang-Communist Partnership*

In March 1919 the Bolsheviks had founded the Third Communist International (Comintern) which was assigned the task of organizing—and controlling—Communist parties throughout the world and which were to assist in the promotion of world revolution. In July 1921 Comintern agents helped organize the first congress of the Chinese Communist party in Shanghai. In line with Comintern policy to work with bourgeois parties, these agents also sought alliances with the leaders of other Chinese political organizations. Among these leaders was Sun Yat-sen, who in the summer of 1922 had been forced to flee from Canton and had sought refuge in Shanghai. His political fortunes were thus at a low ebb when he was approached by a Comintern agent named Adolf Joffe, who proposed the formation of a Communist-Kuomintang alliance. Joffe assured Sun that the Soviet Union had no desire to export Communism or the Soviet political system to China and that it had no imperialist ambitions in Outer Mongolia, recently occupied by Soviet troops. The Soviet occupation was only temporary to prevent the takeover of this area by Japan or other imperialist powers.

Without other offers of foreign support, for which he had pleaded in vain, and having lost his own political base, Sun agreed to the alliance with the Communists which was announced publicly in a joint Sun-Joffe statement of January 26, 1923. Almost immediately afterwards, the Comintern issued orders to the Chinese Communists to join the Kuomintang, which they were to control from within by obtaining key leadership posts. In accordance with Comintern policy, however, the Chinese Communists themselves were to remain strictly independent and preserve their own highly centralized party organization.

Within a month after making his alliance with the Communists, Sun regained war-lord support which enabled him to return as nominal leader of the government in Canton. The Communist alliance had nothing to do with this reversal of his political fortunes, but his reinstatement in Canton increased his potential value to the Soviet government, which now began to give him systematic support.

In September 1923 a Comintern agent named Michael Borodin arrived in China with a letter of introduction to Sun Yat-sen. Moscow had keenly felt the absence in Canton of a permanent and reliable representative, the letter stated, and the appoint-ment of Borodin, who had "worked for a great many years in the revolutionary move-ments in Russia," represented an important step in rectifying this situation. In fact, Borodin had spent many more years outside Russia than within. Born in 1884 of Jew-ish parents (his real name was Gruzenberg), he was exiled from Russia in 1906 and spent the next decade in Chicago, where he worked among immigrants in that city's slums and became headmaster of a progressive school. He returned to Russia after the Bolshevik revolution, but shortly afterwards he was sent abroad once again, this time as a Comintern agent in Mexico and Britain.

Borodin quickly established himself as the dominant force within the Kuomin-tang and the principal architect of its structure and policies. "If we want to achieve success in our revolution," Sun told his colleagues in the Kuomintang, "we must learn the Russian method, organization, and training. . . . So I ask Mr. Borodin to be the ed-ucator of our party, to train our comrades." Borodin responded to this request with skill and energy. Under his direction the party developed from an ineffectual group of individuals and factions into a centralized and well-organized mass movement.

At the advice of Borodin, Sun drafted a party manifesto embodying an ideological program that Borodin considered essential "to arouse the revolutionary fervor of the masses and kindle the flames of nationalist emotions." Besides being an ideological program, the manifesto laid out a plan for national reconstruction, which was to be achieved in three stages: a military stage, essential for the achievement of Chinese po-litical unity; a stage of political tutelage, in which a party dictatorship would prepare the people for self-government; and a third and final stage—self-government itself and the establishment of a genuine constitutional democracy. In the realm of foreign pol-icy, the party's principal goals were the national unification of China, the abrogation of the unequal treaties imposed on China by foreign governments, and the renegotia-tion of agreements which had given foreigners special rights and privileges in China.

The most important Soviet contribution to the Kuomintang was the development of a weapon the party had so conspicuously lacked heretofore, namely, military power. Not long after the dispatch of Borodin to China, the Soviets sent military ad-visers to Canton who set up a military academy on the island of Whampoa, ten miles below Canton, modeled on the officers school of the Red Army. The first superinten-dent of the Whampoa academy was a young officer named Chiang Kai-shek, whom Sun had sent to Russia in the previous year "to discuss ways and means whereby our friends can assist my work in this country." In a letter to Soviet leaders, Sun introduced Chiang as "my chief of staff and confidential agent . . . fully empowered to act on my behalf." Prominent from the first in the Whampoa academy were Chinese Commu-nists, who were intent above all on controlling the school's program for ideological indoctrination. Soon to take a position at Whampoa as deputy head of this indoctrination program was a young Chinese Communist recently returned from France named Chou En-lai.

❑ *Moscow's China Policy*

In its policy towards China, the Soviet government did not rely exclusively on the connection established with Sun and the Kuomintang or its relationship with the Chinese Communist party. While working with Sun and the Communists in Canton, Moscow was negotiating with the government in Peking and with warlords in control of other parts of the country. The Soviets were thus obviously trying to keep a foot in every camp. Given the confusion in the Chinese political situation at the time, this policy was understandable, but it also made for embarrassing contradictions in Soviet policy because each of the governments with which Moscow was negotiating was attempting to destroy the others.

Negotiations with the Peking government produced a treaty of May 31, 1924, reestablishing formal diplomatic relations between Russia and China and recognizing the Peking regime as the official government of the country. The May 31 treaty restated previous Soviet renunciations of rights and privileges obtained by the tsarist regime, and it formally recognized Chinese sovereignty over Outer Mongolia and its status as "a component of the Chinese Republic." The Soviets, however, failed to honor their promise to recognize Chinese sovereignty over Outer Mongolia, for they steadily extended their control over that region and in November 1924 they made it a de facto Soviet protectorate as the Mongolian People's Republic. Symbolic of Soviet overlordship was the change in the name of the capital city of Urga to Ulan Bator (city of the Red Hero).

In the autumn of 1924, the Peking government, which since October had been under the direction of a military triumvirate that included Chang Tso-lin, the warlord of Manchuria, invited Sun Yat-sen to join in working out a plan to unite China and put an end to the country's chronic political instability and civil war. As China's unification had always been Sun's own primary political goal, he accepted this invitation and journeyed to Peking in December 1924. Here he learned that he was mortally ill with cancer of the liver. He died in Peking on March 12, 1925.

With China sorely in need of a national hero and symbolic champion of Chinese freedom and national unity, Sun was now transformed into a cult figure whose achievements assumed legendary proportions and whose writings were revered as fonts of political wisdom. Sun-yat-senism became a far more potent force than Sun himself had ever been, and after his death Chinese leaders representing a wide variety of political persuasions laid claim to his legacy while reinterpreting his ideas to suit their own purposes.

❑ *The Rise of Chiang Kai-shek*

The death of Sun Yat-sen set off a struggle for leadership within the Kuomintang. That party was split between its Left-wing faction, dominated by its Communist members, and rival factions whose leaders appear to have been less concerned with ideology than with power and the promotion of their own interests. Although still young and not yet regarded as a serious contender for party leadership, Chiang Kai-shek, the superintendent of the Whampoa Military Academy, was in the forefront of this struggle from the beginning. In May 1925 he was to acquire a potent weapon for the realization of his ambitions through his appointment as commander of the Kuomintang army.

Chiang Kai-shek, who was to play such a prominent role in Chinese history over the next quarter century, had received his own military training at the Paoting Military Academy in northern China and in Japan. From 1909 to 1911 he served in the Japanese army, whose Spartan ideals he admired and whose ruthlessness may have been a model for his own behavior, though it is doubtful whether in his case any model was necessary. Throughout his career he behaved with unscrupulous brutality towards rivals and opponents when he thought he could afford to do so. In more delicate political situations, on the other hand, he could be a masterful manipulator, capable of winning the cooperation of rivals he was unable to defeat or playing them off against each other to prevent their union against him. He demonstrated comparable talent in dealing with foreign governments.

At home and abroad Chiang cultivated the image of a dedicated patriot. The record of his career, however, suggests that his concern for China was consistently subordinated to his personal ambition, or, to put it more charitably, that he identified his country's welfare with his own, a not unusual association in the realm of power politics. In his personal life, too, Chiang proved an adept manipulator. A notorious womanizer, he set aside two wives and a concubine to seek the hand of Sun Yat-sen's widow, Ching-ling, a daughter of the wealthy and well-connected Soong family, in order to make himself a prime contender for the Sun legacy. When Ching-ling rejected him he courted her sister, Soong May-ling, whom he married in December 1927.

Besides being Sun's sister-in-law, May-ling brought Chiang important connections in the United States and the world of finance. Her brother, T. V. Soong, was a Harvard graduate and already a prominent financier, as was her brother-in-law, H. H. Kung, a graduate of Oberlin College, married to the oldest of the Soong sisters, Ai-ling. All three sisters had attended Wesleyan College in Macon, Georgia, but May-ling had left Wesleyan to go to Wellesley College in Massachusetts in order to be near her brother at Harvard. The Soongs were Christians—their father had been a Methodist minister—and shortly after his marriage to May-ling, Chiang himself converted to Christianity. Conversion and marriage to May-ling, who was to prove a master of the art of public relations, were to generate enormous sympathy and support for Chiang in the United States. Of more immediate assistance were May-ling's male relatives T. V. Soong and H. H. Kung, whose financial operations provided a substantial part of the funds needed to support Chiang's political and military campaigns.

Even more valuable than the Soong connection was Chiang's relationship with crime bosses of the Chinese underworld who controlled the drug trade, prostitution, and protection rackets in China's major cities. Well-organized, wealthy, and immensely powerful, these crime bosses saw in Chiang an ally against the Communists, labor unions, and other organizations they regarded as threats to their interests. They supported Chiang's campaigns against these domestic foes through their own organizations, financial assistance, and the outright assassination of rival leaders. In August 1925 the most likely successor to Sun as chairman of the Kuomintang, the Left-oriented Liao Chung-kai, was gunned down in Canton upon his arrival for a meeting of the party's Central Committee. Chiang made a great display of cooperating with government authorities in tracking down Liao's murderer, but so great was the suspicion that Chiang himself was behind this assassination that another leading candidate for the chairmanship fled Canton to avoid a similar fate. His departure left the way open to the eventual succession of Chiang himself.

With his major rivals for the leadership of the Kuomintang out of the way, Chiang moved to destroy the influence of the Chinese Communists and political Leftists in general. Using the pretext of an alleged Communist coup to declare a state of martial law in Canton on March 23, 1926, he proceeded to carry out sweeping arrests of Communists, Leftists in the Kuomintang, trade union leaders, and others suspected of Leftist inclinations, while placing Soviet agents in Canton under house arrest and dismissing his Soviet military advisers. Two months later he forced through a party resolution excluding Communists from the Kuomintang and from leading positions in the government and army. In July he succeeded in having himself elected chairman of the party.

❑ Chiang-Moscow Relations

Chiang and Moscow now engaged in a game of mutual deception that was to characterize their relationship until after World War II. While proceeding against Chinese Communists and Soviet agents in Canton, Chiang assured Moscow of his own and his party's loyalty to the Soviet alliance and dismissed the Canton unpleasantness as having been the result of a misunderstanding. In seeking to preserve the goodwill and support of the Soviet government, Chiang was aided by the domestic political situation in the Soviet Union, where Russia's China policy had become an issue in the struggle for leadership between Stalin and Trotsky that had been building up since Lenin's death in 1924.

Stalin saw through Chiang's game, but he had convinced himself that Chiang was critical to the success of the "bourgeois" phase of the Chinese revolution. The Chinese Communists must therefore continue to cooperate with Chiang and the Kuomintang in order to crush the provincial warlords and foreign imperialists. Ignoring the coup in Canton, Stalin accepted Chiang's patently dishonest pledges about his continued loyalty to Moscow and instructed Borodin to reach a compromise with Chiang to ensure a continuation of the alliance with the Kuomintang. When Chiang had achieved his goal of uniting China, the time would have come to replace him and the entire Kuomintang apparatus with reliable Chinese Communists controlled by Moscow. Chiang and the Kuomintang were to be used to the limit of their usefulness, "squeezed like a lemon and then thrown away."

Trotsky, on the other hand, was dubious about the desirability of cooperating with Chiang and the Kuomintang because he believed, correctly as it proved, that Chiang's behavior in Canton had revealed the true nature of his attitude toward both the

Chinese Communists and the Soviet Union. Because Stalin prevailed in the domestic struggle in the Soviet Union, his victory ensured the continuation of Soviet support for Chiang.

❑ *The Campaign to Unify China*

In the late spring of 1926 Chiang Kai-shek began a long-planned military expedition to smash the northern warlords (the Northern Campaign), which was to be the first step in his campaign to unify China. By early October his generals had captured the city of Hankow (part of tri-city of Wuhan) on the Yangtze River, and in November the seat of the Kuomintang government was transferred from Canton to the more centrally located Hankow. Borodin and the Chinese Communists now demonstrated that they too could play a duplicitous game. While Chiang and the greater part of his army were campaigning well to the east, they carried out a coup giving them control of the Kuomintang's Central Committee and proceeded to oust Chiang from his positions as party chairman and commander of the party's armies.

Chiang himself was meanwhile advancing against Shanghai, at the mouth of the Yangtze. The Shanghai Communists, still under orders from Stalin to cooperate with Chiang, organized a general strike to facilitate his conquest of the city. Once in control of Shanghai, Chiang displayed his gratitude by ordering a wholesale slaughter of Communists and their supporters in what observers have described as a purge of awesome proportions. Among the few Communists who escaped was Chou En-lai, Chiang's former colleague at the Whampoa Military Academy, who was to become a principal figure in the Communist government of Mao Tse-tung after World War II.

With the Communists in control of the Kuomintang government in Hankow, Chiang established his own Kuomintang government in Nanking. Here he continued to protest his loyalty to the Soviet Union while at the same time moving systematically against Chinese Communists and left-oriented labor unions in areas under his control.

Stalin had finally had enough of Chiang, but he continued to pursue policies that revealed a curious misunderstanding of what was actually happening in China. Vastly overestimating the strength of the Chinese Communists, he ordered the Hankow Communists "to destroy the present unreliable generals" and Communist parties elsewhere in China to take over the governments in their spheres of operation. The results were disastrous. The Chinese Communists and their Soviet advisers, who had done so much to promote the buildup of the Kuomintang army, had failed to establish their control over that army. Thus when China's "unreliable generals" learned of Stalin's orders to destroy them, they seized control of the Hankow government, severed the Kuomintang's alliance with the Communists, and outlawed the Chinese Communist party.

Borodin and his team of Soviet advisers, their influence eliminated and their lives in danger, fled from Hankow and returned to Russia via Mongolia. An "Autumn Insurrection" in Hunan led by Mao Tse-tung, at that time still a relatively unknown Communist leader, was suppressed by forces loyal to Chiang Kai-shek, as were all other Communist uprisings. By 1928 Stalin's China policy was in shambles and Soviet influence south of the Great Wall virtually eliminated, a disaster Stalin blamed on the ineptness of the Chinese Communist leaders. Mao and a few followers survived to create a new Communist movement independent of Soviet influence and control.

Following the overthrow of the Communist Kuomintang regime in Hankow, the Kuomintang was reunited under the chairmanship of Chiang Kai-shek, who was now given extraordinary powers by the party leadership to aid him in carrying out the party's mission to unify China. Besides his chairmanship of the party, he was named chairman of the national government, commander-in-chief of the armed forces, and chairman of the government's military council with authority to issue orders directly to provincial and local governments and to enforce them by military action if necessary.

In the spring of 1928 Chiang resumed his Northern Campaign, his objective the capture of Peking, still China's "official" capital.

❑ *The Japanese Factor*

Alarmed by Chiang's advance to the north, the Japanese sent a contingent of marines to Shantung to protect their still-substantial interests in the peninsula, a violation of Chinese territory and Japanese treaty commitments. The Chinese responded with their most potent economic weapon—a massive boycott of Japanese goods—which was only lifted after the Japanese agreed to withdraw their troops.

Of far greater concern to the Japanese was Chiang's drive to Peking, which threatened their even more substantial interests in Manchuria. In this connection it is necessary to recall that since 1924 the government of Peking was under the direction of a triumvirate that included Chang Tso-lin, the warlord of Manchuria, who, in return for Japanese support, recognized Japan's special position in Manchuria. As the armies of the Kuomintang moved north, the Japanese feared that Chang Tso-lin would be driven from Peking and that Chiang Kai-shek might be tempted to follow up his capture of Peking by pushing ahead into Manchuria. To forestall this danger, the Japanese persuaded Chang Tso-lin to leave Peking of his own accord before the arrival of the Kuomintang forces; the Japanese for their part would protect his position in Manchuria by warning Chiang Kai-shek not to advance beyond the Great Wall.

Chang Tso-lin duly left Peking on June 3, 1928, but at dawn on the following day he was killed by a bomb as his train approached the Manchurian city of Mukden. As we now know from Japanese sources, his assassination was engineered by officers of Japan's Kwantung army who were disgusted by their government's failure to pursue a more vigorous China policy and intended to provoke a crisis to force their government's hand. Their action failed to produce the desired result because the Japanese government, chastened by the effectiveness of the Chinese economic boycott and the hostile reaction of world public opinion to its intervention in Shantung, decided to revert to a policy of restraint. Japan did nothing to prevent the Kuomintang army's takeover of Peking on June 8, 1928, nor did it intervene in Manchuria when Chang Tso-lin's son and successor, Chang Hsueh-liang, rejected Japanese overtures for an alliance and instead declared his allegiance to Chiang Kai-shek's national government.

As a reward, or payment, for his loyalty, Chiang Kai-shek made Chang Hsueh-liang commander-in-chief of China's Northeastern Frontier Defense Forces, and governor not only of Manchuria (the three Eastern provinces) but of the neighboring province of Jehol and a portion of Inner Mongolia as well.

☐ *China on the Eve of the Manchurian Crisis*

Between August and October 1928 the Central Committee of the Kuomintang, meeting in Nanking, established a dictatorship of the party, as envisaged by Sun Yat-sen, that was to guide the Chinese people though a period of political tutelage until they had gained sufficient experience to allow for the introduction of constitutional democratic government. Chiang Kai-shek, who had exercised quasi-dictatorial powers since the previous spring, was elected chairman of the party's Executive Committee.

The official capital of China was now moved from Peking (the northern capital) to Nanking (the southern capital) and Peking was renamed Peiping (the northern peace). As a symbol of this transfer, the body of Sun Yat-sen was brought from Peiping in June 1929 to a sumptuous granite and marble mausoleum on the slopes of the Purple Mountain of Nanking, where it still lies.

With the success of Chiang Kai-shek's Northern Campaign and Chang Hsueh-liang's recognition of Chinese sovereignty over Manchuria, China was ostensibly unified. But Chiang's authority was undermined from the start by factional strife within his government and the Kuomintang party. Moreover, the Nanking regime's authority over the rest of the country was based on a fragile coalition with provincial warlords. Like Chang Hsueh-liang in Manchuria, these warlords accepted the nominal overlordship of Nanking in return for their appointment as governors of their respective provinces with quasi-independent powers. Only five provinces in all of China made any pretense of remitting revenues to Nanking, and two of these supplied the bulk of the funds that supported the national government. Thus China remained deeply divided—and weak.

That weakness was soon to be starkly revealed. In July 1929, angered by Soviet violations of their agreements providing for joint management of the Chinese Eastern railway (running across northern Manchuria through Harbin), Chang Hsueh-liang, the governor of Manchuria, ousted the Soviet managers and took over sole control of the line in the name of the Chinese government. After protesting in vain, Moscow broke off diplomatic relations with Nanking and in November sent a Soviet army into Manchuria. The Soviets easily routed the Chinese forces, and on December 23, 1929, peace was restored with the signature in Nanking of the so-called Khabarovsk Protocol. This treaty provided for the return to Russia of all prewar rights and privileges, the reinstatement of Soviet personnel on the Chinese Eastern railway, the convocation in Moscow of a conference to discuss all other outstanding differences, and the reestablishment of formal diplomatic relations between Nanking and Moscow.

The Soviet action was a striking example of the successful use of force and one that took place at the very time that almost all the countries of the world were signing the Kellogg-Briand Pact outlawing the use of force as an instrument of national policy. (See p. 154.) It was a lesson not lost on the Japanese, who would soon take forceful action of their own to protect their interests in Manchuria.

❑ *Japanese Policy after the Washington Conference*

The fact that the Japanese government pursued a policy of restraint in the years following the Washington Conference did not mean that nationalist fervor and imperialist ambitions had died out or even subsided in Japan. Yet during the relatively prosperous years of the 1920s, the influence of moderates within the Japanese government was generally in the ascendant. Their priorities in foreign affairs were summed up in a 1924 memorandum by Shidehara Kijuro, the Japanese foreign minister, who pointed out that Japan's population was increasing by almost 1 million persons a year. Because of the island empire's own lack of natural resources, Japan had no alternative but to continue its industrial expansion and seek overseas markets for its exports, which were essential for the purchase of food and raw materials from abroad. "If we try to cure our economic problems by territorial expansion," Shidehara said, "we merely destroy international cooperation" on which Japan's overseas trade depended.

The Japanese policy of international cooperation was dealt a bitter blow with the passage by the American Congress in May 1924 of a law prohibiting the entry of Japanese immigrants into the United States. This law represented a unilateral abrogation of the American-Japanese Gentlemen's Agreement of February 1908 whereby the Japanese had agreed to a voluntary restriction on immigration. Infuriated by this humiliating legislation, the Japanese engaged in widespread anti-American demonstrations and boycotts. Although Japanese leaders were similarly incensed, they did their best to ease tensions. After sending a note of protest to Washington, Shidehara instructed his ambassador to the United States to do nothing more: further action would only lead to greater mutual hostility and serve no useful purpose; nothing, however, could dispel the painful impression of this unjust legislation from the minds of the Japanese people.

Important as were Japan's relations with the Western powers, the overriding concern of Japanese foreign policy was China, which was Japan's major export market and its major foreign source of food and raw materials. In his 1924 memorandum Shidehara declared that the preservation of the great market of China must be a priority for Japan, whose proximity to China and low wage scales gave Japan a competitive advantage over its Western commercial rivals. But precisely because of the importance of the China market, Japan was exceptionally vulnerable to China's principal economic weapon, the boycott. Japan must therefore be particularly careful to avoid arousing Chinese hostility.

This advice was disregarded by Tanaka Giichi, a Japanese general who took over the posts of prime minister and foreign minister in April 1927. It was he who in 1927 and again in 1928 had sent Japanese troops into China's Shantung Peninsula to protect Japanese interests, provoking massive Chinese boycotts of Japanese goods, whose effectiveness evidently convinced Tanaka to revert to a policy of restraint. He made no further moves to intervene in China except to warn Chiang Kai-shek, now embarked on his Northern Campaign, that Japan would not tolerate the spread of the Chinese civil war beyond the Great Wall. In other words, Chiang was not to advance into Manchuria.

Tanaka also refrained from intervention in Manchuria following the assassination of the Manchurian warlord Chang Tso-lin on June 3, 1928. (See p. 117.) He was confident that Chang Tso-lin's successor in Manchuria, his son Chang Hsueh-liang, had abandoned all thought of compromise with the government of Chiang Kai-shek, and he assured the new Manchurian warlord that he could count on Japanese support behind the scenes if he maintained this independent posture. In partnership with Japan "Manchuria can be made into the most developed part of China." Although Tanaka's confidence in Chang Hsueh-liang proved to be misplaced—as noted earlier, Chang recognized the sovereignty of the Chinese national government over Manchuria—he still made no move to intervene in Manchuria. Nor did Shidehara, who returned as foreign minister after the fall of the Tanaka government in July 1929 and now resumed his active promotion of good relations with China. "However China treats us," he informed Parliament in January 1930, "we shall endeavor to regulate relations between the two countries in accordance with what we believe to be just and fair." Diplomatic differences would inevitably arise, but the future interests of both countries required that "we must go forward in cooperation."

The coming of the Great Depression, however, was to produce domestic pressures which the Japanese moderates proved unable to resist.

❑ The Impact of the Great Depression

The Wall Street crash (see pp. 158–159) inaugurated a general collapse of foreign markets for Japanese goods, a blow intensified by the erection of tariff barriers on the part of importing countries to protect their own producers. The economic impact on Japan, a country so critically dependent on foreign trade, was catastrophic. As in other capitalist countries, the Japanese government attempted to deal with its economic problems through retrenchment and deflation. The result was a sharp increase in unemployment, a corresponding decrease in domestic purchasing power, and an intensification of domestic economic hardship.

Japan's rural population was especially hard-hit. Farm prices fell precipitously, rice and silk by as much as 75 percent. A succession of unprecedented crop failures dealt further blows to the rural economy and led to outright famine in many areas. Rural economic hardship had a special political significance in Japan because a large proportion of the country's military personnel was recruited from the peasantry. With their families suffering severe hardship or outright starvation, Japanese soldiers were painfully aware of their country's economic plight and the dire need to find solutions to its problems.

Besides its impact on the army, the depression enhanced the popular appeal of Japanese super-patriots, who had long called for drastic changes in their country's domestic structure and foreign policy. The historian Edwin Reischauer, a former American ambassador to Tokyo, has described Japanese nationalist extremists as constituting only a small fraction of the population, "yet, judging by the consequences of their actions, they were undoubtedly the most effective pressure groups in the 1930s." According to Reischauer there were two principal components of this ultra-nationalist lobby: civilian patriotic societies, which began to proliferate with the coming of the great depression, and the army, which, although professionally modern, had remained a stronghold of conservatism.

Military and civilian super-patriots shared a common concern for what they regarded as traditional Japanese values—loyalty to the emperor, the citizen's duty to the state, and social harmony, all of which they saw threatened and undermined by Western influences. They denounced the present Japanese government and constitution, which they regarded as a Western aberration that had spawned divisive party politics and political corruption. They resented the wealthy urban bankers and industrialists with their international association and called for a more equitable distribution of the country's national wealth. But most importantly, they disliked Japan's present foreign policy, with its emphasis on international cooperation and conciliation, which seemed to be conducted on behalf of the country's business interests and ignored the fundamental needs and aspirations of its people.

As the effects of economic depression spread, an ever-growing body of public opinion in Japan came to share the views of super-patriots that their government's pacific and conciliatory foreign policy was mistaken and that they could no longer allow their country's economic welfare to remain dependent on international trade. In view of Japan's own lack of essential agricultural resources and raw materials, its very survival required the acquisition of territories where such resources were available so that access to them could never be cut off by hostile powers or the vicissitudes of the international market. Nor was there any problem as to where the necessary territorial acquisitions could be made. Directly across the Japanese Sea lay Manchuria, where Japan's Kwantung army already had a strategic foothold and where Japan already had substantial economic interests. All that was needed was the will to act.

TEN

❑

The Manchurian Crisis

On the night of September 18, 1931, a bomb destroyed a small section of the Japanese-controlled South Manchurian railway near Mukden. As was suspected at the time and as we now know from Japanese sources, the bombing was arranged by officers of Japan's Kwantung army to provoke a crisis that would serve as an excuse for establishing Japanese control over Manchuria. Blaming the bombing on Chinese saboteurs, the Kwantung army proceeded to take over the entire city of Mukden, allegedly in the interests of law and order, and in the following weeks it rapidly extended the scope of its operations. By the end of the year it had established its control over the greater part of southern Manchuria.

The Japanese conquest of Manchuria was the first great breach in the international treaty system established after World War I, the first blatant example of successful "revisionism," and the beginning of the Western policy of appeasement that was to lead to World War II. The Manchurian crisis has therefore loomed large in the historiography of the interwar years.

❑ The Japanese Interest

To understand the nature of Japanese interests, rights, and claims in Manchuria, it is necessary to look back to the Sino–Japanese war of 1894–1895. Following their vic tory in that war, the Japanese compelled China to cede them the Liaotung (east of the Liao River) Peninsula, which juts into the Yellow Sea at the southernmost end of Manchuria. The Japanese acquisition of this territory was a blow to Russian ambitions in East Asia, for the Russians had hoped to acquire the ice-free harbor of Port Arthur, at the southern tip of the peninsula, as a terminus of their projected Trans-Siberian railway. With diplomatic support from France and Germany, the Russians compelled Japan to retrocede the Liaotung Peninsula to China—and then compelled the Chinese to lease the Peninsula to themselves, a move that caused understandable bitterness in Tokyo.

At about the same time, the Russian government pressured the Chinese into granting a Russian-controlled consortium a concession to build and operate a railway

MAP 6   THE MANCHURIAN CRISIS

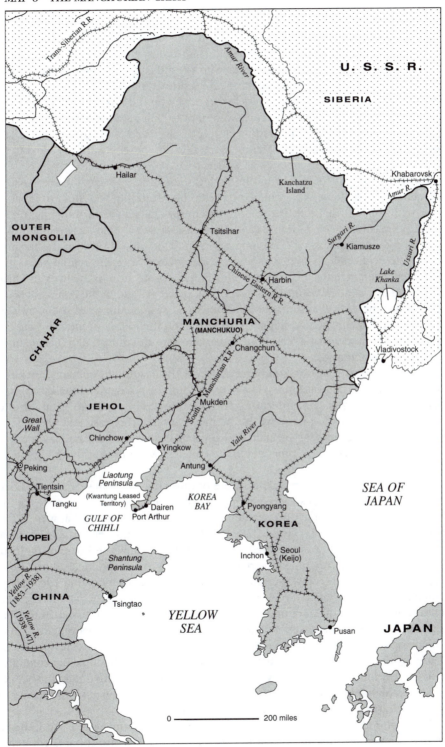

Trans-Siberian R.R.

Amur River

U. S. S. R.

SIBERIA

Hailar

Khabarovsk

Kanchatzu
Island

Amur R.

**OUTER
MONGOLIA**

Tsitsihar

Surgari R.

Kiamusze

Chinese Eastern R.R.

Harbin

*Lake
Khanka*

Ussuri R.

CHAHAR

MANCHURIA
(MANCHUKUO)

Changchun

Vladivostock

*Great
Wall*

JEHOL

South Manchurian R.R.

Mukden

Yalu River

Chinchow

Yingkow

Peking

Antung

Tientsin

*Liaotung
Peninsula*

*KOREA
BAY*

**SEA OF
JAPAN**

Tangku

(Kwantung Leased
Territory)

Dairen

Pyongyang

*GULF OF
CHIHLI*

Port Arthur

KOREA

HOPEI

*Shantung
Peninsula*

Inchon

Seoul
(Keijo)

*Yellow R.
[1853-1938]*

CHINA

*Yellow R.
[1938-47]*

Tsingtao

*YELLOW
SEA*

Pusan

JAPAN

0 ——————— 200 miles

cutting across northern Manchuria from a junction on the proposed Trans-Siberian line to the Russian harbor of Vladivostok. This route (the future Chinese Eastern railway) was some five hundred kilometers shorter and far less rugged than that of the Trans-Siberian, which, confined to Russian territory, followed the large crescent formed by the Amur and Ussuri Rivers before reaching the terminus of Vladivostok. The Russians subsequently also secured the right to build a railway from Harbin, on the Chinese Eastern line, to the harbor cities of Dairen and Port Arthur on the Liaotung Peninsula (the future South Manchurian railway), thereby gaining access to ice-free terminals for the Trans-Siberian as well as their Manchurian railways.

The Japanese got their revenge following their military victory over Russia in 1905, when the Russians were obliged to cede their Liaotung leasehold to Japan together with Russian rights to the South Manchurian railway as far north as Changchun. After making peace with Russia, the Japanese signed a separate agreement with China giving Japan extensive economic rights in Manchuria. In return the Japanese promised to withdraw their troops and railway guards from the region as soon as China "shall become herself capable of affording full protection to the lives and property of foreigners." Such withdrawal never took place. In fact, in the course of World War I the Japanese took advantage of European as well as American preoccupation with the affairs of Europe to compel China to extend their lease of the Liaotung Peninsula to ninety-nine years, a leasehold and extension not contested or altered at the Washington Conference.

Under Japanese rule, the southern sector of the Liaotung Peninsula, including Port Arthur and Dairen, was known as the Kwantung (east of the [Shanhaikwan] pass) Leasehold, though the names Liaotung and Kwantung continued to be used interchangeably. At the head of the Japanese administration in the leasehold was a governor general (whose jurisdiction included the Japanese-controlled railway zones in Manchuria), who was also commander of the Japanese Kwantung army and of the Japanese forces in the railway zones.

It is important to understand the nature of these railway zones, which had been defined in the earlier Chinese agreement with Russia as lands "actually necessary for the construction, operation, and protection of the Chinese Eastern Railway." These lands, as finally delineated, extended some thirty kilometers to either side of the actual railway line. On the basis of their agreement with China, the Russians (and subsequently the Japanese) assumed the right to exercise supreme political as well as economic authority in the railway zones under their control, including the right to maintain military and police forces for their protection. In 1906 the Japanese government formed the South Manchurian Railway Company, which was assigned the management of the railway and supervision over all other Japanese economic interests in Manchuria. The company was a semi state-owned enterprise, its director-general appointed by the prime minister. After its formation, with the influential backing of the Japanese government, it worked systematically and successfully to obtain further concessions in Manchuria, including the right to exploit the region's natural resources, control its transportation systems, and develop its industries.

In the period between their victory over Russia in 1905 and World War I, the Japanese concluded agreements with Russia dividing Manchuria into spheres of interest, whereby the Russians were conceded preponderant influence in the north, the Japanese in the south. After the Bolshevik revolution, the Russians made their dramatic renunciations of all the special rights and privileges in China obtained by the tsarist government (see p. 110), but in the course of the 1920s they managed to recover and even extend their influence in China's frontier provinces, including northern Manchuria. The big difference now was that the Russians, acutely conscious of the weakness of the new Soviet state, were determined to avoid a premature confrontation with Japan.

The Japanese continued the vigorous promotion of their economic interests in Manchuria, where by 1931 they had invested over 1 billion yen, about 75 percent of their total foreign investment. Japanese industry had become critically dependent on Manchurian raw materials, and Japan's rapidly growing population, which could no longer be sustained by its own agricultural production or fishing industry, had become similarly dependent on imports of Manchurian food. The infusion of Japanese capital and entrepreneurship had also contributed substantially to Manchurian prosperity. By the 1930s the region accounted for one-fifth of China's total trade and productive capacity, and the port of Dairen was handling a volume of shipping second only to China's own greatest seaport, Shanghai.

To the dismay of Japanese imperialists, their economic investment was not accompanied by comparable Japanese immigration to Manchuria. The land-hungry Japanese peasants proved surprisingly reluctant to move to the Asian mainland, despite vigorous encouragement from their government and handsome subsidies. Chinese peasants, on the other hand, propelled by civil war and famine and encouraged by their own government, moved in massive numbers to the relatively underpopulated lands of the north, their migration facilitated by the Japanese-developed transportation networks. Between 1900 and 1930 the population of Manchuria had increased from roughly 10 million to 34 million, and of this total 95 percent were Chinese, a mere 1 percent Japanese. In a very literal sense, therefore, the Chinese, not the Japanese, were taking over Manchuria. The Chinese were also beginning to challenge Japan's economic domination in Manchuria by building competing railway lines and harbors and starting their own commercial enterprises, a challenge that led to constant and ever-increasing friction with the Japanese.

❑ *The Japanese Takeover*

The coming of the great depression and the economic hardship resulting from the loss of Japan's international markets gave new impetus to the arguments of Japanese imperialists that their country's economic welfare and future security required the extension of direct Japanese control over territories that could provide the food and raw materials the island empire itself so conspicuously lacked.

Students of Japanese history have been struck by the absence of systematic thinking among Japanese imperialists and their failure to draw up programs defining the nature and scope of their ambitions. In fact, as was the case with imperialists of all countries, there were wide differences of opinion among them, but most Japanese militants probably saw no need for systematic thought or programs. Since 1905 Manchuria had been the most obvious region for further Japanese expansion. All that was required was action and forceful leadership, which the government had so far signally failed to provide.

In the summer of 1931, with the government still deeply divided about the future course of Japanese policy, the army supreme command in Toyko drew up a plan that envisaged three options for dealing with Manchuria, all of which would require the use of force in some form: the ouster of the government of Chang Hsueh-liang in Manchuria in favor of a more compliant ruler, the establishment of a puppet government, or the outright Japanese takeover of the region. As yet, however, the supreme command seems to have had no intention of implementing any of these policies, for early in September it ordered the commander of its Kwantung army to continue to exercise "patience and restraint" in Manchuria.

But the militants among the officers of the Kwantung army could no longer be restrained. Stationed in Manchuria and confronted daily with evidence of growing Chinese influence, they had long since been convinced of the need to establish direct control over the country. Ironically, it was the "patience and restraint" order that spurred them into action. Informed of that order before it was officially delivered, they decided to anticipate its delivery by staging an incident that would justify their abandonment of patience and restraint. That incident was the afore-mentioned bombing of the South Manchurian railway on the night of September 18, 1931. The Kwantung army now went on to extend Japanese control over the greater part of southern Manchuria—some 200,000 square miles of territory and 20 million people—a success greeted by Japanese public opinion with tumultuous acclaim.

The Japanese government, despite the doubts of many of its members about the wisdom of the Manchurian enterprise, found itself helpless to change the course set by the army and could do little more than serve as its apologist before the world. As the British historian Ian Nish phrased it, the Tokyo government "presided over" rather than "steered" Japanese policy during the Manchurian crisis. The great political importance of that crisis was that it inaugurated the takeover of Japanese policy by militant extremists that was to continue until the Japanese defeat in World War II.

❑ *The Chinese and Soviet Reaction*

A remarkable feature of the Manchurian crisis was the failure of the Nanking government and the Chinese people in general to put up greater resistance to the Japanese takeover. The Kwantung army, including the railway guards, numbered just over 10,000 men, reinforced by the end of 1931 to about 60,000. By contrast, the Manchurian warlord Chang Hsueh-liang had about 110,000 regulars under his command in the Tientsin and Peking areas and another 140,000 in Manchuria and Jehol. The armies of Chiang Kai-shek's Nanking government were much larger still.

China, however, despite the claim of the Nanking regime to have unified the country, was still torn asunder by civil war, the Nanking government itself riven by factional strife. Political weakness was compounded by economic catastrophe. In the late summer and autumn of 1931 the Yangtze and Yellow Rivers burst their banks, flooding the greater part of China's most productive agricultural land and killing thousands of peasants.

Despite the rise of Chinese nationalist sentiment during this period, no Chinese leader had proved capable of mobilizing this national spirit effectively for the purposes of establishing a truly centralized national government or creating armies capable of resisting the Japanese. Chiang Kai-shek was clearly more intent on conserving his forces to deal with domestic foes than with resisting the Japanese in Manchuria. Doubtful about the reliability of the Manchurian warlord Chang Hsueh-liang, Chiang ordered him not to risk pitched battles with the Japanese but to withdraw his forces to Chinese territory behind the Great Wall.

The most effective Chinese response to the Japanese takeover was the employment of their by now familiar weapon of an economic boycott, which, as events were to show, was the only resistance that had any appreciable influence on Japanese policy. So severe was the impact of the boycott on the Japanese economy that the Tokyo government risked serious international complications to compel the Chinese to lift it. On January 29, 1932, the Japanese bombed Shanghai, an aerial attack followed by a large-scale ground offensive designed to take the city hostage. It was a dangerous gamble, for Shanghai was a center of Western interests in China, and the Japanese attack might have been expected to stir the Western powers into action. But the Japanese use of force worked. The Western governments did no more than protest, and on May 5, 1932, after protracted negotiation, the Chinese agreed to lift their embargo. Japanese troops thereupon withdrew from Shanghai and this phase of the crisis ended. Thus the Chinese boycott, while provoking a sharp Japanese reaction, was in the end totally ineffective in halting Japanese aggression.

Apart from China itself, the country whose interests were most seriously affected by the Japanese takeover of Manchuria was the Soviet Union. In February 1932, at almost the same time as the Japanese attack on Shanghai, the Japanese took another dangerous gamble by advancing into the Soviet sphere of interest in Manchuria and occupying Harbin and Tsitsihar, key cities on the Soviet-controlled sector of the Chinese Eastern railway. The Soviets, however, were still preoccupied with domestic problems, their massive program of industrialization and rearmament had barely begun, and they were therefore willing to go to great lengths to avoid a confrontation with the Japanese. They permitted the Japanese to use the Chinese Eastern for the transport of their troops, thereby facilitating the Japanese conquest of the north, and in May of the following year they offered to sell Japan their interest in the railway. Negotiations over this offer continued over the next two years, by which time the Japanese had whittled down the original Soviet asking price of 650 million yen to 140 million, one-third of which was to be paid in cash over the next three years, the balance in goods. The final agreement, concluded on March 23, 1935, was described by Maxim Litvinov, the Soviet commissar for foreign affairs, as "a solution to one of the most complicated Far Eastern problems and the greatest positive event in the relations between the Soviet Union and Japan." The Chinese Eastern was now renamed the North Manchurian railway, and with its sale Soviet influence in Manchuria was virtually eliminated.

❑ *The Western Response*

As viewed by Western observers at that time and since, the great historical significance of the Manchurian crisis was not the weakness of the Chinese or Soviet response but the failure of the Western powers and the League to take effective action to halt Japanese aggression. Their failure has been seen as setting the stage for the aggressions of Mussolini and Hitler, the first step on the road of appeasement that was to lead to World War II.

Japan's successful challenge of the League and the Western democracies may indeed have encouraged Mussolini and Hitler to risk similar challenges. There were, however, decisive differences between the appeasement of Japan in East Asia (if one can even call it that) and the subsequent appeasement of the Italian and German dictators in the West. The most important of these differences was geography. In the West, the democracies were in a position to halt Italian and German aggression at a very early stage. But how were the Western powers to stop the Japanese in distant Manchuria?

There were three possible methods for doing so: through diplomatic pressure, through economic sanctions, or through force. For reasons that will be explained later, the Western powers employed only the first of these. Diplomatic pressure, however, unless backed by a believable threat of force, is rarely effective. It was totally ineffective in dealing with Japan. The second method—economic sanctions to cut off all trade with the aggressor as called for in Article 16 of the Covenant of the League of Nations—was never seriously considered. The Western powers were floundering in economic depression, and their governments feared to risk yet another blow to their battered economies by cutting off all trade with Japan. There was the further consideration that if the Western governments did impose economic sanctions, the Japanese would simply turn to the Soviet Union and other nonmembers of the League to supply their economic needs. Worse still, Japan might be goaded into further military aggression if it saw its vital interests endangered.

Finally, Japan might have been stopped through the actual use of force, and here the factor of geography was crucial. It will be recalled that at the Washington Conference, Britain and the United States had agreed not to build new bases west of Hawaii, north of Australia, and east of Singapore. They had thereby conceded Japan naval supremacy in the Western Pacific and thus made it virtually impossible to undertake the only action that might have compelled the Japanese to withdraw from Manchuria: the establishment of a naval blockade between the Japanese islands and the Asian mainland. The Western powers might have been able to establish their own naval supremacy in the Western Pacific through a mammoth program of naval rearmament, but since 1919 public opinion in the West had been nurtured by visions of international disarmament. And during the economic depression, financial retrenchment, not expensive rearmament and military enterprises, was the order of the day.

The most serious objection to the use of force against Japan, however, and one that was rarely honestly addressed, was that the Western powers had no vital interests in Manchuria and therefore no compelling reason to risk a major sacrifice of blood and treasure by taking action there. On the contrary, they had compelling reasons for allowing the Japanese a free hand. For both Britain and France, a Japanese takeover of Manchuria was far preferable to a Japanese thrust into Central or Southern China, where both still had substantial interests, or into the South Pacific or Southeast Asia, where the Japanese might be tempted by the open spaces of Australia and New Zealand, or by the wealth of raw materials in the British, Dutch, French, and Portuguese colonial empires. Further and most importantly, a Japanese-controlled Manchuria would serve as a buffer to the expansion of Russia, Bolshevik or otherwise. That country was already showing alarming tendencies to revert to tsarist imperialist policies, and now, stimulated by the messianic fervor of Bolshevism, Russia seemed to many Western statesmen the greatest potential threat on the international horizon.

The American president, Herbert Hoover, summed up the position of most Western leaders, although few others expressed themselves so forthrightly. At a meeting with his cabinet a month after the Mukden incident, he denounced the Japanese advance into Manchuria as immoral. At the same time he acknowledged that the Japanese had a good case in seeking to preserve order and defend their economic interests in China, over which loomed the menace of Bolshevism. As for the United States, "neither our obligation to China, nor our own interest, nor our dignity, require us to go to war over these questions. . . . We will not go along on war or any of the sanctions, either economic or military, for these are the roads that lead to war."

❑ *The Response of the League of Nations and the Stimson Doctrine*

The Manchurian crisis exposed the inherent weakness of the League of Nations, a weakness that should have been obvious from the beginning. For the League had no army and could only issue diplomatic protests, while exhorting its members to enforce the provisions of the League covenant. But, like the United States, the members of the League proved unwilling to make any move that might involve either political or economic risk. In late October 1931, well over a month after the Mukden incident, the League Council passed a resolution calling upon the Japanese army to withdraw to the positions held before September 18. And in December the Council resolved to send a commission of enquiry to Manchuria to investigate the cause of the conflict and put forward recommendations for its settlement. This resolution was actually proposed by the Japanese who, convinced of the justice of their cause, evidently believed that other powers would be similarly convinced.

If this was indeed their belief, it proved to be mistaken. In January 1932 the American secretary of state, Henry L. Stimson, notified all the signatories of the 1922 Nine-Power Pact that the United States would not recognize any territorial gains achieved through the use of armed force. This principle of nonrecognition, subsequently known as the Stimson Doctrine and formally adopted by the League of Nations, was hailed by the international lawyer Quincy Wright as the most significant development in international law in recent or even more distant times. Stimson himself saw it as "perhaps the greatest constructive achievement" of his public life. The British historian Christopher Thorne described the Stimson Doctrine rather more accurately as "cant in foreign policy," for it did nothing to bring home to the public the inherent difficulties of the situation; instead, it encouraged the expectation that one could exert influence without accepting responsibility. Nonrecognition was a diplomatic gesture that gave scant consolation to the Chinese and had no effect whatever on the policies of Japan.

❑ *The Establishment of the Puppet State of Manchukuo*

Meanwhile the Japanese were endeavoring to legitimize their intervention in Manchuria by claiming that they were aiding the Manchurian people's struggle for self-determination and freedom from China. On February 18, 1932, a puppet government under Japanese control proclaimed the independence of Manchuria, which was now renamed Manchukuo (the land of the Manchus). The last emperor of China, Henry Pu-yi, who had abdicated in 1912 at the age of three, was brought in by the Japanese as titular head of the new state, first as regent and then as emperor. As Pu-yi was a member of the last Chinese imperial dynasty, the Ching, which came from Manchuria, his choice as head of state gave the Japanese-sponsored regime a veneer of legitimacy; and because he was also a drug addict, he was an ideal puppet ruler.

The actual government of Manchuria was run by a highly centralized administration of Japanese advisers under the Japanese ambassador to Manchukuo, who was also governor-general of the Kwantung Leasehold and commander-in-chief of the Kwantung army. In September 1932 the Japanese government officially recognized Manchukuo as an independent state and announced that its independence would be protected by Japanese arms. The Japanese acknowledged among themselves, however, that the chief purpose of the new state was to serve Japanese interests. At a cabinet meeting several months before the recognition of Manchukuo, the Japanese government decided that the new state was to be organized in such a way as to become, in partnership with Japan, "a self-sufficient economic unit" capable of ensuring Japanese political and economic security.

❑ *The Lytton Commission*

The League commission entrusted with the investigation of the Manchurian situation was headed by an Englishman, Lord Lytton, and was made up of members from four other countries—France, Germany, Italy, and the United States, although the United States was not a member of the League. The Soviet Union, another nonmember, was also invited to appoint a representative to the commission but refused to do so in deference to Japan. That invitation, a Soviet official declared, was nothing less than "an attempt to bribe the U.S.S.R. and induce it to join a possible anti-Japanese front."

The Lytton commission arrived in Yokohama at the end of February 1932 and spent seven months assembling evidence about the Manchurian situation. Its final report, circulated to League members in October, concluded that Japanese military action in Manchuria had not been taken in self-defence and that the creation of an independent Manchukuo did not flow from a "genuine and spontaneous independence movement." It therefore recommended that the present Japanese-sponsored government in Manchuria should be replaced by an autonomous demilitarized regime under Chinese sovereignty, with international advisers and police.

In reply, the Japanese trotted out their by now familiar arguments to justify their presence in Manchuria: the need to restore law and order and to protect the lives and property of foreigners from Chinese banditry and sabotage. They emphasized that Japanese intervention had not violated the 1922 Nine-Power Pact (guaranteeing the territorial integrity of China) because Manchuria had never been part of China. The people of Manchuria, in proclaiming their independence, were exercising their right to self-determination, and the Japanese were fulfilling a moral obligation in supporting their efforts to do so.

The Japanese had a strong case. The authority of the Chinese government had not extended to Manchuria for many years. In the absence of a government capable of maintaining law and order, the commercial interests of the Japanese and all other foreigners had indeed suffered. Moreover there were abundant precedents of comparable European and American intervention in China proper, as well as in many other parts of the world. The Japanese therefore found it hard to understand why their action should be condemned by states that had acted — and were still acting — in exactly the same way. As Christopher Thorne observed, the Japanese had learned to play the European imperialist game. "At this point the West then declared that the nature of the game was to be changed. . . . Nor could it escape Japan's attention that by this change of rules the major Western powers did not divest themselves of their own empires — indeed, it could be thought that they were seeking to preserve them by new means."

In February 1933 the Assembly of the League of Nations voted to approve the Lytton commission's report. At the same time it adopted Stimson's formula of nonrecognition with regard to Manchukuo and demanded that the Japanese relinquish their military control of the country. The Japanese protested, pointing out "the absolute necessity of taking into consideration the fact that China is not an organized state; that its internal condition and external relations are characterized by extreme confusion and complexity . . . and that, accordingly, the general principles and usages of international law . . . are found to be considerably modified in their operation so far as China is concerned." The majority of League members, the Japanese declared, "have attached greater importance to upholding inapplicable formulae than to the real need of assuring peace." The Japanese protested in vain. On March 27 they gave notice of Japan's intention to withdraw from the League.

❑ The Japanese Takeover of Jehol and the Truce of Tangku

The demands of the League that the Japanese relinquish their military control of Manchuria were even more futile, for the Japanese remained. Indeed, in January 1933 they had already gone beyond Manchuria and begun the takeover of the neighboring province of Jehol (Rehe). They justified this new invasion on the grounds that the banditry and drug trade that flourished in Jehol threatened the security, interests, and welfare of the Manchurian people and that therefore "the affairs of Rehe are unquestionably an internal problem of Manchuria." As in Manchuria, the Japanese met with little or no resistance. By April they had overrun the entire province.

The Japanese war with China, set off by the 1931 Mukden incident, ended with the signature of the Truce of Tangku of May 31, 1933. The principal provision of this treaty was the creation of a demilitarized zone extending thirty miles south of the Great Wall. The Chinese were allowed to maintain a police force in this zone, provided it remained "friendly to Japan," while the Japanese, thanks to the provisions of an earlier treaty, could maintain a garrison army in the zone to protect the area's major railway lines—a juxtaposition of Chinese and Japanese forces that was to have fateful consequences. For the Japanese, the Tangku truce represented an enormous victory, for it left them in control of the three Eastern provinces that constituted Manchuria together with the neighboring province of Jehol. The Nanking government for its part was now free to deal with the problems of civil war and the Communists.

The Tangku truce brought the volatile stage of the Manchurian crisis to an end. But it also left the Japanese poised on the frontiers of China within striking distance of Peking, confronted with the constant temptation to extend their influence further at China's expense—a temptation the Japanese proved unable to resist.

Was the Manchurian crisis a milestone on the road to World War II, as many historians and other observers have contended? The English historian A. J. P. Taylor has argued convincingly against this theory. "In reality," he says, "the League, under British leadership, had done what the British thought it was designed to do: it had limited a conflict and brought it, however unsatisfactorily, to an end." Taylor goes on to say, however, that the affair nevertheless had great contemporary significance, although not in the way subsequently attributed to it. For "it diverted attention from Europe just at the moment when European questions became acute."

ELEVEN

□

East Asia: From the Manchurian Crisis to the Sino-Japanese War

□ *The Japanese Government and its Policies*

In the course of the Manchurian crisis important changes had taken place in the leadership of the Japanese government. On May 15, 1932, militant naval officers assassinated Prime Minister Inukai Tsuyoshi, the latest in a succession of political assassinations that had taken place over the previous two years. The sentences handed out to the assassins were remarkably lenient, considering the nature of their crimes, and an important result of this atmosphere of intimidation created by Japanese ultrapatriots was the demoralization of Japan's political parties. Indeed, the May 15 "incident" put an end to party government, and over the next months the power of the Japanese parliament was virtually eliminated. The army refused to supply a minister of war to a government headed by a party leader, and though cabinets still included members of Japan's major political parties, the governments were headed by nonparty military and naval officers.

At this point it is important to recall that according to the Japanese constitution the military leadership—the supreme command of the army and navy—was not responsible to the cabinet or to parliament, but only to the emperor. The original intention of the oligarchs who drew up the constitution was to keep the military strictly segregated from domestic politics, a prohibition that prevented political interference in military affairs but which did not prevent the military from interfering and eventually exercising a dominant influence in politics, especially in the conduct of foreign affairs.

Herbert Bix, a biographer of Emperor Hirohito, has convincingly refuted the belief that the Japanese monarch was a figurehead ruler, as he has frequently been described, who sat silent at ministerial meetings and simply endorsed the policies of his advisers. Instead, Hirohito demanded to be kept informed about the formulation of policy and policy decisions, and the need to provide him with information might occupy much of the time of his senior officials.

Bix also demonstrates, however, that the emperor was never the actual initiator of Japanese policy, that his chief responsibility lay in approving or at least condoning the policies formulated by his advisers, and that he generally went along with the aggressive plans that plunged his country into the costly China war and the disasters of World War II. Thus the emperor did not plan the war against China or the attack on the United States; he did not order the use of poison gas against the Chinese or the massacres of Chinese soldiers and civilians perpetrated by his troops. But he was informed early and in great detail about the aggressive plans of his advisers, including the attack on Pearl Harbor, and he knew about the poison gas and the massacres. His responsibility lay in not opposing those plans or intervening to halt the barbarities of his soldiers. After being informed about the decision to go to war with the United States at a meeting that included all the members of his cabinet, his army chief of staff observed that "the emperor nodded in agreement to each explanation that was made and displayed not the slightest anxiety. He seemed to be in a good mood. We were filled with awe." The critical and indeed decisive role of the emperor in all this was that his decisions were held to be divinely ordained, and that, once he approved a policy, that policy itself was considered sacred and could no longer be contravened.

The emperor's advisers, however, did not speak with one voice. There was constant rivalry between the army and navy for funds, power, and prestige; and there were also broad differences of opinion among leaders within both services. In theory, differences were worked out within Ministerial Conferences, made up of the prime minister, the foreign minister, and the ministers of finance, the army and the navy, where agreement was reached on policy decisions. In practice, however, such agreement was achieved all too frequently by incorporating the demands of every party concerned, with the result that national policy directives became a composite of competing and even contradictory programs. The emperor did not resolve those contradictions, but, though he might ask the occasional question, he presided over such composite agreements and allowed competing and contradictory policies to go forward.

The records of a meeting of his army and navy ministers of June 30, 1936, provide a striking example of how agreement on policy was reached by incorporating the recommendations of all interested parties. This document called for the pursuit of a "consistent policy of overseas expansion," the elimination of the menace of the Soviet Union, and "preparations" against Britain and the United States. The army was to be strengthened so as to be able to smash the Soviet army "with one blow, from the beginning." At the same time there was to be a massive buildup of the navy "to maintain command of the Pacific against the United States navy," and plans were to be made "for a future advance into the South Seas" to secure the resources essential to the maintenance of Japanese naval supremacy.

These plans were subsequently endorsed at Ministerial Conferences in August and incorporated in a memorandum entitled Fundamentals of National Policy. Japan's continental policy continued to be based on strengthening the army to eliminate the Soviet threat and thereby safeguard Japanese interests in Manchuria and China. At the same time, however, the navy was to be strengthened and preparations were to go forward to secure the resources of the South Pacific. All such preparations were to be carried on discreetly "so as not to arouse the fears of [Western] powers," and the hope was expressed that Japanese economic expansion in the South Seas could be achieved "by modest and peaceful means" to avoid clashes with other powers.

Great as were their differences over foreign policy and armament priorities, all Japanese leaders agreed about the fundamental importance of China to Japan's political and economic security and the desirability of extending Japanese control over that country. The differences arose over how this control was to be achieved and exercised. In dealing with these differences, we find further examples of how Japanese leaders reached consensus by incorporating the views of all the parties concerned in a single policy recommendation. The first part of a 1934 policy memorandum on China advocated the peaceful and gradual expansion of Japanese commercial interests in China, the avoidance of measures likely to arouse Chinese hostility, and negotiation with the Nationalist government in Nanking to achieve Japanese objectives. But the second part of this same memorandum called for outright Japanese intervention in China's affairs, the suppression of all anti-Japanese activity, the appointment of officials friendly to Japan, "uncompromising" opposition to any Chinese attempt to seek the support of foreign powers, and Japanese encouragement of Chinese provincial leaders to break away from Nanking and form independent governments under Japanese auspices.

Although the Japanese services were enjoined to exercise caution so as not to alarm foreign powers, a massive military and naval buildup could hardly be conducted with discretion, nor did the Japanese make any serious effort to do so. They participated in an international naval disarmament conference that convened in London in December 1935, but only to announce that they no longer intended to be bound by previous naval arms limitation agreements. This gesture may have satisfied the pride of Japanese naval leadership, still smarting from the humiliation of accepting naval ratios lower than those of Britain and the United States, but it could not fail to alarm the Western powers, the very thing the Japanese government had hoped to avoid.

The Japanese aroused further alarm, this time in the Soviet Union, by concluding a treaty with Nazi Germany on November 25, 1936, the so-called Anti-Comintern pact, which, although announced with much fanfare, was little more than an agreement to cooperate in combatting international Communism. The Soviets, however, suspected that the Anti-Comintern Pact was actually a military alliance, and in response they stepped up their armament program as well as efforts to form closer diplomatic and military partnerships with the Western powers.

The Japanese were lucky, or so it seemed at the time, because for some years they were able to pursue their various policies without incurring foreign intervention. Britain and France were still coping with the problems of economic depression and domestic turmoil, while in foreign affairs, much though they might deplore Japan's incursions in East Asia, their attention was focused on crises closer to home engendered by Mussolini, Hitler, and the Spanish Civil War. For the Soviet Union, too, the paramount danger was not Japan but Nazi Germany, whose government was avowedly dedicated not only to the destruction of Communism but to the conquest and absorption of Russia into a Nazi territorial empire. Alone among the Western powers, the United States was free to pursue a more vigorous policy in East Asia. But, as at the time of the Manchurian crisis, the United States still lacked the power—and the will— to do so. America continued a large-scale export of materials vital to Japanese armament production and restricted its displeasure with Japanese policies to innocuous notes of protest.

❑ *China after the Manchurian Crisis*

Although China had ostensibly been unified in 1928 with the establishment of a national government in Nanking under Chiang Kai-shek, the country remained deeply divided. As discussed earlier, the Nanking government itself was torn by factional strife, provincial warlords had been conceded a large measure of independence in return for their nominal recognition of Nanking's suzerainty, and its authority was challenged outright by the Chinese Communists, who had survived purges and military defeats to emerge once again as a formidable political force in several parts of the country.

The Chinese Communists suffered from factional strife of their own, divided between those who remained loyal to the leadership of Moscow and those who chose to pursue an independent course. Further, among the leaders of both camps there was vicious doctrinal controversy as well as competition for authority and power. The Moscow loyalists for the most part had gone underground following their defeats in the late 1920s, but the independents had managed to establish Chinese Soviet governments in the hinterlands of Kiangsi and Hunan in the south and in the province of Shensi in the north.

Between 1930 and 1934 Chiang Kai-shek waged five "campaigns of encirclement and extermination" against the Communists. His obsession with the Communist menace was a major reason for his failure to mount effective resistance to the Japanese takeover of Manchuria and Jehol and their flagrant intervention in other provinces of northern China. In the fifth of these campaigns, he succeeded in driving the Communists from their strongholds in Kiangsi and encircled their southern armies in Juichen, on Kiangsi's southeastern border. But his goal of extermination was not achieved, for on the night of October 15, 1934, the Communists broke through the Nationalist lines.

Therewith began their famous Long March, which was to end a year later after a trek on foot of over 5,000 miles to the northern province of Shensi, where another group of Communist independents had already established a foothold. It was in the course of this Long March that Mao Tse-tung, the leader of the Kiangsi Soviet, secured general recognition as the leader of the Chinese Communist party, though factional strife among the Communists continued. Not until 1938 was Mao's leadership publicly acknowledged by Moscow.

Not all of Chiang Kai-shek's generals or members of his government agreed with his policy of waging war against the Chinese Communists while a large part of their country remained under Japanese control. Prominent among those who disagreed was Chang Hsueh-liang, the former warlord of Manchuria who had been driven out by the Japanese and was now a general in the service of Chiang Kai-shek. In December 1936, while at a spa near the city of Sian, Chiang Kai-shek was confronted by a mutiny led by Chang Hsueh-liang, who had been negotiating with the Chinese Communists to form a united front against the Japanese. Chiang was placed under arrest and presented with demands to end the Chinese civil war and bring all parties together in a new government dedicated to the task of national salvation.

At this point Chiang Kai-shek once again received decisive support from Stalin. With the Nazi menace on his western flank, the Soviet dictator was intent above all on making China a meaningful counterweight to Japan in the east, and he still looked to Chiang as the most useful instrument for this purpose. Upon receiving news of his arrest, he telegraphed the Chinese Communists that Chiang was the only man capable of leading a united front against Japan; they should therefore secure his release and agree to a political alliance under his leadership. After their many betrayals by Chiang and the disasters they had incurred by following Stalin's orders in the past, the Chinese Communists might have been expected to balk at his orders in the present instance, but they too recognized the unique value of Chiang's prestige as a national leader. On December 25 Chiang was allowed to fly back to Nanking. To guarantee his personal safety and as a gesture of Chinese solidarity, Chang Hsueh-liang accompanied him to the capital and was rewarded for his patriotism by being kept under house arrest for the rest of his life.

With the formation of a new Nationalist government in alliance with the Communists, China was ostensibly united, but that unity was still superficial at best. Although Chiang Kai-shek was now obliged to abandon his campaigns against them, he remained deeply distrustful of the Communists, factional strife continued within his own government, and provincial leaders retained a large measure of autonomy. In view of his overall record, there is reason to doubt whether Chiang possessed the leadership qualities or political vision required to mobilize China's people and resources effectively. He was given little opportunity to try, for within six months China was to be overwhelmed by new political and natural disasters.

❑ *The Marco Polo Bridge Affair: the Beginning of World War II in Asia*

World War II in Asia began as a result of a seemingly minor incident in the demilitarized zone south of the Great Wall established by the Truce of Tangku (see p. 132), where the Japanese were allowed to maintain a garrison army to protect the railways and the Chinese were conceded a local police force "friendly to Japan." On the night of July 7, 1937, troops of the Japanese garrison army clashed with the Chinese police force near the Marco Polo Bridge, about eight miles southwest of Peking. The incident was no more serious than others that had taken place in this border zone, and it appeared to have been settled by July 11 through negotiations between the commander of the Japanese garrison army and the local Chinese administration. Instead it developed into a full-fledged war.

The evidence about the Marco Polo Bridge incident is complicated and contradictory, but there are two obvious explanations for its development into a war: Chiang Kai-shek's resolve finally to take a firm stand against the Japanese, and the seizure of the initiative by a Japanese general in the field, who would eventually be backed up by the Tokyo government.

Chiang Kai-shek made the first move towards war by refusing to recognize the July 11 agreement or any other settlement concluded without the participation of his own government and by ordering four divisions of the Chinese Nationalist army to advance toward the demilitarized zone established by the Truce of Tangku. On July 17 he issued what amounted to a call to arms. If Japan continued its aggressive policies,

MAP 7   EAST ASIA, DECEMBER 1941 ON THE EVE OF THE JAPANESE ATTACK ON PEARL HARBOR

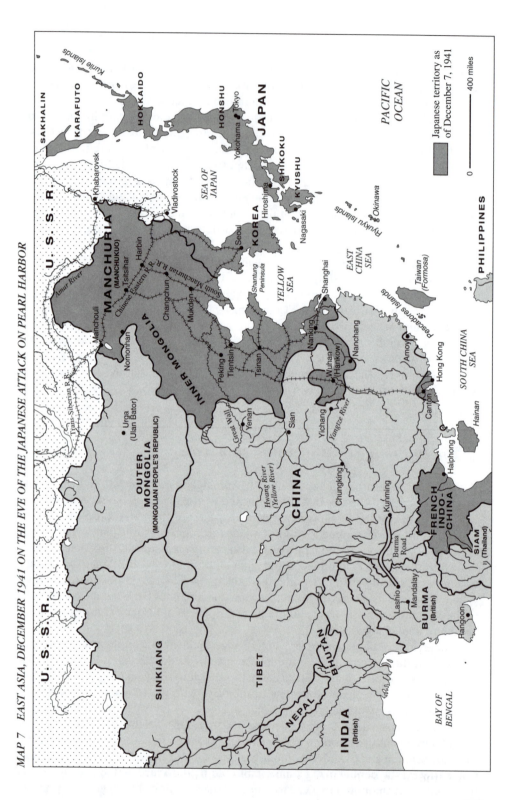

China would have no choice but "to throw the last ounce of its energy into a struggle for national survival no matter how great the sacrifice." To tolerate the loss of even one more inch of Chinese territory would be "an unpardonable crime against our race." The Chinese people must stand united and steel themselves for a long and difficult struggle "to avoid extinction." In response to a Japanese demand that Chiang halt the advance of his armies toward the demilitarized zone and agree to the implementation of the July 11 settlement, Chiang reiterated his own demand that any settlement had to be negotiated with his Nanking government. He refused to halt his military operations and called upon the signatories of the 1922 Nine-Power Treaty for support.

Upon learning of the Marco Polo Bridge incident, the Japanese high command in Tokyo had ordered its garrison army to exercise prudence and avoid an extension of the conflict. With the northward advance of the Chinese Nationalist forces, however, Tokyo authorized the reinforcement of the Japanese garrison army but at the same time repeated its admonition to local officials to seek a peaceful resolution of the affair. At this point the commander of the Japanese garrison army suffered a heart attack and was replaced by a general named Kazuki Kiyoshi, who arrived on the scene on July 12 intent on pursuing a more aggressive China policy. On July 25 he took advantage of another clash between Japanese and Chinese troops to request Tokyo's permission to retaliate with force. Without waiting for Tokyo's authorization, he ordered a Japanese counterattack followed up by an ultimatum, subsequently approved by Tokyo, demanding that the Chinese withdraw their forces beyond the Yungting River, some ten miles west of Peking. The Chinese rejection of this ultimatum gave Kazuki the excuse to attack the Chinese Nationalist troops who had advanced into the demilitarized zone. By the evening of July 28 he had driven out the Chinese and established Japanese control over the entire Peking-Tientsin area.

Already on the previous day, however, the Japanese government, far from recalling or rebuking Kazuki, had sent Chiang Kai-shek the equivalent of an ultimatum calling for "a fundamental solution of Sino–Japanese relations." Japan demanded the enlargement of the demilitarized zone to include the entire Peking-Tientsin area, a treaty of friendship with Japan, the establishment of a common front against Communism, and China's recognition of the independence of Manchukuo. Chiang's response was defiant. "The only course open to us now," he said, "is to lead the masses of the nation, under a single national plan, to struggle to the last."

At this point the Japanese supreme command once again urged restraint. Still preoccupied with the Soviet threat, it persuaded the Tokyo government to take a more conciliatory line in dealing with Chiang Kai-shek. The next terms submitted to Nanking included what seemed to be a major concession: an offer to recognize the authority of the Nanking regime over all of northern China, though with the critical reservation that Chinese officials appointed to administer this area "be sympathetic to the attainment of Sino-Japanese reconciliation."

Whether Chiang Kai-shek would have agreed to negotiate on the basis of these proposals will never be known. Before they could be submitted to Nanking another crisis situation had developed, this time in the great Chinese seaport of Shanghai, where the Japanese and other foreign powers with interests in Shanghai were allowed to maintain small military garrisons. On August 9, 1937, a Japanese marine lieutenant and a seaman were shot by Chinese soldiers, an incident that impelled the Japanese to send an additional two divisions to Shanghai to reinforce the 2,500 marines already stationed in the city. Determined to resist further Japanese encroachments, the Nanking government ordered general mobilization, set up a central command headquarters, and named Chiang Kai-shek commander-in-chief of all Chinese armed forces.

Despite the overwhelming numerical superiority of Chinese forces in the Shanghai area, the Japanese declared their intention to wage a "war of chastisement" until China had lost its will to fight and "reflected on the error of its ways." Thus by mid-August of 1937 the skirmish at the Marco Polo Bridge had developed into an all-out war. The Japanese nevertheless persisted in calling the conflict the "China Incident" so as not to be accused of violating the Kellogg-Briand pact outlawing the use of force for the settlement of international disputes and, more importantly, to avoid Washington's enforcement of its neutrality laws forbidding the sale of arms to belligerents.

Once again there had been conflicting views among Japanese leaders over their country's China policy. The Japanese army high command, still fearful of the Soviet threat, had originally been reluctant to send reinforcements to Shanghai. Not only would a Shanghai campaign divert forces that might be needed for defense against the Soviet Union, but the size of the Chinese army in the Shanghai area and the nature of the terrain in the Yangtze delta would make operations there difficult and costly. But Japan's China policy now assumed a momentum of its own. By the end of September the original two Japanese divisions sent to Shanghai had been increased to fifteen, and the fighting had developed into a major military campaign. The conquest of Shanghai proved more difficult than the most pessimistic Japanese generals had anticipated. By early November, however the Japanese had succeeded in outflanking the Chinese defenders and by November 13 they had established Japanese control over the city.

The China Incident now developed into an outright war of conquest. From Shanghai, the Japanese pressed forward to the Nationalist capital of Nanking, which fell on December 13. There followed a week-long orgy of slaughter and rape by the Japanese soldiers, one of the earliest and ugliest atrocities of the war.

After the fall of Nanking, Chiang Kai-shek's Nationalist government retired into the interior, first to Hankow (part of the tri-city of Wuhan), then to Chungking in the Szechwan province, some 500 miles farther up the Yangtze River. To slow the Japanese, Chiang ordered his engineers to blow up the dikes on the Yellow River. This drastic measure temporarily stalled the Japanese advance from the north, but at catastrophic cost to the Chinese people. For the ensuing floods once again changed the course of the Yellow River, which since 1853 had flowed into the Yellow Sea north of the Shantung Peninsula and now shifted back to its southerly course. As in the previous century, this change of course resulted in the death of thousands of peasants and the destruction of the intricate network of canals and dams that served to make the Yellow River valley one of China's most productive agricultural regions.

Meanwhile the Japanese stepped up the pace of their war with China and advanced with astonishing speed and success, especially considering that they regularly faced much larger armies. By late 1938 they had extended their control over China's most densely populated and productive provinces, its major seaports and inland cities, and its principal rail and river lines of communication. Yet their most important goal eluded them. Despite the vast expansion of their war effort, their military victories, and the extent of their conquests, they failed to end the war with China. Chiang Kai-shek and the Communists continued to hold out in the country's interior, and the Japanese found it necessary to keep a large army in China.

To administer the areas conquered by their armies, the Japanese set up puppet governments similar to the regime in Manchukuo. As nominal heads of these governments they installed leaders with some claim to legitimacy, all of them tightly controlled by Japanese advisers. The bulk of the actual administrative work, however, was performed by Chinese officials, who had no alternative but to collaborate with the Japanese in carrying out the routine tasks of government.

The Japanese clearly hoped to secure popular collaboration as well. Their propaganda stressed their common Sino-Japanese racial and cultural heritage and the need for Asian solidarity to counter the political and economic imperialism of the West. They claimed to have awakened a new spirit in Asia. "Truly the China Incident opens the main chapter in the story of the Asiatic race. . . . The Asian peoples must turn their backs on the self-centered individualistic materialism of Europe, accept the common ideals of Asia, and devote themselves to lives rooted in Asia." Prime Minister Konoe Fumimaro sounded the same theme in a speech of November 3, 1938. Japan had no territorial ambitions in China. Quite the contrary, Japan was fighting for the liberation of China, which had so long been "the victim of the imperialist ambitions and rivalries of Occidental powers." The goal of Japan was to put an end to Western imperialism, bring "eternal peace" to East Asia, and establish a New Order based on true justice.

❏ International Reaction

Despite the horror aroused abroad by reports of Japanese atrocities in China and Japan's flagrant disregard of foreign interests, Japan was spared foreign intervention in its war with China because the attention of the governments of Western Europe, the United States, and the Soviet Union remained focused on the threat posed by Nazi Germany.

As at the time of the Manchurian crisis, the League of Nations condemned Japan's undeclared war with China and called upon the signatories of the Nine-Power Treaty to mediate. A conference of those powers (minus Japan) convened in Brussels in early November 1937, but it accomplished nothing by way of mediation and it adjourned with only a mild statement of support for China. A speech of October 5 by the American president, Franklin D. Roosevelt, which suggested the possibility of a quarantine of aggressor nations, inspired hope that the United States would take the lead in putting international pressure on Japan. But the quarantine speech did no more than provoke heated domestic criticism and was not followed up by action of any kind. Even the Japanese bombing in December 1937 of the American naval vessel *Panay,* escorting American oil tankers on the Yangtze River, failed to provoke the United States into doing anything more than issue renewed, and ineffectual, protests.

Although American public opinion was overwhelmingly sympathetic to China, the United States still made no move to halt its shipments of strategic raw materials to Japan.

As we can see in retrospect, if Washington had in fact "quarantined" Japan by placing an embargo on the shipment of strategic raw materials—scrap metals and, above all, oil—the Japanese might very well have found themselves compelled to accept American or some other foreign mediation of their dispute with China. But, still mired in economic depression, Washington decided that trade with Japan was more important than halting Japanese aggression, a decision that was to prove one of the most costly the American government ever made.

❑ *Changes in the Japanese Government*

As the China war dragged on, the Japanese saw the need for a broader body to coordinate the overall requirements of the army and navy, the distribution of the country's resources, and the policies of the various branches of the government. For this purpose the Ministerial Conference (see p. 134) was expanded in November 1937 into a Liaison Conference that included the army and navy chiefs and vice-chiefs of staff, and the chiefs of the military and naval bureaus of the war and naval ministries. By July of 1940 this body was convened with greater frequency and was strengthened to include the president of the Planning Board, the president of the Privy Council, and others concerned with the mobilization of the country's resources.

By this time the Liaison Conferences had usurped the decision-making functions of the cabinet and become the principal forum for debating and deciding national policies. Final decisions of the Liaison Conference meetings were formally disclosed at Imperial Conferences presided over by the emperor, who had already been informed of the matters to be decided. Herbert Bix describes the Imperial Conference as "*the device for legally transforming the 'will of the emperor' into the 'will of the state.'*" Far from being a passive monarch who merely endorsed policy decisions made by others, Bix describes him as "a dynamic emperor participating in the planning of aggression and guiding the process by a variety of interventions that were often indirect but in every instance determining." As observed earlier, however, the actual formulation of aggressive plans were not the work of the emperor, whose ultimate responsibility lay in the fact he approved them and allowed them to go forward.

❑

TWELVE

Western Europe:
From Versailles to Hitler
1919   1933

Unlike the postwar turmoil in Eastern Europe and East Asia, the armistice of November 11, 1918, brought peace to Western Europe, if only briefly. The principal guardian of that peace was France—a France obsessed by its catastrophic losses in the recent war and determined never to have to fight a war again. French policy was therefore dedicated to the defense of the postwar treaty system that had been designed to ensure the preservation of peace and thus also of French security.

❑ *The French Search for Security*

Of the many threats to peace and French security in the postwar world, the most obvious and the one most feared by French statesmen and public opinion alike was the revival of an embittered and vengeful Germany. The prevention of such a revival had been the major concern of French statesmen during the making of the postwar treaties; it was to remain their major concern throughout the postwar years.

The most effective means of dealing with the German menace would have been a political breakup of Germany—the cession to France of the left bank of the Rhine and the creation of separatist governments elsewhere. But, as discussed earlier, France's Rhineland aspirations had foundered over the opposition of Britain and the United States, whose representatives had objected that such partition would be an excessively flagrant violation of the principle of self-determination. In return for abandoning their claim to the left bank of the Rhine, the French were promised defensive alliances with Britain and the United States, which would thereby share the burden of coping with the crippled but still formidable monster they had refused to kill. But the American Senate refused to ratify the American alliance with France, and because British ratification depended on American participation, the French were left without guarantees from their most powerful allies.

The French had greater success in arranging alliances with the smaller states of Europe which also had reason to fear a revival of German power. In the course of the 1920s France concluded alliances with Belgium in the west and with Poland,

Czechoslovakia, Romania, and Yugoslavia in the east. In this same period France gave its blessing to the formation of the so-called Little Entente, a defensive alliance between Czechoslovakia, Romania, and Yugoslavia. None of these alliances, however, even approached the value of France's prewar ententes with Britain and Russia or the desired postwar alliance with Britain and the United States.

The French also tried to make the League of Nations an effective instrument of international security with a proposal to build up a League army composed of contingents from all its member states. But the member states, jealous of their sovereignty, refused to relinquish troops to an international authority or pay for their equipment and maintenance. Further, League members saw reason to fear that a French-dominated League with effective coercive power would be used by the French as an instrument to serve their own national interests.

Denied guarantees of support from Britain and the United States, and unable to equip the League with effective peace-keeping powers, the French found themselves compelled to rely on their own military strength. Consequently throughout the 1920s they made their acceptance of any limitation of land armies—the subject of a succession of international conferences—conditional on receiving international guarantees they had so far sought in vain.

☐ *The Weapon of Reparations* ➤

As we have seen, the French had acquired a powerful weapon for defending their security in the economic provisions of the Versailles treaty, which required that Germany and its allies pay reparations to atone for their responsibility for starting the war and which sanctioned Allied intervention in Germany in the event of defaults in reparations payments. Because of the immense gulf between what some Allied leaders thought Germany *should* pay and what others believed Germany *could* pay, the naming of a final reparations figure had been turned over to a reparations commission which was to report to the Allied governments on May 1, 1921.

The bill finally presented by the Allied reparations commission called for Germany's payment of 132 billion gold marks, or roughly 33 billion dollars. Once again, members of the commission who regarded themselves as realists believed that this sum far exceeded Germany's capacity to pay, but they feared that anything less would be unacceptable to the French government and public opinion. At the same time, to adjust reparations to what they believed was more in line with Germany's capacity to pay, they set up a complex schedule of payments that in effect reduced the total reparations bill to 50 billion gold marks. This London Schedule of Payments was presented to the Germans on May 5 in the form of an ultimatum. Germany was to agree unconditionally to the payments schedule and was to pay 1 billion gold marks within twenty-five days. In the event of a German refusal, the Allies threatened to occupy the entire Ruhr industrial region.

The London schedule was not unreasonable and the German government could have made the required payments through taxation. The Germans, however, regarded *any* reparations payments as unreasonable, and the demand for the immediate payment of 1 billion gold marks faced the government with a genuine dilemma. This sum was raised by borrowing from abroad at high rates of interest and by resorting to the dangerous expedient of printing money and selling debased German currency on foreign exchanges. The result was that the German mark, already seriously inflated during the war years, plunged in value.

❑ *The Russo-German Rapallo Treaty*

Reparations were closely linked to a multitude of other problems: inter-Allied war debts, Russian debts repudiated by the Bolshevik government, international security guarantees, and international disarmament. To deal with these problems, the Allies convened a succession of international conferences where the efforts to find meaningful solutions foundered over the divergent interests of the participating states. The French refused to make concessions over German reparations or agree to disarmament without ironclad security guarantees from Britain and the United States; the United States refused to provide security guarantees or forgive the wartime debts contracted by the Allies; the British refused to provide guarantees without American participation; the Bolsheviks refused to honor the debts contracted by the tsarist government or recognize the property rights of foreign investors.

The most significant agreement produced by any of these early postwar meetings was an unexpected by-blow of a conference that met in Genoa from April 10 to May 19, 1922, which for the first time included representatives of Europe's two pariah states, Germany and Russia. Each came to the conference intensely suspicious of the other. The Germans feared that the Russians might be tempted to side with France over reparations—to increase the German reparations burden, the French had invited the Russians to claim their share. While the Russians feared that Germany might join a capitalist united front over the foreign debt question—the tsarist government had also borrowed heavily from Germany before 1914. To avoid a mutual sellout, the German and Russian representatives at the Genoa conference withdrew to the nearby resort town of Rapallo, where on April 16, 1922, they signed a separate Russo-German agreement providing for the resumption of diplomatic relations, the mutual cancellation of all debts and claims, and economic cooperation.

The representatives of the Western powers received the news of the Rapallo treaty with stupefied indignation. The *Times* of London denounced it as an unholy alliance, "an open defiance and studied insult to the Entente powers." Entente leaders suspected that the treaty contained secret clauses providing for political and military, as well as economic, cooperation, and that it was a prelude to an alliance they had most reason to fear: a union of German technological proficiency and organizing ability with Russia's manpower and resources. In fact, the Rapallo treaty contained no secret provisions, but it gave new impetus to Russo-German military collaboration, which had already begun in 1921 and was to continue until the advent of Hitler, and the mere threat of a closer Russo-German rapprochement was to prove a valuable diplomatic weapon for both countries.

At subsequent conferences convened to deal with the questions of reparations and inter-Allied debts, the French became increasingly exasperated by what they perceived as a callous disregard of French interests by their negotiating partners. Called upon to grant the Germans a moratorium on reparations, Prime Minister Poincaré accused the Germans of deliberately ruining their currency to give a fraudulent impression of national bankruptcy. Forceful measures were now necessary to put an end to German efforts to sabotage reparations and convince them of the futility of further evasion. On December 26 the French representative on the reparations commission pushed through a motion that Germany was in default on its reparations payments, and on January 11, 1923, French and Belgian troops began the occupation of the Ruhr, the heartland of Germany's industrial economy.

❑ *The Franco-Belgian Occupation of the Ruhr; the German Inflation*

The German government responded to the Ruhr occupation by suspending all payments in kind to France and Belgium and inaugurating a program of passive resistance by forbidding all cooperation with French and Belgian authorities. As the overall German economic situation grew more desperate and to finance the millions of workers idled by passive resistance, the German government once again resorted to the expedient of printing more money, with the result that inflation spun completely out of control. The mark, already 18,000 to the dollar in January 1923, quickly fell to several billion to the dollar and was soon worth literally less than the paper it was printed on.

The immediate consequences of inflation were massive unemployment, the impoverishment of a large proportion of the population, widespread malnutrition, a surge in suicide rates, and a sharp increase in crime. A wave of strikes swept over the country in the summer of 1923. The Communist party in the Ruhr staged a notable revival, and Communists were invited to join coalition governments in Saxony and Thuringia. On October 10 the Berlin Communist newspaper *Rote Fahne* printed a letter from Stalin, who hailed the approaching revolution in Germany as the most important event of our time and predicted that the victory of the German proletariat would shift the center of world revolution from Moscow to Berlin.

A Communist revolution never took place in Germany. The inflation itself, however, was in many ways equivalent to a revolution, for it brought economic ruin to the most stable elements of German society—the middle classes who worked hard, saved their money, and were staunch defenders of law and order. The inflation destroyed the economic status of these guardians of social stability; it shattered their system of values and contributed to an erosion of moral standards that left them receptive to the appeals of extremists of every variety—political, religious, and moral. A small number of entrepreneurs and financial manipulators made immense profits during the inflation, a fact that further embittered the losers. The German government itself, however, was the major beneficiary of inflation, for its domestic debt was virtually wiped out and its foreign debt written down, a success achieved at a terrible political and social cost.

Over the question of reparations, France's tough policy seemed to have triumphed. In September 1923 a German government under the leadership of Gustav Stresemann braved intense domestic disapproval by acknowledging defeat, calling for an end to passive resistance, and announcing his government's intention to resume reparations payments. The French, however, had paid a high price for their victory. Their occupation of the Ruhr had provoked widespread international criticism, and the occupation itself had placed a severe strain on the French economy. Further, with the German economy in shambles, the expectation of France's creditors that the French government could repay its loans at home and abroad through German reparations payments declined sharply, and by the autumn of 1923 the franc too had plunged in value. The French government now came under heavy domestic as well as foreign pressure to cooperate in promoting international economic recovery that would necessarily include the recovery of Germany.

❑ *The End of Inflation; the Dawes Plan*   *Nich*

On November 15, 1923, the Stresemann government initiated a plan to end inflation by retiring all existing currency and introducing a new currency, the Rentenmark (which would have the same face value as the prewar mark), its value guaranteed by mortgages on German industry and agriculture. The German government subsequently imposed rigid restrictions on the amount of currency that could be issued, cut off new credits to industry, and compelled speculators to sell one and a half billion dollars in foreign currency to the Reichsbank, the German national bank.

Later that same month two international committees were formed to deal with the problems of the German economy and assess Germany capacity to pay reparations. The reparations committee included two representatives each from Belgium, Britain, France, Italy, and the United States. Although the American delegation was allegedly unofficial, its members had been selected and carefully briefed by the Washington government. The importance of the American presence was acknowledged with the election of the senior American representative, Charles G. Dawes, the first director of the U.S. Bureau of the Budget, as chairman of the committee, which began its deliberations in January 1924.

The final report of the international financial committee, presented on April 9 and subsequently known as the Dawes Plan, stressed that it was concerned with business, not politics; with the recovery of debt, not the imposition of penalties; and with the economic reconstruction of Germany, which was part of the larger problem of the economic reconstruction of Europe. Noting that the German government's domestic debt "has been practically extinguished by the depreciation of the currency," the plan called for the stabilization of the German currency and a complete reorganization of German finances under Allied supervision. Germany was to be granted temporary relief from reparations payments (though not from payments in kind) and was to be given a loan of 800 million gold marks to provide a gold reserve for German currency and prime the pump of the German economy. In the first year after the plan went into effect, Germany was to pay 1 billion gold marks in reparations, a total that was to increase by the end of five years to 2 billion 500 million. This sum was to be raised from three sources: the income from state railways, industrial debentures, and taxation. The report took into account the possibility of a German economic relapse and the

potential difficulty of transferring German payments abroad. Anticipating such problems, it provided that payments might vary according to changes in the German economy and international monetary rates.

The German government accepted the Dawes Plan on April 16. In May Poincaré
was defeated in French parliamentary elections by a so-called Cartel of the Left (Cartel des Gauches), a setback generally attributed to French anger over the depreciation of their own currency and the high cost of Poincaré's policy of coercion. On August 16, 1924, the government of his successor, Edouard Herriot, joined other powers
represented on the reparations commission in accepting the Dawes Plan and announced that the Ruhr would be evacuated within one year.

The international acceptance of the Dawes Plan has been called the end of French
predominance in Europe. But in reality that predominance had ceased over a century
earlier with the defeat of Napoleon; its brief revival after World War I was due entirely
to the temporary weakness of Germany and Russia. The importance of the Dawes Plan
was that it accelerated the process of German economic recovery and severely restricted France's power to use reparations as a weapon to enforce the terms of the
Versailles treaty.

Why did the French agree to the Dawes Plan? Largely because of their own economic troubles, the pressure of their allies, their realization that an economically prostrate Germany would be unable to pay reparations, and their fear that further recalcitrance might have serious political as well as economic consequences. Most telling of
all may have been the fear—which the German government did its best to exploit—
that the continued deterioration of the German economy might result in a Bolshevik
revolution in Germany.

❑ *The Locarno Treaties*

Through their occupation of the Rhineland, the French still possessed a powerful
weapon to enforce the provisions of the Versailles treaty. Shortly after their acceptance of the Dawes Plan they announced that their evacuation of the Cologne zone
would not take place as scheduled in January 1925 because of German violations of
the treaty's disarmament provisions. Fearful that the French might delay their evacuation of the Ruhr or even undertake new incursions into German territory, the Germans resorted to a bold diplomatic maneuver. Well aware of the French desire for a
British guarantee of their postwar frontiers and of Britain's reluctance to provide it,
the Germans sounded London, confidentially and unofficially, about the desirability of
an international guarantee of the frontiers of France and Belgium that would at the
same time guarantee the western frontiers of Germany. This proposal was warmly received by Austen Chamberlain, the foreign secretary of a Conservative government
that had come into power in November 1924, who saw in it (as the Germans had intended) a means of evading the persistent French demand for a British guarantee of
all European postwar frontiers, eastern as well as western.

Aristide Briand, now French foreign minister, had heretofore opposed a treaty
limited to a guarantee of Germany's western frontiers. But the Ruhr occupation had

aroused widespread international hostility, especially on the part of Britain and the United States, and negotiations over the Dawes Plan had revealed the extent of France's diplomatic isolation. Britain's offer to endorse a guarantee of the Franco-Belgian frontier with Germany seemed better than no guarantee at all, and Briand hoped that negotiations over this frontier might be used to secure more extensive treaty commitments. With this aim in view, he agreed to appoint French representatives to a committee of jurists that was to prepare drafts of the proposed treaties. These were presented to a conference of foreign ministers that convened in the Swiss resort town of Locarno on October 5, 1925.

The Locarno treaties, signed on December 1, 1925, consisted of several separate agreements. The first and most important of these treaties was a mutual guarantee of the frontiers of Belgium, France, and Germany as established by the Treaty of Versailles, a guarantee that included Articles 42 and 43 providing for the demilitarization of the Rhineland. This treaty was underwritten, and thus theoretically guaranteed, by Britain and Italy.

The second and third Locarno agreements were arbitration treaties between Germany and Belgium and Germany and France. The fourth and fifth were arbitration treaties between Germany and Poland and Germany and Czechoslovakia, whereby these states relinquished the right to alter their frontiers by force and were obliged to submit disputes to international arbitration. The weakness of treaties four and five was that they were indeed arbitration treaties that left open the possibility for a revived Germany to alter its eastern frontiers with Poland and Czechoslovakia through diplomatic pressure backed up by the threat of force. To make up for the deficiencies of the arbitration treaties, the French concluded mutual assistance treaties with Poland and Czechoslovakia (the sixth and seventh of the Locarno agreements), which provided that in the event of Germany's failure to observe the terms of its arbitration treaties with those countries, they would act in accordance with Article 16 of the Covenant of the League of Nations "to lend each other immediate aid and assistance, if such a failure is accompanied by an unprovoked recourse to arms."

Following the signature of the Locarno treaties and in accordance with previous agreements, Germany was admitted to the League of Nations on September 8, 1926, and entitled to a permanent seat on the League Council.

❑ Briand and Stresemann

The acceptance of the Dawes Plan to promote Germany's economic recovery, the signature of the Locarno agreements, whereby Germany voluntarily accepted its postwar western frontiers (as opposed to its acceptance under compulsion of the "dictated" terms of Versailles), and the admission of Germany to the League of Nations seemed to have resolved the most difficult problems created by the postwar treaties. Idealists now saw reason to believe that the groundwork had been laid for an era of better international understanding. This belief was reinforced by the image of the men in charge of the foreign policy of France and Germany. Briand and Stresemann seemed to represent a new quality of sensible leadership, a willingness to cooperate and compromise in resolving problems of mutual concern, and to bury or ignore the differences and hatreds of the past.

In the euphoria generated by the Locarno agreements, their principal architects, Briand, Stresemann, and Austen Chamberlain, were awarded the Nobel Peace Prize. All three were to continue to direct their country's foreign policies until the end of the decade, although after Locarno the influence of Chamberlain was eclipsed by his French and German counterparts, who were to play far more significant roles on the international stage. Both Briand and Stresemann suffered the fate of being lionized by idealists as "good Europeans" while being vilified by ultranationalists and denounced as traitors for having betrayed their countries' interests. Their reputations have undergone comparable vicissitudes at the hands of historians, though Stresemann remains by far the more controversial figure.

Briand's most notable quality as a statesman was his flexibility, his ability to adapt his policies to what he perceived to be the needs and possibilities of the moment. He demonstrated this quality early in his career by playing a leading role in resolving the bitter church–state controversy that had threatened to engulf France in civil war in the first years of the century. Maintaining friends and contacts in a broad range of political parties, seemingly without doctrinaire political convictions of his own, Briand succeeded in forming six cabinets under his leadership before and during the war and holding key positions in a variety of postwar governments until his death in 1932.

Briand has been accused of compromise and concession in dealing with Germany and of inaugurating the fateful policy of appeasement that led to World War II. Compromise and concession, however, are essential tools in negotiation, and in the case of Briand they were employed on behalf of his fundamental political objective throughout the postwar years: the security of France. He saw that this security depended in the first instance on maintaining the strongest army in Europe, he was instrumental in negotiating France's alliances with the states of Eastern Europe, and he originally took a hard line in dealing with Germany. It was Briand who made the decision to occupy Düsseldorf, Duisburg, and Ruhrort in March 1921 in response to a German default in reparations payments; and it was Briand again who in May of that year addressed the ultimatum to Germany demanding payment of 1 billion gold marks in reparations by the end of the month or face an Allied occupation of the Ruhr.

In following years, however, Briand became alarmed by the international hostility aroused by France's intransigent policies. He also recognized that Germany could not be held in subjection permanently, that Germany was potentially stronger than France, and that French security was therefore critically dependent on the support of Britain and the United States. Briand's advocacy of France's acceptance of the Dawes Plan was motivated in part by his recognition of the need to regain British and American friendship. He favored the Locarno agreements as a step toward bringing Britain as well as Germany into an international system of guarantees, and he made persistent if vain efforts to secure American guarantees for the postwar international system, which the Americans had done so much to establish. He was to become a leading advocate of a greater degree of European political and economic integration that he hoped would enmesh Germany in such a tightly knit and interdependent international association that war would be eliminated as a practical possibility. The preservation of peace, Briand came to realize, was the most economic as well as most effective way to safeguard French security. It was a tragedy for France and the entire world that his concessions and compromises failed to achieve this purpose.

Gustav Stresemann's reputation as a good European, like that of Briand, derived from the belief that he was dedicated to a policy of compromise and cooperation. But with the capture of Stresemann's unpublished papers and the entire body of German diplomatic documents after World War II, historians discovered that Stresemann, far from being a good European, was a fervent German nationalist, primarily concerned with safeguarding and promoting the interests of his country as he understood them. In this respect he did not differ from Briand or indeed from any other national leader. Unlike Briand, however, Stresemann did not see his country's interests best served by the maintenance of the postwar treaties. On the contrary, he was a revisionist, intent on throwing off the shackles of Versailles and recovering his country's full sovereignty and independence. He sought the removal of foreign troops from German soil, the reduction or outright elimination of reparations, and the elimination of arms restrictions. He promoted the secret rearmament of Germany and its military collaboration with the Soviet Union. More sinister still, he sought the revision of Germany's postwar frontiers in Eastern Europe and did not exclude the possibility that military pressure might be necessary to achieve this purpose.

Anyone familiar with Stresemann's political background should not have been surprised by these revelations. A member of the conservative National Liberal party, Stresemann had always been a staunch defender of the existing political and social order. Before and during the war, he supported expansionist and annexationist policies. After the war he reluctantly abandoned his hopes for a monarchist restoration and gave his allegiance to the Weimar Republic as the only alternative to a military or Communist dictatorship. Appointed chancellor on August 12, 1923, during the Franco-Belgian occupation of the Ruhr and the darkest days of the German inflation, he made the tough decision to yield to French pressure, abandon passive resistance, and seek the stabilization of the German currency. His government fell on November 23, just over three months after taking office, but Stresemann remained in successive cabinets as foreign minister until his death on October 3, 1929.

It was during his period of service as foreign minister that Stresemann acquired his reputation as a good European. Many students of German history believe this reputation has been hopelessly shattered by revelations of his more ambitious political objectives, and some have gone so far as to regard him as a precursor of Hitler whose policies were seen as part of a continuum of German aggression going back to the era of Bismarck and beyond.

The evidence of Stresemann's revisionist ambitions, even when interpreted in the worst possible light, does not justify a comparison to Hitler. Stresemann was no racist, certainly not in the Nazi sense (his wife was of Jewish descent); he never advocated the destruction of Poland and Russia, the extermination of Jews, or the establishment of a German racial state. In marked contrast to Hitler, Stresemann was a pragmatic realist who understood better than any German statesman since Bismarck that politics is the art of the possible, and the very real success he achieved was due above all to his shrewd evaluation and exploitation of the possibilities that opened out before him. Although under constant and savage attack by nationalist extremists who called for the forthright repudiation of Versailles and the public proclamation of an expansionist program—the radical demands that gave the Nazis much of their popular appeal—Stresemann adhered to a more cautious political course. While not ruling out the use of military pressure to secure frontier rectifications, he was, as the leader of a defeated country, acutely aware of the hazards of war and appears to have believed that he could achieve his objectives through negotiation. But his ultimate intentions remain a matter of speculation. Worn out by overwork and the perpetual need to fend off the attacks of his domestic critics, he died at the age of fifty-one before he was able to reveal, through his actual policies, the extent of his revisionist ambitions or what steps he would take to realize them.

Unlike many of their more optimistic contemporaries, Briand and Stresemann did not see the Locarno agreements and Germany's admission to the League of Nations as inaugurating a new era of international understanding. They were painfully aware of how many problems were still unresolved. The eastern boundaries of Germany had been left in limbo, subject to revision through future arbitration agreements; Britain and the United States persisted in their refusal to shore up French security with overall guarantees of the postwar treaties; the German economy remained precariously dependent on foreign loans; the thorny questions of reparations and Allied war debts remained unresolved; and so far no significant steps had been taken toward achieving an international disarmament agreement.

❑ *The Disarmament Problem*

The Treaty of Versailles stated that its purpose in imposing arms restrictions on Germany was "to render possible the initiation of a general limitation of the armaments of all nations." Yet in the years after the signature of Versailles, the only international agreement on arms control had been the 1922 Washington treaty on naval armaments, which was restricted to limiting the construction and retention of capital ships. (See pp. 107–108.) Thereafter nothing further had been done on behalf of international disarmament. In December 1925, however, the League of Nations set up a Preparatory Commission for a Disarmament Conference, a committee of experts that was to examine the problems of disarmament and draw up proposals for an international disarmament agreement. Although not a member of the League, the United States was invited to appoint representatives to this commission, an invitation extended to Germany when it became a member of the League and to the Soviet Union in 1927.

The Preparatory Commission encountered all the obstacles to an international disarmament agreement that have prevented the adoption of effective arms controls to the present day. The leaders of every sovereign state, even if sincerely committed to the principle of disarmament, believe their country must remain capable of defending its national security. Because the means required for defending that security differ widely from country to country, there are inevitably wide differences of opinion among them. Technologically backward countries with large populations favor the abolition of sophisticated weaponry; highly industrialized countries with smaller populations favor limiting the size of armies but insist that they need to retain their arsenals. The Spanish diplomat and historian Salvador da Madariaga compared the negotiations of the Preparatory Commission to a disarmament conference among the animals: the lion proposed the abolition of all weapons except teeth and claws; the eagle, all weapons except beaks and talons; and so on. The animals, however, did not face two other formidable obstacles to international disarmament, namely, the lobby of the munitions industry and the fact that the manufacture of arms makes a substantial contribution to the national income of technologically advanced countries, a source of wealth they have always been reluctant to give up.

At a meeting of the Preparatory Commission in late 1927, Maxim Litvinov, the representative of the Soviet Union, which was taking part in its deliberations for the first time, declared that if people were sincere about disarmament, no elaborate plans were necessary; the only way to achieve genuine disarmament was to disarm. Litvinov's proposal was dismissed as Communist propaganda, which of course it was. But for the Soviet Union this proposal also had its practical side, for, with its own arms industries as yet relatively undeveloped, this large and populous country could only benefit from the disarmament of its rivals.

During the deliberations of the Preparatory Commission, the United States had tried to follow up the limited success of the Washington conference with another naval disarmament conference to limit naval vessels below the capital ship class. This conference met in Geneva in May 1927, but the French and Italians, still smarting from the low ratio on capital ships allotted to them at the Washington conference, refused to attend. The Geneva conference was thus restricted to representatives of Britain, Japan, and the United States, who were unable to reach agreement. The Americans, with widely scattered naval bases, wanted fewer restrictions on large cruisers; the British, with an abundance of bases, were reluctant to limit the number of smaller cruisers; and the Japanese, who had not been enthusiastic about further naval restrictions in the first place, were happy to watch their American and British rivals quarrel. The Geneva conference ended in failure.

❑ *The Kellogg-Briand Pact*

The failure of the Geneva naval conference and the lack of progress of the League's Preparatory Commission provoked bitter criticism from idealists and a particularly angry outcry from Americans, who conveniently forgot their own country's refusal to subscribe to any international guarantees for peace. Consequently France, and all other countries concerned with maintaining the existing international order, had no alternative but to insist on maintaining the weapons they deemed necessary to defend it. The public outcry for some gesture on behalf of international peace was so great, however, that European as well as American statesmen felt obliged to respond.

In June 1927 Aristide Briand, the French foreign minister, sought to take advantage of American public sentiment on behalf of international peace by proposing that

France and the United States conclude a pact of perpetual friendship, a proposal he clearly intended as a lever to secure renewed American participation in the European security system. The American secretary of state, Frank B. Kellogg, was embarrassed by this proposal, which seemed likely to appeal to American peace enthusiasts but was certain to be interpreted by the Senate as an entangling alliance. After delaying a reply for several months, he came forward with a proposal of his own: a multilateral treaty for the renunciation of war, which would sidestep the dangers of Briand's bilateral pact and at the same time satisfy American peace enthusiasts, who would not know the difference. It was now Briand's turn to be embarrassed. What France needed from the United States and Britain were specific guarantees, not general statements of good intentions. But the French statesman was now trapped, unable to reject a proposal that had such obvious popular appeal.

The result of Briand's subsequent negotiations with the Americans was the Kellogg-Briand Pact, signed in Paris on August 27, 1928, whereby the signatory states renounced war as an instrument of national policy. Widely hailed at the time as a decisive step toward the achievement of international peace, the pact was actually little more than a token gesture to meet public demand for some kind of antiwar declaration. It was carefully worded to avoid any commitment the Senate might interpret as an entangling alliance. Even then the Senate only ratified it with an accompanying declaration that it did not curtail the American right to self defense, that it was not inconsistent with the Monroe Doctrine, and that it did not commit the United States to participate in punitive expeditions against aggressor states. Indeed, the pact contained no enforcement provisions of any kind and was thus signed with little hesitation by almost every country in the world. Its only practical result was that henceforth there were fewer formal declarations of war. Nevertheless, the pact was the first formal antiwar declaration to which a majority of the world's sovereign states had subscribed and represented at least a moral recognition that war was no longer a legitimate instrument of national policy.

Not to be left behind in the realm of morality, the Soviet Union, which had also signed the Kellogg-Briand Pact, promulgated an antiwar treaty of its own drafted by the Soviet commissar for foreign affairs, Maxim Litvinov. The Litvinov Protocol for the Renunciation of War was signed in Moscow on February 9, 1929, by the Soviet Union, Poland, Romania, Estonia, and Latvia. In the Soviet document, too, enforcement provisions were conspicuously lacking.

❑ *The Failure of Disarmament Negotiations*

At the final meeting of the League's Preparatory Commission, November 6 to December 9, 1930, a draft convention was adopted as the basis for the deliberations of a League-sponsored international disarmament conference which was scheduled to convene in February 1932. That conference, which included representatives from the United States and the Soviet Union, duly assembled in Geneva, but it was doomed from the start for the same reasons that doomed all similar conferences. The most obvious obstacles to agreement were differences between France and Germany. The French insisted that a disarmament treaty include restrictions on German armaments as provided by the Treaty of Versailles, which they considered essential to French security; the Germans demanded arms equality, which the French saw as an unacceptable threat to their security. The conference was finally scuttled in October 1933 when Hitler announced Germany's withdrawal from both the disarmament conference and the League of Nations.

Siegfried Line

❑ Reparations, the Young Plan, and the Evacuation of the Rhineland

In December 1927, Parker Gilbert, the American agent-general who was supervising the collection of reparations under the Dawes Plan, proposed the formation of a new committee to arrange a final reparations settlement. The German government agreed to this proposal in principle, but asked that the Allies, in return for Germany's acceptance of a final settlement, withdraw their occupation forces from the Rhineland immediately rather than wait until 1935, the date fixed by the Versailles treaty.

The Allied governments agreed to consider this proposal, and in February 1929 a financial committee began its meetings in Paris with the task of drafting a final reparations settlement. It differed from previous reparations committees in that it included representatives from Germany as well as from the Allied countries responsible for the Dawes Plan—Belgium, Britain, France, Italy, and Japan. Once again the United States was represented unofficially, but as in earlier negotiations over reparations, its representatives were selected and carefully briefed by Washington. And once again the importance of American participation was acknowledged with the election of an American, Owen D. Young, to the chairmanship of the committee. Young, chairman of the board of General Electric, had played a leading part in drafting the Dawes Plan and was thus an experienced hand in dealing with the reparations question.

The expectations of the Germans that negotiations over reparations would be accompanied by simultaneous negotiations over the evacuation of the Rhineland were thwarted by Briand, who refused any discussion of the Rhineland until the reparations committee had submitted its report. The cabinet of Chancellor Hermann Müller (Socialist) nevertheless voted unanimously to accept the final recommendations of the Young committee, which submitted its report to the governments concerned on June 7, 1929.

The German government had ample reason to endorse the Young Plan, for it left Germany exclusive responsibility for meeting its reparations payments, it removed virtually all Allied supervisory functions and controls, and it scaled down the payments schedule set up under the Dawes Plan, although Germany's annual payments would still be substantial and would continue until 1988. Because the annual payments proposed by the Young Plan were less than those being made by Germany without difficulty in the final year of the Dawes Plan, economic experts saw reason to hope that the Young Plan did indeed represent a final reparations settlement. To receive and disburse reparations payments, effect transfers, and handle deliveries in kind, the Young Plan provided for the establishment of a Bank for International Settlements, which was set up in the Swiss city of Basel.

Following the delivery of the Young committee report, it remained for the governments represented on that committee to ratify the Young Plan and deal with ending the Allied occupation of the Rhineland, which the Germans had demanded as a condition for agreeing to a final settlement on reparations and Briand had refused to consider until a final reparations agreement had been reached. Briand had hoped that, in return for France's ratification of the Young Plan and its agreement to an early withdrawal of Allied occupation forces from the Rhineland, he could obtain ironclad guarantees from Britain and the United States to ensure Germany's reparations payments and the permanent demilitarization of the Rhineland. But before he could proceed further, he learned that Britain's Labour government, without consulting the French, intended to withdraw all British troops from the Rhineland by Christmas, thereby depriving Briand of the Rhineland as a bargaining counter.

Briand was even more seriously undercut in his quest for guarantees of German reparations payments. A conference on reparations held in The Hague in January 1930 reached the curious decision that defaults be referred to the International Court of Justice, which meant in effect that punishment of defaults could be delayed indefinitely. Thus the reparations weapon to safeguard French security was stripped of virtually all firepower.

The leaders of the Weimar government, instead of reaping domestic political benefits from their success in ending Allied economic supervision and securing the early evacuation of the Rhineland, found themselves subjected to a barrage of denunciation for having sold out German interests. Germans generally had always regarded the charge of war guilt and the burden of reparations as profoundly unjust, and for a large majority of Germans the striking feature of the Young Plan was the obligation to continue substantial reparations payments until 1988, well into the lifetime of their grandchildren.

The plan provided fresh fodder for nationalist extremists, who succeeded in forcing the government to submit the question of ratification to a national referendum. The document that was to be the subject of that referendum, speciously entitled The Law Against the Slavery of the German People, or Freedom Law, called for the unilateral repudiation of the war guilt clause of the Versailles treaty, the immediate and unconditional evacuation of the Rhineland, the abolition of all foreign controls over Germany, and the rejection of the Young Plan. Further, it provided that any member of the government who signed the Young Plan or any other treaty implying recognition of Germany's war guilt could be tried for treason. In the referendum held in December 1929, almost 6 million Germans (approximately 14 percent of the electorate) voted for the Freedom Law, an ominous sign of the radicalization of German politics. The referendum nevertheless upheld the government's decision to ratify the Young Plan, which finally went into effect on May 17, 1930. It lasted little more than a year.

❑ *The Maginot Line*

With the inauguration of the Young Plan, which removed all direct Allied supervision and control over the German economy, and with the Allied evacuation of the Rhineland five years ahead of schedule, the French found themselves compelled to find other means to safeguard their security. In December 1929, the French government made the first of a succession of immense financial appropriations to construct a system of fortifications along the frontier of Germany stretching from the borders of Switzerland to Belgium. This defensive system came to be called the Maginot Line, named for the French minister of war.

The overall conception of the Maginot Line was seriously flawed from both a military and political standpoint. It was flawed militarily because its builders assumed that a future conflict would be similar to World War I, a defensive war of attrition. It thus ignored the possibility that new weapons and new strategies—for example, the use of tanks and aircraft—might render traditional fortifications obsolete. A further and even more obvious military flaw was that the line was never extended along the frontier of Belgium. Thus it could always be outflanked by a German attack through the Low Countries, the very route of Germany's western offensive of 1914.

The political flaws inherent in the Maginot Line were equally glaring. Its construction signaled to the world that France intended to pursue a defensive rather than offensive strategy in a future conflict with Germany. France's Eastern allies would thus be deprived of all prospect of effective aid in the event of a German attack, for such aid could only be provided by a vigorous French offensive that would compel the Germans to deploy a large part of their forces in the west and wage a war on two fronts. With the construction of the Maginot Line, Germany was virtually conceded a free hand in Eastern Europe.

❑ *Briand's European Federation Plan*

While the construction of the Maginot Line was still being debated, Aristide Briand initiated a more imaginative and potentially more effective strategy to safeguard French security. He proposed the formation of a European federal union, a permanent organization that would enable the states of Europe to cooperate on behalf of their mutual political and economic security. Encouraged by what he perceived as a positive reception of his proposal, Briand set forth his ideas in greater detail. Basic to his overall conception was the extension of the Locarno treaties to the whole of Europe, a guarantee of political security which he deemed an essential condition for the restoration of economic stability and future economic progress. The formation of a European political union would open the way to a European common market, a free trade association which would improve the quality of life of the entire European community.

Once the details of Briand's federation plan were presented, the initial enthusiasm it had aroused faded away. Other European governments, in particular France's rivals, saw his proposals as yet another French effort to inveigle them into providing guarantees for French security. Moreover, his common market scheme seemed designed to give France maximum scope to use its economic clout to extend its political influence.

The Briand plan was finally dealt a mortal blow by the German Reichstag elections of September 1930 in which two out of every five German voters cast their ballots for the Nazis or the Communists, political parties that advocated the overthrow of the German republic and the existing international system. Following this demonstration of the strength of extremist parties in the country whose involvement was crucial to his plan, Briand realized that all hope for the establishment of a system dedicated to international cooperation and reconciliation had to be abandoned.

❑ *The Coming of the Great Depression*

In retrospect, Stresemann's death on October 3, 1929, can be seen as marking the end of the era of postwar international reconciliation. It was followed later that same month by the stock market crash on Wall Street, which inaugurated an economic depression that was to engulf the greater part of the world. Scholars differ about the causes of the Great Depression, but there can be no disagreement about the importance of its impact on the domestic and foreign affairs of the world's great powers and most lesser states as well.

There had been numerous indications of worldwide economic trouble well before the Wall Street crash. Agricultural prices had declined steadily, in some cases precipitously, throughout the 1920s, a decline generally attributed to the overexpansion of agricultural production during and after the war and the low cost of shipping agricultural products from the southern hemisphere. A similar decline in the prices of industrial products began later in the decade when industrial production too surpassed consumer demand. The ensuing industrial slowdown was accompanied by rising unemployment and a corresponding drop in purchasing power, which led to further economic decline.

More fundamental was the problem that the prosperity of the later 1920s had been based on unsound economic foundations. All the governments of Europe had financed their participation in the late war by borrowing—from their own citizens and from foreign governments—in the confident expectation that these loans would be repaid through reparations levied on the defeated countries. How the defeated countries were to pay the gigantic sums the war had consumed was a question never given adequate consideration; it was simply assumed that they would and should pay. As we have seen, after the war the defeated countries raised money to pay reparations and to finance their own economic recovery through further borrowing, largely from the United States, which invested immense sums not only in Europe but in many other parts of the world, notably in Latin America. While becoming the world's foremost source of loans, the United States was also a major purchaser of foreign products. A serious American economic crisis was therefore bound to have global repercussions.

The boom in the American stock market preceding the 1929 crash had itself contributed to global economic difficulties. With the spectacular rise in American stock prices, American investors who had previously been attracted by the high interest rates in foreign countries now saw more lucrative investment possibilities on Wall Street. With this diversion of investment to the American securities market, foreign countries found it more difficult to get American loans while confronted with demands for the repayment of American and other short-term loans. To meet their short-term obligations, foreign banks were obliged to call in loans to their own entrepreneurs, a measure that ruined many marginal enterprises and forced others to cut their expenditures to the bone.

After the Wall Street crash, the recall of foreign investments became a matter of grim necessity for numerous American financial institutions. During the boom years of the 1920s they had lent immense sums to stock market speculators, whose securities had plunged in value since the crash and whose consequent inability to repay their loans confronted the banks with disastrous financial losses. The banks faced similar losses in their loans to small businesses and farmers, many of them forced into bankruptcy with the drop in prices for their products. Nor could the banks recoup their losses by mortgage foreclosures because the property that represented security for those mortgages had meanwhile also plunged in value. American bank failures rose from a pre-depression annual figure of about 650 to over 1,300 by 1930 and to roughly 4,000 in 1932. During this same period American industrial production, 40 percent of the world's total, had fallen to 31 percent of its 1929 level and unemployment had risen to the unprecedented figure of almost 14 million.

American foreign credits, which had played so significant a role in the global economy, now dried up almost completely. So did the American market for foreign industrial and agricultural products, a situation worsened by American efforts to protect their economy by raising tariffs on foreign imports to prohibitive levels.

❑ *The Impact of the Great Depression on Germany*

The collapse of the American economy was to have particularly serious political and economic consequences in Germany. The point has already been emphasized that Germany's economic recovery and relative prosperity in the later 1920s had been fueled by foreign loans. Under the Dawes Plan, Germany had paid approximately 8 billion marks in reparations but had borrowed the equivalent of 23 billion marks, about half of it from American investors attracted by high interest rates. Thus the German economy rested on a perilously insecure economic foundation. This situation was rendered even more dangerous by the fact that approximately half of Germany's borrowed money was in the form of short-term credits, which German banks, with a misplaced confidence in their country's continued economic recovery, had lent out as long-term credits. Worse still, much of this borrowed money had not been invested in economically productive enterprises, but had been used instead for public works programs—housing, schools, hospitals, social and recreational facilities—whereby German political leaders and regional authorities had hoped to bolster their own political fortunes and, more generally, to generate support for Germany's postwar republican regime.

With a substantial proportion of Germany's short-term loans tied up in long-term loans and public works projects, the drying up of the American money market and withdrawal of short-term credits had more serious repercussions in Germany than elsewhere. In order to repay American investors, German banks were now obliged to lean particularly heavily on German business enterprises. The result was a proliferation of business failures, sharp increases in unemployment, and the onset of economic depression in Germany even before the Wall Street crash. All the more severe was the blow when that crash actually took place.

The government of Heinrich Brüning, which took office in March 1930, sought to restore the German economy by reduction in government spending, tax increases, and deflation—the economic orthodoxy of that time. Unable to secure Reichstag approval for his package of stringent economic measures, Chancellor Brüning persuaded President Hindenburg to grant him emergency powers under Article 48 of the Weimar constitution which would enable him to enact legislation by decree without having to secure its passage through the Reichstag. When the Reichstag voted on June 18, 1930, to abrogate the decrees enacted in this manner, the chancellor decided to dissolve the Reichstag and appeal to the country by calling for new elections in September, two years before they were required by the constitution.

The call for new elections was a courageous but inept political maneuver, for higher taxes, cuts in salaries and welfare payments, and tight credit restrictions are never popular. Moreover Brüning's stringent deflationary program, far from contributing to Germany's economic recovery, had only hastened the process of decline and led to more business failures, more unemployment, and a further drop in purchasing power. The question is still hotly debated as to how much Germany's economic troubles contributed to the rise of Nazism and the success of the Nazis and Communists in the Reichstag election of September 14, 1930, but the voting results show that there was at least a significant linkage. In 1928, while Germany was still relatively prosperous, the Communists held 54 seats in the Reichstag, the Nazis a mere 12. In the elections of September 1930, Communist representation rose to 77 seats, the Nazis to a spectacular 107.

The success of extremist parties in the September election, while dealing a mortal blow to Briand's European federation scheme, also had serious financial repercussions, because this revelation of Germany's political instability set off another large-scale withdrawal of foreign credits. By this time, too, Germans themselves were sending whatever capital they still controlled to safer investment havens abroad. By September 26, 420 billion marks had been recalled or exported, a financial hemorrhage that was to continue into the following year and hasten Germany's economic deterioration. In a desperate attempt to shore up the prestige of his government and counter the mounting criticism of political extremists, Brüning now resorted to a more nationalistic and aggressive foreign policy.

❑ *The Austro-German Customs Union*

A key feature of Briand's European federation plan had been the removal of European tariff barriers and the creation of a European economic common market. In March 1931 the Briand plan was revived from an unexpected and, from a French point of view, most undesirable quarter. For in that month the Austrian and German governments announced that they were taking what they described as "the first practical step" in breaking down international tariff barriers by establishing an Austro-German customs union which all other countries were invited to join.

This announcement aroused fury and consternation in France. One of the most important provisions of the Treaty of St. Germain between the Allies and Austria had been the prohibition of any kind of Austro-German union. This prohibition had been reinforced by the so-called Geneva Protocol of 1922, an international agreement to promote Austria's economic recovery that expressly forbade any measure that might affect Austria's economic independence.

With the announcement of the Austro-German customs union, the French immediately denounced it as a prelude to political union "no matter how the agreement was twisted and turned," a clear-cut violation of St. Germain and the Geneva Protocol and an action of "major imprudence." As we now know from the German documents, this is precisely what some German officials hoped to achieve through the customs union, though this intention was to be disguised by "dressing it up in a pan-European cloak." More immediately, the Austrian and German governments hoped the customs union would be seen by public opinion in both their countries as a foreign policy triumph that would contribute to a renewal of public confidence, now dangerously undermined by economic depression and the attacks of nationalist extremists.

The customs union proposal was indeed an action of major imprudence, as Austrian and German leaders should have realized from the start. It was certain to arouse fierce international opposition and expose their countries to political and economic attacks that might be—and indeed proved to be—disastrous. The French immediately demanded that Austria and Germany abandon their customs union project, and they were in a powerful position to enforce that demand. Now that the American money market was virtually shut down, France had become the major source for foreign loans. Both Austria and Germany were still dependent on such loans to repay the immense sums borrowed from abroad in more prosperous years. By withholding those loans from Austria and Germany, the French could bring inexorable economic pressure to bear on both countries.

Austrian and German banking crises were to give the French additional economic leverage. News of immense losses suffered by Austria's Creditanstalt bank, which controlled 70 percent of the country's banking business and two-thirds of its industrial enterprises, set off a run on the bank which the Austrian government tried in vain to halt by guaranteeing its deposits. Germany was soon to share in Austria's economic plight, for the run on the Creditanstalt quickly spread to German banks. Loans from the Bank of England provided only temporary relief and contributed substantially to the deterioration of Britain's own financial situation. The call of the American president Herbert Hoover for a one-year moratorium on all intergovernment debt payments was denounced by the French as a "scandalous presumption and an unparalleled interference with French rights," and the eventual agreement to the moratorium failed to stem the Austro-German financial panic.

The French bided their time. Unfazed by the British loan to Austria, the French ambassador to London confidently predicted that the Austrians would soon find themselves compelled to make another request for a French loan, "and that would be the occasion for his government to renew the condition that they had laid down as to the renunciation of the customs union." That was in fact what happened. By mid-August the Austrian and German governments saw that they were beaten, and on September 3, 1931, the Austrian government formally announced that it was abandoning the customs union project. The attempts of the Austrian and German governments to refurbish their image through an aggressive foreign policy had failed disastrously, and the Weimar Republic had suffered yet another damaging blow.

❑ *The End of Reparations*

On November 19, 1931, Brüning announced that further reparations payments would complete the ruin of his country's economy and requested the formation of an international committee of experts to examine Germany's financial situation. The committee established in response to this request recommended the convocation of yet another international conference on reparations. That conference met in the Swiss city of Lausanne in June and July of 1932 and produced an agreement which all but wiped out reparations.

There were numerous reasons for this remarkable development. Political events in Germany had forced the conference participants to recognize at last the reality of the danger of a radical revolution in that country, Communist or otherwise, and that drastic measures were needed to stem the rising tide of German political extremism. They had also come to recognize that Germany's economic plight was having serious consequences for much of the rest of Europe. France as yet remained relatively unscathed, but France was now virtually without support in dealing with international economic issues. French prosperity was seen with considerable resentment by France's former allies, and French economic policies were held to be largely responsible for the German economic collapse and thus for the economic downturn elsewhere.

Yet another and perhaps the most important factor affecting the decision of the statesman at Lausanne was provided by the Japanese, who on September 18, 1931, had begun their takeover of Manchuria. For many European and American statesman, the need to deal with the crisis in East Asia now seemed more important than holding the line on reparations.

❑ *The End of German Democracy*

The Lausanne decision on reparations came too late to save the Brüning government and the Weimar Republic. Without popular support, unable to command a majority in the Reichstag, Brüning had long been dependent on the power conferred on him by President Hindenburg to enact legislation by decree. But by the spring of 1932 Brüning had lost Hindenburg's confidence, his position undermined by the failure of his economic and foreign policies, by the intrigues of political rivals that fed on those failures, and by the virulent criticism of political extremists. Brüning resigned on May 31, 1932. Brüning's two successors, however, also lacked popular support, both failed to revive the economy or quell nationalist and social unrest.

In national elections held in July 1932, the Nazis scored another spectacular gain which swelled their representation in the Reichstag to 230. They fared less well in the November elections of that same year (held after a dissolution of the Reichstag following a no-confidence vote in the government). But they remained the largest single party in the Reichstag and were clearly the party with the broadest and most militant popular support. To enlist this popularity for their own political purposes, Hindenburg's coterie of conservative advisers persuaded the aged president to appoint Adolf Hitler, the leader of the Nazi party, to the chancellorship. Contemptuous of Hitler, a low-born vulgarian with no practical experience in government or foreign policy, they saw him as a figurehead who would provide the necessary popular support for a government they confidently expected would be run by themselves. They were to be quickly and disastrously disillusioned.

THIRTEEN

❑

Western Europe: Mussolini and Hitler to the Spanish Civil War

The term *revisionism* has been used to describe the efforts of the losers in World War I and other disaffected states to revise the postwar treaties for the purpose of relaxing or removing treaty-imposed controls and revising postwar frontiers. But the term is misleading when applied to Japan and Nazi Germany, whose policies were not revisionist but revolutionary. These countries represented a new form of nationalist imperialism dedicated to large-scale conquests designed to ensure the future security and great-power status of their respective countries which would require a radical and permanent alteration of the international power structure.

In comparison with Japan and Germany, the Italian dictator Benito Mussolini, who came to power a decade before Hitler in Germany, was a lesser but nonetheless significant proponent of revolutionary imperialism. His imperialist program was never so clearly defined and certainly never attained the dimensions of Japanese or German expansionist efforts. But his participation in the game of revolutionary imperialism and his opportunistic attempt to elevate Italy to the status of a major imperial power made him a dangerous and incalculable player on the international stage throughout the interwar years.

❑ *Postwar Italy*

Infuriated by not having been awarded all they had been promised in return for their entry into World War I on the side of the Allies, the Italians had denounced the postwar peace treaties as *la vittoria mutilata*. Instead of standing firmly at the side of their wartime allies in defense of those treaties, they joined the ranks of the revisionists, intent on altering the postwar settlements in Italy's favor. It was a foolish and ultimately disastrous policy, for in terms of their national security the Italians had made more significant gains through the postwar treaties than France. The only serious threat to Italian security, Austria-Hungary, had been permanently eliminated as a great power, whereas Germany, the major threat to French security, had been left largely intact. Moreover, for the first time in their modern history the Italians had acquired an easily

164

defensible northern frontier at the Brenner Pass, an extension of their boundaries that went well beyond legitimate ethnic claims.

But the Italians had not been given all they had been promised in Africa, nor were they satisfied with the concessions allotted them in the Balkans and the Middle East. They were alarmed by the creation of the new state of Yugoslavia (the Kingdom of the Serbs, Croats, and Slovenes), which they feared might become a dangerous rival on their southeastern flank. They were especially aggrieved by being denied possession of the coastal city of Fiume, which they had never been promised but which they claimed on the basis of the city's predominantly Italian population. (See p. 51.)

Refusing to accept the verdict of the Allied peacemakers over Fiume, the flamboyant Italian patriot and poet Gabriele d'Annunzio seized Fiume in September 1919 at the head of a band of ultranationalists and war veterans that included black-shirted *Arditi,* Italy's wartime shock troops. But the Italian government was unable to support d'Annunzio's coup. Under heavy international pressure, it concluded a treaty with Yugoslavia in November of the following year that made Fiume a free city and used Italian troops to drive out d'Annunzio.

Italian nationalists were dismayed by this display of weakness on the part of their government, which also seemed incapable of coping with the country's multitude of postwar domestic problems. The economy was floundering and large parts of the country were in turmoil—quasi-anarchic conditions that would eventually produce a consensus among Italians who desired a restoration of law and order. Industrialists and landlords, shopkeepers and peasant landowners, all agreed about the need for strong leadership that could put an end to anarchy and revive the Italian economy. They were to find that leadership in Benito Mussolini.

❑ *Mussolini*

Mussolini was born in the Romagna in 1883, the son of an anticlerical Socialist blacksmith. He was named after Benito Juárez, the Mexican revolutionary who in 1867 had overthrown the French-installed puppet government of Emperor Maximilian. A violent and unruly student, Mussolini nevertheless did well enough in school to receive a diploma in elementary education from a Royal Normal School in 1895, graduating first in his class in history, literature, the Italian language—and music. A confirmed Socialist and antimilitarist, like his father, he went to Switzerland in 1902 to avoid the draft, but after two years of odd jobs abroad he returned to Italy, performed his military service, and became a local organizer and journalist for the Socialist party. His performance was sufficiently impressive to secure his election to the party's executive, and in 1912 he was appointed editor of the party's newspaper *Avanti.*

Mussolini had been jailed in 1911 for his outspoken opposition to his country's imperialist war in Africa, but he abandoned his antimilitarism with the outbreak of World War I and became a passionate advocate of intervention on the side of the Allies. Expelled from the Socialist party and dismissed as editor of *Avanti,* he moved to a prointerventionist paper, *Il Popolo d'Italia,* whose first issue appeared on November 15, 1914. When Italy entered the war in the following year, Mussolini enlisted as a private and was seriously wounded on the Isonzo front (by an explosion of his own artillery). The government obviously thought him more valuable as a propagandist than as a soldier, and upon his recovery he was ordered to return to his position as editor of *Il Popolo d'Italia.*

The postwar treaties were a bitter blow to Mussolini as to other Italian ultranationalists. In March 1919 he formed an organization of nationalist extremists and other disaffected persons called the *Fasci di combattimento,* an offshoot of a prointerventionist lobby known as the *Fasci d'azione revoluzionaria,* founded in 1914. The name came from the symbol of authority of ancient Rome, the *fasces,* an axe enclosed in a tightly-bound bundle of rods. Prominent in the new organization were followers of d'Annunzio who had adopted the black-shirts of the *arditi* shock troops, the future uniform of the Fascist militia. Originally as socialist as it was nationalistic, the Mussolini party made a miserable showing at the polls in the elections of May 1921. Mussolini learned quickly. In November of that year he renamed his organization the National Fascist party and gave it a new party platform which, while retaining its nationalist emphasis, abandoned socialism altogether in favor of a program of law and order.

As Mussolini had clearly intended, his metamorphosed Fascist party attracted the support of property owners and other proponents of law and order. Its nationalist emphasis appealed to patriots generally and, more importantly, to military leaders, while its newly proclaimed hostility to radical anticlericalism won the support of the powerful Roman Catholic hierarchy. Backed by such influential forces in Italian society and now well-financed, the Fascist party quickly gained political momentum.

By the summer of 1922 Mussolini felt strong enough to refuse the offer of a seat in the cabinet and demand the right to form his own government. In October, to back up this demand, the Fascists organized a massive rally in Naples and then proceeded to march on Rome. Prime Minister Luigi Facta appealed to the king to proclaim martial law. The king, however, was persuaded by his advisers that the country needed the kind of forceful leadership Mussolini promised to provide, and on October 29 he offered him the prime ministership. Mussolini came to Rome by train on the following day to become head of the Italian government, a post he was to retain for the next two decades. His appointment was greeted with widespread approval. According to a contemporary Italian historian, the entire Italian parliament, with the exception of the Communists and more doctrinaire Socialists, "welcomed Mussolini's government with a sigh of relief, as the end of a nightmare. The civil war, people said, was over."

Mussolini moved cautiously to avoid uniting the political forces still ranged against him, but one month after taking office he persuaded the king and parliament to grant him quasi-dictatorial powers for one year to enable him to take emergency measures to deal with Italy's manifold problems. At the end of his year's grace as dictator by royal and parliamentary consent, Mussolini introduced a new electoral law in November 1923 which provided that the party receiving the most votes in a national election should get two-thirds of the seats in parliament. By this time members of the Fascist party were solidly entrenched in key positions in the army, police, and city and local governments, while the most prominent anti-Fascists had fled abroad and been imprisoned or otherwise intimidated. With members of the Fascist militia surrounding the polling places, the Fascists had no trouble winning a majority of the votes in the national elections held in April 1924 and were duly awarded two-thirds of the seats in parliament.

Mussolini now had a "legal" majority which assured him permanent dictatorial powers. The Italian parliament became a rubber stamp, the king a powerless puppet. In 1924 Mussolini made himself commander-in-chief of the Italian armed forces, in 1926 he officially abolished all opposition parties, and in 1928 the Fascist party militia was incorporated into the regular army to reinforce that organization's political loyalty. In 1929 Mussolini made peace with the Roman Catholic Church, which had refused to recognize the Italian government's incorporation of Rome and the papal states into the Italian national state in the previous century. In a Concordat of February 1929, the papacy recognized the territorial unity of the national state in return for a monetary indemnity and the Italian government's acceptance of papal sovereignty over the Vatican and the cathedral of St. Peter. The pope now abandoned his self-imposed status of "prisoner in the Vatican," and on July 25, 1929, the pope left the Vatican officially for the first time since 1870.

As the ally of Hitler who led his country to disaster in World War II and ultimately sanctioned many of the Nazi leader's abhorrent racial policies, Mussolini has not enjoyed a good press among students of Italian history. He has been described as a pompous buffoon, ignorant and vain, ill-informed in both domestic and foreign affairs, vacillating and indecisive. Yet this was a man who for the greater part of two decades retained his hold over a people as intelligent and realistic as the Italians and who, at least during the early part of his career, won the admiration of a wide assortment of foreign statesmen and intellectuals. His vigorous anti-Communism may have influenced the opinion of conservatives like Winston Churchill, who declared that if he had been an Italian he would have been a wholehearted supporter of Mussolini "in his triumphant struggle against the bestial appetites and passions of Leninism." But Mussolini was also warmly praised by Bernard Shaw, by the distinguished banker Otto Kahn, by Nicholas Murray Butler, the president of Columbia University, and by Gandhi, who visited him in 1931 (accompanied by his goat) and described him as "the savior of the new Italy."

Whatever admiration Mussolini enjoyed among his contemporaries at home and abroad derived from his success in restoring political stability and relative economic prosperity in Italy, while his dictatorial government and ruthless suppression of political opposition were excused as unfortunate necessities in achieving these objectives. He has since been evaluated more critically, but criticism should not obscure the qualities that made him successful. Far from being an ignorant buffoon, he was a shrewd and agile political manipulator with a keen sense of opportunism. He was also a masterful demagogue, who fueled his domestic popularity through his ability to play on popular prejudices and emotions. Perhaps the greatest source of his appeal was his romantic nationalism, which would eventually lead him to ruin. For his dream of an Italian revival of the glories of ancient Rome, while evoking wild enthusiasm among his compatriots, blinded him to the realities of modern Italy's capacities and interests.

❑ *Italian Fascism*

Mussolini's Fascist government was the first, or at least the most notorious, of the dictatorships of the Right established after World War I. "Fascist" subsequently became a term of opprobrium applied to every kind of Rightist government—and indeed to any government or political movement disliked by the Left—and it has been used so loosely and indiscriminately as to become virtually meaningless. Italian Fascism itself, in marked contrast to Communism or Nazism, had no clearly defined political or ideological program when Mussolini came to power. Early definitions of Fascist policy were vague and contradictory, designed to appeal to a wide range of interests and hopes.

The only official formulation of Italian Fascist ideology was an article, "La Dottrina del Fascismo," published in the 1932 edition of the *Enciclopedia Italiana* and thus a decade after the triumph of the movement. Ostensibly written by Mussolini himself, the article was blessedly brief in comparison with the theoretical writings of Lenin or Hitler. It was nevertheless a disorganized and often incomprehensible potpourri of ideas drawn from the writings of a variety of political theorists.

Fascism, Mussolini explained, was not a doctrine worked out beforehand but was born of a need for action; from the beginning it was practical rather than theoretical. Fascist theory was developed during years of conflict, from violent and dynamic negation to positive construction as realized in the Fascist state's laws and institutions. In Fascism, the state was all-embracing. No human or spiritual values could exist, much less have value, apart from the state. Thus Fascism was totalitarian and the Fascist state a synthesis and embodiment of all values which interpreted, developed, and fulfilled the potential of the life of the people. Fascism repudiated the political and economic doctrines of classical liberalism, socialism, trade unionism, egalitarianism, pacifism, internationalism, and international organizations; it rejected the myth of felicity and indefinite progress, the materialistic conception that equated happiness with well-being.

Apart from its glorification of the state, the only positive concept in Fascist ideology was its glorification of war and imperialism. Fascism rejected the belief in the possibility or even the desirability of perpetual peace. War alone keyed up all human energies to their highest potential and set the seal of nobility on those peoples who had the courage to wage it. Fascism embodied the Roman tradition of imperialism, which in itself was a manifestation of a nation's virility, requiring discipline, coordinated effort, and a profound sense of duty and self-sacrifice. To retain the favor of the church in propounding these far from Christian principles, Mussolini declared Roman Catholicism to be the positive religion of the Italians, which the Fascist state would respect and defend.

❑ *Mussolini's Imperialism*

While extolling imperialism and conjuring up visions of the ancient Roman empire, Mussolini remained realistic enough during the first decade of his rule to recognize that he lacked the means to embark on foreign conquests at the expense of Britain and France or any other major power. His imperialism therefore was as opportunistic as every other aspect of his political program and was not based on any consistent or long-range plan. But all along he dallied with the dream of creating a new Roman empire and extending Italian control once again over the entire Mediterranean basin.

His first imperialist venture was a disaster. In August 1923 he took advantage of a crisis with Greece to seize the island of Corfu. Greece appealed to the League of Nations, which responded with remarkable speed and unanimity. Under heavy international pressure from Britain and other League members, the Italians evacuated the island on September 27—a victory for the League that gave a false sense of optimism about that organization's ability to halt aggression and arrange a peaceful settlement of international disputes.

Mussolini did better in dealing with the new state of Yugoslavia, which from the beginning had been weakened by ethnic and factional strife. In March 1922, before Mussolini came to power, Italian Fascists had once again seized the Adriatic seaport of Fiume. Unlike an earlier Italian government, which had bowed to international pressure to repudiate d'Annunzio's earlier seizure of Fiume and conclude a treaty with Yugoslav making Fiume a free city (see p. 165), Mussolini took advantage of Yugoslav domestic turmoil to secure that country's recognition of Italy's possession of Fiume.

Mussolini did what he could to contribute to Yugoslavia's weakness. Well aware of the resentment of Serbian domination on the part of Croats and other religious and ethnic minorities, Mussolini gave money, arms, and refuge to anti-Serb revolutionaries to promote the dissolution of the South Slav union and open the way for an extension of Italian influence over Yugoslav Dalmatia.

A dissolution of Yugoslavia did not take place until World War II, but already in 1926 Mussolini managed to acquire control over Albania, the state directly south of Yugoslavia's Dalmatian coast. In 1925 he had taken advantage of quasi-anarchic conditions in that country to back the efforts of a tribal chieftain named Ahmet Bey Zogu to claim leadership of the Albanian government. In November 1926 Mussolini compelled Zogu to sign a treaty which reduced Albania to the status of an Italian satellite, and two years later he made him his puppet ruler of Albania as King Zog I. Although Mussolini did not annex Albania officially until 1939, he had long since come to regard Albania as Italian territory and had made plans to settle Italian peasants in the more fertile areas of the country, from which the native Albanians were to be removed. Italian Fascists called Albania "the first stage of our imperial journey" and "the proof by fire for Fascist Italy." Once established there and having subjugated "the decadent Albanian race," Italy could move forward to more distant objects of expansion in the Balkans, Africa, and the Levant.

Italy already had colonies in Africa (Libya, Eritrea, and Italian Somaliland) where the Italians were encountering the same unrest on the part of native populations as other colonial powers. To restore law and order in Libya, the Mussolini government resorted to herding the native population into concentration camps for the purpose of depriving rebel guerrillas of support and food, a strategy the British had employed in defeating the Boer guerrillas in South Africa earlier in the century. But Mussolini hoped to do far more than restore order. He wanted to do away with the nomadism of native tribes and revive agricultural production so as to make North Africa once again the breadbasket of the Mediterranean, as it had been in the days of ancient

Rome. For this purpose his government encouraged the migration of Italian peasants to North Africa, but the project met with little enthusiasm among the Italian peasants, despite offers of generous subsidies. Italian businessmen, too, showed a disheartening reluctance to invest in African colonial enterprises.

All along, however, Mussolini's primary objective in Africa was the conquest of Ethiopia, the only large state in Africa not already under European control and one that had inflicted a disastrous defeat on the Italians when they had attempted to take over the country in the late nineteenth century. Ethiopia was thus not only a tempting prize in its own right but a stain on Italy's military honor which Mussolini was determined to avenge.

So long as France and Britain remained in a position to prevent any major changes in the international status quo, Mussolini found little opportunity to realize his more grandiose ambitions in Africa or elsewhere. But new opportunities opened out after Hitler came to power in Germany in January 1933. At this stage Mussolini was no admirer of the German dictator, but the fears Hitler aroused among the Western powers and his ostentatious desire for an alliance with Italy enabled Mussolini to play Germany off against Britain and France, which were to offer generous inducements to keep Italy out of the German camp.

❑ *Hitler*

Adolf Hitler was born on April 20, 1889, in the Austrian border town of Braunau-am-Inn, the fourth child of the third marriage of an Austrian customs official named Alois Hitler. There was nothing particularly remarkable about Hitler's youth. His school record was uneven and undistinguished, marked by a lack of discipline and perseverance. After the death of his mother in 1907, he moved to Vienna intending to study art. Despite his failure to gain admission to the Vienna Academy of Art, he remained in the Habsburg capital for six years earning a meagre living from the sale of sketches and paintings and living for a time in a hostel for the homeless.

It was in Vienna that Hitler appears to have imbibed most of his theories about race and nationality. In the course of that city's industrialization in the nineteenth century, there had been an influx of non-German laborers from every part of the heterogeneous Habsburg empire, with the result that the social and class tensions common to all industrialized societies were exacerbated by ethnic rivalries. Vienna, far from serving as a national melting pot, was transformed instead into an ethnic cockpit where hatreds flared high and the most extreme theories on the subject of race and nationality found ready acceptance from members of all ethnic groups.

In June 1913 Hitler moved to Munich, evidently hoping that his talent as an artist would win greater recognition in the Bavarian capital. Shortly after his arrival in Germany he was extradited to Austria for failure to register for military service, but he returned to Munich upon being declared physically unfit by the Austrian authorities. His physical disabilities cannot have been serious, for with the outbreak of war in 1914 he volunteered for service in the Bavarian army and served for four years as a courier assigned the hazardous duty of conveying messages to front line positions. He was wounded twice and was awarded the iron cross of the first and second class, rare distinctions for a private soldier at that time. But he was never promoted beyond the rank of corporal because his superior officers believed he could never command the respect of men of lower ranks.

Stunned and embittered by Germany's defeat, Hitler joined a miniscule political organization called the German Workers' party, whose name was changed in 1920 to the National Socialist German Workers' party to reflect its nationalist as well as socialist emphasis. Hitler soon demonstrated that his superior officers had seriously underestimated his leadership talents, for he proved to have a remarkable ability to inspire fanatical devotion among men (and women) of higher as well as lower ranks. By 1920 he was recognized as the undisputed leader of the National Socialist party (now generally known by its abbreviated name, Nazi) and assumed the title of Führer, which remained his preferred title to the end of his career.

In November 1923, encouraged by the success of the miniscule Bolshevik party in Russia, Hitler attempted to take advantage of the economic chaos and nationalist anger aroused by the French occupation of the Ruhr to overthrow the Bavarian government. His attempt at a coup, the so-called Beer Hall Putsch, was easily suppressed. Several of his followers were killed or wounded, Hitler himself was arrested and sentenced to five years in prison. He was released after serving less than one year, but during this time he dictated the first volume of his autobiographical political testament, *Mein Kampf.*

During the years of relative prosperity of the mid-1920s, the Nazi party fared badly. In the Reichstag elections of December 1924, just after Hitler came out of prison, the Nazis won only 14 seats; in 1928 they won only 12. During this period, however, they succeeded in enlarging their party membership from 27,000 to over 100,000 and extending their organization to every part of Germany. They scored their first major breakthrough with the coming of the Great Depression, winning 107 seats and 18 percent of the vote in the Reichstag elections of September 1930 and more than doubling their strength in the elections of July 1932, when they won 230 seats with 37 percent of the vote. The Communists also made impressive electoral gains during the early depression years. Their success at the polls, like that of the Nazis, reflected growing disillusionment with the economic policies of the Weimar government and was directly related to the rise in German unemployment, which grew from about 1 million in September 1929 to well over 6 million in 1932.

In January 1933, persuaded by his advisers that they had imposed conditions on Hitler that would make him a "chancellor in chains," a reluctant President Hindenburg appointed the Nazi leader head of the German government. (See p. 163.) The Nazis liked to refer to the events of January as their seizure of power, but no seizure of any kind was involved. Hitler's appointment was made in accordance with the provisions of the Weimar constitution. The Nazi revolution that took place after that date was not a seizure but a consolidation of power, the extension of party control over the key offices of central and regional government and its use of those offices and the party's own organizational apparatus to impose Hitler's political and ideological program on Germany.

❑ *Nazi Ideology*

In marked contrast to Mussolini, Hitler came to power with a fully developed ideological program which he set forth in detail and with remarkable frankness in *Mein Kampf,* a work dictated and written between 1923 and 1925. It is difficult to understand why some scholars have discounted the importance of *Mein Kampf,* for Hitler himself described it as the embodiment of all his major ideas. Moreover, he reiterated these same ideas with a terrible consistency throughout his career: in a second ideological treatise written in 1928 but not published until after the war, in top secret speeches and policy directives, and in private conversations with his most trusted henchmen. The ultimate proof that he took those ideas seriously and intended to implement them is provided by the record of the policies he actually initiated and pursued in Germany and in the countries that came under German control before and during World War II.

Hitler's central idea was the primacy of the factor of race and nationality in the human social order, and on this idea he built up the entire superstructure of his ideological program. His fundamental premise was that the Germans were the greatest of human races, the founders of all that was best in human civilization, the creators of all stable social and political institutions, the producers of all the world's great culture. From this premise it followed that the Germans were the only nation on earth which deserved to survive in the brutal competition for the world's limited resources of food and raw materials.

Hitler's views about race and nationality represent a tragic fulfillment of the nineteenth-century historian Jakob Burckhardt's prophecy that the next century would very likely be dominated by "terribles simplificateurs." Hitler's proposals to ensure the security and survival of the German race were not only simplistic but appalling. To protect the purity and thus the unique superiority of the German race, he called for the complete removal or extermination of all non-Germanic races from German society—not only the Jews, it is important to emphasize, but Gypsies, Slavs, and anyone else Nazi racial "scientists" decided to classify as an alien race and thus a threat to Germanic racial quality.

Besides purifying the German race within Germany's existing borders, Hitler proposed to extend German control over all territories inhabited by ethnic Germans, beginning with his native Austria, so that all Germans might be included in a Greater German Reich. But German policy could not be restricted to achieving this comparatively modest objective. As Hitler surveyed the global scene, the German race, and therewith human civilization in its highest form, was doomed to destruction if it remained confined to a narrow strip of territory in Central Europe. The Germans were surrounded on all sides by jealous and hostile neighbors. Across the channel lay England, the perennial opponent of any German attempt to improve their international position. Across the Rhine lay France, which sought nothing less than Germany's total destruction. But the gravest and indeed mortal threat to the survival of the Germanic race lay in the east, where a vast expanse of territory provided the breeding ground for an inexhaustible supply of a particularly brutal form of humanity which, inferior though it might be, possessed the manpower and natural resources that would enable it to overwhelm the Germans if they failed to break out of their present narrow territorial confines.

To acquire the lands and resources the Germans would need to ensure their triumph in future contests of strength, Hitler deemed it essential that the Germans engage in territorial expansion on a massive scale—not in faraway colonies across the sea, but in contiguous territories which could be colonized by German settlers and thus made part of the German Reich for all time. From these lands, as from the Old Reich, all alien or non-German elements were to be removed. For Hitler did not propose to repeat the fatal mistake of the Spaniards, whose intermarriage with inferior races had resulted in the weakening and the ultimate destruction of the great Spanish empire, or of his former Habsburg rulers, with their indiscriminate accumulation of peoples of different races and religions. His model instead was that of the European settlers of North America, who had ruthlessly swept aside inferior races in the interest of their own ethnic survival.

Hitler stated bluntly that it would be necessary to wage war to achieve these objectives. He also named the major victim of Nazi imperialism: the territorial conquests needed to ensure Germany's future would have to be made chiefly at the expense of Russia.

Although Hitler looked to the east for the lands and resources needed to guarantee Germany's future, he realized that in all probability he would not be allowed a free hand there. The moment Germany became involved in campaigns in the east, France would seize the opportunity to fall on Germany's flank. The result would be a two-front war, all the more dangerous because of the vulnerability of the Rhine-Ruhr region, the heartland of Germany's industrial economy, which lay perilously close to the French frontier. A successful penetration of Germany's defenses in this area could deal a mortal blow to the country's ability to wage war. The French threat would therefore have to be neutralized or eliminated before Germany could embark on its conquests in the east. For this purpose Hitler proposed to seek alliances with Italy and Britain, which he hoped to secure by recognizing Italy's supremacy in the Mediterranean area and promising German support for the preservation of the British empire. He nevertheless took into account that his efforts to woo the racially related British might fail, and that the British as well as French threat in the west would have to be removed before he could embark on his conquests in the east.

Thus, long before he came to power, Hitler had revealed to the world an ideological program that included territorial conquest on a vast scale together with a detailed description of the strategy he intended to employ to realize his objectives. Further, he made a particular point of his intention to carry out a racial program which would require the elimination or removal of all inferior races from his future German empire.

❑ *Germany's International Position in 1933*

When Hitler came to power in 1933, Germany was enclosed in a network of international treaties and alliances that seemed to provide an impenetrable barrier to Hitler's territorial ambitions. Germany's western boundaries with France and Belgium, fixed by the Treaty of Versailles, had been confirmed by the Locarno treaties of 1925, which the German government itself had negotiated and accepted and which were guaranteed by Britain and Italy. In the east, Germany faced a set of defensive alliances among the smaller states, most of them backed up by France, including specific treaties of mutual assistance between France and Poland and France and Czechoslovakia. At sea, Britain still ruled the waves, at least in the waters of northern Europe. Germany itself was in the throes of economic depression, its financial credit exhausted, its army and navy still far inferior to those of rival powers despite the clandestine and open rearmament that had taken place during the Weimar era.

After the Nazis came to power Germany's international position seemed to deteriorate still further. Whatever foreign sympathy the country may have enjoyed as a defeated and underdog nation was dissipated by the truculence and vulgarity of the new regime, its brutality in dealing with its opponents, and its abhorrent racial program, Soviet Russia, which had formed an alignment of sorts with its fellow outcast during the Weimar period, now looked to the West for support against Germany's new anti-Communist regime. In 1934 the Soviet Union joined the League of Nations and in the following year it concluded defensive alliances with France and Czechoslovakia. Elsewhere, Communist parties were following Moscow's instructions to unite with other parties of the Left to resist Right-wing elements at home and conduct an anti-Nazi foreign policy abroad. The Little Entente powers of Czechoslovakia, Yugoslavia, and Romania drew closer to France and sought to strengthen their own alliances through institutions to coordinate their political and economic policies. Poland, while concluding a nonaggression pact with Germany in 1934, at the same time extended its 1932 nonaggression pact with Soviet Russia for another ten years. Even the Austrians, who since the end of World War I had appealed in vain to be allowed to establish closer relations with their fellow Germans, were alienated by the Nazis' anti-Catholic and anti-Socialist policies, and an authoritarian Austrian government now sought support for its independent status from Italy and Hungary.

Mussolini was eager to provide such support. Hitler had said that the union of Germany with his native Austria was the first objective of his foreign policy, and the Italian dictator had no desire to see the establishment of German power directly on the Italian frontier in place of weak and hapless Austria. During the first years of the Nazi regime, Mussolini worked systematically and effectively to block an Austro-German union and looked with suspicion on all proposals for closer German-Italian relations emanating from Berlin. In March 1934 he concluded treaties with Austria and Hungary, the so-called Rome Protocols, providing for closer political and economic cooperation between these countries, a clear indication of his determination to uphold the independence of these states and prevent their annexation by Germany.

Hitler's own actions did little to reassure the world about his intentions. His brutal treatment of his political opponents and the viciousness of the Nazi anti-Semitic campaign aroused general disgust and consternation. Hitler's concordat with the Vatican of July 1933 promising to respect the rights and privileges of the Roman Catholic Church in Germany did not improve his image abroad, for reports of Nazi religious persecution became even more frequent after the conclusion of that treaty.

In October 1933 Hitler withdrew Germany from the disarmament conference at Geneva and from the League of Nations. His explanations for these acts were masterpieces of sophistry and propaganda, but these demonstrations of his hostility to all institutions designed to ease international tensions and preserve peace only increased the apprehensions of his opponents. On June 30, 1934, Hitler provided a particularly vicious demonstration of Nazi ruthlessness as members of his elite guard, the SS, carried out a massacre of potential rivals to Hitler within the Nazi party and of other German leaders who might threaten his authority. Victims of this "Night of the Long Knives" included Ernst Röhm, the head of the Nazi party militia (the SA) and several of his henchmen, Gregor Strasser, a rival for Nazi party leadership, and General von Schleicher, Hitler's immediate predecessor as German chancellor.

Less than a month later, in July 1934, Austrian Nazis attempted to carry out a coup in Vienna and assassinated the Austrian chancellor, Engelbert Dollfuss. There is convincing evidence that Hitler thought a putsch in Austria at this time would be premature and that the Austrian Nazis acted on their own initiative. But Hitler was inevitably suspected of having ordered the Austrian action, which resulted in a further intensification of foreign hostility.

❑ *The Ethiopian Crisis*

Although Mussolini had concluded a treaty of friendship with the government of Ethiopia (Abyssinia) on August 2, 1928, this was seen later as an attempt to disguise his true intentions, for ever since coming to power he had been making plans for the conquest of that country. With the coming of the Great Depression, that enterprise was no longer merely a desirable end in itself. It had become the most obvious means to refurbish the tarnished image of the Mussolini regime and divert the attention of the Italian people from their economic woes at home to glorious military victories abroad. As observed earlier, Hitler's coming to power in Germany had created a favorable international climate for the realization of Mussolini's ambitions in Africa, for the Western powers were prepared to offer him generous concessions at the expense of Ethiopia to keep him in the anti-German camp.

In January 1935, while concluding an agreement with Italy to cooperate in preserving Austria's independence and oppose any German attempt to violate existing treaties, Pierre Laval, the French foreign minister, gave Mussolini verbal assurances that France would not oppose an extension of Italian influence in Ethiopia. An interdepartmental committee of the British government, assigned the task of coordinating British policy with that of France, reported to the British foreign secretary, Sir John Simon, that "there were no vital British interests in Abyssinia or adjoining countries such as to necessitate British resistance to an Italian conquest of Abyssinia." A copy of this document, sent to the British embassy in Rome, was intercepted by Italian intelligence and provided Mussolini with the assurance he needed that Britain as well as France would not oppose him in Africa. Early in 1935 he began a large-scale buildup of Italian forces in Eritrea and Italian Somaliland that could only have been intended for mounting a war of conquest against neighboring Ethiopia.

❑ The German Diversion: Saar Plebiscite and German Rearmament

Events in Germany provided indirect but nonetheless valuable aid to Mussolini by reinforcing British and French awareness of the German danger and making them all the more eager to preserve good relations with Italy.

The Treaty of Versailles had assigned the resources of Germany's coal-rich Saar Valley to France (under the administration of the League of Nations) for a period of fifteen years. After that, the inhabitants of the region were to decide by plebiscite whether they wished to become part of France, remain under League administration, or return to Germany. The scheduled plebiscite took place in January 1935 and resulted in a 90 percent vote in favor of Germany. As most of the inhabitants of the Saar were German, the result of the plebiscite came as no great surprise. What was remarkable was the size of the German victory, which represented a great moral triumph for Hitler and provided a clear indication that Nazi bestiality had not affected German nationalist sentiment.

A far greater shock came two months later. On March 16, 1935, Hitler took the first of his momentous international gambles by formally denouncing the disarmament clauses of the Treaty of Versailles and announcing Germany's intention to rearm and reintroduce compulsory military conscription. This action was a violation of one of the key provisions of the Versailles agreement, but instead of issuing an immediate ultimatum to Berlin backed up by the threat of an Allied invasion, the Versailles victors did no more than issue protests and confer about what action should be taken.

❑ The Stresa Front and the Franco-Russian Alliance

The first action on the part of Britain and France, if it could be called action, was to secure a reaffirmation of Italian support. In April 1935 British and French representatives met with Mussolini at the Italian resort town of Stresa, where they agreed to issue a public declaration that their countries would act "in close and cordial cooperation" to oppose "any unilateral repudiation of treaties which may endanger the peace." When Mussolini asked that the words "in Europe" be added to this declaration, neither the British or French representatives objected, although the addition of these words was nothing less than a statement that their opposition to unilateral threats to peace did not apply to Africa.

Even after ensuring that Mussolini was on their side, Britain and France did not take a firm stand against Hitler. Shortly after the Stresa conference, the League of Nations condemned Germany's unilateral repudiation of the Versailles disarmament clauses, but neither the League nor the great powers took any further action against Germany.

What Laval did do was to shore up France's diplomatic position by concluding an alliance with the Soviet Union. This treaty, signed May 2, 1935, was to run for five years and provided for mutual military assistance in case either power became the victim of unprovoked aggression. Laval also played midwife to negotiations between the Soviet Union and Czechoslovakia which resulted in a mutual assistance pact of May 16, 1935, whereby the Soviet Union promised to come to the aid of Czechoslovakia in case of unprovoked aggression against that country—but with the critical reservation that the Soviet Union would provide such assistance only after France had done so. Despite this reservation, it seemed that Laval's diplomacy had been eminently successful. Germany remained isolated and was now encircled by a formidable great-power coalition of Britain, France, Italy, and the Soviet Union, and by the lesser powers of Poland and the Little Entente.

The alliance with the Soviet Union seemed a particularly significant diplomatic achievement because the Moscow government, heretofore the self-proclaimed enemy of all "bourgeois-capitalist" regimes and the supporter of subversive Communist movements throughout the world, was now enrolled in a bourgeois-capitalist anti-German coalition. In response to a request from Laval, Stalin ordered the French Communists to end their opposition to French rearmament, which Stalin now described as an urgent necessity. More significant still was Stalin's order to the world's Communist parties to abandon their opposition to parliamentary systems of government and to enter into Popular Front alliances with parties similarly dedicated to halting Nazi aggression.

❑ The Anglo-German Naval Agreement

On June 7, 1935, following a general election in Britain, Stanley Baldwin, leader of the Conservative party, succeeded the Labour leader Ramsay MacDonald as prime minister and head of Britain's National Coalition government in which Conservatives had long predominated. A mere eleven days later Britain dealt the anti-German coalition a damaging blow by concluding a naval agreement with Germany. Through this treaty, signed June 18, 1935—the anniversary of the Battle of Waterloo!—Germany promised to limit the size of its fleet to 35 percent of Britain's, a ratio the British had sought in vain before World War I. (The ratio for submarines was to be 45 percent.) The treaty was a horrendous diplomatic blunder, for in effect it recognized Germany's right to rearm and gave de facto legitimacy to Hitler's violation of the disarmament provisions of the Versailles treaty. It was an especially bitter blow to the French, for it left them with the impression that Britain's sole concern was the maintenance of its naval supremacy and its own security.

As we now know from British documents, this treaty was negotiated by the British Admiralty to ensure British naval superiority in the North Atlantic while leaving Britain sufficient seapower to deal with the Japanese threat in East Asia and the threat of a Italian naval buildup in the Mediterranean. Yet at this very time the British Foreign Office was making concessions to Mussolini to avoid a conflict with Italy in the Mediterranean and keep him in the anti-German camp.

❑ *The Italo-Ethiopian War and World Reaction*

In making their concessions to Mussolini, the French and British governments had failed to reckon with the groundswell of public support for Ethiopia aroused by Mussolini's obvious preparations for war with that country. To deal with the hostility to Mussolini on the part of public opinion, the French and British governments now sought to persuade the Italian leader not to embark on the outright conquest of Ethiopia but to agree instead to various stratagems that would make for the peaceful extension of Italian control. In seeking to avoid a domestic crisis over Ethiopia, however, both governments failed to recognize that Mussolini was not primarily interested in peaceful economic or territorial concessions. What he wanted was the opportunity to stage precisely the kind of show the French and British governments sought to avoid, namely, a dramatic display of Italian national virility and military prowess, a victorious war of conquest that would unify the Italian people and confer glory and prestige on his regime. Far from dissuading him from his war of conquest, the British and French offers made him even more confident that London and Paris were determined to retain Italy as an ally against Nazi Germany and that they would not risk alienating Italy by opposing him in Africa.

On October 3, 1935, Italy began an all-out invasion of Ethiopia for which undisguised preparations had been going on since the beginning of the year. On October 7, with unusual dispatch, the League Council declared Italy to be the aggressor, and on October 11 the League Assembly of fifty-one nations voted to impose sanctions on Italy. The League then settled back to consider how this was to be done.

As was obvious at the time, sanctions were not even necessary. The surest and simplest way to stop Mussolini would have been to close the Suez Canal, for this was the sole route for the transport of his troops and supplies for the Ethiopian campaign. As for sanctions themselves, there was no need for deliberation or delay because Article 16 of the League Covenant had laid down clear and unambiguous rules on this point. Sanctions meant that members of the League immediately sever *all* trade and financial relations with an aggressor. The British and French, however, still determined to avoid driving Mussolini into the arms of Hitler, were able to argue convincingly that League sanctions were useless so long as Italy could get all the supplies it needed from countries that were not members of the League, most importantly the United States. The League therefore voted to impose sanctions "in principle," but these were not to come into force "until conditions for rendering them effective appear to be realized."

With that the responsibility for imposing effective sanctions against Italy was passed to the United States. The response of the U.S. Congress was if anything more flaccid than that of the European democracies. Primarily concerned with avoiding any move that might harm the floundering American economy, it declared that the president had no right to impose an embargo on shipments of raw materials to any nation. The members of the League could therefore continue to argue that there was no point in imposing sanctions on products Italy could obtain from the United States such as oil, iron, and steel.

Meanwhile, a more sinister argument came from Mussolini himself, who threatened war if his supplies of oil were cut off or if Britain closed the Suez Canal. Mussolini's threat placed his most vociferous opponents in the Western democracies in a dilemma. While antifascists, liberals, and pacifists demanded the imposition of effective sanctions against Italy, they were horrified by the prospect of war. Earlier in the year the results of a public opinion poll in Britain, the so-called Peace Ballot, had shown that an overwhelming majority of British voters favored economic sanctions against aggressors, but at the same time they favored a reduction in armaments—and this just after Hitler had announced Germany's intention to rearm.

The British government was particularly sensitive to the mood of public opinion at this time, because on October 25, 1935, Stanley Baldwin had dissolved parliament and called for new elections. To win these elections, Baldwin saw that it was necessary to cater to the large body of public opinion which wanted to halt Mussolini's aggression but which at the same time opposed rearmament and war. The British government therefore made a great deal of fanfare about sanctions, but its policy remained consistent: Mussolini was to be retained in the anti-German coalition at all costs. This was also the policy of the French government, or at any rate that of Pierre Laval, who in May 1935 had become prime minister as well as foreign minister.

In the general election of November 1935, Baldwin's Conservative-dominated National Coalition retained a substantial parliamentary majority. With the election behind him, his government resumed its active wooing of Mussolini, whose Ethiopian campaign was proving more difficult and costly than he had anticipated. Believing that the Italian dictator might now be prepared to accept a compromise over Ethiopia, Sir Samuel Hoare, the British foreign secretary, concluded an agreement with Laval on December 8, 1935, embodying peace terms which they intended to submit to the Italian and Ethiopian governments. These provided for the outright cession to Italy of a large part of Ethiopia and made the rest of the country an Italian sphere of influence. The Hoare-Laval pact remained a dead letter, however, because on the day after its signature its terms were leaked to the press and aroused such indignation in Britain that Hoare was compelled to resign. But public opinion in France, too, was infuriated, and the Laval government fell a month later, the victim of failures in domestic as well as foreign policy.

The government of Laval was replaced by a stop-gap ministry headed by Albert Sarrault, and new elections were scheduled for May 1936. Thus France was in a period of political transition and turmoil when confronted the most critical international crisis of the interwar years: Hitler's remilitarization of the Rhineland.

❏ *The Remilitarization of the Rhineland*

While the British and French governments strove to appease Mussolini abroad and attempted to appease public opinion at home, Hitler took advantage of their preoccupation with Ethiopia and their mounting domestic problems to make one of the boldest and most critical moves of his career—the remilitarization of the Rhineland. For with this action, which he announced on March 7, 1936, he destroyed at one blow the major strategic advantage the Allies had gained through their victory in World War I and brought about a decisive change in the European balance of power in Germany's favor.

Hitler's action affected France most directly, for it meant that in the event of another conflict German forces would be poised directly on the French frontier, while the French would be deprived of the advantage of being able to strike at Germany through a demilitarized zone that was also the heartland of Germany's industrial economy. But Hitler's action was an even greater blow to France's Eastern allies, for a French invasion of Germany from the west was the only effective military aid France could provide in the event of a German attack in Eastern Europe. The remilitarization of the Rhineland not only made such a French invasion more difficult but reduced the effectiveness of any attempt to exercise diplomatic pressure by a threat of invasion.

The remilitarization of the Rhineland was a clear-cut unilateral violation of international treaties, not only of the Treaty of Versailles, which Hitler maintained had been imposed on Germany in violation of the Allies' armistice agreement, but of the 1925 Locarno treaties, which Germany had negotiated with France and Belgium and which were guaranteed by Britain and Italy. France now had every legal right and certainly every military reason to undertake another occupation of the Rhineland. German generals warned Hitler in the most pressing manner not to risk a move that was certain to provoke a French invasion and could only result in national humiliation and disaster. But Hitler disregarded all voices of caution. The fact that his generals were proved wrong only increased his contempt for Germany's old-guard conservative leadership and his confidence this his judgment was better than that of his military experts.

Hitler's gamble was successful. The French and British governments protested, as they had done in the previous year in response to Germany's remilitarization, but again they did nothing. After examining the French government documents on the Rhineland crisis, the Canadian historian John Cairns concluded: "These papers demonstrate again how crucial was this turning point of March 7, how it really was a moment of high decision, and how infinitely much harder it would be for France (and for them all) to recover the ground already lost should she fail to make a stand then and there." Hitler would have agreed. In 1938 he told the Austrian chancellor: "Two years ago when we marched into the Rhineland with a handful of battalions, I took a grave risk. If France had marched then, we should have been compelled to withdraw. . . . But now it is too late for France."

Why did France and Britain fail to act during the Rhineland crisis? The most obvious answer is that public opinion in both countries was not prepared for war, and that both lacked statesmen capable of mobilizing public opinion on behalf of decisive action. Both were still in the throes of economic depression. Feuding factions in France, consumed with hatred for each other, refused to bury their differences or sacrifice parochial interests on behalf of confronting the threat of a foreign foe. Moreover, as we now know from French documents, political as well as military leaders were incomprehensibly negligent in preparing for a crisis situation. They had long anticipated a German attempt to remilitarize the Rhineland, but no military plans were made to deal with this possibility. Not until three days *after* the German move did the

French government ask the army to draw up a preliminary war plan, but even then no attempt was made to implement it. The French military leadership, vastly overestimating Germany's military strength, protested that any action to stop Hitler would mean war. And if it came to war, the army could not muster adequate forces without general mobilization, and it lacked the modern weaponry needed for their equipment. Further, having adopted a defensive strategy built around the Maginot Line, the army was not prepared to undertake offensive operations.

In this crisis, as in all subsequent crises prior to the actual outbreak of war, the French looked for leadership to Britain. They did not get it. The French were informed that the Rhineland did not constitute a major British interest, and that Germany's breach of its treaty commitments in that area was not sufficiently grave to justify the tremendous responsibility of initiating a preventive war.

Finally, to return to a point emphasized earlier, the fundamental consideration for both the French and British governments may have been their fear that an Allied offensive in the Rhineland would result in the overthrow of Hitler and the establishment of a Bolshevik regime in Germany that would enter into an alliance with Bolshevik Russia. There is considerable evidence to suggest that this fear permeated the thinking of French and British leaders throughout the interwar years, even it this fear was not always clearly defined or acknowledged.

As yet the extent of the Hitler danger was not at all clear to foreign observers. Nineteen thirty-six was, the year of the Olympic Games in Berlin, when the Nazis presented a face of respectability to the world, and the prosperity and apparent political stability of Nazi Germany provided an impressive contrast to conditions in the Western democracies. In France, national elections in April and May of 1936 resulted in victory for the Popular Front, a coalition of Leftist parties which included the Communists, and the Socialist leader Léon Blum, a Jew, became prime minister. This victory of the radicals evoked panic among solid bourgeois property owners, and the pamphleteers of the Right proclaimed that these elections had finally exposed the extent of the Red menace. Elections in Spain in the previous February had also resulted in a triumph for Popular Front parties. Could France risk a war with Germany that might provoke a Bolshevik revolution in that country and might very well lead to the Bolshevisation of France?

❑ *The End of Ethiopia*

On May 5, 1936, Italian troops entered the Ethiopian capital of Addis Ababa. That evening Mussolini spoke to hysterically enthusiastic crowds from his famous balcony on the Palazzo Venezia in Rome and announced that Ethiopia was now Italian. On May 9 the king of Italy was proclaimed emperor of Ethiopia and the entire country was annexed. Administratively, Ethiopia was now linked with Eritrea and Italian Somaliland to form Italian East Africa.

The Italian conquest of Ethiopia has generally been regarded as the second dramatic demonstration of successful military aggression during the interwar years (the Japanese seizure of Manchuria having been the first), and critics have bitterly denounced the flaccid policy of appeasement adopted by the Western powers, which simply encouraged further aggression on the part of revisionist states and led inexorably to a major war. As we have seen, however, it would have been very difficult indeed for the Western powers to have halted the Japanese in Manchuria even if they could have agreed on a common policy, which they could not. In the case of Ethiopia, British and French "appeasement" was a calculated effort to retain Italy as an ally against Germany, which they correctly regarded as the principal threat to their interests in Europe. The sacrifice of Ethiopia was not an honorable policy, but it was a policy they had adopted often enough in the past to protect their national interests.

And a case can be made that this policy worked. For, despite all Mussolini's subsequent proclamations of friendship for Germany, he did not burn his diplomatic bridges to the Western powers. Even before his final victory over Ethiopia he had taken steps to restore good relations with Britain. In late April 1936 the Italian ambassador in London was instructed to inform King Edward VIII of his government's desire to reestablish traditional ties with Britain; in May he told Anthony Eden, the new British foreign secretary, that Mussolini hoped to reconstitute the Stresa Front against Germany and collaborate in defense of the Locarno treaties; and later that month, Mussolini told the *Daily Telegraph:* "Not only is the Anglo-Italian rapprochement desirable, but it is necessary, and for my part I will do everything which lies within my power to bring it about." When Hitler went to war in 1939, Mussolini remained neutral, and he finally entered the war on Hitler's side only after a German victory seemed certain, in order to share in the spoils.

The principal victim of British and French policy in the Ethiopian affair, apart from Ethiopia itself, was the League of Nations, which was exposed as a hopelessly inadequate instrument for mobilizing international action to punish aggression and preserve peace. The League even provided an abject conclusion to this sorry chapter in its history. On July 4, 1936, the Council of the League announced that it was dropping sanctions against Italy.

Another loser in the Ethiopian affair, though it certainly did not appear so at the time, was Mussolini, whose policies had dangerously damaged his relations with the Western powers and whose investment of Italian military strength in Africa and later in Spain was to place him at a grave disadvantage in subsequent dealings with Germany. For when Hitler made his move to take over Austria in 1938, Mussolini was no longer able to mount a demonstration of Italian military might at the Brenner Pass or take the lead in organizing international opposition against him, as he had done at the time of the Austrian Nazi coup in 1934.

With the Western powers still in shock following Hitler's reoccupation of the Rhineland and the Italian conquest of Ethiopia, they were faced with yet another crisis: the outbreak of civil war in Spain in the summer of 1936.

❑

FOURTEEN

The Spanish Civil War

In the years between the two world wars, nothing moved public opinion in the West with such emotional force as the Spanish Civil War. And, largely because of its emotional impact, few episodes during this fateful period have given rise to more controversy.

❑ *The Political Background*

Spain had not been spared the painful effects of the world economic depression. Economic distress added fuel to an already volatile political situation, and in April 1931 King Alfonso XIII fled abroad. Although the king let it be known that he was prepared to return if recalled by popular demand, no such desire was ever expressed.

The flight of the king was followed by elections to a constituent assembly which were won by candidates of a republican-socialist coalition. The assembly proceeded to draw up a constitution designed to give Spain a genuine democratic government and improve the social and economic conditions of the country's workers and peasants. It provided for the establishment of a single-chamber parliamentary government elected by universal suffrage and severely restricted the powers and prerogatives of the army and the church. Education was to be secularized, church property nationalized, and the government was given the authority to expropriate private property, redistribute the holdings of large estates, and nationalize public utilities.

The policies of the new republican government provoked the bitter hostility of military and clerical leaders, property owners, and conservatives in general. At the same time, however, the new government failed to fulfill the aspirations of Spanish radicals, who engaged in violent agitation for faster and more sweeping changes in the existing economic and social structure. Nor did they satisfy Basque and Catalonian separatists, chronic opponents of Spanish central government. Although given a large degree of local autonomy by the constitution, Basque and Catalonian separatists established quasi-independent regimes that the central government finally brought under control at the cost of alienating large segments of the population in these critical regions.

Elections in November 1933 resulted in a victory for a coalition of the Right, which was no more successful in maintaining law and order or reviving the economy than its predecessor.

Early in 1936 the parties of the Left in Spain, following the example of their counterparts in France, entered into an uneasy alliance to form a Popular Front coalition. Although this coalition was joined by the Spanish Communists, who had been ordered to do so by Moscow, the Popular Front in Spain was not dominated by Communists. Its political program was reformist, not revolutionary. Yet in Spain as in France, the Popular Front was perceived by its opponents at home and abroad as a political Trojan Horse that would open the way to a Communist regime.

Elections held in February 1936 gave the Popular Front a narrow but clear-cut victory. The new government immediately set about carrying on with the reform program initiated five years earlier, and in doing so it faced the same problems of the reformist regime of 1931: the hostility of the church, army, and property owners; the demands for more sweeping reforms on the part of radical extremists, whose violent demonstrations and provocation of crippling strikes undermined the government's authority; and the agitation of Basque and Catalonian separatists, who wanted nothing less than complete autonomy and thus the breakup of the country. The government was weakened further by the lack of unity among its component parties and their leaders, who, driven by personal jealousies and ideological differences, frequently seemed to expend more energy in fighting each other than their opponents on the Right. In his magisterial work on the Spanish Civil War, the British historian Hugh Thomas writes: "The midsummer of 1936 . . . saw the culmination of one hundred and fifty years of passionate quarrels in Spain," and "from the moment of the elections onwards, a trail of violence, murder, and arson spread across the country."

❑ *The Plot against the Republic*

The Popular Front government has been criticized of criminal carelessness for not taking more energetic measures to guard against a Rightist uprising. Yet one of its first moves was the imprisonment, exile, or removal from office of political and military leaders the government regarded as its most dangerous opponents. All army officers who had been active politically were obliged to retire, and those who had not played a conspicuous political role but were nevertheless seen as threats to the government were transferred to provincial or overseas posts. These potential threats included Francisco Franco, chief of staff of the war ministry, who was appointed military governor of the Canary Islands off the coast of Africa, and Emilio Mola y Vidal, the commander of the Army of Africa in Morocco, who was transferred to what was considered to be the less critical provincial post of Pamplona in northeastern Spain.

The transfer of General Mola to Pamplona proved to be a disastrous mistake, for Mola became the principal organizer of a military conspiracy against the Republic. Mola's recruits were instructed to work out detailed plans to take over public buildings, arsenals, public utilities, and lines of communication in the major cities and strategic centers of Spain. At a given signal they were to move simultaneously to seize power and announce the overthrow of the Republican regime. The order for the uprising was to be sent first to the commanders of Spain's most effective fighting force, the Army of Africa, whose headquarters were in the garrison city of Melilla in Spanish Morocco. The Melilla uprising was to begin on July 17 at 5 P.M., at which time the signal was to go out to set off simultaneous uprisings throughout Spain itself.

The rebels were successful in taking control of the Army of Africa, but their plans broke down in many critical areas of Spain where they met with vigorous civilian resistance. More serious still for the rebel cause, the greater part of the navy and air force remained loyal to the government, as did segments of the army and police. After the first days of the rebellion, over half of Spain, including Madrid and its major industrial cities, were still under government control.

The rebellion also lost its putative leader, General José Sanjurjo, who was living in exile in Portugal and who now embarked for Spain in a small aircraft from a private airfield north of Lisbon, presumably for reasons of secrecy and to avoid embarrassing the Portuguese government. Undeterred by the small size of his plane, the general insisted on taking baggage containing the uniforms and other paraphernalia he would need as chief of state. His overloaded plane, unable to clear the trees at the end of the runway, crashed, and Sanjurjo was killed.

❑ *The Role of Foreign Intervention*

The rebels had launched their uprising in Spanish Morocco to make sure of controlling the Army of Africa, which they regarded as essential to their success, and in the first hours of the rebellion General Francisco Franco, the former army chief of staff, had flown from his post in the Canary Islands to take command of these elite troops. Although the rebels had succeeded in gaining control of the Army of Africa, they were faced with an immediate problem that threatened to doom their entire enterprise. Their failure to take over the Spanish navy meant that the government had the means to block the transport of the Army of Africa across the Straits of Gibraltar to Spain.

To overcome this obstacle, Franco appealed to Germany and Italy, the two states most likely to be sympathetic to the rebel cause. His emissaries flew to Italy on July 19, to Germany on July 22. Both countries responded quickly. German transport and fighter planes arrived in Spanish Morocco on July 28. They were followed two days later by a small contingent of Italian bombers. With their aid the rebels succeeded in conveying a large part of the Army of Africa to Spain over the next two months and establishing their control over the Straits of Gibraltar. On August 6 Franco flew to Seville to take command of the rebel armies in the south.

By enabling the rebels to transport the Army of Africa to Spain, Hitler and Mussolini saved the rebel cause and converted what most likely would have been a failed coup d'état into a civil war. It was once widely believed that Germany and Italy had promised aid to the rebels well before their uprising, and that both countries had played an important role in fomenting the rebellion itself. Although Mussolini had given limited support to anti-Republican forces in Spain in the past, there is no reliable evidence that high-ranking officials of either the German or Italian government were in touch with the leaders of the 1936 rebellion. On the contrary, the evidence we now have from German and Italian archives leaves no doubt that both governments were taken by surprise by the uprising.

❑ *Francisco Franco*

Besides saving the rebel cause, German and Italian intervention contributed enormously to the power and prestige of Francisco Franco, the commander of the Army of Africa and the chief recipient of German and Italian aid.

That Franco should eventually emerge as supreme commander of the rebel forces and head of the rebel Nationalist government was not at all obvious at the beginning of the civil war. His success was due to a combination of luck, accident, and his own political and military skill. His most formidable rivals for leadership were killed or discredited at an early stage of the rebellion. By establishing control over southern Spain, Franco emerged as the most successful of the rebel generals, and his success in securing Italian and German aid enabled him to claim that he enjoyed the support of Mussolini and Hitler. On October 1, 1936, Franco took advantage of his temporary preeminence to have himself declared generalissimo of all the rebel armies and chief of state of what the rebels now chose to call the Spanish Nationalist government. In the following month, the Franco regime was recognized by Germany and Italy.

Franciso Franco was born in 1892 in El Ferrol, a seaport and naval base in the northwestern province of Galicia. His father, a naval paymaster, was an outspoken agnostic who scoffed at conventional forms of morality and in later life deserted his family to live with a mistress in Madrid. Altogether different was his mother, a deeply pious woman and rigorous observer of social conventions. Whether in reaction to the licentious behavior of his father or inspired by the example of his mother, Franco himself is reputed to have adhered throughout his life to quasi-puritanical moral standards. He was a hard and conscientious worker, he drank little, and after his marriage, which is reputed to have been a love match, he remained a devoted husband.

At the age of fourteen Franco was admitted to the Infantry Academy in Toledo and henceforth made the army his career. Short and paunchy, with a receding chin, sallow complexion, and high-pitched voice, Franco was a far from impressive military figure, nor was his performance at the academy distinguished. Upon receiving his commission as second lieutenant in 1910, he was 251st in a class of 312.

Franco soon demonstrated qualities that enabled him to overcome these physical and academic deficiencies. Ambitious, patriotic, with a keen sense of duty, he saw little opportunity to prove himself in Spain and volunteered for service in Spanish Morocco, where the army was suffering heavy casualties in its campaigns to suppress native uprisings. Here he quickly gained a reputation as an able administrator and organizer, but the quality that brought him particular distinction was his cool and competent leadership in combat. While displaying an almost fatalistic personal courage, his leadership was characterized by caution, calculation, and patience, an unwillingness to commit his men to action until he was convinced that action was necessary and likely to be successful. When barely thirty-three, he was promoted to brigadier, the youngest general in the Spanish army and reputedly the youngest in all of Europe.

As he rose in rank, Franco associated increasingly with political as well as military leaders. In dealing with them he displayed the same caution and calculation that characterized his behavior on the battlefield. He was notorious for saying little, playing his cards close to his chest, and refusing to commit himself. "A less straightforward man I have never met," the American journalist John Whitaker wrote after an interview. Franco was the last of the senior generals to join Mola's conspiracy against the government, and he did so only after being promised command of the elite Army of Africa and after having become convinced that a military takeover of the government was the only alternative to anarchy.

Because he was the leader of a revolution, it was only natural that Franco was seen by much of the world as a revolutionary; and because he became the head of an authoritarian government that came to power with the aid of Hitler and Mussolini, he was labelled a Fascist and condemned as the Spanish counterpart of the German and Italian dictators. Political labels are notoriously inexact, but they are particularly misleading in the case of Franco, who was a conservative nationalist and, basically, a counterrevolutionary. He took up arms not to overthrow the existing social and economic order but to defend it and preserve what he regarded as Spain's traditional values, which he saw threatened by the radical forces unleashed by the Popular Front and agents of the Soviet Union.

❑ *The Falange*

In the course of the civil war, Franco and his government chose to become identified with the closest Spanish equivalent to a Fascist political movement, the Falange Española, which took its name from the ancient Macedonian military formation, the phalanx. Founded in 1933, it included fewer than 10,000 members when the civil war began and has been described as being noteworthy only for its insignificance. It lacked competent leadership and was divided into rival factions with fundamentally different conceptions about its program and purpose. The centerpiece of the ideology of all Falangist factions, however, was nationalism, an emphasis expressed in the party anthem *Cara al Sol* (Face to the Sun), which celebrated a united, great, and free Spain (in that order.) Ignoring their own lack of unity, Falangist leaders called for the national unity of Spain and the fulfillment of what they described as their country's "metaphysical mission." This included among other things "the implacable extermination of foreign influences," the suppression of separatist movements and class warfare, and a revival of the Spanish imperial mission, for unity could only be achieved through common participation in a transcendental cause. A special place was reserved for the Roman Catholic Church, which was seen as embodying the Spanish "racial" tradition.

The membership of the Falange increased dramatically in the course of the civil war, largely because it came to be seen as the political party of the Nationalist government. This perception was deliberately fostered by Franco, but he appears to have done so primarily to convince his German and Italian allies of his political reliability and to show them that he too was the leader of an ideologically inspired movement. In April 1937 the Falange was made the official party of the state and Franco himself took over its leadership, assuming the title of Caudillo, an ancient Castilian designation for leader but one that also had a desirable resonance with the titles of Führer and Duce. Once in charge of the Falange, however, Franco put it firmly under state control and did nothing to implement the racist or imperialist features of the party's ideological program.

❑ *The International Dimensions of Foreign Intervention*

If the Spanish insurgents had succeeded in overthrowing the Republican government through a quick and relatively bloodless coup d'état, as they had confidently expected to do, there would have been no opportunity or need for foreign intervention. But as we have seen, at the very outset of their uprising they had been obliged to appeal for foreign aid, so that from the start the Spanish civil war was internationalized and foreign intervention became a matter of international concern.

In considering the problem of foreign intervention, which was to be decisive for the outcome of the war, we are confronted with the perplexing question: why did Germany, Italy, and the Soviet Union engage in intervention, openly and on a large scale; and why did the major Western democracies, Britain, France, and the United States, adopt a policy of nonintervention?

Hitler's reasons for intervention are obvious. He could only welcome the opportunity to overthrow Spain's Popular Front government and the installation of an anti-Communist regime in Madrid. A Spanish government sympathetic to or actually allied with Germany would compel the French to divert part of their army to stand guard at the Pyrenees, open the way to Germany's use of Spanish seaports as submarine bases, threaten Britain's control of Gibraltar, and admit German cooperation in the development and exploitation of Spain's economic resources.

As the rebellion in Spain developed into a protracted civil war, Hitler took advantage of the conflict to test new German weapons and tactics and give German troops combat experience. In October 1936 he authorized the recruitment in Germany of what became known as the Condor Legion, a force of some five thousand men consisting largely of pilots and tank crews. The first German troops arrived in Spain in November 1936, and over the next three years the Condor Legion was to make an important contribution to the insurgents' war effort.

But Hitler resisted appeals to send a sufficiently large force to Spain that might enable Franco to score a quick victory. At a conference in his Berlin chancellery in December 1936, he rejected the proposal of his diplomatic representative to the Franco government to send three additional divisions to Spain. He was interested in keeping foreign attention focused on Spain for a long time, he said, not in a quick Franco victory, especially if this endangered the German rearmament program. He would send sufficient help to make sure Franco was not defeated, but only send additional help if disaster threatened the Nationalist cause.

At the same time, Hitler did nothing to discourage Mussolini from sending a large Italian army to Spain. Large-scale Italian intervention was likely to exacerbate Mussolini's relations with the Western democracies and therewith reinforce his dependence on Germany. Even more important, the diversion of Italian military power to Spain and the consequent drain on Italian resources would reduce the Italian leader's capacity to oppose or even influence German policies in dealing with Austria and Eastern Europe.

Mussolini's initial motives for intervention in Spain were similar to Hitler's. He too wanted the overthrow Spain's Popular Front regime and the establishment a friendly government in Madrid. But unlike Hitler, whose aid to Franco remained rigidly limited, Mussolini provided large-scale and purposely ostentatious aid to impress upon Franco the extent of his obligation to Italy and demonstrate Italy's military might to the world. Unfortunately for Mussolini, the performance of his Italian "volunteers" in Spain was far from impressive and he signally failed to make Spain a base for extending Italian influence over the western Mediterranean.

If German and Italian aid in transporting the Army of Africa to Spain was decisive for the survival of the rebel cause in the first days of the Spanish civil war, Soviet aid to the Republic in the autumn of 1936 was similarly decisive in preventing a quick Nationalist victory and prolonging the war for three years.

Like Hitler and Mussolini, Stalin was caught by surprise by the revolution in Spain, but unlike them he hesitated for many weeks before deciding to send aid to the Republic. There were numerous foreign and domestic reasons for this hesitation. At home he was preoccupied with fear of subversion and about to embark on his remorseless campaign to stamp out all real or imagined threats to his authority. In foreign affairs his primary concern was the threat of Hitler, and to deal with that threat he had formed alliances with other states threatened by Hitler and had ordered the world's Communist parties to join forces with anti-Fascist "bourgeois" parties to form Popular Front governments. Suspicions of Soviet intentions continued to run deep, however, and Soviet agents warned that there was nothing more likely to intensify the distrust of the Western powers than open and large-scale shipments of arms to the Spanish Republic, which they would certainly interpret as a Soviet move to establish a Communist regime in Spain.

In any case, Stalin had every reason to believe that the arms needed by the Spanish Republic would be provided by the Western powers to prevent the establishment of a military dictatorship in Spain tied to Italy and Germany. Instead of providing such aid, however, the Western democracies indulged in the farce of nonintervention (see pp. 191–193), and by the late summer of 1936, with Nationalist forces poised for a final assault on Madrid, Stalin at last decided that Soviet aid was essential if the Republic were to survive. On August 30, Moscow instructed General Walter Krivitsky, chief of Soviet military intelligence in Western Europe with headquarters at The Hague, to extend his operations immediately to cover the Spanish civil war: "Mobilize all available agents and facilities for prompt creation of a system to purchase and transport arms to Spain." Soviet arms were to be paid for with the Spanish government's gold reserves, which were to be shipped to Russia. Still fearful of alarming the Western powers, Stalin attempted to disguise Soviet arms shipments, but by October the Soviet government abandoned its attempts at concealment. Estimates differ widely as to the amount of Soviet aid and its quality, but it was sufficient to enable Republican forces to turn back the Nationalist offensive against Madrid in the autumn of 1936.

At approximately the same time that Soviet arms began arriving in Spain, the first contingents of the so-called International Brigades went into combat. These were made up of volunteers recruited by foreign Communist parties under the direction of the Comintern, they were led by Communist officers, and they eventually included men from virtually every country of Europe and Western hemisphere. Highly motivated and well disciplined, they exercised a steadying influence within the generally undisciplined Spanish Republican forces and have been credited with playing a role scarcely less significant than Soviet arms in enabling the Republic to hold out.

It is noteworthy that the International Brigades, while enlisting numerous Russian émigrés, did not include recruits from the Soviet Union, which remained wary of being seen as playing a significant role in either the Republican army or government. Stalin in fact went to great lengths to reassure the Western powers and Spanish moderates that Soviet aid to Spain did not represent support for revolutionary policies or an effort to install a Communist government in Madrid. The Comintern was instructed to drop all revolutionary slogans as well as all references to the class struggle and the dictatorship of the proletariat, and to adopt new slogans emphasizing the preservation of peace and the common cause against Fascism. The notion that the Comintern had ever advocated revolution or violence was to be refuted as slander spread by Fascist war mongers. Communists were no longer to refer to themselves as such, much less as Bolsheviks, but should call themselves instead anti-Fascists and defenders of democracy.

In December 1936 the Soviet leadership advised Largo Caballero, the Republican prime minister, to issue decrees that would attract the support of the Spanish peasantry, and to seek bourgeois support through promises to protect private property and a free economy. He should also do everything possible to bring moderates into his government to prevent enemies of the Republic from branding it as Communist. Caballero agreed, but at the same time he assured the Soviet leadership that "among us" there were no enthusiastic defenders of the parliamentary form of government.

The Spanish Communist party itself, under firm Soviet tutelage, was ordered to keep a low profile. But behind the scenes the Spanish Communists carried on an unrelenting and ruthless campaign to establish control over the power centers of the state. To control the army, they followed the Red Army model of appointing political commissars at every level of the army's chain of command. They used much the same method to control the government, introducing the equivalent of political commissars at every level of the government bureaucracies. The Italian Communist leader Palmiro Togliatti, who arrived in Spain in July 1937, was able to assure the Comintern's Moscow headquarters that the Spanish Communist party had learned its lessons well and clearly understood its functions, which were first and foremost "to wage a coherent struggle to extend and reinforce its position in the army, the police, and the apparatus of the state."

The Western democracies bore a large share of the responsibility for this development, for their policy of nonintervention and refusal to support the Republic allowed the Soviets to dominate the Republican government by default.

❏ *French and British Nonintervention*

Nonintervention was as important as intervention in the Spanish civil war. It is also far more difficult to explain.

The immediate response of the French government to the Spanish Republic's appeal for aid was in fact positive, and by the end of July 1936 France had sent some fifty World War I military aircraft to Spain together with hastily assembled supplies of guns and ammunition, and hundreds of French volunteers had crossed the border to fight for the Spanish Republic.

But early in August the French government abruptly changed course, blocking the further shipment of arms to Spain and adopting a policy of nonintervention. There were three basic reasons for this policy reversal; fear that intervention in Spain would result in the escalation of the Spanish civil war into a general European conflict, which the French were determined to avoid; the opposition by anti-Communists in France to intervention on behalf of what was widely perceived as a proto-Communist regime in Spain—an opposition so intense that it threatened to plunge France itself into civil war; and the attitude of the British government.

On July 22–23, Blum and his foreign minister went to London to confer with British leaders about restructuring the Locarno agreements in response to Hitler's remilitarization of the Rhineland. When the question of aid to the Spanish Republic was raised, the British leaders left their French visitors in no doubt of their opposition to intervention. Although Anthony Eden, the British foreign secretary, later denied having made any attempt to influence French policy toward Spain, Spanish emissaries who met with Blum immediately after his return from London tell a very different story. According to them, Blum was warned that if French aid to Spain resulted in a general European war, Britain would consider itself relieved of all obligations to come to the aid of France.

The opposition to intervention in France was meanwhile becoming increasingly strident. While Blum was in London, the Spanish request for aid (sent by uncoded telegram) and the French government's positive reply had been published in the French press, which had also been informed in minute detail about proposals for further arms transactions. These reports had provoked a storm of protest in France by anti-Communists and anti-Semites, who detested their own Popular Front government and its Jewish prime minister. But French moderates, too, were deeply disturbed by their government's policy. They shared British fears that intervention in Spain would plunge their country into a general European war, and they argued with some plausibility that France, having refused to accept the risk of war over the Rhineland, where vital French interests had been at stake, had far less reason to risk war over Spain. Upon his return from London, Blum was warned by the president of France, Albert Lebrun, that "what is being planned, this delivery of arms to Spain, may mean war or revolution in France."

Blum resolved to stand firm. After a cabinet meeting on July 25, he confessed that his heart was torn but that he was determined to adhere to his policy of aiding the Republic no matter what the costs or how great the risks. "We must help a Spain that is friendly to us," he said. But Blum did not stand firm. On the very next day, evidently won over by the arguments and warnings of the opponents of his policy, he informed the British that his government had decided on a policy of nonintervention, convinced that intervention would result in disastrous divisions within France and might lead to a general European war. The British were clearly relieved to learn of this change of course. "We agreed to this French decision of policy," Eden wrote in his memoirs. France's Eastern allies were also relieved. Any diversion of French power in Western Europe would mean a corresponding decline in French capacity to intervene in Eastern Europe, which was already dangerously undermined by Germany's remilitarization of the Rhineland and France's adoption of a defensive posture through the construction of the Maginot Line.

On August 2, 1936, France officially submitted a proposal for a nonintervention agreement to the governments of Britain and Italy, a proposal immediately endorsed by Britain and subsequently accepted in principle by Italy, Germany, and the Soviet Union, and all other European states with interests in Spain. The deliberations of the international Non-Intervention Committee, formed to supervise the implementation of the agreement, have been described by Hugh Thomas as graduating from equivocation to hypocrisy and humiliation. In fact, there was little graduation involved because the policy of nonintervention was blatantly hypocritical from the start. As everyone knew, Italy and Germany were already intervening in Spain and they continued to do so, while the Soviet Union was preparing to intervene on a large scale.

Why did the British government take such a strong stand against intervention? The fundamental British concern may have been the one they presented to the French: to prevent the civil war in Spain from escalating into a general European war. In Britain as in France, public opinion was bitterly divided over the question of intervention. Leftists, liberals, and a large majority of intellectuals were for the most part passionate and vociferous supporters of the Republic, and many fought and died in its defense. The attitude of British conservatives was more reserved and ambivalent. Many shared the belief of conservatives generally that Spain's Popular Front government was a prelude to a Communist takeover. They were therefore receptive to the argument of the Spanish Nationalists that they were waging a war against Communism on behalf of the restoration of law and order. The Nationalists certainly seemed more likely to respect Britain's substantial economic interests in Spain.

But perhaps the most telling reason for the British government's opposition to intervention was its belief that British interests would not be greatly affected no matter who won the civil war in Spain. A quick victory by either side would not give a foreign power the time or opportunity to gain decisive influence in Spain. In the event of a long war, the victor, whoever it might be, would be compelled to look to Britain, France, and the United States for financial and other assistance when faced with the tasks of postwar reconstruction. A policy of intervention, on the other hand, besides exposing Britain to the risk of war and any number of unknown dangers, would not necessarily make for the promotion or even defense of British interests. Given traditional Spanish pride, a Spanish government, whatever its politics, could be expected to resist foreign efforts to influence its policies no matter how great its dependence on foreign support. Towards the end of the war, when it was commonly assumed that Franco's debt to Italy and Germany would leave him solidly entrenched in the Axis camp, the British ambassador to Spain, Sir Henry Chilton, expressed complete confidence about Spain's postwar orientation. There was not the slightest possibility, he assured his government, that Germany or Italy would dominate a Spain under Franco's rule.

Franco did his best to foster this belief. Despite German pressure and displeasure, he did not cut off exports to Britain or allow the Germans to take over British economic interests. After his conquest of Bilbao in June 1937, which gave him control over the major ore-producing regions of northern Spain, he continued to direct more iron ore exports to Britain than to Germany.

❑ *German Frustration*

Chilton had analyzed the situation correctly. In a long memorandum of February 1938 on Germany's relations with Nationalist Spain, the German ambassador, Eberhard Stohrer, lamented that the agreements concluded so far had dealt largely with matters of principle and that in return for German support "we have thus far not acquired any positive compensation." Stohrer proposed various measures for putting pressure on Spain to provide such compensation, but he agreed with the instructions issued by the highest German authorities "to avoid any interference in the internal affairs of Spain." "One must always bear in mind that there is hardly a people in the world so difficult to handle as the Spaniards," Stohrer said, and he believed that any attempt to influence Spanish policy would only achieve the opposite. "One must not count on political gratitude," he concluded. "Coercive measures will prove only momentarily successful with the Spaniards, and after the war the country's situation even at best will not be such that there is much left for its allies."

In November 1938, taking advantage of a desperate Franco appeal for more military aid, the Germans at last secured more specific economic concessions. But even now the Spaniards promised little more than opportunities for German investment in mining companies in Spain and Spanish Morocco and duty-free imports of German mining machinery, all of which would benefit Spain quite as much as Germany and left German interests at the mercy of the Spanish government.

Franco was lavish with assurances of friendship and good intentions, but he felt compelled to draw Germany's attention to the Spanish government's need for extreme caution in its international relations. In a letter to Hitler of January 11, 1939, he expressed the fear that overt signs of Nationalist Spain's friendship with Germany and Italy would be exploited by Britain and France to attack Spain. By seeking to safeguard against such an attack, Franco believed he was not only serving the interests of Spain but those of Germany and Italy as well, because the occupation of Spain and the Straits of Gibraltar by their enemies would be a crippling blow in the event of war. In its economic affairs, too, Spain had to conceal its intention to orient its postwar commercial relations to friendly countries, especially Germany. "British suspicion compels us to be very cautious so as not to allow our future economic policy to become too obvious."

With victory in sight, Franco recommended that Germany and Italy reach agreement between themselves about their assistance in rebuilding postwar Spain so as to eliminate competition between them. But the Spaniards also admitted frankly that they would have to look beyond Germany and Italy in dealing with the problems of postwar reconstruction and that they intended to seek aid from a wide range of foreign countries. As little as he liked the idea, the Spanish minister of economics informed the German ambassador, Spain would need credits, and certain countries, in particular Britain, France, and the United States, "will certainly offer us very extensive deliveries on credit." Even now their businessmen were urging Spain to turn to them for assistance, but Spain did not intend to respond to such offers until it learned what Germany and Italy could deliver and to what extent they were willing to help.

Here was blackmail of the crudest sort, but the Germans and Italians were helpless and could do nothing but try to maintain the friendship of Franco on Franco's terms. On March 27, 1939, Spain joined the German-Italian-Japanese Anti-Comintern pact, but this was merely a reaffirmation of common hostility to Communism. And a German-Spanish treaty of friendship signed four days later was little more than a restatement of an earlier treaty expressing the desirability of closer economic cooperation.

With the outbreak of World War II, the British naval blockade virtually ended German-Spanish trade and enabled Britain and France to take over the lion's share of Spanish exports. Between September 1939 and the fall of France, Britain provided Spain with credits of 2 million pounds and Spain agreed to ship the bulk of its ore exports to the Western Allies. Even after the fall of France, Spain ignored German protests and continued its ore shipments to Britain, while rejecting German demands to be allowed to purchase British and French interests in Spanish mines. By far the most important of Franco's services to Britain, however, was his refusal to allow the passage of German troops through Spain to attack Gibraltar, whose capture by the Germans might have changed the course of the war. (See pp. 224–225.)

◻

FIFTEEN

From the Spanish Civil War to the Eve of World War II in Europe

◻ *Italy, Germany, and the Problem of Austria*

The state most critically affected by the Spanish civil war, apart from Spain itself, was Italy. As in the case of his Ethiopian war, Mussolini's intervention in Spain had worsened his relations with the Western powers and proved such a drain on his country's military and economic resources that his overall political and diplomatic position was seriously weakened. Contrary to a widely held assumption, this weakness did not automatically deliver him into the arms of Hitler, but it did make him more amenable to Hitler's offers of friendship and forced him to abandon his uncompromising opposition to a buildup of Nazi influence in Austria.

One of Hitler's most cherished foreign policy objectives was the union (*Anschluss*) of his native Austria with Germany, a task he defined on the first page of *Mein Kampf* as one to be promoted at all times and by every means. This objective, however, conflicted with a major Hitler diplomatic objective, a German alliance with Italy, for no Italian government could welcome an Austro-German union which would install Germany on Italy's northeastern frontier. To allay Mussolini's fears about an Austro-German union, Hitler did not hesitate to lie. On meeting with the Italian leader in Venice in June 1934, Hitler assured him that he now realized there could be no question of a German annexation of Austria. Mussolini was justifiably suspicious of Hitler's assurances, and until the Ethiopian war he remained a staunch defender of Austrian independence, assiduously concerned with blocking any extension of Nazi influence in that country.

As his relations with France and Britain became increasingly strained over the Ethiopian affair, Mussolini evidently believed he could strengthen his hand in dealing with those powers by a more positive response to Hitler's overtures. In January 1936 he informed the German ambassador to Rome that he was now prepared to dispose of the only obstacle to a fundamental improvement in German-Italian relations, namely, the Austrian problem. Since the Germans had always declared they had no intention of infringing on Austria's independence, he would have no objection to an Austro-German treaty that would make for closer cooperation between the two countries.

Hitler quickly took advantage of this opening. On July 11, 1936, he concluded a so-called Gentlemen's Agreement with Austria recognizing Austrian sovereignty and independence and renouncing any intention to annex the country. In that same agreement, however, was a provision allowing for the inclusion of members of the "national opposition" in the Austrian government. Hitler thus prepared the way for the entry into and eventual takeover of the Austrian government by Austrian Nazis and other pro-*Anschluss* elements.

Mussolini must have seen through this stratagem, but with his attention now focused on the revolution in Spain, he evidently decided that he could do no more than take Hitler's word about Austria. The Gentlemen's Agreement, he informed the German ambassador, had removed "the last and only mortgage on German-Italian relations." In October 1936 he sent his foreign minister and son-in-law Count Ciano on a highly publicized official visit to Berlin. After Ciano's return, Mussolini described Italy's new relationship with Germany as the Rome-Berlin Axis, thereby allowing the world to assume that Ciano had laid the groundwork for, or had actually concluded, an alliance with Germany.

In fact, Ciano had done nothing of the sort. His agreements with Germany were merely policy statements on specific problems and not an alliance or even a consultative pact. Hitler had nevertheless used the occasion of Ciano's visit to reassure Mussolini yet again about his intentions. Germany was interested only in Northern and Eastern Europe and would leave the entire Mediterranean area to the Italians. Reinforcing reassurance with flattery, he informed Ciano that Mussolini was "the finest statesman in the world to whom no one else could even remotely be compared."

While trumpeting his friendship with Hitler, Mussolini had no intention of burning his bridges to other countries. In January 1937 he concluded an agreement with Britain whereby both powers promised to respect their mutual rights and interests in the Mediterranean area and to maintain the independence and territorial integrity of Spain. In March of that year he concluded a five-year nonaggression pact with Yugoslavia to counter German influence in the Balkans.

But by now, with so many of his troops bogged down in Spain, there was no longer anything he could do about Austria. When the Austrian chancellor Kurt von Schuschnigg came to Italy in April 1937 to plead for support to preserve Austria's independence, Mussolini was obliged to inform him that he could not count on military aid from Italy and that he would have to make the best bargain he could with Hitler. Deserted by Italy, Schuschnigg turned for support to other states whose national interests would be imperiled by Germany's annexation of Austria. To his dismay he found that fear of Germany and fear of war overshadowed their concern for Austria's independence. He also discovered that the British government's conception of national interests had been significantly revised by Neville Chamberlain, who succeeded Stanley Baldwin as prime minister on May 28, 1937.

❏ *The Policy of Appeasement*

The term *appeasement* has been used to describe the failure of the Western democracies to halt Japanese aggression in Manchuria, Italian aggression in Ethiopia, Hitler's violations of the treaties of Versailles and Locarno, and Franco's overthrow of the republican government in Spain.

With Chamberlain, however, appeasement became a policy with a rationale of its own which drew on the British government's successful use of appeasement in resolving domestic conflict. By extending the franchise and yielding to the demands of laborers in factories and mines for higher wages and better working conditions, a succession of British governments had defused the revolutionary appeal of political demagogues and persuaded the masses to work through the existing political and economic system. Chamberlain believed that a similar strategy could be employed in dealing with Hitler.

In November 1937 Chamberlain sent Lord Halifax, soon to replace Anthony Eden as British foreign secretary, on a mission to Berlin to initiate his policy of taking positive steps to ensure the preservation of peace. Halifax was to sound out Hitler about the nature of German grievances, and he was to inform him that Britain would be prepared to meet Germany's "legitimate" demands as the price of peace. Without waiting to hear what Hitler's demands might be, Halifax proceeded to define the price Britain was prepared to pay. Certain changes in the European order "might be destined to come about with the passage of time," Halifax said. "Among these questions were Danzig, Austria, and Czechoslovakia." Britain insisted only that such changes take place through a process of peaceful evolution. In the new international order that would then be established, Germany was entitled to be regarded as a bulwark of the West against Bolshevism.

There can be no doubt that the maintenance of Germany as a bulwark against Bolshevism was a prime ingredient in Chamberlain's appeasement policy. This, after all, had been a cardinal consideration of many other Western leaders throughout the interwar years. Although by the mid-1930s Stalin was urging the formation of Popular Front governments in Western Europe and the cooperation of foreign Communist parties with parliamentary "bourgeois" regimes, many Western leaders remained convinced that Stalin was still committed to world revolution and that he was trying to foment war among the Western powers as a way to achieve this purpose. Chamberlain confided to his sister his belief that Russia was "stealthily and cunningly pulling all the strings behind the scenes to get us involved in a war with Germany."

Chamberlain was much pleased with the results of Halifax's visit to Hitler, which he considered a triumph in the interests of peace. He summed up his policy in his personal journal. "I don't see why we shouldn't say to Germany 'give us satisfactory assurances that you won't use force to deal with the Austrians and the Czechoslovaks, and we will give you similar assurances that we won't use force to prevent the changes you want, if you can get them by peaceful means.'" It was Chamberlain's (and the world's) tragedy that in pursuing what seemed to him a reasonable policy, he was not dealing with a reasonable adversary. Hitler's ambitions went far beyond anything Chamberlain envisaged by way of removing "justifiable" grievances. So long as Hitler remained in power in Germany, a policy of appeasement had no chance of success.

Early in 1938 Mussolini made a final effort to block a German takeover of Austria, once again showing that he had not burned his bridges to the West. In view of the German threat to Austria, he informed the Chamberlain government, an Anglo-Italian agreement was essential. Chamberlain was eager to take advantage of this renewed opportunity to bring Italy into the Western camp. But Anthony Eden, his foreign secretary, disagreed, convinced at last that Britain's appeasement of Italy had been a mistake. On February 20, 1938, after a heated controversy with Chamberlain, he resigned rather than renew negotiations with Mussolini. His successor as foreign secretary was Lord Halifax, who had already given Hitler such welcome assurances of his own support of appeasement. On April 20, 1938, Britain concluded a treaty with Italy recognizing Italy's annexation of Ethiopia in return for Mussolini's promise to withdraw Italian troops from Spain.

❑ Hitler's Annexation of Austria

In November 1937, at about the same time of the Halifax mission to Berlin, Mussolini told the French as well as Austrian governments that in the event of a crisis over Austria, Italy would stand aside. The French too decided to stand aside. Taking their cue from Britain, they informed Hitler that they would have no objection to a further assimilation of certain Austrian domestic institutions with those of Germany. Hitler would shortly receive similar assurances from the governments of Poland, Yugoslavia, and Hungary.

Having been conceded a free hand in Austria by the major and minor powers most concerned with the problem (with the notable exception of the Soviet Union), Hitler now had only to deal with Austria. The Austrian chancellor Kurt von Schuschnigg, deprived of all foreign support, yielded to German demands for a large-scale coordination of Austrian and German institutions, including the army and the economy—which met Chamberlain's condition of securing control over Austria by peaceful means.

Knowing where Hitler's policy of coordination would inevitably lead, Schuschnigg made a final desperate effort to save Austrian independence. He announced his intention to hold a plebiscite on the question of Austrian independence with the obvious intention of exposing the falsity of Hitler's claims that the Austrian people wanted self-determination in the arms of Nazi Germany. It was a futile move that only hastened the course of events. Hitler was well aware of what the results of a plebiscite conducted by the authoritarian Austrian government would be—he had used the same ploy often enough himself—and he now took immediate steps to prevent it. He demanded that Schuschnigg postpone the plebiscite and change voting arrangements to ensure a proper representation of pro-German sentiment in Austria, a demand backed up by the threat of a German military invasion.

Schuschnigg yielded all along the line, but by this time Hitler, having received renewed assurances that Mussolini would not intervene, decided to go through with the invasion. At daybreak on March 12, 1938, German troops marched unopposed across the Austrian frontier. Even now Hitler appears to have intended no more than

ATLANTIC
OCEAN

WHITE SEA

FINLAND

NORWAY

Lake
Ladoga

SOVIET
UNION

Helsinki   Viborg
SWEDEN   Hanko   Leningrad
Oslo   Stockholm   Tallinn
ESTONIA

NORTH
SEA

Pskov

DENMARK
Copenhagen

LATVIA
Riga

Moscow

Memel
Danzig

LITHUANIA
Kaunas (Kovno)

Smolensk

NETH.
Amsterdam
Dunkirk
BELG.
Brussels

Berlin

EAST
PRUSSIA

Wilno
(Vilna)   Minsk
Grodno

RUHR GERMANY
Ruhr R.
Rhine R.

Warsaw

Pinsk

RHINE-
LAND
LUX.

POLAND

Kiev

FRANCE

Danube R.

① Prague ①
②   ⑤
③

Lvov

N. BUKOVINA

Bern
SWITZ.

Vienna

AUSTRIA
Budapest
HUNGARY

④

BESSARABIA

Kishinev

VICHY
FRANCE

Genoa

ROMANIA

Ploesti

Belgrade

Bucharest

MEDITERRANEAN
SEA

YUGOSLAVIA

BLACK SEA

ADRIATIC SEA

BULGARIA
Sofia

Rome

ALBANIA

TURKEY

ITALY

Tirana

GREECE

Changes in Czechoslovakia, 1938-1939
① Sudetenland, annexed
   by Germany 1938
② Protectorate of Bohemia-Moravia,
   created by Germany 1939
③ Slovakia, German protectorate 1939
④ To Hungary 1938, 1939
⑤ To Poland 1938

Soviet territorial gains, 1939–1941

Axis Powers

Western and northern areas overrun
by Germany, spring of 1940

Under Axis occupation

0   200   400 Miles

a coordination of Austrian and German institutions, but news of the enthusiastic reception of German troops in every part of the country and his own tumultuous welcome in Linz and Vienna convinced him that he need hesitate no longer. On March 13 Austria was officially annexed to the German Reich.

Through his annexation of Austria, Hitler acquired an additional German population of six and a half million, including enough men of military age to form six new divisions. He gained control over an economy with valuable supplies of lignite, iron ore, magnesite (for aircraft production), and timber, plus foreign exchange and gold reserves valued at four hundred million Reichmarks. The annexation also improved Germany's strategic position, for German power could now be brought to bear on Czechoslovakia from three sides. In his propaganda, Hitler might subsequently denounce Czechoslovakia as a menace to German security, an unsinkable aircraft carrier in the heart of the Reich. But in fact, as no one knew better than Hitler, Czechoslovakia was now in the maw of the Nazi dragon.

The Selling Out of Czechoslovakia: Sudeten Crisis and Munich Agreement

Following his annexation of Austria, Hitler shifted his emphasis almost immediately to Czechoslovakia, a second region Lord Halifax had named as one where the British government believed revisions in the existing international order might be justified. The justification in this case was the violation of the principle of self-determination by the inclusion of some three million ethnic Germans in Czechoslovakia when that state was established after World War I. Because a large number of these Germans were concentrated in the Sudeten mountains along the frontier between Bohemia and Silesia, the areas they inhabited were generally called the Sudetenland and the inhabitants themselves became known as the Sudeten Germans.

On March 28, 1938, Hitler received Konrad Henlein, the chief instrument of Nazi policy in the Sudetenland, and assured him of his determination to solve the German problem in Czechoslovakia soon. To prevent all possibility of compromise with the Czechoslovak government, he instructed Henlein to adopt the tactic of constantly stepping up his demands with the ultimate aim of securing the total independence of the Sudeten Germans and the territories they inhabited. The realization of this aim would deprive Czechoslovakia of its strategic frontiers and the fortifications that had been built there and would, in effect, render that state defenseless. Because Hitler could not expect the Czechs to make such suicidal concessions, he took into account from the first that military action might be necessary. But before taking such action, he had to make every effort to ensure that Britain and France would not intervene.

The British had already assured him of their desire for a peaceful solution of the Sudeten problem, and Chamberlain was resolved to continue that policy. He noted in his journal that he no longer saw any possibility of saving Czechoslovakia from being overrun by the Germans, even if he wanted to do so. "I have therefore abandoned any idea of giving guarantees to Czechoslovakia, or the French in connection with their obligations to that country."

The French were less resigned to the abandonment of Czechoslovakia. Quite apart from their treaty obligations, they recognized in Czechoslovakia the most formidable anti-German bastion in Eastern Europe. But in April 1938 the Popular Front government of Léon Blum had given way to the more conservative government of Edouard Daladier, whose foreign minister, Georges Bonnet, took his foreign policy cue from Britain. Like Chamberlain, he regarded Czechoslovakia as a doomed state, and he seemed more concerned with finding loopholes in France's treaty obligations to the Czechs than in seeking means to honor them.

Meanwhile Hitler kept up the pressure on Czechoslovakia. On September 13, 1938, he instructed Henlein to present a six-hour ultimatum to the Czechoslovak government demanding the withdrawal of all state police in districts inhabited by a German majority and the transfer of their powers to local German authorities. When the Czechoslovak government failed to yield within the prescribed time, Henlein broke off negotiations altogether.

Confronted with the imminent possibility of armed conflict, Chamberlain responded according to form. On September 15 he went to Berchtesgaden to meet with Hitler, letting it be known that he was prepared to examine far-reaching German proposals. Taking full advantage of this offer, Hitler for the first time specifically demanded the "return to the Reich of the three million Germans in Czechoslovakia." Chamberlain said that he personally "recognized the principle of the detachment of the Sudeten areas," but he would have to consult his colleagues in the cabinet as well as the French before he could give Hitler specific assurances. He made no mention of consulting the Soviet Union—or the Czechs—and he never did.

Chamberlain now returned to London to convince his colleagues and the French of the need to compel the Czechoslovak government to grant self-determination to the Sudeten Germans, for nothing less could prevent another world war. His efforts were successful, if that term can be used for this operation. On September 19 the French joined the British in advising the Czechoslovak government to give up the Sudetenland. Justifiably infuriated by this betrayal, the Czechs resolved to reject this advice, but under uncompromising Anglo-French pressure they at last gave in. On the morning of September 21 Hitler was informed that Prague had yielded unconditionally.

To Chamberlain's surprise and indignation, Hitler now put forward new demands: German troops were to be allowed to occupy the Czech territories designated by the German government immediately. The Germans would thus be able to take everything they wanted before the Czechs had time to rally international support or build new defensive lines. Chamberlain does not appear to have perceived the implications of Hitler's new demands and, suppressing his annoyance, he agreed to communicate them to the Czechs. The Czechs, however, saw clearly what was at stake and rejected Hitler's demands out of hand "because they would deprive us of every safeguard for our national existence."

Ignoring Czech protests, the British and French governments remained determined to achieve a peaceful solution. In response to their appeals, to which those of Mussolini were now added, Hitler agreed to meet with the leaders of the British, French, and Italian governments in Munich, where Mussolini put forward proposals for a peaceful solution to the Sudeten crisis drafted for him by the German government. The agreement reached at Munich on September 29 met all Hitler's demands, his only concession being that, instead of occupying all the Czech territories designated by the German government immediately, the process should be drawn out for ten days. In an annex to the Munich agreement, the British and French governments guaranteed the new boundaries of Czechoslovakia against unprovoked aggression, a guarantee which the German and Italian governments were to join after the settlement of Polish and Hungarian demands for Czechoslovak territory on ethnic grounds.

Upon Chamberlain's return to England from Munich, he was hailed by enthusiastic crowds as he held aloft a copy of what was assumed to be the Munich agreement (actually it was a declaration of Anglo-German friendship signed by himself and Hitler) and announced: "I bring you peace in our time." The French reaction was more subdued and was best summed up by the comment of Léon Blum: "We were filled with shame, and relief."

The Munich agreement has been defended as another courageous effort on the part of Chamberlain to preserve peace through a negotiated settlement. On a more practical level it has been defended as a purchase of time needed for Britain's rearmament, for in the year after Munich many of the aircraft and weapons were built that enabled the British to defeat the German Luftwaffe in the summer of 1940.

Critics of the Munich agreement have argued more convincingly that whatever Britain may have gained by another year of rearmament could not begin to match what the Western democracies lost by selling out Czechoslovakia. Quite apart from their ignominious loss of moral stature through this sacrifice of the most democratic and best-governed state in Eastern Europe, they lost a military ally which might have been able to hold up the Germans far more effectively than Poland was able to do a year later. Czechoslovakia had a large, well-trained, and well-equipped army, backed up by one of the greatest munitions industries in Eastern Europe. Since 1919 it had built up a powerful network of frontier fortifications which might well have withstood a German attack for an extended period, especially if Germany had been obliged to keep a large part of its army in the West to guard against an Anglo-French threat to its Rhineland industries. Moreover, if France and Britain had gone to war with Germany on behalf of Czechoslovakia, the Soviet Union would have been obliged to do so as well, and Russia was in a geographic position to render immediate and effective aid.

The prospect of Soviet intervention, however, may have been a principal reason why Chamberlain yielded to Hitler over Czechoslovakia. In July 1938 the German ambassador had reported from London of Britain's profound understanding of one of the essential aspects of German policy, "namely to prevent the Soviet Union from deciding the destinies of Europe." Soviet aid to Czechoslovakia would have required the passage of Soviet troops through Poland and Romania. If Soviet forces entered these countries and succeeded in aiding the Czechs in turning back the Germans, who was to turn out the Russians?

Historians sympathetic to the Soviet Union have supported the Soviet claim that the fundamental purpose of the Western appeasement of Hitler was to give him a free hand in Eastern Europe and eventually dissipate Germany's aggressive energies in a conflict with the Soviet Union. This interpretation breaks down over the fact that Britain and France finally took a firm stand against Hitler when he invaded Poland, which for the first time brought him into a direct confrontation with the Soviet Union and thereby established the essential condition for a Nazi-Soviet conflict. Instead of standing aloof at this point, when they might anticipate the fruition of a policy designed to bring about a Nazi-Soviet conflict, Britain and France chose to go to war with Germany themselves—while the Soviet Union joined Germany in carving up Poland into spheres of interest between themselves.

The Soviet factor in Western thinking has already been stressed repeatedly, yet the evidence is overwhelming that the primary concern of the Western leadership during the interwar years was the preservation of peace and that their policy of appeasement was meant to serve that purpose. Western leaders and public opinion were simply not mentally prepared for war, not yet convinced that the inevitable sacrifices of war were necessary or morally justifiable. The enthusiastic reception Chamberlain received upon his return from Munich indicates that his thinking and his policies reflected the attitude of a large number of his compatriots. It would require a major shock to convince British public opinion, and Chamberlain, that the policy of appeasement in dealing with Hitler was a failure, and that if Britain itself was to survive as an independent nation it would have to stand up to the German dictator at last, no matter what the cost.

❏ *Kristallnacht and Hitler's Violation of the Munich Agreement: the Occupation of Bohemia and Moravia*

Actually there were two shocks. The first came on the night of November 10, 1938, following the assassination of a German diplomat in Paris by a Jewish refugee. Following that incident, the Nazi leadership unleashed their anti-Semitic fanatics in what has become known as the Night of the Broken Glass (*Kristallnacht*). The shop windows of thousands of Jewish stores were smashed, synagogues were burned and looted, twenty thousand Jews were arrested, and the true horror of Nazi racism was glaringly revealed.

The second and ultimately convincing shock took place in March 1939 when the Germans invaded the Czech provinces of Bohemia and Moravia, a cynically cold-blooded violation of the Munich agreement. The reaction of public opinion in the West was immediate and vehement. There was a more delayed reaction on the part of Western leaders. Chamberlain in particular took some time to grasp how completely his policy, pursued with such dogmatic consistency and confidence, had failed. But now, disillusioned and determined at last to stand firm, British and French leaders went to another extreme by giving military guarantees to Poland, Romania, Greece, and Turkey, all of which seemed threatened by the Axis. The rationale behind Britain's guarantee policy, conceived in the last week of March 1939, was to form an interlocking system of alliances whereby an attack on any one would bring in all the others. In the overall international picture, the most important consequence of Hitler's violation of the Munich agreement was the Anglo-French guarantee to Poland, for it was this guarantee that propelled Britain and France into war with Germany in September 1939.

In view of the fateful consequences of his occupation of Bohemia and Moravia, an area already within Germany's sphere of influence, why did Hitler choose to take such a step at this particular time? The most obvious answer is that Hitler did not expect the reaction his move would provoke in the West. At Munich, Britain and France had appeared to give him a free hand in Eastern Europe. Prior to his occupation of Bohemia and Moravia, he had pressured the Czech government into appealing for German aid to restore order, and he must have thought that he had therewith supplied ample legal and moral justification for his action. The West had been satisfied with even more specious explanations in the past.

There were, however, more compelling reasons for the occupation of Bohemia and Moravia at this time—reasons Hitler himself put forward to explain his move that were completely in accord with his overall plans and major policy statements. He had always maintained that sooner or later he would have to fight to acquire the territory he thought essential to guarantee the future of the German people. Once the inevitability of war was recognized, the main problem became one of timing, of striking while Germany's military strength was at its maximum in relation to that of its opponents. Early in 1939 he had evidently decided not to wait until 1943 or 1945, the latest time limit he had set himself earlier, but to launch the military phase of his struggle in the near future. German weapons were modern, the very latest in military equipment, but new inventions might quickly render such equipment obsolete. The Western powers, with the economic resources of much of the world at their disposal, were beginning to rearm at a rapidly increasing pace. In a few years their armament might not yet be equal to that of Germany, but it was likely to be proportionately far greater than the ratio in 1939.

In March 1939 Hitler was not yet sure when he would strike, or against whom, but the occupation of Bohemia and Moravia was an essential precondition to military action in any quarter. As a gateway to Eastern Europe, the area was of prime strategic importance, but it possessed prime economic importance as well. The incorporation of Bohemia and Moravia meant the gearing of such concerns as the Skoda munitions works to German military production and the integration of the entire Czech economy with its important coal, iron ore, and timber resources into that of Germany. The Germans obtained gold worth 10 million pounds from the Czech National Bank, an additional 6 million pounds deposited with the Bank for International Settlements at Basel, and the entire Czechoslovak military arsenal. The German occupation also eliminated what was left of Czech army, thereby freeing some thirty German divisions for use elsewhere. Any danger that Czech airfields might be used, however briefly, as bases for bombing attacks on German industry had likewise been eliminated.

❑ *The German Annexation of Memel*

On March 23, 1939, eight days after the German occupation of Bohemia and Moravia, Hitler acquired the territory of Memel, an ancient German Hanseatic city that had been placed under Allied control in 1918 but was seized by Lithuania in January 1923.

On March 22 a Lithuanian delegation arrived in Berlin in response to a German ulti-matum, and that same evening they signed a treaty providing for Lithuania's evacua-tion of the Memel territory and its reunion with Germany.

Memel was only a minor episode in the course of Nazi expansion, but it was to be Hitler's last bloodless territorial acquisition. His move toward his next objective, Poland, was to inaugurate World War II in Europe.

❑ *The Nazi Racial War* — *why?*

Well before the outbreak of the Sino-Japanese war or World War II in Europe, Hitler had been waging another war from the moment he came to power: a racial war to protect the purity of the German race, which called for the expulsion, enslavement, or extermination of all non-Germanic races from German society. (See p. 172.) From the start, however, that war was concentrated and was waged with the most ven-omous intensity against the Jews.

Hitler's primary agents in carrying on that war were the fanatic Nazi ideologues recruited into his elite guard, the SS, headed by the most fanatic ideologue of them all, Heinrich Himmler, who also managed to acquire control of the most important agen-cies of the Nazi police. The tragic fact must be emphasized, however, that the Nazis found collaborators in their racial war, or at least complacent acceptance of their racial policies, among large numbers of ordinary Germans and among the peoples of virtually every country the Germans occupied during World War II.

The campaign against the Jews was not originally conceived as an outright ex-termination program: the Jews were to be expelled from Germany, and until the out-break of war the Nazi government adhered to a program of expulsion, though large numbers of Jews were jailed, sent to concentration camps, or executed on a variety of charges. As we now know from documentary evidence, most German Jews might have been saved from subsequent extermination if the governments of foreign coun-tries that professed to be appalled by the Nazi racial policies had permitted unre-stricted Jewish immigration. As it was, they severely limited immigration, admitting for the most part only Jews with visible means of support or with friends or relatives who could intercede on their behalf.

After the outbreak of war, when all principal avenues of foreign emigration were closed, the Nazis resorted to the mass deportation of Jews to Eastern Europe, where from the beginning they engaged in mass executions of Jews by firing squads. Jews capable of work were herded into labor gangs and factories producing equipment for the German army, but Reinhard Heydrich, the head of Himmler's security police and soon to be entrusted with the "final solution" of the Jewish question, made it clear that mass deportations and the use of Jewish labor were merely temporary expedients. Only three weeks after the German attack on Poland, he issued instructions to his task forces in Poland that left little doubt that what he meant by the term "final solution" was the outright extermination of the Jews. Those instructions, however, were ac-companied by the admonition: "I should like to emphasize once more that the total measures planned (i.e. the final aim) are to be kept strictly secret." A conference in the Berlin suburb of Wannsee on January 20, 1942, has become famous as the occasion when the SS leadership spelled out the program for achieving the final solution, but long before that conference took place the Nazis had initiated their mass extermination policies.

It is uncertain when the decision was made to carry out the mass execution of Jews in gas chambers instead of by firing squads. The first gas chambers, set up in December 1941, were mobile units using carbon monoxide gas generated by trucks. Subsequently several permanent killing centers were established, all of them in former Polish territory, where carbon monoxide was replaced by hydrogen cyanide (prussic acid). Of these, the largest and most notorious was Auschwitz (Oswiecim) in the former Polish district of Kattowitz, which had been incorporated into the Reich province of Silesia.

Gas chambers expedited the mass execution of Jews, but they also enabled the Nazis to carry out their extermination program in greater secrecy. Mass executions by firing squads were having a deleterious effect on the morale of German troops in the east and in some areas were creating serious difficulties with the local populations. Already in the first weeks of the war, Heydrich had ordered that the "total measures planned" be kept strictly secret. As the war dragged on Nazi officials ordered that all publicity about Germany's Jewish policy be avoided and that the "special treatment program" (the Nazi euphemism for extermination) be kept a top secret because the majority of Germans did not understand the necessity for such extreme measures. Finally in July 1943 Hitler himself found it necessary to issue an order prohibiting all mention of the final solution of the Jewish problem; if questions were asked about what had become of the Jews, people were to be told that they had been drafted for labor purposes.

There are still stories in circulation that the mass extermination of the Jews never took place, or that Hitler himself had never ordered a program of mass extermination. These stories are not only false but insulting to the memory of the victims of Nazi persecution. There is abundant and irrefutable evidence that at least by 1943 Hitler and the chief executors of his policies were determined to kill or sterilize all Jews within their power sphere, with the possible exception of Jews who might be used for purposes of exchange or barter. Moreover, this operation was to be carried out, insofar as possible, in the course of the war, while the attention of the German people was focused elsewhere, and with an almost total disregard for political or economic consequences. Hitler's greatest fear was that the German people, and perhaps even his immediate successors as rulers of Germany, would not understand the vital need of a "final solution" of the Jewish problem.

The Jews were only the first and most grievous victims of Hitler's racial war. The Nazis carried out similar policies in dealing with the Slavs and other peoples they regarded as inferior races, policies that turned the populations of Eastern Europe, many of whom had originally greeted the Germans as liberators from Bolshevik tyranny, into fierce opponents of Nazi rule. The historian reads with stupefied amazement of how, while the German armies were engaged in a struggle in which the very existence of the Reich was at stake, Nazi leaders diverted critically needed resources and transport facilities to the roundup and extermination of Jews, including Jews working in vital German war industries. Not only that. To implement Hitler's program to Germanize the conquered territories of Eastern Europe, Himmler's agents carried out massive re-settlement projects, commandeering trains, trucks, and manpower to ship peasants and their livestock from Western to Eastern Europe, disrupting the economy of both regions in the process.

All considerations of the mind-boggling stupidity of Nazi policies, however, are overwhelmed by the sheer horror of their inhumanity.

SIXTEEN

❑

World War II in Europe: From the German Attack on Poland to the Russian Campaign

❑ *The Heat on Poland*

In his early speculations about German expansion in the east, Hitler had devoted surprisingly little attention to Poland. Only Russia was large enough to fulfill German requirements of living space in the east, and in the process of conquering Russia the destruction of Poland was evidently taken for granted. After coming to power, and especially after the conclusion of his ten-year nonaggression pact with Poland in January 1934, Hitler avoided public expressions of hostility. When it suited his diplomatic purposes he even laid particular stress on German-Polish friendship, and during the Munich crisis he invited the Poles to participate in the dismemberment of Czechoslovakia, which they did with considerable enthusiasm.

The Poles soon learned about the dangers of supping with the devil. After the destruction of Czechoslovakia, Hitler began to direct his attention to his partner in spoliation and to voice demands for Danzig and the Corridor as he had recently demanded the Sudetenland. As we have seen, the German occupation of rump Czechoslovakia on March 16, 1939, brought Poland pledges of aid from Britain and France on March 31, which were extended on April 6 into guarantees of mutual assistance. Similar guarantees were subsequently given to Greece, Romania, and Turkey.

Hitler professed to be deeply disturbed by the threat of encirclement implied in these Anglo-French guarantees. On April 28 he denounced Poland's treaties with the Western powers as a violation of the German-Polish agreement of 1934, and declared that his nonaggression pact with Poland as well as his 1935 naval agreement with Britain were therefore null and void. Even before the Anglo-French pledge to Poland, however, Hitler had instructed his generals to work on a plan for "solving" the Polish question, and on April 3 they were told that this plan should be ready to put into execution at any time after September I. This order did not necessarily mean that Hitler had definitely committed himself to a military solution of the Polish question. As in the case of Austria and Czechoslovakia, he believed that he might succeed in eliminating Poland without war, or at least substantially improve his strategic position by securing the peaceful cession of Danzig and the Corridor. Even after the Anglo-French guarantee, Hitler's military directives still emphasized that he did not wish to solve the Danzig question by force and that Germany's relations with Poland should continue to be based on the principle of avoiding disturbances. He had little reason to take the Anglo-French guarantee seriously. Similar guarantees to Czechoslovakia had been disavowed with easy sophistry.

Negotiations with the Poles did not go well, and by August Hitler decided that military action would be necessary to achieve his objectives. He expressed confidence that Britain and France would not intervene—"the men I got to know at Munich were not the kind that start a new world war"—but he nevertheless continued his efforts to ensure that they did not do so. With the obvious intention of having his statements passed on to London and Paris, he explained to Carl Jacob Burckhardt, the League of Nations high commissioner for Danzig, that the whole object of his policy was to gain a free hand in the East. "Everything that I undertake is directed against Russia; if the West is too stupid and too blind to grasp this, I will be obliged to come to an understanding with the Russians, to defeat the West, and then after its downfall, to turn with my assembled forces against the Soviet Union."

On August 23 Hitler made good his threat to come to an understanding with the Russians by concluding a nonaggression pact with Stalin.

❑ *The Nazi-Soviet Pact*

On March 17, 1939, alarmed by false reports of an imminent German attack on Romania, the British government sounded Moscow as to whether the Soviet Union would come to the aid of Romania. This enquiry marked the beginning of Anglo-French negotiations with the Soviet government (about which the Germans were informed in detail through their own intelligence services) designed to bring the Soviet Union into a security system to check further Nazi expansion.

At the same time that Stalin was negotiating with the West, however, he was casting out feelers about the possibility of renewing Russia's traditional political and economic ties with the Germans. On May 3, in the course of these negotiations, Maxim Litvinov, who was Jewish and had an English-born wife, was replaced as Soviet commissar for foreign affairs by Vyacheslav Molotov, a reliable Stalin henchmen, who as a non-Jew was evidently considered more suitable for doing business with Nazi Germany.

By late July Soviet negotiations with Britain and France seemed well on the way to creating the kind of security system all three governments professed to desire. On July 23 the draft of an agreement had been worked out whereby Britain, France, and the Soviet Union undertook to give each other "all effective assistance" if any one of them were attacked by another power. An Anglo-French military mission was then sent to Moscow to determine how this mutual assistance might be rendered.

The Soviet government can hardly have been impressed by Western enthusiasm to implement this agreement, for the Anglo-French military mission was not sent by air but by boat and train and did not arrive in Moscow until August 11. And indeed the British government, or at any rate Chamberlain and his supporters, remained deeply suspicious of Soviet intentions. A British Foreign Office memorandum weighing the pros and cons of a Soviet alliance expressed the fear that the Russians' "real" policy was to get Britain and France involved in war with Germany while staying out of it themselves. Besides, it was unlikely that Russian military assistance would be of much use. This poor opinion of Russia's military capabilities was shared by French as well as British military experts and was backed up by reports of their intelligence services.

The decisive stumbling block to a Western military agreement with Russia, however, was the refusal of the states bordering on the Soviet Union (Poland and Romania) to allow Soviet troops into their territory because of their fear that once Soviet forces had entered their country they would never leave. As Churchill wrote later in his memoirs, "It was this hideous choice that paralyzed British and French policy."

There was no similar stumbling block to Soviet negotiations with Nazi Germany. As early as January 1939 the Soviet government sounded the Germans about the desirability of closer economic relations, and on May 5, directly after Litvinov's replacement by Molotov, the Russians sought a resumption of trade talks with Berlin, stressing the absence of foreign policy differences between them. Molotov himself went further, suggesting that economic negotiations would only make sense if established on a political basis. The Germans agreed about the desirability of a political treaty, and over the next two months the Nazi and Soviet governments conducted simultaneous political as well as economic negotiations. A comprehensive economic agreement was signed on August 19, a political agreement (the Nazi-Soviet nonaggression pact) on the night of August 23-24.

News of the pact was received with stunned disbelief abroad. How was it possible that two seemingly irreconcilable antagonists should conclude a treaty that represented a repudiation of all their professed principles? The Japanese correctly regarded the treaty as a clear-cut violation of the Anti-Comintern Pact (see p. 135), while anti-Nazis the world over felt betrayed by this cold-blooded Soviet sellout to the enemy. Die-hard Communists, on the other hand, condoned this latest shift in Soviet policy, and until the German attack on the Soviet Union American Communists remained staunch isolationists.

Outsiders would have been far more shocked by the secret protocol attached to the nonaggression pact, an agreement not known in the West until the capture of Germany's official documents after World War II and not acknowledged by the Soviet government until 1988. For this protocol was nothing less than a division of Eastern Europe into spheres of interest between Germany and the Soviet Union. Finland, Estonia, Latvia, and Bessarabia (annexed by Romania after World War I) were to go to Russia; Lithuania to Germany; while Poland was to be divided along the lines of the Narev, Vistula, and San Rivers.

Quite as important for Hitler as the nonaggression pact and its secret additional protocol was the economic agreement signed four days earlier, which guaranteed Germany a substantial supply of lumber, cotton, feed grain, lead, zinc, phosphates, platinum, raw furs, and above all petroleum. This treaty, plus the possibility of transshipment via the Soviet Union of other crucial raw materials such as rubber and tin from East Asia, did much to free Hitler from the nightmare of economic blockade which haunted all Germans conditioned by the experience of World War I.

The Nazi-Soviet pact was concluded with cynical calculation by both sides. For Stalin, it represented an opportunity to turn the tables on the Western powers, whose policies seemed designed to give Germany a free hand in the East that would lead to a German war against the Soviet Union. Instead, Stalin was giving Germany a free hand in the West that opened the way for a war between Germany and the Western powers, a war that would exhaust these capitalist states, leave the Soviet Union supreme in Europe, and create conditions that would make for the final triumph of international Communism.

More immediately important were the territorial provisions of the pact, which would improve the Soviet Union's strategic position, and its economic provisions, whereby Germany promised to supply the Soviets with weapons and machinery that would enhance Soviet military strength. A treaty with the Western powers, on the other hand, which promised the Soviet Union support in standing firm against Hitler, would have meant that the Soviets would be involved immediately in the event of war with Germany. Such a treaty might even have been intended by the Western powers to promote the Russo-German war they had so long desired—a treaty which, whatever its provisions, would allow them to remain on the defensive, leaving the Soviet Union to bear the brunt of the conflict. Altogether, the treaty with Germany seemed the safer and far more profitable arrangement.

For Hitler, the pact removed the danger of Soviet intervention on the side of Poland. Far more importantly, the treaty seemed likely to eliminate all possibility of Anglo-French intervention on behalf of Poland, for without Russian involvement they were even less likely to go to war over Poland. Hitler knew in detail of Anglo-French negotiations with the Soviet Union, and, like Stalin, he may have believed that their main objective was to promote a Russo-German war in the hope that such a conflict would eliminate both the Nazi and Soviet menace. But as he exulted to his generals, any such hope had been foiled by his own pact with Russia. "With this I have knocked the weapons out of the hands of these gentlemen. Poland has been maneuvered into the position we need for military success."

❏ *The Outbreak of World War II in Europe: the German Attack on Poland*

With the political stage seemingly so perfectly set, Hitler was dismayed to learn on August 25 that Britain and France, instead of seeking excuses to abandon Poland, had ratified their treaties of mutual assistance with that country. That evening he postponed the date for the attack on Poland "because of the changed political situation." "Is this temporary or for good?" he was asked. Only temporary, Hitler said, "but I must see whether we can eliminate British intervention."

During the next days Hitler used all his familiar and heretofore successful tactics to prevent Western intervention. He wanted the restoration of Danzig to Germany, a route through the Corridor, and the opportunity to end the "Macedonian conditions" on Germany's eastern frontier. Afterwards he would negotiate a treaty with Britain guaranteeing the integrity of the British empire and placing the power of the Reich at its disposal. In response to a British appeal, Hitler agreed on August 29 to enter into direct negotiations with Poland. This, however, was a mere gesture to mollify the British, because Hitler left no time for serious negotiation. The order to attack Poland was issued on the morning of August 31.

At dawn on September I, 1939, German troops crossed the Polish frontier on a broad front, an action German diplomatic representatives were instructed to describe not as war but "engagements caused by Polish attacks." As Hitler had told his generals earlier, he intended to give a propagandist reason for starting the war; it was immaterial whether this was plausible or not. "When starting and waging a war it is not right that matters, but victory. Close your hearts to pity. Act brutally. Eighty million people must obtain what is their right. Their existence must be made secure."

A few hours after the Germans began their invasion of Poland, the British and French governments demanded that Germany suspend its aggressive action, otherwise they would fulfill their military obligations to Poland. The Germans denied that there had been any aggression, their troops did not suspend their activities, and on September 3 Britain and France declared war on Germany. The European phase of World War II had begun.

Unlike the fierce controversy over responsibility for World War I and the question of war guilt, there can be no doubt about the responsibility for World War II in Europe. This was Hitler's war. The leaders of the Western powers went to extreme and, in the view of many, excessive lengths to avoid it. Their guilt, if the word can be used at all in this connection, lay in their failure to honor their treaty commitments (whereby they might have stopped Hitler before he could wage a major war), and in their subsequent frantic efforts to avoid war that allowed him to wage it under such favorable circumstances. The leaders of the Soviet Union have been roundly condemned for concluding the nonaggression pact that freed Germany from the danger of Soviet intervention, but given their understandable suspicion that the policies of the Western powers were designed to divert German aggression to the East, Soviet leaders can hardly be blamed for making their own arrangements to avoid war.

In notable contrast to the general enthusiasm for war in 1914, there was no comparable enthusiasm in 1939 either in Germany or the other belligerent countries. There were, to be sure, Nazi fanatics who welcomed the war, but the general mood in Germany as elsewhere was one of resigned fatalism, a climate of opinion the Nazi leadership contemplated with surprise and dismay.

❑ *The Fourth Partition of Poland*

The German campaign against Poland was spectacularly successful, the first demonstration of the effectiveness of offensive weaponry (mechanized units supported by air power) in carrying out what came to be called a *Blitzkrieg*—a lightning war. On September 17, with the main centers of Polish resistance already shattered by the Germans, the Red Army invaded Poland from the east. Warsaw surrendered ten days later, and by October 6 all organized Polish resistance came to an end.

MAP 9   *WORLD WAR II IN EUROPE. SEE ALSO MAPS 8 AND 12.*

ATLANTIC OCEAN

ICELAND

EIRE

GREAT BRITAIN
London

NORTH SEA

NORWAY
Narvik
Trondheim
Bergen
Stavanger
Oslo

SWEDEN
Stockholm

DENMARK
Copenhagen

FINLAND

Murmansk

WHITE SEA

Archangel

SOVIET UNION
Sverdlovsk
Kazan
Kuibyshev
Gorky
Moscow
Kalinin
Leningrad
Novgorod
Smolensk
Voronezh
Kursk
Kharkov
Stalingrad
Rostov-on-the-Don
Baku

CASPIAN SEA

IRAN

IRAQ

SYRIA

LEBANON

TURKEY
Ankara

CYPRUS

BLACK SEA
Istanbul
Novorossiisk
Sevastopol
Yalta
CRIMEA
Odessa
Dniester R.
Dnieper R.
Dnepropetrovsk
Kiev
Lvov
Minsk
Vilna
Riga

BALTIC SEA
EAST PRUSSIA
Danzig
Oder R.

ESTONIA
LATVIA
LITHUANIA

POLAND
Warsaw
Lublin
Cracow

GERMANY
Berlin
Torgau
Prague
Vienna

SLOVAKIA
HUNGARY
Budapest

ROMANIA
Bucharest
Ploesti
Danube R.

BULGARIA
Sofia

YUGOSLAVIA
Belgrade

ALBANIA

GREECE
Athens

Taranto
Messina
ITALY
Rome
Sardinia (Italy)
Corsica (Vichy French)

MEDITERRANEAN SEA

Malta (Britain)

TUNISIA (Vichy France)
ALGERIA (Vichy France)
Algiers

MOROCCO (Vichy France)
Casablanca

SPANISH MOROCCO

Gibraltar (Britain)

SPAIN
Madrid

PORTUGAL
Lisbon

NETH.
BELG.
LUX.
FRANCE
Paris
Normandy
VICHY FRANCE

SWITZ.

Don R.

MAP 9   *WORLD WAR II IN EUROPE. SEE ALSO MAPS 8 AND 12.*

Soviet boundary prior to Nazi attack on USSR (June 22, 1941)

Germany, 1938

Areas under control of or allied with Axis powers prior to June 22, 1941

Nazi-Soviet line by the end of 1941

Nazi-Soviet line, November 1942

Nazi-Soviet line, June 1944

0   200   400 Miles

213

On September 29 Germany and the Soviet Union concluded an amended version of their partition agreement of August 23 whereby Germany ceded the greater part of Lithuania to the Soviet sphere of interest in return for a larger share of Poland. A supplementary protocol of October 4 defined the new German-Soviet boundary in Poland in detail and set up a commission to mark this boundary on the ground. Additional protocols provided for the voluntary migration of nationals from the German or Soviet spheres and for the suppression of Polish agitation in their respective territories. On October 26 Germany formally annexed Danzig and the lands that had been part of the German and Habsburg empires before 1914 (the Austrian and Prussian shares of the eighteenth-century partitions of Poland). The Polish territory allotted to Germany by the Hitler-Stalin pact that was not annexed to the Reich was placed under a Nazi civil administration under a governor general and was known as the *Generalgouvernement.*

Hitler had made no detailed preparations for the occupation and administration of the occupied Polish territories, but he had very definite ideas about the general line of policy he intended to pursue. In *Mein Kampf* and subsequent pronouncements he had rejected the nationalities policies of earlier "bourgeois" governments which had sought to Germanize non-German peoples in territory under German control. The National Socialist state, he wrote in 1928, "should under no circumstances annex Poles with the intention of making Germans of them." On the contrary, it "must either seal off these alien racial elements to prevent an ever-recurring corruption of the blood of our own people, or remove them without further ado and hand over the territory made available in this way to members of our own racial community."

Hitler's views did not change in 1939. At a conference with his army and intelligence officers on September 12, he announced his intention to carry out large-scale executions of Poles, in particular the nobility, clergy, and intelligentsia. When some of his generals protested, he assured them that if the army refused to carry out his policies, this would be done by the SS and the Gestapo. Further, he intended to establish civil administrations in the occupied territories entrusted with the task of racial extermination and political housecleaning. To his more reliable henchmen, he described his plans to colonize the greater part of the conquered Polish territory with Germans, to clear all annexed territories of "Jews, Polacks, and other trash," and to conduct a racial war that would admit no legal restrictions. These tasks could not be left to the military leadership, which was filled with prejudices and did not understand their importance.

Hitler meant what he said. Directly behind the troops of the regular army came SS and police battalions, which in the name of the pacification of the conquered territories proceeded to carry out mass arrests and mass executions, for the most part quite arbitrarily and in full view of the Polish population and the German troops. He pursued these policies with fanatic consistency, and throughout the war insisted on the need for a ruthless racial policy in all the territories that came under German occupation.

The reports of eye witnesses and German government documents captured after World War II have revealed in grim detail the brutality and scope of German political and racial policies in all territories that came under their control in the Nazi era. As yet there is less documentation available about Soviet policies. The Soviets annexed their share of the 1939 partition of Poland, most of which had been part of the tsarist empire following the eighteenth-century partitions. Like the Germans, they engaged in mass arrests, executions, and deportations to remove all anti-Soviet elements, in particular the Polish nobility, property owners, political leaders, and intellectuals, including large numbers of Jews. In April 1943 the corpses of some 15,000 Polish soldiers and civilians were discovered in mass graves in the forest of Katyn, near Smolensk, a massacre the Soviets blamed on the Germans but which medical evidence revealed (and which the Soviet government later admitted) had been carried out during the Soviet occupation of this area.

❑ *The Decision to Attack in the West*

With the final surrender of the Polish forces on October 6, 1939, Hitler made a speech before a special session of the Reichstag offering to make peace with the Western powers and to settle all outstanding international differences by negotiation, a peace offer rejected by Chamberlain six days later. In all likelihood Hitler's peace bid was nothing more than a propagandistic maneuver designed to convince the German people that the continuation of the war was due to the recalcitrant attitude of Britain and France. For he clearly had no intention of concluding a permanent peace with these states while they were still in a position to threaten Germany's security.

After coming to power, Hitler had reluctantly concluded that for the time being at least he could not hope to make friendship with Britain the cornerstone of German policy, as he had once intended, and that the British as well as the French were hate-filled antagonists who would always oppose the establishment of German hegemony on the continent. In a speech to his military leaders shortly after the conclusion of the Polish campaign, he explained that the fundamental aim of the Western powers in World War I had been the destruction of the German national state and that this was still their primary aim. If the German state were to survive and the German people gain their rightful status on the European continent, they would be compelled to face a showdown struggle with Britain and France sooner or later. It was the task of German leadership to see that this struggle was waged at a time most advantageous to Germany.

That time, Hitler was convinced, had now arrived. The success of the Polish campaign and the treaty with the Soviet Union had made it possible for Germany to wage war on a single front and to throw all its strength against the West while leaving only a few covering troops in the East. This was a situation that could not be expected to endure. By no pact or treaty could the lasting neutrality of the Soviet Union be assured. The trifling significance of treaties, as Hitler was able to state with some authority, had been demonstrated on all sides in recent years. At the moment, German strength was at its peak compared to that of the Western powers, but time would permit a steady increase in the military capacities of Britain and France whose war industries were able to draw on the resources of the entire world. Every increase in their strength would make Germany's inevitable life-and-death struggle more difficult.

But for Hitler the conclusive argument for knocking out the threat from the West at the earliest possible moment was his recognition that Germany had an Achilles heel, the Ruhr, whose industries were essential to the German war economy. Located along Germany's western frontier, the Ruhr industries were perilously vulnerable to attack. Hitler was sure that the importance and vulnerability of the Ruhr must be evident to Germany's enemies—the possibility of an enemy attack in this area had been a primary worry during the Polish campaign—and he was now convinced that Germany must launch an immediate attack of its own to safeguard this vital industrial center. On October 9 Hitler issued the order to prepare for military operations against the West. The primary objective of the operation would be to crush the enemy armies and secure as large an area as possible as a protective zone for the Ruhr and as a base for conducting air and naval warfare against Britain.

Preparations for an offensive in the West were completed early in November, but the weather now forced a long series of postponements. The original German plan of attack had resembled the Schlieffen Plan of 1914 in calling for a major sweep through the Low Countries to encircle the Allied armies, only this time more attention was paid to securing the channel ports to prevent the landing of British and other overseas reinforcements. Believing that a repetition of the 1914 offensive was exactly what the enemy would expect, Erich von Manstein, one of Germany's younger and more innovative generals, conceived of a plan that retained the offensive through the Low Countries. This, however, was to be merely a feint to draw the Allied armies into central Belgium. Meanwhile the main German offensive would be a thrust through the hills and forests of the Ardennes region of southeastern Belgium, where it was least likely to be expected because the terrain was considered unsuitable for the operation of tanks and a massive troop deployment. After some hesitation Hitler endorsed Manstein's plan (later taking credit for having conceived it in the first place), and imposed it on his more conservative and cautious senior commanders.

The German attack in the West was then postponed again because of complications that had meanwhile developed in Northern Europe.

❑ Soviet Expansion: the Annexation of the Baltic States and the War with Finland

Following the Red Army's occupation of the Soviet share of the partition of Poland, the Soviets hastened to take advantage of the other provisions of their partition treaty with Germany to extend the Soviet defense perimeter still farther. On September 29, 1939, the same day that they concluded the revised partition treaty with Germany giving them the greater part of Lithuania, the Soviets imposed a treaty on Estonia giving them military and naval bases on Estonian territory. This treaty was followed up by similar agreements with Latvia and Lithuania. All three countries were subsequently absorbed into the Soviet Union as Soviet Socialist Republics—a grim reminder of why other states of Eastern Europe had refused to conclude mutual assistance pacts with Moscow.

The Soviets next attempted to impose a treaty on Finland, another state the Germans had conceded to the Soviet sphere of interest. They demanded the cession of frontier territory on the Karelian Isthmus and islands in the Gulf of Finland to provide a better defensive perimeter for Leningrad, the lease of the port of Hanko (Hangö) for a Soviet naval base, and an adjustment of the frontier in the north that would give the Soviets the valuable Petsamo nickel mines and provide better safeguards to the approaches of the port of Murmansk. In exchange the Soviets offered Finland a broad strip of Soviet Karelia. On November 26, 1939, the Finns rejected the Soviet demands. Four days later the Soviet Union went to war against Finland.

The Finns' valiant resistance evoked widespread sympathy and admiration. The failure of mighty Russia to score a quick victory over a country with a mere 4 million inhabitants reinforced the belief among Western and German leaders that the Red Army had been gutted by Stalin's purges of the 1930s and was no longer an effective fighting force—the Red Army's victories over the Japanese in East Asia in 1938 and 1939 continued to be ignored. (See p 234.)

But in Finland too the Red Army eventually triumphed. On March 12, 1940, after 105 days of fighting, the Finns were obliged to conclude a peace treaty with the Soviet Union ceding the entire Karelian Isthmus, including the city of Viipuri (Viborg), a strip of territory (the Salla area) along the Russo-Finnish border, the Finnish portion of the Rybachi Peninsula in the far north, and the nearby Petsamo nickel mines. They also agreed to the establishment of a Soviet naval base at Hanko at the entrance to the Gulf of Finland.

In the overall international picture, a major legacy of the Russo-Finnish war was its revelation of the apparent weakness of the Red Army, which undoubtedly influenced Hitler's decision to attack the Soviet Union in the following year. Of more immediate significance to Hitler, however, was the information he received of Allied plans to send an army into Scandinavia to aid Finland, a military operation that would pose a mortal threat to Germany's strategic and economic position. It was this danger that propelled Hitler to take action of his own in Scandinavia.

❑ *The German Attack on Denmark and Norway*

When World War II began, Hitler had no intention of moving against Scandinavia. The Scandinavian people were Nordics who at some future date might be cajoled or coerced into some kind of greater Germanic political organization. But for the time being Hitler counted on the Scandinavian states to remain neutral, as they had in World War I. As the Russo-Finnish war dragged on, however, he received increasingly alarming reports that the Allies were preparing to occupy Norway and Sweden under the cover of coming to the aid of Finland.

Hitler was convinced that such a move must be forestalled at all costs, for if the British succeeded in establishing themselves in the ice-free ports of Norway they would be in a position to close the entrance to the Baltic Sea and dominate the entire German sea coast, including all German naval bases. Quite as serious as the strategic threat was the economic threat. Germany was dependent on Sweden for 51 percent of its iron ore, which, because Swedish ports froze over, was shipped via Norway's ice-free ports in winter and would have been cut off completely during the winter months if Britain occupied those ports.

A detailed Hitler directive to prepare for a Scandinavian campaign went out to his military leadership on March 1, 1940. "The development of the political situation in Scandinavia," he said, "requires that all preparations be made for the occupation of Denmark and Norway." The purpose of the operation was to prevent British encroachment on Scandinavia and the Baltic, guarantee Germany's access to Swedish iron ore, and give the German navy and air force a wider base for operations against Britain. In making his plans for Scandinavia, Hitler at no time mentioned the possibility of occupying Sweden. He evidently assumed that with the occupation of Denmark and Norway, Sweden would be effectively cut off from the West and that German political pressure would suffice to ensure the delivery of Swedish ore.

With the conclusion of peace between Finland and Russia on March 12, 1940, Hitler relaxed the tempo of his preparations for a Scandinavian campaign, which he had previously scheduled to begin on March 15. By now his concern seems to have shifted from fear of an imminent British attack on Norway to the vulnerability of his northern flank when the time came to launch his campaign in the west. Because the moment Germany violated the neutrality of the Low Countries, as envisaged in his campaign plans, the British might seize this excuse to violate the neutrality of Norway.

For a time Hitler was uncertain whether he should strike first in the north or in the west, but on April 2, upon learning that all German preparations for a Scandinavian campaign were complete, he ordered that the invasion of Denmark and Norway begin on April 9. "On principle, we will do our utmost to make the operation appear as a *peaceful* occupation 'for the purpose of preserving Scandinavian neutrality which was threatened by the British.'" Hitler hoped that the governments of Denmark and Norway would submit peacefully to German demands to occupy their countries, but if German forces met with resistance they were to use all military means to crush it.

The Danish government did indeed yield peacefully, although under protest, which meant that the Germans were able to occupy Denmark quickly with almost no losses in manpower.

They were not so lucky in Norway, where the government evaded capture and ordered the army and people to engage in all-out resistance. Thus the illusion of a peaceful German occupation was shattered from the start. The superiority of German strength was overwhelming, however. By the end of April almost all organized resistance in southern Norway had ceased, but stubborn resistance continued in the north until June.

As we now know, Hitler's fears of an Allied move in Scandinavia were justified. As early as September 19, 1939, Winston Churchill, first lord of the admiralty, had proposed the mining of Norwegian territorial waters to stop the transport of Swedish iron ore to Germany. Following the outbreak of war between the Soviet Union and Finland, he urged a major offensive operation that would include the takeover of the major Swedish iron ore mines. But the Allies delayed too long. Not until April 8, 1940, did they finally decide to mine Norwegian waters, an operation that was to be backed up by landing forces at major ports on Norway's western coast—Narvik, Trondheim, Bergen, and Stavanger. When an Anglo-French force finally arrived in Norway, however, they found the Germans already in control of the country's major Atlantic ports.

The British scored some minor victories, including expelling the Germans from Narvik, but the successful German offensive in the West, launched on May 10, 1940, put at end to any Allied hope of driving them from Norway. On June 7 the last Allied forces were withdrawn from Norway. That same day the king and his government left the country to set up a government in exile in Britain.

In their Scandinavian campaign, the Germans had suffered serious naval losses which they could ill afford. But they had safeguarded their northern flank and access to Swedish iron ore, and they had acquired an extensive line of strategic bases for carrying on naval warfare against Britain.

❑ *The Churchill Succession*

Dejected by the failure of his policies and British military defeats, Neville Chamberlain resigned as British prime minister on May 10, 1940, the day the Germans launched their campaign in the West. He was succeeded by Winston Churchill at the head of a Conservative-Labour coalition cabinet. Churchill, for so long a time a voice crying in the wilderness, was to provide the determined and inspirational leadership his country had so conspicuously lacked during the interwar years. (For a brief biography of Churchill, see p. 263–264).

❑ *The German Campaign in the West*

The German campaign plan as finally revised called for a major feint westward through the Netherlands and northern Belgium, while the main attack was to be conducted through the wooded and hilly Ardennes region of southeastern Belgium.

The northern feint achieved just what the Germans had hoped. It drew major Allied forces into Belgium to meet the German offensive and diverted their attention from the German thrust through the Ardennes. But the northern campaign itself was dramatically successful. Within four days the Dutch army capitulated. Parachute troops landing on top of the key Belgian fortress of Eben Emael enabled the Germans to break through the Belgian defensive lines and compelled the Allied forces to retreat to the channel coast.

The main German attack was equally successful. German tanks pushed through the Ardennes, outflanked the Maginot Line, and within three days reached the Meuse River, which they successfully crossed. Now in open country, ideal for tank warfare, they raced down the valley of the Somme and by May 21 reached the Channel. The Allied forces that had advanced to meet the Germans in the north were now surrounded. The Germans could hardly believe their luck. The high command, nervous about the advance of their tanks so far ahead of infantry support, had repeatedly tried to slow down the offensive of their mechanized units. Finally on May 24 Hitler himself gave the order to halt. Unaware of the extent of Allied demoralization, he feared an attack by the large French forces in the south on the weakly held German positions and he hesitated to risk a further advance of his tanks through the canal and river network of the Low Countries.

The halt of the German offensive enabled the Allies to carry out what came to be called the Miracle of Dunkirk: the evacuation of some 200,000 British and 140,000 French troops from the beaches of France to safety in England, though with the loss of the greater part of their equipment.

In retrospect, Hitler's order to hold up his armored divisions has been seen as a major error that allowed the escape of Allied troops, who were to return to France four years later. According to one theory, Hitler deliberately spared the British to make them more amenable to future German peace overtures. A second theory holds that he yielded to the arguments of Hermann Göring, the commander of the German air force, to allow his Luftwaffe to complete the destruction of the trapped Allied troops and therewith enable his Nazi henchman to share in the prestige won by commanders of the regular army.

Both theories are contradicted by existing evidence. Hitler had no intention of sparing the British, for on May 24 he ordered the total destruction of the trapped Allied forces, whose evacuation was to be prevented by the Luftwaffe. Hitler may have been influenced by Göring's arguments, but his senior army officers agreed that the mechanized forces should not be put at risk in the treacherous terrain of Flanders—a viewpoint later hotly contested by German tank commanders, who maintain that the terrain would have been no problem. The operations of the Luftwaffe, however, were hindered by bad weather, their bombs lost much of their impact falling into the soft sand of the French beaches, and Allied aircraft were able to provide temporary cover for the evacuation.

The Belgian army, surrounded and threatened with annihilation, surrendered on May 28. The last evacuations from Dunkirk took place on June 4. The Germans were now free to move against the French forces in the south. At this point they received unexpected—and unwelcome—aid from Mussolini. Confident that the war would soon be over and eager to share in the spoils of victory, the Italian dictator declared war on France and Britain on June 10. On June 16 a new French government was formed under Marshal Henri-Philippe Pétain, the aged hero of World War I, who on the following day asked the Germans for an armistice. That armistice was signed on June 22 in the same railway car in the forest of Compiègne where the German had signed the armistice of November 11, 1918, ending World War I.

The armistice of June 22 divided France into two parts, an occupied and an unoccupied zone. The occupied zone, about three-fifths of the country, covered the northern half of France, including Paris and the entire Channel coast. According to the terms of the armistice, the French government was to be allowed to return to Paris with its authority extended over both the occupied and unoccupied zones. But from the beginning the Germans established their own authority over a large part of the occupied zone and blocked every attempt on the part of the French government to return of Paris. In June 30 that government had moved to the spa of Vichy, where it was to remain until 1944. On July 9 Pétain, still the head of the French government, was given dictatorial powers by the French legislature to enable him to act quickly and authoritatively in this period of national emergency.

Pétain blamed the French defeat on the moral decadence fostered by the Third Republic and called for a French national revival. The slogans of Work, Family, and Fatherland replaced Liberty, Equality, and Fraternity; the Roman Catholic Church was restored to a prominent place in French national life; and the emphasis in education was to be on moral principles instead of mere information.

Scorning the pretensions of the Vichy regime, which they regarded as a Nazi puppet, patriotic French who were in a position to leave the country joined the Free French movement led by General Charles de Gaulle.

❑ *Hitler's Confrontation with Britain*

After the fall of France, there is every indication that Hitler expected even the dogged British would at last be prepared to concede Germany supremacy on the continent, provided they could do so without losing their own position as a world power. Hitler was willing, even eager, to accord them this status. He regarded the British as Nordic cousins and saw in the British empire a cornerstone of Western civilization, a monument to the state-building capacity of the Anglo-Saxon race. In his fundamental considerations on foreign policy, he had consistently advocated a German alliance with Britain, and there can be no doubt of the sincerity of his expressions of regret about his inability to make one. In November 1939 he told a Nazi associate that he still believed in the desirability of an alliance with Britain, especially from a long-term point of view. For his part, he had done eveything possible to achieve it, but a Jewish-dominated minority in Britain had frustrated his efforts. The British would only see the light after they had been taught a terrible lesson.

By June 1940 Hitler believed the British had been taught such a lesson. Their armies had been driven from the continent, all chances for victory over Germany seemed irretrievably lost. Now if ever the British might be expected to see reason, to reverse the disastrous decision of September 1939 and enter into partnership with Germany. On June 2, 1940, Hitler told his generals that if Britain was now prepared to make a sensible peace, as he expected, his hands would at last be free for his greatest and real task, the destruction of Bolshevism.

On June 13 Hitler used the dramatic moment of the entry of his troops into Paris to make the first of several statements about his desire for peace and friendship with Britain, and he was much disturbed by the absence of any positive response to his various overtures. At the end of June he expressed the fear that the British might need another demonstration of German military might before they gave in "and freed our backs for the East." But he was most reluctant to deal Britain such a blow. "If we crush England by force of arms," he told his generals, "the British empire will fall to pieces. But this would be of no advantage to Germany. We would spill German blood only in order that Japan, America, and others might benefit."

On July 19 Hitler made a formal public appeal to the British in a speech before the German Reichstag, but on July 22 the British foreign secretary, Lord Halifax, publicly rejected his peace bid, which he declared was based on no arguments except fear and threats. Hitler was infuriated and issued orders that no further attempt be made to build bridges to Britain. "If the English want their own destruction, they can have it."

Already on June 16, however, three days before his Reichstag speech appealing to the British to see reason, Hitler had issued his first detailed directive to prepare for a landing in Britain. He wanted preparations to be pushed as rapidly as possible so as not to lose his military momentum, but he still hoped that the British might come to terms. He believed that the primary reason for their refusal to make peace was their expectation that Russia and the United States would intervene on their side. Even now Stalin was encouraging the British to continue the war, for Moscow had no interest in seeing Germany grow too powerful. As yet Hitler saw no sign of overt anti-German activity on the part of the Soviet Union, but in late July he nevertheless instructed his military leaders to prepare plans for the destruction of Russia and therewith eliminate Britain's last hope for support on the continent.

Hitler's instructions to prepare for an attack on the Soviet Union at this early date, seen against the background of his ideological program and the fact that he attacked the Soviet Union instead of Britain, have given rise to a theory, supported by the post-war testimony of a number of German leaders, that Hitler was never serious about the invasion of Britain and that all his invasion preparations were mere camouflage for his Russian campaign. This theory is certainly false insofar as it applies to Hitler's policy in the summer of 1940, for there can be no doubt about the seriousness of his invasion plans from July to September of that year.

On July 31 Hitler set September 15 as the target date for the invasion. Everything depended on the success of the Luftwaffe in destroying British air and naval power, for without complete mastery of the air over the invasion route the operation could not be considered. From early August to late September the British and German air forces waged what has come to be known as the Battle of Britain. The Germans made the mistake of not concentrating on the destruction of British air fields, radar installations, and aircraft factories. Instead, they diverted much of their effort to bombing British cities in the mistaken belief—shared by all the belligerents—that bombing could cow the enemy into submission.

But it is doubtful whether the Germans could have gained mastery of the air no matter what strategy they had employed. The British fighter planes proved superior to those of the Germans, and by this time Britain's production of fighter aircraft had also surpassed that of Germany. Thus the British were able to replace their losses more quickly than the Germans, whose losses were in any case approximately one-third higher. Especially telling in this connection was the ratio in losses of trained pilots.

The British had two further important, and perhaps decisive, advantages. They had been quicker than the Germans to recognize the importance of radar (the detection of distant objects through radio waves) for use in early warning systems against air attacks. By the spring of 1939 they had built a chain of fifty-one radar stations along their eastern and southern coasts that were later supplemented by a second chain to detect low-flying aircraft. Radar was subsequently installed on aircraft for battles against enemy aircraft and to locate targets through clouds and darkness for bombing operations, and an underwater detection device, sonar, was installed on ships for defense against submarines.

A second major technical achievement was the British success in breaking the German code machine, Enigma, used by all branches of the German armed forces, military intelligence, the SS and police, merchant vessels, and the railways—an achievement even more remarkable than that of the Americans in breaking the Japanese code and one of the most fascinating stories in the history of international intelligence operations. The British code-breaking operation, Ultra, succeeded in penetrating the principal Enigma code used by the Luftwaffe in the spring of 1940, and from that time to the end of the war that code was broken daily. Ultra provided conclusive evidence about Hitler's decision to postpone the invasion of Britain, thereby allowing the British to send reinforcement to their forces in Africa. It would later play a significant role in enabling the Allies to intercept ships bearing supplies to Axis forces in Africa, and in the end it proved a decisive instrument in enabling the Allies to eliminate the German U-Boat menace.

As Hitler's invasion deadline of September 15 drew nearer, it was obvious that the Luftwaffe had achieved none of its essential objectives. It had not gained mastery of the air, much less broken Britain's will to resist. On October 12, after repeated delays, Hitler ordered the postponement of the invasion of Britain until the following spring. He was convinced by now that, barring major blunders on his part, the military situation in Europe could no longer develop unfavorably for Germany, and an invasion of Britain, with the inadequate means at his disposal and the Soviet menace at his back, was precisely the kind of blunder he was determined to avoid. By December he had come to the conclusion that before proceeding with military undertakings involving any serious risk, he must knock out the Soviet Union.

The directive to make detailed preparations for a campaign against the Soviet Union was issued on December 18, a decision Hitler made without misgivings because he was convinced that the Soviets could be defeated quickly and easily. He had nothing but contempt for the Red Army and its leadership, an opinion that seemed fully borne out by their miserable showing in the war against Finland. The Soviet army, he believed, could be destroyed with a few decisive blows, and the Bolshevik state itself would collapse the moment the first German troops marched into Russia.

In resolving to shift the focus of his military endeavor from west to east, Hitler may also have been influenced by a continuing desire to avoid what he regarded as a racial civil war with Britain. One top-ranking member of the Nazi hierarchy at least seemed to have believed that this was Hitler's intention. Shortly before the German invasion of Russia, Rudolf Hess, the Führer's deputy and head of the Nazi party organization, flew to Britain in an effort to convince influential persons in that country to come to terms with Germany. There is no evidence that Hitler had anything to do with the Hess mission, and his anger about this futile gesture and dangerous blow to German prestige was almost certainly genuine.

Hitler himself seems to have abandoned all expectation of successful negotiation with Britain while the British still had reason to hope for support from the United States or the Soviet Union. In a letter to Mussolini on the eve of the Russian invasion, he explained that he lacked the means to eliminate the United States, but he could eliminate Russia. If, after the defeat of Russia, Britain still failed to bow to the realities of the military-political situation, then, with security at his back and the resources of the entire continent at his disposal, he could consecrate himself to the task of removing this last and most persistent opponent of Germany's continental supremacy.

It was only after December 1940 that German preparations for an invasion of Britain became primarily a camouflage for the preparations being made against the Soviet Union; these in turn were now to be represented as camouflage for the invasion of Britain.

❑ *The Mussolini Intervention*

Well before abandoning his plans to invade Britain in favor of a campaign against the Soviet Union, Hitler found himself obliged to deal with the problems arising from the defeats of his Italian allies in the Balkans and North Africa.

On June 10, 1940, convinced that Germany had won the war, Mussolini had declared war on Britain and France to share in the spoils of victory. The Italian army made a poor showing in France, but Mussolini was saved from embarrassment in this sector by France's surrender on June 22. Jealous of the triumphs of his German counterpart, he now sought some laurels of his own. In August 1940 his armies overran British Somaliland, in September they invaded Egypt, and in October, following the Greek government's rejection of an Italian demand for Greek bases, the Italians invaded Greece from their satellite state of Albania. The Italian attack was launched at an unfavorable season, without adequate manpower and equipment, and by December their invasion of Greece had been transformed into a Greek invasion of Albania. Meanwhile the Italians were also suffering serious reverses in Africa, where the British had launched offensives in Libya, Ethiopia, Italian Somaliland, and Eritrea, and where the Italians were being defeated on every front. The Italian defeats dealt a damaging blow to the prestige of the Axis. Worse, the British, despite the precarious position of their home islands, had sent expeditionary forces to Greece as well as North Africa and were now in a position to launch air and naval strikes from bases in these territories against southern Europe and the Romanian oil fields, which were crucial to the German war economy. This accumulation of dangers convinced Hitler of the need to secure his southern flank before moving against Russia. The simplest and most obvious way to do so was to seize Gibraltar, which controlled the entrance to the Mediterranean, thereby making it impossible, or at least far more difficult, for the British to deploy their sea power in the Mediterranean or make use of their Mediterranean or North African bases.

❑ *The Spanish Card*

The key to the success of any such endeavor was Spain, for owing to his own lack of sea power Hitler could only move against Gibraltar by land and Spain was the only overland route available. Until the Italian debacle in Greece Hitler had questioned the desirability of bringing weak and impoverished Spain into the war, but he now made every effort to enlist Spain's active participation so as to acquire the necessary bases for the conquest of Gibraltar. At the time of the collapse of France and with the defeat of Britain seemingly imminent, Franco had been lavish with offers to cooperate with Germany in return for a share of the spoils of the French and British empires. But Britain's stubborn resistance and Italy's defeats had cooled his ardor, and he met Hitler's demands for Spain's entry into the war with demands of his own. For the defense of Spain, he would require massive supplies of military equipment, fuel, and grain, which, as Franco well knew, Germany could ill afford. Further, he insisted that Spanish troops alone should carry out the conquest of Gibraltar, since Spanish honor would not admit the conquest of Spanish territory by foreigners. Franco's demand for specific assurances regarding the Spanish share of the French and British empires was also awkward. For, while seeking Spain's participation in the war, Hitler was also seeking the participation of Vichy France, and for this purpose his most telling inducement was a guarantee of the French colonial empire plus a French share of the British spoils.

Franco bargained and procrastinated with stubborn tenacity. His resistance to German pressure may well have been encouraged by Admiral Wilhelm Canaris, the head of Germany's counterintelligence service and a principal German emissary to Franco. Canaris detested the Nazis (he was to be executed following the failure of the July 1944 plot to overthrow Hitler), and there is considerable evidence to suggest that he kept Franco informed about Hitler's true intentions. Whether or not influenced by Canaris, Franco persisted in his resistance to German pressure.

By late February 1941 Joachim von Ribbentrop, Hitler's foreign minister, concluded that the Spanish leader had not the least intention of entering the war, because even if Germany met his demands he was posing conditions that would enable him to postpone that entry indefinitely. Hitler reluctantly agreed, but decided against resorting to military action. He has numerous reasons for staying his hand in Spain. He was now faced with the alternative of leaving Spain under the leadership of a benevolent neutral or conquering a hostile nation, a situation that recalled Napoleon's efforts to conquer Spain that had inaugurated the downfall of the French dictator. Even if Franco finally yielded to the threat of a German invasion and entered the war on the side of the Axis, the abandonment of Spanish neutrality would open the way to a British invasion that might require Germany to give Spain substantial military as well as economic support. Spain would thus become, like Italy, a serious military and economic burden.

By mid-February Hitler decided to cancel his timetable for an attack on Gibraltar. Preparations for the capture of the rock were to continue, however, so that an attack could be carried out immediately after the successful conclusion of the Russian campaign.

❑ *The North African Strategy*

The refusal of Franco to enter the war and Hitler's consequent abandonment of plans to attack Gibraltar forced the Germans to consider a more costly and less certain method of combatting British influence in the Mediterranean, namely, to support

Italian military operations in North Africa. By January 11, 1941, with the Italians in full retreat in both the Balkans and North Africa, Hitler decided that for strategic, political, and psychological reasons, Italy would have to be supported in both sectors. Ten days later he arranged with Mussolini to send German troops to Tripoli as soon as possible, but by this time the Italian retreat in North Africa had turned into a rout. The British captured Tobruk on January 22, Derna on January 24, and Bengasi, the capital of Cyrenaica, on February 7. In a campaign of just over two months, the British had captured 114,000 Italian prisoners at the cost of 3,000 casualties of their own.

By now Hitler realized that only large-scale German intervention could save the Italians and wrest control of North Africa from the British. For this purpose he decided to send armored units to North Africa to destroy the British in a battle of movement. These troops were to be under the command of General Erwin Rommel, "the most daring general of armored forces in the German army." The objective of the German Africa Corps, as it came to be called, would be to close off the Mediterranean to the British through the conquest of Morocco and Gibraltar in the west and Egypt and Suez in the east.

On February 11 the first of several contingents of German troops arrived in Tripoli, and by the end of March Rommel felt strong enough to mount a counterattack against the British in Libya. By late May Axis forces had reached the Egyptian frontier, but Rommel never received the manpower or equipment necessary to sustain the Axis offensive. Britain's control of the sea lanes in the Mediterranean proved a formidable obstacle to reinforcing and supplying the Axis troops in Africa (having broken the German code, the British had precise information about Axis shipping), and the bulk of Germany's military power was soon to be employed in campaigns in the Balkans and Russia. Rommel launched a second offensive against Egypt in May 1942, but early in July he was halted at El Alamein, sixty miles west of Alexandria. On October 23, the British launched a major offensive of their own at El Alamein, and on November 8 an Anglo-American army landed in French North Africa. The Axis forces were now surrounded, and doomed. By May of the following year all Axis resistance in North Africa came to an end.

❑ *The Balkan Dilemma*

Hitler's Spanish and North African policies had been designed to close the Mediterranean to the British and secure his southern flank. Meanwhile, a more immediate and serious threat had developed in the Balkans, where Germany had vital economic as well as strategic interests. The Balkans provided Germany with critical supplies of bauxite, antimony, lead, copper, raw textiles, livestock, and cereal. The fundamental consideration here, however, was Romanian oil, which constituted roughly one-third to one-half of Germany's total oil supply and was therefore crucial to the German war economy.

On June 27, 1940, the Soviets had demanded Romania's cession of Bessarabia, conceded to them by the Germans in their August 23 partition treaty of the previous year, as well as Northern Bukovina, which the Germans had not conceded. The annexation of these territories brought the Soviet Union perilously close to the Romanian oil fields. On September 20, to provide greater security for German interests in this area, Hitler ordered the dispatch of a German military mission to Romania, ostensibly to back up a German guarantee of what was left of Romanian territory. Its real tasks, however, were to protect the oil fields and prepare for an invasion of the Soviet Union from Romania. Early in October 1940 German military units began arriving in Romania in force.

The German move into Romania was to have unexpected and dangerous consequences, for it provoked Mussolini into launching his disastrous campaign against Greece. (See p. 224.) As usual he had not been informed of Hitler's intentions, and he was enraged by this further extension of German influence. "Hitler always presents me with a *fait accompli.* This time I am going to pay him back in his own coin. He will find out from the papers that I have occupied Greece. In this way the equilibrium will be reestablished." On October 28, 1940, he issued his ultimatum to Greece demanding strategic bases on Greek soil. The Greeks, however, backed up by a British guarantee, rejected the Italian demands, and Mussolini was obliged to expose his hopelessly inadequate military hand. Instead of occupying Greece, his troops were driven back into Albania, and the British rather than the Italians now established strategic bases in Greece.

Hitler, with unusual restraint, described the Italian action as a "regrettable blunder" that seriously disrupted his diplomatic efforts to bring the Balkan states in line preparatory to his attack on Russia. In some dismay he pointed out to Mussolini that British aircraft based in Greece now posed a direct threat to southern Italy; worse still, they were now only 500 kilometers from the Romanian oil fields. "One things is certain, Duce, there is no effective protection for the oil fields." The fire of antiaircraft guns was as great a danger as assailing aircraft. "From the military standpoint this situation is threatening. From the economic standpoint, so far as the Romanian oil fields are concerned, it is positively terrifying."

By December Hitler concluded that German intervention was required to bring the Greek situation under control. He planned to build up a task force in Romania that was to occupy the Aegean coast by way of Bulgaria as soon as favorable weather set in. He expected the support of Bulgaria against Greece and believed Turkey would remain neutral. The position of Yugoslavia remained to be determined.

❑ *The Attack on Yugoslavia and Greece*

Recognizing that Yugoslavia's fear of Italy was a major obstacle to that country's cooperation with the Axis, Hitler offered to guarantee Yugoslavia's domestic and international position, a guarantee that would protect Yugoslavia from the Italians and undercut Italian support of Yugoslavia's national minorities. As a more concrete inducement, he offered Yugoslavia the Greek harbor of Salonika and therewith an outlet to the Aegean. If Yugoslavia rejected these offers, he could not vouch for the policy of Italy. The Yugoslav government accepted, though on condition that neither Germany nor Italy would demand the passage of troops through Yugoslav territory or any other kind of military assistance. The Yugoslav treaty with the Axis was signed March 25, 1941. With that, Germany's flank for an attack on Greece via Bulgaria, scheduled to be launched on April 1, seemed secured.

Hitler's Yugoslav program was disrupted by Yugoslav army officers. Fearful that their country was about to share the fate of Czechoslovakia or Romania, they carried out a *coup d'état* on the night of March 26–27, overthrowing the regime that had concluded the pact with the Axis and establishing a new government that on April 6 signed a pact with the Soviet Union. Already on March 27, however, Hitler had decided to destroy Yugoslavia "militarily and as a state." The Serb-dominated Yugoslav government would have been an uncertain factor in the campaign against Greece and even more so in the campaign against Russia later on. The blow was to be delivered with unmerciful harshness and lightning speed so as to deter Turkey from intervening. Hitler expected support from Italy, Hungary, and Bulgaria, which were to be promised territorial acquisitions. He also expected support from the Croatians in Yugoslavia, who were to be promised autonomy. The German army was to make every effort to reopen the Danube to navigation as soon as possible and to secure the copper mines at Bor, which were "all-important economically."

At dawn on April 6, 1941, German troops invaded Yugoslavia. Organized resistance lasted only eleven days. The Yugoslav regular forces surrendered unconditionally on April 17. By April 23 Greece, too, was crushed, and the British expeditionary forces were driven from the country. Southeastern Europe was now completely open to German economic exploitation and the southeastern flank secured for the German attack on the Soviet Union.

Following their conquest of Yugoslavia, the Germans and Italians took advantage of the ethnic and religious hatreds that had always simmered under the surface of the Yugoslav union. In Croatia they set up a puppet government under Ante Pavelich, the head of a nationalist terrorist organization known as the Ustashe. Patriotic Serbs joined a guerrilla army known as the Chetniks, led by Draza Mihailovich. In the course of the German-Italian occupation, the Croats and Serbs engaged in a quasi-genocidal civil war, waged with vicious and indiscriminate brutality on both sides.

Calling for war against the German and Italian occupiers instead of war against their fellow Slavs, the Communist leader Josip Broz Tito revived the Yugoslav idea. Tito, himself half-Croatian, recruited a guerrilla army from all segments of the South Slav population under the banner of Communism, making effective use of Communist ideology as a unifying force. It was his appeal to South Slav nationalism, however, which appears to been his most effective weapon in rallying support for his struggle against the foreign invaders.

❑ *The Attack on the Soviet Union*

The German attack on the Soviet Union has been called the greatest blunder of World War II. That Nazi ideology as expounded in *Mein Kampf* called for the conquest of Russia and the destruction of Bolshevism was one thing. But ideology had never fixed a time limit for these accomplishments. Why then did Hitler defy another political principle laid down in *Mein Kampf* and gratuitously plunge his country into a war on two fronts while Britain, backed by the United States, remained a threat in the West?

The explanations from the Nazi point of view are numerous, but they all hinge on the belief that the Soviet Union would never tolerate a definitive German victory in the West. In line with this belief, a question formed itself automatically for Nazi leaders: were the Soviets in a position to prevent or seriously hinder that German victory? The march of events since September 1939 convinced Hitler that they were.

Hitler's primary reason for concluding his nonaggression pact with the Soviet Union had been to avoid a major war on two fronts, but as the price for Soviet neutrality he had been forced to surrender a large part of Eastern Europe to the Soviet sphere of interest. While the Germans were overrunning Poland and Western Europe, the Soviets had proceeded to take over the areas allotted to them. In the autumn of 1939 they had compelled the Baltic states (Estonia, Latvia, and Lithuania) to accept "mutual aid" treaties permitting the establishment of Red Army garrisons in these countries and had subsequently incorporated all three into the Soviet Union. With the successful conclusion of the war against Finland, the Soviets were in control of the entire eastern littoral of the Baltic Sea.

While extending their sphere of influence in the north, the Soviets followed a similar course in the south by bringing heavy diplomatic pressure to bear on Romania, Bulgaria, and Turkey. In late June 1940 they compelled Romania to cede Bessarabia and Northern Bukovina, which gave them control of the principal overland route into the Balkans and the mouth of the Danube—and brought them to within 160 kilometers of the Romanian oil fields at Ploesti. When Hitler sent troops into Romania to protect the oil fields and back up a German guarantee of what was left of Romanian territory, the Soviets sought a similar status for themselves in Bulgaria while sounding the Germans about the possible annexation of all of Finland.

Even more ominous for Germany than the strategic threat represented by Soviet territorial annexations was the Soviet economic threat. Germany's great weakness was its lack of critical raw materials. The significance of the Soviets in this connection lay in the fact that they either supplied the Germans with the bulk of the raw materials they needed from abroad or covered their routes of access to them. From the north of Finland to the Balkan passes there was not an economic cord in the east which the Red Army could not have severed or seriously endangered. The Soviets controlled access to the Petsamo nickel mines, whose output was essential to German war industries. From Finland, they were in a position to cut off Germany's supplies of Swedish iron ore.

Most serious of all was the threat to German imports from the Balkans, especially Romanian oil. "Now, in the era of air power," Hitler told his generals in January 1941, "Russia can turn the Romanian oil fields into an expanse of smoking debris . . . and the life of the Axis depends on those oil fields." Finally there was the importance of the Soviet Union itself to the German economy, both with respect to its own exports and its transshipment of goods from East Asia. From the Soviet Union, Germany was receiving oil, phosphates, iron ore, scrap iron, chrome ore, platinum, manganese ore, timber, and grain. Across the Soviet Union lay Germany's only routes to East Asia, from which the Soviets had contracted to transport crucial supplies of rubber and tin as well as soy beans.

The importance of the Soviet Union to Germany's war economy makes the attack on that country seem very much like killing the goose that lays the golden eggs, and so in a way it was. From Hitler's point of view, however, there were two critical flaws in his trade agreements with the Soviets: they could cut off deliveries to Germany at any time that suited their political or military purposes, and they demanded prompt payment for them of a kind most inconvenient for a nation at war, namely, in war materials. German difficulties in filling Soviet orders began almost immediately. As German deliveries to the Soviet Union began to lag, Moscow warned that if a balancing of accounts were not achieved soon, a suspension of Soviet deliveries to Germany was to be expected.

As Hitler saw it, the Soviet threat to Germany's vital supply lines and their demand for armaments in exchange for raw materials essential to the German war economy made for an impossible situation. His solution to the problem was characteristically direct. "What one does not have, but needs, one must conquer," he said two days before the attack on the Soviet Union. The conquest of the Soviet Union would eliminate in one blow the threat to Germany's economic lifelines and ensure German access to Soviet natural resources without the need to pay for them. Hitler realized that military action might result in a large-scale destruction of Soviet economic assets, but he was confident that the speed of Germany's conquest would prevent excessive damage and that direct German control would make for vastly greater deliveries of food and raw materials than the Soviet Union had provided.

For the timing of Hitler's Soviet campaign, the decisive factor was the refusal of Britain to surrender in the summer of 1940. His various peace feelers had met with no response, and his "final appeal to common sense" of July 19, 1940, had been rejected. The reason for British recalcitrance, Hitler was convinced, was Russia and their hope for Russian intervention against Germany. "Should Russia be smashed, however, then England's last hope is extinguished." To his naval commanders, who favored carrying on the war against Britain in one form or another, Hitler pointed out that the loss of a German expeditionary force in the Channel or a serious setback elsewhere would be the signal for Russian intervention. Russia's entry into the war while Germany was deeply involved elsewhere would constitute a grave danger. "Therefore every possibility of such a threat must be eliminated beforehand. With the elimination of the Russian menace we can continue the war against England under thoroughly favorable circumstances."

The clinching argument for the attack on the Soviet Union was Hitler's certainty that the Soviets could be defeated quickly and completely. The Red Army, he believed, could be destroyed with a few decisive blows, and the Bolshevik state itself would collapse the moment the first German troops marched into Russia. Hitler's ignorance about the real strength of the Soviet Union was shared to a remarkable degree by military experts in other countries and by his own generals. German intelligence reports concluded that the Red Army was no match for an army with modern equipment and superior leadership and that Soviet tanks could not stand up to the demands of a war of movement. The commander-in-chief of the German army estimated that there would be up to four weeks of heavy fighting, after which the war would be little more than a mopping-up operation. Before the invasion of the Soviet Union had even begun, German generals were busy with plans for new campaigns and had set up a timetable for the conversion of the war economy to the production of the warships and planes that would be needed to defeat Britain.

By the end of 1940, with the end of all prospects of peace or a military victory over Britain, Hitler appears to have made the final and definite decision to attack the Soviet Union. On January 2, 1941, he summed up his arguments for the attack in a speech to his generals, concluding with the confident prediction that the conquest of Russia would make Germany impregnable.

Hitler left his military commanders in no doubt about the type of war he intended to wage against the Soviet Union. The forthcoming campaign would be no ordinary conflict, he told them in March 1941, but a life-and-death struggle between two races and two ideologies, between German and Slav, between National Socialism and the criminal code of Jewish Bolshevism, which constituted the greatest threat to the future of civilization. In this struggle the German soldier was not to be bound by the laws of war, nor was there any room for chivalry or out-of-date concepts about comradeship between soldiers. The military power of Russia was to be broken for all time, the entire Bolshevik-Jewish intelligentsia and all Communist political leaders were to be wiped out. For this was to be a fight to the finish, a war of extermination, which would have to be waged with unprecedented, unmerciful, unrelenting harshness.

Hitler, however, had no confidence that his generals fully appreciated the necessity for such ruthlessness, and to make certain that problems of security and ideology were handled with appropriate severity he ordered that the SS and other selected forces accompany the troops of the regular army into the Soviet Union to carry out "special tasks" assigned them by the Führer. Further, as soon as the military situation would allow, the army was to surrender jurisdiction over occupied areas to a civilian (Nazi) administration, to which a senior SS officer and his staff would be attached to complete the work of pacification and ideological purification.

Hitler's diplomatic preparations for the war against the Soviet Union were almost entirely devoted to improving Germany's strategic position in Eastern Europe and safeguarding its access to vital raw materials. Special attention was devoted to Finland and Romania because of their obvious strategic importance on the northern and southern flanks of the invasion, and because the nickel of Finland and the oil of Romania were essential to the German war economy. The neutrality of Turkey was assured, at least temporarily, by a German-Turkish friendship treaty of June 18, 1941, supplemented by a statement calling for closer economic relations that enabled the Germans to step up their purchases of Turkish chrome, another article in short supply in the German war economy. In addition, the Turks promised to cooperate with the Germans in preventing the passage of Soviet ships through the Straits.

So confident were the Germans of victory that they neither sought nor desired the aid of Japan, whose participation in the war against the Soviet Union might have given Hitler the quick victory he expected. Instead, German diplomacy sought to persuade the Japanese to pursue a more active policy in East Asia in order to tie down British forces and focus American attention on the Pacific. The Japanese were given no hint of the forthcoming Russian operation, though they learned about it through their own intelligence services before the German invasion began.

The German attack on the Soviet Union began at dawn on June 22, 1941. By the autumn of that year German forces had pushed to the gates of Leningrad in the north; in the central sector they had overrun the Ukraine, advanced into the valley of the Don, and laid siege to Moscow; and they had entered the Crimea on the southern end of this gigantic front. But an early winter and tenacious Soviet resistance halted the German offensive. On December 1 the Soviets recaptured Rostov near the mouth of the Don, in the following week they relieved the pressure on Moscow, and on December 16 they recaptured the strategic communications center of Kalinin on the Moscow-Leningrad line.

With German forces in Eastern Europe reeling under the impact of Soviet counterattacks and the entire German front in the Soviet Union in danger of cracking, the continued presence of Britain in the field on Germany's western flank could no longer be ignored until final victory over the Soviet Union was achieved. Already British bombing attacks on German cities and British victories in Africa were having a detrimental effect on German morale. Far more serious than the menace of Britain itself, however, was the fact that behind Britain loomed the immense potential power of the United States, whose government was pursuing policies that indicated a determination to support or actually join Britain in the conflict with Nazi Germany.

It was primarily as a counterweight to Britain and the United States that Japan now assumed a prominent role in Hitler's calculations.

❑

SEVENTEEN

World War II in Asia: From the China Quagmire to Pearl Harbor

If the Japanese had confined their attention to resolving the conflict with China, they might have continued to escape foreign entanglements, worn down the resistance of Chiang Kai-shek, and made their puppet governments in China, like that of Manchukuo, effective instruments of Japanese control. Instead, while still bogged down in China, they plunged into war against Britain and the United States that was to bring devastation and defeat to the island empire and result in Japan's total expulsion from the Asian mainland. How can Japanese policy that led to such a fateful turnabout be explained?

Any attempt to answer this question must begin by recalling that Japan had only recently entered the ranks of the great powers, that it was the only non-European state (in terms of ethnicity) to have attained this status, and that it had demonstrated its great power credentials in 1905 by defeating in war one of the greatest of the European powers, Russia. The Japanese people felt intense pride in these achievements and a correspondingly intense bitterness that Europeans nevertheless persisted in regarding them as racially inferior. They saw that attitude clearly expressed by the rejection of their request for a racial equality clause in the Treaty of Versailles, by the American immigration bill of 1924, and by the inferior capital ship ratio imposed on them at the Washington Conference.

All national leaders have fears for the security and welfare of their country. Among Japanese leaders such fears were accentuated by these perceptions of racism; by the size and resources of their most dangerous rivals, Russia and the United States; and by their awareness of their own dependence on foreign trade, a dependence only partially relieved by the resources of Manchukuo and the Chinese areas under Japanese control. It was largely to improve their country's strategic position and to gain greater economic independence that the Japanese had embarked on their imperialist ventures on the Asian mainland. These same concerns remained predominant in their subsequent formulations of Japanese policy.

As emphasized earlier, there were broad differences of opinion among Japanese leaders as to what that policy should be. Successive governments attempted to reconcile and respond to the conflicting demands of military and naval departments, business interests, and civilian and military pressure groups, all of which threatened to lead to a dangerous overextension of Japanese resources and capabilities. The emperor drew attention to that danger with a query addressed to his ministers and the leaders of his armed forces at a Liaison Conference of February 1938. "Is it possible," he asked, "to put into effect a plan which calls simultaneously for long-term hostilities [in China], military preparations against Russia, and the expansion of the navy?" This question was never answered, and the emperor did nothing to halt these programs.

❑ *The Soviet Threat, Germany's Betrayal, and American Economic Pressure*

Japanese concern about the Russian threat had grown steadily over the past decade as the Soviet Union engaged in a massive military and industrial buildup. This concern was powerfully reinforced in summer of 1938 when Japanese and Soviet troops clashed over a frontier dispute at the junction of the borders of Korea, Manchuria, and Siberia. Japanese militants now called for a major military campaign against the Soviet Union so as to eliminate the Russian threat once and for all. Their voices were muted, however, when Japan's proud Kwantung army was decisively defeated in August 1939 at Nomonhan, on the borders of Manchukuo and Outer Mongolia, by the mechanized forces of the Red Army and forced to retire from the disputed frontier districts after suffering heavy losses. From this experience the Japanese learned that Russia had once again become a formidable foe and that its defeat would be a far more difficult undertaking than they had anticipated. This demonstration of Russian military power was a lesson lost on the governments of Western Europe, most especially on Hitler.

After the Japanese–Soviet border clashes, the Japanese explored the possibility of an alliance with Nazi Germany, which had consistently trumpeted its hostility to international Communism and the Soviet Union. Relations with Germany were clouded by Japan's refusal to grant German economic interests preferential treatment on the Asian mainland in return for Germany's withdrawal of its military mission to China and its recognition of Japan's puppet government of Manchukuo. Joachim von Ribbentrop, the Nazi foreign minister, was nevertheless receptive to Japanese overtures, but instead of a pact directed exclusively against the Soviet Union, as the Japanese desired, he proposed its extension to Britain and France, his idea being that the Japanese threat to their Asian interests would deter Anglo-French intervention against Germany in Europe. The German-Japanese alliance negotiations never got anywhere. At this time the Japanese were still wary of a partnership that might involve them in war with the Western powers, and they feared that a Japanese alliance with Nazi Germany might be countered by an American economic embargo.

By the spring of 1939 Hitler evidently decided that all efforts to entice Japan into the kind of military alliance desired by Germany were futile. While continuing to negotiate with Japan, he entered into negotiations with the Soviet Union, and on August 23, 1939, concluded the notorious Hitler-Stalin pact, which he hoped would put an end to any intention Britain and France might have had to honor their treaty commitments to Poland.

The Nazi-Soviet pact, concluded without consulting Japan and a clear-cut violation of the Anti-Comintern agreement (see p. 135), produced shock and consternation in Tokyo, where the pact was seen as an infamous betrayal that left Japan alone to bear the brunt of Soviet hostility. News of the pact brought down the government of Hiranuma Kiichiro. He was replaced as prime minister by the pro-Western General Abe Nobuyuki, who abandoned all negotiations with Germany and sought closer diplomatic ties with Britain and the United States.

The great and, as it proved, insuperable obstacle to better relations with the Western powers was China. The United States persisted in its refusal to recognize Japan's puppet state of Manchukuo or otherwise acknowledge Japan's special interests in China. Further, in July 1939 the United States announced that it would not renew its commercial treaty with Japan that was due to expire on January 26, 1940, but would only continue commercial relations on a day-to-day basis. The threat of an American economic embargo was serious indeed, for the United States purchased roughly 30 percent of Japan's exports and supplied almost 35 percent of its imports. Three-quarters of these imports were raw materials and equipment essential to the Japanese war economy—petroleum, iron and steel, copper, aircraft, automobiles, and machines, together with their parts and accessories.

Had the United States employed this economic weapon in the wake of the Marco Polo Bridge incident, the Japanese might have been successfully pressured into a speedy settlement of their dispute with China. But now, after the investment of so much blood, treasure, and prestige in China and Manchukuo, no Japanese government could have agreed to the abandonment of Japan's dominant political and economic position in these areas. The Japanese thus felt constrained to adopt policies that would enable them to counter the threat of American economic pressure.

❑ *The Correlation of Events in Europe and Asia*

The course of the war in Europe was now to have a decisive impact on Japanese policy. In September 1939 Germany had attacked Poland, thereby setting off World War II in Europe. In the spring and summer of 1940 the Nazi armies overran the Netherlands and defeated France, thereby leaving the Dutch and French colonies in East Asia isolated and without hope of support from their home governments. This situation opened up opportunities for the Japanese that were to prove irresistible, for the Dutch and French colonies possessed many of the raw materials essential to their war economy that were now supplied by the United States. French Indochina produced rubber and rice; the Netherlands East Indies, bauxite, tin, nickel, rubber, and, above all, oil. With the anticipated defeat of Britain by Germany and disintegration of the British empire, the Japanese planned to extend their control over British Burma and Malaya, India, Australia, and New Zealand. A principal objective of this entire expansionist program was the creation of a self-sufficient economic zone that would free Japan from economic dependence on foreign powers.

Following Germany's spectacular military victories in Europe, the Japanese hastened to resume negotiations with Berlin to secure their share of the spoils. In May and June 1940, directly after the Nazi conquest of the Netherlands and France, the Japanese, stressing their considerable service to Germany in tying down the American fleet in the Pacific, asked the German government for an expression of "disinterestedness" in the Netherlands East Indies and recognition of Japan's special interests in French Indochina. Such claims were not at all welcome to Hitler, who hoped to use these territories as bargaining chips in securing the cooperation of the defeated European states in his war against Britain and who was in any case reluctant to give up European colonial possessions.

What Hitler wanted above all at this time was a peace treaty with Britain that would make further military action against this racially kindred nation unnecessary, and a prime bargaining chip for this purpose was a promise to guarantee the preservation of the British empire. Japan's pretensions only reinforced his reluctance to move against Britain and thereby contribute to the destruction of the British empire, for, as he told his generals in July 1940, "we would spill German blood only in order that Japan, America, and others might benefit."

The Germans, however, were in no position to contest Japanese claims in East Asia, and on June 24, 1940, they provided the assurances of disinterestedness the Japanese had requested. Just one day later the Japanese pressured France's Vichy government (established in unoccupied France after the defeat by Germany, with nominal authority over France's overseas empire) into an agreement allowing Japan to occupy the northern part of French Indochina, which provided not only economic but strategic advantages. With this area under their control they could cut off major supply routes to Chiang Kai-shek, pressure Thailand into permitting the passage of Japanese troops toward the great British naval base at Singapore, and acquire better bases for the takeover of the most important prize of all, the oil of the Netherlands East Indies.

❑ *The Adoption of a Southern Strategy*

In response to the Japanese threat to French Indochina, the United States at last began to carry out its threat of an economic embargo by forbidding the sale of high-grade scrap iron and aviation fuel to Japan. American economic pressure only made the Japanese more desperate, and in early July 1940, for the first time since the beginning of the China Incident, Japanese military and naval leaders reached agreement about the future course of Japanese policy: the interests of the empire could be enhanced most effectively through the adoption of a southern strategy, which meant gaining control of the resources of Southeast Asia that would free them from their economic dependence on the United States. When Prime Minister Yonai Mitsumasa expressed disagreement with an exclusive commitment to this policy, he found himself obliged to resign.

He was succeeded on July 17, 1940, by Prince Konoe Fumimaro, who now formed his second ministry, which included General Tojo Hideki, the former chief of staff of the Kwantung army, as minister of war, and Matsuoka Yosuke, who had led the Japanese delegation out of the League of Nations during the Manchurian crisis, as foreign minister. Tojo was something of a compromise candidate. Never particularly distinguished as a military commander or strategist, he was known chiefly as an able administrator, though so obsessed with petty detail that he had acquired the nickname of Private Tojo. Matsuoka, who had gone to the United States at the age of thirteen and earned a bachelor of law degree at the University of Oregon, had been a career officer in the Japanese diplomatic service for seventeen years and more recently had been president of the South Manchurian Railway Company. At the time of his appointment he was a leading advocate of Japan's southern strategy and is credited with having coined the term Greater East Asia Co-Prosperity Sphere to describe the political and economic organization of this region under Japanese auspices.

By the time the Konoe cabinet was formed Japanese political and military leaders had already made the critical decision to pursue the southern strategy. The immediate goal of this policy—the takeover of the French and Dutch colonies—was to be attained "if at all possible" by peaceful means. A peaceful takeover seemed especially necessary for securing the oil of the Netherlands East Indies, because the use of force might impel the Dutch to destroy their oil wells before they could be captured and might well provoke American intervention.

Before the implementation of the southern strategy, every effort was to be made to resolve the China Incident by renewed negotiation with Chiang Kai-shek and by cutting off all avenues of foreign aid to both Chiang and the Chinese Communists, in particular the Burma Road and the routes from French Indochina, Thailand, and the Soviet Union. In the realm of diplomacy, Japan would seek a neutrality pact with the Soviet Union that would free Japan from the danger of a Soviet attack while engaged in operations in the south. Such a pact might also prove useful in settling the China Incident, for it would deprive the Chinese of all hope of Soviet intervention on their behalf and might even persuade Moscow to cut off Soviet supply routes to China. Finally, Japan would seek a military alliance with Germany and Italy whose chief purpose would be the intimidation of the United States. The calculation here was that the materialistic Americans, faced with so formidable a military coalition, would flinch before the risks of intervention and decide that the preservation of neutrality would be both safer and more profitable.

❑ *Towards a German Alliance*

As hopes for a negotiated peace with Britain faded and the danger of American intervention increased, Hitler came to agree with the Japanese that the best way to prevent such intervention would be through a military alliance that would "intimidate the United States into continued neutrality." In September 1940 he authorized the dispatch of a personal representative of his foreign minister, Ribbentrop, to conduct the necessary negotiations. "Germany does not want the present conflict to develop into a world war," Tokyo was told, "and wishes to bring it to an end as quickly as possible. . . . What it wants from Japan is to have Japan play a restraining role and prevent the United States from entering the war at all costs." A clear and unequivocal attitude on the part of Germany and Japan was the only way to prevent American intervention in either Europe or East Asia. At the same time Germany would do everything possible to prevent a German-Japanese alliance from developing into a military confrontation with America.

At an Imperial Conference of September 19, 1940, several Japanese leaders questioned the desirability of a German alliance because they feared it would increase American political and economic pressure. Nor was it certain that Japan could obtain oil from the Netherlands East Indies to compensate for a cutoff of American supplies. In response, Foreign Minister Matsuoka, the leading proponent of a German alliance, stressed that the whole object of the pact was to deter the United States, something that could only be done by a "firm stand on our part at this time." The Americans might adopt a hostile attitude for a while, but he thought they would ultimately take their own interests into account and arrive at a reasonable attitude. In the end, the conference authorized Matsuoka to conclude a military alliance with Germany and Italy, but urged that "every conceivable measure should be taken to avoid war with the United States" and that the southward advance should be carried out "as far as possible by peaceful means."

❑ *The Tripartite Pact and Its International Repercussions*

A Tripartite Pact between Germany, Italy, and Japan was finally signed on September 27, 1940, providing for cooperation among the signatory powers in establishing new orders in Greater East Asia and the "regions of Europe." The American reaction to the Tripartite Pact was a bitter disappointment to its signatories. Instead of being bluffed back into isolationism, the United States took a firmer line than ever in dealing with Japan and the Axis. So uncompromising was the American attitude that the Germans now began to fear that their pact might boomerang, and that Japan rather than the United States might be deterred from further intervention in the war. The great danger for Germany in this situation was that Japan, bogged down in China and at the end of its economic tether, might decide to come to terms with the United States, thereby leaving the Americans free to concentrate the bulk of their power against Germany in Europe. German fears were intensified when in February 1941 Admiral Nomura Kichisaburo, well known as an advocate of better relations with the United States, was sent as Japanese ambassador to Washington. The Germans would have been even more alarmed had they known that Nomura accepted the assignment to Washington only after being assured by both Konoe and Matsuoka that the preservation of peace with the United States took precedence over Japan's commitments to Germany and Italy.

Germany's fear of a possible Japanese-American rapprochement, coupled with Britain's stubborn refusal to come to terms, finally convinced Hitler that he should seek Japan's participation in the war against Britain. Such a move would put added military pressure on the British, but far more importantly, it would put an end to any prospect of an agreement between Japan and the United States. Accordingly, the German ambassador was now instructed to do everything in his power to persuade the

Japanese to attack Singapore. Instead of attacking Singapore, however, the Japanese concluded a neutrality pact with the Soviet Union on April 13, 1941, which freed them from the danger of a Soviet attack from the north. With that, the Japanese had realized a major precondition for the implementation of their southern strategy.

Otherwise Japanese diplomacy was not going well. The various Japanese diplomatic missions to the Netherlands East Indies failed to get the desired commercial guarantees from the Dutch authorities in the islands, a situation that led to increasing frustration in Tokyo and the breaking off of diplomatic relations with the Dutch in mid-June 1941.

Negotiations with the United States were not going well either, although the Japanese seem to have been quite prepared to jettison their pact with Germany and Italy and conclude an agreement with the Americans that would divert their attention from the Pacific and enable them to concentrate their resources against Germany. China, however, remained the great stumbling block to better relations with Washington. Although there were voices in Washington that favored an agreement with Japan in order to get a free hand to deal with Germany, the American secretary of state, Cordell Hull, continued to insist that Japan respect the sovereignty and territorial integrity of all nations and promise not to interfere in their domestic affairs. This was nothing less than a demand for Japan's withdrawal from both Manchuria and China and the abandonment of all Japanese ambitions in Southeast Asia.

❑ *Japan and the German Attack on the Soviet Union*

The entire international situation was dramatically changed with Hitler's attack on the Soviet Union on June 22, 1941. The Japanese government was now confronted with what may well have been one of the most critical policy decisions in modern history: should Japan join the German campaign against the Soviet Union for the purpose of eliminating the Soviet threat once and for all? Or should Japan take advantage of Russia's war with Germany to implement its southern strategy?

The Germans, who up to this time had been urging a Japanese attack on Britain, now urged instead that they join in the war against the Soviet Union. Ribbentrop described in glowing terms the immense advantages for Japan as well as Germany that would result from the destruction of the Soviet Union. With Russia's natural resources and immense oil reserves at its disposal, Germany would be able to move with decisive effect against Britain in the West, thus eliminating at the source what remained of British power in East Asia. Japan, meanwhile, permanently freed from the Soviet menace in the north, would be able to settle the China question at its leisure and then move south when all preparations to guarantee success had been completed. "The need of the hour," Ribbentrop telegraphed the Japanese foreign minister on July 1,

is for the Japanese army to seize Vladivostok as soon as possible and penetrate as deeply toward the west as possible. The goal of these operations should be to have the Japanese army in its march to the west meet the German troops advancing to the east halfway, even before the cold season sets in; then to establish a direct connection between Germany and Japan over Russian territory, both by way of the Trans-Siberian railway and by air; and finally to have the whole Russian question settled by Germany and Japan jointly in such a way as to eliminate for all time the Russian threat to both Germany and Japan.

Ribbentrop argued that the problem of the United States, too, would be solved with the conquest of Russia. "As far as America is concerned, I hope that after Russia has been brought to its knees, the weight of the Tripartite Pact nations . . . will suffice to paralyze any tendency toward intervention in the war that may still arise in the United States."

Once again there were broad differences of opinion among Japanese leaders. Foreign Minister Matsuoka was the principal advocate of joining Germany in the war against the Soviet Union. He was supported by military leaders who had long regarded Russia as the most serious threat to Japanese security and who believed its destruction would also contribute to the solution of the China Incident by ending all Chinese hope of Russian intervention. Matsuoka accepted Germany's sanguine prediction that the war would be short and that, with Japan's aid, Russia would be defeated before the United States could contemplate intervention. The foreign minister acknowledged that he had previously favored the southern strategy as the best way to solve the problem of Japanese economic shortages as well as the China question, but he now favored an advance to the north and west as far as Irkutsk. "If we got even halfway there, our action might have an effect on Chiang that would lead to an overall peace." To strike south, on the other hand, was like playing with fire and would probably mean war with Britain and the United States as well as Russia.

Hara Yoshimoto, the president of the imperial privy council, agreed. The German attack on the Soviet Union was a unique opportunity for Japan, which would have to wage war against that country sooner or later to eliminate the Russian-Bolshevik menace. Further, by joining in the attack on the Soviet Union, Japan might avoid American intervention, whereas American intervention was certain if Japan undertook a campaign in the south.

Japanese military leaders were less sanguine about the prospects of a war with the Soviet Union. Sugiyama Hajime, the army chief of staff, drew attention to the weakness of the Kwantung army and argued that it was not prepared for a northern campaign. Nor would such a campaign be easy, for the Soviet Union had sent only four of thirty divisions of its crack Far Eastern army to the West and "still maintains an absolutely overpowering force, ready for strategic deployment." Sugiyama wanted time to reinforce the Kwantung army so that it could defend itself, provide backing for diplomatic negotiations, and be able to take the offensive "when the opportunity comes," by which he meant when the Red Army had been decisively defeated by the Germans and Japan no longer had to fear a Soviet offensive. "If the development of the German–Soviet war should turn out to be favorable to our Empire, I believe we will have to decide on using force to settle the Northern Problem and assure the security of our northern borders."

A final resolution of the north–south argument was officially endorsed at an Imperial Conference of July 2, 1941. The result was a defeat for Matsuoka and the advocates of joining the German attack on the Soviet Union. The attitude of the Japanese government toward the German–Soviet war would be based on the spirit of the Tripartite Pact. "However, we will not enter the conflict for the time being." Instead, the empire was determined to follow a policy that would result in the establishment of the Greater East Asia Co-Prosperity Sphere. The empire would continue to seek to achieve this objective by diplomacy, but would take specific measures with respect to French Indochina and Thailand for the purpose of "strengthening our advance into the southern regions." In carrying out these plans, "our Empire will not be deterred by the possibility of becoming involved in a war with Great Britain and the United States."

The future course of the war may have turned on this decision. On the basis of what we now know of the Soviet military situation in the autumn of 1941, it seems possible that a Japanese attack from the east coinciding with German blows from the west might have brought about the collapse of the Soviet Union. In the summer of 1941 Japan still had stockpiles of raw materials that would have permitted large-scale military operations for at least another eighteen months, and, as Japan was soon to demonstrate in waging war against Britain and the United States, it still possessed astonishing striking power despite the drain on its resources caused by the war against China (though the China war had given the Japanese access to China's resources and had required a major expansion of the Japanese army and war industries). A Japanese offensive against the Soviet Union, or even the threat of such an offensive, would have prevented the transfer to the west of the Soviet Far Eastern army, which is generally credited with having played a decisive role in halting the German advance toward Moscow. Further, a Japanese advance to the north instead of the south might well have avoided or at least postponed a conflict with the United States.

With the Soviet Union defeated, the Germans would have had the immense military power deployed against the Soviets available for use against Britain, and, even if an actual invasion of the British Isles was still impossible, the Germans could have launched campaigns against Gibraltar and Suez to sever Britain's economic lifelines. As for the Japanese, the defeat of the Soviet Union would certainly have increased the effectiveness of their diplomatic pressure on the Netherlands East Indies and everywhere else in East Asia. More importantly, the plight of Britain in the west might well have compelled the United States to concede Japan supremacy in East Asia, at least temporarily, in order to be able to concentrate its power against Germany, which the Roosevelt administration had always regarded as the most serious threat to American interests.

The Japanese nevertheless had compelling reasons for not entering the war against the Soviet Union. In the opinion of many Japanese policy makers, the German war effort so far had been altogether too successful. Their advance into Russia had been swift and spectacular, and Japanese intervention seemed likely to ensure the quick and decisive victory the Germans themselves so confidently predicted. But what then? Japan would have the Nazi racial state as a neighbor in Asia instead of Communist Russia. The Nazis had downplayed the entire racial issue in their dealings with Japan, but how long would it be before Nazi racist fanatics revived Teutonic ambitions in East Asia, perhaps in alliance with the defeated white races of Europe and the United States? Racism apart, a quick and decisive German victory might make the Germans far less amenable to granting concessions to Japan in East Asia. And was it not possible that Hitler might still sell our Japan in order to make peace with Britain by promising German support for the preservation of the British empire? Hitler's betrayal of Japan in the Nazi-Soviet Pact was still a vivid, and bitter, memory.

There were more immediate practical considerations. The oil and other raw materials Japan so desperately needed were in southeast Asia, not in Siberia. The Germans promised to provide the resources Japan required after victory over the Soviet Union, but the transportation problems would be formidable under the best of circumstances. And would the Germans keep their promises? Even if they did, which was doubtful, the Japanese would have been placed in a position of dependence that would have allowed the Germans to exert a decisive influence on the conduct of Japanese policy. There was the further problem, raised by the army chief of staff, that the Kwantung army was not prepared for a northern campaign. As the Japanese had learned from their border clashes with the Red Army in 1938 and 1939, such a campaign might be far longer and more difficult than the Germans predicted and would leave Japan helpless to withstand American economic pressure. Far better, then, to use the opportunity of Germany's involvement in war with the Soviet Union to stake out Japanese claims in Southeast Asia before Germany was in a position to object or make a deal with Britain. At the same time, Japan could secure the natural resources that would make it economically independent and give it a fighting chance to cope with the opposition of Britain and the United States. If the Germans achieved their quick victory over the Soviet Union as they so confidently predicted, Japan could still mount a campaign in the north to safeguard its interests, and then with minimal risk.

The Japanese decision to implement the southern strategy was communicated to the Germans on July 3, 1941. A southern campaign would tie up the Anglo-Saxon forces in Asia, the Germans were informed, and would thereby make a maximum contribution to their joint war effort. The Germans were in no position to protest. What they still feared most was the possibility of a Japanese bargain with the United States that would allow the Americans to concentrate their power against Germany. Hence the Germans, while still urging Japanese intervention against the Soviet Union, were eager to support a Japanese offensive anywhere that would end the danger of a Japanese-American rapprochement.

The most noteworthy feature about German-Japanese relations at this time, and throughout the course of the war, was the almost total lack of coordination of German and Japanese policies, diplomatic or military.

❑ *From the Southern Strategy to Pearl Harbor*

The first Japanese step in implementing their southern strategy was to pressure France's Vichy government into agreeing to their occupation of southern as well as northern Indochina for the purpose of acquiring better bases for an attack on the Netherlands East Indies.

Japanese forces entered southern Indochina on July 25. The American response was swift. On July 26 Washington ordered the freezing of all Japanese assets in the United States, placed an embargo on virtually all exports to Japan, and forbade Japanese ships the use of the Panama Canal. The American embargo was followed by British and Dutch economic sanctions which closed off all Japanese access to foreign oil. At about the same time Washington recalled General Douglas MacArthur to active duty and placed him in command of all American forces in the Pacific area, and orders went out to the United States Pacific fleet to take "precautionary measures against possible eventualities."

The Japanese had not expected the American reaction to be so immediate or so far-reaching. The American embargo, however, put an end to whatever doubts they still may have had about their southern strategy and convinced them they had no alternative but to take over the territories where the raw materials essential to their war economy could be obtained. They still hoped to avoid conflict with the United States, and throughout the late summer and autumn they continued their negotiations with Washington. The big change in the negotiations now was that Japanese diplomats faced a deadline. With critical foreign imports cut off, the Japanese could not afford to wait indefinitely for a favorable outcome of their diplomatic efforts. Suzuki Teiichi, the president of the Japanese Planning Board, warned that "if the present condition is left unchecked, Japan will find itself totally exhausted and unable to rise in the future." He predicted that the Anglo-American blockade would bring about the collapse of the Japanese economy within two years, and urged that a final decision for war or peace be made at once and without hesitation.

A decision was not reached at once and even then there was still hesitation. A Liaison Conference of September 3, 1941, resolved that Japan should continue to make every possible effort to attain its objectives through negotiation with Britain and the United States. But "in the event that there is no prospect of our demands being met by the first ten days of October . . . we will immediately decide to commence hostilities against the United States, Britain, and the Netherlands."

By the first part of October the Japanese appear to have abandoned all hope for the success of their negotiations. Konoe resigned on October 16 and was succeeded by the more militant General Tojo, who retained his position as minister of war. By this time the Japanese had completely ruled out an attack on the Soviet Union as being too risky and unprofitable. With strategic economic shortages still their most critical concern, they decided that if the United States persisted in its economic boycott, the only possible course for Japan would be to relieve those shortages by a policy of conquest in Southeast Asia. Between the islands of Japan and the southeastern sources of raw materials, however, lay America's Philippine Islands. The fateful question before the Japanese now was whether they could hazard a major drive to the south with the Americans lying athwart their main lines of communication. The decision they reached in answer to this question was that they could not: if they undertook a drive to the south, the threat represented by the American presence in the Philippines would have to be eliminated. This would mean war with the United States.

Strategic considerations, too, played a part in the Japanese decision to risk war with the United States. Japanese planners proposed to extend their conquest beyond the Philippines to include the most important British and American bases in the Western Pacific and the South Seas. Once in control of these territories, they intended to build up a network of strategic bases so formidable that the materialistic Americans would not consider it worth their while to challenge Japan's supremacy in East Asia; or, if they did challenge it, they would find the Japanese defenses impregnable.

Still the Japanese hesitated, and the deadline for negotiations was extended. An Imperial Conference of November 5, however, set a new and final deadline: if the current negotiations with the Americans did not lead to a result satisfactory to Japan by December 1, hostilities against the United States were to begin. At this November 5 conference, Army Chief of Staff Sugiyama Hajime was asked to explain what would happen if negotiations with the United States broke down; what would be the scope of military operations; and how good were Japan's chances for success? Sugiyama responded in some detail. Targets of initial operations were the American, British, and Dutch military, naval, and air bases in Guam, Hong Kong, British Malaya, Burma, British Borneo, Dutch Borneo, Sumatra, Celebes, and the Bismarck Archipelago; at the same time the army and navy were to cooperate in launching simultaneous campaigns in the Philippines and Malaya. The next step would be a campaign against the Netherlands East Indies. The army estimated that fifty days would be required to complete the campaign in the Philippines; one hundred days for Malaya; and another fifty for the Netherlands East Indies. At the start of military operations, Thailand was to be pressured into permitting Japanese troops to enter the country so that the attack on Malaya and Singapore could be launched from there.

It is noteworthy that no mention was made at this conference of Pearl Harbor, although plans for an attack against this major American naval base in the Pacific had been approved by the supreme command in mid-October. The idea for a carrier-based attack on Pearl Harbor had been conceived by Admiral Yamamoto Isoroku, commander-in-chief of the combined fleet, in late 1940 or early 1941. A technical obstacle to this plan was that Pearl Harbor was so shallow that torpedoes dropped from aircraft were likely to sink into sand and mud. This technical problem was solved by attaching fins to the torpedoes, as the British had done recently in an air raid on the Italian naval base at Taranto. The other prerequisite for the Yamamoto plan was surprise, and to ensure secrecy the plan was communicated only to the prime minister and the supreme command.

In the wake of their November 5 decision, the Japanese once again sought closer relations with Germany, and they now put out discreet feelers to elicit a promise from Germany not to conclude a separate armistice or peace in the event of a war between Japan and the United States. The Germans, their policy still determined by fear of a Japanese-American agreement, did not hesitate to give the Japanese the assurances they requested. In case Japan or Germany became involved in war with the United States, no matter for what reason, it was considered a matter of course in Berlin that no separate armistice or peace would be made. If any doubts existed in Japan on this score, Germany was prepared to conclude a special agreement to cover all possible contingencies.

Meanwhile, the Japanese continued their negotiations with the United States and even sent a special envoy to Washington, a professional diplomat named Kurusu Saburo, to support the efforts of their ambassador, Admiral Nomura, to persuade the Americans to resume normal commercial relations and thereby avoid the need for a military confrontation. There was never any prospect that negotiations with the United States would be successful, however, because, as in the past, the Japanese continued to demand the equivalent of a free hand in China, while the Americans continued to demand Japan's withdrawal from both China and Manchuria.

In these final negotiations with the Japanese, the Americans had the great advantage of having broken the Japanese diplomatic code so that they were informed of Japanese proposals before they were officially submitted, including all instructions the Japanese government was sending its envoys in Washington. They therefore knew that the Japanese were desperate, that the Japanese negotiators faced a deadline of November 29 after which "things would automatically begin to happen." Though Tokyo gave no indication of what these "things" might be, there could no doubt that the breakdown of negotiations would mean war.

The Americans now faced a crucial decision of their own: should they continue their firm stand against Japan that would involve them in war in the Pacific, or should they make concessions to the Japanese that would allow them to concentrate American power against Nazi Germany? Several members of the Roosevelt administration favored the latter course, but there never seems to have been any doubt in the mind of Secretary of State Cordell Hull that the United States should reject any form of appeasement. In taking this uncompromising stand, Hull had the backing of Roosevelt, who thought the Japanese would most likely attack the Dutch East Indies or British Malaya. Both Roosevelt and Hull may have been influenced by the views of Secretary of War Henry Stimson and Stanley Hornbeck, a State Department expert on Asian affairs, who were convinced the Japanese were bluffing. If this was the case, Hull was determined to call their bluff. In his reply of November 26 to what he knew to be the final Japanese offers, he dispensed with diplomatic finesse and bluntly demanded that Japan not only halt its campaign southward but abandon all gains made at China's expense since 1931. In return, the United States would admit Japanese imports and allow limited exports of cotton and oil, the latter for civilian use only.

But the Japanese were not bluffing. The Hull response of November 26 confirmed what many Japanese had long feared. At an Imperial Conference of December 1, Prime Minister Tojo observed that the Americans refused to make a single concession and that their demands "not only belittled the dignity of our Empire and made it impossible for us to harvest the fruits of the China Incident, but also threatened the very existence of our Empire." Hara Yoshimoto, the president of the imperial privy council and heretofore a staunch opponent of war with the United States, agreed:

In negotiating with the United States, our Empire hoped to maintain peace by making one concession after another. But to our surprise, the American position from beginning to end was to say what Chiang Kai-shek wanted them to say. . . . The United States is being utterly conceited, obstinate, and disrespectful. It is regrettable indeed. We simply cannot tolerate such an attitude. If we were to give in, we would give up in one stroke not only our gains in the Sino-Japanese and Russo-Japanese wars, but also the benefits of the Manchurian Incident. This we cannot do. We are loath to compel our people to suffer even greater hardships on top of what they have endured during the four years since the China Incident. But it is clear that the existence of our empire is threatened, that the great achievements of the Emperor Meiji would all come to nought, and that there is nothing else we can do. Therefore, I believe that if negotiations with the United States are hopeless, then the commencement of war, in accordance with the decision of the previous Imperial Conference, is inevitable.

The Imperial Conference of December 1 decided that negotiations with the United States were indeed hopeless and war inevitable. Four days earlier the Japanese task force assigned to attack the American naval base at Pearl Harbor had sailed from Hitokappa Bay in the Kurile Islands with instructions that the operation was to be halted if negotiations with the United States were successful. The decision of the Imperial Conference of December 1 ensured that no order to call off the attack on Pearl Harbor would be sent.

Having broken the Japanese diplomatic code, the United States government knew that a crisis was imminent. On November 24 the navy sent warnings to all United States naval commanders in the Pacific, including Hawaii, that they might expect "a surprise attack in any direction." Three days later the navy sent out a more emphatic message. "This dispatch is to be considered a war warning. Negotiations with Japan looking toward stabilization of conditions in the Pacific have ceased and an aggressive move by Japan is expected within the next few days." The navy thought the attack might be launched against the Philippines, Thailand, the Kra peninsula, or possibly Borneo. Hawaii was not mentioned, but all commanders in the Pacific were instructed to "execute an appropriate defense deployment."

On Sunday morning of December 7 (Washington time) the United States government had the complete text of the final Japanese note announcing the breakoff of negotiations. Washington thus knew that an attack of some kind was imminent, though not precisely when or where it would take place. The army chief of staff, General George Marshall, was riding in Rock Creek Park when the final Japanese message was decoded. Informed of the Japanese note when he returned to his office at eleven, he ordered that an additional warning be sent to American commanders in the Pacific. Marshall turned this message over to the army's telegraph network for transmission and was assured it would be delivered in thirty minutes. Instead, apparently because the army network was already overloaded, the message to Hawaii was sent by commercial telegraph and radio, and then by a bicycle messenger, who was caught in the Japanese attack while carrying the still encoded message to Fort Shafter.

❑ *The Pearl Harbor Controversy*

Few events in American history have aroused more consternation and controversy than the Japanese attack on Pearl Harbor. How could that attack have been so successful, and who was to blame? Immediately after the attack, American isolationists put out a theory that Roosevelt, to ensure America's entry into the war, had deliberately goaded the Japanese into attacking the United States and that his government had deliberately withheld information obtained through the broken Japanese code from American military and naval commanders in the field. In short, the principal blame for the entire Pearl Harbor disaster rested with the Roosevelt administration.

This theory, which was subsequently supported and embellished by a number of distinguished scholars and military experts, is patently absurd. There can be no question that Roosevelt wanted to speed America's entry into the war against Nazi Germany, but it is inconceivable that any American leader would have been prepared to sacrifice hundreds of American lives and a large proportion of America's Pacific fleet to overcome American isolationist sentiment and propel the country into war. Roosevelt may be criticized for having failed to do enough to supervise the negotiations of his secretary of state, Cordell Hull, who has been criticized in turn for his excessively moralistic posture, his uncompromising stand in negotiating with the Japanese, and for putting such pressure on them that they believed they had no alternative but to resort to extreme measures.

But by December 1941 the American government had had ample time to observe the consequences of compromise and appeasement in both Europe and Asia. Appeasement in Europe, far from contributing to peace, had only led to further German and Italian aggression; appeasement in Asia had enabled the Japanese to conquer Manchuria and a large part of China. Moreover, as we now know, Japanese territorial ambitions were not restricted to Manchuria and China but included a large part of the former British, French, and Dutch colonial empires. Unless the United States was prepared to concede Japan hegemony in East Asia, war for the Americans, too, was inevitable. The blame for that war, however, lies in Tokyo, not Washington.

In seeking culprits for the Pearl Harbor disaster, it is tempting to look beyond the commanders in the field and seek men in high office engaged in a sinister conspiracy. But, though the subject remains controversial, the evidence now available supports the thesis that the real culprits were the commanders in the field, whose failure to take precautionary measures against a surprise attack amounted to criminal negligence. Secretary of War Stimson's condemnation of General Walter Short, the American military commander in Hawaii, seems thoroughly justified. Stimson noted that Short had received ample warning that hostilities were imminent:

> Under these circumstances . . . to cluster his airplanes in such groups and positions that in an emergency they could not take to the air for several hours, and to keep his antiaircraft ammunition so stored that it could not be promptly and immediately available, and to use his best reconnaissance system, the radar, only for a small fraction of the day and night, in my opinion betrayed a misconception of his real duty which was almost beyond belief.

Even more unbelievable negligence was to follow. On the morning of December 8 General Douglas MacArthur, the American commander in the Philippines, received a warning that left no room for misinterpretation, namely, news of the Japanese attack on Pearl Harbor. Thus every possible preparation should have been made at once to anticipate an attack on American bases in the Philippines. Yet when the Japanese bombed the Philippines shortly before noon, they found all the American aircraft wingtip to wingtip on the ground and were thus able to destroy them all, therewith wiping out the greater part of what was left of American airpower in the Pacific.

☐ *Diplomatic Aftermath*

Immediately after the Japanese attack on Pearl Harbor, the Japanese ambassador in Berlin called on Ribbentrop asking that Germany and Italy honor their pledge to Japan by issuing formal declarations of war on the United States immediately. Ribbentrop replied that Hitler was at that very moment studying means for making such a declaration so as to make the best possible impression on the German people and Germany's allies; he had already sent out orders to German naval commanders to attack American ships wherever they might meet them.

A final treaty between Germany, Italy, and Japan, pledging cooperation in the war against the United States and promising not to conclude a separate armistice or peace, was signed on December 11, 1941. On that same day Germany and Italy declared war on the United States.

Still the Japanese were not satisfied. On December 15 they presented the Germans with the draft of a military convention providing for a division of the world into spheres of military operations along the 70th degree of longitude, with Germany and Italy responsible for the territory west of that line, Japan for the territory to the east. The draft included provisions for mutual aid in either sphere when circumstances seemed to warrant it.

The Germans disliked the Japanese proposal. They feared, quite correctly, that the division of the world into operational spheres was an attempt to establish a precedent for a subsequent delimitation of political spheres, and they regretted the absence of any Japanese commitments regarding the Soviet Union.

Despite their reservations, the Germans decided not to haggle. They believed that the essential thing was to engage the Japanese against Britain to the greatest possible extent, and that the best means for doing so was to leave them maximum prospects for conquest at the expense of the British empire. A military treaty designating their mutual fields of operation, signed on January 18, 1942, by the German, Italian, and Japanese governments, corresponded almost exactly with the original Japanese draft. Not until after the signature ceremony did the Germans express the hope, and then only orally, that the Japanese would endeavor to stop American shipments to the Soviet Union via Vladivostok and do everything possible to tie down Soviet forces in Siberia to prevent their withdrawal for use on the Western front.

The Japanese did not fulfill German hopes in either regard. Shipments to the Soviet Union continued to arrive in Vladivostok without Japanese interference of any kind, and the Japanese took no steps to tie down Soviet forces in East Asia. Soviet troops transferred from Siberia in the months after the conclusion of the Russo-Japanese neutrality pact may have been the decisive factor in halting the German drive on Moscow in December 1941, and the troops which continued to be withdrawn from Asia appear to have played an important role in sustaining Soviet counterattacks during the rest of the winter.

The Japanese motive in seeking German and Italian declarations of war on the United States is obvious. The motives of Hitler and Mussolini, on the other hand, are far more complicated and require detailed examination.

◻

EIGHTEEN

Hitler's Declaration of War on the United States, the War in the Pacific, and the Turn of the Tide

The Japanese had cogent strategic and economic reasons for their attack on Pearl Harbor. The attack opened the way for the Japanese to acquire the raw materials and strategic bases they deemed essential for their national survival. Yet their act of aggression against the United States can only be regarded as a monumental blunder, for in one blow it overcame the still powerful isolationist sentiment in America and united the American people, as they might never have been united otherwise, in support of a war to halt Japanese expansion in East Asia.

But if Japan's Pearl Harbor attack had an understandable rationale and actually brought about a substantial improvement in Japan's strategic and economic position, what can be said for Hitler's declaration of war on the United States? It was an act that brought Germany no appreciable military or economic advantages and that canceled out the greatest single benefit to Germany of the Japanese attack, namely, its diversion of American attention from Europe to the Pacific. Once Japan had committed itself to war with the United States, Hitler might surely have found excuses to procrastinate about fulfilling his pledge to join Japan in that war. At the very least he might have demanded Japanese support against the Soviet Union in return for German support against the United States, if only a promise to stop American shipments to the Soviet Union via Vladivostok.

Hitler certainly seemed to have every reason to procrastinate. For after Japan's dramatic act of aggression, the United States government, however much it might regard Germany as the more dangerous enemy, would have had difficulty convincing the American public that an attack by Japan should be answered by an American attack on Germany. By delaying his own declaration of war on the United States, therefore, Hitler might have gained several months of grace before the Roosevelt government could find cause to direct any large proportion of American power against Germany. As it was, by throwing down his own gauntlet to the United States, he gratuitously placed Germany on an equal footing with Japan in the ranks of America's enemies. In so doing, he ended all possibility of a quick German military victory and created a situation that virtually guaranteed Germany's ultimate defeat.

In attempting to explain Hitler's catastrophic decision to declare war on the United States, analysts of Nazi policy have placed a good deal of emphasis on Hitler's ignorance about America and his apparent contempt for America's military capacities. The evidence of Hitler's low estimate of American power must be treated cautiously, however, for his comments about American weakness were generally intended to instill courage into people justifiably fearful about America's strength. Certainly Hitler's actual policies, in contrast to many of his statements, appear to have been determined by a very realistic respect for American power and by a constant fear that America might intervene in the war before Germany's position on the European continent had been consolidated, an attitude that was to be expected from a man as obsessed as Hitler with the experiences and lessons of World War I.

❑ *Hitler's Initial Caution*

Whatever his real opinions may have been, Hitler's policies in dealing with the United States were characterized by caution. With the coming of war in 1939 this attitude of caution became a cardinal principle of German policy. The Nazi press received strict orders to avoid all statements that might give offense to Americans and to desist from attacks on President Roosevelt, heretofore a favorite target of Nazi polemicists. When these orders were not immediately or strictly enough observed, Nazi journalists received further instructions on September 18 expressly charging them "to treat all questions concerning the United States with even more caution than hitherto." Directives along similar lines were sent to all branches of the German government and armed forces, a policy to which the German government adhered until the eve of Hitler's declaration of war on the United States.

The most numerous and stringent directives concerning the United States were issued to the German navy. Clearly aware that Germany's submarine warfare had been the most important single factor leading to American intervention against Germany in 1917, Hitler instructed the navy to avoid any kind of provocation of the United States at sea, and he consistently rejected the many appeals of his admirals to be allowed greater freedom in waging submarine warfare. In October 1939 he turned down his navy's plea for an all-out naval and submarine blockade of Britain. Two months later he ordered that even those American ships that entered the combat zone were not to be attacked. In February 1940 he refused to authorize German submarines to patrol the Canadian coast off Halifax, an important center for the formation of British convoys, because of the "psychological effect any such step might have on the United States." On March 5 the navy was sent a categorical order not to stop, capture, or sink American ships wherever they might be.

On the eve of the German attack on the Soviet Union in 1941, Hitler forcefully restated the arguments for avoiding incidents with the United States and his belief that the defeat of Russia would discourage American intervention because of the increased threat that would be posed by Japan. Until Germany had achieved the expected decisive victory over Russia, "the Führer desires absolutely to avoid any possibility of incidents with the U.S.A." The navy and Luftwaffe were again forbidden to attack all naval vessels, from the cruiser class upwards, with the exception of ships definitely recognized as belonging to the enemy. In a subsequent order he forbade all attacks on

American merchant ships, including those that sailed into the combat area. Hitler was confident that the collapse of the Soviet Union would have a decisive effect on both Britain and America; therefore, it was "absolutely essential that all incidents with the United States should be avoided. . . . Germany's attitude toward America is therefore to remain as before: not to let itself be provoked, and to avoid all controversy."

❑ American Pressure

The United States government did not make it easy for Hitler to adhere to his policy of restraint. Roosevelt had never made any attempt to conceal his loathing for the Hitler regime or of his desire to aid the opponents of Nazism. For purposes of sending such aid, however, he was severely handicapped by the American Neutrality Act, which forbade the sale or shipment of arms in American ships to all countries involved in war and which was stoutly defended by American isolationists. In November 1939 Roosevelt secured an amendment of the Neutrality Act to permit the sale of arms to the Allies, but only on a cash-and-carry basis.

As German victories in the spring and summer of 1940 made Americans more conscious of the magnitude of the Nazi menace, Congress approved Roosevelt's request for a billion dollars to strengthen America's armed forces and step up the pace of American aircraft production. Islationist sentiment remained powerful, however, and the Roosevelt administration was unable to secure the passage of any major measures to help the hard-pressed British. To circumvent the isolationists in Congress, the president concluded an executive agreement (which did not require Congressional approval) with the British on September 2, 1940, which gave the British 50 overage American destroyers for convoy duty in exchange for a 99-year lease on British naval bases in Newfoundland and the Caribbean. The transfer of these bases in itself gave further aid to Britain, for it relieved British forces stationed there for duty elsewhere. On January 10, 1941, following his election to an unprecedented third term as president, Roosevelt submitted a Lend-Lease Act to Congress asking for 7 billion dollars in credits to nations whose defense was considered vital to the United States, and despite the determined opposition of isolationists, the act was passed on March 11. On March 30 the United States seized all Axis as well as all Danish ships in American ports; on April 4 the Americans announced the extension of the Pan-American security zone to the east coast of Greenland, a possession of German-occupied Denmark, allegedly to prevent Greenland from falling into the hands of the Germans but in fact to use it as an advanced base for sending aid to Britain. In a major speech on foreign policy on May 27, 1941, Roosevelt announced that "our patrols are helping now to ensure delivery of the needed supplies to Britain. All additional measures necessary to deliver the goods will be taken." The United States, the president declared, was now in a state of unlimited emergency.

On June 14 the United States froze all Axis assets in America; two days later the State Department ordered all German consular officials and the employees of other German offices still operating in the United States to leave the country. On July 17 the Americans took over from the British the defense of Iceland, a strategic point in the convoy routes across the Atlantic, and a week later they extended the definition of the territorial waters of the Western Hemisphere to include Iceland. In August Roosevelt and Churchill joined in the promulgation of the Atlantic Charter in which the United States expressed its determination to cooperate with Britain in securing a just and lasting peace, a document that could only be interpreted as an assurance that if necessary the United States was prepared to come to the aid of Britain in order to defeat the Axis powers.

Soon afterwards there occurred the type of incident Hitler had so strenuously sought to avoid. According to American accounts, on September 4 a German submarine fired two torpedoes on the American destroyer *Greer,* which was following the submarine to keep a British plane carrying depth charges informed of its location. The German submarine commander, on the other hand, denied that any torpedoes had been fired because an attack on an American vessel would have been a violation of Hitler's orders. Whatever the truth of the matter, Roosevelt used the incident to issue an order that henceforth all American ships on convoy duty were to "shoot on sight" at all Axis ships encountered in the American neutrality zone. In October he called for the repeal of that section of the Neutrality Act prohibiting the arming of American merchant vessels, and in November Congress repealed all the remaining restrictive provisions of the act.

❑ Hitler's Final Response

With each new American provocation the German navy appealed to Hitler to be allowed to take countermeasures, but he adhered to his policy of restraint. Even if the American Neutrality Act were repealed in its entirety, he said, he intended to do everything possible to avoid incidents, and in fact orders to this effect continued to be issued until December 2, 1941.

While going to great lengths to avoid a German war with the United States, Hitler was encouraging Japan to attack British possessions in East Asia in the hope that such an attack would end all possibility of a Japanese-American rapprochement and focus American attention on Asia. Part of this purpose was fulfilled, with a vengeance, when Japan attacked Pearl Harbor on December 7, 1941.

But the Japanese attack did not divert American attention to Asia, for on December 9, two days after Pearl Harbor, Roosevelt announced that he considered Germany just as guilty as Japan for the Pearl Harbor attack and that a shift of American forces from the Atlantic to the Pacific was not to be expected. On that same day Hitler issued orders for German submarines to begin an immediate all-out attack on American ships wherever they might be, and on December 11 he declared war on the United States.

By declaring war on the United States while the greater part of his army was still bogged down in Russia, Hitler sealed his fate. But by now he was inextricably caught up in the processes he himself had set in motion, and in the context of these processes his declaration of war not only becomes understandable but even assumes a quality of inevitability.

For some time already Hitler had been convinced, certainly correctly, that Roosevelt was only waiting for an opportunity to intervene in the European war. He had already moved the United States a long way from a status of neutrality, and his shoot-on-sight order to American ships would have produced an incident in the near future that would have given him the pretext he needed for intervention. Hitler must therefore have calculated that any delay on his part in honoring his pledge to Japan to join immediately in the war against the United States would accomplish nothing more than a brief postponement of his own inevitable clash with that country. The failure to honor his pledge, on the other hand, might irreparably damage Germany's relations with Japan and permanently end any prospect of Japanese cooperation against the Soviet Union. Moreover, in view of America's steady and obvious abandonment of neutrality, further German delay in responding to American acts of provocation would only delay an all-out German effort to halt American deliveries to Britain. Further, it might create the impression that Germany was afraid of the United States and lower Germany's prestige in the eyes of its satellites and the uncommitted nations. These and similar dangers could all be avoided by an immediate declaration of war, which would have the additional advantage of allowing German aircraft and submarines to strike at American shipping before America's defenses had been properly organized.

After the terrible anxieties Hitler had felt about the course of Japanese policy and the possibility of a Japanese-American rapprochement, Japan's final commitment to war against the United States came as a great relief, "a deliverance," a "new lease on life." "For the first time we have on our side a first-rate military power," Hitler said. Giving Japan a free hand in East Asia was admittedly a turning point in history. "It means the loss of a whole continent, and one must regret it for it is the white race which is the loser." But Hitler would not concede that his alliance with Japan represented a betrayal of National Socialist racial principles. To win, he said, "we are quite prepared to make an alliance with the devil himself."

It should be remembered that Hitler still counted on a short war. If Japan could hold America in check for just a year, then the Russian campaign would be over (if it were not, Hitler must have realized the war would be lost in any case) and Germany could once against shift the bulk of its military might to the West backed by all the resources of Europe—and Asia. Surely then both Britain and America would realize that the task of defeating the Axis powers and Japan was hopeless. But if they still refused to come to terms, Germany could calmly build up its own strength to knock out first one, then the other, at the appropriate moment.

❑ *Japan's Miraculous Six Months*

In Japanese overall military and naval planning, the attack on Pearl Harbor was to be only to be one of a succession of synchronized and simultaneous attacks on other targets in Southeast Asia and the Pacific that were to form part of Japan's defensive perimeter and ensure access to the raw materials that would be required to sustain the Japanese war effort. An hour before the attack on Pearl Harbor, the Japanese army and navy had already launched coordinated attack on Singor and Kata Bharu in Malaya, acquiring the bases they were to use for their attack on Singapore.

The primary purpose of the Pearl Harbor attack had been to destroy so much American seapower as to give Japan naval supremacy in East Asia, an essential precondition to other projected campaigns in this area. The success of that attack had exceeded Japanese expectations. Five American battleships, three cruisers, and large numbers of smaller vessels were sunk or severely damaged, three other battleships were put out of action, 177 aircraft were destroyed, and harbor installations were devastated.

The Americans were lucky to escape further damage, because Admiral Nagumo Chuichi, the commander of the Japanese strike force, fearful for the safety of his own vessels, rejected the appeals of his airmen to continue their attacks in order to destroy the enormous stores of oil at Pearl Harbor (almost equal to Japan's total supplies) as well as its dockyard facilities. The Americans were also fortunate that none of their aircraft carriers was at Pearl Harbor at the time of the Japanese strike—two were delivering aircraft and supplies to Guam and Midway Islands, another was at sea, while a fourth was undergoing repairs in the United States. The survival of the carriers was crucial, because they proved to be the decisive weapons in subsequent naval battles in the Pacific theater.

The Japanese coordinated their attack on Pearl Harbor with simultaneous attacks on American, British, and Dutch bases in Southeast Asia and the Pacific. The speed of their conquests was remarkable. Guam fell on December 13, Wake Island on December 20, Hong Kong on Christmas Day, and Manila, the capital of the Philippines, on January 2, although American and Filipino forces in the Philippines held out until May 6. Already on February 15 the Japanese had captured the British naval base of Singapore, the bastion of British seapower in East Asia. By March 8 they captured Rangoon, the capital of Burma, and by the end of April the last British troops were driven from the country.

The most important economic goal of Japan's initial campaigns was the capture of the oil of the Netherlands East Indies, which was expected to cover all Japanese military requirements. Since the fall of the Netherlands to Hitler's armies in the spring of 1940, the Japanese had tried to obtain guarantees of Dutch oil shipments through peaceful diplomatic pressure because they feared that the Dutch would destroy their oil wells if the Japanese resorted to force. Had the Dutch actually destroyed those wells, they might have altered the course of the war in the Pacific. But they did not. Early in January 1942 the Japanese made their first landings on the Dutch-held islands. The capital city of Batavia fell on March 6, and by the end of the month the greater part of Java was under Japanese control. Lacking confidence in the loyalty of their Indonesian troops, the Dutch surrendered without mounting any kind of serious resistance. Nothing was done to destroy the oil wells or other economic installations.

MAP 10   THE WAR IN THE PACIFIC (SEE ALSO MAP 7)

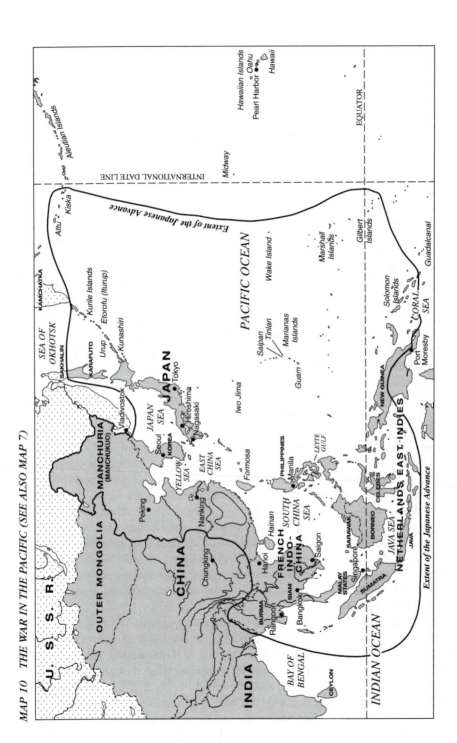

255

❏ *The Turn of the Tide: The Battles of the Coral Sea and Midway*

The Japanese suffered their first serious reverse in early May 1942 when they attempted to capture Port Moresby in southeastern New Guinea, which they hoped to use as a base for attacks on Australia and the New Hebrides. The Japanese invasion force, supported by two heavy and one light aircraft carriers, was met by a much weaker Allied fleet that included two American carriers. In the ensuing Battle of the Coral Sea, the first between Japanese and American carriers, the rival fleets never saw each other for the actual fighting was done by the carriers' aircraft. One American carrier was sunk and the second was badly damaged, though able to return to Pearl Harbor for repairs. But the Japanese suffered even greater losses. Their light carrier was sunk and one heavy carrier was so badly damaged that it was out of action for several months. The second Japanese heavy carrier was undamaged but, owing to the loss of 37 percent of the Japanese combat aircraft, it was no longer fully operational.

Admiral Yamamoto had always been aware that Japan could never match American production and was therefore not likely to win a long war. Further, as the architect of the Pearl Harbor attack, he had also recognized the decisive role of airpower in naval warfare and the corresponding importance of aircraft carriers. The Coral Sea engagement can only have reinforced his views on these questions, for he now decided to stake everything on winning a major naval victory with the primary objective of destroying the American carriers that had escaped the attack on Pearl Harbor. With the American carriers out of the way, he believed Japan could achieve such naval supremacy in the Pacific that the United States might be willing to negotiate, especially if Japan agreed to make major sacrifices for the sake of peace.

The Yamamoto plan was to strike at Midway Island, some thousand miles northwest of Pearl Harbor. He calculated that the Americans would regard this island as a vital strategic interest and that they would therefore muster what was left of their fleet for its defense. In preparing the Midway operation, he put together the largest fleet ever assembled in the Pacific—4 heavy and 4 light aircraft carriers, 11 battleships, 18 heavy and 8 light cruisers, 55 destroyers, and 20 submarines, plus transports, tenders, and tankers. On board the carriers were 433 combat aircraft. While the bulk of this fleet was to converge on Midway, another contingent was to sail to the Aleutian Islands, a feint designed to draw away part of the American naval forces to meet the Japanese challenge in the north.

Although the American fleet was numerically inferior to that of Japan, the Americans had three advantages that proved to be decisive. Once again they had broken the Japanese code and therefore knew that the Aleutian expedition was a feint, that the main Japanese objective was Midway Island, and that they should therefore keep their fleet together to meet the Midway attack. Second, the Americans had radar, which would enable them to anticipate Japanese attacks and locate Japanese targets. And third, the Americans had Midway Island itself, an unsinkable aircraft carrier.

The Battle of Midway began early in the morning of June 4, 1942, with Japanese strikes at American installations on the island. But after their initial strikes, the Japanese made the crucial error of failing to keep their aircraft constantly in position to ward off attacks on their own carriers and the Americans had the incredible luck to arrive at exactly the right time to take advantage of this lapse. While Japanese bombers were refueling and rearming on the decks of their carriers, American dive bombers struck and delivered what has been described as the most stunning and decisive blow in the history of naval warfare. Within just five minutes the entire course of the Pacific war was reversed. Three of Japan's heavy aircraft carriers were set ablaze, a fourth was hit. By the end of the battle all four of Japan's heavy aircraft carriers, 7 battleships (including the flagship *Yamato*), 12 cruisers, and 44 destroyers had been sunk, and 234 Japanese planes had been destroyed. Even more serious than the losses of the aircraft themselves was the irreparable loss of Japan's most experienced pilots. The previous naval advantage of Japan was lost, never to be recovered.

The Pacific war was to continue for another three years. The Japanese fought with fanatic determination, but their defeat was now inevitable.

❑ *The Legacy of the Japanese Victories*

Important as was the American victory at Midway, the Japanese victories over the previous six months had an even greater long-term significance. For during this period the Europeans suffered an irretrievable loss of prestige that hastened the collapse of their colonial empires. As in the case of the Japanese victory over Russia in 1905, the Japanese triumphs over Europeans in World War II gave non-Europeans everywhere a new sense of pride and self-confidence. Before and during the war, Japanese propagandists had done what they could to stimulate anti-European sentiment, and their denunciations of European imperialism had stimulated the national self-consciousness and aspirations for independence among Europe's colonial subjects.

In beating the anti-imperialist drum, however, the Japanese failed to consider that they themselves might be regarded as imperialists by their fellow Asians. And indeed, through their ruthless exploitation of the peoples who came under their control, the atrocities committed by their troops, and the arrogance and brutality of their occupation governments, the Japanese hopelessly compromised their claims to leadership of an Asian New Order.

Even if the Japanese had won the war, there is reason to doubt whether their empire would have long outlasted those of the Europeans. Already they were finding it impossible to subdue the peoples of China. Elsewhere in Asia they would surely have faced the same national revolutions that were soon to drive out the British, French, Dutch, and Americans.

◻

NINETEEN

The Grand Alliance:
To the Fall of Mussolini

◻ *The Beginnings of the Grand Alliance*

The formation of the Anglo-American-Soviet Grand Alliance during World War II was set in motion by Hitler's invasion of the Soviet Union on June 22, 1941. It was completed following Japan's attack on Pearl Harbor and the German and Italian declarations of war on the United States.

When the Germans attacked the Soviet Union, Winston Churchill, despite his deep-seated aversion to Communism and Bolshevik Russia, at once issued a declaration that Britain would do everything possible to aid the Soviet Union and would appeal to its friends and allies to take the same course. "If Hitler invaded hell," he said, "I would make at least a favorable reference to the Devil in the House of Commons." On July 13, Britain and the Soviet Union concluded a mutual aid treaty which included the critical provision that neither power would negotiate or conclude a separate peace with the enemy.

From the beginning of his negotiations with Churchill, Stalin pleaded for the immediate establishment of a second front through a British cross-Channel invasion of France. At that time the British leader could only reply that his country as yet lacked both the manpower and materiel for such an undertaking, as Stalin must have known very well. But his persistent demand for a cross-Channel second front, and the long Anglo-American delay in mounting one, gave him valuable bargaining leverage in securing other concessions from his wartime allies.

◻ *The Atlantic Charter*

In mid-August 1941, Churchill and Roosevelt met on a battleship off the coast of Newfoundland where they drew up the document that became known as the Atlantic Charter, a joint declaration of common principles summing up Anglo-American "hopes for a better future for the world." These principles included a pledge to "respect the right of all peoples to choose the form of government under which they will live . . . and [their] wish to see sovereign rights and self-government restored to those

258

who have been forcibly deprived of them"—a commitment that caused considerable embarrassment in subsequent negotiations with Stalin. The Soviet Union formally adhered to the Atlantic Charter on September 12, but with the critical reservation that "the practical application of these principles will necessarily adapt itself to the circumstances." Churchill was to add another mammoth reservation. In September 1941 he announced in Parliament that the Atlantic Charter applied to the enemy, not to India and Burma.

At their Newfoundland meeting, both Churchill and Roosevelt appear to have had more concrete objectives in view than issuing a statement of principle. Churchill was convinced that after agreeing to their joint declaration, which looked to "the final destruction of the Nazi tyranny," the Americans could not "honourably stay out" of the war. Roosevelt confirmed this belief. As Churchill later informed his War Cabinet, the American president "had made it clear that he would look for an 'incident' which would justify him in opening hostilities."

❑ *Western Aid to the Soviet Union*

In addition to their Atlantic Charter declaration, Churchill and Roosevelt addressed a joint letter to Stalin promising "the very maximum of supplies that you most urgently need" and calling for a conference to discuss long-term policy and strategic planning. In October British and American representatives in Moscow signed an agreement specifying the exact amount of aid that was to be sent to the Soviet Union and the dates for its delivery, and in November the United States extended lend-lease aid to the Soviets. In later years the Soviets were to belittle the importance of Anglo-American aid, thereby contributing to the frictions of the Cold War. It is true that Western aid did not arrive in sufficient quantities to play a critical role in halting the German offensive in late 1941, but it subsequently made a substantial and perhaps even decisive contribution to the Soviet war effort. As of June 1944, the Soviet government acknowledged having received from the United States alone 8,782 aircraft, 3,734 tanks, 206,771 trucks, and well over 2 million tons of food. By the end of the war, American lend-lease to the Soviet Union amounted to some eleven billion dollars.

❑ *The Entry of the United States into the Grand Alliance*

On December 8, 1941, the day after the Japanese attack on Pearl Harbor, the United States and Britain declared war on Japan. Three days later Germany and Italy fulfilled their pledge to Japan by declaring war on the United States, thereby propelling the United States into the war in Europe as well as Asia and into the Grand Alliance. For Britain, America's entry into the war was an even greater relief than the German attack on the Soviet Union. Many Americans, too, were relieved that their country was finally involved militarily in the struggle against Hitler and Japan, though even the most pro-British among them might have been disconcerted if they had heard Churchill hail the American disaster at Pearl Harbor—which "brought America unitedly and wholeheartedly into the war"—as "a blessing." "Greater good fortune has rarely happened to the British Empire."

Immediately after Pearl Harbor, Churchill and an entourage of military and economic advisers met with Roosevelt and the Soviet ambassador in Washington (the Arcadia Conference), where they announced their war aims to be the defense of "life, liberty, independence, and religious freedom" as well as "human rights and justice." On January 1, 1942, representatives of the United States and 25 other nations, including Britain, China, France, and the Soviet Union, signed a Declaration of the United Nations pledging not to make a separate peace with the enemy and to employ all their resources, military and economic, to achieve final victory.

❑ *The Big Three: Stalin, Churchill, Roosevelt*

At their meeting in the Iranian capital of Teheran in November 1943, with victory in sight, Churchill observed that the leaders of Britain, the Soviet Union, and the United States—the Big Three of World War II—presided over the greatest concentration of worldly power ever seen in the history of mankind. These three men were to establish the foundations of the postwar world.

People meeting Stalin for the first time were surprised to find how small he was, about five feet four inches. "A little bit of a squirt," Harry Truman called him after their conference at Potsdam in the final weeks of the war. His face was badly pockmarked, his teeth dark and tobacco-stained, his expression usually impassive and unsmiling. He moved slowly and spoke little, and when he did speak it was in a low and almost inaudible tone. Yet visitors generally found him impressive, a reaction undoubtedly reinforced by their awareness of the power wielded by this squat and otherwise unremarkable figure.

Stalin (the man of steel) was born Joseph Vissarionovich Djugashvili in 1878, in a small town near the city of Tiflis (Tbilisi) in Georgia. His parents were the children of serfs; his father was a shoemaker who had failed in his efforts to run his own shop; his mother earned money as a laundress and seamstress. Hoping that he would become a priest, his mother sent him to the local church school where he did well enough to be awarded a scholarship to the Russian Orthodox theological seminary in Tiflis. He was expelled from the seminary in 1899, most probably because he was already involved in revolutionary activity.

In 1903 he joined the Bolshevik faction of the Social Democratic party after its famous split with the Mensheviks. Nine years later Lenin, evidently impressed by Stalin's loyalty and subservience, co-opted him into membership of the party's Central Committee. Encouraged by Lenin, Stalin wrote a treatise on Marxism and the national question, a subject of obvious importance in the multinational tsarist empire. That treatise, warmly praised by Lenin, established its author's reputation as an expert on the nationalities problem. When the Bolsheviks came to power in 1917, Lenin appointed Stalin commissar for nationalities.

A dogged worker, willing to endure the drudgery of routine administrative tasks, careful to keep himself in the background and never challenge the authority or decisions of Lenin, Stalin was rewarded with the appointment as secretary-general of the Central Committee of the Communist party in April 1922. This position proved to be his stepping stone to power, for it enabled him to supervise and control the selection of the party's personnel and to staff the lower echelons of the party bureaucracy with men who owed their jobs to him. By the time of Lenin's death, Stalin's power within the party was so firmly established that he could no longer be effectively challenged. In January 1925 he maneuvered his most formidable rival, Trotsky, into resigning as commissar for war, and soon afterward he arranged his ouster from the party. Trotsky subsequently fled abroad, first to Norway, then to Turkey, and finally to Mexico, where he was murdered by a Soviet agent in 1940.

In contrast to Trotsky, who held that Communism could only be made secure in the Soviet Union through world revolution, Stalin emphasized the need to make Communism secure in the Soviet Union itself and was convinced this could be done through a policy of Socialism in One Country. To implement this policy he launched a succession of Five-Year Plans that were to transform the Soviet economy and society far more radically than the original revolution of 1917. In industry he inaugurated a crash program of industrial development, with emphasis on heavy industry and the manufacture of armaments, that was to make the Soviet Union secure against the competition and potential aggression of the capitalist world. An important part of his program was the shift of major centers of industrial production from western Russia, where they were exposed to attack from the European capitalist powers, to the Urals and beyond, where they would be virtually invulnerable.

To spur development of agricultural production and at the same time reinforce government control over the peasantry, which still constituted the bulk of the Soviet population, Stalin in 1928 inaugurated a program of collectivization: the amalgamation of individual peasant holdings into collective and state farms. The farms themselves were to be run by state managers, who were to rationalize production methods and were supplied by the government with plans and quotas to ensure the production of food needed to feed the burgeoning industrial cities.

Stalin's programs for the planning and management of industry and agriculture had long been the ideal of political theorists who deplored the waste and social injustice of the capitalist free-enterprise system. These programs were unquestionably impressive in theory and they evoked considerable enthusiasm among foreign observers, in particular those who had long called for a more rational and equitable system of economic production and distribution. In practice, however, Stalin's radical measures to transform Soviet society, implemented with savage ruthlessness, were a human catastrophe. In the words of the British historian Hugh Thomas: "This was the most elaborate, as well as the most brutal, act of social engineering in history."

Urban workers got off comparatively lightly. They were exposed to dangerous and unhealthy working conditions and subjected to compulsory relocation to new industrial cities being created east of the Urals. Housing was cramped and inadequate and consumer goods in short supply. Urban workers nevertheless did have housing, and more importantly, the government saw that they did not go hungry.

Infinitely worse was the lot of the peasants, many of whom—having become landowners for the first time following the Bolshevik revolution—bitterly resented their return to a condition of quasi-serfdom. They resisted their removal to collective farms (some 25 million peasant households were involved), they burned their crops and killed their cattle to avoid having them taken over by the state, and in many areas they engaged in armed resistance. The state responded with a savage program of repression, the removal of recalcitrant peasants to prison camps, and the forced relocation of millions of others that led to famines in many parts of the country comparable to those of the early 1920s. Estimates vary as to how many people died of starvation and how many more died of disease, deportation, exposure, or in forced labor camps, but during the war Stalin candidly admitted to Churchill that in the process of collectivization some 10 million peasants had been "dealt with."

During the 1930s Stalin also "dealt with" all possible rivals, opponents, or suspected opponents. This was the period of Stalin's great purges, the show trails in which hundreds of respected Soviet officials confessed to crimes of treason against the party and state. By the eve of World War II as many as a million civilian party and state officials had been executed, at least ten times that number had been imprisoned or incarcerated in forced labor camps (gulags), and of these another two million appear to have died. The army too, had been decimated by the execution or imprisonment of almost half its officer corps, including the most senior Soviet military commanders.

Following the Nazi attack on the Soviet Union, Stalin's crash program of industrialization, especially his transfer of much heavy industry eastward to the Urals and beyond, could be seen to have saved his country from conquest by the Germans. His apologists have therefore argued that his policies were justified, no matter how great the cost in human terms. The question remains whether similar or even more impressive results might not have been achieved with less brutal methods.

The Yugoslav Communist Milovan Djilas, who fought with Tito against the Nazis and Italians during their occupation of his country and thus had first-hand experience of the brutality of both Hitler and Mussolini, nevertheless thought Stalin's record surpassed that of the Axis dictators. "Whatever standards we use to take his measure . . . to him will fall the glory of being the greatest criminal in history. . . . He was methodical, all-embracing, and total as a criminal. He was one of those terrible dogmatists capable of destroying nine-tenths of the human race to 'make happy' the other tenth."

Stalin's wartime allies chose to overlook his grim political record. Stalin even seems to have persuaded them to doubt its validity, for he proved himself a cunning manipulator of his personal and political image. While negotiating with stubborn tenacity, he managed to convey the impression that he was eager to be cooperative and to present himself as an eminently reasonable, even benign, figure—Churchill and Roosevelt referred to him between themselves as "Uncle Joe." After his return from the Yalta conference in February 1945, Churchill informed the House of Commons that he had come away with the impression that Stalin and all other Soviet leaders wished to live in honorable friendship and equality with the Western democracies. "I feel also that their word is their bond. I know of no Government which stands to its obligations, even in its own despite, more solidly than the Russian Soviet Government." This statement may reflect the euphoria of the Yalta meeting, for it is doubtful whether Churchill was really so confident.

Roosevelt, however, was genuinely sanguine about future relations with the Soviet Union, as was his influential adviser Harry Hopkins. When William Bullitt, a former ambassador to the Soviet Union, warned of the danger of trusting Russia, Roosevelt told him:

> I don't dispute the logic of your reasoning. I just have a hunch that Stalin is not that kind of man. Harry [Hopkins] says he's not and that he doesn't want anything but security for his country, and I think that if I give him everything I possibly can and ask nothing in return, *noblesse oblige,* he won't try to annex anything and will work with me for a world of democracy and peace.

Stalin was to play on these illusions among Western statesmen with masterful skill.

In notable contrast to the humble origins of Stalin, Winston Churchill, the oldest member of the Big Three, was born in Blenheim Palace, one of the most stately of Britain's stately homes, a grandson of John Churchill, first duke of Marlborough and hero of the war against Louis XIV in the early eighteenth century. His father was Randolph Churchill, a brilliant political maverick who failed in his efforts to dominate the Conservative party and spent the last years of his political life in limbo. His mother was the beautiful Jennie Jerome, daughter of a New York financier and horse-racing enthusiast. Thus Churchill was half American and half English, but, as his compatriots would proudly claim in his later years, he was *all* British.

Churchill performed poorly at Harrow, one of England's most prestigious public schools, and was later enrolled in the Royal Military College at Sandhurst because his father did not think he was up to the standards of the bar. His academic difficulties may have stemmed from his refusal to submit to the classical curriculum, the foundation of British education at that time. The books he produced shortly after leaving Sandhurst already demonstrated a keen intelligence and a command of the English language that was to make him one of the finest writers his country ever produced.

Over the next five years, as soldier and journalist, Churchill provided himself with stirring material to write about. In 1895 he spent two months in Cuba reporting the Cuban insurrection against Spanish rule. Volunteering for service on the northwest frontier of India, he sent home dispatches that were were published as *The Story of the Malakand Field Force,* a stirring tribute to British imperial enterprise. In 1897 he took part in the British campaign to establish British control over the course of the Nile River, which he described in *The River War,* another salute to British imperialism. In South Africa when the Boer War began, he became famous for his role in the rescue of an armored train ambushed by the Boers. Taken prisoner in this same engagement, he won fresh laurels by escaping from Boer captivity a month later. He returned to Britain a military hero.

Upon his return from a lecture tour in the United States, Churchill was elected to Parliament as a Conservative. A staunch champion of free trade, he broke with the Conservatives over this issue in 1904 and joined the Liberal party. In view of his later policies and prejudices, it is noteworthy that during his first years as a member of the Liberal party Churchill was a champion of social reform. He denounced the evils of sweated labor, promoted legislation to regulate working hours for miners, and played a role second only to that of Lloyd George in the campaign to curb the power of the House of Lords. In dealing with the pre-1914 industrial strikes that swept over Britain, however, his vigorous defence of public order incurred the hostility of organized labor that he never overcame.

His reputation was also severely damaged by the failure of the Gallipoli campaign in World War I (see pp. 6–7). That failure was due largely to the incompetence of the military and naval commanders assigned to carry it out. But as the most prominent promoter of that campaign, Churchill bore the brunt of the blame. He resigned from the government in November 1915 and volunteered for active service on the Western front. In July 1917, however, he was brought back into the government as minister of munitions by Lloyd George, who had a first-hand appreciation of Churchill's energy and organizing ability. But Churchill could never shake off the stigma of Gallipoli. Nor did he ever overcome the hostility of the Left, a hostility intensified when Churchill, as secretary for war from 1919 to 1921, became a leading proponent of Allied intervention in Russia to bring down the Bolshevik government.

In 1924, alienated by the Liberal party's alliance with Labour, Churchill rejoined the Conservative party and in November of that year he was appointed chancellor of the exchequer in the Conservative government of Stanley Baldwin. By now, however, he was distrusted by both parties for his political vacillations. And, indeed, in the atmosphere of disillusionment and cynicism about traditional values in the years after World War I, Churchill was something of an anachronism: an Englishman who still believed in the unique capacity of England and the English, in the benevolent civilizing mission of the British empire, and in the "vigour of the political conceptions sprung from the genius of the British race."

Out of office after 1929, he used his passionate eloquence to rail against political radicalism at home and the danger of concessions to the colonial peoples. He denounced as a "pillage of the empire" his party's 1935 Government of India Act, which opened the way to greater Indian self-government, while at the same time denouncing appeasement in Europe and calling for unpopular programs of rearmament. His quixotic defense of King Edward VIII during the 1936 abdication crisis undermined the public conception of his credibility still further.

Churchill's persistent crying of wolf on so many fronts in the 1930s unfortunately diluted the effectiveness of his warnings about the menace of Hitler. Yet in the dark days of the spring of 1940, when Churchill was at last seen to have been the only consistent advocate of the policies Britain should have pursued during the previous decade in dealing with Hitler, Parliament turned to him as the only possible choice to succeed Chamberlain as prime minister. Now his eloquence served to rally a despairing country. "I have nothing to offer but blood, toil, tears and sweat." he announced in his first address to the Commons as leader of the nation. "You ask, What is our policy? I will say: It is to wage war, by sea, land, and air, and with all our might and with all the strength that God can give us. . . . What is our aim? I can only answer in one word: Victory—victory at all costs, victory . . . however long and hard the road may be."

Franklin D. Roosevelt was the youngest member of the Big Three. He was born in Hyde Park on the Hudson on January 30, 1882, the only child of James and Sara Delano Roosevelt, who was 26 years younger than her husband. Educated at Groton, Harvard, and the Columbia University School of Law, his academic record, like that of Church-ill, was undistinguished. Nor does he appear to have been enthusiastic about academic work, for after passing the New York bar examination he did not bother to complete his law degree. In 1905, while still in law school, he married a distant relative and first cousin of Theodore Roosevelt, Anna Eleanor Roosevelt, who was to enjoy a distin-guished career of her own in public service.

In 1910 Roosevelt was persuaded to run for the New York state Senate as a Dem-ocrat, the party of his immediate family, after receiving a promise that Theodore Roo-sevelt, a Republican, would not campaign against him. He proved to be as deft a poli-tician as his famous namesake, winning in a district that had been carried by the Democrats only once since the Civil War. Tall (six feet two inches), handsome, an eloquent speaker, charming and persuasive, he could also be tough and ruthless. "I was an awfully mean cuss when I first went into politics," he confessed in later life, a quality that his opponents—and a good many friends—believed he retained through-out his political career, though he became famously adept at disguising it. With his il-lustrious name and influential connections, Roosevelt soon attracted national atten-tion. In 1913 Woodrow Wilson appointed him assistant secretary of the navy. In 1920, as his party's vice-presidential candidate, he campaigned vigorously on behalf of the League of Nations. His party's defeat in this election taught him to respect the politi-cal strength of American isolationism and made him extremely cautious about risking international involvement when he became president.

In 1921, at the age of thirty-nine, he suffered an attack of poliomyelitis that left him crippled in both legs, a handicap that may actually have strengthened his resolve to succeed in public life. In 1928, when Herbert Hoover carried New York by a wide margin, Roosevelt won election as governor of that state by 25,000 votes. Two years later he swept the state by a record majority of 700,000 and thus became an obvious candidate for his party's presidential nomination in 1932. In the ensuing election, with the country plunged in economic depression, the buoyant and radiantly opti-mistic Roosevelt triumphed easily over a dour Herbert Hoover.

Roosevelt was a complex figure who eludes easy evaluation and characterization. By his own admission he was devious and inconsistent, but inconsistency in his case may have been a source of political strength because he was never an ideologue, at least in dealing with domestic affairs. He was willing to experiment with a variety of policies in attempting to find solutions to problems and to adjust to the political cli-mate of the moment. With a finely attuned political instinct, he was sensitive to the pressures and prejudices of public opinion and moved with caution in the political arena. Thus he could make unsavory compromises, procrastinate, assure one influen-tial pressure group of his support while actually deciding in favor of another. His pred-ecessor Herbert Hoover called him "a chameleon on plaid."

Yet throughout his career Roosevelt was guided by a set of idealistic principles, never clearly defined or dogmatic, which grew out of his patrician self-confidence and a sense of obligation to make the world a better place for people less fortunate than himself. His biographer Frank Freidel has compared him to the Tory aristocrats of Vic-torian England, "so certain of themselves that they dared undertake reforms." And he did undertake reforms. He used the power of the government to provide immediate relief to the unemployed, to industrial workers, and to farmers. He introduced legislation to regulate and control the nation's banking system, created the Federal Deposit Insurance Corporation (FDIC) to guarantee bank deposits, a Home Owners' Loan Corporation to refinance mortgages and prevent foreclosures. A National Labor Relations Act gave labor the right to bargain collectively and prohibited employers from blocking union recruitment and organization in their factories. Most important of all was a Social Securities Act of August 1935 that created a system of old-age and unemployment insurance. Although his economic policies failed to end the depression—many of his economic experiments proved to be ineffective—the obvious commitment of his administration to the solution of economic problems and the president's own spirit of buoyant optimism injected new confidence into a dispirited nation.

The record of Roosevelt's foreign policy throughout the 1930s was a good deal less impressive, in part because of his administration's concentration on domestic problems. He undermined the efforts of the International Economic Conference meeting in London in June and July 1933, which had sought to stimulate international economic recovery through an agreement on currency stabilization. He reestablished diplomatic relations with Soviet Russia in November 1933, but otherwise Roosevelt remained largely aloof from the crises developing in Europe and East Asia. He condoned the passage of a Neutrality Act in May 1937 that reaffirmed and enlarged earlier legislation prohibiting the export of arms and munitions to belligerents. And when Chamberlain accepted the invitation to go to Munich in September 1938, Roosevelt personally drafted a telegram to London that contained only two words: "Good man"—an unambiguous endorsement of Chamberlain's policy of appeasement.

Once the war in Europe had begun, however, there can be no question of Roosevelt's determination to aid the Western democracies. His critics have accused him of deceiving Congress and the American public in seeking to bring the United States into the war. There is ample evidence to support this criticism, but it remains a criticism only if one disagrees with Roosevelt's belief that American intervention was necessary to prevent Japanese domination of East Asia and German domination of Europe.

After America's entry into the war, Roosevelt's principal foreign policy objective was the preservation of the alliance with the Soviet Union, which he regarded as an essential condition for victory over Germany. In the course of the war he also became convinced of the need for institutions to ensure the preservation of peace in the postwar world, promote international economic cooperation, and foster the development of democratic governments throughout the world.

In his domestic policy Roosevelt had conspicuously avoided doctrinaire positions, but in his foreign policy he drew on a set of dogmatic assumptions. He regarded imperialism as an unmitigated evil and actively promoted the dissolution of the European colonial empires—a major stumbling block in his relations with Churchill. He disliked the French. But he was positively obsessed by his hatred for Germany and the Germans. He was convinced that Hitler was not the only problem but that the character of Germans in general was deeply flawed: they were Prussianized, militaristic, aggressive, racist, a threat to the international community that could only be removed by the complete revamping of German society and the dismemberment of German political and social institutions.

Roosevelt had no similar qualms about Stalin and the Russian people. On the contrary, he believed that through an understanding and generous policy he could not only maintain the wartime alliance but ensure Soviet cooperation in the postwar world. "I think we are in agreement," he wrote to Churchill shortly before his death, ". . . as to the necessity of having the USSR as a fully accepted and equal member of any association of great powers. It should be possible to accomplish this by adjusting our differences through compromise by all the parties concerned." If this were done, he was confident that a more liberal and more cooperative Soviet Union would emerge from the war whose government would work with the Western powers to ensure the preservation of peace.

So perceptive a critic as the diplomat-historian George Kennan has condemned Roosevelt's foreign policy as that of "a very superficial man, ignorant, dilettantish, severely limited in intellectual horizon." The British historian Donald Watt is even more scathing. He believes Roosevelt's policy decisions were not based on rational calculation but were the product of some intuitive inner voice. "His consciousness was a seething cauldron of misconceptions, *idées fixes,* misunderstandings and prejudices, of which, only too often, no argument could disabuse him."

No aspect of Roosevelt's policy has been criticized more vigorously than his strategy for dealing with Stalin and the Soviet Union, which his critics have condemned as hopelessly naive. Naive or not, Roosevelt succeeded in his immediate objectives: the preservation of the Soviet alliance, which we now know was never in serious jeopardy, and securing Soviet participation in the war against Japan, which in the end proved to be unnecessary and undesirable. Students of international affairs still speculate as to how relations with the Soviet Union might have developed if Roosevelt had lived. Yet in the final weeks of his life, a mortally ill Roosevelt professed to be thoroughly disillusioned with the Soviets, which at this stage may have expressed the opinion of his advisers acting in his name. In any case, there is reason to doubt that even a healthy Roosevelt would have been able to prevent the deterioration that actually took place.

❑ *The Course of the War: General Observations*

There is a commonly held assumption that the Axis powers and Japan came perilously close to winning World War II. This certainly seemed to be the case following the spectacular victories of Germany in Europe and Japan in East Asia between 1939 and the first six months of 1942. But after the formation of the Grand Alliance the Tripartite powers were doomed. With their failure to win a quick and decisive victory, their opponents had time to harness their far greater economic resources and build up overwhelmingly superior military strength. That the Germans and Japanese held out as long as they did against what in the end were immense odds testifies to the human capacity of fortitude and endurance—and to the tragedy that these qualities are so often employed on behalf of inhuman causes.

The Western Allies, besides having access to the greater part of the world's economic resources and America's productive capacity, which surpassed that all of all other belligerents in the course of the war, made more effective use of technological and scientific developments than the Germans. As discussed earlier, the British were quicker than the Germans to recognize the importance of radar, which provided early warning systems against aerial attacks and enabled Britain's own aircraft to bomb enemy targets through fog and darkness. More important still was the British code-breaking operation, Ultra, which penetrated the German code machine, Enigma, and gave the British information about every aspect of the German war effort.

In breaking the Enigma code used by the German navy in the spring of 1941, Ultra enabled the British to contain the U-boat challenge throughout the remainder of that year. In February 1942, however, the U-boats adopted a new form of Enigma, and after that their rate of sinking Allied ships assumed ominous proportions. The penetration of the new German naval code in December 1942 has been called Ultra's greatest triumph, for with that the U-boat menace was finally brought under control and by the summer of 1943 it was virtually eliminated.

The decisive achievement of Western science, however, was the development of a nuclear bomb, which gave the Western Allies a weapon that would have ensured the defeat of the Tripartite powers no matter how great their military success might otherwise have been.

❑ Stalin's War Aims and the Anglo-Soviet Alliance of May 26, 1942

From the start, a major diplomatic task of the members of the Grand Alliance was the preservation of Allied unity until final victory had been achieved. Because of the ideological, political, and economic differences between the Western democracies and the Soviet Union, this task seemed likely to be even more difficult than that of the Allies in World War I. For this reason, as in World War I, Western leaders went to great lengths to reassure their Russian allies of their loyalty, a concern Stalin ruthlessly exploited to Russia's advantage.

As early as December 1941, with Hitler's legions at the gates of Moscow, Stalin sought formal British and American endorsement of his major wartime objectives in return for his agreement to a formal Anglo-Soviet alliance. On December 16 and 17, 1941, he presented to the British foreign secretary, Anthony Eden, an extensive list of demands to be incorporated in a *secret* protocol annexed to a formal alliance treaty. He wanted Britain's immediate recognition of the Soviet frontiers of June 1941 and thus of Soviet territorial gains made in partnership with Hitler. These included the Baltic states of Estonia, Latvia, and Lithuania, the Soviet share of the Nazi-Soviet partition of Poland, the prewar Romanian territories of Bessarabia and Northern Bukovina, and the Finnish territory acquired after the winter war of 1939–1940. In addition, he asked for bases in Finland and Romania beyond the 1941 frontiers.

Poland was to be compensated for the loss of its eastern territories by substantial territorial gains at the expense of Germany. What was left of Germany was to be dismembered and permanently deprived of the means to wage wars of aggression. Austria, Czechoslovakia, and Albania were to be restored as independent states, as were Yugoslavia and Greece, which were to be rewarded for their participation in the war with territorial compensation. In return for Britain's agreement to these proposals,

Stalin promised to support any arrangements Britain might make "for securing bases, etc." in the countries Hitler had overrun in Western Europe.

The demands Stalin set before Eden in December 1941 were substantially the same as those he was to present to his Western Allies in all their subsequent conferences. Thanks to the fortunes of war and the desire of his Western Allies to preserve the Soviet alliance, he was able to secure their agreement to all these demands, and a good deal more.

Stalin's frank statement of war aims hardly reflected a commitment to the principles of the Atlantic Charter to which his government had adhered only three months earlier. His claims over Poland were particularly embarrassing to the British, who had gone to war in defense of Poland and were now allied to a Polish government in exile in London, which demanded the restoration of Poland's prewar frontiers as well as territorial compensation at the expense of Germany. Churchill angrily rejected Stalin's claim to territories acquired "in shameful collusion with Hitler." Acceptance "would be contrary to all the principles for which we are fighting this war and would dishonour our cause." Eden countered that, if the Soviets won the war, their troops were likely to control territory far beyond their 1941 boundaries. "It therefore seemed prudent to tie the Soviet Government to agreements as early as possible." Stalin used a cruder argument that amounted to outright blackmail: if Britain persisted in its refusal to recognize the 1941 frontiers, he would make a separate peace with Hitler.

Churchill not only gave in but appealed to Roosevelt to be allowed to make the concessions Stalin desired to ensure the conclusion of an Anglo-Russian treaty.

> The increasing gravity of the war has led me to feel that the principles of the Atlantic Charter ought not to be construed so as to deny Russia the frontiers she occupied when Germany attacked her. This was the basis on which Russia acceded to the Charter. . . . I hope therefore that you will give us a free hand to sign the treaty which Stalin desires as soon as possible.

In the spring of 1942, however, with the renewal of German offensives in Russia, Stalin dropped his demand that Soviet territorial claims be officially recognized in an alliance treaty. On May 26, 1942, he agreed to a twenty-year Anglo-Soviet treaty that guaranteed the Soviet Union British military support against Germany but made no mention of territorial commitments.

❏ *The Second Front in North Africa*

In November 1942 the Western Allies at last opened a second front—not in France as Stalin had demanded, but in French North Africa. In the spring of that year Germany's African army under the command General Erwin Rommel had mounted a spectacularly successful offensive, and by the end of June his forces were only seventy miles from Alexandria, within striking distance of the Suez Canal. In considerable alarm, Churchill cabled Roosevelt on July 8 saying that now there could be no question of a cross-Channel invasion and stressing the urgent need for an Anglo-American landing in North Africa to relieve the pressure on the British 8th Army in Egypt. On July 27 Roosevelt endorsed plans for a North African campaign drawn up by British

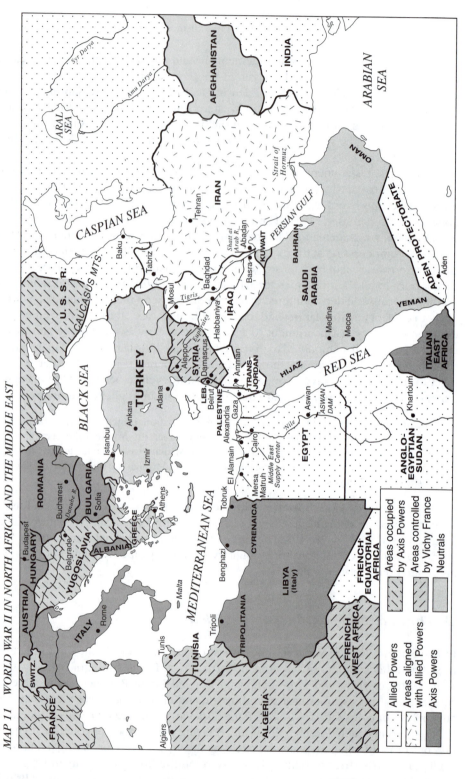

MAP 11 WORLD WAR II IN NORTH AFRICA AND THE MIDDLE EAST

Allied Powers

Areas aligned
with Allied Powers

Axis Powers

Areas occupied
by Axis Powers

Areas controlled
by Vichy France

Neutrals

and American staff officers, and an American, General Dwight D. Eisenhower, was appointed commander-in-chief of the Anglo-American forces.

As it proved, the British 8th Army did not require relief. Already in early July Rommel's offensive had been halted in the first of a series of battles around E1 Alamein that proved to be a turning point in the struggle for North Africa. From the start, however, Rommel had been in a hopeless position. Britain's control of the Mediterranean sea lanes proved a formidable obstacle to reinforcing and supplying Axis troops in Africa, whereas the British were able to carry out a military buildup that gave them air as well as naval superiority in the Mediterranean. By the time the decisive battles in North Africa took place, they had a two-to-one superiority in manpower, tanks, and heavy guns. On October 23, 1942, the British launched the last of their offensives that has since become known as *the* Battle of El Alamein. By November 12 Rommel's forces had been driven from Egypt.

The defeat of Rommel at Alamein did not end Anglo-American preparations for the invasion of French North Africa. Rommel's army was still in the field and the French colonial governments, which had remained loyal to the Vichy regime, still had powerful military forces at their disposal. Because Vichy was under constant pressure from the Germans, the great fear of the Allies was that the French armies in North Africa would oppose an Anglo-American invasion or actually join forces with Rommel. The principal diplomatic task of the Allies in this situation was to persuade the French leadership in North Africa not to oppose the Allied landings, or better still, to join the Allies in driving the Germans and Italians out of Africa.

The Allies were lucky. By what Churchill called a "formidable coincidence," Admiral Jean François Darlan, former deputy leader of the Vichy government and now commander-in-chief of Vichy's armed forces, happened to be in Algiers at the time of the Allied landings visiting his son, who was seriously ill with poliomyelitis. In seeking help for his son, Darlan had been in touch with Roosevelt, crippled many years earlier by the same disease. Besides seeking medical advice, however, Darlan had dropped hints of his willingness to bring France back into the Allied camp if assured of sufficient American military support. Informed of Darlan's presence in Algiers, Roosevelt empowered Eisenhower to conclude an agreement recognizing him as supreme authority in French North Africa in return for a promise not to resist the Allied invasion.

Darlan accepted these terms. On November 9, the day after the first Allied landings, he issued cease-fire orders to French forces in Algiers, and the next day he issued similar orders to French military and naval commanders throughout Algeria and French Morocco. Under the guns of the Germans, Marshal Pétain, the head of the Vichy regime, publicly repudiated Darlan, but in a secret telegram he expressed his confidence in the admiral and empowered him to act on his own authority. Pétain did more. He in effect sanctioned Darlan's cooperation with the Allies by informing him that he, Pétain, enjoyed an *accord intime* with President Roosevelt but could not speak his mind openly because of the presence of the Germans.

Any doubts French officials in North Africa might still have had about obeying Darlan's cease-fire orders were removed when the Germans responded to the Allied landings in North Africa by occupying hitherto unoccupied France on November 11. A major German objective in doing so was the capture of the French fleet at the naval base of Toulon, which Darlan had ordered to sail to North Africa. Unable to escape from Toulon, the French scuttled their fleet to prevent it from falling into German hands.

Appointed high commissioner for French North Africa under Anglo-American auspices in return for his collaboration, Darlan was assassinated on Christmas Eve, 1942, by a young Frenchman, allegedly to avenge Darlan's previous collaboration with the Germans. The most eager aspirant to succeed Darlan as high commissioner was Charles de Gaulle, who had meanwhile moved his Free French government to Algeria in order to be on what he regarded as French soil. But de Gaulle was not popular with the British and Americans, who resented his arrogance and disregard of problems that did not affect France, and the appointment went instead to General Henri Giraud, who had become a national hero by escaping from a German prisoner-of-war camp. Already embittered by constant controversy with his allies, de Gaulle was infuriated by this latest snub, a burning resentment of the British and Americans that was to endure far into the postwar years.

In March 1943 Rommel launched a final desperate offensive to defeat the British 8th Army on his eastern flank before the Anglo-American forces could attack him from the west. In the ensuing Battle of Medenine, he was again decisively defeated by the British, who retained a more than two-to-one superiority in manpower plus control of the sea and air. Rommel was recalled from Africa, and early in April Allied forces defeated what remained of the German-Italian armies in Africa, which finally capitulated on May 11.

❑ *The Casablanca Conference:*
   Sicily and Unconditional Surrender

In mid-January 1943, Churchill and Roosevelt met in the French Moroccan city of Casablanca, where they made two important strategic and political decisions. The strategic decision was to mount an invasion of Sicily in July from their newly acquired bases in North Africa, a course opposed by the American military leadership because it would divert resources from what they regarded as the decisive cross-Channel attack. The British, however, argued that a cross-Channel invasion was still too risky. Preparations for a cross-Channel crossing should be carried on as rapidly and on as large a scale as possible, but meanwhile the best use that could be made of the troops already in North Africa would be to establish secure control over the Mediterranean sea lanes. By compelling the Axis to divert substantial forces to the south, the Sicilian campaign would provide more immediate relief to the Soviets than a mere buildup for a future cross-Channel invasion.

Churchill had more far-reaching objectives in view, which he set forth with multiple variations in subsequent conferences with the Americans. The conquest of Sicily should be followed up by an invasion of the Italian mainland that would knock Italy out of the war and open the Balkans and the Hungarian plain to Allied penetration. A thrust into Romania would be particularly telling, for it would deprive the Germans of vital Romanian oil supplies. A campaign in this region would also encourage Turkey's entry into the war. In any event every effort should be made to secure Turkey's participation, because from Turkish territory the Allies could mount a decisive campaign against the Axis from the south.

With these proposals Churchill intended to accomplish far more than the defeat of the Axis. Deeply concerned about the power structure of the postwar world, he saw in this southern strategy a means of placing the Western allies in control of the Middle East and much of Eastern Europe before these areas could be occupied by the Red Army. The Americans, however, feared that any attempt to implement Churchill's proposals would have disastrous effects on Western relations with the Soviet Union. They therefore turned aside all suggestion for diversionary campaigns in the Eastern Mediterranean and the Balkans, nor would they make definite commitments about future operations in Italy.

The major political decision produced at Casablanca was a demand for the unconditional surrender of the Axis powers and Japan, which Roosevelt announced at a press conference at the conclusion of the conference. This demand was no last-minute improvisation, as Roosevelt alleged at the time. Already in April 1942, a subcommittee of the American State Department had proposed this formula to avoid Wilson's mistake of granting the Germans armistice terms, which had given the Germans a moral base for their protests against the Treaty of Versailles. To eliminate this possibility in the present conflict, the subcommittee recommended that "unconditional surrender rather than an armistice should be sought from the principal enemy states, except perhaps Italy." The unconditional surrender formula, to which Churchill had agreed prior to Roosevelt's announcement, may also have been intended to reassure Stalin as well as Chiang Kai-shek that Britain and the United States would not withdraw from the conflict before final victory was achieved.

Critics have contended that the call for unconditional surrender was a mistake, for it gave Axis and Japanese leaders a propaganda weapon in summoning their people to go on fighting no matter what the cost because they could expect no mercy in defeat. Further, it prevented even a consideration of negotiating with opponents of Hitler, who were plotting his overthrow, and the conclusion of a negotiated peace with Germany that might have saved thousands of lives. There is no way of measuring the validity of these criticisms. In the case of Italy they are unwarranted, for the Casablanca declaration did not affect the Italian decision to surrender. Nor did it put an end to efforts of German opponents of the Nazi regime to assassinate Hitler and seek a negotiated peace, though all those efforts were doomed by Roosevelt's uncompromising stance on this issue with regard to Germany. Unconditional surrender proved to be a serious obstacle to peace with Japan, which was removed when Japan was, in fact, offered conditions.

❑ *The Course of the War: Stalingrad and Kursk*

On February 2, 1943, the Red Army won a major victory over the German army besieging the city of Stalingrad, where twenty-two German divisions, now reduced to 80,000 men and forbidden to retreat by Hitler, were obliged to surrender. The Soviet victory at Stalingrad, achieved despite the failure of the Western Allies to mount a major offensive in the west, proved to be a decisive turning point in the war against Germany. The Germans managed to hold the line in other sectors of the eastern front and even assume the offensive in numerous engagements, but henceforth the history of the war in the east was largely a record of Soviet victories. In early July 1943, the Germans were dealt what proved to be a mortal blow in the Battle of the Kursk Salient, the biggest tank battle in history, which brought to a halt Germany's last major offensive. That battle cost Hitler half a million men and ended Germany's last hope of avoiding defeat. The bulk of Germany's armed forces remained concentrated in the east, however, so that the Soviets continued to bear the principal brunt of the war in Europe.

The tide of battle had long since turned in North Africa, where, as we have seen, the last Axis forces had capitulated on May 11, 1943.

❑ *The Invasion of Sicily and Italy and the Fall of Mussolini*

American, British, and Canadian forces attacked Sicily on July 10, 1943. Within a fortnight half of Sicily, including the capital of Palermo, had fallen. By August 18 all Axis resistance had collapsed, though a substantial number of German and Italian troops managed to escape to the mainland with their equipment.

The decision to follow up the conquest of Sicily with an invasion of the Italian mainland had already been made in mid-May. The British once again took the lead in urging this course of action, using many of the same arguments they had employed in advocating the invasion of Sicily. And once again the Americans opposed further operations in Southern Europe on the grounds that they would delay mounting a second front in France. They finally agreed to an Italian campaign, but only after receiving a British commitment to a cross-Channel invasion of France with a target date of May 1, 1944, together with assurances that further operations in the Mediterranean would not jeopardize the military buildup for the cross-Channel attack.

The Allied invasion of Sicily dealt a final blow to the Mussolini regime, its prestige and popular support already badly eroded by a steady succession of military defeats, the loss of North Africa, and the relentless Allied bombardment of Italy's mainland cities. On July 24, 1943, the Fascist Grand Council, meeting for the first time since 1939, voted to restore a constitutional monarchy and a democratically elected parliament. On the following day King Victor Emanuel III called for the resignation of Mussolini, who was arrested at the king's orders and subsequently moved from one place of detention to another to frustrate possible attempts on the part of his followers or the Germans to liberate him. Mussolini was succeeded as head of the Italian government by Marshal Pietro Badoglio, a hero of the Ethiopian war but dismissed in 1940 following the Italian military debacle in Greece. The king and Badoglio assured the Germans that Italy would remain in the war on their side, but Hitler had no confidence whatever in the word of the Italian leaders. "They say they will fight, but it is certainly treachery," he told his generals on the evening of July 25.

Hitler's lack of faith in the new Italian government soon proved justified. On September 3 the Badoglio government signed a secret armistice with the Allies. Five days later the Western powers took it upon themselves to announce Italy's unconditional surrender, sparing the Badoglio government the need to do so while privately offering him terms to bring Italy into the war on the side of the Allies. The Germans were ready to cope with the situation. They immediately seized strategic positions still held by Italian troops and disarmed all Italian forces that fell into their hands, meeting remarkably little resistance as they did so. On September 12 Mussolini was dramatically rescued by an SS commando unit from his most recent place of detention on the Gran Sasso, the highest peak in the Abruzzi mountains. With German backing, he now formed a government of his own, the Italian Social Republic, but the Italian dictator was henceforth nothing more than a puppet of the Germans, who made no attempt to disguise their intention to annex a large part of northern Italy to the Reich after the war.

On September 2, 1943, one day before Badoglio signed his secret armistice with the Allies, British and American forces crossed the Straits of Messina and began their invasion of the Italian mainland. The swift German takeover of a large part of Italy deprived them of any major advantages they might have gained from the surrender of the Badoglio government, which declared war on Germany on October 13 and soon afterwards was recognized by the Allies as a co-belligerent.

From the time of their invasion of the Italian mainland to the end of the war, Allied troops slogged up the Italian peninsula, where they kept a large number of German troops engaged but never achieved a breakthrough that would decisively affect the outcome of the war. German forces held northern Italy until their final surrender at the end of April 1945.

On April 29, 1945, in the last days of the war, Mussolini and his mistress, Clara Petacci, were shot by Italian partisans while attempting to escape to Switzerland. Their bodies were taken to Milan, where they were hung upside down in the Piazzale Loreto.

TWENTY

Laying the Foundations of the Postwar World

Cold War

□ *The Moscow Conference*

As the tide of battle shifted on every front and the Allies grew confident of ultimate victory, the governments of the Big Three recognized the need to go beyond military planning and to consider the shape of the postwar world. For this purpose the foreign ministers of the Big Three, Eden, Hull, and Molotov, met in Moscow from October 19 to 30, 1943, to work out preliminary proposals that would provide a basis for final agreements to be negotiated by their chiefs of state.

At the Moscow conference, the Russians were still primarily concerned with securing firm Western commitments over a second front in France, and they initially proposed that this be the only item on the agenda. After receiving satisfactory assurances on this point, together with promises of increased deliveries of food and military equipment, they were prepared to deal with other issues.

The three foreign ministers agreed about the need for punitive treatment of Germany, and Hull, warmly seconded by Molotov, called for the summary execution of the principal Nazi leaders. They also agreed that Austria was to be separated from Germany. But beyond that they could only agree that the problems of Germany, and indeed of all countries to be liberated from the Nazi yoke, were too complex to be resolved in a brief meeting. To give adequate consideration to these problems, they established a tripartite European Advisory Commission (EAC), staffed by diplomatic representatives of the Big Three, which was to draw up proposals for the future of Germany and Europe.

The establishment of the EAC was the principal substantive achievement of the Moscow conference, but Hull thought he had achieved a great deal more. He had brought with him to Moscow a joint declaration, previously approved by Roosevelt and the British, embodying a statement of principle to regulate the conduct of all governments after the war. In addition, he had set forth proposals for the establishment of a system of postwar collective security and the creation of an international organization for the preservation of peace. With such principles and organizations in place, he was confident that all other problems could be resolved in due course. His great objective in Moscow had been to secure Soviet adherence to this joint declaration, and he regarded his success in doing so, with only minor Soviet changes of the text, as a major diplomatic triumph.

An obstacle to the Soviet signature of Hull's joint declaration had been the Soviet objection to America's condition that China be one of its sponsors. Molotov had argued that China was too weak and too dependent to be associated on equal terms with the Big Three as a guardian of postwar peace and security. Molotov's argument was valid enough, whatever his ulterior motives may have been, but Hull was insistent. The omission of China, he said, would have "the most terrific repercussions, both political and military, in the Pacific area" and might call for all sorts of readjustments on the part of his own government. After a week of bickering, the Soviets at last agreed to the participation of China. Hull's document thus became a Four-Power declaration.

The entire declaration was so vaguely worded as to be subject to widely different interpretations. It did, however, commit all four signatory powers to the establishment of a postwar international security organization that was to become the United Nations.

At the very end of the Moscow conference, Stalin informed Hull that the Soviet Union intended to enter the war against Japan after the defeat of Germany. Hull professed to be "astonished and delighted" by this unsolicited commitment, offered without reservations or conditions, and he saw in it yet another demonstration of Stalin's loyalty to the Grand Alliance.

Back in Washington, Hull told a joint session of Congress that "as the provisions of the Four-Nation Declaration are carried into effect there will no longer be need for spheres of influence, for alliances, for balance of power, or any other of the special arrangements through which, in the unhappy past, the nations strove to safeguard their security or to promote their interests." In the realm of economics, too, agreements had been reached to prevent the reappearance of barriers to international trade. Hull's speech was greeted in Congress with enthusiastic applause. Roosevelt called the Moscow conference "a resounding success." Churchill hailed its results as "prodigious." Only a few cynics wondered whether Hull's words might not some day sound as hollow as Chamberlain's, who had returned from the Munich conference proclaiming that he had achieved "peace in our time."

The Moscow conference prepared the way, as planned, for the first meeting of the chiefs of state of the Big Three, Churchill, Roosevelt, and Stalin. The Iranian capital of Teheran was chosen as the site of their conference because Stalin insisted that, as commander-in-chief of the Soviet armed forces, he had to remain near the theaters of military operations and could not go farther afield.

❏ The First Cairo Conference, November 22–26, 1943

Before going to Teheran, Roosevelt and Churchill had arranged a meeting in Cairo, to which Roosevelt had invited the Chinese leader, Chiang Kai-shek. Churchill greeted the inclusion of Chiang with some misgivings. Well aware of Roosevelt's anticolonial prejudices, he feared the president might make commitments to the Chinese leader to the detriment of British interests. By associating China in the Four-Power Declaration, the Americans had already elevated China to the status of a major world power, and Eden observed that they were "impressed, almost to the point of obsession, with the merits of General and Mme. Chiang Kai-shek."

Churchill had good reason to be fearful. The Americans had steadfastly opposed British proposals for further operations in the Mediterranean and the Balkans on the grounds that these would interfere with the buildup of a cross-Channel invasion of France. Yet, at the same time, they were advocating large-scale increases of Allied military aid to China and putting forward plans for ambitious new operations in the Pacific.

In his private conversations with Chiang, Roosevelt made commitments to the Chinese leader that may well have exceeded anything Churchill had anticipated. He agreed with Chiang about the desirability of eliminating colonialism in Asia, though he made specific commitments only about the colonialism of the Japanese—China was to recover all territory lost to Japan since the Sino–Japanese war of 1894–1895. In addition, China was to receive massive American military and economic aid to enable that country to take its place as one of the Big Four policemen of the postwar world.

Churchill was not informed about many of the most important features of these conversations, but suspecting their anticolonial drift, he served notice that he would never agree to dismantling the British empire in Asia. Churchill in fact disliked the entire idea of building up China, for there was no way of knowing how China and its government would develop in the future or whether a strong and united China might not become an imperialist power in its own right.

At the conclusion of the Cairo conference, the Americans proposed the release of a public declaration announcing the determination of the three allied powers to destroy Japanese colonialism and restore the territorial integrity of China. Issued on December 1, the Cairo Declaration stated that "the Three Great Allies" were fighting this war "to restrain and punish the aggression of Japan." They coveted no territorial gain for themselves. Japan was to be stripped of all the islands in the Pacific seized or occupied since the beginning of World War I; of "all the territories Japan has stolen from the Chinese, such as Manchuria, Formosa [Taiwan], and the Pescadores" (the fruits of Japan's victory over China in 1895); and of all other territories "which she has taken by violence and greed." Further, the three powers were determined "that in due course Korea shall become free and independent." The declaration made no mention of the East Asian territories "stolen" by the British, French, and Russians, though in their private conversations Roosevelt and Chiang had agreed that not only Korea but French Indochina should be helped to independence.

❑ The Teheran Conference, November 28 to December 1, 1943

On November 28, 1943, two days after their conference with Chiang in Cairo, Churchill and Roosevelt met with Stalin for the first time at the Iranian capital of Teheran. It was here, not at the more famous Yalta conference of February 1945, that many of the most important general agreements among the Big Three over the structure of the postwar world were reached.

In view of the passionate denunciations of these agreements in the West after the war and their exploitation for partisan political purposes, the point should be stressed that the Teheran conference took place while the pressures and passions of war were still intense, while the Soviet Union still bore the chief burden of carrying on the land war against Germany, and while the Western allies were still convinced of the need to secure the Soviets' entry into the war against Japan after Germany's defeat. Among Western leaders, Roosevelt in particular, there was also the longer-range calculation of the need to respond to Soviet concerns about their future security in order to ensure Soviet participation in a postwar international system for the preservation of peace.

In their discussions of military operations, the Big Three were in fundamental agreement from the beginning. Stalin was once again assured, this time personally, that the primary military objective of the Western powers was a cross-Channel invasion of France in the following May (Operation Overlord), which was to be supported by a simultaneous invasion of southern France (Operation Anvil). Stalin for his part promised to mount major offensives on the eastern front to coincide with Western operations in France and to declare war on Japan shortly after Germany's defeat.

The Teheran meeting revealed more clearly than any of Roosevelt's previous actions or pronouncements that coming to terms with Stalin—winning his confidence to ensure Soviet cooperation for the preservation of peace in the postwar world—was the president's principal diplomatic objective. In private conversations with the Soviet leader, he outlined proposals for a United Nations organization that would in effect be controlled and directed by the Big Four policemen—Britain. China, the Soviet Union, and the United States. Stalin, while expressing doubts about the role of China, thought that even more needed to be done to keep Japan and most especially Germany under control.

Roosevelt was not only willing but eager to provide Stalin assurances with respect to Germany, something he was able to do with real conviction because of his personal hatred of that country. He suggested that the very concept of a German *Reich* should be eliminated, the word expunged from the German language. Stalin countered that it was not enough to destroy a word: the Germans should be deprived permanently of the means of waging war, their country should be dismembered, their industry ruthlessly liquidated. He scornfully rejected every suggestion that the German economy might have to be reconstructed after the war for the sake of the economic health of Europe as a whole.

Churchill, who had a rather better record of opposing Nazi Germany than either Roosevelt or the Soviet leader, expressed reservations about the more extreme proposals of his colleagues, and during a dinner at the Soviet embassy Stalin taunted him with having a secret affection for the Germans. Besides imposing permanent and stringent controls on Germany after the war, he suggested liquidating some fifty thousand to one hundred thousand members of the "German commanding staff." Churchill rose to the bait, if bait it was. Denouncing the very idea of "the cold-blooded murder of men who had fought for their country," he rose angrily from the table and left the dining room. Stalin hastened to persuade him to return, assuring him that it was all a joke, and Roosevelt tried to ease the tension with what he evidently intended as another joke by suggesting that they might settle for the liquidation of only forty-nine thousand.

Because of their disagreements over Germany and the sheer complexity of the German question, the Big Three did not formulate final proposals for the future of that country at Teheran. This task was once again left to the European Advisory Commission set up by the Big Three foreign ministers at their earlier Moscow conference.

It was at Teheran, however, that the Big Three made their major territorial decisions about Germany. This was done in connection with the Polish question. Since Eden's mission to Moscow in December 1941, the Soviet government had consistently expressed its intention to regain the Soviet boundaries of June 1941 and thus the territories acquired in partnership with Hitler. The Soviet position was a matter of considerable embarrassment to the British, who had gone to war in defense of Poland. Yet it was none other than Churchill, who had originally indignantly rejected Soviet territorial demands, who now set forth a proposal to yield to those demands and to compensate Poland at the expense of Germany. Using three matchsticks, he illustrated the westward shift of the Soviet, Polish, and German frontiers. Roosevelt heartily approved of Churchill's formula, but he explained that he could not afford to say so publicly for fear of alienating the six- to seven million American voters of Polish descent. While agreeing to Soviet claims to well over half of prewar Poland, Roosevelt put in a plea on behalf of the independence of the three Baltic states, but in what may have been intended as another joke, he assured Stalin that the United States would not go to war over this issue.

The Western leaders themselves thus took the lead in working out a way to meet Soviet territorial demands in Poland, thereby relieving Stalin of the need to take the initiative on the Polish question. By the time of Teheran, however, Stalin was no longer satisfied with the Soviet frontiers of June 1941. He demanded Germany's cession to the Soviet Union of East Prussian territory bordering the Baltic Sea, including the city of Königsberg, while the rest of East Prussia was to go to Poland. He demanded further that Finland, in addition to the territory ceded after the winter war of 1939–1940, should surrender either the harbor of Hanko, on the Gulf of Finland, or the northern region of Petsamo, which would give the Soviet Union a common frontier with Norway as well as the valuable Petsamo nickel mines. Yielding to the pleas of his Allies, he agreed not to absorb the rest of Finland, but he insisted that the postwar government of Finland, like that of all neighboring countries, should be "friendly" to the Soviet Union and that Finland pay a war indemnity of 600 million dollars. "Fair enough," Roosevelt said.

In his efforts to win Stalin's confidence, Roosevelt went out of his way to emphasize his differences with Churchill with the specific purpose of reassuring the Soviet dictator that the Western powers were not "ganging up" on him. He sided with Stalin in opposing Churchill's proposals to restore France as a major European military power. Stalin's motives in not wanting a revival of French power were clear enough: he wanted no rival military power anywhere in Europe, and he must have been delighted when Roosevelt informed him that United States would not maintain a military presence there after the war. Roosevelt's own hostility toward France is more difficult to understand. He seems to have regarded the French defeat in 1940 as proof of the moral degeneration of that country and its leadership. "The French must pay for their criminal collaboration with Germany," he told Stalin, conveniently forgetting that he himself had sanctioned negotiations with France's Vichy government while steadfastly denying recognition to de Gaulle's Free French government in exile.

On no subject did Roosevelt make his differences with Churchill more evident than that of the European colonial empires. Here he allowed his hostility to France free rein, agreeing with Stalin that Indochina should never be restored to France but placed in trusteeship until properly prepared for self-government, a solution he considered valid for other colonial countries as well. After the war the United States intended to grant the Philippines their independence, and Roosevelt obviously hoped other colonial powers would follow the American example. On the mention of India, Stalin observed that this was Churchill's sore point, but this did not deter Roosevelt from suggesting that India should be reformed "from the bottom, somewhat on the Soviet line." When Stalin pointed out that this would mean "going along the path of revolution," the president made no pretense of disagreement.

In dealing with the problems of East Asia in general, Stalin subscribed without reservation to the Cairo Declaration and made no plea on behalf of the Chinese Communists. In return, the Western powers agreed to his own comparatively modest territorial claims on behalf of the Soviet Union: the cession by Japan of the Kurile Islands and the southern half of the island of Sakhalin, obtained by the Japanese after their victory over Russia in 1905.

In dealing with the problems of the Middle East at the Iranian capital of Teheran, the most important negotiations involved Iran itself, where Britain and Russia had competed for influence throughout much of the nineteenth century. To avoid a perpetuation of their rivalry over Iran, the Big Three signed a special agreement to maintain the independence, sovereignty, and territorial integrity of that country—a treaty particularly desired by the Western powers because it promised to forestall a Soviet takeover of this oil-rich country and an extension of Soviet influence to the Persian Gulf.

At the conclusion of the Teheran Conference, the three allies issued a joint declaration stating that they had coordinated their plans for the destruction of the German armed forces; they expressed certainty that their concord would make for an enduring peace; and they looked forward to welcoming all countries, large and small, into a "world family of democratic nations." "We came here with hope and determination. We leave here friends in fact, in spirit, and in purpose."

❑ *The Polish Question*

At Teheran, Churchill had agreed to Stalin's demand for the Polish-Soviet frontier established in 1939 in partnership with Hitler, which would give the Soviet Union the entire eastern half of prewar Poland. As is readily understandable, Stalin tried to avoid any reference to his pact with Hitler, and in making his claims to eastern Poland he referred instead to the Curzon Line, established by an Allied commission after World

War I, which had assigned essentially the same territory to Russia on ethnic grounds. The cession of eastern Poland to the Soviet Union was bitterly opposed by the Polish government in exile in London, recognized by Britain as the official government of Poland, which was composed largely of the aristocrats, landowners, bureaucrats, and army officers who had governed the country since its reestablishment as an independent state after World War I. These London Poles not only expected the British to honor their 1939 guarantees of Poland's prewar territorial integrity, but assumed that they would be accorded international recognition as the legitimate government of Poland after the war.

The Soviets had other ideas. Besides taking over the eastern half of prewar Poland, they had no intention of allowing Poland's prewar government, with its long record of hostility towards the Soviet Union, to govern a postwar Polish state. They therefore began organizing their own Polish government in exile so as to have a pro-Soviet regime ready to install when the Red Army occupied the country.

An unexpected development gave the Soviet government an excuse to sever all relations with the London Poles. In April 1943 the Germans announced the discovery of the corpses of thousands of Polish officers captured by the Russians in 1939 in the forest of Katyn, near Smolensk. The condition of the corpses, their location, and the bullets used in their execution left no doubt that these Polish officers had been murdered by the Soviets. Moscow, indignantly denying all responsibility for the Katyn massacre, accused the Germans of the crime, but representatives of the International Red Cross and other impartial observers confirmed that the mass execution had indeed been carried out by the Russians. (The Russians continued to deny their responsibility until the collapse of the Soviet regime, when researchers in Soviet archives found the order for the execution of the Polish officers, signed by Stalin himself.)

The London Poles were convinced from the start of Russia's guilt and publicly denounced the Soviet government for its perpetration of the Katyn massacre. Although their reaction was understandable, their behavior was a serious diplomatic blunder. The Soviet government, far from admitting its guilt, denounced the London Poles as "criminal purveyors of Nazi propaganda" and could now defend its refusal to recognize their government on the grounds of their hostility to the Soviet Union. The reaction of the London Poles also weakened their position with the British and Americans, who could no longer give them even token support to avoid offending the Russians. The overall result of this tragic episode has been succinctly summarized by the historian Adam Ulam: "Seldom has a crime been translated into a comparable diplomatic and propaganda victory."

The last hope of the London Poles to govern postwar Poland was shattered in the summer of 1944 when the Polish underground army in Warsaw, which owed allegiance to the London organization, was wiped out. On July 29, as the Red Army was driving westward with what appeared to be inexorable momentum, the Soviet-sponsored Polish government broadcast an appeal over Soviet radio stations to the underground army in Warsaw to rise up against the Germans. With the Red Army on the left bank of the Vistula in the outskirts of Warsaw, the Polish underground army, confident of Soviet support, responded to this appeal.

At this point, however, the Soviets halted their advance and for two months remained on the shores of the Vistula as the Germans suppressed the Warsaw uprising with grim brutality. They even denied the Western Allies the use of Soviet airfields to drop supplies to the beleaguered Poles. "Sooner or later," Stalin said in response to Western appeals, "the truth about the group of criminals who have unleashed the Warsaw adventure in order to seize power will become known to everybody." What he meant was that the underground army, had its uprising been successful, might have proclaimed the establishment of a Polish government in Warsaw led by the London Poles. This possibility ended with the annihilation of the Warsaw Poles after a two-month siege. It has been estimated that as many as 300,000 Poles were killed in the conflict, most of them civilians. The city of Warsaw itself was almost totally destroyed.

Prior to the Warsaw uprising, but with the Red Army already in control of a large part of Poland, the Soviets set up a Polish Committee of National Liberation in the city of Lublin headed by a Communist, Boleslaw Bierut. To this body the Soviets turned over the civil administration of all Polish territory conquered by the Red Army *west* of the Curzon Line. On the last day of 1944, the Lublin Committee formally proclaimed itself to be the provisional government of Poland and on the following day it was recognized as such by the Soviet Union. The territory east of the Curzon Line was incorporated into the Soviet republics of Belorussia and Ukraine.

Churchill had long sought to convince the London Poles of the need to seek a reconciliation with Moscow and to accept the Curzon Line; otherwise, the Soviets would simply install a pro-Communist regime in Poland and the London Poles would be frozen out altogether. Exasperated by their obstinacy and procrastination, he became brutally frank. "We are not going to wreck the peace of Europe because of a quarrel between Poles," he told them. "If you want to conquer Russia, we shall leave you to it." Churchill subsequently informed the House of Commons that Britain was prepared to support redrawing Poland's eastern frontiers in favor of the Soviet Union and its frontiers in the west in favor of Poland at the expense of Germany. To forestall criticism, he reminded the House that the Soviets had contributed most to Poland's liberation, and he was prepared to accept the population transfer of several million that would be involved in these frontier shifts. "A clean sweep will be made. I am not alarmed by the prospect of the disentanglement of populations, nor even by the large transfers, which are more possible in modern conditions than they ever were before."

□ *The Course of the War in Europe*

Ever since the surrender of the German army at Stalingrad, the expulsion of Axis forces from Africa, and the defeats of the Japanese at sea, the armies and navies of the Grand Alliance had been victorious on every front, though against stubborn resistance and with varying degrees of success.

The Germans had lost the battle for air supremacy as early as the summer of 1940. After that their principal weapon against Britain was the U-boat, but the British success in breaking the German naval code, which gave them the location and course of enemy submarines, enabled them to bring the U-boat menace under control. Meanwhile, having established their own air supremacy, the Western Allies had stepped up their bombing attacks on Germany aided by the development of a radar system capable of identifying targets through clouds and darkness. By the summer of 1942, besides striking at military and industrial targets, Anglo-American bombers began a systematic destruction of major population centers through the use of incendiary bombs, which created currents of flame at temperatures of 1,000 degrees centigrade, moving at speeds of 100 to 150 miles per hour, which incinerated people above and below ground. Air attacks were mounted against all major German cities, reducing most of them to rubble well before the end of the war. The purpose of this bombing of population centers was to destroy enemy morale, disrupt the German labor force, and divert what was left of the Luftwaffe from offensive operations to the defense of the Reich. Saturation bombing did not achieve the quick and decisive results its advocates had predicted. German morale did not crack and industrial production actually peaked in 1944, as the Nazi government finally organized its economy for total war. But bombing undoubtedly contributed substantially to the precipitate decline of German production in the final year of the war.

On June 6, 1944, Anglo-American forces at last launched their cross-Channel invasion of the continent. To support the Anglo-American operations in the west, the Soviets honored their promise to mount major offensives in the east. By mid-July the Red Army had reached the outskirts of Warsaw, where, as we have seen, it halted for two months while the Germans destroyed the Polish underground army. Elsewhere, however, the Red Army continued its advance. In the south, Romania surrendered on August 23, opening the way to the Red Army's occupation of the lower Danube. On September 5 the Russians declared war on Bulgaria, which, as the ally of Germany, had declared war on Britain and the United States but not on the Soviet Union. Three days later the Bulgarian government asked for an armistice and by mid-September the Red Army had occupied Sofia. In the north, the Finns agreed to an armistice on September 10 and were offered the terms Stalin had proposed at Teheran: the Soviet Union was to receive the territory ceded by Finland after the winter war of 1939–1940 plus Petsamo and the harbor of Porkkala, which the Russians chose instead of Hanko. In addition, Finland was to pay 300 million dollars in reparations.

❑ *The Morgenthau Plan; the Quebec Conference of September 11–16, 1944, and JCS 1067*

While geography and the fortunes of war left the Western allies virtually helpless in deciding the future of Poland and much of the rest of Eastern Europe, they anticipated having an influential voice in the future of Germany. At Teheran the Big Three had agreed in principle to the dismemberment of Germany and the transfer of East Prussia and all German territory east of the Oder River to the Soviet Union and Poland. The task of working out plans for the rest of Germany had been assigned to the European Advisory Commission established by the foreign ministers of the Big Three at their meeting in Moscow in October 1943. The fact that this work had been assigned to the EAC did not deter numerous individual political leaders, government agencies, and private persons from formulating plans of their own over the future of Germany.

Among these many planners was Henry Morgenthau, Jr., the American secretary of the treasury and a close friend of President Roosevelt. Morgenthau, who was Jewish, felt an understandable hatred for Nazi Germany, a sentiment shared by the president. Although the Atlantic Charter and the proclamation of the doctrine of Unconditional Surrender had emphasized that the aim of the Allies was the destruction of the Nazi government, not of the German people, Roosevelt made no such distinction in private. In Morgenthau's diary, Roosevelt is quoted as saying: "We have got to be tough with Germany, and I mean the German people not just the Nazis. We either have to castrate the German people or you have to treat them in such a manner that they can't go on reproducing people who want to continue the way they have in the past." Although expressed only privately by Roosevelt (and Morgenthau may have grossly exaggerated the president's views), similar proposals for the mass sterilization of Germans and mass executions were being advocated publicly at this time by respected men and women in numerous Allied countries, so inflamed were wartime passions and so great was the outrage over reports of German atrocities.

On September 11, 1944, Churchill met with Roosevelt in Quebec, his principal objective to secure promises of a continuation of American economic aid to Britain after the war. Because financial aid was to be a major topic of the meeting, Roosevelt was accompanied by Treasury Secretary Morgenthau, who brought with him his own plan for Germany in a memorandum entitled "Program to Prevent Germany from Starting a World War III." In this plan, Morgenthau proposed that the Ruhr region, by which he meant the entire Rhineland and a large part of western Germany, "should not only be stripped of all presently existing industry but so weakened and controlled that it cannot in the foreseeable future become an industrial area." This program was endorsed by Roosevelt and was subsequently accepted by Churchill, who yielded to the arguments of Roosevelt and Morgenthau "from whom we have much to ask," as Churchill himself expressed it.

After the Quebec Conference, Roosevelt summarized its results in a memorandum to Hull, his secretary of state, informing him that "Morgenthau presented at Quebec, in conjunction with his plan for Germany, a proposal of credits to Britain totaling six and a half billion dollars." Hull, who had not been invited to Quebec or consulted either about the Morgenthau plan or about the aid package for Britain, was appalled. "This might suggest to some the *quid pro quo*," he commented, "with which the Secretary of the Treasury was able to get Mr. Churchill's adherence to his cataclysmic plan for Germany."

Churchill faced scathing criticism from his own foreign secretary, Anthony Eden, who pointed out that the Morgenthau plan not only violated the principles of the Atlantic Charter but undercut the plans for Germany proposed by the European Advisory Commission, which had already been approved by both Roosevelt and Molotov. While bitterly resenting Eden's criticisms, Churchill recognized their validity.

He was spared controversy with the Americans on the subject because Roosevelt withdrew his support of the plan after Secretary of War Stimson and other advisers convinced him of its potentially disastrous consequences. Morgenthau, however, continued to press for a punitive policy towards Germany and succeeded in having the essential features of his plan incorporated in a directive drawn up by the Joint Chiefs of Staff (JCS 1067) that was to be the cornerstone of American occupation policy in Germany until June 1947. JCS 1067 prohibited occupation authorities from taking any step to rehabilitate the German economy except to maximize agricultural production; it was specifically intended to punish the German people collectively through a drastic reduction of their standard of living. The Germans were spared this fate by the coming of the Cold War, when the Soviet Union and international Communism took the place of Germany (in Western eyes) as the great threat to world civilization.

❑ *The Churchill-Eden Mission to Moscow, October 1944, and the Percentages Agreement*

Alarmed by the rapid advance of the Soviet armies and the possibility that they would soon control all of Eastern Europe and the Balkans, Churchill and Eden hastened to Moscow early in October 1944 to rescue what they could on behalf of Western interests.

In an attempt to do something for the London Poles, Churchill proposed that they meet with the Lublin (Soviet-supported) Poles in Moscow, where the two parties would be forced to settle their differences. As Churchill must have realized, however, the most that could be hoped from such a meeting would be a face-saving formula that would give the London Poles token participation in a Soviet-controlled government.

As for the rest of Europe, Churchill and Stalin worked out what amounted to a traditional spheres-of-interest agreement that assigned Romania (90 percent) and Bulgaria (75 percent) to the Soviet sphere and Greece (90 percent) to the British. Influence in Hungary and Yugoslavia was to be divided equally between them. In return for being given what amounted to a free hand in Eastern Europe, apart from Greece, Hungary, and Yugoslavia, Stalin conceded the Western powers the equivalent of a free hand in Italy and France. Otherwise he asked only for an alteration of the Montreux Convention (giving Turkey the right to fortify the Turkish Straits) that would give Soviet ships free access to the Mediterranean. (See p. 316.)

Churchill himself described the negotiation of these percentage agreements as "somewhat rough and ready diplomacy," and as he observed to Stalin, they might be considered crude and callous if exposed to public scrutiny. They therefore could not be made the basis of a public document and he suggested that the paper be burned on which their agreements had been recorded. Churchill nevertheless believed the agreements might serve as a "good guide for the conduct of our affairs" and might perhaps prevent civil war in the countries concerned.

As it proved, the agreement did not prevent civil war in Greece, the only country assigned to the British sphere. Elsewhere, as Churchill must have known very well, civil war against Soviet-installed governments would be prevented by the Red Army, hardly an ideal outcome for a war of liberation. Nevertheless, he could not resist trying to cloak the entire arrangement with Stalin in a mantle of morality by declaring that "our broad principles should be to let every country have the form of government which its people desire."

❑ *The Yalta Conference, February 4–11, 1945*

Early in February 1945, Churchill, Roosevelt, and Stalin met for the second and last time at Yalta on Russia's Crimean Peninsula. Yalta has become the most famous of the Allied wartime conferences because it was here, according to the interpretation offered later by partisan politicians and superpatriots, that a sick and dying president, under the pernicious influence of Soviet sympathizers or outright Communists in the American government, sold out the interests of the United States and those of the "free world" in general.

Insofar as Europe was concerned, these accusations are without foundation. Many of the major decisions affecting the postwar world had been made earlier, most notably at Teheran. Moreover, by the time of Yalta the West had little more to sell out: the Russians were in possession of all the territories they intended to incorporate into the Soviet Union, and the Red Army occupied most of the countries where, for purposes of their postwar security, they demanded the establishment of "friendly" governments. As Churchill had told the London Poles with brutal frankness, the only way to eliminate Soviet control or influence in these areas would be to go to war with Russia, and the Western Allies had no intention of doing so.

As in the case of the Teheran conference, it is necessary to bear in mind the political and military background of the Yalta negotiations. In the final weeks of 1944, the Germans had launched a major counterattack against Anglo-American forces in the west (the Battle of the Bulge). To relieve the pressure on his Western Allies, Stalin responded to their appeal to step up Soviet offensive operations in the east, a gesture greeted with effusive thanks by Western leaders. Although the German offensive in the west had been turned back by the time of Yalta, Anglo-American forces had not yet crossed the Rhine, whereas Soviet troops had reached the Oder River, less than forty miles from Berlin. Soviet forces controlled most of prewar Poland, they occupied Bulgaria and Romania, and they appeared to be on the verge of taking over Hungary and Czechoslovakia.

The Soviet bargaining position was made even stronger by the perceived need on the part of Western leaders to ensure the Soviet Union's entry into the war against Japan after the defeat of Germany. As yet there was no certainty that the atom bomb would work. In view of the fanatic resistance of the Japanese in defending their Pacific conquests, the Americans anticipated even greater difficulty in conquering their home islands and were predicting major losses when the final invasion of Japan took place. Securing a firm Soviet commitment to join in the war against Japan was thus seen as a matter of vital importance. Finally, at Yalta as in all wartime negotiations with the Soviet Union, Western leaders, most especially Roosevelt, were determined to avoid any confrontation that might undermine the wartime alliance or jeopardize future Soviet cooperation in the postwar world.

Much of the work at Yalta was devoted to the coordination of military plans for the defeat of Germany. But, with victory over Germany now imminent, the most important negotiations and decisions made at Yalta were those dealing with the structure of the postwar world.

The Yalta decisions about Germany were essentially an endorsement of the demands of Stalin. The Big Three were to possess supreme authority over Germany and were to take whatever steps they considered necessary for future peace and security, "including complete disarmament, demilitarization, and the dismemberment of Germany." They also intended to "exact reparations in kind for the destruction wrought by the Germans," with reparations going in the first instance to countries that had borne the main burden of the war and suffered the heaviest losses." As an estimate of the total sum of reparations, Roosevelt subscribed to the Soviet figure of 20 billion dollars "as a basis for discussion," 50 percent of which was to go to the Soviet Union. Eighty percent of these reparations were to be paid with German industrial equipment, commodities, and slave labor, rather than in currency.

At Yalta, the Allied leaders endorsed the Teheran decision that East Prussia and all German territory east of the Oder and Neisse Rivers were to go to the Soviet Union and Poland, but once again they left to a committee the task of working out the details about the future of what was left of Germany: how the country was to be dismembered and how its various segments were to be governed. This committee, made up of representatives to the European Advisory Committee, endorsed the EAC's earlier recommendation that Germany be divided into zones of occupation among the Big Three pending a final decision on that country's dismemberment. At the insistence of Churchill, the conference agreed that an occupation zone be allotted to France, to be carved out of the American and British zones.

The clearest demonstration of the determination of Western leaders to avoid a disruption of their wartime coalition with the Soviet Union was their negotiations over the thorny Polish question. With the Red Army already in control of the country, the Western leaders realized that the most they could hope for was to save face. Stalin allowed them to do so. After a week of controversy, he offered what appeared to be an unusually favorable compromise over the composition of a future Polish government. The provisional government now operating in Poland, installed under Soviet auspices, was to be "reorganized on a broader democratic basis with the inclusion of democratic leaders from Poland itself and from Poles abroad." The Soviet foreign minister together with the American and British ambassadors to Moscow were to act as a consultative commission for this purpose. Reorganization was to be followed as soon as possible by "free and unfettered elections" on the basis of universal suffrage and the secret ballot in which all "democratic and anti-fascist parties" were to have the right to put forward candidates.

The failure of the Soviet Union to honor the letter of these agreements was to provide critics of Yalta with their prime example of that conference's sellout of the interests of the free world. The only sellout involved here, however, was that there were decisive differences between Soviet and Western definitions of democracy, free elections, and antifascist parties. Most Western leaders were well aware of this problem, but idealists among them cherished the hope that Soviet policies would change, and even the most cynical were faced with the question: what else could they have done?

They could do even less about Poland's postwar frontiers because the principal decisions on that subject had already been made at Teheran. Poland's eastern frontier was to follow the Curzon Line, with minor modifications, which meant that approximately half of prewar Poland would be ceded to the Soviet Union. In the north and west, Poland was to receive "substantial accessions of territory" at the expense of Germany. Although the Big Three had agreed that Poland's western frontier should be established at the Oder River, the Russians and the Western allies differed as to whether the southward extension of that frontier should follow the western or eastern branch of the Neisse River. The choice of the Western Neisse would involve the relocation of another three to five million Germans to a shrunken postwar Germany and exacerbate the already grim refugee problem in the zones under Allied occupation.

In dealing with this problem too, however, the Western leaders were powerless because the Red Army was in control of the territory surrounding both branches of the Neisse. Six months earlier Molotov had promised the Lublin committee Soviet support for the Western Neisse frontier. Besides bolstering the prestige of the Lublin Poles, the Soviet government had every interest to honor this commitment. Fixing the Polish boundary at the Western Neisse would deprive the Germans of still more territory and valuable economic assets, it would contribute to German–Polish animosity, and it would leave postwar Poland even more dependent on Soviet support. The Russians were not impressed by the argument that Germans had inhabited these lands for centuries. Stalin pointed out that the Germans in this region had already fled and Poles had moved in to take their place, so the area was now effectively Polish.

A separate treaty of February 11, 1945, "Regarding Entry of the Soviet Union into the War Against Japan," was the Yalta agreement that came closest to being a genuine sellout. Although nominally trilateral, this treaty was negotiated exclusively between Roosevelt and Stalin and their deputies—and was kept a top secret. Churchill, who eventually signed it, was not consulted in its formulation. Neither were the Chinese.

The February 11 treaty committed the Soviet Union to enter the war against Japan two or three months after the surrender of Germany. In return, the Soviet Union was promised that the status quo in Outer Mongolia would be preserved, meaning that the Soviet satellite government there—the Mongolian People's Republic—would be maintained and that nothing would be done to restore the area to China. Already at Teheran, Russia had been promised the cession by Japan of the Kurile Islands and the southern half of the island of Sakhalin and its adjacent islands.

Elsewhere in East Asia "the former rights of Russia violated by the treacherous attack of Japan in 1904" were to be restored. In fact, these were rights the tsarist government had extorted from China in the nineteenth century which Russia had ceded to Japan after their defeat by Japan in 1905. The Russians were to regain their former lease of Port Arthur, at the southern tip of Manchuria's Liaotung Peninsula, and the nearby port of Dairen was to be internationalized, with safeguards for the preeminent interests of the Soviet Union. The Chinese Eastern and the South Manchurian railways, the principal avenues of transportation through Manchuria that linked Russia's Trans-Siberian railway to Dairen and Port Arthur, were to be operated by a joint Soviet-Chinese company, with the understanding that here, too, the preeminent interests of the Soviet Union were to be safeguarded, though China was to retain full sovereignty over Manchuria.

The February 11 treaty "understood" that the articles concerning Outer Mongolia and the Manchurian railways required the concurrence of Chiang Kai-shek, but "on the advice of Marshal Stalin," the president of the United States was to "take measures to obtain this concurrence." The Soviet Union for its part "expressed its readiness to conclude with the National Government of China a pact of friendship and alliance . . . in order to render assistance to China for the purpose of liberating China from the Japanese Yoke"—a condition the Americans understood to mean that the Soviet Union would support the government of Chiang Kai-shek rather than the Chinese Communists.

The February 11 treaty was not included in the protocols of the Yalta conference and was to be kept secret until the Soviet attack on Japan, at which time the Chinese were to be informed of its terms and, presumably, coerced into accepting them.

Critics of Yalta have greater reason to question the need for Western concessions in East Asia than in Eastern Europe, but once again the overriding consideration was America's determination to secure Soviet participation in the war against Japan. General Douglas MacArthur, commander-in-chief of the Allied forces in the Pacific and later one of the bitterest critics of his government's "betrayal" of China, seems to have had no doubt at the time that the Soviet entry into the war against Japan was essential. In working out his own military strategy, he consistently estimated an immense loss of life and warned against any American invasion of Japan until the Red Army had been committed to an invasion of Manchuria. After the defeat of Japan, he anticipated that Stalin would want to take over Manchuria, Korea, and part of northern China, but he was obviously prepared to pay this price. It was not even a question of paying a price, for he regarded the Soviet seizure of this territory as inevitable.

At Yalta, the Big Three produced yet another statement of principle: a Declaration on Liberated Europe in which they proclaimed their intention to assist the liberated peoples to solve their political and economic problems by democratic means and create democratic institutions of their own choice. Where in their judgment conditions existed that made assistance necessary, the Big Three would establish conditions of internal peace and form interim governments broadly representative of all democratic elements of the population, pledged to the earliest possible establishment through free elections of governments responsive to the will of the people.

These were noble pronouncements, but what they amounted to in effect was that each great power was given the right to intervene in the internal affairs of the weaker states of Europe whenever "in their judgment" (and thus, in their self-interest) it seemed expedient to do so.

❑ *International Monetary Fund and World Bank*

During the first three weeks of July 1944, a conference of economic experts from forty-four states, including the Soviet Union, met at Bretton Woods in the White Mountains of New Hampshire. Recognizing the need for an institutional mechanism to preserve stable rates of exchange among different currencies to ensure the free flow of international trade, the conference proposed the establishment of an International Monetary Fund (IMF), a monetary pool to which all members would contribute that would provide loans to countries whose economic difficulties threatened the value of their currencies. With emergency loans available, these countries would not have to resort to exchange controls or currency devaluation, which would restrict the free flow of international trade. "Commerce is the lifeblood of a free society," Roosevelt said in a message to the conference. "We must see to it that the arteries which carry that blood stream are not clogged again." In addition, the conference established an International Bank for Reconstruction and Development (later known as the World Bank), in this case a monetary pool of the resources of wealthy nations that would extend loans to stimulate the economic growth or revival of poorer countries and "promote the long-range balanced growth of international trade."

From the start both institutions were dominated by the economic might of the United States, and both were branded by America's critics as vehicles of American economic imperialism and the capitalist system. These criticisms were valid enough, yet these institutions served to prevent the international economic anarchy that flourished after World War I, though it was soon evident that more far-reaching economic measures would be required to revive the economic ravages of war.

As was to be expected, the Soviet government refused to join either organization. The Soviet Union intended to maintain its own centralized state-regulated economic system, free from foreign supervision or control.

❑ *The Establishment of the United Nations*

Roosevelt believed that one of the major achievements at Yalta had been the success of the Western Allies in securing Soviet agreement over the formation and operation of a United Nations organization, which was to protect international peace and security in the postwar world.

The major preliminary work on the structure of the United Nations had been done at the Dumbarton Oaks estate in Washington, where representatives of Britain, China, the Soviet Union, and the United States met in the late summer of 1944. There were to be five principal structural components: (1) a Security Council made up of five permanent members and six other members elected by the General Assembly for two years terms, which was to investigate disputes and take action to ensure the preservation of peace; (2) a General Assembly, in which all members of the United Nations were to be represented, each with one vote, which could discuss all questions within the scope of the UN charter and make nonbinding recommendations to the Security Council; (3) an Economic and Social Council, empowered to initiate studies and reports "with respect to international economic, social, cultural, educational, health, and related matters" and to make recommendations to the General Assembly, member states, and specialized agencies; (4) an International Court of Justice, to replace the Permanent Court of International Justice established in 1919 but entrusted with essentially the same task: the adjudication of international disputes; and (5) a Secretariat, the administrative staff of the UN, headed by a Secretary-General appointed by the General Assembly on the recommendation of the Security Council.

In considering the Dumbarton Oaks proposals the Big Three were sharply divided over the membership and voting procedures of the Security Council. The United

States insisted that China should be a permanent member of the Security Council despite Soviet objections that China lacked the power to fulfill its peacekeeping role and Churchill's scornful reference to China's membership as a "faggot vote on the side of the United States." To secure what he hoped would be an ally in the Security Council. Churchill demanded that France, too, be made a permanent member of that body. Final agreement over membership and voting procedures was reached at Yalta. The Soviets agreed to the inclusion of both China and France. After securing American and British agreement that each member of the Security Council should have veto power over any decisions reached, the Soviets accepted the Western position that *procedural* questions should be decided by majority vote.

The question of membership in the General Assembly was also decided at Yalta. To balance what they believed would be a solid bloc of Commonwealth votes on the side of Britain and Latin American votes on the side of the United States, the Soviets had originally demanded that all sixteen Soviet republics be represented. At Yalta, however, they settled for only three: Russia, the Ukraine, and Belorussia. Roosevelt hailed Soviet concessions on these issues as "a great step forward which would be welcomed by the peoples of the world."

The final achievement at Yalta was an agreement among the Big Three to convene a conference of all members of the United Nations in San Francisco on April 25, 1945. That conference was to draw up a charter for the UN organization based on the proposals made at Dumbarton Oaks and modified by the membership and procedural agreements reached at Yalta. The San Francisco conference duly met on the designated date, and over the next two months delegates of fifty nations drew up a final charter for the United Nations that was signed on June 26, 1945.

❑

TWENTY-ONE

Victory in Europe and Asia

❑ *The Death of Roosevelt*
and the Truman Succession

On April 12, 1945, thirteen days before the United Nations conference convened in San Francisco, Franklin D. Roosevelt died of a massive cerebral hemorrhage. Though his death seemed sudden, the president had actually been dying for months, and had been less and less able to function.

The new American president, Harry S. Truman, was a former senator from Missouri who had been selected as vice-presidential candidate in the previous year because he seemed less likely to damage the Democratic ticket than the Left-leaning Henry Wallace, Roosevelt's running mate in 1940, or other contenders for the vice-presidential nomination.

Roosevelt had done nothing to prepare Truman for the presidency. After the 1944 election, he saw him privately only three times, on each occasion only briefly and over minor matters. He did not invite Truman to accompany him to Yalta; he did not consult or even inform him about major policy decisions. In later life Truman told his daughter Margaret that Roosevelt "never did talk to me confidentially about the war, or about foreign affairs or what he had in mind for peace after the war." Thus when Truman assumed the highest office in the land at one of the most critical moments in its history, he knew little more about the international problems with which he was now obliged to deal than what he had learned from newspapers and the political gossip of the capital.

Although he had been a hardworking and competent senator, Truman had not impressed the Washington political community, where the general reaction upon learning of Roosevelt's death had been: "Good God, Truman will be president." To Americans in general Truman was known, if at all, as a brash midwestern politician, undistinguished in manner or appearance, a former haberdasher and a product of the Kansas City political machine of Tom Pendergast. Few men have ever assumed high office with so little preparation or so little public confidence and support.

Truman's great strength was that he did not allow himself to be daunted by the responsibilities of his office, by hostile public opinion, or by the prestige of foreign statesmen. As he had demonstrated as a member of the Senate, he had an immense capacity for hard work and an ability to cut through detail to the essentials of a particular problem. To compensate for the failure of Roosevelt to inform him about affairs of state, he made a rigorous study of official documents, and unlike his predecessor he sought the advice of professional bureaucrats and men with greater knowledge and experience than his own in dealing with particular problems. Once he was confident that he understood a problem, he was not afraid to make decisions he considered necessary and to assume full responsibility for them. Impatient with procrastination and verbosity, he liked to reach decisions quickly in order to get on with the next items of business.

❑ *The End of World War II in Europe*

On April 30, eighteen days after the death of Roosevelt, Hitler committed suicide in his underground bunker in the rubble of Berlin. On May 8, 1945, representatives of a post-Hitler German government signed terms of unconditional surrender which became effective the next day. In June supreme authority in Germany was vested in an Allied Control Council consisting of representatives of the American, British, French, and Soviet governments. Germany was divided into occupation zones in accordance with the recommendations of the European Advisory Commission and endorsed by the Big Three at Yalta, where the Russians had agreed to allot the French an occupation zone carved out of the American and British zones. This partition was not meant to be permanent and was regarded at the time as nothing more than an expedient to deal with immediate military and administrative problems.

Critics of Anglo-American policy have raised the question as to why their governments conceded the Soviet Union control over approximately 40 percent of Germany, including Berlin (though Berlin too was to be subject to quadrupartite division and control), and why they halted the advance of Western troops into Eastern Europe, which would have prevented the establishment of Soviet control over Czechoslovakia. The answer to both questions is simple enough and has nothing to do with yet another Communist-inspired betrayal of the interests of the "free world" as many critics of the Truman administration have charged. We were still at war with Japan as well as Germany, and both American and British leaders did not wish to jeopardize our relations with the Soviet Union, whose cooperation was deemed essential to speed the defeat of Japan.

In Germany, the Western Allies did no more than withdraw to the zones previously established by the EAC. As Truman wrote later, "We were about 150 miles east of the border of the occupied zone line agreed to at Yalta. I felt that agreements made in the war to keep Russia fighting should be kept and I kept them to the letter." Elsewhere, General Eisenhower, the supreme Allied commander, was more concerned with saving the lives of his soldiers and avoiding controversy with the Soviets than with the occupation of territory, and once the defeat of Germany was assured, he was content to allow the Red Army take credit for the capture of Berlin as well as Prague, the Czech capital. Whether this was a politically wise decision remains a matter of controversy, but the men whose lives were saved thereby would not have considered it a mistake.

❑ *Truman's Introduction to International Politics*

On April 20, shortly after Truman took office, Averell Harriman, the American ambassador to Moscow, returned to Washington to warn the new president against taking an excessively sanguine view of Soviet policies, as some of Roosevelt's advisers had done. In the weeks after Yalta Roosevelt himself had regretfully observed that the Russians were breaking their promises. Far from allowing the peoples of Eastern Europe to choose their own governments through free elections, the Russians were extending their control over neighboring states by unilateral action and making their governments subservient to Moscow.

Harriman's warning was followed by a telegram from Churchill of May 6 saying that "matters" could hardly be carried further by correspondence and urging a meeting of the heads of the three major Allied governments as soon as possible. What Churchill meant by "matters" was set forth in detail in two long telegrams to Truman of May 11 and 12, just a few days after Germany's final surrender. He warned in starkest terms against American withdrawal from the territory they presently held in Germany to the occupation lines established by the European Advisory Commission, for this would mean "the tide of Russian domination sweeping forward 120 miles on a front of 300 or 400 miles" and open the way to a Russian advance to the waters of the North Sea and the Atlantic. To prevent this fearful development, the Western Allies must not retreat from their present positions until they were satisfied about Russian intentions, something that had to be done before the American armies were weakened. "It is to this early and speedy showdown and settlement with Russia that we must now turn our hopes," Churchill said. This was an issue that "seems to me to dwarf all others."

Truman agreed about the desirability of a meeting with Stalin, but he was not panicked by the warnings of Harriman or Churchill's gloomy prognostications, though by this time he had made a careful study of the records of Soviet-American relations and understood the nature of the Soviet threat. He nevertheless still hoped to maintain good working relations with the Soviet government. For this purpose he persuaded Harry Hopkins, Roosevelt's own favorite go-between with the Soviets, to undertake a mission to Moscow "to straighten things out with Stalin." Hopkins was to impress upon the Soviet dictator Truman's intention to carry on the policies of his predecessor, in particular his resolve to cooperate with the Soviet leadership, and to arrange another meeting of the Big Three to enable Truman to present his views personally. At the same time, Truman rejected Churchill's proposal for a prior meeting between the two Western leaders because, like Roosevelt, he wanted to avoid arousing Stalin's suspicion that the British and Americans were "ganging up" on him.

Hopkins' mission to Moscow seemed to be a brilliant success. He not only secured Stalin's agreement to a meeting of the Big Three, but struck what appeared to be a favorable bargain over Poland. Stalin promised that the London Poles would be represented in a new Polish government, that the Soviet government would not interfere in Polish affairs, and that the Soviets would cooperate with the Americans and British to see that the reorganized Polish government held free elections and respected individual rights and liberties.

Because representatives of the London Poles were duly included in a Polish government formed on June 28, that government was recognized by Britain and the United States on July 5. Their representation, however, proved to be a mere token. Moscow continued its blatant intervention in Polish affairs, and no free elections were held. As a result, the Polish question soon resumed its place as a major bone of contention with the Western powers.

❑ The Potsdam Conference, July 17 to August 2, 1945

Potsdam, the site of what proved to be the last conference of the leaders of the Big Three, was an old Prussian garrison town, which, though embellished by the palaces and city planning projects of its Prussian rulers, had remained a symbolic center of Prussian militarism. Potsdam was not chosen for its symbolism, however, but because Stalin wanted the conference held in territory under Soviet control and because Potsdam, unlike Berlin, still retained undamaged palaces to serve as meeting rooms for the conference and housing for its participants.

On the first day of the conference, July 17, President Truman received a report of the successful explosion of an atomic bomb in New Mexico. Truman did not inform Stalin of this event until a week later, and he did so then with deliberate nonchalance. Stalin received the news with equal nonchalance. He was glad to hear it, he said, and hoped the Americans would make good use of it against the Japanese, but he did not question Truman further on the matter. He did not need to. The Russians had been working on an atom bomb of their own since June of 1942, and they were kept accurately informed about the progress of the Americans by pro-Soviet scientists working on the bomb in Britain and the United States. Molotov, who had been in charge of the Soviet atomic development program, took immense pride in the success of Soviet intelligence operations, which had supplied the missing links in the Soviets' own research. "They neatly stole just what we needed. And just at the right moment, when we were beginning this work." Truman's news therefore did not come as a surprise. In any event, Stalin could not afford to reveal that he was in any way disturbed by the existence America's new weapon. He carried on the negotiations at Potsdam as though that weapon did not exist, and in dealing with the affairs of Europe he succeeded masterfully in preventing the Americans from deriving any diplomatic advantage from their newly won military superiority.

Eight days after the conference opened, the Big Three lost the second of its original members. On July 5 there had been a general election in Britain, but because of the time needed to count the votes of British service personnel scattered throughout the world the results were not known until July 26, while the Potsdam conference was in session. On July 25 Churchill and Eden returned to Britain to await the election results. To the surprise of much of the rest of the world, Labour scored a landslide victory—the British electorate chose to remember Churchill's prewar political record rather than his wartime leadership. On the day the results were announced, Churchill resigned.

His successor was Clement Attlee, leader of the Labour party, who had served as deputy prime minister in Churchill's War Cabinet. As his foreign secretary, Attlee selected Ernest Bevin, minister of Labour in the War Cabinet, inexperienced in international diplomacy but a veteran negotiator of labor disputes. As members of the War Cabinet, both Attlee and Bevin were well informed about the fundamental problems of British foreign policy. And both, after years of bitter battles with Communists in Britain, were staunchly anti-Communist. Far from initiating an abrupt change in British policy, as many Americans feared they might, they pursued essentially the same course as their Conservative predecessors in dealing with the Soviet Union. In colonial questions, on the other hand, they held radically different views, and to Churchill's dismay they were prepared to cede a large measure of self-government or outright independence to India and other parts of the British empire.

At Potsdam as at Yalta, the Big Three postponed making final decisions about the fate of the Axis powers and their satellites. To carry out the necessary preparatory work in drawing up final peace settlements, they established a Council of Foreign Ministers that was to include the ministers of China and France as well as those of the Big Three. As its first task, the Council was authorized to draw up draft peace treaties with Italy, Romania, Bulgaria, Hungary, and Finland. When a German government "adequate for the purpose" was established, the Council was also to prepare a peace settlement with Germany.

By the time of Potsdam, and contrary to the advice of Churchill, American and British troops had withdrawn to the occupation zones of Germany established by the European Advisory Commission, the French were occupying a zone carved out of the American and British sectors, and the Red Army was established in East Germany. The principles promulgated at Potsdam for the governance of the four zones were essentially the same as those formulated at Yalta: Germany was to be disarmed, demilitarized, denazified, and democratized. The German economy was to be rigidly controlled and decentralized, but kept sufficiently productive to provide the goods and services required to meet the needs of the occupation forces and the German population, whose average living standards were not to exceed those of other European countries.

Besides this reiteration of general principles, the Potsdam conference dealt with two major issues left hanging at Yalta: Germany's eastern frontiers and reparations. At Yalta, the Russians had demanded that the frontier between Germany and Poland should be established at the Oder River and the western branch of the Neisse River, and that Germany pay reparations totalling 20 billion dollars whose collection was to begin immediately through the expropriation of German economic assets in all four occupation zones. As noted earlier, the British had objected to both demands. Extending the Polish frontier to the Western Neisse would swell the number of German refugees by several million, who would become a burden on Allied occupation governments; and naming a figure for reparations was irresponsible until some estimate could be made of what the Germans would be able to pay. Further, the Soviet expropriation of economic assets in all four occupation zones would destroy what was left of the German economy and impose upon the Western Allies the obligation of supporting the German people.

Both the territorial and reparations questions were resolved, if so benign a term can be employed, by a bargain struck between the new American secretary of state, James Byrnes, and Molotov, a bargain the British were unable to scuttle and which they reluctantly endorsed. The West agreed to Poland's administration over former German territory to the Western Neisse "pending the final determination of Poland's western frontier" in a final peace settlement. In return, the Soviets agreed to drop their demand for 20 billion dollars in reparations and to scale down their claims to reparations in the Western zones of occupation.

Though Western leaders had balked at shifting the boundary of Poland as far as the Western Neisse, they raised no objections to the Soviet annexation of a large segment of East Prussia, including the capital of Königsberg (later renamed Kaliningrad), or to the assignment of the rest of East Prussia to Poland. The Potsdam conference also recognized "that the transfer to Germany of German populations, or elements thereof, remaining in Poland, Czechoslovakia and Hungary will have to be undertaken." Though the conference stipulated that such transfers were be effected in an orderly and humane manner, in most areas they were carried out with a brutality and ruthlessness that emulated the worst excesses of the Nazis. On November 20, 1945, the Control Council for Germany approved the final transfer/expulsion of some 6.5 million Germans from the former German territories to be administered by Poland and the Soviet Union, and of Germans still living in the other countries of Eastern Europe.

Not content with the immense Western concessions in Europe and Asia (see pp. 288–290), the Soviet leaders at Potsdam sought still more concessions in the Middle East and North Africa: Soviet military bases at or near the Turkish Straits; Soviet trusteeship over one of Italy's African colonies, preferably Libya; Soviet membership in the international consortium governing the strategically important city and zone of Tangier, on the coast of North Africa opposite Gibraltar.

Western leaders managed to postpone decisions on all these points. They contended that the Turkish Straits should be the subject of direct conversations between the Big Three and Turkey. The disposal of Italy's former colonies was to be settled in a final peace treaty with Italy. Tangier would be discussed at a future meeting of the representatives of the Big Three, plus France. Stalin was prepared to wait, but he issued the ominous warning that "when the time came around, the Soviet government would resume its talks with the Turks."

❑ *The Course of the War in the Pacific*

In June 1942 the Japanese campaign to destroy the American aircraft carriers that had evaded their Pearl Harbor attack had ended in a crippling defeat in the Battle of Midway, which marked a turning point in the war in the Pacific. (See p. 256.) By this time

American shipyards and industries had begun to make good the losses sustained at Pearl Harbor and to build up the arms superiority that would ensure Japan's ultimate defeat.

Lacking bases for an attack on Japan from the Asian mainland, American strategists planned an offensive against the principal strong points of Japan's defensive perimeter in the Pacific. In mid-June 1944 they scored a decisive victory with the conquest of Saipan in the Marianas, a cornerstone of that defensive perimeter, which provided a base for the disruption of communications between Japan and its remaining outposts in the Pacific. Saipan also brought the Americans within bombing range of the Japanese home islands.

In October, after their capture of Guam and the Palau Islands, the American forces in Pacific converged for the reconquest of the Philippines. Following the first American landings at the Philippine island of Leyte on October 20, the Japanese mounted their last desperate effort to overcome American naval supremacy. In the ensuing Battle of Leyte Gulf, the largest naval battle of all time, the Japanese lost the greater part of what was left of their navy: four aircraft carriers, two battleships, six heavy and three light cruisers, and over 400 aircraft. The Americans now had virtually uncontested naval and air supremacy.

Well before the reconquest of the Philippines, the Americans had dealt damaging blows to the Japanese economic lifelines through submarine warfare. Considering their critical dependence on the import of food and raw materials, the Japanese had done surprisingly little to expand their merchant fleet or develop their shipyards in the years before the war. The Japanese merchant fleet in 1941 was less than one-third the size of Britain's—barely 6 million tons. More surprising still, the Japanese did little during the war to protect their merchant vessels by organizing them in convoys or providing them with naval escorts. The Americans thus found them easy targets. Altogether, American submarines sank approximately 60 percent of the shipping lost by the Japanese in the course of the war. By the time the Americans regained their bases in the Philippines, a large part of the Japanese merchant fleet had already been destroyed. From their Philippine bases, however, the Americans were able to establish an impenetrable naval blockade to stop the shipment of strategic raw materials to the Japanese home islands.

America's large-scale air offensive against the Japanese home islands began in November 1944 with the construction of airfields on Saipan suitable for the use of Boeing B-29 bombers, the so-called Superfortress, far larger and capable of carrying far greater loads than the B-25s previously in use. The air raids were carried out at night to take advantage of the weakness of Japan's night-time defenses, and American bombers were equipped with incendiary instead of explosive bombs. The results were horrifyingly effective, generating a holocaust as great as those inflicted on the cities of Germany, with even more terrible results owing to the vulnerability of Japanese wooden housing. In the first full-scale incendiary attack on Tokyo on the night of March 9–10, 1945, one-fourth of the city was burned out, an estimated 100,000 died in the flames, and as many more suffered incapacitating burns. From that time until the end of the war, the Americans dropped incendiary bombs on all major Japanese cities with the exception of Kyoto, which was spared because of its artistic importance. In these raids, which wrought as much destruction as the nuclear bombs later dropped on Hiroshima and Nagasaki, no attempt was made to single out military or industrial targets. They were a deliberate effort to break the will of the Japanese people and were nothing less than indiscriminate mass murder. But, as the Japanese themselves had demonstrated, the wholesale destruction of the enemy's cities and economic assets, which included the civilian population, had become a feature of modern warfare. The era when civilians, women, and children were not considered legitimate targets of warfare had long since passed.

❑ *The Use of the Atom Bomb*

On August 6, 1945, the Americans dropped an atom bomb on the Japanese city of Hiroshima; three days later they dropped a second bomb on the city of Nagasaki.

The American decision to use the atom bomb in the war against Japan is one of the most controversial and emotionally charged issues of World War II, and it requires a consideration of questions that have been raised about the military necessity and morality of its use. Why was the bomb dropped without giving the Japanese warning of its effects or adequate opportunity to surrender? Why was a second bomb dropped before the Japanese had been given a proper chance to react to the first? Or was the primary purpose of dropping the bomb not the defeat of Japan at all, but rather an attempt to intimidate the Soviets, to make them more amenable to concessions in Europe, to prevent their participation in the postwar government of Japan and their expansion on the Asian mainland?

As is the case with so many decisions in history, the implications of their motivation and morality are often less clear to those involved in making them than to later observers. From the time the bomb project was inaugurated in 1939, there was never any question that the bomb was being made to be used. Moreover, at that time it was difficult to see why the use of an atom bomb should be considered more immoral than the mass bombings of civilian populations by "conventional weapons"—the dire effects of radiation fallout were not yet fully apparent. The suggestion that the use of the bomb against the Japanese but not against the Germans was racially motivated is invalidated by the facts of the case. Germany had surrendered before the bomb was fully developed, the Germans had been subjected to merciless bombardment by conventional weapons, and Roosevelt had actually issued orders to use the atom bomb against the Germans if they had not surrendered by the time it was operational.

American leaders knew at the time the bomb was dropped that its use was not essential to defeat Japan. They could have continued to bomb Japan into submission by conventional weapons; they could have set up a naval blockade around the Japanese islands that would have starved out the Japanese and deprived them of crucial raw materials; they could have awaited Japan's reaction to the Soviet Union's entry into the war against them; they could have done more to explore the possibility of a negotiated peace; or they could have carried out their original plans for invading the Japanese home islands. These and other methods to secure Japan's surrender would have taken time, however, and an invasion in particular would have involved an immense loss of American lives. The overriding consideration for American decision-makers was to end the war as quickly as possible and to save lives, and the evidence is overwhelming that their principal reason for using the atom bomb was that this seemed the most effective means to achieve this purpose. As Truman asked later in justifying that decision: how could he have explained to the American people that he allowed the war to continue when they learned that he had a weapon available to end it immediately?

The question whether to warn the Japanese about the nature of the new weapon or stage a demonstration of its effectiveness was seriously debated prior to its use. As yet, however, the Americans possessed only two such bombs, and their weapons experts were not certain whether an atom bomb dropped from a plane would actually explode. As Secretary Stimson wrote later, "Nothing would have been more damaging to our effort than a warning or demonstration followed by a dud—and this was a real possibility." American scientists, moreover, doubted whether a test demonstration would be effective. Summarizing the divided views of a scientific panel, Robert Oppenheimer, the leading American physicist involved in the project, wrote: "We can propose no technical demonstration likely to bring an end to the war; we see no acceptable alternatives to direct military use." As Oppenheimer testified later, "We did not think exploding one of those things as a firecracker over a desert was likely to be very impressive."

The only move the Americans made to warn the Japanese and give them an opportunity to surrender prior to their use of the bomb was to send them an ultimatum on July 26, the so-called Potsdam Declaration, issued in the name of the American, British, and Chinese governments, calling for the unconditional surrender of their armed forces and warning that the alternative for Japan was "prompt and utter destruction." American fears that the Japanese government was still controlled by military die-hards seemed confirmed with the brusque dismissal of the Potsdam Declaration by the Japanese prime minister, Admiral Suzuki Kantaro: his government did not find anything of value in the Potsdam Declaration and therefore had no recourse but to ignore it and fight resolutely for the successful conclusion of the war. As we now know, Suzuki had in fact drawn up this statement under pressure from military extremists, and though the English translation may not have conveyed the ambiguity inherent in the Japanese original, as Japanese language experts have since pointed out, the statement could only be interpreted as a rejection of the Potsdam ultimatum.

❑ The Bomb and the Soviet Declaration of War on Japan

Some time before the Potsdam conference the Japanese government had authorized its ambassador to Moscow, Sato Naotake, to seek the mediation of the Soviet Union, which had abrogated its neutrality pact with Japan in the previous April but was still officially neutral. The Soviet leaders had temporized; then they had gone off to Potsdam. On August 6 the atom bomb was dropped on Hiroshima. Two days later, when the Soviet leaders had returned from Potsdam, Sato was at last granted an audience with Molotov. But, instead of receiving a positive reply to his government's appeal for mediation, Sato was handed a Soviet declaration of war, effective August 9.

The dropping of the bomb on Hiroshima had precipitated but not caused the Soviet declaration of war. Since the surrender of Germany, the Soviets had been moving troops to East Asia on a large scale preparatory to an invasion of Manchuria, but they had held off going to war against Japan until the Chinese accepted the secret treaty Roosevelt had negotiated with the Soviets at Yalta embodying the manifold concessions China was to make to the Soviet Union. (See pp. 289–290.) With the dropping of the bomb, however, the Soviets saw they would have to act quickly; otherwise the war might be over before they had a chance to take advantage of the Yalta concessions. In his memoirs, the future Soviet leader Nikita Khruschev records that Stalin was urging his military leadership to start action against Japan as soon as possible. "Otherwise . . . Japan might capitulate to the armed forces of the United States before we entered the war." In that case, he doubted whether the Americans would honor their Yalta commitments regarding East Asia.

There is abundant evidence that numerous American leaders, notably Byrnes and Stimson, were thinking along similar lines: in dropping the bomb on Hiroshima and the second bomb on Nagasaki only three days later, they hoped to hasten the surrender of Japan, thereby forestalling a Soviet invasion of Manchuria. After examining official and unofficial American records, the historian Gar Alperowitz has concluded that "the over-riding reason for the use of the bomb was that (implicitly or explicitly) it was judged necessary to strengthen the United States's hand against Russia."

While it is certainly true that the Russian factor played an important role in the calculations of American leaders, it is questionable whether Russia was indeed the "over-riding reason" for their use of the bomb. Indeed, all available evidence suggests that the bomb would have been used even if Russia had not been in the picture. Truman, far from seeking to forestall Soviet involvement in the war against Japan, regarded his success in securing Stalin's reiteration of his pledge to enter the war as his major achievement at the Potsdam conference. After seeing Stalin before the conference even began, he recorded triumphantly in his diary that he had already achieved his main objective: "He'll be in the Jap War on August 15. Fini Japan when that comes about." Truman said much the same thing in a letter to his wife from Potsdam, written early in the morning of July 18, a few hours before learning of the successful explosion of a nuclear bomb in New Mexico. "I've gotten what I came for—Stalin goes to war on August 15 with no string on it. . . . I'll say that will end the war a year sooner now, and think of the kids who won't be killed! That is the important thing."

Intent above all on ending the war, Truman believed his own responsibility lay in showing the Japanese that the Americans meant business. On August 7 and 8, following the destruction of Hiroshima, American bombers continued their massive day-and-night attacks on other Japanese cities by conventional weapons. Truman saw no need for fine moral distinctions. "I regarded the bomb as a military weapon and never had any doubt that it should be used." Churchill took the same view. "The decision whether or not to use the atomic bomb to compel the surrender of Japan was never even an issue. There was unanimous, automatic, unquestioned agreement around our table."

A more complex moral question arises as to why the American dropped a second atom bomb without awaiting the Japanese reaction to the first. Incredible as it seems in retrospect, the use of the second bomb was apparently never the subject of a special decision. It was dropped in accordance with a standing order: "additional bombs will be delivered . . . as soon as made ready by the project staff." A third bomb would presumably have been "delivered" but for the fact that Japan surrendered before it was made operational.

The Japanese have skilfully exploited the horror evoked by the American use of the atomic bomb to pose as martyrs to Western ruthlessness and racisim. They have received substantial support from Western moralists and historians who share the view of Alperowitz that the main purpose of using the bomb was to intimidate the Soviet Union and serve as the ultimate weapon of American imperialism.

The Japanese assumption of the mantle of martyrdom conveniently ignores the precedents the Japanese themselves set in the perpetration of atrocities: their bombing of enemy cities and civilian populations; their massacre, torture, and rape of civilians; their starvation and torture of prisoners of war and captured enemy civilians; their use of Korean women as "comfort girls" for their troops; their use of biological and chemical weapons.

□ *The Japanese Surrender and the End of World War II*

The combination of America's atom bombs and the Soviet declaration of war did not put an end to disputes within the Japanese government about the decision to surrender. But they did provoke the emperor to take the unprecedented step of convening an Imperial Conference where he expressed his wish to end the war. The result was a formal cabinet resolution on August 10 to accept the Potsdam Declaration with but one reservation: "that the said declaration does not comprise any demand which prejudices the prerogatives of His Majesty as a Sovereign Ruler." After hasty consultation, the Allies responded on August 11 that the future government of Japan would be left to the freely expressed will of the Japanese people.

Once again it was the emperor who made the final decision. He did not think the condition regarding the future Japanese government was intended to subvert the national polity of Japan, "but unless the war be brought to an end at this moment, I fear that the national polity will be destroyed and the nation annihilated." On the night of August 14 the Japanese acceptance of the Allied terms was handed to the Swiss minister in Tokyo. It was received on the afternoon of that same day, local time, in Washington. The emperor himself informed the Japanese people of his government's decision to surrender in a radio broadcast of August 15.

On September 2, 1945, General Douglas MacArthur, the American commander-in-chief of Allied forces in the Pacific, received Japan's formal capitulation in a ceremony on board the battleship *Missouri* (President Truman's home state) in Tokyo Bay. World War II was over. But the war in East Asia itself was far from over.

TWENTY-TWO

□

The Breakdown
of the Grand Alliance

❏ *The Great Powers in 1945*

The lineup of the great powers had changed remarkably little after World War I. (See pp. 66–69.) Only one, the multinational Habsburg empire, was broken up and permanently eliminated as a major power. All the others managed to retain or regain their great-power status during the interwar years. But already well before 1914 a great change had taken place in the *relative* strength of the great powers, a change that did not become fully apparent until the final interwar years and World War II itself.

Very different was the situation after World War II. Germany and Japan were decisively defeated—this time it would be impossible for German nationalists to claim that their army had been stabbed in the back by traitors on the home front—and both powers now became the subjects rather than the movers and shakers of international politics. Italy too was defeated, its great power pretensions shattered by its miserable wartime performance as the ally of Hitler.

But the war had also exposed with cruel clarity the relative decline in the strength of Britain and France. In the case of France, that decline was tragically revealed by its swift defeat in the summer of 1940. Britain, which had gallantly stood alone against the Nazi juggernaut after the fall of France, claimed a position of global leadership as a member of the Big Three during and after the war. But well before 1945 it was obvious that the power of Britain too had been badly eroded as a result of its participation in two global conflicts. Nor was the great-power status of Britain and France sustained by their overseas empires. It would soon be evident that both countries lacked the resources and manpower to retain their overseas empires, and that they too now seemed destined to play a secondary and dependent role in international affairs.

The change in the status of Britain and France, already foreshadowed by developments before 1914, seemed to confirm the validity of the theories of Hitler and the Japanese leadership about the need for a large contiguous territorial base to sustain a country's great-power status in the modern world. Hitler had sought such a base through the conquest of Russia, Japan through the conquest or control of the East Asian mainland and its adjacent islands. Both had failed, and now, reduced to a terri-

304

torial base even smaller than their prewar status, they were seemingly relegated to a position that would leave them permanently at the mercy of stronger powers.

The geopolitical theories of Hitler and the Japanese seemed all the more valid because the only states that had unquestionably survived as great powers after World War II (or so it appeared at the time) were the Soviet Union and the United States, both established on a large contiguous territorial base firmly controlled by their respective governments. And only those states that possessed a similar territorial base seemed likely to become major powers in the future once they had harnessed and developed their natural and human resources: for example China, India, Argentina, or Brazil.

The great surprise, both during and after World War II, was the Soviet Union. Hitler had confidently expected the swift collapse of that state under the first blows of his Nazi legions, an expectation shared by informed observers in much of the rest of the world. But the Soviet Union had survived. Despite immense losses of territory and concomitant losses of economic resources, the Soviet Union managed to outproduce Germany in the later stages of the war in the crucial fields of guns, tanks, and aircraft. And after the war, despite the devastation wrought by the German invaders, it remained by far the strongest military power in Europe and Asia, strategically poised to extend that power east or west thanks to its wartime territorial gains and the defeat of Germany and Japan, its major adversaries on both flanks.

In terms of overall strength, however, no country could compare to the United States in 1945. That country had escaped invasion, bombing, and all the other wartime devastation suffered by the major Asian and European belligerents; it faced no major hostile power in its own hemisphere; its most dangerous enemies in Europe and Asia lay prostrate in defeat; its major economic rivals had been destroyed or incapacitated by war. Between 1939 and 1945 America's industrial output had increased by 90 percent, agriculture by 20 percent. By 1945 the United States was producing almost half as much as the rest of the world put together, it controlled two-thirds of the world's gold reserves, three-quarters of its invested capital, and half of its shipping. The American fleet was larger than the combined fleets of all other countries; it possessed the world's most formidable strategic air force; its aircraft carriers made possible the projection of American power to every part of the globe. And in 1945 American power was immeasurably enhanced by having exclusive control of the world's most formidable weapon, the atom bomb.

The rapid postwar recovery of Japan and West Germany and their emergence as major economic powers despite their small size and relatively meager natural resources seemed to demonstrate that an industrious and technologically proficient population was more important than a large territorial base, especially in view of the failure of large and bountifully endowed countries like Argentina and Brazil to experience comparable economic growth. The economic growth of smaller states did not transform them into great powers, however, because their dependence on foreign imports and sales left them even more vulnerable to the vagaries of global politics than underdeveloped countries. The Japanese economy, for example, can be ruined within weeks if deprived of its imports of foreign oil, its overall prosperity remains dependent on the maintenance of a global free market economy, and its security remains dependent on the armed forces of the Western powers.

ICBM
atomic - propulsion
Jet prop.

❑ *The Weaponry Revolution*

To the dismay of many Americans, their country's military and economic power and its exclusive possession of the atom bomb did not give the United States irresistible clout in international affairs or even military security. On the contrary, the bomb and development of increasingly effective weapons systems for its delivery was to render the United States vulnerable, for the first time in its history, to swift and large-scale military destruction. By 1949, far sooner than most experts expected, the Soviet Union had produced a bomb of its own. The ensuing nuclear arms race led to the development of the far more powerful hydrogen bomb and long-range missiles that could be fired from moving bases on land and sea, capable of hitting targets thousands of miles away.

The new weaponry threw into confusion traditional views about the world's power relationships as well as traditional conceptions of military strategy and security. The expanse of two oceans could no longer allow Americans to indulge in the luxury of isolationism or protect the United States from a nuclear holocaust. Neither the vastness of Russian territory nor the rigors of the Russian winter could safeguard the Soviet Union from similar destruction. The Suez and Panama canals, the fortresses guarding Gibraltar and the Turkish Straits, strategic military and naval bases and centers of economic productivity in every part of the world—all could be rendered useless or wiped out within minutes after the outbreak of a nuclear war. Because of their very size, states with a large territorial base were less vulnerable to nuclear annihilation than small states, but any state equipped with atomic or even the latest conventional weaponry could now become a formidable player in global politics.

Surprisingly, however, the new weaponry did not have so revolutionary an impact on the conduct of foreign affairs as at first seemed likely. While the Americans still possessed a monopoly on the atom bomb, the Soviet government did not hesitate to stand up to and even challenge the United States on numerous international issues, apparently confident that the Americans would not risk outraging world opinion by launching a nuclear strike against the Soviet Union. As we now know, this confidence was powerfully bolstered by the reports of agents working for Soviet intelligence in the highest levels of the American and British governments. When the Soviets developed their own bomb in 1949, a balance of power of sorts was reestablished. Washington and Moscow could not help but recognize that the new weaponry was so destructive that its use by either side would have resulted in a mutual holocaust.

The new balance of power has been accurately described as a balance of terror, and up to the present time it has effectively deterred the great powers from engaging in all-out war. But it has not deterred any power, great or small, from waging wars with conventional weapons, nor has it enabled the great powers to put a stop to aggressive and irresponsible policies on the part of smaller and weaker states. On the contrary, the great powers have frequently been prepared to condone or even support the reckless policies of weaker states to gain or retain their friendship, safeguard access to their raw materials and markets, or retain the use of their strategic bases. The leaders of the weaker states, for their part, have gambled successfully that the great powers would not dare to employ their nuclear weapons in the routine game of power politics because of their fear of setting off a nuclear war.

But nuclear arms are only part of the weaponry revolution. Less spectacular but nonetheless lethal are biological and chemical weapons, which can be produced and delivered by countries without nuclear or long-range missile capabilities.

Meanwhile the very existence of such weaponry hangs like a sword of Damocles over the entire human race.

❑ *The Cold War* — *during WW2 — 1989*

The Cold War is the name that has been given to the postwar standoff between the Soviet Union and the United States and their respective adherents.

There has been a great deal of controversy, much of it ill-informed and infused by passion and ideological preconceptions, about the origins of the Cold War, how and when it began, and who was to blame for shattering the hopes of humankind for a peaceful and harmonious postwar world. Much of this argument has been the product of unrealistic expectations nourished by wartime propaganda. As in World War I, this propaganda portrayed the wartime enemies as uniquely evil and militaristic and fostered the belief that their defeat would eradicate militarism and permit the creation of a peaceful new world order.

The record of human experience should have served as a warning to idealists who harbored such illusions, for crises and wars have been chronic features of human behavior long before the Germans and Japanese exploded on the international scene. Sanguine expectations were particularly out of place when contemplating future relations between Russia and the West, which have been marred by fear and suspicion ever since the emergence of Russia as a major player in international power politics. This antagonism was muted but never completely quelled when Russia was sought as an ally by the Western powers to deal with a more immediate danger, as happened in the two world wars of the twentieth century. But even during these wars the alliances between Russia and the West were subject to serious strains and conflicts of interest. They endured only so long as the common danger existed and was clearly perceived. They broke apart with the elimination of that danger and the revival of mutual suspicion.

Thus the Cold War could be considered simply part of the long and continuing history of human crisis and conflict, this one revolving around the long-standing hostility between Russia and the West. But it was more than that. The Bolshevik revolution, with its promulgation of a program calling for world revolution and the destruction of Western political and economic systems, had introduced a new and particularly virulent ideological hostility into Russo–Western relations. An even more critical difference, however, was the existence of the new weaponry, which gave each side the capacity to destroy the other and thereby raised the conduct of international relations to entirely new levels of risk and danger.

❑ *Peacemaking, 1945: the London and Moscow Meetings*

Despite the differences between the Soviet Union and the West that were already evident at the time he became president, Harry Truman recognized the desirability—indeed, the necessity—of carrying on his predecessor's efforts to cooperate with the Soviet Union in restoring peace in Europe and Asia. But he never succeeded in reaching agreement with the Soviet Union over the terms of a peace treaty with Germany and Japan, and it was only after acrimonious and lengthy negotiation that peace treaties were finally concluded with Germany's European allies.

At their Potsdam conference, the Big Three had provided for the establishment of a Council of Foreign Ministers, made up of the representatives of Britain, the Soviet Union, the United States, China, and France, whose "immediate and important" task would be to draft treaties of peace with Italy and Germany's four European satellites— Bulgaria, Finland, Hungary, and Romania. The Council was also to prepare a peace settlement with Germany, "to be accepted by the Government of Germany when a government adequate for this purpose is established." The first meeting of the Council of Foreign Ministers took place in London from September 11 to October 2, 1945. The London negotiations were in difficulty from the start. Fearing that the representatives of France and China would side with Britain and the United States, Molotov, the Soviet foreign minister, sought to restrict the participation of France to the affairs of Western Europe and to exclude China from the discussions of Europe altogether. The London meeting broke up over this issue without any substantive agreement having been reached over a host of other problems.

The American secretary of state, James Byrnes, disappointed by the failure of the London meeting, decided that a bold new initiative was needed to restore the good working relations with the Soviet Union that had existed during the Roosevelt era. Without consulting Ernest Bevin, the British foreign secretary, he approached Molotov with a proposal for another foreign ministers' meeting, this one to be held in Moscow without the participation of representatives from France and China. Molotov readily agreed to this proposal, and Bevin, although infuriated by Byrnes's unilateral action, saw no alternative but to agree as well.

At the Moscow meeting, December 16 to 26, 1945, Byrnes went to extravagant lengths to secure Soviet cooperation in dealing with problems of the postwar world. He offered the Soviets de facto representation in a United Nations Atomic Energy Commission to control the use of this new source of power, participation in the occupation of Japan, and cooperation in arranging the reunification of Korea, which had been divided into Soviet and American occupation zones. In return, Byrnes secured Molotov's agreement to the convocation of a peace conference in Paris and to somewhat vague arrangements to include non-Communists in the governments of Bulgaria and Romania. He failed to secure a Soviet commitment to withdraw their troops from Iran.

George Kennan, the State Department's Soviet expert who had accompanied Byrnes to the Moscow meetings, had nothing but contempt for the secretary's policies. His primary purpose, Kennan said, was to secure "some sort of agreement, he doesn't much care what," in order to enhance his prestige at home, unconcerned about the realities of the situation "since they concern only such people as Koreans, Rumanians, and Iranians, about whom he knows nothing."

Byrnes himself was elated about his achievements. Upon returning from Moscow he issued a communiqué about the results of the conference before informing or consulting the president. Infuriated by Byrnes's bland assumption of responsibility for the conduct of American foreign policy, Truman ordered the secretary to report to him personally—and immediately. Only then did Byrnes give the president a documentary record of the conference. "As I went through these papers," Truman wrote in his memoirs, "it became abundantly clear to me that the successes of the Moscow conference were unreal. . . . Byrnes, I concluded after studying the entire record, had taken it upon himself to move the foreign policy of the United States in a direction to which I could not, and would not, agree."

Truman was particularly outraged that Soviet troops remained in Iran, and he predicted that Soviet treaty violations over Iran would be followed by an invasion of Turkey and the seizure of the Turkish Straits. "Unless Russia is faced with an iron fist and strong language another war is in the making. . . . I do not think we should compromise any longer. . . . I'm tired of babying the Soviets."

In the end, the "concessions" made by both sides at Moscow proved to be meaningless. Soviet-controlled Communists continued to dominate the governments of Bulgaria and Romania; the Americans did not surrender control over atomic energy to a UN commission; General MacArthur, the head of the American occupation government in Japan, did not allow his authority to be diluted or restricted by newly established Allied control commissions; and Korea remained divided. Indeed, Byrnes's only failure at Moscow turned out to be his only success, for on April 5, 1946, the Soviet Union agreed to pull its troops our of Iran.

❑ Stalin's "Declaration of World War III" and Kennan's Doctrine of Containment

Truman's dire predictions about Soviet intentions seemed confirmed by a speech delivered by Stalin on February 9, 1946, on the eve of elections to the Supreme Soviet. While acknowledging the contribution of the West to the victory over fascist forces in the recent war, he reaffirmed the validity of the Marxist-Leninist analysis of the capitalist system, its inherent instability, and the inevitability of future war so long as the capitalist system existed. He extolled his own wisdom in inaugurating the five-year plans whose crash program of industrialization had enabled the Soviet Union to defeat Germany, and he warned the Soviet people to gird themselves for the sacrifices that would be required by another succession of five-year plans that would enable the Soviet Union to meet the challenges of the future. The most sinister part of his speech, however, was his prediction that the confrontation with the capitalist world might come as early as the 1950s, when America would again be in the depths of economic depression.

Stalin's speech aroused alarm and consternation in Washington. The liberal Supreme Court justice William O. Douglas called Stalin's speech a "declaration of World War III." Similarly alarmed, the State Department turned to George Kennan with a request for an "interpretive analysis of what we may expect in the way of future implementation of these announced policies."

Kennan was an American career diplomat and student of Russian history who had spent several years in Moscow as a member of the American embassy staff in the 1930s. He returned to Moscow as minister-counselor at the embassy in July 1944, and in September of that year he wrote a long evaluation of Soviet policy warning his government of the threat Russia might pose to Western interests after the war and putting particular emphasis on the continuity of tsarist and Soviet policies. The Soviet government, he said, was pursuing the same program of territorial expansion as its tsarist predecessors, with the same objective of extending Russian control over the greater part of Eastern Europe, the Balkans, and the Turkish Straits.

In the autumn of 1944 Kennan's warnings had little impact on American policy, but in 1946, as many Americans became increasingly alarmed about Soviet intentions, Kennan found that he was no longer a voice crying in the wilderness but was hailed, somewhat to his embarrassment, as an oracle on Soviet affairs. Kennan's response to the State Department's request for an "interpretive analysis" of Soviet conduct was a document of February 22 that has become known as the Long Telegram. As in his 1944 analysis, Kennan predicted that future Soviet policy would be dedicated to increasing Soviet strength at home and expanding Soviet influence abroad in every possible way. In achieving this purpose, the Soviet government had the invaluable aid of the world's Communist parties "tightly coordinated and directed by Moscow," which would seek to stir up the resentment of colonial and dependent peoples against the Western powers. But even as these peoples were being encouraged to seek independence, Soviet-dominated puppet political machines were being prepared to take over power in areas where independence was achieved.

Kennan proceeded to suggest how the United States should deal with the Soviet menace, and he expressed the belief that the problem could be handled without recourse to war. "Soviet power, unlike that of Hitlerite Germany, is neither schematic nor adventuristic. It does not work by fixed plans. It does not take unnecessary risks. Impervious to logic of reason, it is highly sensitive to logic of force. For this reason it can easily withdraw—and usually does—when strong resistance is encountered at any point."

Kennan's Long Telegram set forth views that became (or already were) articles of faith for many American leaders: a belief in the inexorable quality of Soviet-Communist imperialism and the existence of a monolithic international Communist conspiracy directed from Moscow. The part of the Long Telegram that had the greatest impact on the formulation of American foreign policy, however, was Kennan's argument that Soviet leaders, although impervious to the logic of reason, understood the logic of force and could be stopped if their adversary possessed sufficient force and made clear his readiness to use it. This analysis was to become a basic principle of American foreign policy over the next three decades and became known as the doctrine of containment.

In later years, after the United States had diverted a large part of its budget to a military buildup and plunged into costly and, in the case of Vietnam, disastrous international controversies to uphold the doctrine of containment, Kennan deplored the serious deficiencies—indeed, the egregious errors—of his arguments. He regretted his failure to discuss the weaknesses of the Soviet political system and the strains imposed on that system by the overextension of Soviet involvement in Eastern Europe; his failure to distinguish between various geographical areas or to make clear that "containment" was not a strategy that could be employed successfully everywhere. Over the years it had also become evident that the Communist parties of the world were not an international monolith directed from Moscow, and that there were major differences between them as well as factional strife among their leaders.

Yet in the end Kennan's analysis of the effectiveness of containment proved more correct than he realized, for he predicted that in the long run, if the Soviet Union were held in check and not allowed to extend its dominion over the greater part of Europe and Asia, its rigid and tyrannical political system and its centralized economy would collapse as a result of its inherent weaknesses and that the Soviet empire itself would break apart.

❑ *Churchill's Iron Curtain Speech and the Soviet Reaction*   *Westminster*

Kennan's Long Telegram was an official document that remained restricted to circulation among government departments. A public and far more dramatic expression of Western apprehensions about the Soviet Union was provided by Britain's eloquent wartime leader, Winston Churchill, now out of office. In a speech at Westminster College in Fulton, Missouri, on March 5, 1946, which he described to Truman as the most important of his career, Churchill declared: "From Stettin to the Baltic to Trieste in the Adriatic, an iron curtain has descended across the Continent. Behind that line lie all the capitals of the ancient states of Central and Eastern Europe . . . and the populations around them lie in what I must call the Soviet sphere, and all are subject in one form or another, not only to Soviet influence but to a very high and, in many cases, increasing measure of control from Moscow. . . . This is certainly not the Liberated Europe we fought to build up. Nor is it one which contains the essentials of permanent peace." The Soviets did not want war, Churchill said, but rather the fruits of war "and the indefinite expansion of their power and doctrine." What was needed in response was a union of the Western democracies, specifically an English-speaking union of Britain and the United States.

Truman was taken aback by the hostile reaction in America to Churchill's speech, especially his call for an Anglo-American alliance and the implied disregard of the United Nations. This reaction served as a warning to Truman that isolationism was still a powerful force in American political consciousness, that feelings about Russia were still conditioned by wartime solidarity, and that American public opinion was not yet prepared to support broad international commitments.

As was to be expected, the most virulent denunciation of the Churchill speech came from Moscow. Stalin called it a "call to war," a slanderous attack on Russia's Eastern European allies, all of which were governed by "exemplary democratic regimes, more so than Britain's." He announced the inauguration of a new Five-Year Plan, and stepped up his ideological campaign to eliminate Western cultural influences and reinforce Communist dogma. Further, he rejected the terms of an American offer of a billion dollar loan, which he denounced as an attempt to lure the Soviet Union into a capitalist-controlled economic system, and he refused to become associated with the World Bank and the International Monetary Fund, which he saw as instruments for undermining Soviet influence in Eastern Europe.

In his actual conduct of foreign affairs, however, Stalin played a cautious game. Alarmed by the prospect of a showdown with the West over Iran, he announced on March 26, 1946, that Soviet troops would be withdrawn from Iran within six weeks. Nor did he send them back to Iran when the Iranian government rejected Soviet requests for economic concessions and brutally suppressed political parties and separatist regimes supported by Moscow. Stalin continued to exercise restraint when confronted with America's de facto exercise of sole authority in the occupation of Japan, the rejection of Soviet claims to reparations from West Germany, and British intervention in the civil war in Greece.

❑ Peacemaking, 1946, and the Crucial German Question

On July 29 a general peace conference convened in Paris to negotiate final peace treaties with Germany and its European allies. The negotiation of a German treaty broke down, however, because of fundamental differences over the German question.

By the spring of 1946, American observers in Europe were sending home apocalyptic accounts of the complete economic, social, and political collapse that had taken place in Central Europe and warnings of the potential disastrous consequences for Europe as a whole if anarchic conditions were allowed to continue. Much though one might wish to punish Germany for its wartime sins, the awkward fact remained that the economic rehabilitation of France, the Low Countries, and indeed of all of Western and Central Europe depended on a revival of the German economy, especially the large-scale mining of coal. It would therefore be necessary to relax the stringent restrictions on German economic activity laid down in JCS 1067 (see p. 286) and scale down Allied demands for reparations.

Byrnes made a determined effort to remove Soviet objections to a treaty that would allow for Germany's economic recovery. To allay Soviet fears about potential German threats to Soviet security, he revived an earlier proposal for a four-power treaty guaranteeing the demilitarization of Germany for twenty-five years. Molotov commented that this plan aroused "serious objections," but did not spell out what these might be. One such objection was obvious. Byrnes's proposal would extend the maintenance of American troops in Germany far beyond the two years Roosevelt had predicted as the maximum time American public opinion would tolerate American military presence in Europe. If American, as well as British and French, troops remained in Germany, Soviet influence would be correspondingly diminished.

Seeking a specific exposition of Molotov's views, Byrnes asked him at a private dinner what his government really wanted with respect to Germany. "The Soviet Union wants what it asked for at Yalta," Molotov replied. "Ten billion dollars in reparations—and . . . to participate with the United States, the United Kingdom, and France in a four-power control of the industries of the Ruhr." From the Soviet viewpoint these conditions were eminently reasonable: the Soviet Union was entitled to generous compensation for the devastation and suffering caused by the German invaders. Now, however, it was the turn of the British and Americans to have serious objections. Massive reparations and joint control of the Ruhr would give the Soviet government a decisive voice in the German economy and allow for the extension of Soviet influence over Germany as a whole. They would enable the Soviet Union to delay or prevent altogether Germany's economic recovery, leaving the West with the responsibility of feeding the German people and thus also contributing indirectly to Germany's reparations payments. If economic anarchy in Germany were allowed to continue, the restoration of political and economic stability would be delayed indefinitely not only in Germany but in the greater part of Europe, leaving the peoples of Europe an easy prey to Communist propaganda—which, Western statesmen suspected, might indeed be a principal objective of Soviet policy.

In a speech delivered in Stuttgart on September 6, Secretary of State Byrnes reaffirmed America's intention to promote Germany's economic revival and called for the prompt formation of a provisional German government with authority to administer the entire country so that Germans could again manage their own affairs. At the same time, Byrnes put an end to any expectations the Soviets might still entertain that American troops would soon be leaving Europe. On this point, he declared, there must be no misunderstanding. "We are not withdrawing. As long as an occupation force is required in Germany, the army of the United States will be part of that occupation force."

Because Molotov refused to accept the decision of a majority vote over the German question, the negotiations over Germany remained deadlocked and the peace conference in Paris adjourned on October 15. At yet another meeting of the Council of Foreign Ministers, this time in New York in December 1946, Molotov at last agreed to a compromise: he would accept the verdict of a majority vote if his Western counterparts would abandon specific points his government found impossible to accept. What this compromise amounted to in practice was that the peace conference set aside the controversial German question and dealt only with the drafting of peace treaties with Germany's allies.

❑ Peace with Italy and Germany's Satellites

The peace treaties worked out at subsequent meetings of the Paris Peace Conference were signed on February 10, 1947, in the clock room of the French Foreign Ministry where the Covenant of the League of Nations had been adopted in 1919 and the

MAP 12   EUROPE AFTER WORLD WAR II

ICELAND

Rybachi
Peninsula

PETSAMO
SALLA
Salla

NORTH
SEA

SWEDEN

NORWAY

FINLAND

Karelian
Isthmus

GULF OF BOTHNIA

Hanko Helsinki
Porkkala Vilpuri
Turku
Åland
Islands

Lake
Ladoga

Leningrad

Oslo

Stockholm

GULF OF FINLAND

BALTIC SEA

ESTONIA

Moscow

GREAT
BRITAIN

EIRE

DENMARK

Copenhagen

LATVIA

Kaliningrad
(Königsberg)

LITHUANIA

Minsk

London

ATLANTIC
OCEAN

NETH.

BERLIN

EAST
PRUSSIA

Oder Neisse

POLAND

Warsaw

Pinsk

U.S.S.R.

Bonn

EAST
GERMANY

BELG.

Paris

LUX.

WEST
GERMANY

Prague

CZECHO-
SLOVAKIA

Kiev

Lvov

GALICIA

NORTHERN
BUKOVINA

FRANCE

SWITZ.

Vienna

AUSTRIA

HUNGARY

Budapest

RUTHENIA

BESSARABIA

Trieste

VENEZIA
GIULIA

Fiume

Belgrade

ROMANIA

Bucharest

BLACK SEA

S.
DOBRUJA

PORTUGAL

Lisbon

Madrid

YUGOSLAVIA

BULGARIA

Sofia

SPAIN

Rome

ITALY

ALBANIA

GREECE

Ankara

TURKEY

AEGEAN
SEA

Athens

ALGERIA
(France)

TUNISIA
(France)

MEDITERRANEAN SEA

GERMANY, 1946

DENMARK

U.S. Zone

Bremen

AIR ROUTE

Berlin

(Formerly
part of
Germany)

NETH.

British
Zone

POLAND

BEL.

Bonn

AIR ROUTE

Russian
Zone

LUX.

Frankfurt

U.S. Zone

CZECHOSLOVAKIA

FRANCE

French
Zone

SWITZ.

AUSTRIA

Venezia Giulia: ceded by
Italy to Yugoslavia; S. Dobruja:
ceded by Romania to Bulgaria

Soviet-annexed territories of
1939–1940, reclaimed in 1945

Former Czechoslovakian and
German territory annexed
by USSR in 1945

Soviet zone of occupation in
Austria prior to 1955

Soviet satellite states by 1950

"Iron Curtain"

0   200   400 Miles

Kellogg-Briand Pact outlawing war as an instrument of national policy had been signed in 1928. The signatories in 1947 were the representatives of the twenty-one states that had waged war against the Axis in Europe and by representatives of the defeated states—Bulgaria, Finland, Hungary, Italy, and Romania. Byrnes had resigned on January 7, 1947, to be succeeded by General George Marshall.

Although the Italian government bewailed the harshness of the Allied peace terms, the Italians got off remarkably lightly. Italy was obliged to cede the greater part of Venezia Giulia, with Fiume, and all its Adriatic islands to Yugoslavia; to cede to Greece the Dodecanese Islands and Rhodes (acquired after its victory over the Ottoman empire in 1913); and to agree to minor modifications of its frontier with France. Italy was also obliged to renounce its annexation of Albania and Ethiopia, which were both declared to be independent and sovereign states.

The complicated question of Trieste, a predominantly Italian city surrounded by a predominantly Slavic hinterland, was settled by a compromise arrangement which made Trieste and its hinterland a free territory under the trusteeship of the United Nations. A final settlement over Trieste was not reached until 1954, when the city of Trieste itself was awarded to Italy while the greater part of the city's hinterland was awarded to Yugoslavia.

Italy's former African colonies, apart from Ethiopia, were placed under the trusteeship of the United Nations, which meant that the Soviet Union abandoned its claim to be awarded the trusteeship of an Italian colony on the Mediterranean. Libya (Tripolitania and Cyrenaica) was granted full independence in December 1951. In 1949 the UN actually placed Italian Somaliland under Italian administration, but in 1960 it was joined to British Somaliland to form the independent Republic of Somalia. A federal union of Eritrea with Ethiopia, arranged by the UN in 1950, took place in 1952.

Italy was obliged to agree to a restriction of its armed forces and to the payment of reparations. The Western powers, eager to promote Italy's economic recovery and prevent the spread of Communism in that country, renounced all claims to reparations. They also managed to scale down the considerable claims of the Soviet Union and those of the victims of Italian aggression. The Soviet Union finally settled for 100 million dollars in reparations, as opposed to their original claim of 6 billion dollars, while another 260 million dollars were to be divided among Greece, Yugoslavia, Albania, and Ethiopia. The greater part of these reparations were eventually paid through loans from the United States.

The treaties with Bulgaria, Hungary, and Romania also included restrictions on their armed forces and an obligation to pay reparations. Otherwise all three states were reestablished within their post–World War I boundaries, with several important exceptions. Romania was obliged to reaffirm the 1939 cession of Bessarabia and Northern Bukovina to the Soviet Union and of Southern Dobruja to Bulgaria. Hungary gave up all territory acquired in partnership with Hitler, but otherwise lost only a minor strip of territory to Czechoslovakia (the Bratislava bridgehead). Bulgaria, which was allowed to retain Southern Dobruja, was the sole gainer.

Finland, besides being forced to pay substantial reparations, was obliged to reaffirm its cession of territory to the Soviet Union following the winter war of 1939–1940: the Karelian Isthmus, the strategic strongpoint of Viipuri, all Finnish holdings on the shores of Lake Ladoga, and a thirty-year leasehold of the Hanko Peninsula. In addition, Finland was now obliged to cede the Petsamo area, with its important nickel mines, which gave the Soviet Union a common frontier with Norway, and to grant the Soviets a fifty-year lease of a naval base at Porkkala, which they relinquished as a good-will gesture in 1955.

❑ *The Truman Doctrine, Aid to Greece and Turkey, and the Greek Civil War*

On February 21, 1947, just eleven days after the signature of the five European peace treaties in Paris, the U.S. State Department received an urgent message from the British ambassador, Lord Inverchapel, informing the American government that owing to Britain's economic crisis—more than half of Britain's industries were idle following one of the most severe winters in living memory—Britain could no longer provide military and economic aid to the anti-Communist government of Greece or the support required by Turkey to resist Soviet pressure. Britain intended to withdraw 40,000 troops from Greece and end all economic aid to that country by the end of March. Would the United States be prepared to take over British commitments in this strategically important area?

This announcement came as no surprise to the Americans, though Truman acknowledged that it came "sooner than we expected." They were well aware of Britain's economic difficulties, and had realized for some time that they might have to take over Britain's role as guardian of Western interests in the eastern Mediterranean.

Western concern for Turkey (the nucleus of the former Ottoman empire) had a very long history. For centuries, Russian rulers had sought control over Constantinople and the Turkish Straits, the strategic waterway between the Black Sea and the Mediterranean, that would enable them to bring Russian power and influence to bear in the Mediterranean basin. And for centuries they had been turned back by the Turks, often with the support of one or more of the Western powers that feared Russia's penetration into the Mediterranean.

The Soviet government had now taken over this ancient tsarist objective. During the war, Stalin had sought the support of his allies for a revision of the 1936 Montreux Convention, which allowed Turkey to fortify the Turkish Straits, and to pressure Turkey into giving the Soviet Union naval bases on the Straits. Failing to gain such support, the Soviet government had taken unilateral action. On March 19, 1945, it denounced its twenty-five year nonaggression pact with Turkey and demanded the cession of bases on the Straits, a demand that Turkey, with tacit Western encouragement, had so far successfully rejected.

Western concern for Greece derived from essentially the same fears that prompted concern for Turkey: the possibility that the Russians would gain control of Greece and therewith acquire bases on the Mediterranean. At his meeting with Churchill in Moscow in October 1944, Stalin had conceded Britain predominant influence in Greece (see p. 286). Two years later, however, the British saw reason to fear that Greece, like the rest of Eastern Europe, would fall under Soviet control. A pro-Western government in Athens, installed under British auspices, was engaged in a de facto civil war with a Leftist movement that was receiving substantial military aid from Communist Yugoslavia and that appeared to enjoy the support of the Soviet Union. This was the situation when the British appealed to the United States to take over the burden of holding Greece and Turkey for the West.

There was remarkable unanimity among American leaders about the need to respond positively to this British appeal. On February 23, 1947, two days after the reception of this appeal, Secretary of State Marshall and Undersecretary Dean Acheson met with Truman and urged immediate action to step into the breach. Secretary of War Robert Patterson regarded the independence of Greece and Turkey as vital strategic interests of the United States. And Navy Secretary James Forrestal described the civil war in Greece as part of a fundamental struggle between the American and Russian ways of life, proof-positive that the Russians would not respond to anything except force.

While agreeing about the need to provide aid to Greece and Turkey, the leaders of the Truman administration realized that they would have difficulty persuading an economy-minded Republican Congress to vote the necessary funds and overcoming the isolationist sentiment that remained a powerful force in the country. In dealing with these problems, the administration received invaluable help from the Republican Senator Arthur Vandenberg, who was to engineer bipartisan support for the aid bill in Congress and who advised Truman to break down isolationism by "scaring the hell" out of the American people.

The Truman administration lost no time in acting on this advice. On February 27 Secretary of State Marshall told Congressional leaders that he was not being alarmist in saying that the United States was now confronted with the first of a series of crises which might extend Soviet domination over the rest of Europe, the Middle East, and Asia, and that America now faced the choice of "acting with energy or losing by default." The same theme was taken up by Undersecretary Acheson, who warned that a Communist-dominated government in Greece would open three continents to Soviet penetration and therewith pose a mortal threat to American security.

Truman himself sounded the most strident note of alarm. In a speech of March 12 before a joint session of Congress, he drew a grim picture of the international situation. The existence of the Greek nation was threatened by several thousand Communist guerrillas, but this was only part of a global struggle "between alternative views of life." The fall of Greece to Communist dominion would set off a fall of other governments that would tumble like dominoes across the map. To forestall such a catastrophe, Truman called for 250 million dollars to provide economic and military aid for Greece, and another 150 million for Turkey. At the same time he set forth principles for the future conduct of American foreign policy. American support should be provided primarily through economic and financial aid "which is essential to economic stability and orderly political progress." But more than that, "it must be the policy of the United States to support free peoples who are resisting subjugation by armed minorities or by outside pressures" and to "assist free peoples to work out their own destinies in their own way."

This commitment to support free peoples everywhere was soon to be known as the Truman Doctrine, a harkening back to the Monroe Doctrine (which had only

cold War

committed the United States to defend the Western Hemisphere against foreign interference.) The scare tactics worked. The House approved the aid bill to Greece and
Turkey by a vote of 287 to 107, the Senate by a vote of 67 to 23.

Criticism began at once and still continues. Almost immediately after the delivery
of the Truman Doctrine speech, the influential journalist Walter Lippmann denounced
the administration's policy as a strategic monstrosity. Calling as it did for the indiscriminate support of free peoples everywhere, no matter how freedom might be defined,
it failed to distinguish between America's vital and peripheral interests and made limitless global commitments that would dangerously overextend America's resources.

Other contemporary observers leveled more specific criticism against Anglo-
American policy in Greece, which they held responsible for the civil war in that
country and the installation of a repressive, corrupt, and incompetent regime. This criticism was countered by the argument that the Greek Communists, like their counterparts in Eastern Europe, had been even more brutal in suppressing rival factions in areas under their control. By supporting a non-Communist regime in Greece, no matter
how incompetent and corrupt, the Western powers remained in a position to press
for reform and prevent Greece from becoming an outpost of Soviet power.

By October 1949, after three years of fighting, the civil war in Greece ended with
the defeat of the Greek Communists. It is surprising that they held out so long, for already in February of 1948 Stalin had demanded that Tito, the dictator of Communist
Yugoslavia, end all support to the Greek Communists, ostensibly to avoid complications with the West.

☑ *The Marshall Plan*

On March 10, 1947, two days before Truman's speech to a joint session of Congress
calling for aid to Greece and Turkey, Secretary of State Marshall was in Moscow to attend a session of the Council of Foreign Ministers, his primary objective to secure Soviet agreement to measures to promote the economic recovery of Germany. The economic situation in Germany and Europe had by now assumed crisis proportions. To
allay Soviet fears about Germany, Marshall revived Byrnes's proposal of a four-power
treaty guaranteeing Germany's demilitarization. But the Soviet government showed
no more interest than heretofore in a guarantee that would ensure America's continued military presence in Europe, and it continued to insist on reparations from Germany that would doom any practical economic recovery program. When the Moscow
meeting broke up on April 24, the only agreement reached over Germany was to abolish the state of Prussia. There was no agreement of any kind over Austria.

Marshall returned from Moscow convinced that Stalin was not so much concerned about reparations in themselves as to use them to hasten the political and
economic disintegration of Western Europe. He had shown no interest whatever in a
settlement over Germany, and seemed quite content to allow the present chaotic conditions to continue. Upon the receipt of Marshall's pessimistic appraisal of Stalin's intentions, Truman was persuaded that further negotiation with Moscow over Germany
was futile; the United States must now pursue an independent course in seeking the

economic rehabilitation of Europe. Truman has been accused of acting hastily, but it had taken him two years to arrive at this conclusion.

After reporting to Truman upon his return from Moscow, one of Marshall's first moves was to instruct George Kennan to put together a Policy Planning Staff that was to draw up a plan for the economic rehabilitation of Europe. Kennan had long argued that Western Europe should be the centerpiece of American concern and that bold steps must be taken to prevent the Soviet destruction of Europe's industrial infrastructure. He was worried most about Germany, and in this connection he voiced a familiar Western fear: "The only really dangerous thing in my mind is the possibility that the technical skill of the Germans might be combined with the physical resources of Russia." Should that happen, "then there would come into existence an aggregate of economic and military industrial power which ought to make every one of us sit up and take notice damn fast."

Kennan's alarm about Germany was shared by leaders of other American government agencies. On April 29, 1947, the Joint Chiefs of Staff issued a policy statement that in effect reversed JCS 1067, which had prohibited occupation authorities from taking any steps to rehabilitate the German economy apart from agricultural production. (See p. 286.) The April statement called for immediate American aid to Germany as well as to Britain and France, and stressed the need for an alignment of the economies of all three countries. The resurgence of German industry, particularly coal mining, was essential for the economic recovery of France, which in turn was fundamental to French national security and hence also to the security of Britain and Canada—and the United States.

The program of American aid for European economic recovery that became known as the Marshall Plan was announced by Secretary of State Marshall in a commencement address at Harvard on June 5, 1947. The fundamental American aim was "the revival of a working economy in the world so as to permit the emergence of political and social conditions in which free institutions can exist." This policy was not directed against any country or doctrine, "but against hunger, poverty, desperation and chaos." Any government that was willing to assist in the task of recovery would receive the full cooperation of the United States. The initiative, however, had to come from Europe. "The program must be a joint one, agreed to by a number, if not all, European nations." The initial role of the United States would be restricted to friendly aid in drafting a European program and of supporting such a program as far as seemed practical. Marshall also issued a warning: "Any government which maneuvers to block the recovery of other countries cannot expect help from us. Furthermore, governments, political parties, or groups which seek to perpetuate human misery in order to profit therefrom politically or otherwise will encounter the opposition of the United States."

Undersecretary of State Dean Acheson, fearing that a commencement address was not a forum that would convey the full significance of Marshall's statement to foreign governments, saw to it that a copy was delivered to Foreign Secretary Bevin in London immediately after its release, whatever the time of day or night. As Bevin was to say later, "We grabbed at the lifeline with both hands." Directly after receiving the Marshall speech, he telegraphed Georges Bidault, the French foreign minister, and arranged to meet with him in Paris on June 17. Together they decided, with the agreement of the Americans, to issue an invitation to Molotov to join them in drawing up a collective response to the American initiative.

Molotov arrived in Paris on June 26 accompanied by an entourage of eighty-nine economic experts and clerks. After four days of abrasive discussion, during which Molotov spent much of his time conferring by telephone with Moscow, the Soviet minister put forward a proposal that each nation set up its own recovery program. As this was precisely what the Marshall Plan was designed to avoid, Bevin and Bidault proposed instead that the European states should work together in formulating a program to present to the Americans. Brusquely rejecting this proposal, Molotov left the conference and announced his government's refusal to have anything to do with the Marshall proposal, which he denounced as a vicious American scheme for using dollars to buy its way into the affairs of Europe. The plan would undermine national sovereignty, revive Germany, and make for American control of the participating states. Besides, America's real aim was not European economic recovery at all but to use its credit facilities to enlarge its foreign markets and stave off the inevitable coming crisis of the capitalist system.

Long after his retirement, Molotov still maintained that the Soviet government had been right to reject the Marshall Plan. Soviet leaders had decided at first to propose that all socialist countries participate, "but quickly realized that was wrong. The imperialists were drawing us into their company, but as subordinates. We would have been absolutely dependent on them without getting anything useful in return."

On July 4, 1947, following Molotov's departure from Paris, Bevin and Bidault issued an invitation to all the states of Europe apart from the Soviet Union and Spain (still excluded from the councils of Europe because of the Franco government's association with Hitler and Mussolini) to a conference that was to convene in Paris on July 12. Under pressure from the Soviet Union, all of its East European satellites declined except Czechoslovkia, which did not get its orders from Moscow in time and accepted. There followed grim retribution. Jan Masaryk, the Czech foreign minister, was hastily summoned to Moscow and ordered to rescind his government's acceptance. Early in the new year, a Communist coup put Communists in firm control of that government, and shortly afterwards Masaryk himself was dead, whether a victim of suicide or assassination has never been determined. (See p. 324.)

The conference of sixteen European states that met in Paris on July 12 set up a Committee on European Economic Cooperation to prepare a coordinated response to the American aid offer. On September 22 this committee submitted a four-year recovery program specifying the immediate and future needs of each of the participating European states and proposing the establishment of a permanent organization of those states. The recovery program itself called for measures to increase production, a general reduction of tariffs, and currency stabilization that would make for currency convertibility and thus facilitate international trade.

Moscow's rejection of the Marshall Plan and the Communist coup in Czechoslovakia proved of immense help to the Truman administration in securing Congressional approval. In March 1948 Congress passed the Foreign Assistance Act (the Marshall Plan) and authorized an initial 5.3 billion dollars to support Europe's economic recovery. In that same month, the countries participating in the recovery plan set up permanent machinery for economic cooperation and the allocation of American aid, the Organization for European Economic Cooperation (OEEC). Between 1948 and 1952 the Marshall Plan supplied grants and credits totalling 13.2 billion dollars: 3.2 billion to Britain and its dependencies, 2.7 to France, 1.5 to Italy, and 1.4 to West Germany (admitted as a full member of the OEEC in October 1949). By 1952, industrial production in Western Europe had risen to 35 percent, agriculture to 10 percent, above their prewar levels.

The Marshall Plan was hailed by Winston Churchill as "the most unsordid act in history," and "one of America's greatest contributions to the peace of the world." And indeed, the European economic recovery associated with the Marshall Plan was so successful that up to the present day there has been no *economic* threat to European peace and stability.

Like all other aspects of America's postwar policies, however, the Marshall Plan has been the subject of intense criticism. Western analysts have echoed the Soviet complaint that the plan was designed to bring the states of Europe into the American political and economic orbit and to stave off the coming crisis of the capitalist system. Others have questioned the plan's actual contribution to Europe's economic recovery, which they contend was already well under way by 1947.

There can be no question that the Americans tried to use their economic clout to influence the policies of the states enrolled in the Marshall Plan, or that the plan contributed to America's own economic prosperity. It is also true that Europe's economic recovery had already begun, at least in some areas, before the plan's enactment. But these criticisms seem both irrelevant and ungenerous when the Marshall Plan is viewed in the light of the circumstances of the time, for they fail to appreciate the immense moral as well as economic boost the plan gave to the countries of Western Europe, or the overall benefit to the Western economy as a whole resulting from European and American economic integration.

TWENTY-THREE

The Formation
of Rival Alignments

❑ The Extension of Soviet Influence in Eastern
Europe; The Creation of the Cominform

In its wartime and postwar agreements with the West, the Soviet Union had promised the installation of representative democratic governments in all the countries liberated by the Allied armies. The Soviet failure to honor these agreements, or rather the differences between the Soviet and Western interpretation of what constituted a representative democratic government, had played a major role in the breakdown of amicable relations between the Soviet Union and the West and the inauguration of the Cold War. The Baltic states of Estonia, Latvia, and Lithuania had been reincorporated into the Soviet Union as Soviet Socialist Republics. Elsewhere in Eastern Europe, the Soviets had sponsored the installation of Communist dictatorships (euphemistically entitled Peoples' Democracies) that by 1947 had transformed Poland, Bulgaria, Romania, and Hungary into reliable Soviet satellites whose governments carried out ruthless purges of opposition leaders and parties. Only Finland had escaped Sovietization—provided it maintained friendly relations with Moscow.

At a conference in Poland in October 1947, Communist representatives from Bulgaria, Czechoslovakia, France, Hungary, Italy, Poland, Romania, the Soviet Union, and Yugoslavia set up the Communist Information Bureau (Cominform). At this conference the Marshall Plan was denounced as yet another American imperialist scheme to subject the countries of Europe to the tyranny of Wall Street. The Cominform, its founders proclaimed, would foil this nefarious plot. It would serve as a coordinating agency to ensure the political and ideological solidarity among the European Communist parties, and was dedicated to the destruction of "bourgeois capitalism." To ensure ideological correctness, the Cominform conference called for the elimination of all independent socialist, labor, and peasant parties, whose deviationist policies were undermining true Marxian socialism.

Stalin selected Belgrade as the headquarters of the Cominform, ostensibly to honor the role of the Yugoslav party in the war against the Axis. The Yugoslavs suspected, however, that his real purpose was to bring the various European Communist parties, most especially that of Yugoslavia, under tighter Soviet control and to make them all more servile instruments of Soviet policy.

It was soon evident that Yugoslav suspicions of Stalin's real intention had been correct: that the Cominform was indeed being used as an instrument of Soviet control over the satellite states of Eastern Europe. In France and Italy, the Comintern became a mechanism for directing the Communist parties to foment strikes and other disruptive activities for the purpose of discrediting their bourgeois governments and ensuring the failure of the Marshall Plan.

❏ *The February 1948 Coup in Czechoslovakia*

For a time it seemed that Czechoslovakia, like Finland, would be allowed to retain a certain amount of domestic independence. During World War II Eduard Beneš, who had resigned as president of Czechoslovakia after the 1938 Munich crisis, set up a government in exile in London, but he was sufficiently realistic about the future power structure in Eastern Europe to seek accommodation with the Russians. In December 1943 his government in exile signed a treaty of friendship and alliance with the Soviet Union whereby the Soviets recognized Czechoslovakia's pre-1938 frontiers and promised not to intervene in that country's domestic affairs. In return the Czechs promised that a postwar Czechoslovak government would include Communists and that it would speak and act in a manner agreeable to the Soviet Union. In addition they agreed to cede Ruthenia (the Carpatho-Ukraine, at the easternmost tip of Czechoslovakia) to the Soviet Union, which would give the Soviets a common frontier with Czechoslovakia and thus enable Moscow to bring direct pressure to bear on that country.

In March 1945 Beneš met in Moscow with Czech Communists who had gone into exile in the Soviet Union. With them he organized a provisional government to administer the country as it was liberated by the Red Army. Seven out of twenty-five posts went to Communists, including the premiership, the ministry of the interior (with jurisdiction over the police), and the ministries of information, labor, and agriculture. Apart from Beneš, the president, the most prominent non-Communist member of the government was Jan Masaryk, the son of Thomas Masaryk, the first president of independent Czechoslovakia, who was awarded the post of foreign minister.

The Soviet Union had reason to hope that Czechoslovakia would be a reliable and subservient partner in Eastern Europe. Unlike the Poles, with their long tradition of hostility to Russian rule, the Czechs and Slovaks had been ruled by Germans and Hungarians before 1918, they still recalled with bitterness their sellout by the West at the time of the Munich crisis, and during World War II they had seen the Red Army rather than the Western powers as the chief instrument of their liberation. Czech and Slovak sympathy for Communist Russia seemed confirmed by the results of elections held in May 1946, which foreign observers generally agreed had been free and fair, in which Communist candidates received 38 percent of the vote, more than twice as much as the party of Beneš, which came in second in the polling. There followed the formation of a coalition government under the premiership of Klement Gottwald, the

Communist leader, whose cabinet included members of the Socialist and Liberal parties. Beneš retained his position as president, and Jan Masaryk was kept on as foreign minister.

Soviet illusions about Czech subservience were dealt a nasty blow in July 1947 when the Czech government accepted an invitation to participate in the Marshall Plan. As noted earlier, Soviet retribution was swift and harsh. Masaryk was summoned to Moscow and summarily ordered to withdraw his government's acceptance. It was a signal to the West, if any were needed, that Beneš and Masaryk had merely provided camouflage for what was essentially a Soviet-controlled regime.

Early in the following year even the camouflage was removed. In February 1948, prior to new general elections scheduled to be held in May, Gottwald took advantage of the resignation of twelve non-Communist members of the government to call upon Beneš to accept the resignation of his "bourgeois" ministers and form a government "without reactionaries." Beneš yielded. All important cabinet posts were now assigned to Communists except the foreign ministry, which remained in the hands of Masaryk. On March 10 Masaryk's body was found beneath the window of his office, ostensibly the victim of suicide, though it was widely suspected that he had been murdered.

Elections were duly held on May 30 and resulted in a landslide Communist victory, thanks to a change in the constitution establishing a system of voting from a single list. Beneš resigned eight days later (he died on September 3), and was succeeded as president by Klement Gottwald. These events were accompanied by a wholesale purge of opposition leaders and groups that continued well into the next decade. From having been the most democratic of the East European states, Czechoslovakia became one of the most oppressive Communist dictatorships.

❏ Cracks in the Iron Curtain: Yugoslavia and Albania

In the course of World War II, Communist dictatorships had also been established in Yugoslavia and Albania, with the significant difference that these governments did not owe their authority primarily to Soviet support. Instead, they were products of native Communist movements that had acquired power and prestige through their leading role in the resistance during the German-Italian occupation.

Although the Red Army had entered Yugoslavia in the last stages of World War II and helped in the final expulsion of the Germans, the Yugoslavs themselves had played the major role in their liberation under the banner of the Communist Josip Broz Tito, who assumed the leadership of Yugoslavia's postwar government. Geographically separated from the Soviet Union and with a powerful battle-hardened army of its own, the Yugoslav government from the first took a more independent stance in dealing with Moscow than its Eastern European neighbors.

Relations with Moscow were strained early when Stalin failed to provide the support Tito had expected to establish his claims to Trieste and southern Austria. (See p. 315.) Stalin did, however, encourage other Yugoslav expansionist ambitions.

During a visit to Moscow in January 1948, Tito's emissary, Milovan Djilas, sounded the Soviet dictator about the possible inclusion of Albania in the Yugoslav federation. Stalin was all in favor of such a move. "We have no special interest in Albania," he said. "We agree to Yugoslavia swallowing Albania." Djilas protested: "It is not a matter of swallowing, but unification!" Molotov: "But that is swallowing!" Stalin: "Yes, yes. Swallowing! But we agree with you: you ought to swallow Albania—the sooner the better."

At a subsequent meeting with Stalin on February 10 that included Edvard Kardelj, the Yugoslav vice-premier, and Georgi Dimitrov, the prime minister of Bulgaria (and former head of the Comintern), Stalin encouraged the formation of a federation between Yugoslavia, Bulgaria, and Albania. Djilas suspected that Stalin's purpose in proposing this minifederation was to make it a prelude to federation with the Soviet Union. In reflecting on Stalin's remarks about swallowing Albania, he recalled how the Soviet Union had swallowed the Baltic states and concluded: "However obscure and hypothetical all these plans may have been, one thing is certain: Stalin sought solutions and forms for the East European countries that would solidify and secure Moscow's domination and hegemony for a long time to come."

At this same February 10 meeting, Stalin demanded an end to Yugoslav aid to the Greek Communists, although he had originally encouraged such aid and welcomed the ensuing deterioration of Tito's relations with the West. Djilas was unclear about Stalin's motives in opposing the Greek uprising, and speculated that he feared the creation of a Communist state that owed more to the support of Belgrade than to Moscow. "Not to speak of possible international complications, which were assuming an increasingly threatening shape and could, if not drag him into war, endanger his already-won positions."

Djilas's speculations about Stalin's Balkan policies were well founded. For a long time already the Soviet dictator had resented Tito's popularity in the Communist world and his refusal to assume a suitably subservient position in his relations with Moscow. In February 1948, to eliminate what Stalin called Yugoslavia's bad habit of acting without consulting the Soviet government, Molotov pressured Kardelj, the Yugoslav vice-premier, into signing an agreement providing for mutual consultation prior to any foreign policy decision affecting both countries. On March 1, however, the Yugoslav Central Committee rejected a Soviet demand for the immediate formation of a Bulgarian-Yugoslav federation, suspecting that Stalin desired such a union as an instrument to control Yugoslavia through the more pliable and more pro-Russian Bulgarians. Stalin's response was unexpectedly drastic. He withdrew all Soviet military and technical advisors from Yugoslavia. There followed an angry exchange of letters between Moscow and Belgrade, capped on June 28 by the Cominform's expulsion of Yugoslavia from that organization on the grounds of doctrinal errors and hostility to the Soviet Union. Condemning the "despotic and terrorist" nature of the Yugoslav government and its nationalism, the Cominform called upon the "healthy elements" within the Yugoslav Communist party to rid themselves of their delinquent leadership.

Stalin proceeded to set in motion a coup by the "healthy elements" in Belgrade. His loyal supporter, Anna Paucker, the foreign minister of Romania, predicted that "everything will be in order in Yugoslavia in a few days," and Stalin himself boasted that he had beaten Tito "simply by wriggling his little finger." His little finger did not do the job, however. The Yugoslav Communists remained loyal to Tito, and Stalin's attempted coup, instead of securing Tito's ouster, exposed the open rift within the Communist camp.

Stalin's East European satellites had followed the Soviet lead in breaking off all economic relations with Yugoslavia and denouncing their treaties of friendship with that country, but the only result of this demonstration of subservience to Moscow was to propel Tito into closer political and economic ties with the West. And the West, despite the opposition of doctrinaire anti-Communists, responded with military and financial aid to Yugoslavia and warnings of intervention in the event of a Soviet invasion.

A less dramatic but nonetheless significant crack in the Communist front took place in Albania. The Soviets had hoped to make this predominantly Muslim country a model Communist state that would be attractive to the Muslim world, especially to Muslim states of the Middle East and Africa.

But Soviet expectations about Albania were to be disappointed. In 1961, fearful that Soviet leaders were seeking to reestablish friendly relations with Yugoslavia at Albania's expense, Albania denounced its alliance with the Soviet Union and looked for support to Communist China. They did so just as China, too, was turning against Moscow—by far the most significant breach of Communist international solidarity. (See pp. 444–446.)

Already in June of 1948, however, the break between Moscow and Belgrade should have been enough to expose the fallacy of the belief that Communism was a global monolithic movement controlled by Moscow. It was some time before the significance of that break was fully appreciated in the West, however, because it took place just as a crisis over Berlin was arousing renewed Western fears about the Communist menace.

❑ The Berlin Blockade *1948*

Djilas had speculated that Stalin's call for an end to Yugoslavia's support of the Greek Communists in February 1948 had been motivated by fear of international complications. But only four months later, on June 24, 1948, Stalin risked far more serious international complications by imposing a blockade on all rail, road, and canal communications to the Western occupation zones of Berlin.

West Berlin had become an object of acute embarrassment to the Soviets, who referred to it among themselves as a bone in their throat. By 1948 West Berlin was already far more prosperous than the countries of Eastern Europe, its prosperity and atmosphere of freedom clearly evident to the most casual visitor from the Soviet bloc. West Berlin had also become an avenue for a mass migration of East Germans to the West that included large numbers of skilled workers whose services were sorely needed in East Germany.

But, as a Western enclave deep in Soviet-controlled territory, West Berlin was also extremely vulnerable. On March 20, 1948, the Soviets signaled their intention to dismantle the quadrupartite administration of Berlin by withdrawing from the Allied Control Council. Three days later they cut off supplies of electricity and coal to West Berlin, and soon afterward they began a systematic interference with all travel and trade with the West by checking the papers and luggage of travelers and requiring special permits for the transport of goods. With the Western initiation of a German currency reform on June 18, the Soviets evidently thought the time had come to wipe out this Western showpiece altogether. By imposing a blockade on all communications with West Berlin, they set off what some historians have called the first great battle of the Cold War.

The West responded to the Soviet blockade by making use of the only access routes to Berlin guaranteed by treaty: air corridors. On June 28, 150 transport planes from the West landed at Berlin's Tempelhof airport with 400 tons of supplies. The Soviets made no attempt to interfere with air traffic, confident that the airlift would fail. But it did not fail. By July 22, 130 planes had been assigned to the airlift, each making two round trips daily and bringing in 2,400 tons of food and fuel per day. By December daily shipments had risen to 4,500 tons, by the spring of 1949 to 8,000 tons, as much as had been carried by road and rail before the blockade. By the time the blockade was finally lifted, some 275,000 flights had delivered 2.5 million tons of supplies to the city.

The Berlin airlift was a remarkable technical achievement and proved to be a major symbolic, as well as political, triumph for the West. The blockade that was intended to throttle West Berlin had instead drained the resources of East Germany and dealt a crippling blow to the economy of the Soviet bloc. By May of 1949, a little less than a year after initiating the blockade, the Soviet government in effect conceded defeat by announcing the blockade would be lifted.

The Soviet blockade was not only a failure but a serious diplomatic blunder. In the West it was seen as a crass violation of treaty agreements and a justification of the Western policy of containment. The blockade crisis also did much to overcome the objections of the French and other Europeans to the establishment of a West German state and the incorporation of that state in a Western security pact.

❑ *Towards a North Atlantic Alliance*

In pleading for passage of the European Recovery Program, Secretary of State Marshall had repeatedly reminded Congress that the restoration of Europe required a revival of the economy of Germany. "But we must be very careful to see that a revived Germany cannot again threaten the European community."

The European Recovery Program itself, however, had been designed from the beginning to minimize the possibility of any future German threat to the peace of Europe. For, with the German economy integrated into that of Europe as a whole and thus subject to permanent European and American supervision, the Germans would be unable to launch a secret rearmament program or take any kind of unilateral action that would threaten the political or economic security of its European partners.

To overcome French fears about Germany, Marshall assured the French that the United States did not intend to repeat the mistakes of the prewar era and would now be prepared to consider military as well as economic commitments. The British, too, were determined to avoid their prewar mistakes. On March 4, 1947, they concluded a pact with France pledging mutual support in the event of an attack by Germany and common action if Germany failed to meet its economic obligations, a British commitment the French had sought in vain during the interwar years.

The British were prepared to do even more. Speaking to the House of Commons on January 22, 1948, Foreign Secretary Bevin put forward a plan to expand the Anglo-French partnership into a more comprehensive European security pact, with the significant difference that this one would no longer be designed exclusively for defense against Germany but against aggressive action on the part of *any* country, whereby Bevin clearly had the Soviet Union in mind.

The Communist coup in Czechoslovakia in February 1948 gave new and seemingly urgent impetus to the Bevin proposal and was followed by the conclusion on March 17 of the so-called Brussels Pact, a fifty-year military alliance between Britain, France, and the Benelux countries (Belgium, the Netherlands, and Luxembourg) that provided for mutual support against armed aggression in Europe, as well as closer economic, social, and cultural collaboration. Truman hailed the Brussels treaty as an expression of "the determination of the free countries of Europe to protect themselves," and promised that this would be matched "by an equal determination on our part to help them protect themselves."

Bevin seized on this statement to sound the Canadian and American governments about extending the Brussels treaty into a North Atlantic security system that would include the United States and Canada. This idea was taken up and advocated publicly for the first time on April 28 in the Canadian House of Commons by the Canadian prime minister, Louis Saint-Laurent. Negotiations between the United States, Canada, and the members of the Brussels Pact began on July 6, and invitations to a conference to establish a North Atlantic security system went out to the governments of Denmark, Iceland, Ireland, Italy, Norway, and Portugal. All except Ireland, still smarting over differences with Britain, accepted. Sweden had indicated from the first that it preferred to maintain its traditional neutrality.

Once again Soviet actions hastened the negotiations for a European alliance. The February 1948 coup in Czechoslovakia and the Berlin blockade took place during a period when Communists were taking further steps to consolidate their hold over the governments of Poland and Hungary and purging their rivals and opponents. For Westerners these purges were highlighted by the flight in October 1947 of the token non-Communist member of the Polish government, Stanislaw Mikolajczyk, and the purge of his followers, and by the arrest in December 1948 of the Hungarian Cardinal Josef Mindszenty on charges of conspiracy to overthrow the government. In January 1949 the Soviet Union created a Council for Mutual Economic Assistance (Comecon), a response to the Marshall Plan, to coordinate the economic and trade policies of its East European satellites and reinforce Soviet control. Then in September 1949 came the alarming news of the Soviet explosion of an atom bomb that was to give further impetus to the implementation of Western security arrangements.

News of the Soviet atom bomb evoked a reaction in the United States comparable to that of Stalin's "Declaration of World War III," when George Kennan had been called upon to provide an analysis of Soviet policy. (See p. 310.) This time the task was entrusted to State and Defense Department officials under the direction of Paul Nitze, Kennan's successor as head of the State Department's Policy Planning Staff. Their final analysis, National Security Council Document No. 68, was presented to President Truman in April 1950. NSC-68 was a shrill blowup of Kennan's Long Telegram, an amalgam of the most extreme features of anti-Communist rhetoric. The apocalyptic tone was intentional: to convince Truman, who had heretofore opposed large-scale increases in military spending, of the need for a massive American buildup to counter the Soviet threat.

Critics of the United States have described NSC-68 as the seminal document that transformed the United States into a warfare state, and they suggest that Truman heartily endorsed it. This was not the case. The president passed the document along to a committee of economic experts, who initially estimated that the full implementation of the NSC-68 recommendations would require an increase in military spending from 13.5 million dollars to as much as 40 million dollars. There is clear evidence to suggest that Truman deliberately procrastinated, reluctant to approve a measure that would undermine his Fair Deal domestic policies and require raising taxes, always a hazardous political course. But a bare two months after receiving NSC-68, his hand was forced by the outbreak of the Korean War on June 25, 1950. (See Chapter 26.)

Meanwhile, well before the drafting of NSC-68 and the Korean War, negotiations for shoring up Western defenses in Europe had gone steadily forward.

❑ *The North Atlantic Treaty Organization (NATO)*

The agreement establishing the North Atlantic Treaty Organization was signed in Washington on April 4, 1949, by the representatives of all the governments that had taken part in its formulation: the United States, the members of the Brussels Pact, plus Canada, Denmark, Iceland, Italy, Norway, and Portugal. The preamble stated that the treaty was not directed against any nation or group of nations, but only against the forces of aggression in order to safeguard freedom, democracy, and the rule of law. It was intended "to promote stability and well-being in the North Atlantic area" and to unite the efforts of its members "for collective defense and for the preservation of peace and security." An armed attack against one or more of the signatory states (including the Algerian departments of France, all islands north of the Tropic of Cancer under the jurisdiction of the signatory states, and the armed forces of any party in Europe—and thus Western forces in Germany) was to be considered an attack against them all. By unanimous consent of the signatories, other European states could be invited to accede to the treaty, which was joined by Greece and Turkey in 1952, by the Federal Republic of Germany in 1955, by Spain in 1982, and, after the collapse of the Soviet empire, by the Czech Republic, Hungary, and Poland.

In the United States, the treaty was ratified by the Senate on July 21, 1949, by a vote of 82-13 and signed by Truman on July 24. On that same day, Truman asked Congress to approve a Mutual Defense Assistance Program—a one-year military aid package of 1.5 billion dollars for America's new allies in Europe.

As the first peacetime military alliance in United States history. NATO represented a radical departure from American political tradition and marked the formal end of American isolationism. It also represented a radical change in traditional military alliances, for it provided not only for a pooling of national military units under international command, but for close collaboration in training, strategic planning, and arms production, and thus for a greater overall integration of the resources of the member states than any previous military agreement. A major American objective here was to create a framework that would enable Washington to overcome objections to the enrollment of German troops into the NATO army. On December 18, 1950, General Dwight D. Eisenhower was appointed commander-in-chief of the North Atlantic treaty forces with headquarters in Paris.

The Partition of Germany

To stave off the danger of further German integration with the West, the Soviets called for the creation of a unified and neutralized Germany independent of either the American or Soviet bloc. The Americans and their European allies had numerous reasons to object to this Soviet proposal. A unified and neutralized Germany would be able to maneuver between East and West and, by securing concessions from both sides, regain a preponderant position in Europe. Or, more dangerous still, it might look eastward for markets and raw materials and see its interests best served by entering into an alliance with the Soviet Union. The Americans therefore replied that unification could only occur "on the basis of consolidating the Eastern zone into ours," a condition they were confident the Soviet government would reject.

Meanwhile, the Western governments had gone ahead with the implementation of their own policies in the Western occupation zones, even if this might result in the continued or permanent partition of Germany. On April 8, 1949, the Western powers published an Occupation Statute that defined their future relationship with their German occupation zones, the rights they reserved to themselves, and the powers they were prepared to concede to a future German government. One month later a West German parliamentary council promulgated a constitution for the government of a Federal Republic of Germany, the so-called Basic Law, which was approved by the Western powers four days later—the same day that the Berlin blockade was officially lifted, May 12, 1949. Parliamentary elections on August 14 resulted in a narrow victory for the Christian Democratic part led by Konrad Adenauer, who became the first chancellor of the new West German government. Bonn, a small city on the Rhine and the birthplace of Beethoven, was chosen as the capital of the Federal Republic. On September 21 the functions of the Allied Military Government were transferred to an Allied High Commission, which was to supervise the operations of the new German government over the next three years.

A parallel transformation took place in the Soviet occupation zone, where in May 1949 an East German People's Council, elected from a single list of Communist-approved candidates, adopted the draft of a constitution for a government of East Germany. On October 7, this time without the luxury of elections of any kind, the German Democratic Republic was installed under Soviet auspices as the government of East Germany, its capital, Berlin. With that the division of Germany under two separate governments was complete.

On June 6, 1950, the German Democratic Republic concluded an agreement with Poland recognizing the Oder-West Neisse line as the final boundary between Germany and Poland, "an inviolable frontier of peace and friendship which does not divide but unites both nations." The West German government protested vigorously at the time—the Oder-Neisse line had been provisional pending a final peace treaty—but on November 18, 1970, the Federal Republic signed a similar treaty with Poland in Warsaw. Thus the eastern boundaries of Germany established at Potsdam were finally recognized by both postwar German governments.

❑ The Creation of a Supranational Economic Organization: The European Coal and Steel Community (ECSC)

Since 1945 the French had been the most vigorous opponents of the economic re habilitation of Germany and its integration into a European economic or political union. But the French now took the lead in putting forward bold and imaginative new integration proposals, originally conceived by Jean Monnet, an early proponent of European economic integration who, as head of a government planning agency, had laid the basis for France's postwar economic resurgence. At a press conference on May 9, 1950, the French foreign minister, Robert Schuman, outlined a plan "to place all Franco-German coal and steel production under a common High Authority, in an organization open to the participation of the other countries of Europe." By transferring coal and steel, the essential ingredients of a military economy, from national to international authority, war between France and Germany would become "not merely inconceivable but physically impossible." The Schuman Plan, which he described as the first step toward a European federation, was designed to appeal to the Germans as a means of bringing their country back into the European community and giving them an influential voice in the future fate of the Ruhr and the Saar, still major objects of contention with France.

The plan also had obvious advantages for France quite apart from its value as a peacekeeping mechanism. It would give French industry access to the rich German coal fields, thereby providing a powerful boost to the French economy; and by excluding the United States it would restrict American economic influence in Europe while enhancing that of France, an influence that promised to be even greater when Britain rejected participation in the Schuman Plan. The British disliked the infringements the plan would impose on their sovereignty and were reluctant to jeopardize their privileged economic relationship with North America and the British Commonwealth.

The Americans might have been expected to have reservations about the Schuman Plan, especially after learning of Britain's nonparticipation. Instead, however, they supported the Schuman Plan from the start as a step toward the integration of

Germany into a European defense system, and, especially after the outbreak of the Korean War on June 25, 1950, they encouraged the Europeans to develop their own military and economic power to stave off the Communist threat. The Schuman Plan was also endorsed by the Benelux countries and Italy, which joined France and West Germany in negotiations over its implementation. On April 18, 1951, representatives of these six states signed a treaty in Paris based on the Schuman Plan to establish the European Coal and Steel Community (ECSC). The treaty went into effect in July of the following year after ratification by the governments of its signatories.

As Schuman had intended, the Coal and Steel Community was a supranational organization that was to serve as a model for the internationalization of other institutions and lead in the end to the creation of a European federation.

❑ *The Western European Union (WEU)*

As the Americans continued to press for German participation in a European defense system, the French responded with a plan that would avoid creating a separate German army but would bring the Germans into a supranational army with common uniforms, a common budget, common armaments, and common leadership under the overall authority of NATO. A treaty creating a European Defense Community (EDC) was signed in Paris on May 27, 1952, by the six members of the Coal and Steel Community, but once again Britain refused to relinquish British sovereignty to a supranational organization. The treaty was then killed by the French themselves. Beset by domestic and colonial problems (see pp. 499–450), the French government did not submit the EDC treaty to the French Assembly for ratification until August 1952. By then, the political balance of power had shifted and, with the Communists leading the opposition, the treaty was defeated on a procedural motion.

The initiative for creating a supranational European army was revived at an international conference that convened in London on September 28, 1954, this time with the participation of Britain, Canada, and the United States. After five days of hard bargaining, the conference reached a set of comprehensive agreements that were put into treaty form and signed in Paris on October 23. These provided for a European defensive alliance that was essentially no more than an extension of the 1948 Brussels Pact, with the crucial difference that the alliance now included Germany and Italy. Now called the Western European Union (WEU), it differed from the European Defense Community in that it would include British troops and, instead of a complete integration of the forces in a common army with a common uniform and the rest, each member state would contribute separate military contingents.

Besides creating the WEU, the Paris treaties included agreements to end of the occupation of Germany and restore German sovereignty, establish an agency for European arms control, and recommend the immediate admission of Germany into NATO. The Paris treaties were ratified by the signatory states and went into force on May 5, 1955. On that day the Allied occupation of West Germany came to an end and the Federal Republic of Germany regained full sovereignty over its domestic affairs, though its rearmament would remain under international control. Four days later West Germany was officially enrolled in NATO.

❑ *The Warsaw Pact*

On May 6, 1955, the day after the Paris agreements were ratified, the Soviet Union denounced its 1942 alliance treaty with Britain, and on May 14 representatives of the Soviet Union, Albania, Bulgaria, Czechoslovakia, the German Democratic Republic, Hungary, Poland, and Romania, signed the Warsaw Pact, a twenty-year political and military mutual defense alliance. Described as a treaty of "friendship, collaboration, and mutual assistance," the Warsaw Pact was actually an instrument for formalizing Soviet political and military control over its East European satellites.

There followed the establishment in January 1956 of a United Military Command of the Warsaw Pact armies under a Soviet commander-in-chief, and the Soviets' conclusion of bilateral treaties with Poland, the GDR, Romania, and Czechoslovakia to justify the stationing of Soviet troops in these countries. At the same time the Soviet government proudly announced the successful firing of an intermediate-range ballistic missile (IRBM) capable of delivering Soviet nuclear warheads to any part of Western Europe.

So it was that by the mid-1950s the greater part of Europe had been divided into two rival camps, the one dominated by the Soviet Union, the other by the United States. This domination was by no means absolute. The states within the American orbit continued to pursue independent policies, and within the more tightly controlled Soviet sphere there were periodic unsuccessful uprisings against Soviet dominion. An uneasy equilibrium had nevertheless been established, and for the next thirty years both sets of alliances proved sufficiently stable to prevent the escalation of European crises into major threats to world peace. By this time, too, the balance of terror had been intensified with the development by both the United States and the Soviet Union of a hydrogen bomb, many hundred times more powerful than the original atom bomb exploded over Hiroshima. In addition, both countries were now equipped with long-range bombers and ballistic missiles capable of delivering the new bomb to distant targets.

World War II had ended in May 1945 in Europe. Ten years later, although divided into two rival treaty organizations, Europe had settled into an uneasy but relatively stable equilibrium. The war in East Asia, however, had not ended with the defeat of Japan. China, the major victim of Japanese aggression, remained engulfed in civil war, while elsewhere in East Asia revolts against the European colonial powers spawned new international conflicts that were to make East Asia the world's major conflict arena in the later part of the twentieth century.

TWENTY-FOUR

❑

Japan: From Surrender to Final Peace Agreements

1. relinquish all terr. since 1895
2.

❑ **The Specifics of the Japanese Surrender**

In East Asia as in Europe, the immediate postwar fate of a particular country or territory was determined by the wartime agreements among the Allied powers, by the actual position of the Allied armies at the time of the enemy's surrender, and by the Allies' regional arrangements for the actual surrender of enemy forces and the transfer of power to Allied authorities.

In East Asia, however, the postwar political configuration was considerably more fluid than in Europe because of the wholesale revolt of the peoples formerly under colonial rule, the internecine conflicts among the Asian peoples themselves, and the efforts on the part of European imperial powers to reestablish their former authority. Thus, whereas in Europe most of the prewar states were reestablished after 1945, albeit with numerous boundary changes, there appeared in Asia a new galaxy of states, many of them carved out of the European and Japanese colonial empires, that were to experience wild fluctuations in their governments as well as their territorial configurations.

At their wartime conferences at Teheran and Yalta, the Allies had agreed that Japan was to be stripped of all territories acquired since that country's emergence as an imperial power in the late nineteenth century. China was to recover all territory lost to Japan since the Sino-Japanese War of 1894–1895. The Soviet Union, however, was to regain the rights and privileges in Manchuria that tsarist Russia had extorted from the Chinese imperial government in the nineteenth century but had surrendered to Japan following Russia's defeat by Japan in 1905. The Soviet Union was also to enjoy special rights in Outer Mongolia—a further impingement on territories that had been part of the ancient Chinese empire. In addition, the Soviet Union was to be allowed to annex outright the Japanese-held southern part of the island of Sakhalin and the strategically important Kurile Islands, an archipelago between the Japanese islands and Russia's Kamchatka Peninsula.

Despite Roosevelt's outspoken aversion to colonialism and his agreement with Chiang Kai-shek about the desirability of eliminating colonialism altogether in Asia,

334

the Allies made no specific arrangements about the future disposition of the European colonies in Asia that had been conquered by the Japanese. Churchill served notice that he would never agree to dismantling the British empire in Asia, and with that the entire question of Europe's Asian colonies had been set aside. The Allies agreed only that Korea, which had been annexed by Japan, should eventually be granted complete independence, though only after a certain period of tutelage.

Of particular importance for postwar developments in East Asia were the regional arrangements for the Japanese surrender in the areas under Japanese occupation. To avoid conflict and confusion over this complex problem, the American government sought and secured the agreement of its allies to a General Order No. 1, issued August 15, 1945, specifying which Allied commanders in the various theaters of war should be authorized to accept the Japanese surrender. As future developments were to show, the most critical of these surrender specifications involved Korea, French Indochina (Vietnam, Laos, and Cambodia), and China. In Korea, Japanese forces were to surrender to the Soviets in the area north of the 38th parallel; to the Americans south of that parallel. In French Indochina, they were to surrender to the Nationalist army of Chiang Kai-shek north of the 16th parallel; to either British or Australian military authorities south of that parallel. In China, south of the Great Wall, and on the island of Formosa, they were to surrender to the Chinese Nationalists; in Manchuria, to the Soviets.

The division of authority in Korea at the 38th parallel and in French Indochina at the 16th parallel were both presumed to be temporary, but their partition, like that of Germany, was to have fateful consequences in the future.

Stalin agreed to General Order No. 1 provided that it was clearly understood that the Liaotung Peninsula, at the southern tip of Manchuria, was considered part of Manchuria and thus part of the area that would be surrendered to Soviet authorities. In addition, however, he asked that the territory to be surrendered to a Soviet commander include the Kurile Islands and northern Hokkaido, the northernmost of the Japanese home islands. Truman agreed about the Kurile Islands, which had been allotted the Soviet Union at Yalta; however, after the bitter altercations with Moscow over the occupation of Germany and Austria, he was determined to prevent Soviet participation in the occupation of Japan. He therefore rejected Stalin's bid to occupy northern Hokkaido, which, as part of Japan proper, was to be surrendered to General MacArthur. All he would concede to Stalin was that "Allied token forces, which of course would include Soviet forces," would be used to implement the terms of surrender on the Japanese home islands—but only "as the American commander considered necessary."

The surrender of the Japanese armies was generally carried out in accordance with the provisions of General Order No. 1. But even as the Japanese surrender was taking place, the European colonial powers, having just joined in a war to free the world from German and Japanese imperialism, took steps to restore their own imperial authority in East Asia, where they were immediately confronted with wars of liberation against themselves.

Hirohito

❑ *The American Assumption of Authority in Japan*

In their final wartime negotiations with Japan in August 1945, the Allies had made a significant concession in their demand for unconditional surrender: the ultimate form of the government of Japan would be left to the freely expressed will of the Japanese people. This provision had left open the possibility for the Japanese to retain their "celestial imperial government" and may well have been decisive in persuading the emperor himself to make the decision to surrender. The surrender document itself, however, left no doubt where the ultimate postwar authority in Japan would reside: "From the moment of surrender the authority of the Emperor and the Japanese Government to rule the state shall be subject to the Supreme Commander for the Allied Powers."

Following the Japanese government's acceptance of the Allied surrender terms on August 14, 1945, American troops and token Allied contingents occupied the Japanese home islands, where on September 2 the formal final surrender took place on board the battleship *Missouri* in Tokyo Bay. With that, supreme authority in Japan passed to Douglas MacArthur in his capacity as supreme commander for the Allied powers (SCAP). MacArthur himself was subject only to the authority of the president of the United States and the joint chiefs of staff. He might also consult with America's allies, but "in the event of any differences of opinion among them, the policies of the United States will govern."

Although Britain and the Soviet Union subsequently secured concessions that appeared to give them an influential voice in the occupation government of Japan, General MacArthur allowed nothing to interfere with his supreme authority. When Stalin renewed his claim to Soviet control over northern Hokkaido, backing it up with a threat to send Soviet troops to the island, MacArthur's response was brusque: any Soviet troops landing in Hokkaido would immediately be placed under arrest. Unable to match American sea power or airpower in East Asia, the Soviet government did not press the matter.

America thus succeeded in retaining virtually exclusive control over the occupation government of Japan, thereby arousing resentment not only in the Soviet Union but among its other allies. Soviet and other critics of American policy have argued that, in assuming quasi-exclusive authority in Japan, the Americans had no grounds to complain when the Soviet Union sought to exercise similar authority in Eastern Europe and other areas under Soviet occupation or control. This criticism is certainly justified, but there were to be decisive differences between American and Soviet occupation policies.

❑ *The American Occupation and the Reconstruction of the Japanese Government*

Under the rule of the arrogant and authoritarian General MacArthur, and to the surprise of many observers, the occupation of Japan was conducted with remarkable tact and effectiveness. In accordance with his instructions to work through agencies of the Japanese government, MacArthur undertook the reconstruction of those agencies and subsequently empowered them to enact decrees designed to make Japan a democracy. Fundamental to this purpose were guarantees of civil liberties and freedom of religion, and the extension of the franchise to all persons over twenty years of age, women as well as men. A National Diet, elected the basis of this franchise, drew up a constitution in the name of the Japanese people embodying the principles and institutions that should henceforth be the cornerstones of the Japanese government.

That constitution, promulgated on November 3, 1946, went into effect on May 3 of the following year. Officially termed an "amendment" of the old Meiji constitution, presumably as a sop to Japanese sensibilities, the constitution was in fact a revolutionary document that was drawn up in accordance with American specifications. Its most notable feature was its transfer of sovereign power from the emperor to the people. Henceforth the emperor was to be only "the symbol of the state and the unity of the people," his powers limited to those of a constitutional monarch. The constitution guaranteed human rights, but it went beyond the familiar life, liberty, and pursuit of happiness by including "the right to maintain the minimum standards of wholesome and cultural living, academic freedom, and the right of workers to collective bargaining." It provided for an independent judiciary, and for a Supreme Court with powers to pass on the constitutionality of government legislation. The Japanese government renounced war as an instrument of national policy and forbade the maintenance of armed forces—a prohibition that was to cause the Americans considerable embarrassment when, in response to what they perceived as the Communist menace in East Asia, they called for the reestablishment of a Japanese army.

In East Asia as in Europe, the perception of the Communist menace produced profound changes in Western policies in dealing with the countries defeated in World War II. Much of the impetus for promoting Japan's economic recovery was provided by events in China, where, already by mid-1948, there could no longer be any doubt that the Communists would win the Chinese civil war. Earlier in that year, Washington announced that the fundamental task of the occupation government from now on would be to aid Japan's economic recovery, which was described as an essential step toward that country's independent development and political stability. But it was the outbreak of the Korean War in June 1950, with the demand it created for Japanese goods and services, that provided the decisive stimulus for Japan's economic recovery and set Japan on the road toward becoming an economic superpower.

The occupation government's emphasis on economic recovery was marked by a shift in policy to favor big business, a sharp decline in the breakup of large business combines, and a growing hostility toward the labor movement when strikes and industrial sabotage threatened to disrupt Japanese production. To deal with this problem, the Americans encouraged the Japanese government to curb the power of the unions, prohibit strikes, and move aggressively against the Communist party and its leaders. This policy shift was greeted by Japanese business leaders with understandable enthusiasm. Critics of the American occupation, on the other hand, denounced the new policy as a flagrant abandonment of democratic principles.

Principles seemed to be violated even more flagrantly after the Communist victory in the Chinese civil war, when the Americans sponsored the creation of a 75,000-man Japanese national police force, ostensibly to be used to deal with domestic disturbances. In his New Year's Day message to the Japanese people in January 1950, MacArthur declared that the Japanese constitution's renunciation of war did not mean the renunciation of the "inalienable right of self-defense against unprovoked attack." With the outbreak of the Korean war in June 1950 the Americans began urging the Japanese to assume a greater share of the responsibility for their defense. A major difficulty now was the reluctance of the Japanese themselves to assume that responsibility. When a senior American official proposed the creation of a 350,000-man army to defend Japan in the event of a Soviet invasion, the Japanese prime minister told him not to joke. And, indeed, after so many years of America's self-righteous vilification of Japanese and German militarism, the American admonitions about the urgent need for the rearmament of Japan and Germany were greeted with bitter amusement in both countries.

❑ *The Peace Treaty with Japan, September 8, 1951*

While seeking to promote Japan's economic recovery, the American government was taking steps to conclude a final peace treaty with that country. The Soviet government agreed about the desirability of a peace treaty, but Moscow had very different views as to how that treaty should be drawn up and what it should contain. Over the question of the actual terms of a Japanese peace treaty, the Americans found themselves opposed not only by the Soviets but by their other wartime allies in the Pacific, notably Australia, New Zealand, and the Philippines (independent since July 4, 1946), whose governments agreed with the Soviets in favoring far harsher peace terms than those being proposed by Washington.

Truman foresaw yet another difficulty in the United States itself: would the Senate Republicans ratify *any* peace treaty his administration negotiated with Japan? To overcome this difficulty, he assigned the task of negotiation to a prominent Republican leader, John Foster Dulles, a distinguished lawyer with wide experience in international diplomacy. Dulles proved to be an admirable choice. He not only secured Republican support for a treaty, but adopted a strategy at the beginning of the negotiations that avoided the most obvious obstacles to their success. Instead of convening a peace conference or working through any kind of international forum, he arranged with the British that Britain and the United States alone should negotiate with the Japanese, thus by-passing the two-China problem (whether Nationalist or Communist China should represent China at the peace conference), Soviet obstructionism, and whatever objections might be raised by America's other wartime allies. The great problem here, of course, would be to persuade the other countries involved to accept terms worked out exclusively by the Americans and the British.

The invasion of South Korea by Communist North Korea and the subsequent Korean War helped Dulles overcome some of these difficulties. To persuade the Japanese and America's non-Communist allies to accept Anglo-American peace terms, he played on the fears raised by the renewed specter of a Soviet-Communist threat in the Pacific, holding out the promise of a security pact guaranteeing all these countries American support in the event of foreign aggression.

On July 20, 1951, Britain and the United States sent formal invitations to the states that had declared war on Japan to attend to a peace conference in San Francisco. Prior to that conference the terms of the treaty negotiated by London and Washington were submitted to fourteen co-belligerents, including the Soviet Union. But to by-pass the thorny two-China question, no invitation was sent to either the Nationalist or Communist governments of China. Because of the exclusion of Communist China, India refused the invitation to attend.

The Japanese peace conference convened in San Francisco on September 4, 1951, and only four days after the conference convened the peace treaty was signed by Japan and the majority of the conference participants. It was not signed by Burma and Indonesia because it did not specifically recognize their claims to reparations, or by India. Most importantly, it was not signed by the Soviet Union, whose representative had walked out of the conference on September 3. The San Francisco conference thus ended with Japan still in a nominal state of war with the Soviet Union and with both the Nationalist and Communist governments claiming authority over China.

The Japanese peace treaty recognized "the full sovereignty of the Japanese people over Japan and its territorial waters." Japan was required to recognize the independence of Korea and renounce all claims to Formosa (Taiwan), the Pescadores Islands, the Kurile Islands, the Spratly and Paracel Islands (in the South China Sea), Southern Sakhalin, and Japan's former mandates in the Pacific. The Bonin and Ryukyu Islands, including Okinawa and their adjacent islands, were to be placed under U.S. trusteeship by the United Nations. Although the Soviet Union had annexed the Kurile Islands and Southern Sakhalin, in accordance with the Yalta agreements and the terms of the Japanese surrender, the treaty did not grant the Soviet Union title to either of these territories. Nor was Communist China granted title to Formosa, where the Nationalist government had established itself after its defeat in the Chinese civil war.

The sensitive issue of reparations, which affected all of Japan's former enemies, was set aside. The treaty recognized that Japan *should* pay reparations for the damage and suffering it had caused, but it also recognized that Japan *could* not pay adequate reparations if it was to maintain a viable economy. The treaty provided only that negotiations over reparations were to continue on behalf of a final settlement of claims.

The treaty required that Japan refrain from the threat or use of force against any other state, but at the same time, citing Article 51 of the Charter of the United Nations, it recognized that Japan as a sovereign nation possessed the "inherent right of individual or collective self-defense" as well as the right to enter into collective security arrangements. As part of its recognition of Japanese sovereignty over its home islands, the treaty provided that all occupation forces were to be withdrawn from Japan ninety days after the treaty came into effect. This was done with the exchange of ratifications on April 28, 1952. On that same day, April 28, Japan signed a peace treaty with Nationalist China ceding Formosa and the Pescadores Islands to that government.

❑ *The Soviet Peace with Japan, October 19, 1956*

In his memoirs, the Soviet leader Nikita Khrushchev expressed understandable bitterness about America's high-handed policy in dealing with the Soviet Union over Japan. No Soviet representative had been invited to the ceremony of the Japanese surrender in 1945, and in the subsequent occupation of Japan the Americans had treated the Soviet Union like a poor relation at a rich man's wedding. Khrushchev believed that things might have been different if Roosevelt had lived, but Truman, "a stupid man," carried on "an unstinting, unbridled reactionary policy toward the Soviet Union. . . . A clever president would not have behaved so provocatively."

The Soviet government finally made its own peace with Japan on October 19, 1956, ending an eleven-year state of war and reestablishing diplomatic relations between the two countries. This was done through a declaration, not a treaty, whereby the Soviet Union relinquished its right to reparations and agreed to support Japan's application for membership in the United Nations.

❑ *The American Security Pacts in the Pacific*

Prior to the signature of the peace treaty with Japan, the United States honored its promise to conclude a security pact with the Philippines (on August 30, 1951) and with Australia and New Zealand (on September 1). The so-called ANZUS treaty with Australia and New Zealand did not include specific pledges of mutual military aid, largely because these states did not want to be committed to supporting the United States against Soviet or any other aggression that might take place outside the Pacific area. Instead, each party recognized that armed attack against another "would be dangerous to its own peace and safety and declares it will act to meet the common danger in accordance with its constitutional processes." That Britain was not a party to this treaty was a sad indication of its decline as a global power: Australia and New Zealand no longer looked to Britain but to the United States as the prime guarantor of their security.

On September 8, 1951, five hours after signing the Japanese peace treaty, the United States honored its promise to conclude a security pact with Japan. This treaty granted the United States the right to place armed forces "in and about" Japan, and required that Japan not grant similar facilities to other states without America's consent. The security treaty, like the peace treaty, specifically granted Japan the right to rearm in the obvious hope that Japan take increasing responsibility for its own defense.

TWENTY-FIVE

The Powers and China: From World War II to the Korean War
1945 - 1950

The surrender of Japan did not bring peace to China, which remained engulfed in a de facto civil war between the Nationalist armies of Chiang Kai-shek and the Communist forces of Mao Tse-tung. Another belligerent appeared on the scene following Moscow's declaration of war on Japan on August 8, 1945, as Soviet forces swept into northern China to secure the spoils promised the Soviet Union at Yalta and to establish control over a broad strip of Chinese territory along their southern frontiers. This Soviet offensive, launched on an immense scale on a broad front, continued well after Japan's final surrender and gave the Soviets control over Manchuria, the border regions of northern China, and North Korea.

❏ America's China Policy prior to the Japanese Surrender

The United States had long been concerned by the rift between the Nationalists and Communists in China, who were dissipating much of their military strength in fighting each other instead of the Japanese—the American embassy in the Nationalist capital of Chungking estimated that some 400,000 of Chiang's best troops were deployed against the Communists. That concern became acute in the spring and summer of 1944, as the Japanese launched an offensive that threatened to overrun the American air bases in China and perhaps knock China out of the war altogether.

After futile efforts on the part of the American ambassador to Chungking, Clarence Gauss, to persuade Chiang to establish a united front with the Communists, President Roosevelt sent Vice President Henry Wallace to Chungking to bring more impressive pressure to bear on the Nationalist leader. Wallace had no more success than Ambassador Gauss. After long discussions with Chiang and Communist representatives in Chungking from June 21 to 24, he concluded that both sides were "so imbued with prejudice" that he could see little hope for a long-term settlement.

Chiang had rejected American proposals to form a coalition government with the Communists unless he were given full authority over that government, including absolute command of all Chinese armies, Communist as well as Nationalist—a condition that doomed all negotiations with the Communists from the start. To explain his intransigence in dealing with the Communists, Chiang warned Wallace not to be taken in by their portrayal of themselves as democratic agrarian reformers; in reality they were diehard Marxists, more Red than the Russians. Convinced of the need to work with Chiang, Wallace agreed to convey to Roosevelt the generalissimo's request to send a personal representative to Chungking to act as a liaison between himself and the president and thus bypass the State and War Departments. Wallace also passed on Chiang's request to replace General Joseph Stilwell, the American officer serving as Chiang's chief of staff, whom he accused of impeding his cooperation with the Americans. This accusation was thoroughly justified. The able but acerbic Stilwell, who came honestly by his nickname "Vinegar Joe," had long been critical of Chiang's government and his conduct of military operations, nor had his relations with Chiang been improved by his scornful references to the generalissimo as "the Peanut."

In his personal report to Roosevelt, Wallace endorsed Chiang's request for a personal presidential representative as well as his plea to replace Stilwell with an officer capable of winning the Chinese leader's confidence. Although alerted to the corruption and incompetence of the Chiang government by members of the American embassy staff, Wallace blithely predicted that "with the right man to do the job it should be possible to induce the Generalissimo to reform his regime."

❑ *The Stilwell Debacle*

Chiang's request for the recall of Stilwell was blocked by Roosevelt's own chief of staff, General Marshall, who recommended exactly the opposite course. Instead of replacing Stilwell, he proposed to raise him to the rank of a full general and compel Chiang to give him command of all the Chinese armies, both Nationalist and Communist. This demand was incorporated in a message to Chiang of July 6, 1944, drawn up by the War Department in Roosevelt's name and signed by him without change. "The critical situation which now exists." Chiang was told, "in my opinion calls for the delegation to one individual of the power to coordinate all Allied military resources in China, including the Communist forces."

It seems likely that Roosevelt, already ill and with his attention focused on the war in Europe (the Allied landings in Normandy had begun just a month earlier) had not been aware of the implications of the document he had signed, for it represented a complete turnabout in his attitude toward Chiang, whom he had previously seen as head of a Chinese government acting as one of the Four Policemen in the postwar world.

Upon receiving Roosevelt's (or Marshall's) demand, Chiang expressed his willingness to yield completely on the question of the supreme command. But once again he posed the impossible condition: if Stilwell "used the Reds," they should acknowledge the authority of the Nationalist government. Marshall grew impatient. Another note to Chiang, once again drawn up by the War Department and signed by Roosevelt, brutally criticized him for his failure to press military operations against the Japanese and demanded that he immediately place Stilwell "in unrestricted command of all your forces." Stilwell, delighted that Roosevelt's eyes had at last been opened to the true situation in China, appears to have been even more delighted to present this message to Chiang personally. As he described the scene, he "handed this bundle of paprika to the Peanut and then sank back with a sigh. The harpoon hit the little bugger in the solar plexus and went right through him." Chiang's only reply was, "I understand."

❑ *The Hurley Mission*

In the end, however, it was Chiang who won this particular game, saved by Roosevelt and by General Patrick Hurley, who had been appointed to serve as the president's personal representative to Chungking in response to Chiang's request. Hurley had been recommended by Marshall, who feared that Roosevelt would appoint one of Chiang's many American admirers, whereas Hurley had professed his admiration for Stilwell. The choice of Hurley was warmly endorsed by Secretary of War Stimson, who described him as loyal, intelligent, and diplomatic, "the only man either Marshall or I could think of to revolutionize the situation of backbiting and recrimination and stalemate that has been surrounding poor Stilwell." It was a singularly inappropriate description, for Hurley, an oil magnate from Oklahoma who had been Hoover's secretary of war, knew nothing about China, he ignored the advice of men on the American embassy staff who did, and in the end he sabotaged the efforts of his own War Department to reinvigorate the Chinese war effort by placing the Chinese armed forces under more capable leadership.

Hurley had been present when Stilwell presented his "solar plexus" message, but he too was evidently won over by Chiang's warnings about the Communists and decided that Chiang was more important to American interests in China than Stilwell. In forwarding Chiang's complaints to Washington, he endorsed his demand for Stilwell's recall on the grounds that the two men were "fundamentally incompatible." "If you sustain Stilwell in this controversy," he warned the president, "you will lose Chiang Kai-shek and possibly you will lose China with him."

Roosevelt agreed. Assured by Chiang that he would accept another American commander, he gave "direct and positive" orders to remove Stilwell from China without delay. Stilwell had been warned about what was coming. "If Old Softy [Roosevelt] gives in on this as he apparently has, the Peanut will be out of control from now on." Stilwell was formally dismissed on October 19, and upon his return to the United States he was silenced to prevent his making any criticism of American policy in China that might influence the outcome of the forthcoming presidential elections. He was replaced by General Albert C. Wedemeyer, who was made commander of the American forces in China and chief of staff to Chiang—but not commander of the Chinese armed forces. In November Hurley was rewarded with the appointment of ambassador to the Nationalist government. The civil war in China continued.

❑ *The American Failure to Establish a Communist Connection*

During Henry Wallace's mission to China in June 1944, Chiang Kai-shek had agreed to allow an American military mission to go to the Communist capital of Yenan to evaluate the Communist military potential. A military mission was duly sent to Yenan a month later under the command of Colonel David Barrett, reputed to be the only American capable of telling jokes convincingly in Chinese to a Chinese audience. As his political adviser, he selected John S. Service, a professional foreign service officer who also spoke Chinese fluently and had a thorough knowledge of Chinese history and politics. In their discussions in Yenan, Barrett and Service found the Communist leaders prepared to join a coalition government. But the Communists continued to reject Chiang's demand to be given absolute authority over that government and command over the combined Chinese armies, and they urged the Americans to pressure Chiang into compromising on these issues.

Hurley, however, refused to put pressure on Chiang. On the contrary, with Roosevelt's approval he announced publicly that the United States would continue its exclusive support of the Nationalists and would not recognize or provide aid to any other Chinese faction.

The Chinese Communists did not give up their efforts to secure American aid and support. In January 1945 the Communist leader Mao Tse-tung and his foreign minister Chou En-lai sounded the Americans about the possibility of going to Washington to confer with Roosevelt "as leaders of a primary Chinese party." In relaying this proposal to his government, Hurley argued that a reception of Communist leaders in Washington would constitute a recognition of the Chinese Communists as an armed belligerent and lead to the "destruction of the National Government . . . chaos and civil war, and a defeat of America's policy in China"—as though China had not long since been engulfed in civil war. Roosevelt, preoccupied with preparations for the Yalta Conference and anxious to avoid new complications in his relations with Chiang, accepted Hurley's estimate of the situation. And Hurley, left to his own devices, did nothing to respond to the Communist overtures.

Political observers still speculate about how America's relations with China might have developed if Washington had opened the way to talks with the Chinese Communist leaders.

❑ *America's Postwar China Policy*

During World War II, the immediate objective of American policy in China had been to unite the Chinese for the common struggle against Japan. After the Japanese surrender, Truman pursued the long-range goal already adopted by the Roosevelt administration to restore peace to China, end the civil war, and, in the words of Truman's secretary of state James Byrnes, establish "a strong, united, and democratic China." Not yet obsessed with fear of Communism, the American government still believed this goal could be achieved by brokering an agreement between the Nationalists and the Communists and the formation of a coalition government under the leadership of Chiang Kai-shek.

In pursuit of this objective, Ambassador Hurley was sent to the Communist capital of Yenan directly after the Japanese surrender, where he succeeded in persuading Mao to return with him to Chungking to negotiate directly with Chiang. Those negotiations, begun on September 3, 1945, once again foundered over Chiang's demand for absolute control over a coalition government and Hurley's unwillingness to pressure him into agreeing to a compromise the Communists might accept. On November 27, after the failure of this latest round of negotiation, Hurley resigned, charging that his mission had been sabotaged by the Truman administration and the "dudes" in the State Department, whom he accused of being sympathetic to the Communists—as indeed some of them were.

❑ *The Marshall Mission*

On the afternoon of Hurley's resignation, President Truman asked General Marshall, the venerable and highly respected American chief of staff during World War II, to go to China as his special representative. He was assigned essentially the same task as Hurley: to work for the unification of China and the establishment of a strong, united, democratic government. To eliminate what was now perceived as a major reason for the failure of previous American emissaries to Chiang—their unwillingness or inability to pressure him into agreeing to a compromise settlement with the Communists—Marshall was empowered to apply the necessary pressure by threatening to withdraw American aid to the Nationalist government. Truman's instructions also stated, presumably to dispel any illusions Chiang might have on that score, that American aid "would not extend to United States military intervention to influence the course of any Chinese internal strife."

Marshall arrived in China on December 20, 1945, where he was greeted by news that Chou En-lai, the foreign minister of the Chinese Communist government, had proposed a truce with the Nationalists that would permit a renewal of negotiations to establish a coalition government. Delighted by this promising development, Marshall used his authority to pressure Chiang into agreeing to a truce. On March 11 this truce was extended to Manchuria, which had been occupied by Soviet forces since the final days of the war. In the course of their occupation, Soviet authorities had permitted the entry of large number of Chinese Communist "civilians" into Manchuria and allowed them to arm themselves with military equipment surrendered by the Japanese. Thus, by the time of the extension of the truce, a powerful Chinese Communist army had been established in Manchuria under Soviet auspices.

This was a situation Chiang decided he could not afford to tolerate. Taking advantage of the withdrawal of Soviet forces from Manchuria in the spring of 1946 and ignoring Marshall's advice to consolidate his position south of the Great Wall, he violated his truce with the Communists and launched an offensive in Manchuria designed to bring that region under Nationalist control. In response, the Truman administration made good its threat to cut off American aid by imposing an embargo on shipments of arms to the Nationalists.

Truman, however, was no longer in control of America's China policy, which was now engulfed in the murky bogs of American domestic politics, undercut by the powerful China Lobby (a consortium of Chiang's American supporters and opponents of the Truman administration) and by politicians eager to exploit differences over China to further their own careers. Spurred on by the China Lobby and convinced that the United States could not afford to abandon him, Chiang Kai-shek stubbornly resisted Marshall's appeals to return to the negotiating table. By October Marshall concluded that further mediation efforts were useless. He returned to the United States in January 1947, his mission to China a failure. Truman's confidence in Marshall's judgment and ability was in no way shaken. Upon his return from China he appointed him secretary of state in place of James F. Byrnes.

In accepting the position of secretary of state, Marshall also accepted the task of dealing with Truman's formidable domestic opponents. Five months after taking office, he succumbed to the pressure of the China Lobby to lift the arms embargo on the Nationalists and to send yet another mission to China to assess the military situation. To head this latest China mission he selected General Wedemeyer, Stilwell's successor as Chiang's chief of staff, who was thoroughly familiar with the incompetence and corruption of the Nationalist government. Marshall evidently hoped that Wedemeyer could be counted on to support his policy of pressuring Chiang into agreeing to a negotiated peace and the formation of a coalition government. If this was indeed his expectation, he was to be disappointed. Wedemeyer's final report, although severely critical of Chiang and the Nationalist government, was essentially a recommendation to restore large-scale military and economic aid to the Nationalists. Wedemeyer's only novel proposal was downright fatuous. To remove Manchuria as a bone of contention between the Nationalists and the Communists, he suggested that the region be governed by a United Nations mission.

Marshall, staunchly supported by Truman, turned down Wedemeyer's proposals and kept his report under wraps. So great were the political pressures brought to bear by the China Lobby, however, that Truman found himself compelled to agree to a renewal of American aid to Chiang.

❑ The China Policy of the Soviet Union

Stalin's policy in dealing with China after World War II remained as cautious; and to outside observers as enigmatic, as it had been in the prewar decades. At Yalta he had expressed his "readiness to conclude a pact of friendship and alliance with the Nationalist Government of China." And on August 14, 1945, the same day as Japan's acceptance of the Allies' terms of surrender, he actually concluded such a pact, reaffirming Soviet recognition of the Nationalist regime as the legitimate government of China as well as Chinese sovereignty over Manchuria. Further, the Soviet Union promised not to aid or deal with any Chinese political faction other than the Nationalist government, to refrain from interference in China's domestic affairs, and to withdraw from

Manchuria at the end of the war with Japan. In return, the Nationalist government was obliged to agree to all the concessions to the Soviet Union that Roosevelt had made at China's expense at Yalta and to recognize the independence of the Soviet client state of Outer Mongolia.

In concluding this pact with the Chinese Nationalist government, Stalin had ostensibly abandoned the Chinese Communists, but this was not the case. While steadfastly proclaiming his loyalty to his pact with the Nationalists, he gave the Communists substantial support after the Japanese surrender, notably by enabling them to take over the arms surrendered by the Japanese in Manchuria. How this was done was candidly described in the memoirs of Nikita Khruchshev, one of Stalin's successors as head of the Soviet government.

> We had certain agreements with our allies [the Chinese Nationalists] concerning the transfer of captured weapons, so we had to avoid giving the impression that we were giving these arms [to the Chinese Communists] directly. As it was explained to me, our method was to collect the weapons and leave them somewhere for the Chinese [Communists] to find. In that manner, we managed to equip the [Communist] Army in Manchuria with arms which our own army had captured from the Japanese.

Stalin, however, remained cautious. While flagrantly violating his pact with the Nationalists by providing arms to the Communists, he piously protested his adherence to that pact and went so far as to offer to help the Nationalists reestablish their authority in Manchuria. It may be that Stalin was simply trying to keep a foothold in both camps, but it is more likely that he did not want an all-out victory for either side in the Chinese civil war. A strong Chinese central government capable of harnessing the resources of that immense and populous country would make China a dangerous threat to the security of the Soviet Union. Moreover, a Communist head of such a government would have sufficient prestige and power to challenge his own leadership of the Communist world. Soviet interests were best served by keeping China weak and divided, a continuation of anarchic conditions that would allow for the steady penetration of Soviet influence but at the same time prevent China from emerging as a major power in its own right.

There is evidence to suggest another theory—namely, that Stalin underestimated the strength of the Chinese Communists and believed that Chiang, with his powerful American support, would crush them if they persisted in waging their civil war. This would explain his advice to the Chinese Communists to seek accommodation with Chiang and participate in a coalition government, a policy that would leave their organization intact and give them a wedge for the gradual extension of their influence within that government—the very reason why Chiang so stubbornly resisted their inclusion in a coalition.

The meager available evidence now available suggests that Stalin was genuinely surprised by the quick and complete triumph of Mao. But once that triumph was achieved he worked with characteristic caution to establish a relationship with Mao that would ensure Soviet influence in China while leaving himself in the position of senior partner. A partnership of sorts was indeed established, but it was an uneasy partnership from the beginning and it broke down altogether after Stalin's death.

❑ Outer Mongolia Becomes a Soviet Satellite

On October 20, 1945, the Soviets honored one part of their August 14 treaty with the Nationalists, namely, the promise to hold a plebiscite in Outer Mongolia to determine whether that country should become part of China or remain "independent." The plebiscite, conducted under Soviet auspices, resulted in a vote of 483,291 to zero in favor of independence (even Hitler had not rigged his plebiscites quite so crudely), which meant that Outer Mongolia would remain a Soviet satellite. In the following February, the government of Outer Mongolia concluded a ten-year mutual assistance pact with the Soviet Union, complemented by an agreement to promote economic and cultural collaboration.

❑ The Chinese Civil War: the Kuomintang Nationalists

Even the most sympathetic visitors to the headquarters of Chiang Kai-shek deplored the corruption and incompetence of his government, its repressive policies, and its refusal to introduce reforms that might have won it a greater measure of popular support. During the war against Japan, having lost the most productive parts of China to the Japanese, the Nationalists imposed all the greater demands on the population they did control. After the war, they extended their policies of extortion to provinces recovered from the Japanese, where they behaved more like conquerors than liberators. Still without adequate revenue, and much of that dissipated by waste and corruption, the Nationalists resorted to printing money, an expedient that led to rampant inflation and destroyed the economic base of the very people who might have been expected to support them against the Communists.

Nationalist troops were treated scarcely better than the peasantry. Raised by forced recruitment, poorly paid (if at all) and poorly fed, they were regularly compelled to live off the land and terrorized the peasantry as they indulged in indiscriminate looting of food and property. They suffered a long succession of defeats at the hands of the Japanese, and were little more effective in their battles against the Communists except when they possessed decisive superiority in numbers and the quality of their equipment. Faced with defeat or determined opposition, they deserted, surrendered, or went over to the Communists.

Little wonder that in the Nationalist camp morale was low, the government without popular support, the economy in shambles.

❑ The Chinese Communists and Mao Tse-tung

According to visitors to the Chinese Communist capital at Yenan, an altogether different atmosphere prevailed in the Communist camp. As we now know from government documents as well as from recent revelations from Soviet archives, many of these visitors were prepared to be sympathetic to the Communists and their reports were certainly colored by their preconceptions. They described an honest and efficient Communist leadership, armies that were disciplined to protect rather than expropriate the peasants, a revitalization of the economy that enabled the Communists to feed their armies without imposing oppressive burdens on the local population. The Communists seemed genuinely concerned with improving the quality of life of the peasants and of the urban masses as well. They had introduced political and economic reforms the Americans had vainly sought from Chiang and, perhaps more importantly, they seemed to be instilling a new sense of pride and patriotism in the Chinese people. Foreign admirers of the Yenan regime believed that much of the credit for the Communist achievement should be assigned to the party's leaders, above all to Chairman Mao Tse-tung. They praised his sense of purpose and his capacity for decision making, his disciplined control over his troops and his ability to inspire their loyalty and fighting spirit. Most of all they admired his human qualities, the warmth and simplicity behind his dignified reserve, his willingness to sacrifice personal comfort for an ideal, and his quasi-puritanical lifestyle, which contrasted so sharply with the venality and self-indulgence of the Nationalist leadership.

Foreign admiration for Mao was not shared by the Soviet leader, Nikita Khrushchev, who in 1956 astounded the world with a passionate denunciation of the crimes of Stalin. After several meetings with Mao, Khrushchev was convinced that the Chinese leader suffered from the same megalomania and the same diseased contempt for the human race as Stalin. Unlike some of his Soviet colleagues, Khrushchev did not think that Mao had gone mad. On the contrary, he thought him highly intelligent and predicted that he would defeat any opposition mounted against him. He played the game of politics "with Asiatic cunning, following his own rules of cajolery, treachery, savage vengeance, and deceit . . . a master of concealing his true thoughts and intentions."

This characterization was shrugged off by admirers of Mao, who believed it was motivated by personal dislike and anger over Mao's repudiation of Soviet leadership. Impossible to explain away, however, is the evidence provided by Dr. Li Zhisui, Mao's personal physician from 1954 until his death in 1976. Dr. Li, an ardent admirer of Mao upon entering his service, was to be quickly and permanently disillusioned. In his memoir of his years with Mao, he describes the Chinese dictator as an egomaniacal monster and dangerous psychopath: paranoid, cruel, cunning, and deceitful, a sexual predator who fondled his handsome male guards and transmitted his venereal infections to hundreds of young women who shared his bed. Instead of the Spartan simplicity that so impressed foreign visitors, he lived in imperial splendor, isolated from human contact, "devoid of human feeling, incapable of love, friendship, or warmth . . . [and] ruthless in disposing of his enemies." In formulating his policies, he was oblivious to twentieth-century science and technology, and oblivious as well to the manifest failure of those policies, their disastrous consequences for his country, and the suffering they inflicted on the Chinese people.

Even during the era of the civil war, Mao must have employed cunning and terror in maintaining his ascendancy over the Chinese Communist party and its armies. But cunning and terror alone do not account for the affection and veneration he inspired among the Chinese masses, a veneration that has continued after his death as is evident from the pilgrims who still come in their thousands to pay homage to his memory at his tomb in Tienanmen Square. Khrushchev has supplied a simple but perhaps the key explanation for this phenomenon. "One thing I know for sure about Mao. He's a nationalist. . . . His chauvinism and arrogance sent a shiver up my spine." To the Chinese masses, humiliated for so many years by foreign encroachments, Mao's chauvinism may also have set off spinal shivers. But in their case these were surely shivers of excitement over Mao's success in finally throwing off all foreign controls, uniting the country, and giving the Chinese people reason to believe that their country was once again the Middle Kingdom, the leader of world civilization and font of all authority. There is no way of measuring the ingredients of popular emotion, but a strong case can be made that Mao's nationalism, not his Communism, was the prime ideological force behind his popular appeal.

Mao Tse-tung was born on December 26, 1893, in a village near Changsha, capital of the Hunan province. He was the son of an affluent peasant and grain dealer who is said to have valued education only as training for keeping records and accounts. Withdrawn from school by his father at the age of thirteen to work full-time on the family farm and help with the accounts, Mao rebelled against parental authority and left his family to continue his studies. He completed his secondary school education in Changsha, where he came into contact with the ideas of Chinese political reformers, including those of the nationalist revolutionary Sun Yat-sen.

In 1911 Mao became a revolutionary himself, taking part in the uprising against the Manchu dynasty and serving briefly in the revolutionary army. His real political education began when he came to Peking during the heady days of the May 4th Movement of 1919—the mass protest against foreign encroachments at China's expense, which is generally seen as a landmark in the development of Chinese nationalism. Already at this time, however, many Chinese intellectuals were turning to the theories of Marxism-Leninism in seeking solutions to their country's problems.

In the summer of 1920 Mao himself embraced Marxism as the philosophical basis for revolutionary action, but at an early stage in his career he developed theories that deviated from those of orthodox Marxists. Deeply impressed by mass peasant protest demonstrations in the winter of 1924, he became aware of the revolutionary potential inherent in the peasantry. Whereas orthodox Marxists regarded the urban proletariat as the essential vanguard of a genuine Communist revolution, Mao came to the conclusion that this role could be played by the peasantry quite independently of the urban population. In his most famous public pronouncement on this subject, a political report of 1927, he extolled the Chinese peasantry as an elemental revolutionary force that would sweep everything before it, including urban intellectuals (i.e., orthodox Marxists) who were unwilling or unable to unite with the peasant masses.

Mao soon had occasion to put his theories about the revolutionary potential of the peasantry into practice. Following Chiang Kai-shek's purge of the Communists from the Kuomintang in 1926–1927 and the failure of the various Communist uprisings during those years, including Mao's own autumn revolution in Hunan (see p. 116), Mao began organizing rural Soviets and building up a peasant guerrilla army in Hunan and the neighboring province of Kiangsi. Once again he met with defeat. In October

1934 Chiang Kai-shek launched the fifth and most successful of his anti-Communist campaigns. With his larger and better-equipped army, he surrounded the Communists and seemed on the verge of wiping out their forces in southern China.

But, as noted earlier, a small band of Communist soldiers, including Mao Tse-tung, broke through the Nationalist lines. Therewith began the great saga of the Chinese Communist revolution, the legendary Long March of the southern Communists to join their comrades in the Communist enclaves that had managed to survive in the north. It was during this Long March that Mao established his authority over the Chinese Communist party. Following his arrival in the north, he used that authority to build up the party organization and a formidable army which would eventually triumph in the Chinese civil war.

— 1949 —

❑ *The Chinese Civil War: The Course of the Conflict*

The Chinese civil war between the Kuomintang Nationalists and the Communists may be said to have begun with Chiang Kai-shek's purges of the Communists in the 1920s, and it continued throughout the war against the Japanese. The civil war was halted briefly by the truce brokered by General Marshall early in 1946. (See p. 345.) It was resumed with renewed ferocity in March of that year following the withdrawal of Soviet forces from Manchuria, when Chiang launched his offensive to wrest Manchuria from Communist control. In fighting the larger and better-equipped Nationalist armies—the Japanese weaponry turned over by the Soviets could not match the quality of the American arms supplied to the Nationalists—the Communists adopted a strategy of withdrawal to lure the Nationalists ever farther from their supply bases and extend their lines of communication. At the same time, relying on local peasant support and using tactics previously employed against the Japanese, Communist guerrillas operated behind the Nationalists' lines, cutting their communication and supply routes, and conducting probing thrusts against their military outposts.

By the spring of 1947 the Communists had extended their control over the Manchurian countryside so effectively that the Nationalist armies, which still controlled the major cities, were actually under siege, cut off from each other and from outside sources of supply. By this time, too, the Communists, their own armies enlarged by rural recruitment and Nationalist desertions, began to risk pitched battles. While still laying siege to the cities of Manchuria, they mounted a major offensive into central and eastern China. In the winter of 1948, after a two-month battle in the valley of the Huai River involving half a million men on each side, the Communists encircled the greater part of the Nationalist army, which surrendered on January 10, 1949. With all prospects of relief now gone, the Nationalist garrisons in Tientsin and Peking also surrendered. In April the Communist armies crossed the Yangtze River, they entered Shanghai in May, Canton and Chungking in October and November. By the end of the year 1949 they had driven the last of the Nationalist armies from the Chinese mainland.

Chiang Kai-shek had long since abandoned the struggle. On January 21, 1949, he "retired" as president of China, and on April 23 he fled to the island of Taiwan taking with him a horde of Chinese art treasures from the mainland. The withdrawal of what remained of the Nationalist forces to Taiwan was completed by December, their evacuation covered by the American navy. Foreign observers noted with wry amusement that the only foreign dignitary to have remained with Chiang until his flight to Taiwan was the ambassador of the Soviet Union. The Americans had dropped him a good deal earlier. On August 5, 1949, the State Department issued a White Paper formally announcing the end of all aid to Chiang and attributing his defeat to the incompetence and corruption of his regime.

❑ *Mao Leans toward the Soviet Union*

In the spring of 1949, as Communist troops crossed the Yangtze on their way to conquering southern China, Mao Tse-tung once again made what appeared to be conciliatory gestures to the United States. The new Communist government of China, he said, would be prepared to establish diplomatic relations with any foreign government if it severed its relations and cut off aid to Chiang Kai-shek. "The Chinese people wish to have friendly cooperation with the people of all countries and to resume and expand international trade in order to develop production and promote economic prosperity."

This statement was warmly welcomed by the American ambassador to China, John Leighton Stuart, the former president of Yengching University, who had asked his government to allow him to remain in Nanking after the Communists occupied the city for the purpose of opening a channel of communication to the Communist leadership. Upon learning of Mao's overtures, he asked Secretary of State Dean Acheson for permission to go to Peking, now the Communist capital, to meet with Communist leaders. Acheson agreed, as did Truman, who evidently hoped the Stuart mission would further their own efforts "to exploit every possibility of rifts between the Chinese Communists and the Soviet Union." On June 30, however, Washington abruptly canceled Stuart's visit to Peking, a move deplored by critics of the Truman administration who accused Truman and Acheson of failing to take advantage of Mao's overtures, thereby virtually driving the new Chinese government into the arms of Moscow.

It was Mao himself, however, who made the decisive move towards Moscow. At the same time that he was talking about friendly cooperation with all foreign countries, the Chinese leader was indulging in heated anti-American rhetoric. In April 1949 he joined with the Communist governments of Eastern Europe in condemning NATO. On June 19 his government accused the American consul-general in Shenyang (under house arrest since the previous November) of sabotage, and Mao called upon the Chinese Communist party to mobilize in exposing the reactionary nature of American and British diplomacy. To make sure that his government's agreement to the Stuart visit should not be interpreted as a friendly gesture to the United States, Mao proclaimed that solidarity with the Soviet Union would henceforth be the cornerstone of the new China's foreign policy. In an official statement of July 1, before learning that Stuart's visit had been canceled, he announced that the new China would lean toward socialism and the Soviet Union. China did not need assistance from either Britain or the United States. In future China should look only to the anti-imperialist front headed by the Soviet Union for "genuine and friendly help." With that, Mao himself shut the door to cooperation with the United States and put an end to any hope Washington may have had of playing off China against the Soviet Union.

Several reasons have been suggested for Mao's "leaning to one side" declaration: belief in the need for solidarity among the world's Communist parties, belief that solidarity with the Soviet Union would shore up his position within his own party, fear that Stalin would seek an independent status for China's western province of Sinkiang similar to that of Outer Mongolia, and fear that Stalin would reassert the claims over Manchuria conceded to the Soviet Union at Yalta. Mao had particular reason to be concerned about Manchuria, for in July 1949 Stalin signed a trade agreement with the chairman of the Communist administration in Manchuria without troubling to consult the government of Peking, an ominous portent of Soviet intentions to make Manchuria another Soviet satellite state.

❏ American Domestic Reaction to the Victory of the Chinese Communists

Even if Mao had not made his ostentatious turn to the Soviet Union and had made sincere efforts to establish better relations with the United States, Truman and Acheson would very probably have found it impossible to follow them up, whether to drive a wedge between China and the Soviet Union or for any other purpose. Because on the American home front, Chiang's defeat was being exploited by opponents of the Truman administration, who accused the president, Marshall, Acheson, the State Department, and the entire Democratic party of having "lost" China to the Communists. It required a poisonous combination of arrogance and ignorance to believe that China was ever America's to win or lose, but accusations of this kind were to have a powerful political impact.

❏ The Establishment of the People's Republic of China   *1949*

The People's Republic of China (PRC) was officially proclaimed in the Chinese capital of Peiping (now officially renamed Peking) on October 1, 1949, with Mao Tse-tung as chairman of the Central People's Administrative Council and Chou En-lai as premier and foreign minister. The PRC was almost immediately recognized by the Soviet Union, which at the same time broke off diplomatic relations with the Chinese Nationalist government. Soviet recognition was followed by recognition on the part of the Soviet satellites and most nonaligned nations. Britain recognized the PRC in December, to the intense annoyance of the United States—a move defended by Winston Churchill (now out of power) with the cogent argument that "the reason for having diplomatic relations is not to confer a compliment, but to secure a convenience."

☐ *The Sino-Soviet Treaty of February 14, 1950*

Having expressed his intention to lean toward the Soviet Union and his hostility to the United States, Mao journeyed to Moscow in December 1949 to consolidate China's ties with the Soviets and to secure Soviet capital and technical aid for China's economic rehabilitation. He may also have hoped to persuade Stalin to relinquish the concessions made to the Soviet Union at China's expense by Stalin's wartime allies and Chiang Kai-shek. Upon his arrival at the railway station in Moscow, Mao made a speech calling attention to the Soviet government's previous abolition of the unequal treaties imposed on China by the tsarist regime, and announcing that he expected much from Stalin's "just" foreign policy.

There followed two months of hard bargaining, which Mao later recalled with bitterness and which revealed fundamental differences between Chinese and Soviet interests that eventually led to the Sino–Soviet rift. The Treaty of Friendship, Alliance, and Mutual Assistance that was finally hammered out and signed on February 14, 1950, replaced the treaty of August 1945 with the government of Chiang Kai-shek. The treaty was a simple military alliance directed against Japan and any state collaborating with Japan, and it committed both partners to conclude a peace treaty with Japan at the earliest possible date, to be signed jointly with their allies in World War II. A treaty between Communist China and Japan, however, was not arranged until August 1978. The Soviet Union never did sign a peace treaty with Japan, but only a declaration ending the state of war between them. (See p. 340.)

Appended to the February 14 treaty were a set of subsidiary agreements that were more important than the treaty itself. The Soviet Union agreed to return without compensation all property acquired from the Japanese by Soviet military and economic organizations in Manchuria as well as all property acquired by Soviet agencies in Peking. Further, upon the conclusion of a peace treaty with Japan, but no later than 1952, the Soviet Union promised to "transfer to China without compensation . . . all its rights to the joint administration of the Chinese Chungking Railway (the former South Manchurian Railway); to withdraw its troops from Port Arthur and turn over all installations there to China." The status of Dairen was also to be postponed pending a peace treaty with Japan, but a joint commission was to be set up to supervise the transfer to China of all property in Dairen administered by or leased to the Soviet Union. Finally, the Soviet Union promised to provide a credit of 300 million dollars at 1 percent interest, to be used over a five-year period and to be repaid by deliveries of raw materials.

These were significant concessions, and Mao later boasted that "one can after all take meat out of the tiger's mouth," but there was much in the agreements that rankled. The Chungking Railway, Dairen, and Port Arthur were to remain under Soviet control for at least two more years (Port Arthur, in fact, was not restored to China until 1955). And, like Chiang, Mao had been compelled to recognize the "independence" of Outer Mongolia. Most obnoxious of all was a subsidiary agreement of March 27 whereby China was obliged to agree to the establishment of joint Sino-Soviet stock companies in Sinkiang to develop the mineral resources of that region. The Soviet Union had used similar agreements to exploit the resources of its satellite states of

Eastern Europe, and the Chinese feared the agreement over Sinkiang would be used for a similar purpose. Nor can Mao have been mollified by the promise of 300 million dollars in loans (the Soviets had granted Poland 450 million dollars in the previous year), an insultingly paltry sum that suggested the Soviet Union intended to maintain tight control over China's economic development.

The signature of the Sino-Soviet treaty nevertheless seems to have been regarded in both Moscow and Peking as a genuine expression of friendship between the two Communist countries, and its publication reinforced the belief in Washington and other non-Communist states that China had now become part of the Communist monolith controlled and directed from Moscow. This belief in Communist solidarity seemed confirmed eight months later when Communist China entered the Korean war on the side of Communist North Korea, seemingly with the blessing and encouragement of the Soviet Union. (See p. 362.)

TWENTY-SIX

❏

Containment in Asia:
The Korean War

The Forgotten War (handwritten)

❏ *Korea's Postwar Partition*

Korea, which had been formally annexed by Japan on August 22, 1910, had not figured prominently in the wartime deliberations of the leaders of the great powers. At the Cairo Conference of November 1943, Chiang Kai-shek, Churchill, and Roosevelt had issued a declaration that their three nations, "mindful of the enslavement of the people of Korea, are determined that Korea shall, in due course, be free and independent." As Roosevelt told Stalin at Teheran, however, he did not think the Koreans were as yet capable of self-government and believed they would need some period of apprenticeship before being granted full independence, perhaps forty years. At Yalta he secured Stalin's agreement to a four-power trusteeship for Korea that would include Britain, China, the Soviet Union, and the United States, but nothing had definitely been decided when the war suddenly came to an end with Japan's capitulation.

At an emergency meeting of the State-War-Navy Coordinating Committee in Washington on the evening of August 10–11, 1945, to deal with the overall problem of the surrender of the Japanese troops, the committee recommended the 38th parallel as the dividing line for the surrender of Japanese forces in Korea: those north of the parallel were to surrender to the Soviets, those south of the parallel to the Americans. This line was chosen because the committee thought it important to include Seoul, the capital of Korea, in the area of American responsibility. The committee had some doubt, however, as to whether the Soviet Union would accept that line because it was "further north than could be realistically reached [by American troops] in the event of Soviet disagreement."

There was ample reason to expect Soviet disagreement. In Korea as in China, the Soviet occupation was carried out swiftly and on a massive scale, enabling Soviet forces to advance well below the 38th parallel before any American troops landed on the peninsula. The Soviets, moreover, had far greater interests at stake in Korea than did the United States. Vladivostok, the major Soviet port on the Pacific, lay only seventy miles from the Korean frontier. Vladivostok, however, had the drawback of

356

being ice-bound several months of the year, and the Russians had long looked hungrily at the ice-free harbors of the Korean Peninsula. Here they had found their way blocked by Japan, a country that had only recently emerged from isolation to become a major power in the Pacific. In 1896 Russia concluded a treaty with Japan dividing Korea into spheres of influence between them and fixing the dividing line at the 38th parallel—a precedent which may have determined the American decision to make that same parallel the dividing line between the American and Soviet occupation zones. Continuing differences over Korea were a major cause of the war between Russia and Japan that began in 1904. Following their victory over Russia in 1905, the Japanese assumed exclusive control of Korea, and on August 22, 1910, Korea was formally annexed to Japan.

To escape Japanese rule, thousands of Koreans had fled as refugees to China and Russia, where as early as 1922 the Soviet Communist party had set up a special Korean section in its East Asian bureau to train Koreans for positions of political and military leadership in their native country after the revolution so confidently anticipated by Marxist prophecy. The value of these preparations was apparent after the Japanese surrender in 1945, for the Soviet occupation army that entered Korea on August 8 was accompanied by a contingent of Korean Communists who were to serve as the nucleus of the Soviet occupation administration.

Given the Soviet advantage in the occupation of Korea, politically as well as militarily, and Russia's preponderant interests in that country, the Americans were agreeably surprised when Stalin accepted without argument the American proposal to divide Korea at the 38th parallel for occupation purposes and ordered the withdrawal of Soviet troops south of that parallel. There is still speculation why Stalin agreed to this arrangement. The most likely explanation is that he wanted to leave the door open to a comparable division of occupation responsibilities in Japan.

When they first took over the occupation of Korea, both the Americans and Soviets regarded the partition of that country as temporary. The partition made no sense politically or economically. Under Japanese rule, Korean industrial development had been concentrated in the north, where most of the coal mines and power stations were located, while the south remained primarily agricultural and the major source of the country's food supply. The difficulties created by this economic imbalance were accentuated by a demographic problem. The industrial north, unlike the industrial areas of most other countries, had not become a magnet for the Korea's rural population. In 1945 only 8 million Koreans were living in the north as compared to some 18 million in the south, a number swollen to well over 20 million with the postwar repatriation of Koreans from Japan and by the migration to the south of people fleeing from the Red Army, whose soldiers indulged in pillage and rape on a scale comparable to their worst excesses in China and Germany. The wartime disorder was eventually brought under control by the Communist government installed in North Korea under Soviet auspices, but the establishment of that government had inaugurated another large-scale exodus to the south by Koreans who feared the political and economic consequences of Communist rule.

❑ *Soviet North Korea*

The man chosen by the Soviets to head the native government of North Korea was Kim Sing-choo, a member of the Korean cadre trained in Moscow, who had taken the name of Kim Il Sung after a fabled Korean guerrilla leader who had fought the Japanese earlier in the century. The latter-day Kim arrived in Korea with the Soviet army in September 1945, and in February of the following year the Soviets arranged his election as chairman of North Korea's Provisional People's Committee. Kim was duly grateful: "All our conquests, all our successes in economic, political, and cultural life were to an overwhelming measure dependent on the sincere and disinterested assistance given us by the Soviet Union."

A significant part of this assistance was the creation of a North Korean army, which the Soviets equipped with weaponry captured from the Japanese and subsequently provided with the most modern Soviet military equipment. Under the guidance of Soviet military advisers, compulsory military conscription was introduced, military training schools established, new airfields built. By 1948 North Korea had a well-trained and well-equipped army of 200,000 men, which was soon to be reinforced by battle-hardened Korean veterans who had fought with the Chinese Communists against the Japanese and the Nationalists in the Chinese civil war.

❑ *American South Korea and <u>Syngman Rhee</u>*

In contrast to the Soviets, who had brought with them a Korean army and the nucleus of a Korean government, the Americans arrived without a corps of trained administrators, Korean or otherwise, and without even an adequate supply of translators. The head of the American military government, General John R. Hodge, a man without administrative experience who regarded the Koreans "as the same breed of cats as the Japanese." He was not enlightened by members of his staff, most of whom knew as little as Hodge about the country they were called upon to administer.

Two days before the arrival of the Americans, representatives of "peoples' committees" from North Korea and South Korea had met in the capital city of Seoul, where they proclaimed the establishment of a Korean People's Republic. General Hodge, convinced that this government was dominated by Communists, which it was, refused to recognize its authority. Instead, he secured Washington's permission to leave the Japanese administration in place to carry on the routine functions of government and to retain the Japanese police to protect the Japanese troops and the 600,000 Japanese civilians still in Korea until they could be returned to Japan.

These affronts to Korean national pride, which blindly ignored the resentment of the Japanese built up over the past half century, provoked such widespread protest that Washington ordered a reversal of its previous policy. The Japanese were summarily removed from all positions of responsibility, including Japanese technicians who were still needed for the operation of Korea's industrial enterprises.

The overall problem, to be sure, was formidable. In Washington's first directive on the subject of Korea, General MacArthur was instructed "to foster conditions which will bring about the establishment of a free and independent nation." But how were the Americans to find Koreans able and willing to foster such conditions—who could be trusted by the Americans, and whose authority would be respected by their compatriots? Large numbers of Koreans had served in the Japanese army, many others had collaborated with the Japanese during their long occupation, still others had become members of anti-Japanese underground organizations, many of which were avowedly Communist. In his search for Korean leaders with the qualifications he considered necessary, MacArthur turned for advice to the Chinese Nationalist leader Chiang Kai-shek, who had given refuge to a Korean government in exile in China. Chiang proposed two candidates: Kim Koo, the leader of the Korean exile government in China, and Syngman Rhee the head of an exile government in the United States. In October 1945 Kim and Rhee were returned to Korea under American auspices. After a spate of infighting, it was Rhee who emerged as the dominant political figure in South Korea.

Syngman Rhee had spent the greater part of his life in jail or in exile campaigning for his country's independence. Born in 1876, he had fled his country at an early age after being jailed and tortured by the Japanese. During his years of exile, Rhee had worked with fanatic persistence to secure foreign support on behalf of Korean independence. He had appealed in vain to Theodore Roosevelt after the Russo–Japanese war of 1904–1905, and to Woodrow Wilson after World War I. His luck did not seem to improve during World War II. His government in exile, for which he sought recognition as the sole legitimate government of Korea, was contemptuously dismissed by the State Department as a "self-constituted club with limited membership among a group of expatriates," and Rhee himself came to be regarded as something of a nuisance in Washington. He was rescued from political limbo by Chiang Kai-shek and MacArthur. Like Chiang, Syngman Rhee had converted to Christianity, and, again like Chiang, he was a dedicated opponent of the Communists, qualities he was to exploit in winning the favor of the Americans.

❑ *The Establishment of Separate South and North Korean Governments*

In September 1947, unable to reach agreement with the Soviet Union as to which political groups in Korea, north and south, could be considered "democratic" and thus eligible for consultation in the formation of an all-Korean government, the United States called upon the United Nations to supervise elections in North and South Korea to a constituent assembly that would draw up a constitution for an all-Korean government. The Soviet bloc objected that the UN had no jurisdiction in Korea because Korea was not a member of that organization. Outvoted on this issue, the Soviet government announced that it would not participate in a UN electoral supervisory commission, and Soviet authorities subsequently barred the entry of that commission into North Korea. Elections held under UN auspices in May 1948 therefore took place only in South Korea. These resulted in victory for the supporters of Syngman Rhee, who now emerged for the first time as a significant political figure.

The Korean elections had not only been opposed by the Communists but by Korean nationalists, who argued, correctly as it proved, that elections confined to South

Korea would solidify the partition of the country. The various attempts to disrupt or boycott the elections failed, however, and though Rhee's opponents charged that his victory had been achieved through fraud and police coercion, a UN investigation commission concluded that the elections had been "a valid expression of the electorate in those parts of Korea which were accessible to the Commission" and voted unanimously to accept the election verdict.

On July 12, 1948, the assembly elected by the people of South Korea adopted a constitution drafted by a special committee of that assembly, and eight days later the assembly elected Syngman Rhee president of the Republic of Korea. Formal inauguration ceremonies were held in Seoul on August 15 in the presence of General MacArthur. American military government now came to an end, and sovereignty over Korea was transferred to the government of the Republic of Korea, which claimed authority over North as well as South Korea.

Not to be outdone, the Soviet-sponsored administration in North Korea held Soviet-style parliamentary elections to a Supreme Peoples Assembly in August 1948, which resulted in victory for the candidates on the Communist electoral lists and the faction led by Kim Il-sung. An interesting feature of these elections was their inclusion of seats in South as well as North Korea, a device to legitimize North Korean claims to jurisdiction over both parts of the country. On September 9 the Peoples Assembly proclaimed the establishment of the People's Democratic Republic of Korea under the leadership of Kim, whose government was promptly recognized by the Soviet Union and its satellites. With the establishment of separate sovereign governments in both North and South Korea, the division of the country was formally institutionalized.

❑ The Soviet-American Military Withdrawal and North Korea's Invasion of the South

Since the beginning of the Soviet-American occupation of Korea, the Soviets had pressed for the early withdrawal of both occupation armies. This withdrawal finally took place after the establishment of Korean governments in their respective client states. The Soviet withdrawal was completed by the end of December 1948, the American by June of the following year, though not without serious misgivings on the part of American political and military leaders.

The Soviets, however, besides providing the North Koreans with their most modern tanks, artillery, and aircraft, left an estimated 3,000 military advisers in North Korea, and as many as fifteen Soviet officers remained attached to every division of the North Korean army. In 1949 the North Korean army was strengthened further by the return of some 50,000 to 70,000 veterans who had fought with the Chinese Communist armies of Mao Tse-tung against the Japanese and the Chinese Nationalists.

The Americans did not provide similar support for South Korea, in part because Syngman Rhee, to avoid the appearance of dependency on the Americans, demanded full control over any aid the Americans might provide. Altogether, Rhee proved to be a difficult and embarrassing partner. His regime was autocratic, corrupt, and incompetent. The South Korean parliament, torn by fictional strife, proved incapable of enacting constructive legislation to alleviate economic misery or quell popular discontent, which was systematically stoked by local Communists and agitators sent in from the north. Confronted with an increasingly volatile situation, the Rhee regime resorted to political repression and martial law, which only made his government more unpopular.

American advisers made sincere and determined efforts to put together a coalition of political moderates to reform the South Korean government, but besides the difficulties they encountered in South Korea itself, they were handicapped by Washington's ambivalence about Korea's overall importance to American interests. A State Department analysis of July 1949, endorsed by Truman, described Korea as "an ideological battleground upon which our entire success in Asia may depend." But a Joint Strategy Survey Committee reached exactly the opposite conclusions, ranking Korea next to last among the countries whose security was vital to American security. State evidently came to agree with this negative view. In August the State-War-Navy Coordinating Committee recommended that "every effort should be made to liquidate or reduce the U.S. commitment of men and money in Korea as soon as possible"—though with the critical (and quasi-contradictory) qualification that this should be done "without abandoning Korea to Soviet domination."

In their public pronouncements, too, American leaders seemed to go out of their way to inform the world of America's lack of interest in Korea. In an interview published in the *New York Times* on March 3, 1949, General MacArthur defined America's defensive perimeter in the Pacific as running from the Philippines through the Ryukyu Archipelago, Japan and the Aleutian Island chain to Alaska, thus leaving out both Korea and Taiwan. The most influential public statement along these lines was a major address before the National Press Club in Washington in January 1950 by Secretary of State Dean Acheson, who also conspicuously left out Korea and Taiwan in defining America's defensive perimeter—though with the significant proviso that an invasion of South Korea would invoke "the commitments of the entire civilized world under the Charter of the United Nations."

During their occupation of Korea, the Americans had done far less than the Soviets to shore up the army of their client state. At the time of Acheson's Press Club speech, they responded to a Syngman Rhee appeal for aid by sending 500 military advisers to South Korea plus a modest increase in military aid. American military authorities expressed confidence that the South Korean security forces were sufficiently well-equipped and trained to withstand an attack from the North.

This appraisal was either the product of a ludicrously incompetent intelligence service or an attempt to cover up the inadequacy of America's military commitment. Although the South Korean security forces were sufficiently strong to suppress the numerous efforts of North Korean agents and guerrillas to topple the Rhee regime, they proved to be utterly incapable of withstanding an attack from the North. For, within hours of launching a full-scale invasion of the south on June 25, 1950, troops of the North Korean regular army broke through the South Korean defenses and seemed poised to win the all-out victory.

❑ *The Korean War: the Question of Responsibility*

The North Korean invasion abruptly ended the vacillations of the American government over Korea. The senior members of the Truman administration were never in any doubt that the invasion was an act of aggression on the part of the North Koreans, or that this aggression had been instigated by the Soviet Union.

Circumstantial evidence bore out the American belief in North Korea's responsibility and Soviet culpability. The North Korean forces were equipped with Soviet tanks, artillery, and combat planes, they had been trained by Soviet advisers, their invasion was carried out on a large scale and had obviously been carefully planned. It was therefore inconceivable that their invasion was a response to South Korean aggression, as the North Koreans contended at the time and revisionist historians were to argue later. Syngman Rhee, to be sure, had been eager to launch an invasion of the north, but he lacked the means to do so and the United States did not provide them.

Soviet and Chinese sources and the depositions of Soviet and Chinese leaders have now provided irrefutable evidence that the attack of June 25 was indeed a carefully planned initiative on the part of the North Korean government. Like Syngman Rhee, Kim Il-sung was determined to unify his country, if necessary by force of arms, and he was in a far more favorable military and political position to do so. Soviet documents reveal that he had appealed long and persistently to both Stalin and Mao to agree to his invasion of the south. He had finally received Stalin's consent during a visit to Moscow in March 1950. He obtained the blessing of Mao while in Peking a month later. By the end of May the North Korean army had begun major troop deployments along the 38th parallel, and its military leaders confidently predicted that they could complete their conquest of the South within 22 to 27 days.

The evidence from Soviet and Chinese sources buttresses the credibility of the memoirs of Khrushchev, who says that the invasion was undertaken at "the initiative of Comrade Kim Il Sung, and it was supported by Stalin and many others—in fact, by everybody." Kim had first proposed an invasion to Stalin in 1949, claiming "that South Korea was blanketed with Party organizations and that the people would rise up in revolt when the Party gave the signal." Stalin consulted Mao, who endorsed the invasion plan. It would be unwise to ignore the possibility of American intervention, he said, but he considered it unlikely because the war would be a Korean internal matter. Stalin had greater fears on this score but was "inclined to think that if the war were fought swiftly—and Kim Il Sung was sure it could be won swiftly—then intervention by the USA could be avoided." But, cautious as ever, he withdrew the Soviet military advisers from North Korea at the time of the invasion so there could be no obvious link with the USSR.

While remaining cautious, Stalin had abundant reason to give Kim the green light. By unleashing Kim, he was employing a favorite Soviet stratagem: to allow a surrogate to take the risks—and the blame—in extending Communist influence without the overt involvement of the Soviet Union. Once Kim had conquered the South, the time would have come to impose Soviet control over a Korean government which, having thrown down the gauntlet to the United States, would be more dependent than ever on Soviet support.

Mao Tse-tung, too, had ample reason to sanction Kim's invasion of the south. He owed Kim a debt of gratitude for his support during the Chinese civil war—Kim is said to have sent as many as 150,000 Korean "volunteers" to fight with the Chinese Communists. More importantly, the conquest of South Korea would eliminate this outpost of American influence on the Asian mainland, contribute to the security of China, and further the cause of the Communist world revolution.

There remains the question why the *United States* intervened, after so many government analyses and public statements about America's lack of interest in Korea. The answer seems obvious when this question is viewed in the light of contemporary foreign and domestic problems. In July 1949 the Soviet Union had exploded an atomic bomb, ending America's atomic monopoly far earlier than most experts had expected, and later that same year China had fallen to the Communists. These shocks were accompanied by revelations about traitors who had occupied sensitive government positions. In January 1950 Alger Hiss, a high-ranking State Department official accused of transmitting documents to Soviet agents, was found guilty of perjury; Klaus Fuchs, a leading research scientist in Britain's atomic program, was found guilty of betraying atomic secrets to the Soviets; from Canada had came intelligence reports of a massive Soviet espionage ring operating in North America. Leading a campaign of irresponsible vilification of American government officials, Senator Joseph R. McCarthy of Wisconsin claimed to have a list of 205 card-carrying Communists in the State Department. The Truman administration was blamed for having "lost" China, for being soft on Communism, and for failing to deal firmly with the Soviet Union while the United States still had a monopoly on atomic weaponry.

There is every reason to believe, however, that Truman would have acted as he did over Korea even if his government had not been under such heavy domestic attack. In his memoirs, he records how impressed he was by "the complete, almost unspoken acceptance on the part of everyone that whatever had to be done to meet this aggression had to be done. . . . This was the test of all the talk of the last five years of collective security." Failure to act would have had incalculably disastrous consequences. "If we let Korea down, the Soviet[s] will keep right on going and swallow up one piece of Asia after another. . . . If we were to let Asia go, the Near East would collapse and no telling what would happen in Europe." Failure to act would destroy the credibility of American commitments elsewhere, encourage neutralism, and set back hopes to wrest the initiative from the Kremlin. Truman saw Korea as the Greece of the Far East. "If we are tough enough now, if we stand up to them like we did in Greece three years ago, they won't take any next step." All along, Truman and his advisers were acutely conscious of the lessons of recent history. This time there was to be no appeasement. Korea was not to be another Manchuria, another Ethiopia, Austria, or Czechoslovakia.

Truman acted decisively and with dispatch. On June 25, after conferring briefly with his advisers, he ordered that South Korea be supplied with arms, he authorized MacArthur to give the South Korean army naval and air support, and he instructed the military chiefs in Washington "to prepare the necessary orders for the eventual use of American units." On June 27 he ordered the submission of a resolution to the Security Council asking the members of the UN "to provide the Republic of Korea all necessary aid to repel the aggressors"—a maneuver to make resistance to North Korean aggression not merely an American but a United Nations operation on behalf of the principle of collective security. This resolution was adopted by a vote of seven to one (Yugoslavia) with two abstentions (India and Egypt). It was not blocked by a Soviet veto because since January the Soviet delegate had boycotted Security Council meetings to protest the fact that China's seat on the Council was occupied by a representative of the Nationalist instead of the Communist government.

❑ *The Course of the Conflict*

On June 30, MacArthur reported to Washington that air and seapower alone would not be able to check the North Korean advance and that it would be necessary to send American ground troops to Korea. Two American divisions were promptly dispatched to the mainland, but even these reinforcements failed to stem the advance of the North Koreans, who by the beginning of September controlled the entire peninsula with the exception of a beachhead around Pusan in the southeast.

The military situation was soon to change dramatically. On September 13 MacArthur carried out a daring and brilliant military maneuver. Having steadily built up his forces at Pusan, he launched an amphibious flank attack at the port city of Inchon, southwest of Seoul, designed to cut off North Korean communications with the south. The Inchon landing was coordinated with a massive counterattack by the heavily reinforced South Korean and American army from the Pusan perimeter. The North Koreans, facing attack on two fronts, their supply routes cut by Americans advancing from Inchon and heavy aerial bombardment, fell back in confusion. By the end of the month a large part of their army had been destroyed, the rest driven back beyond the 38th parallel.

For the Americans, the military objective now was the destruction of the North Korean army, and MacArthur was given a free hand to wind up the war as swiftly as possible. "We want you to feel unhampered, tactically and strategically, to proceed north of the 38th parallel," he was told by General Marshall, now secretary of defense. A few voices of caution were raised in Washington, notably those of Soviet experts George Kennan and Charles Bohlen, but the general opinion was expressed by Dean Acheson: "Troops could not be expected . . . to march up to a surveyor's line," which as a boundary was meaningless in any case.

Until now MacArthur had been empowered to operate north of the 38th parallel provided there was no threat of Chinese or Soviet intervention. The Joint Chiefs seemed to abandon this sensibly cautious restriction in an instruction to the general of October 9: "In the event of an open or covert employment anywhere in Korea of major Chinese Communist units, without prior announcement, you should continue the action as long as, in your judgment, action by forces now under your control offers a reasonable chance of success." Their only remaining reservation was that MacArthur must "obtain authorization from Washington prior to taking any military action against objectives in Chinese territory."

Already on October 2, however, the Chinese government had issued clear warnings that if UN forces crossed the 38th parallel, China would send troops to aid North

MAP 13   THE KOREAN WAR

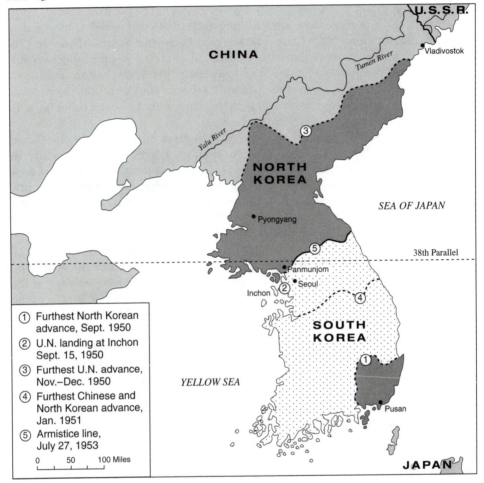

① Furthest North Korean advance, Sept. 1950
② U.N. landing at Inchon Sept. 15, 1950
③ Furthest U.N. advance, Nov.–Dec. 1950
④ Furthest Chinese and North Korean advance, Jan. 1951
⑤ Armistice line, July 27, 1953

0   50   100 Miles

Korea. As warnings of Chinese intervention continued to flow into Washington, including reports that Chinese troops were actually fighting in Korea, Truman became sufficiently alarmed to fly to Wake Island on October 15 to confer personally with his commander in the Pacific. MacArthur remained breezily confident. He assured Washington that he had the situation in Korea under control, "formal resistance" would end by Thanksgiving, and the American 8th Army would be back in Japan by Christmas. He was no longer afraid of Chinese intervention. The Chinese had no air force, they could get at most 50,000 to 60,000 men across the Yalu River separating China from Korea, and if they tried to get down to the North Korean capital of Pyongyang "there would be the greatest slaughter."

It was soon evident that MacArthur had disastrously underestimated the Chinese threat. On November 6 he wired Washington in some panic that "men and materiel in large force are pouring across all bridges over the Yalu." To stem the Chinese advance, he asked for permission to destroy those bridges by aerial bombardment. Permission was granted, but bombing was to be restricted to the Korean end of the Yalu bridges, nor was there to be any bombing of the dams and power plants on that river. This did not satisfy MacArthur, who believed it essential to strike bases on Chinese soil which were providing sanctuary for enemy aircraft now appearing over Korea in increasing numbers—a belated acknowledgment that China had an air force after all. But here Truman drew the line. He feared that an attack on Chinese territory might result in a full-scale war with China and perhaps with the Soviet Union as well, and he refused to take a risk of that magnitude.

The first Chinese troops had crossed the Yalu River on October 19, 1950, and within a few days they had driven UN forces from the border region. But with that they broke off their offensive and retreated along a broad front. As this retreat took place just as American planes began to bomb the Yalu bridges, MacArthur apparently assumed that he had overestimated the Chinese danger. For he now resumed his own offensive, announcing grandly on November 24 that this campaign would end the war and "bring the boys home by Christmas."

In tragic contrast to the Inchon landings in September, MacArthur's November offensive was disastrously ill-conceived. He had grossly underestimated the scope and strength of the Chinese intervention, and had failed to take adequate account of the rigors of the Korean winter. Instead of keeping his forces united, he sent separate armies up the two sides of the peninsula. They were thus divided by the rugged mountains of the interior and unable to support each other.

The Chinese had deliberately played on MacArthur's overconfidence. Their retreat after their initial offensive was part of a carefully planned strategy of "purposely showing ourselves to be weak, increasing the arrogance of our enemies, letting them run amuck, and luring them deep into our areas." MacArthur plunged into the trap the Chinese had set for him. On November 25, the day after his confident prediction of total victory, the Chinese launched a massive counterattack that turned the tide of battle as decisively as the Inchon landings had done, only this time it was the Americans who were surrounded and driven back.

With the UN armies in full retreat and in danger of annihilation, the American government at last accepted the offers of Asian and Arab countries to negotiate a ceasefire. Now it was the turn of the Chinese to balk, confident that they were in control of the situation. Declaring that the 38th parallel had been obliterated forever, the Chinese foreign minister Chou En-lai demanded the removal of all foreign troops from Korea, America's abandonment of Taiwan, and China's admission to the United Nations with the seat on the Security Council now occupied by the Nationalists.

MacArthur blamed his military disasters on the restrictions his own government had imposed on his operations, presumably its refusal to allow him to carry the war to China, for otherwise he had been left with all too free a hand. Denouncing China's intervention in Korea as "one of the acts most contrary to international law that had ever been recorded," he called on Washington for "political decisions and strategic plans" adequate to meet the realities of what was now "an entirely new war." What MacArthur proposed was nothing less than all-out war with China: a naval blockade of the Chinese coast; the dropping of atom bombs on air bases and other sensitive points in Manchuria; the landing on both sides of the Sino-Korean border of a half-million Chinese Nationalist troops from Taiwan supported by two divisions of U.S. marines; and the "introduction" of another Chinese Nationalist army into southern China, perhaps via Hong Kong.

Informed of MacArthur's extravagant proposals by British intelligence, Prime Minister Clement Attlee hastened to Washington in early December to sound out the intentions of the American government. Even more disturbing to the British was a statement by the president himself. At a press conference on November 26, Truman declared that United States would take whatever steps were necessary to deal with the military situation. A reporter asked whether that included the atom bomb. That includes every weapon we have, Truman replied. In a private conversation with the president, a worried Attlee asked whether the press conference statement was intended as a hint that the United States was actually thinking of using the bomb. "I assured him that nothing of that sort had been intended," Truman wrote in his memoirs, and in a communiqué issued after his meetings with the British leader he expressed the hope that world conditions would never call for the use of the bomb. His government would do everything possible to avoid war with China, he said, and "we are ready, as we have always been, to seek an end to hostilities through negotiation."

The Chinese did not rush to the negotiating table. In the final days of 1950 Chinese and North Korean forces crossed the 38th parallel; on January 5 Seoul fell for the second time to the northern invaders. But by late January, with their overextended lines under constant American air attack, the Chinese offensive stalled and the fighting front was stabilized. By March the tide of battle had turned once again as Communist forces were driven back beyond the 38th parallel after suffering heavy losses. With the prewar territorial status quo essentially reestablished, Truman made a renewed bid to end hostilities through negotiation. To clear the way for a settlement and forestall any attempt on the part of MacArthur to block it, the Joint Chiefs sent the general a directive on March 20 informing him that the UN was now preparing to discuss conditions of peace; he should therefore not undertake another advance beyond the 38th parallel.

❑ *The Dismissal of MacArthur*

MacArthur had not been chastened by his recent defeats, and he evidently decided that if peace was to be made, he should be the one to make it—and on his terms. On March 24, without consulting Washington or the UN, he released a statement entirely at cross-purposes with the policies of his government. He declared that the Communists had been disastrously weakened by recent UN operations, so much so that the Chinese must now be painfully aware that "an expansion of our military operations to [China's] coastal areas and interior bases would doom Red China to the risk of imminent military collapse." Thus there should be no insuperable difficulty about arriving at decisions over Korea without being burdened by "extraneous matters not directly related to Korea, such as Formosa or China's seat in the United Nations." As military commander, he stood ready at any time to confer in the field with the commander-in-chief of the enemy forces on behalf of realizing the political objectives of the United Nations without further bloodshed.

In his memoirs Truman called this "a most extraordinary statement for a military commander of the United Nations to issue on his own responsibility." It represented an open defiance of the orders of the president of the United States and a challenge to presidential authority embodied in the constitution. "By this act MacArthur left me no choice—I could no longer tolerate his insubordination."

Truman had already made up his mind to dismiss MacArthur when he was confronted by yet another act of subordination. On April 5 Joseph Martin, the Republican minority leader in the House of Representatives and a bitter critic of Truman's East Asian policies, read a letter to the House addressed to him by MacArthur in which the general expressed his agreement with Martin's view about the desirability of using Chinese Nationalist troops. MacArthur implicitly criticized the Truman administration for not allowing him to extend the war to China or even the Soviet Union to eliminate the Communist menace once and for all. "It seems strangely difficult for some to realize that here in Asia is where the Communist conspirators have elected to make their play for global conquest," MacArthur said, and " . . . that here we fight Europe's war with arms while the diplomats there still fight with words; that if we lose this war to Communism in Asia the fall of Europe is inevitable. . . . As you [Martin] point out, we must win. There is no substitute for victory."

To this Truman commented: "But there is a right kind and a wrong kind of victory, just as there are wars for the right thing and wars that are wrong from every standpoint." Although Truman had already made up his mind, he consulted with the Joint Chiefs and found they were unanimous in recommending that MacArthur be dismissed. On April 10 Truman relieved MacArthur of his several commands and appointed General Matthew Ridgway to succeed him.

There was a howl of protest in the United States and a fresh round of denunciations of Truman, capped by a typically elegant statement by the redoubtable Senator McCarthy: "The son of a bitch ought to be impeached." MacArthur returned home to a hero's welcome, he was invited to address a joint session of Congress, and he stirred patriotic hearts with renewed calls for an expansion of the war and victory. But Truman continued to receive the support of the Joint Chiefs, who agreed that the enlargement of the war would not guarantee victory, that it might bring Russia in, and that the United States would lose allies in every part of the world. Truman himself had long since decided that if victory in Korea meant risking a world war, he would settle for no victory.

❑ *The Long Road to an Armistice*

China, too, was ready to make peace. A second major Chinese offensive in May 1951 had been repulsed with immense losses. On June 23 the Soviet representative to the UN Security Council indicated that his government believed discussions should be started between the belligerents in Korea, a proposal endorsed two days later by the Chinese government and accepted by the United States.

Truce talks began in July, but another two years were required before an armistice was finally signed at the tiny village of Panmunjom near the 38th parallel. Each side accused the other of stalling, while the governments of both North and South Korea insisted they would settle for nothing less than a unified Korea. There was also the knotty problem of North Korean prisoners of war. After World War II, the Western Allies, at Stalin's insistence, had sent Soviet prisoners of war back to the Soviet Union, where they were treated as traitors, shot, or sent to the notorious Soviet gulags as slave laborers. Truman was determined that North Korean prisoners of war (or defectors) should not suffer a similar fate, and the differences over this question made for unexpectedly serious obstacles to peace. Meanwhile, the war not only continued but was being waged with mounting intensity as each side attempted to gain ground to improve its bargaining position.

The election of General Eisenhower to the American presidency in November 1952, followed by his warning that unless the war were ended quickly the United States might have to retaliate "under circumstances of our choosing," may have had a moderating effect on the Communist position. But the decisive factor in breaking the deadlock was the death of Stalin on March 5, 1953. Just three days earlier, Molotov, the Soviet foreign minister, had told the UN political committee that no Korean armistice would be acceptable except on Communist terms. Stalin's successors, however, were prepared to bargain.

An armistice was finally signed at Panmunjom on July 26, 1953, establishing a demilitarized zone along the borders of the two Koreas, a joint UN-Communist military armistice commission, and a supervisory commission of neutral states to enforce the armistice terms. On October 10 Washington concluded a mutual defense treaty with South Korea promising to keep American troops in Korea and to provide American military aid—but only "in case of an external armed attack . . . against territory which has been recognized by the United States as lawfully brought under the administrative control of the Republic of Korea."

Negotiations for a final peace treaty between North and South Korea were begun after the conclusion of the armistice, but so far all such negotiations have failed and Korea remains divided.

❏ *The Mutations of Interpretation*

During the first year of the Korean war, Truman was fiercely denounced by his more militant compatriots for his restraint: for not following MacArthur's prescription for all-out victory, including extending the war to China and even the Soviet Union; for not waging it with all available weapons, including atomic bombs; for not using the Nationalist Chinese troops of Chiang Kai-shek. After the armistice negotiations began and the war dragged on, Truman was blamed for the continuation of the conflict. General Ridgway, MacArthur's successor as commander of the UN troops in Korea who successfully held the line during the long armistice negotiations, was branded "Butcher Ridgway," and the conflict itself became "Truman's War." During the presidential campaign of 1952, General Eisenhower, the Republican candidate, was persuaded by his advisers that it would be good politics to promise to go to Korea and finally end what had become a thoroughly unpopular war. They were right. The promise enhanced Eisenhower's already formidable popularity, and he won the election handily.

From the start of the Korean conflict there had been another body of critics who denounced Truman for having gone to war at all. Their number was soon to be swelled by opponents of the Vietnam War, who came to conclusion that American intervention in Korea, too, had been a mistake. The more moderate among them restricted themselves to describing Truman and Acheson as incompetent bunglers, they argued that the entire Korean question could have been settled through negotiation, and they decried the immorality of supporting the repressive regime of Syngman Rhee, conveniently ignoring the far more repressive regime of Kim Il Sung in North Korea and the atrocities perpetrated by that government.

More strident critics have gone much further, denouncing American intervention as an outright war crime that subjected the Korean people to a veritable holocaust— the slaughter of two million Korean civilians (over 20 percent of the country's prewar population) and indiscriminate bombing. The most extreme among these critics have seen the Korean War as part of an overall pattern of American foreign policy. They accuse the United States of being a hegemonic power seeking to contain Communism and all other revolutionary impulses, not only in Korea but in every other part of the world. They maintain that the long-range American goal, in Asia as elsewhere, is the creation of a new order conducive to American security and economic interests. America's role in Korea, these critics contend, "took no heed of Korean needs and demands for a full restructuring of colonial legacies," but was rather a new imperialism working out the logic of its own interests.

Fair-minded foreign observers, including a large number of Koreans, may question whether such extreme criticism of America's Korean policy is justified. In the decade after the Korean war the United States poured 6 billion dollars of foreign aid into South Korea, laying the basis for one of the most prosperous economies in East Asia. American troops have prevented China and the Soviet Union from reasserting their own influence over South Korea, and the American government has been, if anything, too scrupulous in not intervening in that country's domestic affairs. Meanwhile, the Communist government of North Korea remains one of the world's most oppressive regimes, a police state whose government-controlled economy has upon occasion reduced the country to outright famine.

Ironically, America's most extreme anti-Communists have also deplored the results of the Korean War. South Korea was saved from Communist domination, to be sure, but Communist regimes were left in power in North Korea—and China—where they have remained in a position to foment subversion and mount further campaigns of Communist aggression throughout the rest of Asia. They think MacArthur was right in advocating carrying on the war to ensure the destruction of all Asian Communist governments, and that there was indeed no substitute for victory.

As noted earlier, however, by the time the conflict had bogged down into a stalemate, most Americans had become heartily sick of the war, and as the armistice negotiations dragged on, influential voices in Congress were proclaiming, to widespread approval, that there should be no more Koreas.

In the light of the tragedy of Vietnam, we can now see that the most fateful legacy of the Korean war may well have been its relative success. The non-Communist government installed under American auspices in South Korea had been successfully defended. Why should a similar policy not work in Vietnam, which had also been artificially divided after World War II? The differences in the situation in the two countries would not become fully apparent until many years after the Americans began to transfer the "lessons" of Korea to the peninsula of Southeast Asia.

*

TWENTY-SEVEN

❑

The End of Empire:
India and Pakistan

In the perspective of world history, one of the most far-reaching developments in the years after World War II was the dissolution of the European colonial empires and the emergence of a galaxy of independent states in Africa and Asia. Because of their sheer number, I have dealt with these independence movements only when they played a critical role in the foreign relations of the great powers. The case of the Indian sub-continent merits special attention, however, because India was not only the most valuable component of the British empire—the Jewel in the Crown—but because Britain's recognition of the independence of India broke the dam of British rule, which now yielded to demands for independence in every other part of the empire. The Indian revolution is noteworthy in itself because the weapons employed by its most eminent leader, Mohandas K. Gandhi, were not guns and terror but love and nonviolent civil disobedience. Further, with their acquisition of nuclear weaponry in 1998, India and Pakistan have become decisive players in global politics.

❑ *The Gandhi Revolution*   *Father of India*

Gandhi was born in 1869, the son of a prime minister of a minor Hindu state, who trained as a barrister at London's Inner Temple. An unimpressive figure, shy and awkward in manner, Gandhi was unable to find employment upon his return to his native India and in 1893 he accepted a position in South Africa, where he was to remain for twenty-two years. Here he was to develop remarkable skill as a political activist in confronting the racial discrimination and outright oppression the nonwhite races encountered in that country. Equally impressive and perhaps even more important was his talent to generate publicity, which enabled him to bring his various causes to the attention of a global audience. Gandhi's most formidable political attribute, however, was an extraordinary moral force that, while incomprehensible to many Westerners, persuaded hard-headed Indian politicians to welcome his leadership and won him the adulation of the Indian masses. Among those who came under his spell was India's Nobel laureate, the poet Rabindranath Tagore, who hailed him as a Mahatma (Great Spirit), a name by which he became known throughout the world.

372   *S Africa*

Gandhi called his autobiography *The Story of My Experiments with Truth,* and while still in South Africa he developed the strategy of nonviolent political action he was to call *Satyagraha* (hold fast to the truth), a movement inspired by his belief that injustice and oppression could be overcome by a forthright stand on behalf of principles which he held to be the Truth. In practice, *Satyagraha* was a strategy of civil disobedience that called for a refusal to obey laws held to be unjust because they did not conform to the Truth and refusal to cooperate in any way with the oppressive authority.

Already famous throughout India for his work on behalf of the Indians in South Africa, Gandhi was greeted by jubilant crowds upon his return to India on January 9, 1915, four months after the outbreak of World War I. Despite his abhorrence of war, he loyally supported the British war effort, as did Indians generally—over 1 million Indian soldiers and noncombatants served with distinction on the Allied side on every front. Gandhi confessed in his autobiography that the war confronted him with a complicated spiritual dilemma, but he believed that unequivocal support of the empire in its hour of danger was the stepping-stone to home rule.

At this time Gandhi still looked upon the British empire as a benevolent institution and believed that it was guiding its subject peoples toward the kind of democratic government he had observed and admired in Britain itself. He was encouraged in this belief by British wartime declarations on behalf of national freedom and self-determination, and as the war drew to a close, Gandhi joined leading Indian political and intellectual figures in calling upon the British to honor these wartime commitments. In a prescient letter to the British viceroy he wrote that "in your just and timely treatment of India's claim to Home Rule lies the safety of the Empire."

The British responded with promises of institutions that would make for limited self-government, but this meager concession did not satisfy Indian political activists who believed they deserved more in return for their generous wartime support. Frustrated and angry, they engaged in mass protests and other forms of political agitation. The British reaction was curiously inept. Instead of seeking accommodation with Indian political leaders, they extended wartime emergency measures with the so-called Rowlatt Acts of March 18, 1919, which empowered provincial governments to jail suspected subversives without trial and allowed judges to try sedition cases without juries.

This legislation went into effect at a time when India was overwhelmed by a natural disaster of truly horrifying proportions: an influenza epidemic which took the lives of 5 million people, more than the losses sustained by all the Allied armies in four years of war. It is impossible to evaluate the impact of this catastrophe on the overall political situation, but there can be little doubt that it intensified Indian anger and resentment.

❑ *Gandhi's Leadership Role*

In the surge of popular protest that followed the promulgation of the Rowlatt Acts, Gandhi emerged for the first time as a dominant force in Indian politics and demonstrated his extraordinary power to mobilize the masses. Up to this time the principal vehicle for the expression of Indian political aspirations had been the Congress party, organized in 1885, which Gandhi was to transform from a coterie of high-caste Hindus into a mass movement.

Gandhi was uncertain how best to challenge the Rowlatt Acts, but as he tells us in his autobiography, he was inspired by a dream to inaugurate this "sacred fight" with a day of self-purification: to call upon the people of India to observe a general *hartal* and to suspend their business on that day, which was to be spent in fasting and prayer. The day chosen for this work stoppage was April 6, 1919, which gave him little time to get the word out, and Gandhi professes to have been astonished by the response to his appeal: "The whole of India from one end to the other, towns as well as villages, observed a complete *hartal* on that day."

But Gandhi's joy turned into anguish when on April 10 riots broke out in the city of Amritsar, where an angry mob set fire to British banks and murdered five Englishmen. The British response was even more unfortunate. On April 13, to teach the people of Amritsar a lesson and "produce the necessary moral and widespread effect," a British officer ordered his Gurkha and Baluchi troops to fire at will on thousands of Punjabi peasants celebrating the spring harvest, killing 379 and wounding over 1,200. Shocked by the massacre at Amritsar but dismayed even more by the Indian violence ignited by the Amritsar affair, Gandhi confessed that he had made a "Himalayan miscalculation" in assuming that his illiterate followers were sufficiently purified and disciplined to adhere to his principle of nonviolence. He now realized that a stronger and more tightly organized leadership was required.

The British sought to make amends. They repealed the Rowlatt Acts and in December 1919 they introduced a Government of India Act that once again offered the Indians limited self-government. But this legislation too fell far short of Indian expectations, and at the December meeting of the Congress party in Amritsar the British offer was dismissed as "inadequate and unsatisfactory." In his autobiography, Gandhi described this meeting as "my real entrance into Congress politics." He would have been more accurate in describing this meeting as the entry of the Congress party into Gandhian politics, for it was here that Gandhi began the party's transformation into an instrument capable of mobilizing the masses. He convinced the party leadership of the need for a full-time bureaucracy to conduct its operations and for a party constitution formalizing its organization and defining its objectives. Foremost among these objectives was the attainment of Indian self-rule (*swaraj*), which was to be achieved through the Gandhian strategy of nonviolent civil disobedience—within the British empire if possible, outside that empire if necessary.

❑ *Gandhi's First Campaign for Self-Rule*

Gandhi launched his campaign for self-rule on August 1, 1920, calling upon Indians nationwide to boycott all British products; to end all participation in the British government, British law courts, and British schools and colleges; and to refuse all British honors and titles. Gandhi himself returned two medals awarded for his services with an ambulance unit during the Boer War. Central to Gandhi's political calculations was his awareness of British dependence on Indians in carrying out the routine functions of government and administration. On the eve of World War I, there were a mere 4,000 British officials in India to govern a country of 300 million, a task made possible only through the cooperation of a half-million Indians who staffed the government offices and the Indians who made up the bulk of the British military and police forces in India. Gandhi reasoned that, by the nonviolent withdrawal of that cooperation, the machinery of government would grind to a halt and the British would be obliged to yield to Indian demands for self-rule.

It was at this time that Gandhi, to identify himself more closely with the peasant masses, permanently abandoned Western dress for a peasant's homespun loincloth (*dhoti*) and chose to live in poverty. Convinced that industrialized society and Western methods of mass production, whether carried on by British or Indian entrepreneurs, eroded the human soul, Gandhi urged his followers to follow his example in acquiring a spinning wheel, which would free them from dependence on Western goods and services. Gandhi himself spent two hours daily at his spinning wheel, which was to become a symbol of his movement and which, as the centerpiece of the Indian national flag, has since become a symbol for India itself.

Gandhi's civil disobedience campaign failed. Unwilling to risk their jobs and prospects, a majority of Indian government employees remained at their posts, and after a brief exodus, Indian students, too, returned to their schools and universities. Most importantly, the Indians in the army and the police remained loyal to the British crown. For Gandhi personally, the most discouraging blow may have been the failure of his call for nonviolence, for his self-rule campaign had set off nationwide riots. On February 4, 1922, insurgent peasants at Chauri Chaura, spurred on by Indian nationalists, attacked and burned the local police station, killing 22 Indian policemen. After that incident, a saddened Gandhi once again called off his civil disobedience campaign, but this did not save him or his followers from a massive government crackdown. Tens of thousands were were thrown into jail, and Gandhi himself received a six-year sentence.

Gandhi was released after two years for reasons of health and did not return to active political life until the end of the decade. He now retired to his village ashram where he devoted himself to social reform on behalf of the outcasts of Indian society, the untouchables. A prime objective in this connection was the abolition of the Indian caste system, which Gandhi had long regarded as India's great crime, "a blot upon humanity and therefore upon Hinduism."

❑ *The Rifts in Indian Society*

All along, the Indian self-rule movement was handicapped by the social, religious, and political cleavages among the Indians themselves. The political organization of India was in itself extremely complex. The British exercised direct authority over only 60 percent of the country. Elsewhere, British control was based on treaty relationships with native princes, who ruled over 565 states of widely different size. For the most part these princes had become loyal supporters of British rule, for they recognized that the British were now the principal guarantors of their own status and authority.

The British could also count on the support of India's more prosperous merchants and manufacturers who depended on British markets, and on members of the professional classes who operated through British law courts or taught in British schools and universities.

Throughout India, however, the most significant divisive force was the hostility between the Hindus and Muslims. Muslim political leaders resented the claim of the Congress party, dominated as it was by Hindus, to speak for all India, a resentment fueled by fears that any self-rule achieved by the Congress would leave the country's Muslim population at the mercy of the Hindu majority. Although Muslims had always been welcome in the Congress party and for a time exercised substantial influence within it, in 1906 they established their own political organization, the Muslim League, which, under the able and uncompromising leadership of Mohammad Ali Jinnah, was to wage a campaign for an independent Muslim state altogether free from Hindu control. Within the Congress itself there were serious rifts between political moderates, who favored a gradualist approach to self-government, and radical extremists, who demanded immediate and complete independence. These differences were clearly revealed at an all-party convention and a concurrent session of the Congress party in late December 1928.

Believing that Gandhi alone had the moral authority to restore some measure of unity to the Indian self-rule movement, Muslim as well as Hindu leaders persuaded him to return to the political stage. To heal the differences between Hindus and Muslims, Gandhi appealed to the humanity of both and to their joint interest in the common cause of self-rule. And to deal with the rifts between the moderates and radicals in the Congress party, he proposed a compromise resolution: Congress would call upon the British to grant India Dominion status within one year; if the British still refused to yield, Congress should demand outright independence.

❑ *Gandhi's Salt March*

A year passed with no response to the Congress appeal for Dominion status. Never one to neglect an opportunity for drama, at midnight of December 31, 1929, Gandhi led Congress in a vow to achieve complete independence through nonviolent civil disobedience, which was to include the nonpayment of taxes and a total boycott of British products and institutions. He followed up this vow-taking ceremony with an even more dramatic political demonstration. At six in the morning of March 12, 1930, he left his village ashram at the head of 78 followers to begin a 200-mile march to the sea with the avowed purpose of making salt from seawater, a symbolic gesture of civil disobedience that challenged the government monopoly on salt production and the government salt tax. The dramatic effect was all Gandhi could have hoped for. Thousands of supporters lined the route of his Salt March, strewing his path with leaves. Better still, the event attracted journalists from every part of the world.

Once again the British struck back with a campaign of repression. Gandhi and 60,000 of his followers were arrested. Gandhi, however, had achieved his purpose of evoking international sympathy for his cause, a sympathy enhanced by reports of brutal beatings of unarmed civilians, including women and children, who refused to retaliate or defend themselves. In January 1931 Gandhi was released from jail to enable him to him to represent the Congress party at ongoing round-table conferences in London. These conferences, however, did little more than expose the rifts among the Indians themselves. Hindus, Muslims, the Indian princes, Sikhs, untouchables, and political moderates and radicals all had their own programs and put forward separate and conflicting demands.

Frustrated and confessing a sense of impotence, Gandhi returned to India on December 28, 1931, where he met with a new wave of British repression. Within a week of his return he was jailed once again, as were other leaders of the Congress and thousands of their supporters. While in jail, he returned with renewed resolve to the task of breaking down the Indian caste system, and undertook two fasts on behalf of obtaining equal political and social rights for the untouchables, whom he called *Harijans,* or the Children of God. These fasts twice secured his release from jail, the second time in August 1933, because the British evidently feared that his death in jail would rekindle mass unrest. Meanwhile, his campaign on behalf of the untouchables had alienated large numbers of Hindus, including leaders of the Congress party, who resented his attack on their ancient social institutions. By this time he had also lost the support of political radicals, who had grown impatient with nonviolence and advocated a more militant policy.

With the decline of his political influence, Gandhi resigned from the Congress party in October 1934, but he continued to seek a working relationship between the Hindus and Muslims, which he regarded as essential to the achievement of self-rule and the preservation of India's unity. On August 2, 1935, the British parliament passed a second Government of India Act, which would have provided a large measure of Indian self-rule within an all-Indian federation, but this plan too foundered over differences between Hindus and Muslim over how and by whom such a federation was to be governed. Jinnah, the head of the Muslim League, denounced the leaders of the Congress party for making the "preposterous claim that they are entitled to speak on behalf of the whole of India" and declared that the Muslims could never expect justice or fair play at their hands. These differences had not been resolved when Britain went to war with Germany in September 1939.

Sir Stafford Cripps

❏ India, World War II and the Cripps Mission

On September 3, the British viceroy, without consulting Indian leaders, declared India to be at war with Germany. Infuriated by the viceroy's presumption, the Congress party proclaimed its withdrawal of all support for the British Raj and ordered all members of the party who held office under the British to resign from their posts. A jubilant Mohammad Jinnah hailed the Congress proclamation as "a day of deliverance" which had freed the Muslims from the tyranny of Hindu rule. Early in 1940 he declared the goal of the Muslim League to be the creation of an independent state which was to be called Pakistan, the Land of the Pure—Pak being the Persian-Urdu word for Pure, Stan the word for Country.

The British bastion of Singapore fell to the Japanese in February 1942, and a large part of its 60,000-man Indian garrison enrolled in an Indian National Army fighting on the side of Japan on behalf of India's liberation. Churchill had previously opposed the appeasement of India as fervently as he had opposed appeasement of Hitler, but faced with these disasters, his government was prepared to make major concessions. In March 1942 he sent Sir Stafford Cripps, a Left-leaning member of the Labour party and leader of the House of Commons, to India with an offer to grant the country Dominion status immediately after the war—but with the significant reservation that individual provinces should have the right to secede from India.

The Congress party saw this reservation as nothing less than a provision for India's partition, and Gandhi, once again in the forefront of the self-rule movement, asked Cripps why he had come so far to offer so little. He dismissed Churchill's offer as "a post-dated cheque on a failing bank" that would open the way to the "vivisection of India." India did not intend to wait until the end of the war for its liberation, Gandhi said, nor would it ever agree to partition. On August 7 he submitted a Quit India resolution to an All-India committee and called for another campaign of mass civil disobedience. "I want freedom immediately," he said, "this very night—before dawn," a resolution passed unanimously by the Congress.

What Gandhi got before dawn was not freedom for India but jail for himself, the leaders of the Congress party, and thousands of their followers. Churchill, who may have welcomed the failure of the Cripps mission, responded to Gandhi's Quit India resolution with a ringing declaration: "We intend to remain the effective rulers of India for a long and indefinite period. . . . I have not become the King's first minister in order to preside over the liquidation of the British Empire. . . . Here we are, and here we stand, a veritable rock of salvation in this drifting world."

❏ *The British Capitulation and the Decision to Partition India*

Churchill was spared presiding over the loss of India by being voted out of office in July 1945. The Labour government of Clement Attlee which succeeded him yielded at last to the Congress demand to "quit India" by offering India complete independence. Now, however, the problem arose once again of what form an independent India would take: Congress resolutely held out for a united India under a central government; the Muslim League, under the leadership of Mohammad Jinnah, just as resolutely held out for an independent Pakistan.

Disgusted with long and inconclusive negotiations and to hasten the establishment of a state of Pakistan, Jinnah proclaimed August 16, 1946, to be "Direct Action Day," therewith igniting the bonfires of Hindu–Muslim hostility that had been building up over the past half century. Muslim mobs in Calcutta engaged in four-day slaughter of their Hindu neighbors (the Great Calcutta Killing), to which Hindus responded with brutality on a comparable scale.

Convinced that Britain would have to withdraw from India or be trapped in an Indian civil war, the Attlee government issued a statement on February 20, 1947, announcing Britain's intention to hand over power to a representative Indian government, "or to governments Britain regarded as representative," no later than June of 1948. The task of overseeing the transfer of power was entrusted to Admiral Louis Mountbatten, the wartime commander of the South East Asia Command, who was instructed to do everything possible to preserve a united India.

Mountbatten did his best. He proposed that the Indian government be reconstituted as a parliamentary federation, but with the angry rejection of his federation plan by all parties he concluded that partition could not be avoided. He now put forward a second plan calling for the transfer of power to two separate states, India and a new entity (Pakistan was not yet identified by name), each of which was to be given Dominion status, and the individual Indian provinces were to be given the option of choosing to join one or the other. Meanwhile, as the threat of civil war loomed ever larger, Mountbatten resolved to hasten Britain's withdrawal and announced that the transfer of power was to be implemented by the following August, a full ten months earlier than the date originally set by Attlee.

For the Muslim League, which had long since made clear that it would accept nothing less than partition, Mountbatten's plan was a major political victory. For the Congress party it was a corresponding setback. But, faced with Mountbatten's deadline and the possibility that the rejection of his plan might open the way to an even greater fragmentation of their country, the Congress leaders saw no alternative but to agree. Gandhi alone was willing to risk all on behalf of preserving a united India.

❑ The Implementation of Partition

By June of 1947 Mountbatten had secured the agreement of Hindu and Muslim leaders over the implementation of partition. In the provinces under British rule, the decision to join India or a "new entity" was to be made by the provincial legislatures and by plebiscite, while in the states under princely rule the decision was to be made by the princes. Two of India's largest states, Punjab and Bengal, which contained large Hindu as well as Muslim populations, were to be partitioned between India and Pakistan unless their assemblies could agree on joining one state or the other.

As was to be expected, the provinces with legislatures controlled by the Hindu-dominated Congress party chose to remain part of India, while those under Muslim control opted for Pakistan. In Punjab and Bengal, too, the communities with a Hindu majority voted to stay with India, those with a Muslim majority voted to join Pakistan, thereby ensuring the partition of these provinces. From the start, the rulers of the princely states had opposed Mountbatten's partition plan, for the need to opt for either India or Pakistan meant the loss of their nominal independence. But, threatened and cajoled by Mountbatten and now deprived of British protection, they all finally agreed to go along with the plan with the exception of the rulers of Kashmir, Hyderabad, and the tiny state of Junagadh.

As finally established, the state of Pakistan consisted of two widely separated parts: a West Pakistan, the region flanking the frontiers of Afghanistan, and a much smaller East Pakistan in the delta of the Ganges, which, with only 15 percent of the

MAP 14   INDIA AND PAKISTAN

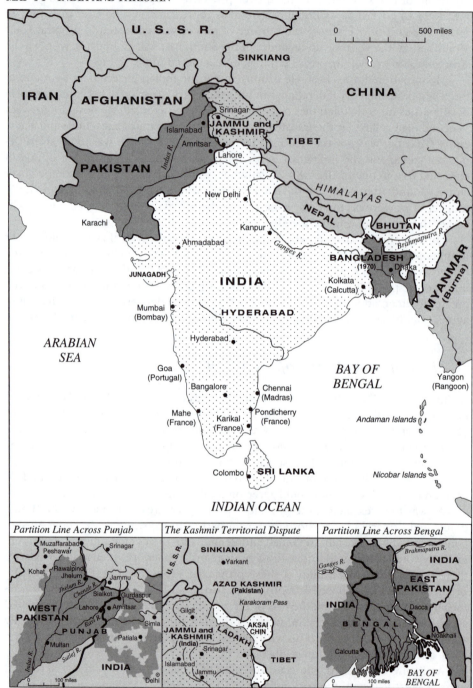

territory, included 55 percent of the population. In 1970 East Pakistan, with India's support, seceded from the Pakistan union and became the independent state of Bangladesh. (See p. 387.)

The most fateful legacy of the Mountbatten partition plan was the division of Punjab and Bengal. Because of the broad overlap of the Hindu and Muslim populations in both provinces, there would inevitably be large Hindu and Muslim minorities in the divided sectors no matter how the boundaries between India and Pakistan were drawn.

There was the further problem of the boundary lines themselves. As both sides put forward extravagant claims and could not reach agreement on this issue, the task of establishing the boundaries was assigned to a commission under a British chairman, Sir Cyril Radcliffe, who had earned a reputation as a brilliant and scrupulously honest barrister in London's law courts. He was chosen as chairman of the boundary commission, however, because he knew nothing whatsoever about India and would therefore be free of prejudices or preconceptions. To avoid outside influence, the unfortunate Radcliffe worked largely on his own, without informed advice, without accurate ordinance maps or population statistics (many of these were deliberately falsified to support rival claims) so that in the end lines were drawn that separated a factory from its sources of raw materials, a reservoir from the fields it was intended to irrigate.

Mountbatten made the boundary situation even worse. To prevent delay in the transfer of power, he held off announcing the decisions of the boundary commission until India and Pakistan had officially proclaimed their independence.

❑ India and Pakistan Become Independent as British Dominions

The transfer of power took place as scheduled at the stroke of midnight on August 14, 1947. The inauguration of the new Dominion governments took place on the following day. Jawaharlal Nehru, a leading member of the Congress party who had been agitating for Dominion status since 1928, became the first prime minister of India, and at Nehru's urgent request, Mountbatten took the position of governor-general, a more prestigious but largely ceremonial office—Gandhi had proposed that this post go to an untouchable girl. In Pakistan, Jinnah assumed the position of governor-general, and the prime ministership went to the deputy leader of the Muslim League, Liaqat Ali Khan. Mountbatten had reminded Jinnah that under the British constitutional process, the prime minister had the power and the governor-general was little more than a figurehead. But Jinnah insisted on having the more prestigious post. "In Pakistan, I will be governor-general," he said, "and the prime minister will do what I tell him to do."

The inaugurations were celebrated with wild rejoicing, but two days later the festive mood was dampened by Mountbatten's announcement of the boundary commission's decision for the partition of Punjab and Bengal. As Mountbatten had expected, that decision was furiously denounced by the governments of both India and Pakistan.

What he had not expected was the violence of the reaction to that decision that would shortly baptize the new states in blood.

The implementation of the boundary decision meant that overnight the lines dividing Punjab and Bengal had become international frontiers, and overnight Hindus and Muslims, freed from the restraints of British control, took advantage of their newly won sovereign status to indulge in the indiscriminate slaughter of what were now their Muslim or Hindu minority populations. To escape these purges, an estimated 5.5 million Muslims crossed from the Indian sectors of Punjab and Bengal into Pakistan, while another 5.5 million Hindus crossed from the Pakistani sectors into India. Further slaughter accompanied these mass migrations. Estimates of the number who fell victim to religious and racial fanaticism run as high as 2 million. Entire villages were exterminated, trainloads of migrants butchered. Among the martyrs was Gandhi himself, who on January 30, 1948, was assassinated by a Hindu Brahmin who regarded Gandhi as an obstacle to practical nation-building and who condemned his message of nonviolence and soul force as "old superstitious beliefs" which were leading the country to ruin.

❑ The Gandhi Legacy

Gandhi's life appeared to have ended in failure. There can be little doubt that the British would have been obliged to relinquish their control over India, as they did over almost every other part of their empire, even if Gandhi had never existed. Gandhi had been willing to stake all to prevent India's partition, but India had nevertheless been divided. He had dedicated his life to achieving India's independence through nonviolence, yet independence had taken place amid a veritable orgy of violence. His vow to fast to the death to stop the slaughter had temporarily shamed both sides into reaching a settlement, yet violence, often on a major scale, was to continue.

Gandhi's very failures, however, would seem to confirm the validity of his message of love and forgiveness, for what have hatred and violence achieved except to perpetuate hatred and provide fuel for further violence? Gandhi devoted his life to breaking this vicious circle. He called upon the peoples of the world to recognize their common humanity. He lived and worked among the outcasts of Indian society, the untouchables, a group so much despised that they were not even given a place in the Hindu caste system. By his identification with the poor and oppressed, he gave a new sense of self-respect to the Indian masses, who rewarded him with their love, though not, as he bitterly acknowledged, with adherence to his doctrine of nonviolence.

With his campaigns of peaceful civil disobedience, Gandhi gave the world an alternative to violence in confronting oppression and injustice and provided the poor and powerless with a weapon and an inspiration. After his martyr's death, Hindus and Muslims alike mourned him as a saint, and the world's leaders paid him tribute. Einstein wrote that "generations to come . . . will scarce believe that such a one as this ever, in flesh and blood, walked upon this earth." Sir Stafford Cripps declared that he knew of no other man "who so forcefully and convincingly demonstrated the power of the spirit over material things." And General George Marshall, now American secretary of state, mourned the loss of "the spokesman for the conscience of mankind." No word of praise or regret came from Stalin.

❑ *Junagadh, Hyderabad, and Kashmir*

As noted earlier, three states under the rule of Indian princes—Junagadh, Hyderabad, and Kashmir—had not opted to join either India or Pakistan. In the tiny Junagadh and the much larger state of Hyderabad, the rulers were Muslims, but their subjects for the most part were Hindus. The ruler of Junagadh finally opted for Pakistan, while the ruler of Hyderabad chose to remain independent. The Indian government did not allow them to exercise either option. The Indian army occupied Junagadh in November 1947, and in September of the following year Indian troops moved into Hyderabad "to restore order." Both states were subsequently incorporated into India.

The ruler-population situation was reversed in Kashmir, where a Hindu prince, Hari Singh, ruled over a predominantly Muslim population. Hari Singh, too, wanted to remain independent and make his beautiful mountainous country the Switzerland of Asia, but his state also fell victim to the Hindu–Muslim rivalry. Mohammad Jinnah was determined to make Muslim Kashmir part of Pakistan, but, wary of provoking British intervention, he used Muslim irregular forces to oust Hari Singh. He could then send units of his regular army to Kashmir to restore order.

The Muslim irregulars, however, succumbed to the temptation of looting on their way to the capital of Srinagar. Their delay gave the Indian government time to send airborne troops to Kashmir to intercept them. With Indian forces now in control of Srinagar, a representative of the Indian government, V. K. Krishna Menon, pressured Hari Singh into signing a treaty ceding Kashmir to India. Upon his return to Delhi, Menon exulted: "Here it is. We have Kashmir, the bastard signed the Act of Accession. And now that we've got it, we'll never let it go."

The Indian takeover of Kashmir set off an undeclared war with Pakistan which ended early in 1949 with an armistice negotiated by the United Nations and the establishment of a cease-fire line that divided Kashmir between India and Pakistan. Pakistan called its sector Azad, or Free Kashmir. Nehru subsequently kept 100,000 Indian troops in the Indian sector, and although he promised to allow the final fate of Kashmir to be settled by plebiscite, no such plebiscite has ever taken place. The dispute over Kashmir, punctuated by a steady round of frontier skirmishes and two further undeclared wars, continues.

❑ *The End of the Portuguese and French Enclaves*

Shortly after India achieved its independence, the Nehru government demanded that Portugal and France turn over the miniscule territories they held in India (the Portuguese since the sixteenth century, the French since the eighteenth) to Indian control. The French relinquished their sovereignty over Indian territory in 1956, but the Portuguese held out until forcibly ejected by Indian troops in December 1961.

❑ Nehru's Foreign Policy and the Sino–Indian War

In his overall foreign policy, Nehru chose to pursue a course of nonalignment to avoid involvement in the controversies of the Cold War, and he aspired to a position of moral leadership among the new nations of Africa and Asia. In a formal policy statement, Nehru proclaimed that his policy of nonalignment did not stand for "neutrality" or "neutralism," as was sometimes alleged, but was on the contrary "a positive, active and constructive policy seeking to lead to collective peace, on which alone collective security can really rest." Basic to his foreign policy were his so-called Five Principles, which have been called the ideological heart of Nehru's vision of the world. These principles, which Nehru regarded as fundamental to peaceful coexistence, required that states respect each other's sovereignty and territorial integrity, that they renounce aggression, and that they pledge mutual noninterference with each other's domestic affairs.

Nehru's hope that these principles would guide the policies of the countries of Asia and Africa was dealt a rude blow by China's invasion of Tibet in October 1950. The Chinese takeover aroused intense indignation in other parts of the world, and more importantly for India, it brought Mao Tse-tung's China to the frontiers of India along a thousand-mile front. Nehru, however, was determined not to allow this action to disturb India's friendly relations with China. In a treaty of April 29, 1954, the Indian government acknowledged Tibet to be an integral part of China and agreed to give up its extraterritorial privileges in Tibet inherited from the British. Incorporated in this treaty were Nehru's Five Principles for Peaceful Coexistence, which were endorsed by an Afro-Asian conference meeting in Bandung in April of the following year.

Before the decade was out, however, India's peaceful coexistence with China was disrupted by boundary disputes involving territories at the eastern- and western-most ends of India's thousand-mile frontier with China/Tibet. These were areas where no internationally recognized boundaries had ever been established, but which the Indian government assumed had always been part of India. In the mid-1950s China had begun building a military road across the Aksai Chin plateau of Ladakh in the southeast corner of Kashmir, a route that would provide easier access from Tibet to the western sector of the Chinese province of Sinkiang that lay along the Soviet frontier. Ten years earlier the Soviets had supported an independence movement in Sinkiang, and, with the present deterioration of China's relations with the Soviet Union (see p. 444), the Chinese believed it necessary to improve their avenues of communication to this area.

Whether ignorant of China's road-building enterprise or still determined to maintain good relations with that country, Nehru did nothing to protest or otherwise challenge China's de facto takeover the Aksai Chin region, some 12,000 square miles of territory. His attitude changed following China's brutal suppression of a rebellion in Tibet in March of 1959 and the flight of Tibet's Dalai Lama and thousands of his followers to India, where they were given political asylum by the Indian government. Now fully alerted to the threat that China posed to his own country, Nehru was increasingly disturbed by reports of clashes between Chinese and Indian border patrols.

In September 1959, claiming that the frontier territories where these clashes had taken place had been part of India for centuries, Nehru demanded that the Chinese withdraw their forces from the areas in dispute and rejected Chinese offers to negotiate because there was nothing that needed to be negotiated. Over the next two years Nehru undertook a steady reinforcement of Indian troops in the disputed areas in the evident belief that China, beset by domestic troubles and at loggerheads with the Soviet Union, would have neither the strength nor the will to challenge the Indian claims.

This proved to be a disastrous miscalculation. On October 10, 1962, the Chinese for the first time actively resisted a forward thrust by the Indian army, and ten days later they struck with overwhelming force, defeating the Indians on every front. After five days they suspended their military operations, but as Nehru procrastinated over their demand for negotiations, they renewed their offensive on November 18 and within two days were in full control of all the disputed areas. On November 21 the Chinese announced a unilateral cease-fire and proceeded to impose their conditions on India.

These conditions were surprisingly lenient. The Chinese returned most of the disputed territory to India, retaining only the strategic Aksai Chin plateau, the route of the Tibet-Sinkiang military highway. Having achieved their most important objective, the Chinese had every reason to end the war with India quickly. They were alarmed by America's prompt response to Nehru's appeal for military aid, and there remained the threat of the Soviet Union.

The China war put an end to Nehru's policy of nonalignment. Following the initial Indian defeats, he had appealed in some panic to Washington and London for military aid, and President Kennedy was eager to exploit this opportunity to bring India into the Western camp. Nehru, however, was even-handed in his abandonment of nonalignment. For, while turning to the United States for military aid, he also sought better relations with the Soviet Union, which he saw as a more valuable counterweight to China than the Western powers.

❑ *The Nehru Legacy*

India had emerged comparatively unscathed from the conflict with China, but India's defeat seems to have been a devastating blow to Nehru personally. He was already suffering from ill health, and his foreign policy failures may have hastened his physical decline. He suffered a stroke on January 6, 1964, and died on May 27.

Nehru's principles for peaceful coexistence, like Gandhi's principle of nonviolence, appeared to have been discredited by failure. But, just as Gandhi provided an alternative to hatred and violence, Nehru had set forth fundamental conditions for conducting a policy of peaceful coexistence, an invaluable contribution, for, in our era of nuclear weaponry, peaceful coexistence has become a condition for human survival.

As prime minister of India, Nehru made a significant contribution to the cause of democracy by not succumbing to the temptation of cutting through the tedious procedures of democratic government and assuming autocratic power. Under the guidance of Nehru, India, in notable contrast to Pakistan and so many other states emerging from colonial rule, adhered to the institutions of democratic government. Equally important was Nehru's recognition of the need to deal honestly and fairly with India's large Muslim population, not only from a human point of view but because the preservation of India itself required that its substantial Muslim minority be made to feel secure. Convinced that Hindu extremism constituted a threat to the very fabric of Indian unity, he devoted much of his political energy to curbing Hindu pretensions to political and moral supremacy. After the horrors that accompanied the partition of Bengal and Punjab, the fact that Hindus and Muslims in India live together in relative harmony may well have been Nehru's supreme achievement.

❑ The Undeclared Wars between India and Pakistan and the Creation of the State of Bangladesh

The border skirmishes between Indian and Pakistan in Kashmir, which had gone on steadily since the cease-fire of 1949, escalated in the summer of 1965 into a second undeclared war. That war ended with another cease-fire negotiated by the United Nations and the conclusion of a formal peace treaty in January 1966 that restored the prewar status quo. The question of Kashmir remained unresolved.

A third undeclared war between India and Pakistan began in the final weeks of 1971. At issue this time was East Pakistan, situated in the delta of the Ganges at the opposite side of India from West Pakistan. Since attaining their independence as part of the Muslim state of Pakistan, the people of East Pakistan, who made up 55 percent of Pakistan's population, had become increasingly resentful of West Pakistan's monopolization of political and economic power. In March 1970 the Pakistani strong man, General Yahya Khan, alarmed by popular unrest and East Pakistan's agitation for independence, placed both East and West Pakistan under martial law. In November of that year a natural disaster in East Pakistan swelled the forces of popular discontent when a cyclone swept over the flat and thickly populated Ganges delta, raising tides by as much as twenty-five feet and wreaking massive material and human destruction. An estimated 200,000 people perished.

General elections in December 1970, the first to be held in Pakistan since independence, resulted in a major victory for the East Pakistan independence party, the Awami League. With a majority of 136 in the Pakistan National Assembly, Mujibar Rahman, the leader of the Awami League, should have been installed as prime minister of both sectors of Pakistan. But General Yahya Khan refused to accept the election results, and on March 15, 1971, he sent his army into East Pakistan to arrest Rahman and suppress the independence movement. His troops proceeded to wage a vicious campaign of intimidation and engaged in a wholesale slaughter of East Pakistan's civilian population. There followed yet another mass migration as 10 million refugees fled to India.

India's prime minister, Indira Gandhi, the daughter of Nehru, appealed to President Nixon to persuade Yahya Khan to end the slaughter and agree to negotiations. But Nixon and his security adviser, Henry Kissinger, were more concerned at this time with preserving the friendship of Yahya Khan, who was a crucial go-between in their campaign to establish better relations with China (see pp. 449–450). Ignored by Nixon, Indira Gandhi turned to Moscow and in August 1971 she concluded a Treaty of Peace, Friendship, and Cooperation with the Soviet Union, which Kissinger described in his memoirs as a "bombshell."

Mrs. Gandhi refrained from taking action of her own in East Pakistan, held off by fear of Chinese intervention and by the advice of her generals that any Indian action be delayed until November, when the weather in the Himalayas would make Chinese intervention more difficult. Mrs. Gandhi followed this advice, so it was not until November 22, 1971, that she ordered Indian troops into East Pakistan, thereby setting off another undeclared war with the Pakistan state. With a far larger army and superior military equipment, India scored a quick victory, and on December 15, after vowing to fight to the last man, the commander of the Pakistani troops in East Pakistan surrendered with his entire army. Mujibar Rahman, released from prison, returned home to become prime minister of an independent East Pakistan, which took the name of the Peoples' Republic of Bangladesh.

Henry Kissinger has called the India–Pakistan crisis of 1971 "perhaps the most complex issue of Nixon's first term," and he takes pride in having kept that conflict localized and preventing the total destruction of Pakistan, "our only channel to China." He fails to mention, however, that the entire crisis might have been avoided had Nixon persuaded Yahya Khan to seek a peaceful accommodation with East Pakistan and end the horrors perpetrated by his troops.

❑ *India and Pakistan Become Nuclear Powers*

The relations between India and Pakistan were to assume critical international significance toward the end of the century. In May 1998 both India and Pakistan conducted nuclear tests demonstrating to the world that both were now nuclear powers. In April of the following year both states revealed that they also had ballistic missile delivery systems. Both refused to sign the international Comprehensive Test-ban Treaty. Fighting continues over Kashmir, where the Pakistan government persists in its efforts to liberate that province from Indian "occupation."

❑

TWENTY-EIGHT

North Africa and the Middle East: From World War II to the Suez Crisis

The revolutionary movements and great power rivalries that had kept East Asia in turmoil after World War II were to contribute to similar turmoil in North Africa and the Middle East. After World War I, as we have seen, Britain and France had cavalierly disregarded their wartime promises to the Arabs to grant them independence and had divided the Arab provinces of the former Ottoman empire into spheres of influence between themselves. In the postwar decades Britain had found it necessary to promise Egypt, Iraq, and Transjordan independence in one form or another, but on terms that left Britain a large measure of control.

The era of World War II seemed to offer the Arabs a golden opportunity to overthrow the last vestiges of European imperialism. The anti-Semitic government of Nazi Germany appeared to be a natural ally of the Arabs in quashing the aspirations of the Jews in Palestine and ousting the British and French altogether from North Africa and the Middle East. But even after the defeat of France and the victories of Rommel in North Africa, the Arabs failed to align themselves in a united front on the side of Germany, much though they might sympathize with Nazi policies. For Arab leaders, justifiably fearful about substituting German-Italian for Anglo-French overlordship, played a cautious game, hoping to extract maximum concessions from both sides. More importantly, the British retained enough military clout in the Middle East to crush whatever pro-Axis movements the Germans had been able to foster. In May 1941 the British crushed a pro-Axis government that had taken power in Iraq. In June British and Free French forces invaded Syria and Lebanon, ousting the French administrations that had remained loyal to the French Vichy government and quashing any possibility of a German takeover. In August the British and Russians imposed joint control over Iran to ensure their access to Iranian oil. And in January 1942 the British compelled Egypt's King Farouk to dismiss a ministry suspected of pro-German sympathies and to appoint a government professing loyalty to Britain.

The danger that the Arabs would align themselves with Nazi Germany receded rapidly after the German offensives in Russia and North Africa had been turned back in 1942. But the final defeat of the Germans did not open the way to the restoration of British and French control in either North Africa or the Middle East. Bled white by two world wars, Britain and France no longer possessed the resources to deal effectively with Arab independence movements, which had been growing steadily in strength and influence since the dissolution of the Ottoman empire. After World War II they could no longer be contained.

❑ *The End of the French Empire in the Middle East and North Africa*

The French tried desperately to hold on. Their attempt to reassert their authority in Syria and Lebanon was mercifully brief. After World War II, disregarding earlier promises of his Free French government to grant both states their independence, the passionately patriotic General de Gaulle had used French troops stationed in the Levant in a futile attempt to reestablish French control. But the French campaign of repression failed, and under intense international pressure de Gaulle at last agreed to honor French commitments to recognize the independence of Syria and Lebanon. The last French troops left Syria by April 15, Lebanon by August 31, 1946.

The agonizing French struggle to retain their empire in Indochina (Vietnam, Cambodia, and Laos) is discussed in chapter 33. Here it is only necessary to note that that struggle ended with the defeat of the French and their ouster from Indochina in 1954.

The success of the Indochinese revolution undoubtedly encouraged the uprising that began that same year in Algeria, which the French had annexed in 1848 and made an integral part of metropolitan France. In 1954 the unrest that had long been simmering in Algeria broke out into open rebellion. In their effort to retain control of Algeria, the French waged an all-out and particularly savage eight-year war. It was de Gaulle who finally recognized that the war in Algeria could not be won and who possessed the requisite courage and prestige to end it. He crushed a revolt of French generals who refused to concede defeat and undertook a reorganization of the French government, which finally recognized Algeria's independence on July 1, 1962. The French had long since given up their efforts to retain control over Morocco and Tunisia, whose independence they had recognized in 1956.

❑ *The British and Egypt*

Egypt had been a cornerstone of British interests in the Middle East since the opening in 1869 of the Suez Canal, which quickly became the principal route to British India and the markets of East Asia. In 1875 the Disraeli government purchased controlling shares in the canal from the impoverished Khedive of Egypt, and in 1882, to quell an Egyptian nationalist threat to British control of the canal, British troops occupied Egypt and established de facto British control over the entire country. In 1936, after the Italian conquest of Ethiopia and the emerging Italian threat to British interests in North Africa, the British transformed their relationship with Egypt into a twenty-year treaty of alliance, which called for the withdrawal of all British troops from Egypt proper but allowed the British to retain their naval base at Alexandria and the right to keep a 10,000-man force in the Suez Canal zone.

During World War II a British army once again took control of Egypt, which became Britain's foremost military and naval base in the Mediterranean. Under British prodding, the Egyptian government broke off diplomatic relations with Germany, the country was placed under martial law, and all officials suspected of seeking accommodation with the Germans were dismissed, jailed, or executed. After the war, however, nationalist agitation was resumed with with ever-increasing ferocity. In 1954 the British yielded to Egyptian nationalist pressure and agreed not only to withdraw their troops from Egypt proper but from the Suez Canal zone. A final blow to Britain's position in Egypt was delivered in 1956, when the Egyptian government nationalized the Suez Canal. (See pp. 406–408.)

❑ *The Palestine Problem*

In their mandate of Palestine, the British were obliged from the beginning to cope with the consequences of the contradictory Balfour Declaration, which promised the Jews a national homeland in Palestine while stipulating that nothing should be done to prejudice the civil and religious rights of existing non-Jewish communities. The British tried, but their various proposals for solving the Palestine question through partition or through representative institutions were rejected by the Palestinian, the Jews, or both. (For the background of the Palestine question, the Balfour Declaration, and Zionism, see pp. 15-17, 93-95.)

The violent confrontations between Arabs and Jews, which had begun well before the inauguration of the British mandate, increased in violence and intensity with the rapid increase of Jewish immigration into Palestine resulting from Hitler's persecution of the Jews in Germany. The British had attempted to calm the fears of the Arabs and control the violence by limiting Jewish immigration. But, as the Nazi armies overran Europe and the Nazi persecution developed into outright extermination, the Jews became desperate about being granted a safe haven in Palestine. A Zionist conference meeting in the Biltmore Hotel in New York in May 1942 urged that the gates of Palestine be opened, that the Jewish Agency (responsible for coordinating with the mandatory power in establishing a national home for the Jews in Palestine) be vested with control of immigration, and that Palestine be established as a Jewish Commonwealth integrated into the structure of the new democratic world.

The British were caught in a cruel dilemma. With their own survival at stake in their war against the Germans, the plight of the Jews had to be weighed against the danger of propelling the Arabs to the side of Germany and jeopardizing British access to Arabian oil. Jews for the most part appear to have recognized this problem. If the British lost the war, the last hope of the Jews, too, would be lost. But after the United States entered the war and the Germans were halted in Russia and North Africa, Zionist militants in Palestine, appalled by the Allies' failure to take more effective action on behalf of the Jews in Nazi-occupied Europe, saw no further reason for restraint. They formed underground armies, raided British arsenals for weapons, and resorted to assassination and sabotage to force Britain's hand on the immigration issue. With the end of the war, Zionist militants stepped up their campaign of terrorism. On

July 22, 1946, they blew up the King David Hotel in Jerusalem, where most British administrators were housed, killing 91 people.

❑ *The End of the British Mandate*

The British tried in vain to negotiate, but their various proposals for a compromise settlement were either rejected outright by both Arabs and Jews or met with demands for revision that would make them unacceptable to one side or the other. By 1947 the British government resolved to give up the struggle. Ernest Bevin, the British foreign secretary, announced this decision to the House of Commons on February 18. The British government, he said, was

> faced with an irreconcilable conflict of principles. There are in Palestine about 1,200,000 Arabs and 600,000 Jews. For the Jews the essential point of principle is the creation of a sovereign Jewish state. For the Arabs, the essential point of principle is to resist to the last the establishment of Jewish sovereignty in any part of Palestine. The discussions of the last month have quite clearly shown that there is no prospect of resolving this conflict by any settlement negotiated between the parties. . . . We have, therefore, reached the conclusion that the only course now open to us is to submit the problem to the judgment of the United Nations. . . . We do not intend ourselves to recommend any particular solution.

To the surprise of no one, the United Nations was no more successful than the British in providing a formula for a Palestine settlement or even a platform for Arab–Jewish negotiation. With the failure of their own negotiation efforts, UN officials predicted that as soon as the British left Palestine "large-scale fighting between the two communities can be expected." In fact, large-scale fighting had been going on for some time, but as the British withdrew the fighting increased in scale and intensity.

❑ *The Arab–Israeli Conflict and the Establishment of the State of Israel, May 14, 1948*

In the struggle between Arabs and Jews it seemed probable that the Arabs, with their numerical superiority and the support of their Arab neighbors, would win. The Arabs, however, despite all their rhetoric about Arab solidarity, were bitterly divided among themselves, their armed forces were poorly trained, poorly armed, and poorly led, and the various Arab armies operating in Palestine failed to coordinate their strategies. In March 1945 the governments of Egypt, Iraq, Lebanon, Saudi Arabia, Syria, Transjordan, and Yemen joined together to form an Arab League. The League charter, however, lacked any provision for collective security or mutual defense, and the league itself proved to be a cockpit rather than a coordinating committee.

In marked contrast to the Arabs, the Jews, despite their own deep political and ideological differences, had a clear sense of purpose as well as daring and resourceful leadership. Their soldiers were well-trained, with educational skills that enabled them

MAP 15   THE ARAB–ISRAELI CONFLICT (SEE ALSO MAP 10)

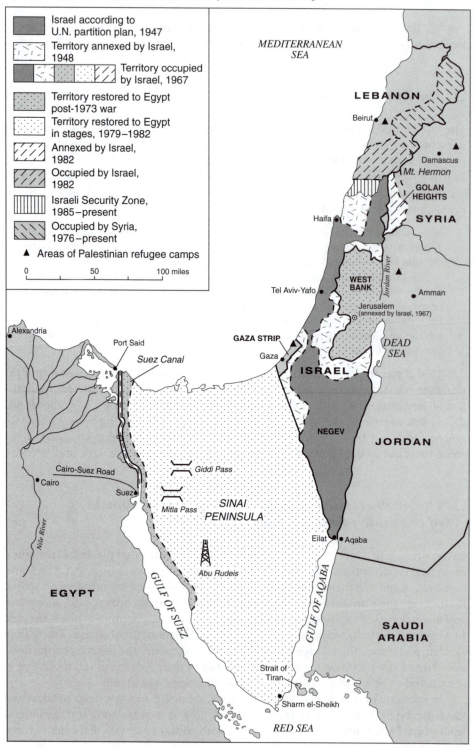

Legend:

- Israel according to U.N. partition plan, 1947
- Territory annexed by Israel, 1948
- Territory occupied by Israel, 1967
- Territory restored to Egypt post-1973 war
- Territory restored to Egypt in stages, 1979–1982
- Annexed by Israel, 1982
- Occupied by Israel, 1982
- Israeli Security Zone, 1985–present
- Occupied by Syria, 1976–present
- ▲ Areas of Palestinian refugee camps

0 — 50 — 100 miles

MEDITERRANEAN SEA

LEBANON

Beirut ▲

Damascus ▲

Mt. Hermon

GOLAN HEIGHTS

SYRIA

Haifa

WEST BANK

Jordan River

Amman ●

Tel Aviv-Yafo

Jerusalem ◎
(annexed by Israel, 1967)

GAZA STRIP ▲

Gaza

ISRAEL

DEAD SEA

NEGEV

JORDAN

Alexandria ●

Port Said ●

Suez Canal

Cairo-Suez Road

Cairo ●

Suez ●

Giddi Pass

Mitla Pass

SINAI PENINSULA

Abu Rudeis

Nile River

EGYPT

GULF OF SUEZ

Eilat ● Aqaba

GULF OF AQABA

SAUDI ARABIA

Strait of Tiran

Sharm el-Sheikh ●

RED SEA

to make the best use of modern weaponry. The Jews had another inestimable advantage: the moral, political, and material support of the world's Jewish communities and from sympathizers throughout much of the Western world, appalled by the tragic fate of the European Jews during the Nazi era. The Jews also had unexpected support from the Soviet Union, which saw the Palestinian conflict as an opportunity to insert Soviet influence in the Middle East and arranged to supply the Jews with modern weaponry from Czechoslovakia.

On May 14, 1948, one day before the deadline the British themselves had set, the British government announced the end of the British mandate in Palestine. On that same day the Jewish leadership proclaimed the establishment of the State of Israel, which was immediately accorded official recognition by both the United States and the Soviet Union.

❑ *The Arab–Israeli War of 1948–1949*

On May 15, 1948, the governments of Egypt, Iraq, Syria, Lebanon, and Transjordan, whose troops had long since been involved in the conflict in Palestine, declared war on Israel "to put an end to massacres and establish respect for the laws of universal morality and the principles recognized by the United Nations." This official declaration of war did nothing to improve the showing of the Arab armies on the battlefield. A disillusioned Palestinian summed up the reasons for their ineffectiveness.

> In the face of the enemy the Arabs were not a state, but petty states; groups, not a nation; each fearing and anxiously watching the other and intriguing against it. What concerned them most and guided their policy was not to win the war and save Palestine from the enemy, but what would happen after the struggle, who would be predominant in Palestine, or annex it to themselves, and how they could achieve their own ambitions.

The Israelis took full advantage of Arab disunity to concentrate their forces against individual Arab armies, defeat them one by one, and then conclude armistice agreements with individual Arab governments. Egypt, the first Arab state to give up the struggle, signed an armistice agreement with Israel early in 1949, and over the next several months the other Arab governments at war with Israel followed the Egyptian example.

The territorial boundaries established by the 1949 Arab–Israeli armistice agreements have been correctly described as fronts rather than frontiers. A de facto state of war continued as both sides engaged in raids and counterraids over the newly created borders. Arabs for the most part continued to deny Israel's very right to exist and vowed to drive the Israelis into the sea. But the Israelis, too, were dissatisfied with their postwar boundaries. Zionist militants aspired to control not only the entire area of Britain's Palestine mandate but a vaguely defined Greater Palestine, which they claimed had been bequeathed to them by God.

❑ *Transjordan Becomes Jordan*

Among the Arab states, the only winner in the 1948–1949 war was Transjordan, which in the course of that war had occupied a broad swathe of territory west of the Jordan River (subsequently known as the West Bank) plus the eastern sector of Jerusalem. On June 2, 1949, the Transjordan government formally announced its annexation of the West Bank, and on that same day it proclaimed that Transjordan would henceforth be called the Hashimite Kingdom of Jordan (Hashim being the name of the Jordanian royal house.)

By annexing the West Bank, Jordan dealt a mortal blow to the Arab contention that Palestine should remain a united state governed by its Palestinian Arab majority population. Emir (now King) Abdullah of Jordan was denounced as a traitor to the Palestinian cause, and two years after his annexation of the West Bank he was assassinated by one of his new Palestinian subjects.

❑ *The Fate of the Palestinian Arabs*

The major victims of the Arab–Israeli war were the Palestinian Arabs. Well before the official Arab declaration of war, an estimated 300,000 Palestinians had fled their homes to escape the advancing Israeli armies. By the end of the war another 600,000 had become refugees, most of them living under deplorable material and moral conditions in refugee camps maintained by the United Nations in the countries of their Arab neighbors.

The Palestinian refugees did not meet with a warm welcome from their fellow Arabs, who feared the threat posed by this large body of immigrants to the economic and political stability of their own countries. But the refugees themselves for the most part did not seek assimilation in other Arab societies, for to do so would have been tantamount to accepting the permanent loss of their Palestine homeland. They chose instead to remain in refugee camps, confident that this situation was temporary and that they would soon be able to reclaim their heritage in Palestine.

The flight of the Palestinians ensured that Israel could become a Zionist state dominated by a Jewish majority at the expense of the approximately 100,000 Arabs who remained. When the war ended, the Israeli government refused to permit the return of the Arab refugees, whose lands they confiscated and made available for purchase by Jews.

❑ *Egypt from the 1948–1949 War to the Suez Crisis*

Egypt's humiliating defeat in the war with Israel stoked the fires of patriotic anger against Britain, which was seen as having played a decisive role in the Israeli victory. Egyptian rage was intensified when Britain announced its intention to promote the independence of the Sudan, which had been under joint Anglo-Egyptian control since January 1899 and which the Egyptians claimed as an integral part of Egypt. In October 1951 Egypt unilaterally abrogated the 1899 treaty with Britain, which had established the Anglo-Egyptian condominium over the Sudan, and at the same time it renounced its 1936 alliance with Britain, which had allowed Britain to maintain an army in the Suez Canal zone.

On July 23, 1952, the army, long a fountainhead of Egyptian nationalism, overthrew King Farouk, who was denounced as a puppet of the British, and conferred dictatorial powers on the nominal leader of the coup, General Muhammad Naguib. The real power behind the coup, however, was another army officer, Colonel Gamal Abdel Nasser, who ousted Naguib in April of 1954. Two years later, under the terms of a new constitution, Nasser was elected president of Egypt.

Nasser had meanwhile gained enormous prestige by negotiating a treaty with Britain of October 19, 1954, providing for the withdrawal of British troops from the Suez Canal zone, which would henceforth be defended exclusively by Egyptian forces. The British, however, were to be allowed to return "in the event of an armed attack by a power outside the Middle East"—by which only the Soviet Union could have been meant.

To retain some measure of Western influence over the Egyptian government, the Eisenhower administration arranged to provide Egypt with loans that, it was hoped, would preserve Egyptian political as well as economic ties with the West. Eisenhower's request for funds for Egypt, however, met with fierce opposition in Congress, which was angered by Nasser's recognition of the government of Communist China, and from supporters of Israel, who contended that Nasser would use American aid to purchase arms for another war against Israel.

Denied aid from the United States, Nasser turned to the Soviet Union, confident that the Soviets would welcome the opportunity to extend their influence in the Middle East. He was not disappointed. On September 27, 1955, he announced that his government had concluded an agreement with the Communist bloc that would provide Egypt with Czech arms in return for Egyptian rice and cotton.

In securing Soviet aid against Israel and the West, Nasser thrust his country into the vortex of the Cold War. But the problems of the Middle East had in any case long since transcended the Arab–Israeli conflict, and the Suez Canal crisis of October 1956, which set off the next Arab–Israeli war, can only be understood in the context of the Cold War rivalries of the great powers and their Middle East clients. These problems are discussed in the next chapter.

TWENTY-NINE

□

Waging the Cold War: From the Korean War to the Cuban Missile Crisis

❏ *Leadership Changes*

In the final stages of the Korean war, significant changes in leadership had taken place in the governments of the world's superpowers. In America, the presidential elections of November 1952 resulted in a victory for the Republican candidate, Dwight D. Eisenhower, who succeeded Harry Truman as president of the United States on January 20, 1953.

An even more significant change took place in the Soviet Union, where Stalin died on March 5, 1953, a bare six weeks after Eisenhower's inauguration. The succession in the Soviet Union was considerably more complicated than in the United States because there was no machinery in place to deal with the problem. Stalin's death was followed by a succession struggle among the henchmen who had survived the grim dictator's political purges. That struggle was eventually won by Nikita Khrushchev, who maneuvered his way to the top, as Stalin had done, through his control of the machinery of the Communist party organization.

❏ *The Eisenhower-Dulles Foreign Policy*

After leaving the White House, Harry Truman remained convinced that the policy of containment, which he had adopted as the guiding principle of his foreign policy, was not only a sound but a winning strategy. He predicted that the slave world of Communism, despite its great resources, could not survive in competition with the free world. As Soviet hopes for easy expansion were blocked, "then there will have to come a time of change in the Soviet world. Nobody can say for sure when that is going to be, or exactly how it will come about, whether by revolution, or trouble in the satellite states, or by a change inside the Kremlin." But Truman, expressing a deep and abiding faith in the destiny of free men, had no doubt that the change would come: "With patience and courage, we shall one day move on into a new era."

The Republicans did not share this optimistic view. In their victorious presidential election campaign in the summer and autumn of 1952, they accused Truman and the entire Democratic party of having been soft on Communism, of having sold out American interests at Yalta and Potsdam, of allowing the Soviet Union to take over Eastern Europe, of losing China to the Communists. Their party platform condemned "the negative, futile, and immoral policy of 'containment' which abandons countless human beings to . . . despotism and godless terrorism," and called for a repudiation of all commitments such as those made at Yalta that had opened the way to Communist enslavements.

The most prominent Republican spokesman on foreign policy, John Foster Dulles, Eisenhower's future secretary of state, joined in the condemnation of containment, which he denounced as "a policy which is bound to fail because a purely defensive policy never wins against an aggressive policy." To replace the stagnation of containment, Dulles advocated a policy of boldness to seize the initiative from the Communists, roll back the Iron Curtain, liberate the captive peoples of Eastern Europe, and make known publicly that the United States "wants and expects liberation to occur." To back up a bold foreign policy, Dulles called for a bolder military strategy: the United States must "develop the will and organize the means to retaliate instantly against aggression by Red Armies, so that, if it occurred anywhere, we could and would strike back where it hurts, by means of our own choosing." These means, Dulles made clear, would include the use of nuclear weapons, and to make the nuclear threat more credible the Eisenhower administration engaged in a massive buildup of America's nuclear weaponry and delivery systems.

Eisenhower had condoned his party's rhetoric in the heat of an election campaign, and his critics feared that the new president, seemingly inexperienced in the field of foreign affairs, would allow himself to be guided by the forceful and strident Dulles. Apart from a brief stint as president of Columbia University, Eisenhower had spent his entire professional career in the army. He had been commander-in-chief of the Allied armies in Europe during World War II, and more recently he had served as supreme commander of the armed forces of the newly formed NATO alliance. It was therefore generally expected that he would be heavily dependent on the advice of politicians versed in the ways of Washington and on experts in all fields not directly related to the military, including foreign policy.

Eisenhower himself contributed to the impression that he would be a hands-off president. With his broad grin and genial manner, he cultivated the image of a benign solder-hero who stood above the sordid world of partisan politics, seemingly happy to delegate authority to members of his cabinet and professional administrators. Often incoherent in his public policy pronouncements, he was seen by many as out of his element in the White House, more at home on the golf course than at the desk in the Oval Office. The very ordinariness of his manner, which gave him the appearance of a simple man of the people, contributed to his immense personal popularity and served to deflect criticism of his administration to his advisers.

The real Eisenhower was very different, as his associates and perceptive observers had always realized. As supreme commander in Europe, he had demonstrated outstanding ability in dealing with the bitter rivalries among the various Allied commanders, a talent that served him well as president in coping with comparable rivalries within and between political parties and government agencies. He was similarly adept in delegating authority. But, while ostensibly giving his subordinates a large measure of independence in formulating and conducting policy, he kept a tight control over all aspects of his administration. Far from being easygoing and benign, he was a hard worker, quick to grasp the essentials of complicated problems, with a fierce and intimidating temper. Like Truman, he was also a jealous guardian of presidential authority. Richard Nixon, who served as his vice-president for eight years, realized early on that Eisenhower was "a far more devious and complex man than most people realized."

In the field of foreign policy, Eisenhower had a far sounder sense of the realities and complexities of international affairs than was evident from the simplistic slogans put forward by the Republican party. He was to acknowledge later that a major reason he consented to run for the presidency had been to save the party from falling into the hands of isolationists or doctrinaire anti-Communists. John Foster Dulles, who as secretary of state was generally regarded as the real author of Eisenhower's foreign policy, was on the contrary scrupulously careful to consult with the president on every issue and to defer to him over all policy decisions.

But Dulles, too, was far more cautious and pragmatic than his contemporaries were led to believe by his public pronouncements. He brought impressive family and personal credentials to the position of secretary of state. A grandfather and uncle has preceded him in that office, and Dulles himself, although a lawyer by profession, had been active in foreign affairs throughout his life, most recently as Truman's special representative in negotiating America's peace treaty with Japan. As the official documents of his service as secretary of state have become available, scholars have recognized that Dulles was not an inflexible Cold Warrior, that he hoped to settle differences with the Soviet Union through negotiation, and that he saw a nuclear war as an incalculable disaster.

The public perception of Dulles, however, was inevitably shaped by his rhetoric, and all too often he did in fact emerge as a doctrinaire ideologue who challenged the world to choose between America's crusade on behalf of moral righteousness or submitting to godless Communism. His skill and expertise were offset by an arrogant assumption of moral superiority, which was frequently even more exasperating to his allies than to his adversaries. Winston Churchill is supposed to have remarked that Dulles was "the only case I know of a bull who carried his own china shop with him."

Throughout his years in the White House, Eisenhower never publicly repudiated the inflammatory rhetoric of his secretary of state or the Republican party, and his administration took some pride in claiming that it had provided American foreign policy with a "new look." But in retrospect we can see that Eisenhower and Dulles actually adhered closely to Truman's strategy of containment and that their actual policies differed from those of the Truman administration chiefly in being even more cautious and restrained.

Very early into the Eisenhower presidency it became evident that the rhetoric about liberating the peoples of Eastern Europe was in fact only rhetoric. In mid-June 1953, when Soviet tanks moved in to smash anti-government demonstrations in East Berlin, his administration did not even undertake some kind of diplomatic intervention. His government remained similarly quiescent when revolts broke out in other parts of Eastern Europe, notably during the major uprising against Communist rule in Hungary in October 1956. (See pp. 404–406.) Cynics concluded that the Republican call to roll back the Iron Curtain had been nothing more than a ploy to lure American voters of Eastern European descent away from the Democratic party. Perhaps that is all that it was, or perhaps Dulles believed that that nuclear threat alone would be sufficient to ensure the triumph of anti-Communist causes. If this was indeed his belief, he proved to be disastrously mistaken. For the nuclear threat did nothing to deter the brutal Soviet suppression of popular uprisings in Eastern Europe, and it signally failed to prevent the defeat of the French in Vietnam. The nuclear threat was simply not credible in situations where the military use of nuclear weapons would have been ineffective, as in Vietnam, or where their use was likely to unleash World War III, as in Europe. Moreover, realistic statesmen were aware that nuclear weapons were likely to be as dangerous to their users as to enemy.

The Eisenhower-Dulles adherence to the policies of the Truman administration was most evident in Western Europe, where they continued America's support for maximum political, economic, and military integration. Dulles's most significant contribution to European integration was his sensitive management of relations with the politically vulnerable government of West Germany and the West German chancellor, Konrad Adenauer, whose personal confidence in Dulles did much to ensure that West Germany remained solidly in the Western camp.

Elsewhere, Eisenhower and Dulles continued a de facto policy of containment. They extended America's anti-Communist alliances in Asia with the formation of the Southeast Asia Treaty Organization (SEATO). In the Middle East they concluded a bilateral security treaty with Pakistan and encouraged the formation of treaties between Britain and the countries of the Middle East that became known as the Bagdad Pact. In seeking to prevent the spread of Communism, Eisenhower again resembled Truman in being as much concerned with economic as with political and strategic considerations. "The minimum requirement," he told Dulles, "is that we are able to trade freely, in spite of anything Russia may do, with those areas from which we obtain the raw materials that are vital to our economy."

The one significant change in the Eisenhower-Dulles foreign policy strategy was their greater use of the Central Intelligence Agency for carrying out covert operations to overthrow or undermine foreign governments believed to be a threat to American interests. While Eisenhower was in office, the CIA assisted in ousting anti-American governments in Iran and Guatemala, it trained the troops of anti-Communist governments in South Vietnam and Laos, and it organized an expeditionary force of Cuban refugees who were to invade Cuba to overthrow the Communist government of Fidel Castro.

❑ *The Post-Stalin Succession: Nikita Khrushchev*

The initial victor in the succession struggle following the death of Stalin on March 5, 1953, was Georgi Malenkov, already widely regarded as Stalin's heir apparent, who took over the top positions in both the Communist party and the Soviet state. Only nine days after Stalin's death, however, Malenkov was forced by his rivals to give up the chairmanship of the party, a position occupied in September by Nikita Khrushchev, a newly appointed member of the party secretariat. Over the next five years, Khrushchev managed to survive frequent bouts of political infighting, and in March 1958 he took over the chairmanship of the Council of Ministers, the top position in the Soviet state, while retaining his position as party chairman. Unlike Stalin, Khrushchev did not acquire or hold these positions by liquidating his political rivals or by the use of systematic terror to snuff out any hint of opposition. Instead, he relied on his political skill and on his success in conducting his country's domestic and foreign affairs. In the field of foreign policy, this quest for success was to involve him in frequent and dangerous political gambles.

Nikita Khrushchev was born in 1894 in the Kursk province near the Ukrainian border. The son of a coal miner, he himself had worked in the pits for a brief period. He was thus a genuine member of the proletariat, unlike so many Soviet leaders. As he told a visiting British dignitary with some pride, he had attended "the working man's Cambridge."

Endowed with immense physical energy, quick intelligence, retentive memory, and keen political instincts, Khrushchev had risen rapidly in the ranks of the Communist party, which he joined in 1918. In 1934 he was elected to the party's Central Committee and in the following year he was appointed party chief in Moscow, just as Stalin began his savage purges of the Soviet political and military leadership. Khrushchev probably owed his own survival to his appointment in 1938 as chairman of the Ukrainian Communist party with headquarters in Kiev, a position that removed him from the deadly world of political intrigue in Moscow and provided him scope to develop his talents as an administrator. Recalled in 1949 to his former post as party chief in Moscow, he was in a strategic position to take part in the power struggle that took place after Stalin's death.

As is evident from his voluminous and fascinating memoirs, dictated after his fall from power in 1964, Khrushchev's service under Stalin and his personal association with the brutality of the Stalinist regime had not made him a cynic or shaken his faith in the Communist political system. To the end of his life he remained a dedicated Marxist, convinced that he was assisting in a glorious, albeit frequently painful and harsh, transformation of his country into the most just and equitable society yet seen on earth.

❑ *Post-Stalin Soviet Foreign Policy*

From the time they took over, the new Soviet leaders expressed their desire to relieve the international tensions that had built up during the Stalin era. As early as March 16, 1953, only eleven days after Stalin's death, Prime Minister Malenkov announced his government's intention to conduct a more conciliatory foreign policy and to engage in negotiations to settle all outstanding differences with foreign countries. "At present there is no litigious or unsolved question which could not be settled by peaceful means on the basis of mutual agreement among the countries involved. This concerns our relations with all states, including the United States." In August in a speech before the Supreme Soviet, Malenkov reiterated his belief that all international problems could be resolved through negotiation. The Soviet government stood "as we have stood in the past, for peaceful co-existence between the two [Communist and capitalist] systems."

And indeed, the new Soviet leaders went to impressive lengths to reduce international tensions. They supported American efforts to arrange a negotiated settlement in Korea. They moved to repair relations with Communist Yugoslavia, abandoned Soviet territorial claims on Turkey, restored the port of Porkkala (strategically located at the entrance to the Gulf of Finland) to Finland, established formal diplomatic relations with the pro-Western government of Greece, and reestablished diplomatic relations with Israel. To strengthen their ties with Communist China, they promised to provide China with further technical and economic assistance and to give up advantages they had secured after World War II, including relinquishing Soviet control over the naval base of Port Arthur and dissolving the joint stock companies that gave them a foothold in the economy of the border province of Sinkiang.

The purpose of these conciliatory gestures was not entirely altruistic. For, as Malenkov frankly informed the Supreme Soviet, they were also calculated to reduce foreign fears and suspicions of the Soviet Union that had provided the United States with its most formidable diplomatic weaponry in building up its anti-Soviet alliances. What the Soviets feared most was the rearmament of West Germany, and in stressing their desire for peaceful coexistence, they hoped to convince Western leaders that their fears of the Soviet Union were unwarranted and that the rearmament of Germany was therefore as unnecessary as it was undesirable.

A parallel Soviet stratagem in dealing with the German danger was to pay court to the West Germans themselves, dangling before them the lure of German reunification, which would only be achieved with the consent of Moscow, and offering them the prospect of lucrative commercial opportunities in Eastern Europe. This tactic was designed not only to wean the West Germans from the West, but to sow suspicions in the West about West Germany's political reliability.

The prime objective of the Soviet German policy, however, was a final peace treaty with Germany that would guarantee the permanent disarmament and neutralization of that country. In pursuit of that objective, Malenkov reverted to a proposal put forward by Stalin a year before his death: a four-power peace treaty with Germany providing for the eventual reunification of Germany and the withdrawal of all occupation forces within one year, but with the inclusion of a German pledge not to enter into any kind of alliance directed against any state which had fought against Germany in World War II.

What the Soviets were offering, in effect, was the relinquishment of Soviet control over East Germany in return for the neutralization of Germany as a whole. Truman and Acheson, however, had fundamental objections to the creation of a united, independent, and neutralized Germany. The underlying purpose of their German policy was the integration of Germany into an international structure which would keep Germany firmly under international control and supervision. An independent Germany, on the other hand, would be free to maneuver between East and West, as it had done so often in the past. But there were other fundamental objections to the Stalin proposal. Even if it were accepted as a basis for a German settlement, negotiations were bound to founder over a definition of German neutrality. Finally, a neutral Germany would be at the mercy of the Soviet Union, for with the withdrawal Western troops there would be nothing to deter Moscow from exploiting an incident to send the Red Army into Germany, West as well as East.

In reviving the Stalin proposal, Malenkov had hoped that differences among the Western allies over the question of German rearmament would generate support for a treaty guaranteeing Germany's permanent neutralization and disarmament. Instead, he was faced with a Western demand for free elections in both East and West Germany to an all-German parliament, because only a government representing all the German people would have legitimate authority to conclude a peace treaty. Because the Soviets found this demand unacceptable, the stalemate over the German question continued.

❑ *The Peace Treaty with Austria, May 15, 1955*

On April 15, 1955, Nikita Khrushchev, the victor in the post-Stalin succession crisis, proposed a four-power peace treaty with Austria, whereby the Soviet Union would withdraw its occupation forces, renounce its claims to the Austrian oil fields, and restore to Austria control over the Danube Shipping Company. In return, Austria was to pay 150 million dollars in reparations and pledge to remain neutral in perpetuity. In making this offer, there can be little doubt that Khrushchev's primary purpose was his expectation that a treaty ensuring the permanent neutrality of Austria would serve as a model for a similar treaty over Germany, and that the Germans, too, would be persuaded of the advantages of nonalignment.

Because the status of Austria was far less critical to their overall European policies than Germany, the Western powers responded positively to the Khrushchev proposal. By May 12 they had reached agreement with the Austrians on the terms of a treaty based on that proposal, and three days later a final peace treaty with Austria, the so-called *Staatsvertrag,* was signed by the foreign ministers of Austria and the four occupation powers: Britain, France, the Soviet Union, and the United States.

❑ *The Continuing Stalemate over Germany*

As Khrushchev evidently hoped, the signature of a peace treaty with Austria in May 1955 opened the way to an agreement with Western leaders to attend a summit conference in Geneva in July—the first meeting of Big Four heads of state since Potsdam ten years earlier—to deal with the far more complicated German question and other matters of mutual concern.

But nothing was settled at Geneva. As in the past, the Soviets rejected the Western demand that a peace treaty with Germany be concluded with the government of a reunified Germany chosen by free all-German elections, because, as Khrushchev candidly admitted later, the East Germans had not yet had time "to be educated to the great advantage of Communism." Free all-German elections would have meant the liquidation of socialism in East Germany and the creation of a single capitalist country integrated with NATO. Instead, the Soviets wanted a peace treaty confirming the existence of both German states and guaranteeing "that each state would be allowed to develop as its own people saw fit."

❑ *Khrushchev's Renewed Call for Peaceful Coexistence and His Denunciation of Stalin*

In his General Report to the Soviet Communist party at its 20th Congress on February 14, 1956, Khrushchev once again emphasized his government's intention to pursue a conciliatory foreign policy. The Soviet Union was now sufficiently powerful to make peaceful coexistence the basis of its foreign policy, confident that the socialist system would eventually triumph through peaceful competition. Reactionary capitalist forces might yet try to unleash war, but war should no longer be regarded as fatalistically inevitable.

At this same party congress, Khrushchev acknowledged the validity of Tito's claim that there were many roads to socialism, as was evident from the example not only of Yugoslavia but of the People's Democracies of Eastern Europe and China. The Soviet Union should endeavor to strengthen the bonds of friendship among all members of the socialist camp, but it should also extend its hand to the "peace-loving" countries of the Third World and indeed to every other country in the world, in particular the United States and its allies. Throughout, the fundamental objective of Soviet foreign policy should be to eliminate the "breeding grounds" of war, prevent the development of new sources of conflict, and explore new ways of dealing with such issues as European security, disarmament, and the German question.

For a party membership still imbued with Stalinist ideological principles, these were revolutionary pronouncements, but Khrushchev delayed delivering his truly revolutionary manifesto until February 25, the final day of the congress. Citing extensive research by Soviet officials in government records, Khrushchev launched into an uncompromising denunciation of the Stalin regime, describing at length and in minute detail his reign of terror and repression, his elimination of loyal members of the Communist party, and his crimes against the Soviet people. Far from being an infallible and beneficent genius, as he was portrayed in his own carefully cultivated personality cult, Stalin was in reality a pathological mass murderer who had liquidated the best cadres of the party in his great purges and violated every principle of socialist legality by obtaining false confessions through psychological and physical torture and odious falsifications of evidence. During World War II, he was anything but the all-knowing strategist to whom the Soviet people owed their victory over Germany. Instead, he had ignored all warnings of the impending German attack and pursued near-fatal military strategies. In the course of the war he had been guilty of monstrous violations of Soviet basic principles with regard to nationality policy, and had deported entire ethnic populations—the Karachai, the Chechen and Ingush, the Balkars and the Kabardinos—to the outer reaches of the Soviet land mass.

Although Khrushchev professed to be surprised and appalled by the discovery of Stalin's crimes, there can be no doubt that he and other Soviet leaders—and a host of lesser party and government functionaries—were familiar with much of the Stalinist record. But Khrushchev's stark revelation of that record nonetheless came as a shock to most of his listeners. To many members of foreign Communist parties it was devastating, undermining their faith in the Soviet leadership and the entire Communist system.

☐ The Repercussions of Destalinization in Eastern Europe: Poland

In June 1956 Tito paid a "fraternal" visit to the Soviet Union, at whose close a communiqué was issued reaffirming Moscow's willingness to allow other Communist governments to pursue an independent course of "national" Communism.

The consequences of this new tolerance were quick in coming. Only a week after Tito left Moscow, strikes and street fighting broke out in the Polish city of Poznan to protest rises in food prices, setting off developments that led to important changes in the Polish government. In mid-October the Central Committee of the Polish Communist party sought to calm public agitation by inviting Wladyslaw Gomulka to rejoin the committee. Out of favor since 1947 for opposing the collectivization of Polish agriculture and jailed from 1951 to 1956, Gomulka had become the leading representative of Polish national Communism. Gomulka posed stiff conditions. He demanded to be conceded the leadership of the Central Committee, that pro-Soviet hard-liners be expelled, and that the Soviet general, Marshal Konstantin Rokossovsky, be dismissed as Poland's defense minister. At its meeting on October 19 the Central Committee agreed to Gomulka's terms. Two days later he was installed as the party's first secretary, Rokossovsky was dismissed, and the Central Committee issued a proclamation that Poland would henceforth pursue "a national road to socialism."

Meanwhile Soviet troops had moved toward the Polish frontier, and Khrushchev and the entire top echelon of Soviet leaders flew to Warsaw. Gomulka handled the situation adroitly. He assured the Soviet leaders of his government's desire, indeed its need, to preserve the friendship of Moscow. "Without the Soviet Union we cannot maintain our borders with the West. We are dealing with our internal problems, but our relations with the Soviet Union will remain unchanged." Convinced that Gomulka's assurances were sincere, Khrushchev told the Polish leader that the Soviet troop movements were merely routine maneuvers. "Nobody believed this false explanation," Khrushchev confessed in his memoirs, "but everyone was pleased that an explanation had been given."

There followed a relaxation of Soviet control over Poland, but Poland itself remained firmly in the Soviet political orbit.

☐ The October 1956 Revolution in Hungary

Events took a very different turn in Hungary, where a Stalinist-style government attempted to quash demonstrations of sympathy for the Gomulka regime in Poland. On

October 23, two days after Gomulka's return to power, a crowd of 200,000 took part in demonstrations in Budapest calling for far more extensive concessions than the nationalists had been conceded in Poland. They demanded the dismissal and trial of Mátyás Rákosi, the Stalinist chairman of the Hungarian Communist party, together with other members of his puppet government; the withdrawal of Soviet troops from Hungary; and the recall of Imre Nagy, a Communist nationalist, as head of the Hungarian government. Unlike the demonstrations in Poland, those in Hungary spun out of control. The crowds burned Soviet flags, overturned statues of Stalin, set fire to Soviet tanks, and occupied public buildings. On October 24 Nagy was installed as prime minister.

Soviet authorities decided to settle for a Polish solution to the Hungarian problem. But the Hungarians were not prepared to settle for the concessions made to Poland, nor did Nagy show the same sense of reality as Gomulka. Swept along by nationalist fervor, he formed a multiparty government, demanded the immediate withdrawal of all Soviet troops, announced that Hungary was pulling out of the Warsaw Pact, and appealed for support from the United Nations.

As was widely assumed at the time and as we now know from Hungarian records, Nagy and his supporters had been encouraged to take these revolutionary measures by America's liberation rhetoric, in particular by a Dulles speech in Dallas on October 27 declaring that any Eastern European country that broke with Moscow could count on American support. Nor would this support be dependent on that country's adoption of a democratic form of government; it would be sufficient if it followed the Tito model and left the Warsaw Pact. Four days later, Eisenhower admitted in a radio address that, much as the United States might hope for an end to the Soviet domination of Eastern Europe, "we could not, *of course,* carry out this policy by resort to force" (emphasis added). Dulles himself, however, was surely aware that the United States could not support a revolution in Eastern Europe without using force and that his government had no intention of providing such support. His speech of October 27 was therefore cruelly irresponsible.

On November 4 a quarter-million-man Soviet army equipped with 5,000 tanks swept into Hungary and suppressed the Hungarian revolution. As Soviet troops went about their bloody business of repression, some 200,000 Hungarians, almost two percent of the entire population, fled to the West via Austria. Nagy and members of his government took refuge in the Yugoslav embassy. Upon being promised amnesty, they left the building and were promptly arrested and taken to Romania, where they were held incommunicado for two years. In the spring of 1958 they were returned to Budapest, secretly tried, and hanged.

Khrushchev insists in his memoirs that he was certain at the time that they were dealing with a counterrevolution in Hungary and that the Soviet-sponsored government, not the Nagy regime, had the support of a majority of the population. Because Hungary had no effective army, "our army took upon itself the function of maintaining order" and to serve "as a covering force against Austria [!] to halt the use of this counterrevolution by hostile forces against socialist Hungary."

The Eisenhower administration was spared the full brunt of the public condemnation of its Eastern European policy by the outbreak of a crisis over the Suez Canal, which diverted public attention from the tragic events in Eastern Europe and developed into a more serious threat to the Atlantic alliance than any diplomatic offensive mounted by the Soviet Union.

❑ *The Suez Canal Crisis*

In September 1955 the nationalistic Egyptian prime minister, Colonel Gamel Abdel Nasser, denied the loans he had been led to expect from Britain and the United States, concluded an agreement with the Communist bloc that would provide Egypt with Czech arms in return for Egyptian rice and cotton. (See p. 395.) In some alarm, British and American agents hastened to counter this potential incursion of Communist influence in Egypt. In cooperation with the World Bank, they worked out an arrangement to finance a 1.3-billion-dollar project to build a dam at Aswan, on the Upper Nile, to harness the waters of the Nile for hydroelectric power and irrigation purposes. By February 1956 the World Bank had concluded its financial negotiations with Nasser, who now sought Washington's confirmation of the agreement.

Five months later he was still waiting for an answer because Secretary of State Dulles was having trouble selling the dam project in Washington. Southern congressmen objected to financing a dam that would enable the Egyptians to produce more cotton, and pro-Israel politicians objected to any project that would strengthen Egypt, especially after Egypt refused to repudiate the Czech arms deal and concluded military alliances with Saudi Arabia, Syria and Yemen. Dulles himself finally abandoned the dam project after Nasser severed relations with the Nationalist regime of Chiang Kai-shek and recognized the government of Communist China.

On July 19, just as the Egyptian foreign minister was arriving in Washington to complete arrangements over the Aswan dam, Dulles announced that the United States was withdrawing its support from the project. Confident that the Soviets lacked both the capital and technical expertise to supplant Western sponsors of the dam, he calculated that the withdrawal of American support would deal Nasser a disastrous political blow and provide Washington with the leverage to compel him to sever his connections with the Communist bloc and the enemies of Israel.

Dulles's appraisal of the situation could not have been more mistaken. On July 26, 1956, Nasser, in an impassioned appeal to Arab nationalist sentiment, announced Egypt's nationalization of the Suez Canal Company. "Citizens, this is a battle against imperialism and against Israel, the vanguard of imperialism. Arab nationalism marches forward, knows its own road and own strength, knows who are its enemies and friends." At this very moment, Nasser said, Egyptian forces were taking over the canal "which is situated on Egyptian territory, which is . . . part of Egypt and owned by Egypt."

The country most immediately affected by Nasser's nationalization of the Suez Canal was Britain. Britain owned a controlling interest in the Suez Canal Company, approximately one-quarter of Britain's imports came through the canal, and one-third of the ships passing through the canal were British. By the mid–twentieth century, however, the status of the canal had become a vital concern not only to Britain but to the entire industrialized world, because the canal was a principal route for the transport of Middle East oil, which was essential to the operation of every industrial economy.

The British government, under the leadership of Anthony Eden since Churchill's retirement in April of 1955, was determined to compel Nasser to restore the canal to international control. On this issue Britain had the full support of the French, who believed that Nasser was a prime supporter of the Algerian revolution against French rule and saw his seizure of the canal as an opportunity to topple his government. To prepare the way for doing so, they concerted with the British to send Nasser an ultimatum to restore the canal to international control: acceptance would deliver a fatal blow to his prestige; rejection would justify the use of force to overthrow him. Both London and Paris were confident that the military action for the latter purpose would amount to little more than a parade drill.

Eisenhower and Dulles, while sympathizing with Britain and France over the canal issue, proclaimed their opposition to the use of force, fearing that an attack on Egypt would revive the specter of European imperialism and unite the peoples of the Third World against the West. Dulles proposed instead a conference of the principal maritime nations to devise a system of international control over the operation of the canal. To the obvious relief of Britain and France, this proposal was rejected by Nasser on September 10. They could now go ahead with plans to take military action.

There remained the difficulty of getting around Washington's opposition to the use of force and the even greater danger that the Arab oil-producing countries would cut off their oil shipments to Europe in the event of an Anglo-French attack on Egypt. To disguise their real intentions, they worked out a script in conjunction with the Israelis, whose ships had been denied use of the canal, contrary to international law. The plan was that Israel would attack Egypt and advance toward the Suez Canal; Egypt would be certain to counter this attack by sending its own troops into the canal zone; Britain and France would then send an ultimatum to both belligerents to withdraw their troops from the zone; Israel would comply, and when Egypt failed to do so Britain and France would send their own troops into the zone with the ostensible purpose of separating the belligerents and protecting the canal.

This transparent scheme was set in motion on October 29, 1956, by an Israeli offensive into the Sinai Peninsula. The next day Britain and France delivered their ultimata. As arranged, the Israelis accepted. As expected, Nasser refused, whereupon British and French planes began bombing Egyptian military targets. It was not until November 6, however, after a succession of hopelessly bungled operations, that British and French forces actually landed in Egypt. By that time the Eisenhower government, which had seen through the Anglo-French collusion with Israel, had taken decisive steps to end their Egyptian operation.

On October 30 the United States submitted a resolution to the Security Council of the United Nations demanding that Israeli forces withdraw immediately behind an established armistice line, and in a radio address the following day Eisenhower condemned Anglo-French military intervention: "For we do not accept the use of force as a wise and proper instrument for the settlement of international disputes." Under intense American economic as well as diplomatic pressure, Britain and France agreed to withdraw their troops from North Africa upon the arrival of a United Nations peacekeeping force, which was to occupy a neutral buffer zone along the armistice line between Israel and Egypt. The UN peacekeepers remained in Egypt until May 1967, when they were withdrawn in response to a Nasser demand for their removal. (See p. 506.)

The Suez affair was a godsend to the Soviet Union. It muted international indignation over the suppression of the revolution in Hungary and augmented Soviet prestige in the Middle East. In seeking to divert attention from Hungary, the Soviet Union had threatened nuclear war if the Western powers did not withdraw from Egypt, and the Arab countries, ignoring the role of the United States, chose to credit the Soviets for frustrating this latest demonstration of Western imperialism.

The position of the Western powers was correspondingly weakened. The Suez debacle destroyed what was left of Anglo-French prestige in the Middle East, and it came close to destroying the Atlantic alliance. Anthony Eden, his career ruined by Suez, resigned as British prime minister on January 9, 1957. His successor was Harold Macmillan, the chancellor of the exchequer, who swallowed his indignation over America's role in the crisis on behalf of maintaining Britain's "special relationship" with the United States and securing a badly needed loan from the International Monetary Fund, which the United States had blocked as part of its campaign of economic pressure. America's uncompromising treatment of its allies had more serious repercussions in France, whose leaders drew the conclusion from the Suez experience that they could not rely on the United States. France would therefore have to build up its own military power and strengthen its diplomatic ties with its European neighbors so as to enable France, and Europe as a whole, to pursue an independent course.

Having ousted the British and French from their historic role in the Middle East, the United States found itself obliged to assume primary responsibility for defending Western interests in that region. Early in the new year, following Eisenhower's reelection in the previous November, Dulles asked Congress to approve a declaration of America's intention to defend the entire Middle East against Communist aggression and to agree to the use of American troops for this purpose (so much for the Eisenhower administration's opposition to the use of force). This declaration, approved by the Senate on March 5 and subsequently known as the Eisenhower Doctrine—every president now seemed to require a doctrine bearing his name—was an obvious effort to deter any effort on the part of the Soviet Union or its clients to exploit the cleavages in the Western alliance exposed by Suez, and represented yet another link in the chain of security commitments the Eisenhower administration had assumed since taking office.

❑ Europe's Move toward Greater Independence; Euratom and the Common Market

The European statesman who made the first move to make Europe more independent of the United States was the leader of a country not directly involved in the Suez crisis. On November 6, 1956, one day after the United Nations ordered the withdrawal of British and French troops from Egypt, the West German chancellor, Konrad Adenauer, put it to the French that the only way the states of Europe could still play an effective role in world affairs was to unite. For that purpose he proposed that West Germany and France work together on behalf of greater Western European political as well as economic integration. He did not think that England was as yet ripe for so bold a program, but he believed that France would be receptive to the idea. A united Europe independent of the United States would be France's revenge for Suez.

Adenauer was right about Britain. In late March 1957 Prime Minister Macmillan and his foreign secretary, Selwyn Lloyd, met with Eisenhower and Dulles in Bermuda to heal wounds in Anglo-American relations resulting from Suez. Britain was clearly opting to stand with the United States rather than draw closer to Europe.

In continental Europe, however, Adenauer's proposal of November 6 bore fruit. On March 25, the day after the Anglo-American meetings in Bermuda, the members of the European Coal and Steel Community—France, West Germany, Italy, and the Benelux countries (Belgium, Luxembourg, and the Netherlands)—signed the so-called Treaties of Rome establishing two new supranational agencies: the European Atomic Energy Agency (Euratom) and the European Economic Community (EEC), better known as the Common Market.

The Common Market treaty, which went into effect on January 1, 1958, marked the beginning of a new era of European integration. Its purpose was to make Western Europe a single free-trade area to allow for the free movement of goods, capital, and labor within a territory comparable in size to the United States. The treaty established a schedule for the elimination of tariffs over the next twelve to fifteen years, and it provided for the creation of a supranational governing board, headquartered in Brussels, that would soon have a civil service of several thousand members. As conceived by their signatories, the Rome Treaties were to prepare the way for closer European political as well as economic integration.

As Adenauer had expected, Britain declined to join the Common Market for fear of jeopardizing its special relationship with the United States and to maintain its profitable preferential trade arrangements with the countries of the British Commonwealth. France, on the other hand, took an increasingly independent stand vis-à-vis the United States, especially after de Gaulle's return to power, first as prime minister in May 1958, then as president of a newly formed Fifth French Republic in December.

❑ ICBMs and Sputnik

Less than a year after the Hungarian and Suez crises, the international prestige of the Soviet Union and of Khrushchev personally were powerfully reinforced by two dramatic technological breakthroughs. In August 1957 Soviet technicians developed the world's first intercontinental ballistic missile (ICBM), an achievement followed two months later by the launching of the world's first artificial satellite, a 184-pound spheroid named Sputnik (fellow traveler). A jubilant Khrushchev assured a Danish journalist that the global balance of power had shifted in favor of the socialist countries, and he predicted that, having achieved technical and military superiority, they would soon outstrip the capitalist countries in industrial production as well. In China, Mao

Tse-tung hailed the Soviet achievement in more poetic terms: "The East Wind was prevailing over the West Wind."

In the United States, where official as well as public opinion had always assumed America's scientific and technological superiority, news of the ICBM and Sputnik was received with stunned disbelief and provoked a reaction bordering on panic. Over the next year, Congress created the National Aeronautic and Space Administration (NASA) to coordinate America's own space program, and passed a National Defense Education Act, a crash program to revivify America's educational establishment with emphasis on the sciences, mathematics, and foreign languages.

Khrushchev's initial use of his country's newly won prestige was an attempt to restore the solidarity among the world's Communist parties and secure a reaffirmation of their recognition of Soviet leadership. His efforts were successful, or so it seemed. During the celebrations of the fortieth anniversary of the Bolshevik Revolution in November 1957, Mao Tse-tung made a special point of recognizing the Soviet Union as leader of the socialist camp. At the close of those celebrations, the representatives of the Communist-bloc countries signed a communiqué calling for unity in opposing capitalism and imperialism abroad and for the elimination of deviationist elements within the Communist movement itself.

This same communiqué included an endorsement of Khrushchev's policy of peaceful coexistence, which was described as "the sound basis for the foreign policy of the socialist countries and the dependable pillar of peace and friendship among peoples." This declaration appears to have been yet another effort to reassure the peoples of Western Europe that the Soviet Union was no longer a threat and that they could afford to loosen their ties with the United States.

In March 1958 Khrushchev assumed the post of head of the Soviet state in addition to his chairmanship of the Soviet Communist party, but political rivalries continued to seethe within the ranks of the state and party leadership and during the summer of that year there was a rapid deterioration in the Soviet Union's relationship with China. (See p. 444.) In November, faced with mounting domestic as well as foreign policy problems, Khrushchev made a new bid to settle the German problem.

❏ Khrushchev's Berlin Ultimatum, November 1958

The status of West Berlin had long been a dangerous embarrassment to the Soviet Union and its client state of East Germany. (See p. 326.) Every year thousands of East Germans, including a large number of highly trained professionals sorely needed by the East German economy, were escaping to the West through West Berlin, an exodus that posed a threat not only to the East German economy but to the very viability of the East German state. West Germany and the United States had poured billions of dollars into West Berlin, making it a showcase of capitalist prosperity, a striking contrast to the drab dreariness of East Berlin and all the countries of the Soviet bloc. Similarly striking was the contrast between the atmosphere of freedom in West Berlin compared with the fear and repression prevalent in the East. Quite apart from these considerations, the very existence of West Berlin was a menace to the Soviet bloc. Situated in the heart of the East German state, it was a haven for Western espionage and for the dissemination of Western propaganda via radio and television.

On November 27, 1958, Khrushchev issued the equivalent of an ultimatum to the Western occupation powers. He called for negotiations to end the four-power occupation of Berlin and the withdrawal of all occupation forces so as to make Berlin a demilitarized free city. If agreement over Berlin were not reached within six months, the Soviet Union would conclude a peace treaty with East Germany that would end the Soviet occupation and transfer Soviet occupation rights, including control over access routes to West Berlin, to the East German government. If the West resorted to violence, the Soviet government would regard an attack on East Germany as an attack on itself and "modern technology" would ensure that the flames of war would spread to North America.

As was evident from the text of his ultimatum, Khrushchev intended negotiations over Berlin to lead to what had long been a fundamental objective of Moscow's German policy: the neutralization of West Germany. "The best way to solve the Berlin question," he said, " . . . would be the withdrawal of the Federal German Republic from NATO, with the simultaneous withdrawal of the German Democratic Republic from the Warsaw Treaty Organization. . . . Neither of the two German states would have armed forces in excess of those needed to maintain law and order at home and to guard their frontier."

Khrushchev had ample reason to believe that the West would agree to negotiate over Berlin. Eisenhower, who had ruled out fighting a ground war in Europe, was unlikely to risk a nuclear war over Berlin. The West European states were even less likely to do so. Moreover, there were clear indications that many Europeans remained dubious about the desirability of an armed West Germany, especially if that armament included nuclear weapons.

Khrushchev, however, had overestimated the differences among the Western powers and underestimated the importance they attached to Berlin. At a meeting of their foreign ministers in December, they coordinated a reply unanimously rejecting his November ultimatum. "Since the agreements [over Berlin] can only be terminated by mutual consent, the government[s] of [the United States, Britain, and France] will continue to hold the Soviet government directly responsible for the discharge of its obligations undertaken with respect to Berlin under existing agreements."

Khrushchev backed down. In the course of a visit by Prime Minister Macmillan to Moscow in February 1959, he reasserted his demands over Berlin in uncompromising fashion. But he then conceded that his six-month deadline need not be taken literally and agreed to refer the problem to the foreign ministers of the Big Four.

The foreign ministers' negotiations over Berlin that took place in the spring and summer of 1959 all ended in deadlock, as had all previous meetings. But meanwhile an important change had taken place in the government of the United States. On April 15, 1959, John Foster Dulles, mortally ill with cancer, resigned as secretary of state (he died on May 24) and was succeeded by Christian Herter, undersecretary of state since 1957 and acting secretary during Dulles' final illness. Eisenhower now assumed a more visible role in foreign policy with the apparent objective of easing international tensions on every front. He damped down his government's Cold War rhetoric, paid goodwill tours to Europe and Latin America, and even as the foreign ministers' negotiations over Berlin collapsed, he announced that he and Khrushchev had agreed to an exchange of visits.

Khrushchev seemed eager to improve relations with the United States. During his visit to America in September 1959 he promised Eisenhower that he would drop any suggestion of an ultimatum over Berlin, and he secured Eisenhower's agreement to attend a four-power summit meeting in Paris in the following spring. Khrushchev's policy prior to the Paris summit is puzzling, however. He himself had suggested the meeting, he had dropped his Berlin ultimatum, and he had given every indication that he intended to use the meeting to settle differences with the United States. Yet a bare three weeks before the Paris summit, he renewed his threats over Berlin and his demand for a general peace settlement with Germany, warning that any Western attempt to maintain their position in Berlin by force would be matched by Soviet force.

Then on May 5, eleven days prior to the summit, Khrushchev announced triumphantly that an American U-2 spy plane had been shot down over the Soviet Union. After the conference in Paris convened, he refused to be satisfied with Eisenhower's promise that there would be no more flights of this kind, he withdrew his invitation to Eisenhower to visit the Soviet Union, and stalked out of the conference. At the time, Khrushchev's anger over the U-2 flights seemed understandable, but we have since learned that the Soviets had known about these flights from the time they first began in the summer of 1956.

Krushchev's behavior is especially puzzling when one considers that just over a month later, at the third Congress of the Romanian Communist party, Khrushchev defended his policy of peaceful coexistence, fully aware that in doing so he was risking a final break with Mao. The Chinese delegation at the congress decried the futility of that policy, pointing to the U-2 incident as evidence of the evil nature of the capitalist system and the inevitability—indeed the desirability—of a final military showdown with the capitalist world. Khrushchev had been alarmed for some time by the bellicose pronouncements emanating from Peking. Earlier, he had reneged on his promise to aid the Chinese in the development of their nuclear program, declaring publicly that they could not be trusted with nuclear weapons. He now abruptly recalled the 1,390 Soviet technicians and military advisers who had been working in China and who took with them their plans and blueprints.

Meanwhile, Khrushchev did nothing to reestablish good relations with the West. He kept the Berlin question on the boil by sanctioning a new set of petty restrictions on travel to East Berlin. In September, while attending a meeting of the United Nations in New York, he ostentatiously courted the representatives of the newly independent states of Asia and Africa and made a spectacle of himself by banging his shoe on the table during a speech by Harold Macmillan at the General Assembly. He went out of his way to annoy the Americans by his courtship of Fidel Castro. He embraced the Cuban leader, wildly applauded his address to the UN, and visited him at his hotel in Harlem, where Castro had chosen to stay to demonstrate his solidarity with the Third World.

During the summer and autumn of 1960, however, the attention of American leaders was focused on the presidential election campaign to select a successor to Eisenhower, who was barred by a constitutional amendment from seeking a third term. In the elections of November 8, the Democratic candidate, Senator John F. Kennedy of Massachusetts, won a narrow victory over Richard Nixon, Eisenhower's vice-president during the past eight years.

❑ *The Kennedy Succession*

The Kennedy administration took office with even more rhetorical fanfare than the Republicans had employed eight years earlier. "Let every nation know, whether it wishes us well or ill," Kennedy said in his inaugural address, "that we will pay any price, bear any burden, meet any hardship, support any friend, oppose any foe, in order to assure the survival and success of liberty. This much we pledge—and more." This was stirring but dangerous rhetoric, for it made commitments that went beyond those of than any previous administration, without regard to America's ability—or willingness—to assume them.

The new president was handsome, articulate, and endowed with an exuberant vitality which he communicated to all who worked with him. He brought into the government men like himself—young, brash, arrogant, supremely self-confident, but short on experience as well as modesty. Adlai Stevenson, defeated twice by Eisenhower in his own bid for the presidency, referred to them scornfully as the boy commandos. "The torch has passed to a new generation," Kennedy declared proudly, a generation "tempered by war" and "disciplined by a hard and bitter peace." Despite all his talk about representing a new generation, however, Kennedy's view of the Cold War was remarkably similar to that of Dulles. He too saw it in terms of a spiritual dichotomy, "a struggle for supremacy between two conflicting ideologies: freedom under God vs. ruthless, godless tyranny."

Unlike Eisenhower, who had appeared to delegate a large measure of authority to his subordinates, Kennedy never left any doubt that he intended to be a hands-on president, especially in the field of foreign policy. In conferring with an aide about the appointment of a secretary of state, he rejected several obvious possibilities. Finally the aide was driven to ask: "Do you want a secretary of state or an *under* secretary?" Kennedy laughed: "Well, I guess I really want an under secretary." His choice fell on Dean Rusk, a Rhodes scholar, currently head of the Rockefeller Foundation, with extensive experience in dealing with foreign affairs as a former member of the State Department but without a political base or any strong political allies of his own.

During the 1960 presidential election campaign, Kennedy had accused the Republicans of allowing a missile gap to develop between the United States and the Soviet Union. The missile gap, however, proved to be a myth, a product of Khrushchev's bluffing and Soviet propaganda. As Eisenhower knew from U-2 flights over the Soviet Union, and as Kennedy learned after he became president, it was the Soviet Union, not the United States, which suffered from a missile gap.

Kennedy was on firmer ground in criticizing Eisenhower's excessive reliance on nuclear weapons, which tied the country's hands when dealing with limited wars or minor crises. To be able to deal with a wide variety of crisis situations without threatening and thereby risking nuclear war, the Kennedy administration adopted a strategy of flexible response, which involved a buildup of the country's conventional forces.

"We must be in a position to confront [a crisis] at any level with an appropriate military response," he said. But Kennedy wanted more than a military buildup. He wanted to restore American leadership in science, technology, and indeed in every other field. America must be first again, "not first *if,* not first *but,* not first *when,* but first *period.*"

❏ *The Vienna Summit, June 1961*

Although it was Khrushchev who had broken up the Paris summit in the previous May, he had let it be known at the time that he still believed such a meeting would be desirable, perhaps in six or eight months—that is, when Eisenhower would be out of office and a new president installed.

Eisenhower had never expected much from a summit meeting unless the basis for a settlement of the major issues on the agenda had been worked out beforehand. Kennedy, on the other hand, was confident that a meeting of heads of state could be an effective forum for the resolution of international problems. On February 22 he sent a message to Khrushchev suggesting such a meeting in late spring, either in Vienna or Stockholm.

The Soviet leader did not reply officially until May 12. Soviet sources have not revealed why Khrushchev took so long to reply, but his decision to agree to a meeting in Vienna was certainly influenced by a humiliating fiasco Kennedy had suffered some five weeks earlier: the defeat of an army of Cuban emigres at Cuba's Bay of Pigs—a botched CIA plan to topple Castro, which Kennedy had inherited from the Eisenhower administration. (See p. 420.) Khrushchev may have believed that the brash and inexperienced young president, humbled by the Cuban disaster, would be vulnerable to pressure.

At their summit meeting in Vienna on June 3 and 4, 1961, Khrushchev certainly behaved as though he thought Kennedy could be bullied. He renewed his ultimatum over Berlin with its six-month time limit, he demanded America's acceptance of Soviet conditions for banning nuclear testing, and he demanded the transformation of the office of the UN secretary general into a committee of three, which would allow for greater Soviet influence. To Khrushchev's evident surprise, Kennedy refused to be browbeaten, but otherwise the new president's first personal venture in summit diplomacy was a failure, for nothing at all was settled at Vienna. On taking leave of Khrushchev, Kennedy observed that it was going to be a long winter.

❏ *The Berlin Wall, August 1961*

In the months that followed the Vienna meeting, Khrushchev kept up the pressure. In July he announced a suspension in reductions of the Soviet armed forces and an increase in military spending. In August the Soviet government broke a three-year Soviet-American moratorium on nuclear testing and resumed testing in the atmosphere. Carried out over the next two months, these tests culminated in the explosion of a bomb estimated to have been 20,000 times more powerful than the bombs exploded over Hiroshima and Nagasaki, the most potent weapon yet tested by any country.

The Western powers were not intimidated by the Soviet military buildup, nor did they allow their own numerous differences to break up their united front on the German question. On July 17 they refused once again to yield to Khrushchev's ultimatum over Berlin. Kennedy reaffirmed America's commitment to defend West Berlin, and to match and overtrump the Soviet military buildup he asked Congress for a 3.4-billion-dollar increase in America's military budget, a doubling of draft call-ups, and authority to call up military reservists.

Confronted with this latest rejection of his Berlin ultimatum, Khrushchev did not wait for his six-month time limit to expire. To end the hemorrhage of the East German population through West Berlin, he authorized the construction of a wall between East and West Berlin and a barrier along the entire border between East and West Germany. Begun before dawn on August 13, 1961, the wall when completed was a high barrier of concrete blocks topped by barbed wire. Strung out along its entire length were watch towers guarded by sentries with orders to shoot to kill anyone who tried to cross it. The wall, which Khrushchev described as a "border control," served its purpose of stopping the flow of East German refugees. Khrushchev may have been right in claiming that the wall saved the East German state, but it also contributed to the ultimate collapse of that state. For it was nothing less than a gigantic billboard advertising the failure of the Communist system and a grim symbol of the oppressive nature of the Communist regime.

With the building of the Berlin Wall, however, Khrushchev withdrew his ultimatum over Germany and called for the negotiation of another nuclear test ban agreement. Further, he proposed the creation of nuclear-free zones "in the first place in Europe *and in the Far East*" (emphasis added.) Khrushchev was playing for high stakes. What he evidently hoped to achieve was America's agreement to a nuclear-free Germany in return for Soviet cooperation in preventing China's acquisition of nuclear weapons. This was a trade-off the Americans might be expected to explore because a nuclear-free China was surely as much in America's as Russia's interest.

It was a dangerous gamble, for the proposal of a nuclear-free zone in Asia was certain to produce a dangerous escalation of Sino–Soviet hostility. And, indeed, the Chinese reacted as could have been expected. Already angered by Khrushchev's attacks on Stalin and on the Albanian Communist party, which they recognized as disguised attacks on themselves, the Chinese foreign minister, Chou En-lai, ostentatiously led the Chinese delegation out of the October 1961 Congress of the Soviet Communist Party and returned to Peking—but not before depositing a wreath at the tomb of Stalin.

While infuriating the Chinese, Khrushchev failed to secure America's agreement to a new test-ban treaty and to a nuclear-free Germany. He was embarrassed further by the Kennedy government's public announcement that America's missile gap had been a myth. Far from being inferior to the Soviet Union, the United States had a decisive missile superiority—"a second strike capability which is at least as extensive as what the Soviets can deliver by striking first."

It was to offset this American advantage—and secure additional leverage for his diplomatic initiatives—that Khrushchev decided to install Soviet missiles with nuclear warheads in Cuba, a decision that led to the most dangerous East–West confrontation of the Cold War: the Cuban Missile Crisis.

THIRTY

❑

The Cuban Missile Crisis

The Cuban Missile Crisis of October 1962 was a dramatic demonstration of how a small and relatively weak state can play a pivotal role in the international relations of the great powers.

The Castro revolution in Cuba, out of which the the missile crisis developed, was a demonstration of a different kind: the importance of the human factor in history—an importance which Castro in his Marxist mode might deny, but which he convincingly demonstrated in putting his personal stamp on his revolution and maintaining sole control over his government. Unlike most Latin American revolutions, which have amounted to little more than changes in leadership, the Castro revolution produced a radical transformation of Cuban society, the nationalization of the Cuban economy, and Cuba's emancipation from American political and economic domination.

❑ *Fidel Castro*

Whether for personal or political reasons, Castro has deliberately misled investigations into his family background and the development of his political ideas. On this last subject he has been particularly devious, but it hardly matters when he became a convinced Marxist-Leninist or that his interpretation of Marxist doctrine differed in many respects from the Moscow party line. The crucial point is that he made his version of Marxism central to his policies after his takeover of power.

Castro was born on August 13, 1926, in Cuba's Oriente province, the illegitimate son of Angel Castro y Argiz, a Galician Spaniard who migrated to Cuba as a penniless orphan at the age of thirteen and who, by dint of hard work and a good deal of luck, succeeded in becoming a wealthy landowner.

Unruly and resentful of parental authority, Fidel was shipped off to school in Santiago at the age of five and eventually went to a Jesuit school, where his energy and competitive spirit were successfully channeled into studies and sports. He completed his secondary education at Cuba's most prestigious Jesuit educational establishment, the Belén School in Havana, where he compiled an outstanding academic record while starring in the school's basketball, baseball, football, and track teams. These achievements were duly recorded in his graduation yearbook which predicted a brilliant future for him: "He has won the admiration and affection of us all."

Upon entering the law school of the University of Havana in 1945, Castro plunged into the raucous and violent world of politics, including participation in an unsuccessful revolution against the Trujillo dictatorship in the Dominican Republic. Awarded the degree of doctor of laws in September 1950, he founded a law firm in Havana, which concentrated on representing the interests of the poor. He made his first bid for political office in 1951, running for parliament as a candidate of the Cuban Peoples' Party, otherwise known as the Ortodoxos because it claimed to represent the ideological orthodoxy of the Cuban revolutionary hero José Martí. The platform of that party—"nationalism, anti-imperialism, socialism, economic independence, political liberty, and social justice"—very probably summed up Castro's own political views at that time.

An election was never held. On March 10, 1952, Fulgencio Batista, the strongman of the Cuban government since 1933, carried out a coup to forestall the possibility of a victory by the Ortodoxo presidential candidate and installed himself as chief of state and premier. The Batista coup has been called the most consequential event in Castro's life, for it ended any prospect of a political career through the electoral process and propelled him into the politics of revolution.

❑ The Castro Revolutions

On July 26, 1953, Castro made his first attempt to topple the Batista regime. At the head of a corps of just over a hundred volunteers, including his brother Raúl, he attacked the Moncada barracks in Santiago. His plan was to seize the arms stored there and distribute them to the people, confident that this action would set off a general uprising. But no general uprising took place. Castro's small band was quickly defeated, he himself was taken prisoner and narrowly escaped execution. Released through a general amnesty after less than two years, he fled to Mexico where he continued his revolutionary activity, joined by his brother Raúl and by a young Argentine medical doctor, Ernesto "Che" Guevara. Raúl and Che were already firm believers in the principles of Marxism-Leninism, but Fidel himself did not yet admit to ideological commitments.

On November 25, 1956, Fidel mounted his second armed attack on the Batista regime, an enterprise even more reckless and ill-conceived than the Moncada uprising. With a pathetically small invasion army of eighty-two men, which included Raúl and Che, he embarked from Mexico in a boat designed to hold no more than twenty-five, its timbers leaky, its engine unreliable. On December 2 his vessel ran aground before arriving at the point in Cuba where he had planned to meet up with a rebel force already on the island. He landed instead at a mangrove swamp, where his small band was surrounded by a Batista army and virtually wiped out. By some miracle, which reinforced Castro's belief in his destiny, he himself, Raúl, Che, and eight others escaped and eventually made their way into the Sierra Maestra mountains, where for twenty-three months they carried on a guerrilla war against the Batista regime.

Castro's small body of guerrillas probably would not have survived had it not been for the support of the Sierra Maestra peasants, who provided the food and shelter indispensable to a guerrilla army. Castro also received unexpected help from a *New York Times* journalist named Herbert Matthews, whose romantic description of the Castro guerrillas—"fighting hard and successfully in the rugged, almost impenetrable mountains of the Sierra Maestra"—captured the imagination of the Cuban people and brought Castro a good deal of popular support. But it was Castro himself who was largely responsible for his eventual success. It was his energy, unflagging confidence, and inspirational leadership that transformed the recruits who joined him in the mountains into an effective fighting force.

Meanwhile, Batista's own support was crumbling. His corrupt and repressive regime had alienated almost every segment of Cuban society, and his army too was in disarray, its morale sapped by futile campaigns against Castro's guerrillas and the army itself weakened by mass desertions. On the last day of the year 1958, Batista, realizing that his cause was doomed, resigned and fled to the Dominican Republic. Four days later Castro's troops entered Havana.

In marked contrast to his rash behavior as a revolutionary leader, Castro played a cautious political game. Instead of taking over the leadership of the government himself, he installed men who might be expected to enjoy widespread popular confidence and he put together a coalition cabinet made up of some of Cuba's most respected political figures. At the same time, however, he took care to retain control of the real source of political power in the country—namely, the army—and on January 6 he announced that the government he had set up would rule by decree for the next eighteen months, which meant that it would be a de facto dictatorship. On January 7, 1959, the new Cuban government was recognized by the United States. The Cuban shadow government did not last long, however. Unwilling to carry out the policies Castro demanded of them, the entire cabinet resigned in mid-February. Castro himself now took over the post of prime minister and therewith became the head of the government in name as well as in fact.

❑ *Castro and the United States*

In April 1959, two months after making himself prime minister, Castro paid an unofficial visit to Washington at the invitation of the Society of Newspaper Editors. From a public relations standpoint, his trip was a triumph. He avoided including anyone in his entourage who could be identified as a Communist and assured the Americans that his regime was not Communist but humanist, by which he presumably meant that it was primarily concerned with improving the quality of human life in Cuba. Eisenhower evaded a meeting with the Cuban leader by pleading ill health and going to Georgia to play golf, but Castro was received by Vice President Nixon and other government dignitaries and was enthusiastically greeted by audiences at his numerous public appearances. By seeming to have snubbed Castro, Eisenhower has been accused of having triggered, or at least reinforced, Castro's hostility to the United States.

Castro's hostility needed little reinforcement. He had long resented America's domination of the Cuban economy and its long-standing support of the Batista regime. On June 5, 1958, while still fighting in the mountains, he wrote to one of his most devoted supporters: "I have sworn that the Americans will pay very dearly for what they are doing. When this war is ended, a much bigger and greater war will start for me, a war I shall launch against them. I realize that this will be my true destiny."

During the April 1959 visit to America, Castro had obviously thought it worth his while to court American public opinion, but he avoided dealing with the American government and turned aside tentative offers of economic aid, which would leave him vulnerable to American influence. Vice President Nixon, although his meeting with Castro appears to have been friendly enough, came away from that meeting convinced that the new Cuban leader was profoundly hostile to the United States. He was certain that Castro was a Communist, or under Communist influence, and he addressed a memorandum to the State Department warning that the Castro government posed a significant threat to American interests.

A month later, Nixon's evaluation of Castro seemed confirmed when his government enacted an agrarian reform law providing for state expropriation of large landholdings, including over 1.5 million acres belonging to American sugar companies. Castro subsequently appointed his brother Raúl and other leading members of the Communist party to top positions in his government and used its highly disciplined party organization to implement his policies. But Castro, while making use of the Communist party apparatus, did not become their tool, and his associates soon learned that allegiance to the Maximum Leader, not to any political party or organization, was the touchstone for political survival.

Well before the end of the first year of his revolution, large numbers of Cubans began to flee from the island, fearful that economic expropriations would be followed by outright purges of opponents, or suspected opponents, of the Castro regime.

❑ *Castro and the Soviet Union*

Khrushchev records in his memoirs that when Castro came to power, the Soviet government knew virtually nothing about him. Cuba had never established diplomatic relations with the Soviet Union, and the information gap had not been filled by the Cuban Communist party. The Soviet leadership therefore had to rely completely on press and radio reports to find out what was happening.

It was not until well over a year after Castro came to power that Moscow established official contact with him. This was done in the course of a visit to Cuba by Deputy Premier Anastas Mikoyan, who on February 13, 1960, concluded the first of a series of trade treaties with Cuba guaranteeing the Soviet purchase of a large portion of the Cuban sugar crop and promising large-scale technical and economic assistance, including a 100-million-dollar loan. Even now the Kremlin leaders remained cautious. They promised to establish diplomatic relations with Cuba on terms of complete equality and independence, but they intended to wait for an "opportune moment" before doing so.

That opportune moment arrived with the downing of an American U-2 spy plane over Soviet territory on May 1, 1960, which had provoked Khrushchev to break up his summit meeting with Western leaders in Paris and cancel his invitation to Eisenhower to visit the Soviet Union. (See p. 412.) Seven days after the U-2 incident, the Soviet Union established formal diplomatic relations with Cuba.

Now assured of Soviet support, Castro stepped up the pace of government expropriations over the next four months, nationalizing all major business enterprises, the banks, and the bulk of American-owned property. "Castro was no longer sitting on the fence," Khrushchev recalled in his memoirs. "He was beginning to behave like a full-fledged Communist, even though he still didn't call himself one." The Americans retaliated in July by halting the import of Cuban sugar, and in October they placed an embargo on all exports to Cuba except food and medical supplies, actions which Castro denounced as American "economic aggression." On March 23, 1960, Castro repudiated the 1947 Rio Pact, which had enrolled the states of the Western Hemisphere in an American-sponsored defensive alliance, and appealed for Soviet military support.

Khrushchev made the most of this opportunity to extend Soviet influence into what had heretofore been an exclusively American sphere. Promising to purchase the sugar no longer sent to the United States, he denounced America's "perfidious and criminal" plots against the Cuban people and threatened to use Soviet rockets "should the aggressive forces in the Pentagon dare to intervene in Cuba." The Monroe Doctrine, he declared, had died a natural death. Khrushchev did more than threaten. He supplied Cuba with tanks, artillery, antiaircraft guns, and fighter planes, and he sent thousands of technicians and advisers to train Cuban troops in their use and maintenance. With some pride he observed that by the end of 1960, thanks to Soviet aid, Castro had a large and well-trained army equipped with the best of modern weaponry.

❏ *The Bay of Pigs Invasion*

On January 3, 1961, the United States severed diplomatic relations with Cuba, one of the last diplomatic actions of the Eisenhower administration, which bequeathed to the new American president, John F. Kennedy, a legacy of hostility to Castro and a secret CIA program to train Cuban exiles for an invasion of Cuba to overthrow the Castro regime.

The CIA's Cuban program was based on the assumption that only a small invasion force would be needed, because the moment the exiles landed on Cuban soil they would inspire a mass uprising against the Castro government. Under pressure from the CIA and fearful of political repercussions if his rejection of this Eisenhower anti-Communist initiative became known, Kennedy allowed the invasion plan to go forward. On April 17, 1961, the Cuban exile army, some 1,400 strong, landed at Cuba's Bay of Pigs. Although the operation was supposed to have been kept a secret, Castro's agents had kept him fully informed of the invasion preparations and had ample time to make defensive arrangements.

Kennedy has been blamed for refusing to authorize air strikes to take out Castro's air force, but there was no way that the CIA invasion plan, based on false premises and fatally flawed from the start, could have succeeded. Castro had a regular army of 25,000 well-trained and well-equipped troops, plus some 200,000 militiamen. Against so formidable an opponent the emigre invaders, even if they had been given all the support envisaged in the original CIA plan, never had a chance. They were quickly and decisively defeated; approximately 100 were killed, the rest taken prisoner. Kennedy's efforts to conceal America's involvement failed as miserably as the invasion itself, so that the Bay of Pigs disaster dealt a serious blow to the prestige of his fledgling administration.

❑ *The Soviet Decision to Install Missiles in Cuba*

In his memoirs Khrushchev states repeatedly that he was convinced the Americans would make another attempt to topple Castro, this time with a large and well-equipped American army. "They feared, as much as we hoped, that a Socialist Cuba might become a magnet that would attract other Latin American countries to Socialism." To defend Castro against the Americans, Khrushchev believed that a tangible and effective deterrent would have to be established, and for that purpose he came upon the idea of installing missiles with nuclear warheads in Cuba, whose installation was to be kept secret until it was too late for the Americans to do anything about them. Faced with the prospect of a nuclear strike against themselves, the Americans would think twice before launching an attack on Cuba.

Khrushchev has consistently maintained that his sole purpose in sending missiles to Cuba was to protect the island from an American invasion: "to prevent any encroachment on Cuban sovereignty and to assure the capability of the Cuban people to be masters of their own country." But he acknowledges in his memoirs that he had another purpose in view. "In addition to protecting Cuba," he says, "our missiles would have equalized what the West like to call 'the balance of power.'" There is reason to believe that Khrushchev intended the missiles to serve a wide range of other purposes. A nuclear strike force in Cuba would strengthen his hand in dealing with the Berlin question and the negotiation of a German peace treaty. It would serve as a bargaining counter to prevent the nuclear armament of West Germany, bolster Soviet prestige in turning back the Chinese challenge to Soviet leadership in the Communist world, strengthen Khrushchev's position in dealing with his domestic rivals. And, of course, it would project Soviet power into the Western Hemisphere.

❑ *The American Response*

American U-2 spy planes had meanwhile kept a close watch on shipments to Cuba from the Soviet bloc, but as of September 1962 they had found no evidence that these shipments included offensive weapons. "Were it to be otherwise," Kennedy warned on September 4, "the gravest issues would arise."

The "gravest issues" arose a little over a month later. On October 14 a U-2 plane flying over Cuba brought home the first evidence that missiles were being installed on the island. As Kennedy and his advisers realized, once those missiles were in place and operational they would be a mortal threat to American security. Missiles fired from Cuba would give America little more than a minute of warning time and would be capable of destroying all American nuclear installations and all American cities short of Seattle.

The most obvious and seemingly the only certain way of dealing with this threat was to take out the missiles before they became operational through an air strike, delivered without warning, followed up by an invasion of Cuba, which would take out both the missiles and the Castro regime. Listening to the advocates of these proposals, Attorney General Robert Kennedy passed a note to his brother, the president: "I now know how Tojo felt when he was planning Pearl Harbor." It was Robert Kennedy who argued most persuasively, and ultimately successfully, against an air strike. "For the United States to attack a small country without warning would irreparably hurt our reputation in the world—and our own conscience," he said.

Besides reputation and conscience, there was the problem that air strikes might not take out all the Soviet missiles, and that enough might remain to enable the Soviets to unleash a nuclear attack on the United States. Further, the Soviets would still be in a position to respond to an American attack on Cuba with an attack, nuclear or otherwise, on America's European allies. Any precipitate military move was therefore likely to set off a chain reaction that would engulf the greater part of the world in a nuclear holocaust.

After two days of deliberation, Kennedy and his advisers rejected the idea of air strikes and an invasion in favor of a naval blockade around Cuba, which left open the option of using other measures if these should prove necessary. A blockade would avoid the danger of what Kennedy called a "spasm reaction" on the part of the Soviets, and would give them time to calculate the risk to themselves if they failed to respond to American demands for the removal of their missiles from Cuba.

In a nationally televised address on the evening of October 22, the president informed the nation about the presence of Soviet missiles in Cuba and how his administration proposed to deal with the situation. He intended to impose a strict quarantine (a less provocative term than blockade) on all offensive military equipment under shipment to Cuba, and to summon emergency meetings of the Organization of American States (OAS) and the Security Council of the UN to support the American action. Finally, he called on Khrushchev "to halt and eliminate this clandestine, reckless, and provocative threat to world peace."

On October 23, having obtained OAS approval, Kennedy announced that the quarantine would go into effect on October 24 at 10:00 A.M. Late in the afternoon of October 24, Washington received reports that some of the Soviet ships sailing toward Cuba had altered course and that the rest had stopped dead in the water. The Americans greeted this news with relief, but they were uncertain what these moves implied: did the Soviets intend to respect the quarantine, or were they merely waiting for the arrival of submarines to escort their merchant vessels? Meanwhile, the Americans still faced the far more difficult question of how to deal with the weapons already sent to

Cuba, a problem that had been central to the deliberations of Kennedy and his advisers from the start.

❑ *The Resolution of the Crisis*

Khrushchev himself opened the way to a solution of this problem. He did so through an unusual but by no means untypical Soviet diplomatic ploy. On the afternoon of Friday, October 26, Alexander Fomin, known to be the head of the secret intelligence unit at the Soviet embassy in Washington (and the agent who "ran" Julius Rosenberg, later condemmed to death for spying for the Soviet Union), approached John Scali, the State Department correspondent of the American Broadcasing Company, with a proposal which Fomin declared had come directly from Khrushchev. Scali was to sound out his contacts at State as to whether Washington would be interested in resolving the crisis along the following lines: the Soviets would withdraw all offensive weapons from Cuba and permit UN supervision and verification of their removal; in return, the United States was to pledge publicly not to invade Cuba. That same evening Kennedy received a four-part cable from Khrushchev with the following proposal: if the United States would lift its blockade, promise not to attack Cuba, and restrain others from doing so, the Soviet Union would promise "that our ships bound for Cuba will not carry any kind of armaments."

The October 26 cable said nothing about the missiles already in Cuba, but the next day a second message arrived from Khrushchev expressing his willingness "to remove those weapons from Cuba which you regard as offensive," but with the condition that the United States agree to "evacuate its analogous weapons from Turkey." This trade-off had been proposed earlier by Kennedy's advisers—the American missiles in Turkey were obsolete and Kennedy had already intended to remove them— but it was rejected because such a trade-off at this time might be interpreted as a surrender to Soviet threats and a sellout of America's NATO allies, who had originally requested the installation of the missiles in Turkey.

Now that the trade-off had become the key to resolving the entire crisis, however, Kennedy was prepared to agree. Still hoping to avoid making this concession public, he authorized his brother Robert Kennedy to promise the Soviets that the American missiles in Turkey would be removed. But if a private promise did not satisfy the Soviet leader, Kennedy arranged that the secretary general of the United Nations would propose the trade-off, to which Kennedy would then agree, but his agreement would now appear to be a concession to the UN rather than to Moscow.

This subterfuge proved unnecessary, however, for Khrushchev accepted the president's private assurance. At 9:00 A.M. Sunday morning, October 28, a message from Khrushchev arrived in Washington via Radio Moscow: "In order to eliminate as rapidly as possible the conflict which endangers the cause of peace . . . the Soviet Government . . . has given a new order to dismantle the arms which you described as offensive, and to crate and return them to the Soviet Union." Kennedy replied at once reiterating his own earlier pledge to end the quarantine and his promise not to invade Cuba. With that, the Soviet-American phase of the Cuban Missile Crisis was over.

Kennedy ordered members of his staff to avoid any show of elation or any tendency to gloat or claim a victory in the crisis. Khrushchev would later claim that it was he who had won a great victory: he had extracted a promise from Kennedy that neither the Americans nor their allies would invade Cuba. "The Caribbean crisis was . . . a personal triumph in my own career as a statesman and as a member of the collective leadership. We achieved, I would say, a spectacular success without having to fire a single shot!"

❑ *Castro's Reaction*

Castro did not see it that way. He had not been consulted or informed about Khrushchev's negotiations with the Americans, and on hearing of his decision to withdraw the Soviet missiles, he is said to have gone berserk. He kicked the wall, shattered a mirror, and denounced Khrushchev as a "son of a bitch . . . a bastard . . . an asshole, a man with no *cojones* [balls], a *maricon* [faggot, the ultimate in Latin insults]." He protested to the Soviet leader that the Cuban people had been prepared to accept annihilation on behalf of the struggle against imperialism. Countless Cuban and Soviet men had been willing to die with supreme dignity, and he had shed tears upon learning of the decision to withdraw the weapons. To this, Khrushchev replied that he had no doubt that the Cuban people would have died heroically "but we are not struggling against imperialism in order to die, but to take advantage of our opportunities." A nuclear war had been avoided and the United States had made a commitment before the world not to attack Cuba. "We view this as a great victory."

Castro was not to be mollified. He refused to allow a UN team to inspect the Soviet missile sites in Cuba and refused to return the Soviet bombers that had been sent to Cuba. To avoid a showdown over the inspection issue, the Soviets agreed to allow American naval vessels to verify the withdrawal of their missiles by counting them at sea, and under heavy Soviet pressure Castro finally agreed to return the bombers. On November 20, 1962, Kennedy announced that the blockade of Cuba would be lifted.

Castro's anger about the peaceful resolution of the Cuban crisis was not a momentary reaction to what he regarded as a sell-out by Khrushchev. Many years later, he still declared with considerable pride that he would have agreed to use nuclear weapons and that the Cuban people were prepared the pay the price of total annihilation. "I wish we [the Cubans] had had the tactical nuclear weapons," he said. "It would have been wonderful."

THIRTY-ONE

❑

Waging the Cold War: From the Cuban Missile Crisis to the Helsinki Accords

In considering the relations between the superpowers in the wake of the Cuban Missile Crisis, it is essential to bear in mind events in other parts of the world (to be discussed in later chapters) that had a significant impact on the policies of Moscow and Washington:

> The Sino-Soviet rift, China's acquisition of nuclear weapons, and China's emergence as a nascent superpower in its own right, which decisively altered the global balance of power.
>
> The Americanization of the Vietnamese civil war, which became the central preoccupation of American leaders and increasingly absorbed American military resources.
>
> The Arab–Israeli wars, the rise of Islamic fundamentalism, and the perennial crises over Middle East oil, now crucial to the economies of the industrialized world.
>
> The Sino–Indian war of October 1962, the India–Pakistan war of August 1965, and the further extension of superpower rivalry in the Third World.

The Cuban crisis had provided a dramatic reminder to the superpowers—and to all the states caught between them—of the cataclysmic consequences of a nuclear conflict, the need to avoid crises which could set off a nuclear war, and the desirability of controlling the testing and proliferation of nuclear weaponry. After the crisis the American and Soviet governments had installed a so-called Hot Line between the Kremlin and the White House to reduce the danger of accidents or misunderstandings that might set off a nuclear war.

But, apart from the Hot Line, the more immediate results of the crisis were less fortunate. Soviet leaders, intent above all on avoiding another international humiliation, engaged in a major military buildup to achieve parity with the United States. Britain and France were already nuclear powers, and other states hastened to join them, convinced they would have to develop nuclear arsenals of their own if they were to retain their ability to conduct an independent foreign policy and resist the diplomatic coercion which nuclear powers were able to exert.

425

❑ De Gaulle's Move toward Greater Independence

The French had suffered the bitter experience of diplomatic coercion during the 1956 Suez crisis, and France's president, Charles de Gaulle, much like the Russians after Cuba, was determined to build up his own nuclear deterrent—what he called a *force de frappe*—to avoid a similar diplomatic humiliation. Nor had de Gaulle forgotten or forgiven the wartime humiliations suffered at the hands of Roosevelt and Churchill.

A year before the explosion of the French bomb, de Gaulle had withdrawn the French Mediterranean fleet from NATO command; in 1963 he withdrew France's Atlantic fleet; and in March 1966 he severed all ties with NATO, demanding that American and Canadian troops leave French soil and that the NATO headquarters be moved from Paris. Meanwhile, he went ahead with France's independent nuclear development, scornfully rejecting an American proposal to create a multilateral nuclear force within NATO.

De Gaulle had long since tried to make France, and Europe generally, more independent of the United States. It will be recalled that in the wake of the Suez Canal crisis, France had joined with West Germany to form the nucleus of a European Economic Community (the Common Market). The British had initially refused to join this European economic union to preserve their special relationship with the United States and the British Commonwealth, and in January 1960 they had formed an economic union of their own, the European Free Trade Association (EFTA), which included Austria, Denmark, Norway, Portugal, Sweden, and Switzerland—a group which became known as the Outer Seven as compared to the Inner Six of the Common Market (France, West Germany, Italy, and the three Benelux countries.) The Outer Seven, however, failed to match the economic success of the Inner Six, and in August 1961 a chastened British government formally applied for admission to the Common Market.

Britain's application was vetoed twice by President de Gaulle, in 1963 and again in 1967, on the grounds that Britain's membership would open the way to American influence and lead to the formation of "a colossal Atlantic community dependent on and controlled by America, which would not take long to absorb the European Community." On January 22, 1963, eight days after his first veto of Britain's entry into the Common Market, de Gaulle concluded a treaty with the Federal Republic of Germany whose declared purpose was the reconciliation of the French and German people. Left undeclared was the French president's intention to make this treaty the basis of a French-controlled European security system in which France's nuclear deterrent would take the place of the nuclear shield provided by the United States.

❑ Kennedy's "Ich bin ein Berliner" Speech, June 26, 1963

The Americans saw clearly enough what de Gaulle was up to, and took countermeasures. On June 23, 1963, President Kennedy went to West Germany, pointedly bypassing Paris on the way. He was greeted by immense and enthusiastic crowds, and in a speech delivered in the West German capital of Bonn he reiterated America's pledge to stand by and defend West Germany because "your liberty is our liberty; and any attack on your soil is an attack upon our own. . . . The United States will risk its cities to defend yours because we need your freedom to protect ours." Kennedy arrived in West Berlin on June 26, the fifteenth anniversary of the Berlin Air Lift, where he aroused an enthusiasm verging on hysteria by making Berlin the symbol of the struggle between the Free World and Communism. With ringing oratorical effect, he challenged anyone who had any doubt that this was the great issue of that struggle or anyone who thought that Communism was the wave of the future: "*Let them to come to Berlin.* . . . Freedom has many difficulties and democracy is not perfect. But we have never had to put a wall up to keep our people in. . . . All free men, wherever they may live, are citizens of Berlin, and therefore, as a free man, I take pride in the words *Ich bin ein Berliner.*"

The enthusiasm generated by Kennedy's visit doomed de Gaulle's effort to lure West Germany out of the Atlantic alliance and create a European security system independent of the United States. The elderly Konrad Adenauer stepped down as West German chancellor in October 1963, but his resignation did not change West Germany's diplomatic orientation. His successor, Ludwig Erhard, the architect of postwar Germany's economic miracle, was, if anything, even more committed to the Atlantic alliance.

De Gaulle persisted in his efforts to make France and Europe more independent of the United States. On January 27, 1964, he established diplomatic relations with the People's Republic of China; in March 1966 he withdrew from NATO; and in June of that year he paid a state visit to Moscow, where Kremlin leaders, as if to reward him for breaking away from the Atlantic alliance, gave him an enthusiastic welcome. The political results of his Moscow visit, however, were disappointing to both parties. The Soviets failed to secure French recognition of their puppet government of East Germany. And de Gaulle was unable to persuade the Soviets to relax their grip on Eastern Europe, thereby frustrating his hope to demonstrate that France was a more effective advocate of European interests than the United States.

❑ *The Nuclear Test Ban Treaty, August 5, 1963*

The most unfortunate result of de Gaulle's quest for political and military independence was his rejection of the appeal by the members of the nuclear club—Britain, the Soviet Union, and the United States—to join them in their efforts to reduce the threat to the world's atmosphere through a nuclear test ban treaty. The Cuban crisis had reinforced the awareness of the nuclear powers of the cataclysmic consequences of a nuclear war, but the scientific world had long since recognized that even the testing of nuclear weapons posed a serious health hazard because of the contamination effects of nuclear fallout. All test ban proposals had foundered over mutual suspicions among the powers, as had more ambitious efforts to integrate a test ban treaty into more comprehensive disarmament and security agreements. Nor had the awareness of the dangers of testing prevented either the Soviets or Americans from continuing their tests in the atmosphere. The Soviets had carried out two series of tests after the explosion of their megaton bomb in September 1961, and the Americans had countered with tests of their own from April to November 1962.

The Americans and the Soviets were finally driven to negotiate a test ban treaty by their mutual fear of the Chinese nuclear program. Serious negotiations began in late 1962. They stumbled temporarily over the question of on-site inspections of nuclear facilities, which Khrushchev opposed on the grounds that these would be nothing more than spying missions. By April 15, 1963, the British and Americans agreed to drop the inspection issue and informed Khrushchev that they were prepared to send high-level negotiators to Moscow. Their negotiating teams arrived in Moscow on July 15.

In his secret instructions to the veteran diplomat Averell Harriman, the head of the American team, Kennedy emphasized that a primary objective of the Moscow negotiations was to find ways to prevent China from going nuclear, which might include joint military action: "Radical steps, in cooperation with the USSR, to prevent further proliferation of nuclear capabilities. . . . Soviet, or possibly joint US-USSR use of military forces against China, presumably a joint air strike against China's nuclear facilities."

The Soviet government seemed prepared to consider such radical measures. On July 14, the day before the arrival of the Western negotiators and while a Chinese negotiating team was in Moscow to discuss a settlement of differences with the Soviet Union, the Soviet Central Committee published an open letter in *Pravda* addressed to all Soviet party organizations. The letter was a bitter attack on the Chinese Communist government, especially its cavalier attitude toward a nuclear war. According to that article, responsible Chinese leaders had expressed their willingness to sacrifice hundreds of millions of lives to win a nuclear war. But who could emerge a winner in such a war? "The nuclear bomb does not adhere to class principles—it destroys everybody who falls within range of its devastating force."

As Harriman had anticipated before arriving in Moscow, the negotiations with the British and Soviets went forward rapidly since agreement in principle had already been reached. The completed treaty, initialled on July 25 and signed on August 5, 1963, prohibited the testing of nuclear weapons in the atmosphere, outer space, and underwater. Over the next two years this limited test ban treaty—limited because it did not prohibit underground testing—was signed by another ninety states. It was not signed by France or China.

Kennedy urged Harriman to pursue further negotiations with Khrushchev over China. Harriman reported back: "It is clear that the Soviets' primary objective in signing the treaty was to isolate the Chicoms. Therefore they place maximum importance on France's adherence to the test ban treaty." Kennedy pleaded with de Gaulle to agree, but the French leader refused. So long as Russia and the United States retained the capacity to destroy the world, "France would not be diverted from equipping itself with the same sources of strength."

The test ban treaty has been widely hailed as a major breakthrough in halting the arms race, but it signally failed to achieve this objective. The arms race not only continued but accelerated sharply as the Soviets strove for military parity with the United States. The treaty also failed to fulfill its primary purpose—halt the proliferation of nuclear weapons. China acquired nuclear weapons in October of the following year, France continued to test nuclear weapons in the atmosphere, and other countries carried on with their own nuclear programs. France and China eventually agreed to stop atmospheric testing, but their agreement was not due to the test ban treaty but to the overwhelming evidence of the destructive effects of nuclear fallout.

The test ban treaty, however, exposed more glaringly than ever before the rift within the Communist camp. The Chinese diplomats in Moscow at the time of test ban negotiations were snubbed and ignored. The Chinese government responded to news of the treaty's signature with a new wave of anti-Soviet vituperation, denouncing the test ban treaty as a Soviet sellout of the interests of the Soviet people, the Socialist countries, and peace-loving peoples everywhere.

❑ *Changes of the Guard*

On October 19, 1963, Harold Macmillan resigned as prime minister of Great Britain, allegedly for reasons of health. It was widely believed at the time, however, that the real reason for his resignation was his government's involvement in one of the century's more lubricious scandals. His secretary for war, John Profumo, was found to have associated with call girls in parties that had included a Soviet military attaché. Called upon to tell his own version of the affair, Profumo lied to the House of Commons and was subsequently forced to resign. Shortly afterwards Macmillan himself stepped down. He was succeeded by his foreign secretary, Alec Douglas-Home, who undertook no significant changes in British foreign policy.

A far sadder change in leadership took place in the United States, where on November 22 President Kennedy was shot while riding in a motorcade in Dallas, Texas. At the time and since, there was an abundance of theories about plots and conspiracies involved in the Kennedy assassination, but the conclusion of an official investigation committee—that Kennedy was shot by a single gunman operating on his own for unknown reasons—has never been convincingly refuted.

❑ *The Johnson Succession*

Vice-president Lyndon Baines Johnson, the successor to the young, handsome, and eloquent Kennedy, was a very different type of leader. A Texan who had presided for many years over the United States Senate, Johnson had more political experience than Kennedy and was far more adept at securing the passage of his legislation through Congress. He was as energetic and forceful as his predecessor, with a quick and retentive mind, but he lacked Kennedy's charm and eloquence. In pushing his political agenda, he relied heavily on flattery and cajolery, larded when necessary with intimidation and threats of political retribution. There was nothing subtle about Johnson. In dealing with his political associates, he couched his arguments in the basic vocabulary of the barnyard and the brothel, but even in dealing with foreign dignitaries he could be embarrassingly crude.

The story of Johnson's ruthless and relentless struggle to achieve political power is far from edifying. But once he had gained that power, he sought to use it to prove himself a worthy successor to the man he professed to admire most in American public life, Franklin Delano Roosevelt. The supreme objective of his domestic policy, he declared, was the creation of a Great Society in which all Americans could have the opportunity to lead decent lives freed from the perils of poverty. Equality of opportunity in turn would gradually reduce the racial and ethnic tensions endemic in American society and create a more unified and harmonious nation, a shining example to the rest of the world.

In foreign policy, however, Johnson pursued a doctrinaire anti-Communist course. Despite all the evidence about the rifts within the Communist camp by the time he became president, he clung to the belief that world Communism constituted a monolithic political movement controlled from Moscow and intent on world domination. The primary task of Western policy must therefore be to reject every form of appeasement and to stop every kind of Communist aggression in its tracks.

When Johnson moved into the White House, Washington had already identified Vietnam as the most conspicuous contemporary evidence of Communist aggression. Johnson's Vietnam policy was therefore no new departure but rather a continuation of the policy of his predecessors. It was carried out with the full approval and support of the holdovers of the Kennedy administration, most notably Secretary of State Dean Rusk and Secretary of Defense Robert McNamara, who shared Johnson's belief in the need to take a firm stand in Vietnam. If America deserted its Vietnamese ally, America's other allies would lose confidence in America's reliability and be tempted to make the best bargain they could with the Communist aggressors. Johnson, Rusk, and McNamara were all firm believers in the domino theory: if Vietnam fell, so would the other countries of Southeast Asia. The power vacuum in that region would be filled by Russia and China, and America would then face the task of stopping the Communists elsewhere—in the Middle East, Europe, or even in the Western Hemisphere. "I am not going to lose Vietnam," Johnson declared. "I am not going to be the President who saw Southeast Asia go the way China went."

Johnson's obsession with Vietnam was to prove disastrous for his presidency. In November 1964, he scored one of the most decisive electoral victories in American history. Four years later, he found his authority so eroded by Vietnam that he took himself out of the presidential race.

❑ *The Ouster of Khrushchev, October 14, 1964, and the Brezhnev Succession*

Eleven months after the assassination of Kennedy, the political rivals of Khrushchev succeeded in removing him from office. He was succeeded as first secretary of the Communist party by Leonid Brezhnev, and as chairman of the Soviet Council of Ministers by Aleksei Kosygin.

Although the posts of party secretary and council chairman were now separated, Brezhnev, following the example of Stalin and Khrushchev, used his position as head of the party to make himself the de facto supreme authority in the Soviet state.

Born in 1906, the son of a smelter, Brezhnev took pride in the fact that he had risen from these humble beginnings to earn a degree as an engineer and move steadily upward in the Communist party hierarchy. Appointed secretary of the party's Central Committee under Stalin, then ousted in Stalin's later years, he was reinstated by Khrushchev—whom he repaid by manipulating Khrushchev's own ouster in 1964.

In his long acquaintance with Brezhnev, the West German statesman Willy Brandt observed an obvious growth in his "sweeping self-assurance" as he consolidated his political authority. But Brandt thought he was fundamentally a party hack, a stolid and unimaginative bureaucrat. His stubborn adherence to out-of-date Communist political and economic programs was responsible for maintaining repressive regimes in the Soviet satellite states of Eastern Europe and for the fact that the economies of those states and of the Soviet Union itself were being left ever farther behind those of the Western and Asian industrialized countries.

In confronting the United States and the ever-growing menace of China, Brezhnev continued a major buildup of the Soviet armed forces. By the late 1960s the Soviets had trebled their ICBM arsenal, surpassed the Americans in the number of their missile-carrying submarines, and challenged American superiority in long-range bombers. In 1969 the American government acknowledged that the Soviets had achieved "essential equivalence" in the realm of armaments. That equivalence, however, was achieved at a cost that was to have disastrous consequences for the Soviet economy as a whole.

During the Brezhnev era some remarkable advances were made in settling the German Question, but the initiative in doing so came not from Brezhnev but from the West German statesman Willy Brandt.

❑ *Willy Brandt and Ostpolitik*

In November 1966, following the breakup of his political alliance with the Free Democratic Party, Ludwig Erhard resigned as West German chancellor. He was succeeded as chancellor and leader of the Christian Democrat party by Kurt Kiesinger, the prime minister of Baden-Württemberg. Seeking a broad consensus to deal with the country's domestic problems, Kiesinger formed what became known as the Grand Coalition through an alliance with the major opposition party, the Social Democrats. In this coalition government, the leader of the Social Democrats and former mayor of Berlin, Willy Brandt, was given the position of foreign minister.

In the field of foreign policy, Chancellor Kiesinger concentrated on reviving Germany's close relationship with France. Brandt on the other hand was primarily concerned with resolving the issues that were the prime ingredients of the German Problem: West Germany's relationship with East Germany and the states of Eastern Europe, a policy that became known as *Ostpolitik.*

Willy Brandt was born in 1913 as Herbert Frahm, the son of an unwed Lübeck saleswoman. A confirmed socialist from an early age, he signed the articles he wrote for socialist publications as Willy Brandt to disguise their real authorship. He fled to Scandinavia when the Nazis came to power but returned to Germany after the war, having formally adopted the name of Willy Brandt. Elected mayor of Berlin in 1957, he became the leader of Social Democrats in 1964 and transformed that party's somewhat doctrinaire ideology into a more pragmatic program with broader popular appeal. In his foreign policy, he dedicated his efforts to the preservation of international peace, the settlement of divisive issues, and the promotion of international economic as well as political cooperation.

Brandt inaugurated his *Ostpolitik* in January 1967 with the establishment of diplomatic relations with Romania, a break with the policy of the Adenauer administration, which prohibited West German diplomatic relations with any state (apart from the Soviet Union) that recognized the government of East Germany. Over the next year, Brandt sponsored trade missions to other countries of Eastern Europe, opening the way to West Germany's commercial and financial penetration into the economies of the Communist bloc.

In 1968, however, Brandt's *Ostpolitik* suffered a serious setback when East German authorities resumed their obstruction of traffic to East Berlin and the Soviets ruthlessly suppressed a liberalization movement in Czechoslovakia.

❑ Czechoslovakia's Prague Spring, 1968

The economy of Czechoslovakia, once the most productive in Eastern Europe, had declined steadily under Communist rule. A joke at the time—humor being one of the few things that may flourish under a tyrannical regime—asked the question: what would happen if the Czech minister of economics were given control of the economy of the Sahara Desert? Answer: in the first year nothing; in the second year they would start importing sand.

In January 1967 the Czechoslovak Communist government responded to demands for economic reform by introducing a more decentralized market-oriented economic program, but these changes only stimulated demands for greater political as well as economic freedom. In January 1968 the Czechoslovak Communist party ousted Antonin Novotny, a hardline Stalinist who had held the post of first secretary of the party since 1953, and elected Alexander Dubček, a champion of economic reform, to replace him.

To implement economic reform, Dubček put competent experts in charge of recommending changes in the country's economic structure. But Dubček wanted more than economic reform. Convinced that the Communist party was "capable of exercising political direction by other than bureaucratic or police methods," he was resolved to introduce Communism with a human face. He encouraged greater popular participation in politics, calling upon intellectuals and artists to put forward proposals for improving the existing system. To make sure fresh voices could be heard, his government abolished censorship on June 25, 1968. The result was a profusion of proposals, including calls for an end to the Communist party's political monopoly, the creation of a multiparty system, neutrality in foreign policy, and the country's withdrawal from the Warsaw Pact.

The sudden burgeoning of these popular demands for change, hailed by the advocates of reform as Czechoslovakia's Prague Spring, was regarded with apprehension in the Kremlin. On July 15 representatives of the Soviet Union and the Warsaw Pact countries (minus renegade Romania) warned the Dubček government that "the developments in your country have aroused profound anxiety among us." They accused Dubček of conducting a reactionary policy supported by international imperialism, which "threatens to push your country off the socialist path and consequently imperils the entire socialist system."

A month later, alarmed by Dubček's announcement of his intention to hold party elections by secret ballot, Brezhnev had decided that the time had come to go beyond warnings and to intervene directly in Czechoslovakia. On the night of August 21, 1968, an estimated half million Soviet troops moved into Czechoslovakia, supported by token contingents from East Germany, Poland, Hungary, and Bulgaria. The Soviet leadership explained to the world that it had taken this action in response to an appeal from the Czechoslovak Socialist Republic for aid in suppressing a "conspiracy of external and internal forces . . . against the existing social order." As the East Bloc armies swept across their frontier, the Czechs for the most part accepted the inevitable and the invaders met with little more than scattered resistance. Dubček and four of his colleagues were arrested and carted away to a prison near Moscow.

Surprised by the vehemence of international condemnation of their Czech operation, even by foreign Communist parties, the Soviets released the Czechoslovak leaders, but only after they had promised to annul much of their reform program and agreed to stationing of Soviet troops on Czech soil. Dubček was actually reinstated as the party's first secretary, only to be ousted once again in April 1969 and subsequently expelled from the party altogether.

The Soviet leadership responded to the Prague Spring with what became known as the Brezhnev Doctrine: no socialist country could be allowed to take any action likely to harm socialism in that country or the fundamental interests of other socialist states. "This means that each Communist party is responsible not only to its own people but also to all socialist countries and to the entire Communist movement." What the Brezhnev Doctrine meant in practice was that the Soviet Union reserved the right to intervene in any Communist country if it saw any threat to Communist—or Soviet—control.

The most significant result of the Soviet suppression of the Prague Spring was the profound disillusionment it aroused among left-wing intellectuals in the West, including those who had consistently made the Communist cause their own and propagandized on behalf of the Soviet Union. But the tragedy of the Prague Spring had little impact on the foreign policies of the superpowers which were preoccupied with problems in East Asia—Washington with Vietnam, Moscow with China.

Soviet relations with China had deteriorated into bitter hostility. Khrushchev had been terrified by the apparent willingness of Chinese Communist leaders to use nuclear weapons. (See p. 445.) The Chinese nuclear threat was all the more serious because the Chinese were demanding a rectification of the "unequal treaties" imposed on China by tsarist Russia in the mid-nineteenth century, whereby Russia had acquired immense tracts of territory in Northcentral and Northeastern Asia. To back up this demand, the Chinese had heavily reinforced their armies along the Soviet frontier, and in 1969 Chinese and Soviet forces had engaged in a succession of border clashes. (See p. 446.)

As Sino–Soviet hostility became steadily more intense, both Moscow and Peking sought to improve their international position, a situation that opened out new diplomatic possibilities for Willy Brandt and for the new American president, Richard Nixon.

☐ *The Nixon Succession*

Nixon was not the first American statesman to perceive that Communism was not a monolithic movement or to recognize the rift that had developed between China and the Soviet Union. But he was the first to initiate policies to exploit that rift. Reversing the myopic refusal of previous administrations to deal with Communist China, he sought instead a working partnership with that immense and populous country so as to enable Washington to play off Peking against Moscow in the international arena.

Nixon was one of the few American statesmen who could have risked a diplomatic approach to China without committing political suicide. For he owed much of his early political success to branding his opponents as being soft on Communism while establishing his own anti-Communist credentials. Elected to Congress in 1946 on a wave of anti-Communist and antilabor sentiment, Nixon won national celebrity by his dogged pursuit of the case of Alger Hiss, a respected former high-level member of the State Department, who had been accused of being a Communist spy. Although the statute of limitations had run out on the spy charge, Hiss was ultimately convicted of perjury and went to jail, protesting his innocence to the end of his life. As we now know from Soviet documents, Hiss had indeed been a spy, as had a substantial number of other high-level officials in the Roosevelt government.

Riding high on his triumph in the Hiss case, Nixon was elected to the Senate in 1950, and in the presidential elections of 1952 Eisenhower was persuaded to select the young and energetic Nixon as his running mate. After eight years as vice-president, Nixon was defeated in his own bid for the presidency by John F. Kennedy in 1960. When he lost the race for governor of California two years later, he seemed to concede that his political career was over, commenting bitterly to the press that they wouldn't have Nixon to kick around anymore.

But Nixon stayed in the political arena and staged a remarkable comeback by campaigning tirelessly for Republican candidates and building up political obligations on a nationwide scale. He was rewarded by being nominated once again as his party's presidential candidate in 1968. As one political observer commented at the time, all those chicken dinners on the campaign trail had finally come home to roost. This time Nixon won, scoring a narrow victory over Vice-President Hubert Humphrey, the Democratic candidate. (On the issue of Vietnam in the 1968 election campaign, see p. 473.)

Richard Nixon was born in Yorba Linda, California, in January 1915, the son of a devout Quaker fundamentalist mother and a father who became an enthusiastic convert to the evangelical brand of Quakerism. There is little in Nixon's political career to suggest his Quaker background, at least not the Quakerism associated with kindness, tolerance, and pacifism. Quite the contrary, as a politician Nixon resembled the very un-Quakerish Lyndon Johnson. He was ambitious, vindictive in dealing with opponents, suspicious, and constantly on guard against real or imagined enemies. Like Johnson, he was insecure in dealing with intellectuals and members of America's version of a political aristocracy, yet pathetically eager to gain intellectual and social acceptance. He also shared one of Johnson's more attractive features: a genuine desire to use his political power on behalf of the public good, as he understood it.

As described by Henry Kissinger, who knew him well, there was no "true" Nixon. Several warring personalities struggled for preeminence in the same individual. One was idealistic, thoughtful, generous; another was vindictive, petty, emotional. There was a reflective, philosophical, stoical Nixon, and there was an impetuous, impulsive, and erratic one.

In the end, ambition and impulse prevailed. During Nixon's 1972 reelection campaign, there had been a raid on the headquarters of the Democratic Party in the Watergate apartment complex in Washington in an apparent attempt to find documents revealing that party's strategy. Whether Nixon had ordered or condoned this "third-rate burglary attempt," as Nixon's press secretary described it, has never been established, but Nixon's attempt to cover up the evidence of that burglary provided his many enemies with ammunition to bring him down. Confronted with the threat of impeachment over the Watergate scandal, Nixon resigned in August 1974.

The great difference between Nixon and Johnson lay in the focus of their political interests. Whereas Johnson had hoped to concentrate on domestic reform, Nixon's primary interest lay in the field of foreign policy. Nixon was determined from the start to bypass the cumbersome diplomatic machinery of the State Department and to conduct foreign policy from the White House. The most obvious instrument for this purpose was the office of the national security adviser, an official appointed by the president and not responsible to Congress. Nixon's selection of a Harvard professor, Henry Kissinger, for this post was not the repayment of an election debt, as some of their detractors have thought, but rather Nixon's need for a well-connected and formidably intelligent agent, a man without a political base of his own whose position was totally dependent on presidential favor.

Kissinger was in many ways an ideal choice. Arrogant, a shameless self-promoter with a monumental ego, Kissinger also had qualities that complemented those of the president. Whereas Nixon was shy, uncomfortable with people, and deeply suspicious of journalists, Kissinger was gregarious, he delighted in social occasions where he could display his intellectual brilliance and wit, and he carefully cultivated relations with the press.

Kissinger and Nixon shared similar views about the fundamentals of foreign policy. Both endeavored to see international politics in global perspective; both considered themselves pragmatists capable of discarding ideological prejudices in favor of what they perceived as the realities of power politics; both believed the prime objective of foreign policy was to serve national interests. American relations with the Soviet Union and all other states should be determined by the international behavior of those states, not by a messianic zeal to transform them in the American image or by concern for their violations of human rights.

The most notable achievement of the Nixon-Kissinger partnership was their success in reestablishing normal relations with China while remaining on relatively good terms with the Soviet Union. Otherwise, their diplomacy was more notable for its virtuosity than its success. They failed in their efforts to use the leverage of Peking and Moscow to secure peace with honor in Vietnam, and after expanding that conflict into Laos and Cambodia, they finally settled for terms that amounted to an acceptance of defeat. In the Middle East, Kissinger's global perspective turned increasingly parochial as his negotiations bogged down in detail, and despite his frenzied activity in that region, his actual achievements were meagre. (For the Nixon-Kissinger policies in dealing with China, Vietnam, and the Middle East, see Chapters 32, 34, & 36.)

The major international settlements that took place during the Nixon years—Berlin and Eastern Europe—were largely the work of Willy Brandt and the Europeans, a success which Kissinger signally fails to acknowledge in his self-congratulatory memoirs in which he actually denigrates Brandt's contribution.

❑ *Arms Control: Salt I*

Although Nixon and Kissinger made much of their success in negotiating arms control agreements, their actual achievements in this field too were meager.

On July 1, 1968, Britain, the Soviet Union, and the United States signed a Nuclear Non-Proliferation Treaty prepared by a United Nations disarmament committee and approved by the UN General Assembly. By the terms of this treaty, the nuclear powers pledged never to furnish nuclear weapons or the technology to build them to non-nuclear states, which in turn promised never to acquire or produce them. To monitor compliance, an international inspection team was established with headquarters in Vienna.

The Non-Proliferation Treaty, eventually signed by 133 states, did nothing to prevent nuclear stockpiling or the improvement of delivery systems, nor did it prevent the deployment of nuclear weapons on the territory of non-nuclear states. It was not signed by two nuclear powers, France and China, which resented any curb on their nuclear programs, or by Israel, India, Pakistan, or Brazil, which aspired to acquire nuclear weapons of their own.

The Non-Proliferation Treaty had been concluded while Johnson was still in office, and it was not until the second year of the Nixon administration that serious negotiations on behalf of a further arms control treaty were resumed. For this purpose Nixon authorized Kissinger to conduct "back channel" talks with the Soviet ambassador, Anatoly Dobrynin. Another two years were required before all details and differences had been worked out for a Strategic Arms Limitation Treaty. Signed in Moscow on May 26, 1972, that treaty was known from the first as SALT I because more treaties were envisaged. Kissinger described SALT I as "a major contribution to strategic stability" as well as "a significant step toward further arms limitations." For the purpose of actual arms limitation, however, the treaty was a very weak instrument indeed. It froze for five years the level of intercontinental ballistic missiles (ICBMs), but not that of multiple independently targeted reentry vehicles (MIRVs), which could give each ICBM three to ten separately targeted nuclear warheads—a provision the historian Stephen Ambrose has compared to freezing cavalry but not tanks. SALT I did not limit aircraft or cruise missile systems, nor did it prohibit the development of improved

ICBMs. Thus, even the freeze on ICBMs did no more than shift arms competition from the assembly line to the drawing board.

Nixon and Kissinger, elevated to the position of secretary of state in the autumn of 1973, paid a second and final visit to Moscow in June 1974, six weeks before Nixon's resignation. Here they signed an agreement on economic cooperation and a treaty banning underground nuclear tests over 150 kilotons, hardly a disarmament breakthrough.

Negotiations for a Salt II treaty were carried on by Gerald Ford, who became president upon Nixon's resignation in August 1974 and who retained Kissinger as his secretary of state. In November 1974 Ford and Kissinger met with Soviet leaders in Vladivostok, where they established guidelines for a SALT II treaty that would set limits on the size of missile systems not covered in SALT I. Even though the limits agreed upon in Vladivostok were fixed at an astonishingly high level, the SALT II negotiations faced bitter opposition in Congress, and the negotiations themselves bogged down in controversies over new Soviet and American weaponry. They were finally shelved altogether following Soviet intervention in a civil war in the former Portuguese colony of Angola. With this apparent revival of Soviet Cold War tactics, Ford announced that he intended to drop the word *détente* from his political vocabulary.

❑ *Brandt Resumes Germany's Ostpolitik and the Treaty of Moscow, August 12, 1970*

In his inaugural address as Federal Chancellor, Willy Brandt, who succeeded Kurt Kiesinger in that office in October 1969, declared that his primary foreign policy objective would be the improvement of relations with Eastern Europe.

His first move in renewing his policy of *Ostpolitik* was to relieve the states of Eastern Europe and the Soviet Union of their greatest fear about West Germany, namely, a West German army equipped with nuclear weapons. On November 28, 1969, his government signed the Nuclear Non-Proliferation Treaty, thereby renouncing West Germany's right to acquire, develop, or use nuclear weapons. Ten days later Brandt went to Moscow for the purpose of negotiating a comprehensive settlement with the Soviet government. The first fruit of his negotiations was a major economic agreement whereby West Germany agreed to provide 1.2 million tons of pipeline in return for Soviet deliveries of natural gas over a twenty-year period starting in 1973.

Eight more months were required before Brandt secured a comprehensive political settlement with the Soviet Union. By the terms of the Treaty of Moscow, signed August 12, 1970, Germany recognized the inviolability of all postwar European boundaries, including specifically the Oder-Neisse line as the western boundary of Poland. Bonn thereby renounced all the eastern territories Germany had lost after World War II. In the light of later events, one of the most significant points of the Moscow treaty was the Soviet government's acknowledgement of a West German "Letter on German Unity" stating that the Moscow treaty "does not conflict with the political objective of the Federal Republic of Germany to work for a state of peace in Europe in which the German nation will recover its unity through free self-determination."

Brandt went to Moscow personally to sign this epochal agreement, which finally broke the deadlock over the German Question and laid the foundation for a final pan-European peace settlement. On December 7 he journeyed to Warsaw to sign a similar treaty with Poland, but it was not until three years later, in December 1973, that he concluded a boundary treaty with Czechoslovakia.

❑ *The Four-Power Treaty over Berlin, September 3, 1971*

At the time of the signature of the Treaty of Moscow, the West Germans pointed out that they were not legally entitled to offer the frontier guarantees embodied in that treaty until the four occupation powers had concluded a final settlement over Berlin. A settlement was delayed by de Gaulle's resignation as president of France on April 28, 1969, and Soviet concern over border clashes with China. But by September 3, 1971, negotiations finally produced a Four-Power treaty which was signed by representatives of Britain, France, the Soviet Union, and the United States. The four occupation powers recognized each others' existing rights and pledged not to alter the status of Berlin unilaterally. "Disputes are to be settled by peaceful means. . . . There shall be no use or threat to use force." The significance of the Berlin treaty, as Brandt explained in a television address, was that from now on there would be no more Berlin crises. The status of and access to Berlin were now guaranteed by the Soviet Union as well as by the Western powers.

With the signature of the Four-Power Berlin treaty, the West German government was able to proceed with the ratification of the Moscow and Warsaw boundary treaties. As Brandt had expected, his renunciation of so much prewar German territory met with fierce domestic opposition. The treaties were not ratified by the Bundestag until May 17, 1972, and then only after the opponents of the treaties agreed to abstain. The final vote on the Moscow treaty was 248–0, with 238 abstentions; on the Warsaw treaty, 248–17, with 230 abstentions.

❑ *The Bases of Relations Treaty, December 21, 1972*

The Four-Power treaty over Berlin paved the way to an agreement between the governments of East and West Germany, the Bases of Relations Treaty, signed December 21, 1972, which resembled the Berlin treaty in being little more than a recognition of the status quo: each side pledged to respect the other's boundaries and territorial integrity. The treaty also provided for increased commercial and cultural relations and for a further easing of travel restrictions. A critical part of the Bases treaty, as of the earlier Moscow treaty, was its provision for East Germany's acknowledgement of a Federal Republic statement "that this treaty does not conflict with the political objective of the Federal Republic of Germany to work for a state of peace in Europe, in which the German nation will recover its unity through free self-determination."

❑ *The Helsinki Accords, July 30 and August 1, 1975*

Willy Brandt's Moscow and Warsaw treaties, the Four-Power Berlin settlement, and the Bases treaty between the two Germanies, opened the way for the overall European peace treaty which Brandt had been working for all along. On November 22, 1972, representatives of all the states of Europe (except Albania), Canada, and the United States met in the Finnish capital of Helsinki to open a Conference on Security and Co-operation in Europe.

In course of Helsinki negotiations, two of their principal protagonists were removed from the political scene. Brandt was forced to resign in May 1974 following the revelation that an East German spy had been working in his office as one of his chief deputies, and in August Nixon resigned as president of the United States. These changes in leadership did not disrupt the negotiations, however. Brandt was succeeded as chancellor by Helmut Schmidt, another Social Democrat, who strengthened his party's alliance with the Free Democrats by appointing that party's leader, Hans-Dietrich Genscher, to the post of foreign minister. Together they adhered to the foreign policy course set by Brandt. Nixon was succeeded by Gerald Ford, who had retained Henry Kissinger as his secretary of state, thereby ensuring continuity in American foreign policy.

The negotiations in Helsinki concluded with the ceremonial acceptance of the Helsinki Final Act on July 30 and August 1, 1975. This Final Act was not a formal treaty, but it represented a moral obligation by the participating states to observe its provisions and was thus the closest the powers ever came to a peace treaty between the belligerents of World War II. In Section I, Questions Relating to Security in Europe, the participating states pledged to "regard as inviolable one another's frontiers as well as the frontiers of all States in Europe and therefore will refrain now and in the future from assaulting these frontiers." These territorial provisions were not inflexible, however, for Section I included a statement that the signatory states "consider that their frontiers can be changed in accordance with international law, by peaceful means and by agreement."

The participating states pledged further to refrain from any kind of intervention in the internal or external affairs of another participating state. With these provisions, the Soviet Union secured what it had long been seeking on behalf of its postwar satellite empire: a guarantee against Western attempts to roll back the Iron Curtain. These same provisions, however, also guaranteed the states of both Western and *Eastern* Europe against Soviet aggression, thereby nullifying the Brezhnev Doctrine, which asserted the Soviet right to intervene in other states to safeguard socialism. They thus opened the way for the people of the Soviet Eastern European empire to modify or overthrow their "socialist" governments free from Soviet interference.

Section II of the Final Act dealt with cooperation in the fields of economics, science, technology, and the protection of the environment.

The most novel and potentially explosive provisions of the Final Act were embodied in Section III, which obliged all the participating states to observe certain designated human rights in the territories under their jurisdiction. Henry Kissinger summed up the importance of these provisions in a later speech: "At Helsinki, for the first time in the postwar period, human rights and fundamental freedoms became recognized subjects of East-West relations and negotiations. The conference put forward our standards of human conduct which have been—and still are—a beacon of hope to millions."

Alas, for a large part of the world's population, the principle of human rights remains no more than a beacon, though it is interesting to note that the other major provisions of the Helsinki Accords—not to violate the frontiers of participating states or intervene in their internal or external affairs—were to be violated in Yugoslavia, where foreign powers have intervened *on behalf of* human rights.

☐

THIRTY-TWO

East Asia: From the Korean War to the Sino-American Diplomatic Revolution

☐ *Sino-Soviet Relations*

The American belief that Communism was a monolithic global movement intent on world domination was reinforced by Mao Tse-tung's declaration in June of 1949 that solidarity with the Soviet Union would henceforth be the cornerstone of the new China's foreign policy. This intention seemed confirmed by the Sino-Soviet alliance treaty of February 14, 1950. In October of that year China intervened in the Korean War on the side of Communist North Korea. In that same month Chinese troops moved into Tibet, which the Chinese claimed was an integral part of China and which Washington saw as further evidence of Communism's inexorable expansionist ambitions.

All evidence seemed to confirm the reality of Sino-Soviet solidarity. In their February 14 treaty with China, the Soviets had promised to return to China virtually all the territorial and other gains made at China's expense after World War II. Although these restorations took place somewhat later than the treaty had stipulated, the Soviets in the end not only honored these promises but transferred to China the Soviet share in the joint stock companies set up under the terms of the February 14 treaty to develop the mineral resources of the Sinkiang province. In addition to these substantial concessions, the Soviets were providing China with economic and military aid together with a large corps of technical and military advisers.

In December 1956 Mao reaffirmed China's policy of "leaning to one side," which he had first announced in 1949. It might appear to China's advantage to stand independently between the United States and the Soviet Union, he said, but this would be a mistake. The Americans could not be trusted, and their political and economic system was at odds with the values of the Socialist world. China and the Soviet Union must stand together against the forces of imperialism.

In November 1957 Mao came to Moscow to celebrate the fortieth anniversary of the Bolshevik Revolution and attend a meeting the world's Communist parties. He admitted that he still had a "belly full of pent-up anger" over the way Stalin had treated him during his visit in 1949, and was pleased to observe that the attitude of the Soviet comrades had changed for the better. He dismissed such personal considerations as irrelevant, however, for the requirements of world revolution remained the same: the world's Communist parties must remain united in the struggle against capitalism and imperialism abroad and against deviationism at home. In carrying on that struggle, they must also have a leader "and that leader must be the U.S.S.R."

The Soviet demonstration of their technological achievements in the autumn of 1957 (the production of an intercontinental ballistic missile and the launching of the first and second artificial satellites) inspired Mao to declare during his November visit that the "East Wind was prevailing over the West Wind," and to conclude a wide-ranging agreement with Moscow that would enable China to take advantage of the Soviet scientific and technological breakthroughs.

Besides Mao's readiness to acknowledge Soviet leadership over the global Communist movement, his government continued to foster economic and cultural ties between the two countries. An agreement of February 1959, giving China even more extensive Soviet economic and technical aid, was followed by a trade treaty in March of the following year providing for a multibillion-dollar exchange of goods. Thus, to all appearances Sino–Soviet solidarity was more solid than ever at the end of the 1950s.

Accounts from Soviet and Chinese sources have now revealed that this solidarity was not at all solid. Mao had been angered by Khruschchev's denunciation of Stalin in February 1956 and by the Soviet leader's presumption of ideological leadership over the Communist world, and he thought the Soviets had been slack in not pushing the cause of world revolution more forcefully after the Korean armistice.

❑ Sino-American Relations: Quemoy, Matsu, and the Taiwan Question

Meanwhile the relations between China and the United States were steadily deteriorating. After China's initial intervention in the Korean War in October 1950, Chinese troops continued to confront the Americans throughout the long negotiations leading to the Panmunjom armistice of July 23, 1953.

America's relations with China did not improve during the Eisenhower administration. While Washington persisted in recognizing the Nationalist regime in Taiwan as the sole legitimate government of China, the Peking government proclaimed its determination to "liberate" Taiwan and denounced the Nationalists as lackeys of American imperialism. Twice, in September 1954 and again in August 1958, the Chinese began bombing islands off the coast of mainland China still held by the Nationalists, among them Quemoy and Matsu, at the entrance of two major Chinese harbors, Amoy and Foochow. The Eisenhower administration reacted in each case by reinforcing the American fleet in the Taiwan Straits and warning that the United States would fight to prevent a Communist takeover of Taiwan, nor would Washington rule out the use of nuclear weapons.

The Taiwan crisis died down without further incident, however, because in the late 1950s Mao's attention once again focused on China's domestic affairs.

❑ *China's Domestic Convulsions*

In May of 1956 Mao Tse-tung ostensibly opened the way to a freer expression of opinion in China under the slogan "let a hundred flowers all bloom; let a hundred schools of thought contend." As he explained to his propaganda department, he wanted "all people to express their opinions freely, so that they dare to speak, dare to criticize, and dare to debate."

Was Mao's Hundred Flowers Campaign a cynical maneuver to expose opponents of his regime or a genuine desire to generate new ideas and initiatives? Khrushchev had no doubts on this score. "He wanted to goad people into expressing their innermost thoughts . . . so that he could destroy those whose thinking he considered harmful." Whatever his real intentions, Mao was shocked by the extent and intensity of the criticism he had released. In June 1957 he abruptly changed course and began a virulent attack on the "rightists and reactionaries" who had spoken out. In the ensuing Anti-Rightist Campaign, a half million critics of government policies confessed to doctrinal errors and were sentenced to labor camps or made to work as peasants on the land.

The Anti-Rightist Campaign was directed in large part against persons the government chose to classify as intellectuals, who were blamed for China's continuing economic difficulties and for undermining the single-minded zeal required for economic development. To overcome these difficulties and restore the requisite zeal, the party in May 1958 adopted Chairman Mao's crash program for economic development, the Great Leap Forward, which was to dispense with the dross of intellectualism and be replaced by a massive mobilization of the people and the people's willpower. The entire population was to be organized in military-style People's Communes, which were to serve as the "basic units of Communist society" and "prepare actively for the transition to Communism." Political zeal, not technical expertise, was to be the key to China's economic recovery. Villages were to become industrial centers, peasants were to set up backyard steel furnaces to raise steel production to the level of Western countries.

The Great Leap Forward proved to be a great leap in the opposite direction, resulting in economic chaos and a famine of major proportions. By conservative estimates, approximately 30 million people perished between 1959 and 1961. This disaster was not due to natural causes, as the Chinese government was to claim later, but to fanatic doctrinal zeal. In late 1961 and early 1962 the party finally abandoned the Great Leap Forward in favor of a policy of "readjustment and consolidation," which once again accepted the contribution of intellectuals and technicians to economic development.

Mao Tse-tung managed to survive the disasters of his ill-conceived economic program thanks to his immense personal prestige and his control of the army and police, the ultimate instruments of power in an authoritarian state. Unlike his ruinous economic policies, Mao's measures to maintain control of the army had positive results. In September 1959 he ousted his defense minister, Marshal Peng Teh-huai, who had made a biting criticism of the "petty-bourgeois fanaticism" of the Great Leap, and replaced him with General Lin Piao, an able and ambitious man who had made a career of linking his fortunes with those of the Great Helmsman. Acutely aware that his own position depended on the favor of Mao, he obsequiously supported the chairman's policies and assembled his quotations in the famous Little Red Book, which became part of the standard equipment of every Chinese soldier and party member. Lin was more than a sycophant, however. He proved to be an exceptionally capable administrator who carried out a wholesale reorganization of the army, improved its training and discipline, and made it a center of scientific and technological research. The research center of the army was to play a leading role in the development of China's atom bomb.

❏ *Revolt in Tibet and War with India*

The value of Lin's reorganization of the army was soon to be demonstrated in combat. In March 1959 it suppressed a Tibetan uprising against Chinese rule with ruthless efficiency. The Dalai Lama, the spiritual leader of the Tibetan people, fled to India, and in late June the Chinese installed a puppet government in Tibet charged with remolding the country in the Communist image.

The Chinese army was soon put to a more severe test. As discussed earlier (see p. 384), the Nehru government of India had hoped to maintain friendly relations with China, but in the late 1950s Sino–Indian relations disintegrated in a flurry of boundary disputes that in October 1962 flared up into outright warfare. On October 20, in the evident belief that China would not have the strength or will to resist an Indian military takeover, Nehru sent the Indian army into the disputed areas with instructions to "free our territory."

The Chinese did more than resist. They launched an offensive of their own and defeated the Indians on every front with surprising ease. By November 20 they had conquered all the disputed territory, and the next day they announced a unilateral cease-fire and offered India surprisingly generous terms. The Chinese had obvious reasons for restraint. They were still dealing with the ravages of the Great Leap Forward and they feared foreign intervention—India had appealed for American support and Washington had responded with transport planes manned by American crews and had dispatched an aircraft carrier to Indian waters. China's most serious concern, however, was the deterioration of its relations with the Soviet Union. (On the Sino–Indian war, see p. 385.)

❏ *The Sino–Soviet Rift*

During his visit to Moscow in November 1957, Mao Tse-tung had seemed to solidify China's relations with the Soviet Union by calling for unity among the Communist states and acknowledging Soviet leadership over the Communist world. At the same time, however, he had alarmed the Soviet leadership by denouncing Khrushchev's policy of peaceful coexistence and the Soviet belief that there could be a peaceful transition to Socialism. "So long as imperialism exists, there will always be soil for aggressive wars," he said. "Lenin teaches, and experience confirms, that the ruling classes never relinquish power voluntarily." Socialism could only triumph through violent revolution. Even more alarming to the Kremlin leadership was Mao's professed willingness to risk a nuclear war. China might lose more than 300 million people, but what did that matter? "The years will pass, and we'll get to work producing more babies than ever before."

Khrushchev was horrified by Mao's callous acceptance of mass destruction on this scale. His differences with Mao became glaringly apparent during the Soviet leader's visit to Peking in September 1959. Khrushchev had just returned from a trip to the United States, and observed that the capitalist countries were showing a realistic understanding of the need to relax international tension. "Therefore we on our part must do all we can to exclude war as a means of settling disputed questions, and settle these questions by negotiation." Any attempt to "test by force the stability of the capitalist world would be a mistake." Mao made no attempt to conceal his scorn. He derided peaceful coexistence as a "bourgeois pacifist" notion, and accused the Soviet leader of "emasculating, betraying, and revising" Marxist-Leninist doctrine in a way that could only lead the Communist movement to disaster.

In July 1960, angered by Mao's campaign to discredit Soviet policy and justifiably fearful of what the Chinese might do if they obtained nuclear weapons, Khrushchev abruptly recalled the 1,400 Soviet military and economic advisers working in China and ordered them to bring with them their blueprints for construction projects already under way. At a meeting of the world's Communist party leaders in Moscow in November of that year, the Chinese joined all 81 participants in signing the so-called Moscow Declaration recognizing the Soviet Union as "the vanguard of the world Communist movement." But the Chinese ostentatiously broke ranks at a similar meeting in October 1961 when Soviet delegates criticized the Albanians for taking the side of China on numerous critical issues.

With a dramatic display of indignation, Chou En-lai led the Chinese delegation out of the meeting and returned to Peking. Mao expressed his own indignation at a secret meeting of the Chinese Communist party. The Soviet leadership had been warped by revisionism, he said, but the Soviet masses would soon see the light and "the rule of the revisionists won't last long."

The two great crises of October 1962—the Sino-Indian war and the Cuban missile crisis—added fuel to the Sino-Soviet dispute. The Chinese accused the Soviets of secretly supporting India, and they were bitterly critical of the Soviet retreat over Cuba. At the anniversary celebrations of the Bolshevik Revolution at the Soviet embassy in Peking, Chinese leaders were conspicuous by their absence.

The Chinese indulged in a fresh round of indignation following the Soviet signature on August 5, 1963, of a limited nuclear test ban treaty with the two other members of the nuclear club, Britain and the United States. Still bitter about the Soviet violation of their promise to aid China's nuclear development, they interpreted the test ban treaty as a move to keep China a second-class military power and dependent on Moscow's nuclear shield. They were right. When Khrushchev was informed a little over a year later that the Chinese were nearing completion of their own nuclear bomb, he seriously considered destroying China's nuclear installations. Whether he would actually have done so will never be known, for on October 14-15, 1964, his political rivals ousted him from his positions of leadership. On the day after Khrushchev's ouster the Chinese exploded their first atom bomb.

The Soviets had ample reason for concern over China's emergence as a nuclear power. China was larger and more populous than all the states of Europe. Lying as it did directly along the 4,000-mile Soviet frontier in Asia, China represented a potential threat to Soviet national security far greater than postwar Germany or even the United States.

As noted earlier, the magnitude, as well as imminence, of that threat was starkly brought home to the Soviets when on March 8, 1963, the Chinese government published a list of the vast territories "lost" to Russia over the past century. Apart from Outer Mongolia, which had only recently become a Soviet satellite, all these territories had been ceded to tsarist Russia in the mid-nineteenth century through what the Chinese called the "unequal treaties," imposed on the weak and hapless Chinese imperial government in the heyday of European imperialism. China now demanded a rectification of the existing Sino–Soviet frontier, based as it was on these unequal and therefore illegal treaties. "About one hundred years ago the area east of Baikal became Russian territory," Mao told a visiting Japanese delegation in July 1964, "and since then Vladivostok, Khabarovsk, Kamchatka, and other areas have become Soviet territory. We have not yet presented our bill for this list." The Chinese had in fact presented their bill with the publication of their list of "lost" territories. The question of how much of that bill they intended to collect—and when—remained to be answered.

The territorial dispute was the most intractable problem dividing the two countries. The Siberian and Central Asian lands that China had ceded to Russia had now been part of Russia for over a century, and the Russians took their possession as much for granted as Americans took for granted their possession of the lands wrested from Mexico in 1848 only a few years earlier. A critical difference between the situation in America and East Asia was that a massive American population had moved into the territories ceded by Mexico, whereas comparatively few Russians had migrated into the areas ceded by China. And the Chinese, with their teeming overpopulation, could not help but gaze with covetous eyes at the vast open spaces of what were now Russian Central and East Asia. There was the further critical difference that Mexico had always been too weak to challenge the legitimacy of its treaty with the United States, whereas China was now a major military power.

Even before the Chinese put forward their territorial claims, the Soviets had begun a massive buildup of their forces along their frontier with China. In January 1966 they concluded a treaty with Outer Mongolia permitting the stationing of Soviet troops along the Sino–Mongolian frontier, and they began the transfer of elite combat units equipped with nuclear missiles from Eastern Europe to East Asia. In the spring of 1969 Soviet and Chinese troops clashed in a succession of frontier skirmishes along the Amur and Ussuri Rivers in eastern Siberia and in Sinkiang in central Asia.

❑ America's Failure to Adjust to the Changing Situation in East Asia

Already by the early 1960s there could no longer be any doubt among foreign observers that the Sino–Soviet rift was no temporary or superficial ideological dispute and that it involved fundamental national differences. The most puzzling feature of

American foreign policy during this period is how little attention the American leadership paid to this radical transformation of the power structure in East Asia. By now heavily involved in Vietnam, the American government continued to base its policies on the assumption that China as well as Soviet Russia stood solidly behind the Communist government of North Vietnam, and that failure to halt a Communist takeover of Vietnam would open the way to an extension of Communist influence over the rest of Asia, the Middle East, and Africa.

This assumption is all the more remarkable in that it was contradicted by so much evidence that should have led to altogether different conclusions. Besides the Sino–Soviet rift, there were clear indications of still more conflict within the Communist camp. The meeting of the world's Communist parties in Moscow in March 1965 was boycotted not only by China and Albania but by North Vietnam, North Korea, Japan, Indonesia, and Romania. In August, a war broke out between India and Pakistan in which China took the side of Pakistan, the Soviets that of India, a situation which once again exposed China's differences with both New Delhi and Moscow.

In September 1965 a military coup overthrew the Chinese-backed Communist government in Indonesia, where a new military government proceeded to massacre some 300,000 Communist party members, including a large segment of the country's ethnic Chinese population. The anti-Communist coup in Indonesia was a dramatic demonstration that Communism was anything but an irresistible force in East Asia. Moreover, the Indonesian massacres and the India–Pakistan war had revealed an intensity of hatred among the Asian peoples which should have put an end to American fears that they would unite under the banner of Communism—or anything else. The danger of China itself began to recede at about this time, for Mao Tse-tung was about to plunge his country into new political convulsions that would immobilize China's foreign policy for the rest of the decade.

Even this remarkable concatenation of events failed to convince American policymakers that they might have miscalculated America's stake in Vietnam. There were Americans within and outside the government who appreciated what was happening in Asia and called for a reappraisal of America's East Asian policy, but they signally failed to bring about a change of course.

❑ *The Great Proletarian Cultural Revolution*

The Great Proletarian Cultural Revolution, the second major Chinese political upheaval of the 1960s, was a curious amalgam of ideological fanaticism and power struggle. As numerous analysts have pointed out, this revolution was not great, proletarian, or cultural. It was not even a revolution, for in the end it did little to change the Chinese government. What it did do, however, was subject the unfortunate Chinese people to yet another agonizing bout of turmoil and civil strife.

In the summer of 1965 Mao Tse-tung was confronted with increasing criticism within his government for his handling of foreign affairs and for continuing to push the pace of collectivization to the detriment of economic productivity. The Great Helmsman chose to interpret this criticism as a challenge to his authority and an abandonment of revolutionary fervor by party and state leaders, whom he accused of

becoming an entrenched "revisionist" hierarchy incapable of carrying on the proletarian revolution to its ultimate egalitarian conclusion. To crush his opponents and at
the same time save the revolution, he called for a massive purge of the state and party
leadership "to extirpate nauseous bourgeois and bureaucratic excrescences," eliminate the last remnants of traditional thought and culture, and conduct policy on the
basis of correct revolutionary principles as laid down by Chairman Mao.

The shock troops chosen to carry out this revolution were an assortment of youth
groups known as the Red Guards, zealot promoters of the ideas of Chairman Mao,
who threw themselves into the job of overthrowing persons in authority with fanatic
fervor. They invaded ministries and other sanctums of authority, and they beat and humiliated officials, intellectuals, technical experts, and anyone else who might be considered guilty of "revisionist" thought, by which they meant all traditional forms of
culture. By the summer of 1967 Mao decided to rein in the Red Guards. They were
ordered to stop "beating, smashing, burning, invading, and obstructing," but by this
time they had reduced large parts of the country to a condition of chaos and anarchy.

The Cultural Revolution was brought to an end, officially at least, at the meeting
of the Ninth Party Congress in April 1969 with the unanimous reelection of Mao as
party chairman, the election of a new Central Committee, and the adoption of a new
party constitution that stressed the guiding role of Mao's thought and the continued
importance of the class struggle. The composition of the new Central Committee
reflected the preeminent role now played by the army, which had been assigned the
task of restoring order. General Lin Piao, vice-chairman of the party and minister of
defense, was formally designated Mao's successor as party chairman. Lin expressed
his gratitude by saluting Mao's victory in the Cultural Revolution and hailing the Great
Helmsman as "the greatest teacher of the proletariat of our time."

Well aware of the tenuous nature of his role as Mao's successor, Lin worked systematically over the next two years to strengthen his own position by perpetuating
the army's dominance in civilian affairs. In doing so, however, he aroused Mao's suspicions, and at a party meeting in August 1970 Mao used the familiar tactic of indicating his displeasure with Lin by attacking one of his supporters. Convinced that both
his position and his life were now in jeopardy, Lin, allegedly with Soviet encouragement, planned a military coup that would include the assassination of Mao. Betrayed
by a co-conspirator, he attempted to flee to the Soviet Union on September 13, 1971,
but was killed when his plane crashed in Outer Mongolia under circumstances that
have never been clarified.

❑ *The Sino–American Diplomatic Revolution*

It is one of history's many ironies that the first American president to explore the possibility of establishing closer relations with Communist China was Richard Nixon,
who had built his political career on his loudly proclaimed hostility to Communism.
As observed earlier, however, given the political climate prevailing in the United States
during the Cold War, only a politician with solid anti-Communist credentials could
have risked an approach to China without committing political suicide.

Nixon proceeded with great caution, using secret diplomatic as well as public channels to sound the Chinese government about a Sino-American détente and to test the climate of opinion in America itself. His diplomatic channels were shrewdly chosen: one of these was Pakistan, which had enjoyed Chinese support in its war with India; the other was Romania, a Soviet satellite state with pretensions to independence. In the summer of 1969, Nixon asked the leaders of the Pakistan and Romanian governments to convey to Peking his belief, "not completely shared by the rest of his government," that Asia could not "move forward" if a nation as large as China remained isolated, and that his administration would not be party to any agreement to maintain China's isolation.

Nixon's public bid for better relations with China took the form of a relaxation of American trade and travel restrictions and a major speech by Secretary of State William Rogers on August 8, 1969, appealing to the Chinese leaders to abandon their introspective view of the world so as to enable the United States to "open up channels of communication." Calling attention to America's unilateral economic concessions, Rogers expressed the hope that they would "remind people on mainland China of our historic friendship for them."

The road to a Sino-American détente was strewn with obstacles, however. Foremost among these was the American commitment to the Chinese Nationalist government on the island of Taiwan, which the Chinese insisted was an integral part of China and should come under the sovereignty of Peking. The Chinese were also concerned about America's ultimate intentions in Southeast Asia, a concern considerably intensified by Nixon's authorization on April 30, 1970, of an invasion of Cambodia to destroy Vietcong-North Vietnamese bases along the Cambodian border. (See pp. 475-476.)

It was not until sixteen months after Nixon's initial approach via Pakistan and Romania that the Chinese government responded to his overtures. This response took the form of two letters from the Chinese foreign minister Chou En-lai, delivered through the same intermediaries employed by Nixon, Pakistan and Romania. In the letter sent via Pakistan, dated December 8, 1970, Chou emphasized that he spoke not only for himself but for Chairman Mao. China had always been willing to negotiate over its differences with the United States, he said, and a special envoy from President Nixon would always be welcome in Peking to discuss America's withdrawal "from the Chinese territory called Taiwan." The only difference in the message Washington received via Romania—but a significant difference—was that China would not only welcome a special envoy but President Nixon himself. The precondition, however, remained the same: such visits would only be welcome if Washington were prepared to settle the Taiwan question, which Chou described as "the one outstanding issue" between China and the United States.

Undeterred, Nixon accepted the invitation to visit Peking on behalf of both a special envoy and himself. To prepare an agenda for the presidential visit, he informed Chou that he was sending his national security adviser, Henry Kissinger, to Peking for a preliminary exchange of views "on all subjects of mutual interest." He insisted only that the Kissinger visit be kept strictly secret to forestall the criticism his approach to China was certain to arouse at home. Chou remained rigidly on course. Chairman Mao had been pleased to learn that Nixon was prepared to visit Peking, he said, but "it goes without saying that the first question to be settled is the crucial issue between China and the United States . . . the withdrawal of all the U.S. Armed Forces from Taiwan and the Taiwan Straits."

Kissinger arrived in Peking, via Pakistan, on July 9, 1971, and in one of his most successful diplomatic maneuvers, he eased his way around the Taiwan problem by contending that this issue admitted no rapid solution and that it should therefore be set aside in order to concentrate on clarifying mutual purposes and perspectives. Kissinger, however, had paid a price for this evasion of the Taiwan question. The United States gave up its opposition to the admission of the People's Republic of China to the United Nations and agreed that the People's Republic should occupy the seat heretofore held by the Republic of China (Taiwan) as well as its seat on the Security Council.

On the evening of July 15, 1971, Nixon stunned the world with his revelation of Kissinger's secret mission to Peking. He had taken the initiative to establish more normal relations with China, the president said, because, as he had emphasized on numerous previous occasions, there could be no stable and enduring peace without the participation of the People's Republic of China with its 750 million people. He then read out an announcement (drafted by Kissinger and the Chinese) that was being issued simultaneously in Peking. The Chinese government had invited him to visit China, and he had accepted the invitation with pleasure. His purpose would be to seek a normalization of relations and an exchange of views on questions of concern to both sides. This would not be done at the expense of old friends (Kissinger's evasion of the Taiwan issue), nor was it directed against any other country. "We seek friendly relations with all nations."

As Kissinger observed with considerable self-satisfaction, Nixon's announcement about his approach to China, far from souring relations with the Soviet Union as the State Department's Soviet experts had predicted, dramatically improved them. Within a week of his trip to Peking the Soviet government, which had been stalling for over a year about a Nixon-Brezhnev summit meeting, suddenly came up with an invitation to Nixon to visit Moscow, and all other negotiations with the Soviets began to accelerate.

Nixon arrived in Peking on the morning of February 21, 1972, taking care to descend from the plane alone so that the cameras could record his handshake with Chou En-lai, a gesture intended to ritualize the change in Sino-American relations since John Foster Dulles's refusal to shake Chou's hand eighteen years earlier. That same afternoon Nixon and Kissinger were brought into the presence of Mao Tse-tung, an audience denoting that the Sino-American détente had the approval of the Great Helmsman. Although Mao was by now very old and could scarcely stand, both Nixon and Kissinger professed to having been overwhelmed by the force of his personality. The far from humble Nixon wrote in his memoirs that he was "humbled and awed in a rare way." Kissinger made no such profession of humility, but he acknowledged that he had met no one, with the possible exception of de Gaulle, "who so distilled raw, concentrated willpower." That evening Chou hosted a state banquet in Nixon's honor in the Great Hall of the People. In his formal toast he once again called for a normalization of Sino-American relations, to which Nixon responded with a quote from the Great Helmsman himself: "Seize the day, seize the hour."

Kissinger was to write later that the Chinese leaders, for all their ideological fervor, "were the most unsentimental practitioners of balance-of-power politics I have ever encountered." In fact, however, now that their ideological bond with the Soviets had been shattered, there was nothing for the Chinese to be sentimental about. They sought détente with the United States to balance the power of the Soviet Union, nothing more.

The document that emerged from this latest round of Sino–American negotiations was the so-called Shanghai Communiqué. Issued on February 28, 1972, the last day of Nixon's visit, the communiqué noted that there were essential differences between the Chinese and American social systems and foreign policies. The two governments nevertheless agreed that all countries, regardless of their social systems, should conduct their relations on the following principles: respect for the sovereignty and territorial integrity of all states, noninterference in the domestic affairs of other states, equality and mutual benefit, and peaceful coexistence. With these principles in mind, the two sides agreed to normalize relations and reduce the dangers of international conflict. Neither would seek hegemony in the Asia-Pacific region; both would oppose efforts of others to achieve such hegemony; neither would negotiate on behalf of a third party or enter into agreements directed against other states; both would seek to broaden the understanding between their peoples and facilitate the development of trade.

The sharpest statement of differences, as was to be expected, concerned Taiwan. The Chinese objected to any suggestion that there were two Chinas or that "the status of Taiwan remains to be determined." The Americans went a long way to bridge the differences with China on this issue. They recognized the Chinese view that there is but one China, that Taiwan is part of China, and they declared that the United States "does not challenge this position." They reaffirmed America's interest in a peaceful settlement of the Taiwan question by the Chinese themselves and stated that their ultimate objective was the withdrawal of all American forces from Taiwan. Meanwhile, they would progressively reduce their forces as tension in the area declined.

In effect, the Shanghai Communiqué represented a Sino–American partnership to block Soviet expansionism and maintain a balance of power in East Asia. The Americans were assured that China would not use force to take over Taiwan or exacerbate American problems in Indochina. The Chinese were assured that the Americans would not support the Soviets in Asia in return for concessions in Europe. The communiqué also opened the way to a major exchange of goods and services giving both countries access to the markets of the other, an especially important provision for China, which would now have access to American science and technology, and, with its cheap labor, would have an immense trading advantage.

A year later Washington and Peking upgraded the Shanghai Communiqué. The two countries now agreed to *resist* (as compared to oppose) *jointly* (as compared to a separate commitment) any attempt on the part of any country (i.e., the Soviet Union) to achieve *world* (as compared to Asian) domination.

❑ *Peace between China and Japan*

America's apparent write-off of Taiwan and the apparent bonanza for American business created by the opening of the China market convinced the Japanese of the need to make a settlement of their own with Peking. In August 1972 the Japanese prime minister, Tanaka Kakuei, made a formal request to visit China. He arrived in Peking in September.

The Sino-Japanese communiqué issued on September 29 at the conclusion of Tanaka's visit closely resembled the Sino-American Shanghai Communiqué. The two countries agreed to reestablish diplomatic relations and would seek a durable peace and friendship. Their agreement was not directed against third countries, neither would seek hegemony in the Asia-Pacific region, each would oppose the efforts of others to establish such hegemony. Over Taiwan, the Japanese adopted the same formula as the Americans: Japan recognized the People's Republic of China as the sole legitimate government of China; China reaffirmed that Taiwan was an inalienable part of the territory of the PRC; Japan understood and respected this position. Japan, however, reserved the right to continue economic relations with Taiwan (as the United States was to do later) and was not obliged to abrogate its earlier peace treaty with Nationalist China.

The communiqué included two other items specifically related to the recent Japanese war with China: Japan expressed a keen awareness of its responsibility for causing enormous damage to the Chinese people and "deeply reproached itself." China, as an answering gesture, retracted its demand for Japanese war indemnities. A final peace treaty between China and Japan, signed August 12, 1978, included essentially the same provisions as the September 29 communiqué issued six years earlier.

❑ *The Final Stages of the Sino–American Diplomatic Revolution*

The official establishment of diplomatic relations between China and the United States did not take place until January 1, 1979, a delay resulting from domestic difficulties in both countries and fresh misunderstandings in the field of foreign affairs.

In the United States, Nixon's role in foreign policy ended altogether with his resignation in August 1974. The cause of Sino–American reconciliation suffered a number of setbacks during the presidency of Nixon's successor, Gerald Ford. In November 1974 Ford agreed to a summit meeting with Soviet leaders—in Vladivostok of all places, the major city in the territories ceded by China to Russia in the nineteenth century, which China was now seeking to reclaim. To the Chinese, a Soviet–American summit was disturbing enough, but the location of that meeting in Vladivostok seemed to signal America's recognition of the Soviet claim to these territories. The Chinese were disturbed further by the Helsinki Accords of the summer of 1975 which, by resolving major Soviet differences with the West in Europe, seemed to leave the Soviet Union a free hand in Asia.

Most alarming of all was Ford's position on Taiwan. There was still a powerful pro-Taiwan and anti-Communist sentiment in the United States, especially among members of Ford's own Republican party. During the presidential election campaign in the summer of 1975, Ford attempted to exploit that sentiment by indicating a willingness to abandon the Taiwan policy of his predecessor. Nor can the Chinese have been reassured by the defeat of Ford, because the successful presidential candidate, Jimmy Carter, was to them a completely unknown quantity.

All this while the Chinese were in the throes of domestic upheavals of their own. Chou en-lai and Mao Tse-tung both died in 1976, Chou on January 9, Mao on September 9. The struggle over the succession, which had begun long before their deaths, was to continue until the restoration of relative stability under the leadership of Teng Hsiao-p'ing in the final years of the decade.

Nixon's efforts to normalize America's relations with China were resumed by President Carter, spurred on by his national security adviser, Zbigniew Brzezinski, a native of Poland who made no attempt to disguise his preference for Peking over Moscow. To clear away differences that had arisen since Nixon's resignation, Brzezinski visited Peking in May of 1978.

He came at a propitious time, for China's relations with Vietnam had deteriorated sharply since the end of the Vietnamese war with the United States. Following the victory of Vietnam's Communist government, the centuries-old hostility between the Chinese and Vietnamese had once again flared up. They were involved in a number of territorial disputes, and Vietnam's Hanoi government indulged in a veritable reign of terror in dealing with its ethnic Chinese population. In the spring of 1978 the Chinese severed all remaining economic and technical links with Vietnam, which they accused of acting in collusion with Moscow. (See p. 482.)

At odds with both Moscow and Hanoi, the Chinese leadership was a good deal more receptive to American overtures than at the time of Kissinger's initial visit and was prepared to be more flexible over Taiwan. In a communiqué of December 15, 1978, the United States recognized the People's Republic as "the sole legal government of China and acknowledges the Chinese position that there is but one China and Taiwan is part of China." Peking, however, allowed the Americans to soften the blow to Taiwan. In a separate statement the United States announced that it was terminating its diplomatic relations and mutual defense treaty with Taiwan on January 1, 1979 (the date for the establishment of formal diplomatic relations with the People's Republic of China), and that it would be withdrawing all its remaining military personnel from the island within four months. The American *people,* however, would be allowed to maintain cultural, commercial, and other unofficial relations with the *people* of Taiwan. Further, the United States would continue its interest in a peaceful resolution of Taiwan's status. To reinforce this point, the American Congress passed a Taiwan Resolution Act declaring that any effort to resolve the Taiwan issue by force would be regarded as a matter of "grave concern to the United States."

On January 28, 1979, the Chinese leader Teng Hsiao-p'ing paid a nine-day visit to the United States, the first such visit by the head of a Chinese Communist government. His visit was a triumph of public relations and his enthusiastic reception, following so many years of American vilification of the Chinese Communists, was a dramatic demonstration of that familiar phenomenon, the volatility of public opinion. In addressing a joint session of Congress, Teng seemed intent on reassuring the Americans on the subject of Taiwan. "We fully respect the realities on Taiwan," he said. "We will permit the present system on Taiwan and its way of life to remain unchanged." He was confident that present policies would lead to the peaceful unification of the island with China. But he then added the disturbing warning that "China cannot commit herself not to resort to other means." In the euphoria of the moment, surprisingly little attention was paid to this potentially explosive reservation.

THIRTY-THREE

❑

Containment in Asia: Vietnam, Part I

The cry of No More Koreas did not determine American policy for long, for the United States was soon to be involved in a far longer and far more bloody conflict than Korea. This one was the result of a decision to implement the doctrine of containment in Indochina, a French colony/protectorate in Southeast Asia consisting of the states of Cambodia, Laos, and Vietnam, which had been conquered and occupied by the Japanese during World War II.

❑ *The Postwar Partition*

As in Korea, postwar events in Indochina were decisively affected by the arrangements made by the victorious Allies for the surrender of the Japanese. On the final day of the Potsdam Conference, August 1, 1945, the American and British governments decided that "for operational purposes" the Japanese forces in Indochina should surrender to the Chinese Nationalist army of Chiang Kai-shek in the area north of the sixteenth parallel, and to the British and Australians south of that line. This decision was incorporated in General MacArthur's Order No. 1 of August 15, 1945, setting out the procedures for the Japanese surrender in all the Pacific theaters of war. Nothing was said at this time about the interests of the French in Indochina, but the French lost little time in making their interests known.

Under the leadership of the ultrapatriotic General Charles de Gaulle, the French government was determined to erase the humiliation of recent defeats in Europe and initiate a revival of French glory, which included the restoration of France's overseas colonial empire. The British Labour government, although it included many professed opponents of colonialism, nevertheless recognized the French claims to Indochina and ordered the commander of their occupation forces in Indochina to prepare for the return of the French.

In seeking to restore their authority in Indochina, the French faced two major obstacles: the Chinese Nationalists, who had been authorized to occupy Indochina north of the sixteenth parallel; and a native Vietnamese Communist government,

455

MAP 16 VIETNAM, LAOS, AND CAMBODIA

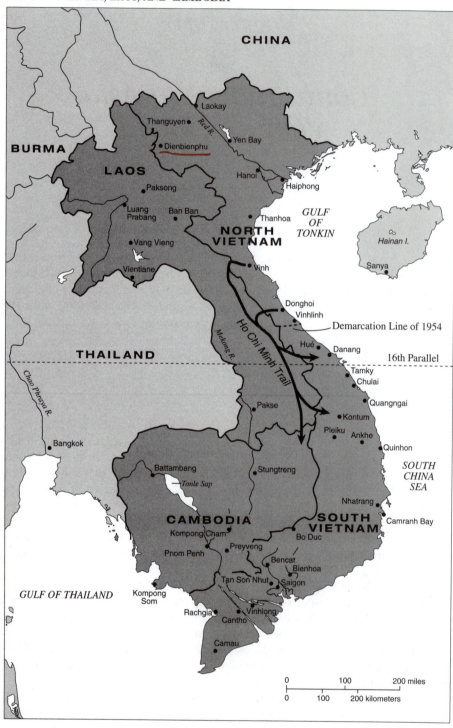

CHINA

Laokay

Thanguyen •

Yen Bay •

• Dienbienphu

BURMA

LAOS

Paksong •

Luang
Prabang •   Ban Ban •

Hanoi •

Haiphong •

Thanhoa •

GULF
OF
TONKIN

NORTH
VIETNAM

Hainan I.

• Vang Vieng

Vientiane •

Sanya •

Vinh •

Donghoi •
Vinhlinh •

Demarcation Line of 1954

THAILAND

Mekong R.

Ho Chi Minh Trail

Hué •   Danang •

16th Parallel

Tamky •
Chulai •

Chao Phraya R.

Pakse •

Quangngai •

• Kontum
Pleiku •   Ankhe •

Bangkok •

Quinhon •

Battambang •

• Tonle Sap

Stungtreng •

SOUTH
CHINA
SEA

Nhatrang •

CAMBODIA

SOUTH
VIETNAM

Camranh Bay

Kompong Cham •

Bo Duc •

Preyveng •

Pnom Penh •

Bencat •
Bienhoa •

Tan Son Nhut •

Saigon •

GULF OF THAILAND

Kompong
Som •

Rachgia •

Vinhlong •
Cantho •

Camau •

0   100   200 miles

0   100   200 kilometers

which claimed jurisdiction over both North and South Vietnam and which on September 2, 1945, had proclaimed Vietnam's independence from France. It was the existence of this Communist government that originally drew the attention of the Americans to Vietnam and eventually persuaded American leaders of the need to support French efforts to suppress it.

❑ *The Historical Background*

Until comparatively recent times, Vietnam was known in the West by its Chinese name, Annam, meaning Pacify the South. And indeed, Chinese efforts to "pacify" the South have been a prominent theme in the history of Chinese–Vietnamese relations since the third century B.C. when the Chinese first established a protectorate over the country. Although the Vietnamese managed to break away from direct Chinese control for long periods of time, Vietnam remained a Chinese tributary state until the late nineteenth century, when Vietnam and the neighboring kingdoms of Cambodia and Laos came under the rule of the French, a region they were to consolidate into a single administrative unit they called French Indochina.

During World War II the Japanese took advantage of the French defeat in Europe to establish their own control over the peninsula. But, with their own administrative resources stretched to the limit by their other conquests, the Japanese left the French in charge of the administration of Indochina until the last months of the war. On March 9, 1945, after France was liberated from German rule and the tides of war had shifted against Japan in Asia, the Japanese put an abrupt end to French administration and sponsored the formation of native governments in Indochina in the hope of winning the support of their fellow-Asians against the Americans and Europeans. In Vietnam, they turned over nominal control to a puppet administration under Bao Dai, the Vietnamese emperor, who had served as puppet ruler under the French. Had the Japanese sought meaningful native cooperation earlier, they might have given some substance to their slogan of Asia for the Asiatics. Now their appeal to fellow-Asians proved a futile gesture.

Meanwhile, a genuine native Vietnamese government was being created by a Communist-led nationalist movement in the mountains near the Chinese border. On August 19, four days after the Japanese surrender, the leaders of this government, with widespread support from the native population, took control of Hanoi, the capital of Tonkin, where they met with no resistance from the 30,000 Japanese troops still stationed in that city. This was the government which on September 2, 1945, had proclaimed Vietnam's independence from France and which the Chinese and British found in place when their forces entered Indochina to accept the surrender of the Japanese.

❑ *Ho Chi Minh and Vietnam's Communist-Nationalist Revolution*

In his proclamation of Vietnamese independence, the leader of the new Vietnamese government, Ho Chi Minh (Ho Who Enlightens), quoted from America's Declaration of Independence and the French Declaration of the Rights of Man in appealing for the support of the victorious Allies. "We are convinced," he said, "that the Allied Nations which have acknowledged the principles of self-determination and equality of states at Teheran and San Francisco will not refuse to acknowledge the independence of Vietnam." He was wrong. Twenty more years of war were required, first against the French and then against the Americans, before that acknowledgment finally took place.

The record of Ho Chi Minh's career establishes him as one of the outstanding leadership personalities of our era. As a political activist and chief of state, he demonstrated outstanding administrative and organizational talents. His most extraordinary achievement, however, was his success in inspiring his compatriots to keep up the fight for Vietnam's independence over so many years and against such staggering odds. Visitors sympathetic to his cause have described Ho as a frail and gentle man who radiated warmth and sincerity. Sincere he undoubtedly was, but he could never have accomplished what he did had he been either frail or gentle. His appearance of fragility disguised a tough physique endowed with immense energy and stamina. Far from being gentle, he was a fanatic ideologue willing to employ the most cold-blooded and ruthless methods on behalf of the cause to which he devoted his life.

There are few reliable records of Ho Chi Minh's early life because a large part of it was spent in exile in foreign countries under a variety of assumed names. He was born in 1890, the son of a peasant scholar and patriot whose hatred of French rule is said to have been so intense that he refused to learn their language. The father nevertheless encouraged his son to go to France for the purpose of finding out as much as possible about that country so as to be able to fight more effectively against it.

Following his arrival in France in the summer of 1911, Ho joined the circle of Vietnamese émigrés who shared his nationalist aspirations. Here he also associated with French political activists and became a founding member of the French Communist party, which broke away from the Socialists by condemning the futility of mere denunciations of capitalism and calling for violent revolution to achieve its goals. A decisive influence in Ho's turn to Communism were Lenin's theses on national and colonial questions, which convinced him that "only Socialism and Communism can liberate the oppressed nations and the working people of the world from slavery." Ho's prominence among Asian radicals soon caught the attention of Soviet leaders, who in the summer of 1923 brought him to Moscow for intensive political training. Two years later he went to Canton, where he became an associate and interpreter for Mikhail Borodin, the Comintern envoy to the Chinese government. (See p. 112.)

Throughout his subsequent service as a Comintern agent in Asia, Ho remained dedicated to the cause of Vietnamese independence. While paying lip-service to the usual Communist political and social goals, Ho's own primary objective remained the overthrow of French rule in his own country. The opportunity to do so seemed to have arrived with the defeat of France by Germany in the summer of 1940. In February 1941 Ho returned to his native land after thirty years of exile, and in the mountains near the Chinese frontier, out of reach of the French and Japanese, he established the nucleus of a Vietnamese government—the League for Vietnamese Independence (Vietminh). Founded in May 1941, the League's platform emphasized a nationalist rather than Communist agenda—a deliberate move on the part of Ho to downplay his association with Communism and overcome the suspicion of his fellow nationalists that he was a pawn of Moscow.

Over the next four years, Ho attempted unsuccessfully to obtain the support of the Chinese Nationalists and the Americans in fighting against the Japanese. American agents reported with some enthusiasm about the desirability of collaborating with Ho against the Japanese. They supplied him with weapons and medicine, and in return he provided the Americans with information and helped in the rescue of pilots shot down over Indochina. The American government, however, to avoid antagonizing the French and suspicious about Ho's Communist background, made no meaningful efforts to cooperate with this obscure revolutionary leader. Neither did the government of Chiang Kai-shek, involved as it was in a civil war against the Chinese Communists.

Ho's calls for a Vietnamese revolution were more successful than his diplomacy. Although his army, which had grown from about 500 in March to 5,000 in mid-August, would have been no match for the Japanese, Ho nevertheless resolved to use it as a vanguard and organizing nucleus for a countrywide revolution and to seize power before the arrival of Allied occupation forces. On the evening of August 18, 1945, military units quietly entered Hanoi to direct an uprising scheduled for the following day, confident that they would have support of a large proportion of the city's inhabitants. Neither the Japanese nor the provisional native government installed by the Japanese offered any resistance. By sundown on August 19, Hanoi was in the hands of the Vietminh in what had been a virtually bloodless takeover.

On August 21, the Vietminh demanded the abdication of Emperor Bao Dai, whose seat of government was in Hué, the old imperial capital, and the next day, backed up by a massive popular demonstration, a local revolutionary committee took over power in Hué. As in Hanoi, there was virtually no resistance on the part of the Japanese or the Bao Dai government. On August 25, revolutionary assault teams seized the government buildings in Saigon, the capital of Cochin China, the southernmost province of Vietnam. Here too they met with virtually no opposition, and shortly after noon representatives of the Vietminh government were sworn in as the provisional government of Cochin China. On the same day that the Vietminh took over Saigon. Ho arrived in Hanoi where on September 2 he issued his declaration of independence.

The Vietnamese, however, were not given the opportunity to work out their own destiny.

❏ *The Chinese Nationalist Occupation of North Vietnam*

On September 9, 1945, one week after Ho Chi Minh issued his Declaration of Independence, the main body of the Nationalist army of Chiang Kai-shek began the Chinese occupation of Indochina north of the sixteenth parallel, a region that included northern Vietnam and northern Laos. Much though he loathed the French, Ho Chi Minh had far greater reason to fear the Chinese and the possibility that they might attempt to restore their ancient suzerainty over Vietnam. For the Chinese were potentially far more powerful than the French, and in a far better geographical position to exert their authority.

During their occupation, the Chinese Nationalist forces had rekindled the long-standing Vietnamese hostility to China by their ruthless exploitation of the country. Their occupation proved to be unexpectedly brief, however. Less than six months after his troops entered Indochina, Chiang Kai-shek, finding that he needed those troops for his civil war against the Chinese Communists, ended the Chinese occupation by an agreement with the French. In a treaty with France of February 28, 1946, Chiang recognized French sovereignty over all of Indochina and agreed to withdraw his troops within three months. In return, the French abandoned their substantial treaty rights in China—their concessions in Canton, Hankow, and Shanghai, and their control over the Chinese portion of the railroad linking China with Indochina.

By the time of their withdrawal, the Chinese had not yet finished the evacuation of Japanese troops from either Vietnam or Laos, ostensibly the primary purpose of their occupation. More importantly, in the course of their occupation the Chinese had allowed the Vietminh to carry on the routine tasks of administration, with the result that after the Chinese withdrawal the Vietminh government, installed in Hanoi after the Japanese surrender, once again exercised authority over North Vietnam.

❏ *The British Occupation of South Vietnam and the Return of the French*

The Vietminh were not given a similar opportunity in the south. On September 12, 1945, three days after Chinese Nationalist forces moved into North Vietnam, British troops—the 20th Indian Division under the command of Major General Douglas Gracey—entered Saigon, the capital of Cochin China, where they found a Vietminh administration in control of that city. Instructed by London to prepare for the restoration of a French administration, Gracey announced that responsibility for the maintenance of law and order was to be transferred to the French as soon as they were in a position to take charge.

To facilitate the French takeover, Gracey rearmed the 5,000 French soldiers who had been interned by the Japanese since the previous March. On September 22 French troops occupied the capital's government buildings, ousted the Vietminh officials, and proclaimed the restoration of French rule. When the Vietminh responded with a call to revolution, Gracey moved quickly to restore order, using not only his own Anglo-Indian forces but the Japanese troops still in Saigon to suppress the Vietminh-inspired uprising.

The French were soon to be heavily reinforced. By the end of October they had 25,000 troops in Cochin China under the command of de Gaulle's trusted lieutenant, General Philippe Leclerc. Provided with an army far better equipped than the Vietminh (and three times larger than the army France had maintained in all of Indochina before the war), Leclerc succeeded by the end of the year in reestablishing French control over the major Vietnamese cities south of the sixteenth parallel. Confident that the situation in South Vietnam had now been stabilized, Gracey began the withdrawal of British forces.

Recognizing the extent of France's temporary military superiority, Ho Chi Minh tried to negotiate a compromise settlement that would avoid a military confrontation. Greatly relieved by the departure of the Chinese, he was willing to put up with the continued presence of the French, confident that in the long run they would be unable to maintain their position in Indochina. "It is better to sniff French dung for a while," he said, "than to eat China's all our lives."

In his negotiations with the French, Ho frankly acknowledged that his ultimate objective was the removal of all French control over Vietnam, but meanwhile he had another purpose in view. "I still need your professors, your engineers, and your capital in order to build up a strong and independent Vietnam." To secure that kind of relationship with France, Ho himself went to France, where from June to September of 1946 he attempted to negotiate a settlement that would give him the French expertise he desired but open the way to complete independence. His efforts were frustrated by the seemingly uncompromising position of the French, and on December 18, believing that there was no longer any alternative to violence, Ho ordered that an attack on French positions be launched on the following day. That attack proved to be the beginning of an eight-year war.

❏ *The Vietnamese War with France*

As was evident from their initial military operations, the Vietminh forces under the command of the brilliant Vietminh General Vo Nguyen Giap had long been preparing for war. For in their December 19 offensive they launched simultaneous attacks on French garrisons in Hué, Danang, Hanoi, and other major cities, an impressive demonstration of coordinated military planning and the ability of the Vietminh army to conduct military operations in every part of the country. After two months of heavy fighting, the French regained control of Vietnam's major cities, but the Vietminh remained in control of the countryside, which enabled them to carry on a guerrilla war. From their rural bases they struck at French outposts and lines of communication, suffering heavy casualties but inflicting losses on the French which the French were far less able to endure.

The Vietminh war was very similar to that waged by the Communists against the Nationalist forces in China, and indeed the Vietminh consciously took over the tactics of the Chinese Communists, who provided training for Vietnamese troops and invaluable supplies of Japanese and American arms captured from the Chinese Nationalists.

By the autumn of 1953, the French military leadership in Vietnam, faced with mounting opposition to the war at home, a declining morale among their own troops, and the frustrations of guerrilla warfare, adopted a strategy designed to lure the Vietminh into open battle, where France's superior firepower and technology would provide the decisive military victory the French so desperately needed. Informed that the Vietnamese were preparing a major thrust into northern Laos, they constructed what they confidently believed to be an impregnable ring of fortresses in the valley of Dien Bien Phu, which lay at the intersection of the main routes along the Laotian border.

The valley of Dien Bien Phu had been chosen because it provided the landing fields essential for the aircraft which were to supply the French garrison. Although a valley fortress would be vulnerable to fire from the surrounding mountains, the French were confident that the Vietminh would be unable to install artillery with sufficient firepower in these distant mountains to threaten their fortifications. The French calculations proved to be disastrously wrong. While they were constructing their fortresses, the Vietminh used their manpower to drag artillery supplied by the Chinese into positions that would command the valley of Dien Bien Phu. Their artillery destroyed the French landing fields, and under cover of artillery fire their troops steadily advanced into the valley and surrounded the French positions. By mid-March 1954 the French recognized that Dien Bien Phu would fall unless they received immediate and substantial aid from the United States, which by this time was already bearing approximately three-quarters of the costs of the French war in Vietnam. What the French wanted now was nothing less than American military intervention.

The French had every reason to believe their appeal would be successful. American leaders, including President Eisenhower, had stated repeatedly that America's own security would be jeopardized if Vietnam were allowed to fall to Communism. The previous January Eisenhower's secretary of state, John Foster Dulles, had announced that the United States, if challenged, had both the power and determination to react instantly, if necessary with atomic weapons, against targets of its own choosing.

But now, when called upon to act in accordance with their rhetoric, Eisenhower and Dulles turned cautious. Army Chief of Staff Matthew Ridgway, fresh from his dismal experience in Korea, argued that any advantage achieved through air strikes would be "altogether disproportionate to the liability it would incur." Eisenhower agreed. Air strikes alone were unlikely to raise the siege of Dien Bien Phu, and nuclear strikes would inflict at least as much damage on the French as on the Vietminh. Their most compelling reason for restraint, however, was the possibility that American military action might provoke Chinese intervention, as had happened in Korea. And behind China stood the Soviet Union, which now possessed atomic weapons of its own—in Washington the belief still prevailed that Communism was a monolithic movement bent on global conquest.

Eisenhower decided to procrastinate and, in effect, do nothing. Dien Bien Phu fell on May 7, 1954. The only way the French could now salvage something from the debacle in Vietnam was to reach some kind of negotiated settlement.

❑ *The Geneva Accords, July 1954*

The stage had meanwhile been set for negotiation. At their meeting in Berlin in early 1954, the foreign ministers of the four occupation powers had agreed to convene an international conference in Geneva in April to arrange a final peace treaty for Korea and consider the problem of restoring peace in Indochina. Communist China and "other interested states" would be invited to attend. In the end the conference included representatives of the Big Four (Britain, France, the Soviet Union, and the United States), the People's Republic of China, the State of Vietnam (the French-supported government in South Vietnam), the Democratic Republic of Vietnam (the Vietminh government), and the royal governments of Laos and Cambodia.

The final settlement reached at Geneva on July 20 and 21, 1954, took the form of three bilateral armistice (cease-fire) agreements between the military commands of the Vietminh and the French, who acted on behalf of their puppet governments of Vietnam, Cambodia, and Laos. Besides the armistice agreements, the major document produced in Geneva was a so-called Final Declaration, subscribed to but not signed by all the conference participants except South Korea and the United States, who did not sign *or* subscribe. The dividing line between the State of Vietnam and the Democratic Republic was fixed at the seventeenth parallel, where a temporary demilitarized zone was to be established. The crucial part of the Final Declaration as it concerned Vietnam was its provision for "free general elections by secret ballot" in both parts of Vietnam, which were to be held in July 1956 under the supervision of an International Supervisory Commission made up of representatives from Canada, India, and Poland. Even the most fervent anti-Communists conceded that the Vietminh were certain to win those elections handily, so that the Geneva settlement in effect provided for the reunification of Vietnam under a Vietminh government within two years.

Although the Vietminh were infuriated by this delay, they had reason to be satisfied with the results of the Geneva Conference. As Khrushchev wrote in his memoirs, all would have been well if everyone had adhered to the Geneva Accords: after two years general elections were to be held, "and we had no doubt that Ho Chi Minh— that is the Communists . . .—would have emerged victorious. But then that sinister man [Secretary of State] Dulles and the United States stepped in and imposed a long, bloody war on the Vietnamese people."

Dulles did indeed step in. As convinced as Khrushchev that all-Vietnam general elections would result in a Vietminh victory and lead to a Communist takeover of the South, he was resolved from the beginning to prevent these elections from being held. His decision to torpedo the elections can be seen in retrospect as a crucial turning point for American policy in Southeast Asia, for in doing so he deprived the Vietminh of the principal prize of their victory over the French. This was a setback the Vietminh would be certain to challenge, if necessary by force of arms.

Speaking to congressional leaders while the Geneva conference was still in session, Dulles had observed that any agreement reached at the conference would be "something to gag about." The United States might nevertheless still be able to salvage something in Southeast Asia "free from the taint of French colonialism." This would involve taking over from France the responsibility of defending Cambodia, Laos, and South Vietnam, and fighting subversion within this area "with all the strength we have."

Besides the United States and South Korea, another participant at the Geneva Conference had refused to be a party to the Geneva Accords. This was the State of Vietnam (South Vietnam), under the nominal rule of Emperor Bao Dai, the puppet ruler installed by the French in the 1930s, installed by the Japanese after their ouster of the French administration in March 1945, and in March 1949 once again installed under French auspices. On June 14, 1954, while the Geneva Conference was still in session, Bao Dai had turned the premiership of his government over to Ngo Dinh Diem, the most prominent figure among his country's anti-Communists. At the conclusion of the conference, the Bao/Diem regime rejected the armistice agreement with the Vietminh as well as the provision to hold general elections in Vietnam on the grounds that the Geneva Accords had been negotiated and signed by the French, not by a representative of the State of Vietnam, the country most affected by these provisions. Dulles warmly supported the decision by the Bao/Diem regime, because it provided an obvious way to avoid elections altogether.

dissolved 1977

❑ **The Southeast Asia Treaty Organization (SEATO)**

In line with the policies he had outlined to Congress, Secretary of State Dulles now pursued two parallel lines of strategy: the strengthening, economically and militarily, of the non-Communist regimes in Indochina; and the formation of an international security pact for Southeast Asia. After the Geneva Conference, he issued invitations to the non-Communist governments with interests in Southeast Asia to attend a conference in Manila to discuss measures to counter the Communist menace.

The result of that conference was the formation of the Southeast Asia Treaty Organization, signed in Manila on September 8, 1954, by the governments of the United States, Britain, France, Australia, New Zealand, the Philippines, Thailand, and Pakistan—India, Burma, Indonesia and Ceylon had turned down the invitation to participate. The SEATO treaty was hailed by the Eisenhower administration as an Asian counterpart to NATO and a triumph of Dulles's diplomacy. The agreement was far too loosely worded, however, to be an effective diplomatic instrument. The signatories agreed that an armed attack against any one of them constituted a danger to them all, but they carefully avoided making specific commitments in the event of an attack (or defining what constituted an attack). They promised only to meet a common danger in accordance with their own constitutional processes. Each signatory was thus left a broad avenue for evading any action whatever.

In terms of international law, the most important provision of the SEATO agreement was a separate protocol listing Cambodia, Laos, and the "free territory under the jurisdiction of the State of Vietnam" among the territories covered by the treaty. The SEATO signatories thus joined the United States in ignoring the major provisions of the Geneva Accords, which had specified that the partition of Vietnam was provisional and envisaged the eventual reunion of the country through free general elections. In the realm of practical politics, however, this protocol was virtually meaningless because the signatories, not being bound by specific commitments, did not consider themselves obliged to join the United States in defending the territories listed therein.

The SEATO treaty proved to be far more significant for the conduct of American foreign policy than as an instrument for collective security. Its ratification by the Senate was subsequently interpreted by the White House as conferring on the president the authority, indeed the obligation, to take whatever measures he considered necessary for the defense of the Southeast Asian countries listed in the treaty's protocol.

Ho Chi Minh

❑ *The United States, South Vietnam, and Ngo Dinh Diem*

Even while the Geneva Conference was still in session, the Eisenhower administration had initiated its policy of strengthening the government of South Vietnam by the creation of a Saigon Military Mission, its assignment to bolster the military capacity of South Vietnam and prepare for eventual "paramilitary operations" against the Vietminh. In October 1954 Eisenhower appointed a military officer, General Lawton Collins, as ambassador to Saigon. Collins brought with him a presidential letter to Prime Minister Diem assuring him of American aid "in developing and maintaining a strong and viable state capable of resisting attempted subversion and aggression by military means." Ambassador Collins expressed misgivings about Diem from the time of his arrival in Saigon, but by April 1955, after an outbreak of violent uprisings by opponents of his regime, Diem had succeeded in restoring order and a relieved Dulles observed that "we have no choice but to continue our support of Diem. There is no other suitable leader known to us."

Critics of American policy in Vietnam have speculated whether there could have been anyone *less* suitable. Diem was a member of the Vietnamese aristocracy that had prospered under the French. He was also a Roman Catholic in a predominantly Buddhist country and was thus part of a religious as well as social minority. From the start, his regime made a mockery of American claims that their mission in Southeast Asia, besides keeping Communism at bay, was to bring the blessings of democratic government to the peoples of this region. Though he made the occasional democratic gesture, Diem's government was and remained a dictatorship, which relied on repression, censorship, and political chicanery to maintain and extend its authority. Instead of introducing reforms that might generate popular support for his regime, he remained myopically content to rely on the support of the minority Roman Catholic population, on business leaders and property owners with a stake in the existing political and economic system, and on his family, who were installed in key positions in the central and provincial administrations.

In October 1955 Diem's personal authority was strengthened, or so it seemed at the time, when Emperor Bao Dai, in a move to reassert his own authority, dismissed Diem and appointed a new prime minister. Refusing to step down, Diem announced a referendum to enable the South Vietnamese to choose between himself and the emperor. That referendum, held on October 23, resulted in an overwhelming victory for Diem who received 98.2 percent of the vote, including some quarter-million more votes in Saigon than there were registered voters. Three days later Diem declared South Vietnam a republic with himself as president. Bao Dai was formally deposed and retired to France, where he lived the rest of his life in luxurious leisure.

The failure of the Bao Dai coup hastened the withdrawal of French troops from Indochina, which had begun immediately after the Geneva Conference and was completed in April 1956. By that time the United States had taken over full responsibility for training the South Vietnamese army and building it up into an effective fighting force. The Americans had also assumed responsibility for scuttling the all-Vietnam elections. When the North Vietnam government proposed starting preparations for these elections, as stipulated by the Geneva Accords, Diem, with the approval of

Washington, publicly rejected this proposal. He reminded his critics that his government had never subscribed to the Geneva Accords, and argued further that free elections were in any case impossible under a Communist regime because it denied its people the requisite freedom.

❑ *The Vietminh Response to the Refusal to Hold All-Vietnam Elections*

In view of the impressive military showing of the North Vietnamese in their war with the French, foreign observers were surprised that Ho Chi Minh did not threaten immediate military action to compel South Vietnam's compliance with the Geneva Accords. He had two compelling reasons for holding off: domestic difficulties and fear of American intervention.

In the summer and early autumn of 1954 the Hanoi government, following the example of Communist China, had initiated land reforms which required the confiscation of holdings from a broadly defined "landlord" class. Hanoi's ruthless implementation of this program had caused a serious disruption of the North Vietnamese economy and led to widespread peasant unrest. Over the next two years an estimated half-million peasants fell victim to famine, economic dislocation, and outright government purges. Indeed, as we now know from Vietnamese records, Ho carried out the equivalent of mass murder on a scale comparable to that of his Communist counterparts, Stalin and Mao Tse-tung. This quasi-revolutionary situation had continued into the spring and summer of 1956, hardly an ideal platform for launching a war.

The international situation was also unpropitious. Ho was being sent sharp warnings from Moscow and Peking to avoid measures that might give the Americans an excuse to intervene. If his policies involved him in war with the United States, he could not expect either Soviet or Chinese support.

With elections and military action ruled out, Ho considered using Communist agents in South Vietnam to unleash a revolution against the Diem regime, but he was advised by his Central Committee that the situation in the South was not yet "ripe." For the time being Communists in the south should restrict their activities to hastening the ripening process. This was to be done through a systematic program of terror, the assassination of local administrators and other supporters of the Diem regime (to be justified as the "extermination of traitors"), and the organization of cadres among disaffected members of the population. The entire campaign was to be carried out in such a way as to avoid giving the "imperialists and feudalists" any excuse to provoke a war with the North.

It was not until some four years later that the Vietminh Central Committee decided to initiate a more overt militant policy. At its meeting in January 1959, it authorized the formation of armed units in the South and the systematic infiltration into the South of North Vietnamese troops trained to organize and lead the southern insurgents. To facilitate this infiltration, Hanoi undertook major improvements in what came to be called the Ho Chi Minh trail, a network of paths and roads through the jungles of Laos and Cambodia along Vietnam's western frontier. The Ho Chi Minh trail became the principal avenue for the transport of men and supplies from the North to the South, for, running as it did through nominally neutral territory, it bypassed the demilitarized zone between North and South Vietnam established by the Geneva Accords.

Over the years, the Vietnam Communists had found that the Communist label had been an obstacle to their mobilization of popular support in the South, and to deal with this prejudice they formed a new party on December 20, 1960—the National Liberation Front (NLF), which was portrayed as being free from Communist ties and was designed to attract "all patriotic classes and all sections of the population." Its central objective, set forth in the new party's program, was the overthrow of the "Diem lackeys of American imperialism" and the formation of a national democratic coalition government dedicated to the liberation of the country and its reunification.

Hanoi had another purpose in advising the southern Communists to form the National Liberation Front. Heretofore North Vietnam had discouraged large-scale military operations in the South to avoid provoking American intervention. But if such operations were carried out by the National Liberation Front they could be portrayed as a genuine popular mass movement totally independent of Hanoi. The Americans could thus no longer intervene in the name of halting the spread of Communism, but could instead be charged with suppressing a revolution on behalf of national freedom and self-determination.

Diem scornfully dismissed the NLF as a Communist front organization and denounced its members as Viet Cong, a pejorative label for Vietnamese Communists which was soon to be taken up by the Americans. The NLF nevertheless achieved what its founders had desired. Within a year it had recruited close to half a million members, an indication of the degree of hostility Diem had built up over the years. The party was more than a protest movement, however. Besides its appeal to national and patriotic sentiment, it promised a broad range of social and economic reforms, including a redistribution of property to the peasantry, an agricultural program that attracted widespread support, though the actual implementation of this breakup of larger agricultural units was to result in a decline in productivity.

As the NLF membership grew, the Communists stepped up their revolutionary activity in the South, their operations facilitated by the NLF's popular support, particularly in rural areas. The number of assassinations of government officials rose from 700 in 1958 to 2,500 two years later, and earlier hit and run operations developed into full-scale attacks on government-controlled villages and exposed units of the South Vietnam army. Soldiers of the North Vietnamese army who had come South over the Ho Chi Minh trail played a central role in organizing and directing these operations. They brought with them large supplies of weaponry, much of it provided by the Chinese. With them, too, came a cadre of native South Vietnamese Communists who had moved North after the Geneva Accords and who now returned, after intensive training, to take over positions of leadership in the South. Within two years the NLF had gained control over a large part of the South Vietnam countryside, creating a situation very similar to that which had confronted the French: government forces still controlled the cities, but these had now become islands in a sea of rural revolution.

❑ *The Laos Problem*

Despite the deteriorating situation in Vietnam, President Eisenhower did not even mention Vietnam when he briefed President-elect Kennedy on Southeast Asia shortly before Kennedy took office in January 1961. He concentrated instead on neighboring Laos, which he described as the linchpin of the domino theory. "The fall of Laos to Communism," he said, "could mean the subsequent fall—like a tumbling row of dominoes—of its still-free neighbors, Cambodia and South Vietnam and, in all probability, Thailand and Burma. Such a chain of events would open the way to Communist seizure of all Southeast Asia." Eisenhower considered Laos so crucial that he was prepared to go to war in its defense, "with our allies or without them."

The Kingdom of Laos had been granted its independence by the French in October 1953. Its independence was reaffirmed by the 1954 Geneva Accords, which had stipulated that the country should be neutralized and that its government should not request foreign military aid or provide military bases for foreign powers. But the 1954 accords had signally failed to prevent violations of Laotian neutrality, as did another set of accords formulated in 1962. For the North Vietnamese were regularly sending men and supplies through neutral Laos via the Ho Chi Minh trail. But the Americans, too, regularly violated Laotian neutrality in seeking to disrupt the Ho Chi Minh trail and support anti-Communist factions in Laos.

❑ *The Kennedy Escalation*

In his inaugural address of January 20, 1961, John F. Kennedy had brashly proclaimed that "the torch has passed to a new generation." But, at least in foreign policy, it proved to be the same old torch, only kindled with more inflammatory rhetoric. While scathingly critical of Eisenhower's policies, Kennedy pursued many of the same policies with exactly the same objectives. As defined by Kennedy's national security adviser, McGeorge Bundy, these objectives were to prevent Communist domination of South Vietnam; to create in the country a viable and increasingly democratic society; and to initiate, on an accelerated basis, a series of mutually supporting covert actions—military, political, economic, and psychological—to achieve this objective.

Khrushchev's threatening behavior in dealing with European questions in the summer of 1961, which Kennedy interpreted as an effort to take advantage of his inexperience, made the young president all the more determined to prove his toughness in Vietnam. The gut issue was not whether Diem was a good ruler, he told his staff on November 14, but whether the United States could accept Communist aggression in South Vietnam with impunity. The moves that Washington now made would be examined on both sides of the Iron Curtain "as a measure of the administration's intentions and determination."

Kennedy was already being urged to do far more than supply South Vietnam with aid and advisers. General Maxwell Taylor, soon to become head of the Joint Chiefs of Staff, proposed sending an American task force (combat troops) to South Vietnam "as a visible symbol of the seriousness of American intentions," warning that "our program to save SVN will not succeed without it." Secretary of Defense Robert McNamara and Secretary of State Dean Rusk went even further, arguing that it might be necessary for U.S. forces to strike at the source of the aggression, namely, at North Vietnam itself. Kennedy drew the line over attacking North Vietnam, but he did approve massive increases in American military aid and a steady escalation of the American military presence in South Vietnam.

Early in 1962 the Diem government launched a new campaign against the Vietcong: a Strategic Hamlet program whereby the entire peasantry would be relocated in fortified compounds where they could be defended against—and prevented from giving food and shelter to—the Vietcong. The Strategic Hamlet program, far from curbing rural unrest, only served to increase it. The peasants resented being compelled to leave their homes and gardens and herded into stockades, which they were forced to build without compensation. Masses of peasants fled from their villages and went over to the Vietcong, and the fortified villages not directly controlled by government troops readily opened their gates to insurgent forces.

The Diem government was arousing more dramatic opposition in the cities. In May 1963 the Buddhists staged mass rallies to protest government curbs on religious freedom. The vicious response of government security forces commanded by Diem's brother, Ngo Dinh Nhu, provoked further protests, including the self-immolation of Buddhist monks. Western observers were horrified by television pictures of these incidents, a horror considerably reinforced by Madame Nhu's scornful references to the immolations as Buddhist barbecues. In August, after Diem had assured the Americans that he would take no further action against the Buddhists, Nhu's security forces carried out a massive raid on Buddhist temples, vandalizing the temples, roughing up monks who resisted, and arresting some 1,500 protesters.

❑ *The Overthrow of Diem*

By this time Kennedy appears to have been prepared to condone a coup by South Vietnamese generals to overthrow the Diem regime. On October 6, 1963, Henry Cabot Lodge, the American ambassador to Saigon, was informed by a senior official in the State Department, that, while the United States did not wish "to stimulate a coup," it would not "thwart a change of government or deny economic and military assistance to a new regime if it appeared capable of increasing effectiveness of military effort, ensuring popular support to win war, and improving working relations with U.S." Lodge agreed. On October 25 he wired Washington that the plotting among the Vietnamese generals was now so far advanced that "we should not thwart a coup." He thought it was "at least an even bet that the next government would not bungle and stumble as much as the present one has."

The coup took place on November 1. Diem and his brother, Ngo Dinh Nhu, were assassinated, and a new government was formed under the nominal leadership of General Duong Van Minh. The overthrow of the Diem regime aroused wild enthusiasm among the people of South Vietnam. Lodge, however, proved to be wrong about his "even bet" that a new government would be an improvement over the old. The generals who now assumed power were hopelessly incompetent. Corruption and coercion continued as before, coup followed coup, and government followed government.

❑ *Johnson Holds Course*

A bare three weeks after the murder of Diem, Kennedy himself was assassinated. America's Vietnam policy did not change under the leadership of his successor, Lyndon Baines Johnson. He too was determined to prevent the fall of South Vietnam to Communism, but he soon learned that even greater American military intervention might be required. In August 1964, taking advantage of attacks (or alleged attacks) on American warships in the Gulf of Tonkin, Johnson secured what amounted to a congressional blank check for whatever policies he considered necessary in Southeast Asia. The so-called Gulf of Tonkin Resolution, passed unanimously by the House and by an 88-2 vote in the Senate, authorized the president as commander-in-chief of America's armed forces "to take all necessary measures to repel any armed attack against the forces of the United States and to prevent further aggression." The United States regarded the maintenance of international peace and security in Southeast Asia to be "vital to its national interest and world peace" and was therefore prepared, as determined by the president, to take "all necessary steps, including the use of armed force" to assist any member of the Southeast Asia Treaty Organization "requesting assistance in defense of its freedom."

Johnson did not make immediate use of these powers. His opponent in the forthcoming presidential elections was Senator Barry Goldwater, who supported the most extreme measures advocated by the Joint Chiefs of Staff, including the use of nuclear weapons. Johnson decided that the more prudent political course was to pose as a champion of caution and moderation. His strategy paid off, for in the elections of November 3, 1964, he won a landslide victory.

The Johnson administration now entered what Secretary of Defense McNamara subsequently considered to be the most crucial phase of its Vietnam policy and one that he described as a decisive "fork in the road." On January 27, 1965, he and National Security Adviser McGeorge Bundy presented the president with a memorandum setting forth two policy alternatives: to use American military power in the Far East to force a change in Communist policy, or to salvage whatever possible through negotiation and thereby avoid further military commitments. Among the senior members of the Johnson administration, only Undersecretary of State George Ball appears to have favored the second course and to have urged a compromise settlement.

After a personal inspection tour to Saigon, Bundy reported on February 4 that the situation in Vietnam was steadily deteriorating: the Vietnamese were unable to defend themselves, but negotiations too were impossible. "Any negotiated withdrawal today would mean surrender on the installment plan." Bundy therefore recommended a policy of graduated and sustained bombing of North Vietnam, a policy Johnson approved in the hope that bombing would defeat aggression "without escalating into war." Before going ahead with the bombing, however, Johnson consulted Eisenhower. The former commander of the Allied forces in Europe warned that a military escalation might indeed be required. He reminded Johnson that his first duty was to contain Communism in Southeast Asia. The time had come to adopt a policy of pressure. Eisenhower hoped that a large force would not be needed for this purpose, but if it were, "so be it."

The bombing campaign, Rolling Thunder, began on March 3, and over the next three years more bombs (in terms of tonnage) were dropped on Vietnam than on all of Europe in World War II. The bombing campaign also triggered the introduction of American ground forces. On March 7 and 9 two battalions of marines, the first American forces openly acknowledged to be combat troops, landed in Vietnam to defend the Danang air base. By mid-March the American commander in Vietnam, General William Westmoreland, strongly supported by the Joint Chiefs, was asking for two army divisions. The process of the escalation of the Vietnam conflict into an American war had begun.

In early 1965 there were some 23,000 American "advisers" in South Vietnam, a number that gradually swelled to well over a half-million by March of 1969. According to public opinion polls, this escalation was supported by a majority of the American people. More significantly, it was supported by some of America's most distinguished elder statesmen, a bipartisan group which came to be known at the Wise Men, who were virtually unanimous in advising Johnson to commit whatever forces were necessary to prevent South Vietnam from falling under Communist control. A lone call for negotiations by Paul Hoffman, who had headed the Marshall Plan, was firmly resisted by former Secretary of State Dean Acheson and Arthur Dean, Eisenhower's negotiator at the Korean armistice talks. This was no time "to turn over our Far East policy to the U.N."

The crucial problem remained, as it had all along, that the fundamental condition for American success in Vietnam had not been met, namely, the establishment of a stable government in Saigon supported by a population determined to resist a Communist takeover. Indeed, the opposite was true. After another mission to Saigon in November 1965, McNamara described the U.S. presence as resting on a bowl of jelly. Political instability had increased, pacification efforts had stalled, desertions from the South Vietnam army had skyrocketed. Nor did the situation improve with the arrival of large-scale American reinforcements and a stepped-up bombing campaign. As McNamara acknowledged many years later: "External military force cannot substitute for the political order and stability that must be forged *by* a people *for* themselves."

The Vietnamese *had* in fact created a stable political order, but that order had been established by the Communists who had rallied a substantial part of the Vietnamese population to their banner in the name of national unity and independence. The Americans found themselves fighting a guerrilla war in which the Vietcong, not they, enjoyed the support of the native population. American bombing failed to disrupt the supply routes to the South nor did it halt the flow of supplies from China and the USSR, which more than made up for the destruction caused by the bombing. Further, as had been the case in Germany and Japan during World War II, bombing signally failed to break the morale of the Vietnamese people. The American ground forces fared no better. Though the Communists suffered immense losses, their numbers actually increased as the war went on thanks to their ability to raise recruits among the local population and their steady reinforcement by North Vietnamese military units and Chinese "volunteers." Meanwhile American casualties, too, were steadily increasing—as was domestic opposition to the war.

❑ *The Impact of the Tet Offensive on American Policy*

At the end of January 1968 during the Tet (lunar new year) holiday, traditionally observed by a cease-fire, Hanoi mounted coordinated attacks against the major cities of South Vietnam. Although the Tet Offensive was eventually turned back everywhere with heavy losses, it proved to be a major psychological triumph. For this demonstration of the ability of the North Vietnamese to coordinate an attack on so broad a scale—reported in grim and often exaggerated detail in the American media—had a shattering impact on American public opinion. It reinforced the already powerful feelings of frustration about the war and spurred renewed calls for withdrawal from a conflict on behalf of a government that seemed so lacking in popular support and was manifestly incapable of defending itself.

American military leaders continued to urge a still greater military buildup in Vietnam, but by now Secretary of Defense McNamara, up to this time a firm supporter of the war, was urging the president to seek a negotiated peace. He argued that, if the war were allowed to continue, the president would be faced by a steady demand for more troops. He saw no prospect, however, that further escalation would bring victory, whereas it was certain to lead to a further erosion of public support.

Disgusted with McNamara, Johnson arranged for his appointment as president of the World Bank and his replacement as secretary of defense by Clark Clifford, who continued to favor military escalation. Before he officially took over at the Pentagon, Clifford bluntly asked the military to justify their request for additional troops. Accustomed to hearing optimistic prognostications, he was shocked to be told that they could provide no assurance that more troops or more bombing could ensure victory, nor did they know whether, if ever, the South Vietnamese would be ready to carry the main burden of the war. Although there were strong differences of opinion among the many experts he consulted, Clifford concluded that the war could not be won except at a cost disproportionate to whatever might be gained, and that from the standpoint of domestic politics a further escalation of the war would be suicidal. Clifford therefore could do no more than offer the president essentially the same advice that had decided him to get rid of McNamara: the United States must seek a negotiated peace.

❑ *Johnson's Final Peace Initiative and the 1968 Presidential Election*

Sick at heart, Johnson saw no alternative but to accept this advice. On March 31, 1968, he went on national television to announce that, on behalf of a negotiated peace, he was sharply cutting back the bombing of North Vietnam. He was prepared to discuss peace at any time and at any place, and was "designating one of our most distinguished Americans, Ambassador Averell Harriman, as my personal representative for such talks." He had also decided that the presidency should not be involved in the partisan divisions that were developing this election year; he would therefore not seek or accept his party's nomination for another term as president.

A mere three days later the North Vietnamese agreed to peace negotiations, which began in Paris on May 13. The chief of the American delegation, Averell Harriman, approached the negotiations with a good deal of skepticism. As far back as 1962 he had told an aide: "I don't agree with you that these people are dying to negotiate. They are dying to accept an honorable defeat on our part." Moreover, even if they did sign an agreement, Harriman doubted whether they would honor it for long.

Harriman's skepticism was justified. The talks bogged down immediately. The North Vietnamese demanded an unconditional stoppage of all bombing before they would even consider "substantive" negotiations. Beyond that, the two sides were deadlocked over who should represent South Vietnam at the negotiating table: the Saigon government, as demanded by the Americans, or the National Liberation Front, as demanded by Hanoi. In early October they reached a compromise of sorts by agreeing that both Saigon and the NLF should be represented. On October 31 President Johnson ordered the unconditional bombing halt demanded by Hanoi so that "substantive" negotiations could at last proceed. But on the very next day, Nguyen Van Thieu, president of South Vietnam since June 12, 1965, declared he would not take part in any negotiations if the NLF were allowed to participate as a separate delegation. With that the peace talks were aborted before they had a chance to begin.

Vietnam and the Paris peace talks had long since been major issues in the 1968 presidential election campaign. The Republican candidate, Richard Nixon, had announced that he had a secret plan to end the war and promised to begin withdrawing American troops. According to public opinion polls, he held a commanding lead over Vice President Hubert Humphrey, who remained associated with the policies of the Johnson administration. It was to offset this Nixon advantage that Harriman and other leading Democrats finally persuaded Johnson to announce the bombing halt on October 31, less than a week before the elections, which would allow the Democrats to claim that they had more than a peace plan; they were actually making peace. The strategy almost worked. The polls showed that in these final days Humphrey was rapidly narrowing Nixon's lead and might even be drawing ahead. Then came the news that President Thieu refused to negotiate on the terms Harriman had arranged in Paris. On November 5 Nixon won a narrow election victory.

Americans were to learn later that Thieu's refusal to negotiate had actually been encouraged by Nixon to ensure that the Democrats would not be able to make political capital out of any success they might achieve in Paris. Henry Kissinger, who was to become Nixon's national security adviser, was feeding Nixon information about the Paris negotiations from friends on the Harriman negotiating team, while Nixon was sending signals to Thieu through a variety of channels, assuring him that a Republican administration would provide firmer and more reliable support for his government than the Democrats. Thieu, however, was well aware of the antiwar sentiment in the United States, and fearful of being sold out in Paris, he needed no prompting from Nixon to sabotage the Paris negotiations. Nevertheless, although the contribution of Nixon and Kissinger to the Paris debacle cannot be considered decisive, their role in subverting the Paris peace talks was a scandalous betrayal of their own country's policies on behalf of partisan politics.

THIRTY-FOUR

□

Containment in Asia: Vietnam, Part 2

□ *Nixon's Vietnam Policy*

Although Nixon prided himself on his willingness to pursue bold and innovative programs, his Vietnam policy remained the same as that of his predecessors: the preservation of an independent, non-Communist state in South Vietnam. Failure to honor America's commitments to South Vietnam would destroy America's credibility with its other allies, open the way to Communist domination of Southeast Asia and beyond, and make for a bloodbath of major proportions in Indochina itself.

During the 1968 election campaign, Nixon had announced that he had a secret plan for ending the war in Vietnam with honor. As his critics complained, he should have made this plan public instead of using it as an election ploy. Had he done so, however, he would very probably have lost the election, for his plan was quite simply to threaten North Vietnam with nuclear warfare.

Nixon was convinced that this threat, used by Eisenhower in 1953, had been decisive in ending the Korean war, and he believed it could be used with equal effect in dealing with North Vietnam. To be effective, however, the threat had to be credible: the Communists had to be convinced that the new president would actually use nuclear weapons. For this purpose, he gave his staff orders to "slip the word" to the North Vietnamese, reminding them of his reputation as a political extremist. "I call it the madman theory," he told one one his aides, but in his case "a madman who has his hand on the nuclear button." Nixon confidently predicted that once Hanoi was confronted with this threat, "Ho Chi Minh himself will be in Paris in two days flat begging for peace."

But the North Vietnamese gave no sign of being intimidated by the threats of the new president. Ho did not appear in Paris to beg for peace, nor did his negotiating position become any more conciliatory or resilient. Informed by Kissinger of Nixon's commitment to a negotiated settlement, Ho responded with the same conditions that had doomed all previous negotiations: the unconditional withdrawal of all American forces from Indochina and the ouster of the "clique" now running the government of South Vietnam.

Once it became evident that Hanoi was not about to wilt under the threat of nuclear warfare, Nixon resorted to a combination of stratagems which had already been used or considered by his predecessors. Central to these was a program which became known as Vietnamization: the gradual withdrawal of American troops from Vietnam and shifting the responsibility for fighting the war to the South Vietnamese. This policy required Saigon to draft an ever-larger proportion of its country's male population into the army and a massive increase in American military aid to enable South Vietnam to carry on the war without American combat support.

The new burdens imposed on the people of South Vietnam only made the South Vietnam government more unpopular, and the Nixon administration was no more successful than earlier American governments in persuading South Vietnam to adopt policies that might generate public support. Nixon nevertheless assured the American people that Vietnamization was working, thereby generating popular support for his own government. American soldiers were coming home, the draft was abolished in favor of a volunteer army, and draft-age American students, freed from the threat of having to fight in Vietnam, no longer formed the vanguard of the antiwar movement. In the presidential election of 1972, the antiwar candidate, George McGovern, suffered a crushing defeat.

❑ *The Extension of the War to Cambodia and Laos*

Besides building up the army of South Vietnam, Nixon's Vietnamization program called for a systematic weakening of the enemy. This was to be done by stepping up the air war to destroy North Vietnam's military and economic installations and lines of communication, and by bombing enemy sanctuaries and supply routes in the neutral states of Cambodia and Laos.

As discussed earlier, since the beginning of the war the North Vietnamese had been sending men and supplies to the South through the territory of the nominally neutral states of Cambodia and Laos along a transport network known as the Ho Chi Minh trail, which enabled them to circumvent the demilitarized zone separating North and South Vietnam. Within the Cambodian frontier zone the North Vietnamese had also set up strategic bases from which they could carry out attacks on South Vietnam and then retire to "neutral" territory. Besides the Ho Chi Minh trail, the North Vietnamese were using Cambodia to transport supplies via the Cambodian port of Sihanoukville (Kompong Som) on the Gulf of Thailand.

Until Nixon's election, the Americans had held off taking action in Cambodia to avoid the international criticism that such an extension of the war would provoke and because of the danger of Soviet or Chinese intervention. Nixon accepted the risk of intervention, but to avoid a domestic outcry he ordered that the bombing be kept a top secret, a procedure which required a falsification of the records of American bombing operations.

Nixon gave the order to bomb Cambodia on March 16, 1969, and over the next fifteen months American B-52 bombers carried out 3,600 attacks on Cambodian territory. American military leaders described these bombing raids as "the most telling

operations of the entire war," claiming that they disrupted enemy logistics and reduced his capacity to use Cambodian staging areas for attacks on South Vietnam. According to eye-witness reports, however, the bombing did little more than drive the
North Vietnamese deeper into Cambodia. Bombing, no matter how intense, was incapable of disrupting a transportation system operating on human backs and bicycles.

In March 1970 Prince Noradoum Sihanouk, the head of the Cambodian government, who had chosen to ignore the North Vietnamese incursions to keep country out
of the conflict, was overthrown by his long-time political associate, General Lon Nol,
while Sihanouk was on a visit to China. Kissinger insists that the American government had nothing to do with the Cambodian coup. Lon Nol must nevertheless have
counted on American support, for one of his first acts was to send Hanoi an ultimatum demanding the withdrawal of North Vietnamese troops from Cambodia within
forty-eight hours. Disaster followed. Poorly trained and poorly equipped, the Cambodian army was no match for the veteran North Vietnamese, who now advanced farther than ever into Cambodia with the apparent objective of toppling the Lon Nol regime and installing a government under their Cambodian Communist proteges.

Confronted with the possibility the North Vietnam might soon have all of Cambodia as a military staging area, Nixon decided to "go for broke" in Cambodia and to
send American as well as South Vietnamese troops into the country to prevent its takeover by the Communists. This time there was no way he could keep the operation
secret. On April 30, 1970, Nixon went on national television to announce that American and South Vietnamese forces were moving into the nominally neutral state of
Cambodia. This was not an invasion, the president explained, but an incursion, a response to the aggression of the North Vietnamese, who had been violating Cambodia's neutrality for years for use as supply routes and staging areas for attacks on South
Vietnam. The target of the operation was the nerve center of North Vietnamese operations in Cambodia "to protect our men who are in Vietnam and to guarantee the
continued success of our withdrawal and the Vietnamization program."

According to reporters on the spot, the Cambodian invasion was not only politically damaging but militarily futile. The "nerve center" of North Vietnamese operations in Cambodia turned out to be little more than a scattering of empty huts. When
the invasion began, the North Vietnamese simply moved their operational bases farther into the Cambodian interior. The enemy supply routes, too, were only temporarily disrupted. The foot and bicycle paths were quickly repaired and new ones were
built. By the late spring and summer of 1970, men and supplies were again pouring
down a network of Ho Chi Minh trails.

From his own army, however, Nixon received glowing reports of the success of
the Cambodian operation, which encouraged him to cut the Ho Chi Minh trail running through the territory of neutral Laos. To avoid the domestic outrage provoked by
the Cambodian incursion, he ordered that the invasion of Laos be carried out exclusively by South Vietnamese troops. American participation was to be restricted to providing air and artillery support.

In Laos, however, there was nothing the American army leadership could do
to disguise the disastrous nature of the operation. The South Vietnamese invasion,
launched February 8, 1971, was met by a massive counterattack by a larger North

Vietnamese army equipped with the most modern Soviet tanks. Within six weeks the South Vietnamese were driven from Laos after suffering crippling losses, leaving the country more firmly than ever under North Vietnamese control.

❑ *Diplomatic Breakthrough?*

While implementing their program of Vietnamization and extending the Vietnam war to Cambodia and Laos, Nixon and Kissinger had never abandoned their endeavors on the diplomatic front. Although Kissinger's negotiations with the North Vietnamese were conducted in strictest secrecy to prevent leaks and the kind of sabotage that had scuttled the Harriman efforts, he had been no more successful than previous American negotiators in breaking the diplomatic deadlock. Hanoi continued to insist on complete and unconditional American military withdrawal from Indochina, the ouster of the present clique in Saigon, and the installation of a coalition government that would include representatives of the National Liberation Front.

With the death of Ho Chi Minh on September 3, 1969, the Americans had hoped that Hanoi would become more amenable to compromise, but nothing of the sort happened. Nixon too, however, although eager to get the Vietnam albatross off his back, still insisted on conditions that would ensure the independence of South Vietnam and allow him to claim that he had achieved "peace with honor."

On October 8, 1972, one month before another American presidential election, Kissinger's secret negotiations with Hanoi finally produced an agreement which has all the appearance of having been another election ploy. True, the agreement met America's fundamental condition: the North Vietnamese dropped their demand for the ouster of the Saigon government. Otherwise, however, the October agreement gave the North Vietnamese everything they could have desired. It provided for a cease-fire and for the withdrawal of all American troops within sixty days after the cease-fire went into effect. But, while all American troops were to be withdrawn, the North Vietnamese were to be allowed to remain in the positions they already occupied in South Vietnam—a quite incredible concession that suggests Kissinger was determined to secure an agreement at any price. The agreement did not even include nominal North Vietnamese guarantees to respect the independence of South Vietnam. Instead, the future arrangement for the government of South Vietnam was to be under the supervision of a National Council of Reconciliation and Concord, a tripartite commission representing the Thieu regime, the Hanoi-controlled National Liberation Front, and the Neutralists, whoever they might be. This National Council was to oversee elections in South Vietnam and assume responsibility for implementing the terms of the agreement. Thus, although the Thieu regime was to be left in place, Hanoi was granted the coalition government in South Vietnam which it had always demanded and one in which the National Liberation Front and the "neutralists" would have a majority position.

President Thieu, who had not been consulted in the course of Kissinger's negotiations and whose consent had not been sought for the October 8 agreement, was naturally outraged, and he now attempted to skewer the Kissinger negotiations as he had those of Harriman four years earlier. Kissinger professed to be enraged by Thieu's threat to what he claimed to be a major diplomatic achievement, conveniently forgetting his own role in Thieu's sabotage of Harriman's negotiations. On October 26, to forestall any further obstructionism on the part of Thieu, Kissinger went on national television to announce proudly that "peace is at hand." On November 7 Nixon won a landslide victory over the antiwar Democratic candidate George McGovern, a victory Kissinger interpreted as a landslide rejection by the American voters of the "candidate urging capitulation."

Having contributed to Nixon's election victory by holding out the prospect of peace through his agreement with North Vietnam, Kissinger had no qualms about repudiating some essential features of that agreement. When negotiations with Hanoi were resumed on November 20, he demanded the withdrawal of North Vietnamese troops from South Vietnam and the reestablishment of a demilitarized zone separating the North from the South. To back up these demands, he warned Hanoi that the president, with a landslide national mandate behind him, would not hesitate to take whatever action he considered necessary to protect American interests.

Once again the North Vietnamese refused to be intimidated. Rejecting any significant modification of the October 8 agreement, they broke off the negotiations until the Americans were prepared to honor their earlier commitments. Nixon's reaction was true to form. On December 18 he accused Hanoi of "deliberately and frivolously delaying the talks," and that same day he ordered a resumption of the bombing of North Vietnam and the mining of its harbors. The so-called Christmas bombing, halted on Christmas Day itself, was resumed on December 26 and continued for another four days. These attacks were the most intensive of the entire war, exceeding in tonnage all the bombs dropped from 1969 to 1971. As explained by Kissinger's aide Winston Lord, "The President felt he had to demonstrate that we couldn't be trifled with—and, frankly, to demonstrate our toughness to Thieu—that was the rationale for the bombing."

The bombing brought the North Vietnamese back to the negotiating table in Paris, but it accomplished little else. The Paris Accords of January 27, 1973, included essentially the same provisions as those of the October 8 agreement. This time they were imposed on President Thieu—a demonstration of sorts of Nixon's toughness, for the Paris Accords did no more than furnish some window dressing on Thieu's behalf. They provided for the maintenance of the demilitarized zone between North and South Vietnam and prohibited the infiltration of North Vietnamese troops and supplies to the South. But, as they left 150,000 North Vietnamese troops in the South, that prohibition seemed particularly pointless. Further, as in the October 8 agreement, they once again placed a National Council of Reconciliation in charge of a final political settlement in South Vietnam. Kissinger expressed complete satisfaction with the settlement. "We had achieved far better terms than most had thought possible."

Thieu did not agree. So far as his government was concerned, the terms could hardly have been worse. His sole consolation was Nixon's promise, made in writing on several occasions, that the United States would back up the agreement and respond in force to any violation of its provisions. Given the climate of opinion in Congress and the country at large, Nixon must have known that this was a promise he would not be able to keep. Nor did he.

❑ *The Collapse of the Saigon Government*

The January 1973 Paris Accords (for which Kissinger and his North Vietnamese counterpart, Lu Duc Tho, were awarded the Nobel Peace Prize) proved to be little more than a fig leaf covering America's withdrawal. The fighting between North and South Vietnam continued, and a genuine cease-fire did not take place in Vietnam until the final defeat of the Saigon government on April 30, 1975.

Kissinger blamed the failure of his peace agreement on the refusal of the American Congress to provide for its enforcement. Washington was maintaining large armies in Korea and Western Europe to uphold international treaties and American interests in those areas, but no combat troops were left in Vietnam. Kissinger does not remind us that American troops were withdrawn from Vietnam in accordance with terms he himself had negotiated. But even if American troops had remained in Vietnam, the war would simply have gone on as before with no better prospect of preserving the South Vietnam government. As the Americans had learned through bitter experience, no amount of American aid would have been sufficient to generate popular support for the Saigon regime or offset the incompetence and corruption of its leadership.

Meanwhile the North Vietnamese, although proceeding with caution to avoid provoking renewed American intervention, prepared systematically for a final showdown with the South. At a meeting of senior North Vietnamese political and military leaders, Lu Duc Tho, Hanoi's principal negotiator of the Paris Accords, reported with some pride his government's success in violating them. Since their signature, the Vietcong had regained control of the greater part of the South Vietnamese countryside, and he foresaw no danger of resistance on the part of the local population. There remained the danger of American intervention. Early in 1975, to test the American reaction, the North Vietnamese army launched an attack from Cambodia into the South Vietnam province of Phuoc Lang, sixty miles north of Saigon. The Hanoi leaders did not think the Americans would reenter the war or even resume their bombing, though they were prepared to adopt a different strategy if their calculations proved wrong. As it was, they estimated that two to three more years would be needed before the South Vietnamese army was finally defeated.

They were right about the Americans. Nixon had resigned in disgrace in the previous August, and the new Ford administration did not even threaten American intervention in Vietnam. But Hanoi had vastly overestimated the Saigon government's capacity and will to resist. Within a fortnight North Vietnamese forces had overrun the Phuoc Lang province. From here they swept to the coast, cutting South Vietnam in half. Their northern offensive was equally successful. The ancient capital of Hué fell on March 25, the great naval base at Danang surrendered five days later, just thirty-two hours after being surrounded. By the end of March the roads of South Vietnam were clogged with millions of refugees, virtually halting the movement of South Vietnamese troops and creating a panic atmosphere among them.

Encouraged by their unexpectedly easy victories, the North Vietnamese leadership resolved to strike at Saigon itself before the spring rains set in. President Thieu resigned on April 21 and fled to Taiwan, denouncing the desertion of the Americans as an "inhumane act by an inhumane ally." On the morning of April 30, 1975, North

Vietnamese forces stormed into Saigon, bringing to an abrupt end a war that had lasted for almost thirty years.

The war had taken the lives of at least one and a half million Vietnamese, hundreds of thousands had been maimed, millions more had become refugees. Over 58,000 Americans had died in Vietnam, the United States had spent 170 billion dollars and would spend another 200 billion in pensions and compensation to Vietnam veterans. But the American government did nothing to prevent the final fall of Saigon, and given the state of American public opinion, there was nothing it could have done. In the 1976 presidential elections, hardly a word was said about Vietnam. Central to American concerns for so many years, Vietnam was no longer an issue.

❑ *Southeast Asia after the American Withdrawal*

There could hardly have been a more telling revelation of the ignorance and misconceptions that had fueled American intervention in Vietnam than the events in Southeast Asia that took place following the American withdrawal. The dominos did not fall, at least not in the way American interventionists had predicted. Instead, the ethnic hatreds and rivalries that had played so large a role throughout the history of Southeast Asia flared up with renewed intensity.

Hanoi originally allowed South Vietnam to retain its separate identity under a Provisional Revolutionary Government, but in July 1976 North and South Vietnam were merged to form the Socialist Republic of Vietnam. Observers sympathetic to North Vietnam reported with some satisfaction that the fall of Saigon was not followed by a bloodbath, as Nixon and so many other supporters of the Saigon government had predicted. Instead, a "disciplined" Hanoi government was concentrating on the tasks of reconstruction and reconciliation.

The records of the Hanoi government itself tell a different story. Although the North Vietnamese did not indulge in massacres on a Stalinist or Maoist scale, they nevertheless carried out large-scale executions of South Vietnamese officials accused of war crimes. The fate of thousands of others was in many respects worse than a bloodbath. Some 400,000 South Vietnamese civil servants and army officers, as well as physicians, teachers, technicians, journalists and others who could be classified as intellectuals, were herded into "re-education" camps, where, according to Amnesty International, they were beaten and tortured and deprived of adequate food and medical care. Later, in an outburst of xenophobic zeal, the government was to conduct brutal campaigns against Vietnam's ethnic minorities, which in the case of the Chinese developed into outright genocide.

In undertaking the formidable task of reconstruction in a land devastated by so many years of war, the Hanoi leadership looked for guidance to the social and economic policies introduced by other Marxist governments. These called for a centralized state-controlled economy, the transfer of private property to state and communal ownership, and the mobilization of the population for service to the state. A currency reform, which destroyed the old "capitalist" currency, was deliberately designed to promote the creation of an egalitarian society, as was a taxation system that wiped out the profits of anyone still engaged in "bourgeois" business enterprises. A Five-Year Plan, introduced in December 1976, concentrated on industrial development at the expense of agriculture, but the government's fiscal policies had left the country without adequate financial resources for industrial expansion. The situation was made even worse by the government's purge of professional administrators and technicians, and by the ideologically driven procedures of bureaucrats entrusted with the central direction of a planned economy who snarled production in a hopeless maze of directives and regulations.

While the industrialization program faltered, agricultural production plummeted. In the countryside, peasants resisted their transfer to collective farms, in many areas they killed their livestock rather than have them confiscated by the government, and collectivisation itself deprived them of any incentive to produce. To stimulate agriculture production, the government included in its Five-Year Plan a program to remove a large proportion of the urban population from the cities to new economic zones, which were to supply food for what remained of the urbanites—a program that was to involve the forced relocation of six million people. The theory behind this mass urban relocation program was that bourgeois shopkeepers and hawkers who trafficked for a living had performed no useful work for the state.

The new economic zones proved to be yet another disaster. Government planners made virtually no preparations to accommodate the new settlers, many of whom had indeed been employed in bourgeois occupations and had never before done agricultural work. Without adequate tools or training, in many cases without even a minimum supply of food or seeds for cultivation, their contribution to agricultural production was minimal, their suffering intense; thousands starved.

Nothing demonstrated more clearly the revulsion of the population to the government's policies than the mass exodus from Vietnam that took place after the fall of Saigon. One hundred thousand fled in the first wave of refugees. They were eventually followed by 1.5 million others. Their flight, whether by land or sea, was difficult and dangerous. Nor did their suffering end with their escape, for the majority of those who survived found themselves penned in squalid refugee camps where thousands were to remain for years.

❏ The Fate of the Ethnic Chinese and the Response of China

No segment of the Vietnamese population was subjected to more humiliation and misery than the ethnic Chinese. The traditional hostility of the Vietnamese toward the Chinese had been dampened but not extinguished by China's support of the Vietnamese in their wars against France and the United States. But even before the fall of Saigon that hostility had flared up again, initially over disputed claims to the Spratly Islands in the South China Sea and frontier territories along the Sino-Vietnamese border. In these territorial controversies with China, the Vietnamese looked to the Soviet Union for support, while at home they turned against the ethnic Chinese as enemy aliens in their midst. As the controversy with Peking intensified, the Vietnamese introduced measures specifically directed against the Chinese community. In late 1976 the Hanoi government closed all Chinese newspapers and schools. Early in the following year it began the expulsion of ethnic Chinese from disputed frontier territories and the forcible relocation of Chinese in economic development areas.

In the spring of 1978, to protest this persecution, the Chinese government severed all remaining economic ties with Vietnam and withdrew its technical and economic advisers. China chose to blame the Soviet Union for Vietnam's hostility to China and the ethnic Chinese. "Behind every anti-Chinese step taken by the Vietnamese authorities is the large shadow of Soviet imperialism," the Chinese declared. "Moscow needs . . . a 'forward post' to dominate Southeast Asia [as part of its] strategic plan . . . to outflank and encircle Europe and isolate the United States."

Chinese fears of collusion between Moscow and Hanoi seemed confirmed with the signature on November 3, 1978, of a Soviet-Vietnam Treaty of Friendship and Cooperation, which was in effect a military alliance. In return for a continuation of Soviet military and economic aid, Vietnam allowed the Soviets to use the former American military and naval station at Cam Ranh Bay, which gave Moscow a forward post to outflank China, if not Europe.

There followed a succession of bizarre episodes, as the Communist Vietnamese, supported by the Communist Soviet Union, invaded Communist Cambodia, supported by Communist China, to install a Communist Vietnamese puppet government in Pnom Penh. Communist China responded with an invasion of Communist Vietnam, which set off another mass expulsion of Vietnam's ethnic Chinese by the Vietnamese government.

By the end of the decade, an estimated 260,000 of Vietnam's ethnic Chinese population had fled, or been driven, to China. Another 400,000 had joined the hundreds of thousands of ethnic Vietnamese fleeing their country by boat.

❑ *The Agony of Cambodia* 1975-79

The bloodbath Nixon had predicted for Vietnam in the event of a Communist victory took place with a vengeance in Cambodia.

On April 17, 1975, thirteen days before the fall of Saigon to the North Vietnamese, the army of the Cambodian Communists, the Khmer Rouge, swept into the capital of Pnom Penh and overthrew the American-backed Lon Nol government. That very day the Khmer Rouge leader, Pol Pot, inaugurated a revolution even more radical than anything attempted so far in the Soviet Union or China. Once in control of Pnom Penh, he ordered the immediate evacuation of all inhabitants from "this wasteful and consuming city" and from all other urban areas. In a single week after April 17, some 2 million people were driven from the cities of Cambodia and relocated in work camps in the countryside.

Determined to eradicate all vestiges of the old regime and traditional values, the Khmer Rouge engaged in a mass killing of former leaders, intellectuals, priests, and even peasants who adhered to "family-oriented" methods of production. A constitution promulgated in January 1976 established the Democratic Republic of Kampuchea, which was declared to be a state of "workers, peasants, and other laborers." The entire population was drafted into restructuring society, private property was nationalized, the use of money abolished, the Buddhist religion proscribed, and the people forced to live in government-controlled communes. The destructive fury of the Khmer Rouge laid waste a large part of the country, ruined the economy, and ultimately caused the death of an estimated 2 million people—one-quarter of the entire prewar population—through starvation, exposure, disease, or outright murder.

An integral feature of the Khmer Rouge revolution was its extreme xenophobia, which was directed against all foreign influences but especially against the Thais and the Vietnamese. Although the Khmer Rouge owed their very survival to Communist Vietnam's support, they now proclaimed their intention to root out all Vietnamese influence by every possible means. A resolution of the party's Central Committee of June 1976 declared Vietnam to be the Number One enemy of Kampuchea, and the army was ordered to wipe out Cambodia's own Vietnamese population so as to "to strike terror in the hearts of the Vietnamese people."

❑ *The Vietnamese Occupation of Cambodia*

Infuriated by the persecution and massacre of Cambodia's ethnic Vietnamese population and by Khmer Rouge attacks on Vietnamese military outposts and settlements along the Cambodian frontier, Hanoi decided the time had come to crush their erstwhile Communist proteges. On Christmas Day 1978 the North Vietnamese launched a full-scale invasion of Cambodia. Within a fortnight they had swept aside the Khmer Rouge army, entered Pnom Penh, and ousted the Pol Pot government. In its place they installed a native Cambodian puppet government made up of Cambodian exiles who had fled to Vietnam to escape the Khmer Rouge.

The Soviet Union hailed the liberation of Cambodia from the "Pol Pot clique" and proclaimed the inauguration of a new era of peace and freedom in Indochina. A very different note was sounded in Peking, which denounced the Vietnamese invasion as part of a Soviet plot to conquer Southeast Asia and "an important part of the global strategy pursued by Moscow in its quest for world hegemony."

❑ *The Chinese Invasion of Vietnam*

The Chinese did more than denounce the Vietnamese invasion of Cambodia. Their anger at the boil over Vietnam's treatment of the ethnic Chinese and Hanoi's ingratitude for China's earlier support, the Chinese invaded Vietnam on January 30, 1979. Fearful of Soviet intervention, however, they announced that their action was a "defensive retaliatory strike" designed to do no more than "teach Hanoi a lesson" and that their invasion would be limited in scope and time.

Now it was the turn of the Vietnamese to throw out charges of hegemonism and imperialism. They accused China's "reactionary rulers" of "plotting with the United States imperialists to annex our country in a bid to realize their great power expansionism and hegemonism." "They have now thrown off the revolutionary mask . . . to collude with the imperialists. . . . They have become a dangerous and direct enemy of the whole Socialist system." The Soviets joined in the chorus, branding the Chinese invasion as a brazen bandit attack and hailing Vietnam as "the mighty obstacle to Peking's expansionism in Southeast Asia."

The Chinese kept their word so far as Vietnam was concerned. They broke off their offensive within two weeks. As a "lesson" to Hanoi, their invasion did no more than hasten the exodus of Vietnam's remaining ethnic Chinese. Somewhat surprisingly, the Chinese also left Hanoi in control of Cambodia, where the Vietnamese maintained a 170,000-man occupation army to support their puppet regime in Phnom Penh and carry on the fight against Pol Pot's guerrilla army.

The Vietnamese withdrew their troops from Cambodia in September 1989, a move directly connected with political crises in Eastern Europe and the sharp curtailment of Soviet and East European aid. Without this aid, Hanoi was finding the occupation of Cambodia an intolerable economic burden. Even after the withdrawal of Vietnamese troops, however, the Vietnamese continued to exercise a dominant influence in Cambodia, whose government remained dependent on Vietnamese support in combatting domestic opposition. *1977-81*

 Throughout the crisis over Cambodia, the Carter government in the United States had sided with China in support of the Pol Pot regime, blandly ignoring its bestiality and the fact that it had ousted the pro-American government of Lon Lol. Carter's bitterly anti-Russian national security adviser, Zbigniew Brzezinski (see p. 453), saw the conflict in Cambodia as a proxy war between China and the Soviet Union. Already in May 1978 he had inaugurated a diplomatic alignment with China on behalf of the Pol Pot regime. With Vietnam's invasion of Cambodia, the United States branded Vietnam as the aggressor, which of course it was, and joined China and Thailand in retaining Cambodia's seat in the United Nations for representatives of the Pol Pot regime.

☐ *The Communist Triumph in Laos*

Although the Paris Accords of January 1973 had called for the withdrawal of all foreign troops from Laos and Cambodia, the North Vietnamese had not even made a gesture to honor this agreement but had kept a substantial force in both countries. Their attempt to retain control over Cambodia had been temporarily frustrated by the Khmer Rouge. They had better luck in Laos, where their troops supported the Communist Pathet Lao Party, whose leaders made no attempt to disguise their subservience to Hanoi.

Laos's satellite status was sealed in a twenty-five year Treaty of Friendship with Vietnam of July 18, 1977, which gave Hanoi the right to maintain an army in Laos "to assist in defending the country against foreign threats and domestic sabotage. Although less extreme than the Communist governments of Cambodia and Vietnam, the People's Republic of Laos carried out similar purges of its opponents and instituted a government-controlled economy. This government has survived into the 1990s, and its behavior suggests that Laos has remained a Vietnamese satellite.

◻

THIRTY-FIVE

Waging the Cold War: From the Helsinki Accords to the Ouster of Gorbachev

❑ Carter's Foreign Policy

In the presidential elections of November 1976, Gerald Ford was defeated by the Democratic candidate, Jimmy Carter. A wealthy peanut farmer from Georgia, Carter had graduated from the Naval Academy, served on a nuclear submarine, entered politics as a state senator in the 1960s, and was elected governor of Georgia in 1970. He had little experience in domestic politics on the federal level or in foreign affairs, but in the atmosphere of disillusionment following the Watergate scandals and the Vietnam disaster, Carter successfully extolled his very lack of involvement in Washington politics in his run for the presidency. He came to the Oval Office with a Wilsonian sense of morality and mission. "I don't want to do anything as President," he said, "that would be a contravention of moral and ethical standards that I would exemplify in my own life as an individual."

Carter intended to apply these same moral standards in his conduct of foreign policy. He expressed the belief that "the demonstration of American idealism was a practical and realistic approach to foreign affairs, and moral principles were the best foundation for the exertion of American power and influence." He rejected the doctrine of containment and announced his desire to put the Cold War behind him, reestablish normal relations not only with China but with Cuba and Vietnam, withdraw American troops from Korea, suspend production of the B-1 bomber and the neutron bomb, and in the field of arms control, to go beyond mere limitation to actual arms reduction. He declared that it was necessary to see international problems on a global scale, to go beyond petty bickering over parochial issues in order to work out global settlements of global problems. Prominent among these was Carter's concern for human rights. "Our commitment to human rights must be absolute," he proclaimed in his inaugural address. But Carter aspired to do far more. He hoped to improve the life of all the peoples of the world through the implementation of international agreements over clean air, clean water, safe supplies of energy, and laws governing the exploitation of the seas.

Carter was unquestionably sincere in declaring his intention to keep his political as well as personal conduct in line with moral principles, and his ability to convey this sense of decency to a jaded electorate undoubtedly contributed to his political success. Unfortunately, in Carter's case, morality and goodwill were not sufficient to overcome political inexperience or the pitfalls of practical politics. Moreover, Carter himself lacked the very qualities that were essential to seeing problems on a global scale. Intelligent, with an enviable capacity to absorb and retain information, he had difficulty interpreting this information and placing it in a global context. Instead, he hunkered down in dealing with individual issues with a myopic parochialism he professed to deplore. Asked whether the president had trouble seeing the woods for the trees, one of his aides complained that Carter had trouble seeing the trees for the leaves.

In the end, owing to a combination of monstrous bad luck and failure to appreciate many of the practical difficulties involved in foreign policy, virtually all his original noble objectives were abandoned or hopelessly compromised. Despite his pledge to cut military spending and America's military presence abroad, military spending increased 14.5 percent during his administration and more American soldiers were posted overseas. Carter found it impossible to withdraw American forces from Korea. To bolster a sagging economy, he authorized increases in American arms sales abroad. While advocating nuclear nonproliferation, he agreed to ship 38 metric tons of enriched uranium to India despite India's refusal to sign the nonproliferation treaty. He failed to secure Senate ratification of the SALT II arms limitation treaty (see p. 436). He failed to normalize relations with Cuba. Toward the end of his administration America's relations with the Soviet Union had sunk to a new low. The most grievous blow to his presidency, however, was the seizure of hostages at the American embassy in Teheran by irate Iranians, who were infuriated that Carter had allowed the deposed shah of Iran to come to New York for treatment of the cancer that would shortly kill him. The Iranian hostage crisis was to be his overriding concern during his last months in office. (See p. 519.)

To offset this catalogue of failure, the Carter administration could point to several notable achievements. Carter himself was proudest of the Camp David Accords of September 1978, his personal brokerage of an agreement between Egypt and Israel, which eventually led to peace between these two countries. But this success did not lead to an overall peace settlement in the Middle East, as Carter had hoped, and Israel's relations with all the countries of the Middle East, including Egypt, remain tense. (See Chapters 36 and 37.)

❑ *The Panama Canal Treaties, July 9, 1977*

Carter's most enduring achievements were his treaties with Panama, which provided for the eventual reversion of the Panama Canal to Panamanian control—though many Americans regard even these as yet another Carter disaster.

In November 1903, after engineering a revolution through which Panama broke away from Colombia to become an independent state, the United States had concluded a treaty with the new Panamanian government that gave the Americans full jurisdiction, in perpetuity, over a zone five miles wide on both sides of a future canal, whose "neutrality" was to be guaranteed by the United States. By the time the Panama

Canal was constructed and opened to shipping on August 15, 1914, the Panamanians had already begun agitating for a revision of the 1903 treaty and demanding America's recognition of Panamanian sovereignty over the Canal Zone. After World War II, Panamanian agitation assumed dangerous proportions, and on January 10, 1960, following large-scale riots, the Panamanian government formally denounced the 1903 treaty and broke off diplomatic relations with the United States. Fearful that the Panamanians might go so far as to destroy the canal if Washington remained obdurate, the Johnson, Nixon, and Ford administrations all agreed on the need for a negotiated settlement of the canal issue.

Negotiations had heretofore broken down over the Panamanian demand for unfettered control of the canal and the elimination of any possibility of American intervention in Panamanian affairs, a demand rejected by the Americans, who insisted that the successful operation and security of the canal required that they share in its administration and defense. To circumvent these differences, the Carter administration negotiated two treaties with the Panamanians. The first met the Panamanian demand for unfettered control of the canal by providing for a mixed American-Panamanian administration until 1999, after which full control would be exercised by the Panamanians. The second, the so-called Neutrality Treaty, dealt with the major American concern by giving the United States the permanent right to defend the canal and keep it open under all circumstances.

The two treaties were signed in an elaborate ceremony in Washington on September 7, 1977. Zbigniew Brzezinski, Carter's national security adviser, says in his memoirs that Carter regarded these treaties "as the ideal fusion of morality and politics; he was doing something good for peace, responding to the passionate desires of a small nation, and yet helping the long-range United States national interest."

Neither the American nor Panamanian parliaments, whose ratification was necessary for the treaties to come into effect, shared Carter's enthusiasm about them. Americans objected that Panamanian control of the canal would threaten American security, while Panamanians contended that giving the Americans the right to defend the canal would allow for continued American intervention in Panamanian affairs. To close the gap between American and Panamanian perceptions of the treaties, Carter and the Panamanian chief of state, General Omar Torrijos, issued a formal statement reiterating that the Neutrality Treaty gave both countries the right to keep the canal open against *any* threat, "but this does not mean, nor shall it be interpreted as a right of intervention of the United States in the internal affairs of Panama." American opponents of the treaties were still not satisfied, and over the next six months the Carter administration devoted more time to overcoming the objections of American senators than to any other foreign policy issue. The Senate finally ratified the Neutrality Treaty on March 16, 1978, but only after being given yet another government statement that the United States had the right to take any action, including the use of force, to keep the canal open. In the end the Panamanian parliament, too, ratified the treaties, but any goodwill the Carter government hoped to reap from ceding the canal to Panamanian control was blighted by the Panamanian fear (thoroughly justified by later events) that the Americans would continue to use the excuse of defending the canal to intervene in their country's domestic affairs.

❑ Arms Control and SALT II

In negotiating a SALT II treaty, as had been envisaged in the SALT I agreement (see p. 436), Carter intended to go beyond a mere limitation on the possession and deployment of nuclear weaponry—and the very high ceilings on those limitations. Instead, Carter called for an arms *reduction* treaty whereby the two superpowers would make deep cuts in their respective nuclear arsenals, restrict weapons testing, and ban further weapons deployment altogether. In putting forward these proposals, Carter revealed his political inexperience, for he failed to take into account their political implications, at home and abroad, and announced them publicly before presenting them to the Soviets. He was saved embarrassment at home by Brezhnev, who dismissed the president's proposals out of hand, calling them "unconstructive and one-sided" and "harmful to Soviet interests."

Disarmament negotiations nevertheless continued between Carter's secretary of state, Cyrus Vance, and the Soviet foreign minister, Andrei Gromyko, but another two years were required before Vance and Gromyko finally reached agreement on the terms of a SALT II treaty, which was signed by Carter and Brezhnev in Vienna on June 18, 1979. SALT II had been called one of the most complicated treaties ever negotiated, but once again it did no more than limit weaponry (still at very high levels) and the deployment of weapons systems. In the United States the treaty was bitterly attacked by both the Left and Right—by the Left because it did nothing to reduce nuclear arsenals; by the Right because it was seen as conceding too much to the Soviets. SALT II was finally killed by the Soviet invasion of Afghanistan in December 1979 (see p. 520), which ended any chance of the treaty's ratification by the American Senate.

Arms control negotiations nevertheless continued in Geneva until December, 1981, when the Soviets walked out after failing to halt the deployment of American Pershing II missiles in Western Europe. Meaningful arms talks were not resumed for another four years.

❑ Enter Ronald Reagan

Running on a platform calling for large-scale tax reductions, a massive increase in military spending to restore America's global supremacy, and a repudiation of a policy of détente, Ronald Reagan easily won the Republican nomination for the presidency in 1980 and trounced Jimmy Carter in the elections held in November of that year.

Ronald Reagan was born in 1911 in Tampico, Illinois, the son of an alcoholic and frequently unemployed shoe salesman who possessed the Irish flair for telling a good story—"the best raconteur I ever heard," his son recalled admiringly. This was a talent Ronald inherited and used to good effect in his political career. After attending Eureka College, a small church-affiliated institution in Illinois, Reagan became a sports broadcaster and eventually a successful motion picture actor. Handsome and genial, Reagan was always well-liked. He had been president of his high school senior class, and in Hollywood he was elected president of the Screen Actors Guild, which he led to victory in its only strike.

At that time Reagan was still a liberal-leaning Democrat and a fervent admirer of Franklin Roosevelt. In the 1960s, however, he was drawn into the burgeoning neo-conservative movement; he joined the Republican party and won lasting credit among Republican conservatives by his staunch support of Barry Goldwater's unsuccessful bid for the presidency in 1964. He reaped the fruits of that credit with his election as governor of California in 1967, and in 1976, after two terms as governor, he came close to defeating the incumbent president Gerald Ford for his party's presidential nomination. He won the nomination on his second bid four years later and went on to score a landslide victory in the November presidential elections.

Henry Kissinger has described Reagan's political success as an astonishing per-formance and one that has been nearly incomprehensible to academicians. Reagan was certainly no intellectual. He was ill at ease in answering questions unless supplied with cue cards, and his public performances were elaborately stage-managed. His knowledge of history seemed rudimentary, and what he did know appeared to have been boiled down to a few simplistic ideas about the evils of Communism, the dan-gers of appeasement, and the virtues of America.

Academicians may have been astonished by Reagan's political success, but the reasons for that success were obvious enough. Kissinger himself makes the point that Reagan had an extraordinary intuitive rapport with a large majority of the American people. Weary of Carter's moral sermons, his impotence in dealing with the Iranian hostage crisis, the apparent decline in American prestige and influence abroad, and the soaring rate of inflation at home, the American electorate turned with obvious re-lief to the buoyantly optimistic Ronald Reagan, who repudiated the Carter legacy and promised a revival of American greatness. Called the Great Communicator by his ad-mirers, Reagan was able to generate immense popular support for his policies by his simple and readily comprehensible explanations, made all the more convincing by their appeals to American patriotism, prejudice, and self-interest.

To the delight of American patriots and taxpayers, Reagan honored his campaign promises. He cut taxes and launched the largest peacetime arms buildup in American history. He approved the construction of 100 B-1 bombers, at the cost of 3 billion dol-lars each, and ordered the assembly and stockpiling of neutron bombs. He revived the production of chemical weapons, expanded the weapons research program, enlarged the navy and the special forces for counterinsurgency warfare, and increased the num-ber of American troops overseas. With his tax cuts and military spending program—a five-year 1.5-trillion-dollar defense budget—he ran up a federal debt larger than the combined total incurred by all previous administrations. In their patriotic euphoria, most Americans were happy to overlook the significance of that debt burden, and even Reagan's critics found it inexpedient to attack him on this issue because of his personal popularity and public support for his policies.

❑ *Reagan's Contradictory Soviet Policy*

Reagan had little trouble securing support for his arms buildup, which he explained to the American people as essential to the security—indeed, the very survival—of a Free World confronted as it was with an ever-growing threat from the Communist world. In his first press conference after becoming president, he denounced détente as a one-way street which had been exploited by Soviet leaders to promote world revolution and enable them to realize their ultimate goal of establishing a one-world Communist state. In their fanatic quest for world domination, the Soviet leadership reserved the right to commit any crime, to lie, and to cheat. With this evaluation of Soviet motives and policies, Reagan was saying, in effect, that all negotiation with the Soviets was futile because any agreement reached was certain to be violated.

Reagan seemed to cling to this view of the Soviet leadership. In March 1983, after two years in office, he told the National Association of Evangelicals that "if history teaches us anything, it teaches that simple-minded appeasement or wishful thinking about our adversaries is folly." He denounced the idea of a freeze on nuclear weapons, and urged his audience not to ignore "the facts of history and the aggressive impulses of an evil empire." We are enjoined by scripture and the Lord Jesus to oppose sin and evil, he said, and the simple fact was that the Soviet Union was "the focus of evil in the modern world."

There is an astonishing contradiction between these simplistic pronouncements and Reagan's actual policies in dealing with the Soviet Union. This contradiction can best be explained by that fact that Reagan, like all successful politicians, was never altogether consistent and adjusted his rhetoric to the audience he was addressing. A speech before the British parliament in June 1982, for example, was a remarkably perceptive analysis of the problems facing the Soviet Union, whose accuracy would soon be borne out by events. Referring to current antigovernment demonstrations in Poland, he saw the Soviet Union as being gripped by a "great revolutionary crisis," and Poland, "magnificently unreconciled to repression," as the pivot of that crisis. "The global campaign for freedom," he predicted, "will ultimately prevail. . . . It is the Soviet Union that runs against the tide of human history by denying human freedom and human dignity to its citizens." Reagan noted that the Soviet Union was also in deep economic trouble. The rate of Soviet economic growth had been declining steadily since the 1950s and was less than half of what it had been then. "The dimensions of this failure are astounding. A country which employs one-fifth of its population in agriculture is unable to feed its own people. . . . Overcentralized, with little or no incentives . . . what we see here is a political structure that no longer corresponds to its economic base, a society where productive forces are hampered by political ones." Reagan predicted "repeated explosions against repression" in Eastern Europe, and warned that "the Soviet Union itself is not immune to this reality."

In his first press conference after becoming president, Reagan had scornfully rejected a policy of détente, yet as early as April 24, 1981, in the first weeks of his administration, he formally lifted the grain embargo imposed on the Soviets by President Carter. This was not done merely to curry favor with American farmers, for on that same day he addressed a handwritten letter to Leonid Brezhnev reminding the Soviet leader that the United States had used its power after World War II to rebuild the war-ravaged economies of the world, including those of countries that had been America's enemies. "It is in this spirit, the spirit of helping the people of both our nations, that I have lifted the grain embargo. Perhaps this decision will contribute to creating the circumstances which will lead to the meaningful and constructive dialogue which will assist us in fulfilling our joint obligations to find lasting peace."

This conciliatory policy was at odds with the views of Reagan's secretary of state, Alexander Haig, a bumptious general who had served on the staff of Henry Kissinger and as White House chief of staff during the final crisis of the Nixon administration. Nixon described Haig as "the meanest, toughest s.o.b. I ever knew," a quality about which Nixon spoke with some authority. During the Carter administration, Haig had expressed contempt for Carter's "experiment in obsequiousness" in dealing with the Soviet Union and deplored his failure to match the Soviet arms buildup. Moscow, he declared, was the "greatest single source of international insecurity today," and he warned that the Soviets' "tremendous accumulations of armed might has [sic] produced the most complete reversal of global power relationships ever seen in a period of relative peace."

Disagreeing with Reagan's April 24 letter to Brezhnev, Haig persuaded the president not to send a second letter in which he expressed his desire for a nuclear-free world and nuclear disarmament—an even more remarkable departure from Reagan's campaign rhetoric. Whether because of differences with Haig over these or quite different issues, Reagan, who ordinarily tried to avoid unpleasant personal confrontations, fired Haig in June 1982 and replaced him with George Shultz, a successful corporate executive with a reputation for integrity and efficiency. Shultz came to State with a good deal of government experience, having served as Nixon's secretary of labor, director of the Office of Management and Budget, and secretary of the treasury. Because Shultz had been reluctant to support Nixon's crackdown on his opponents, Nixon regarded him as a "candy ass" and had not recommended his appointment to Reagan.

Although Shultz was a firm supporter of Reagan's arms buildup, he was also a believer in negotiation. Convinced that personal encounters would produce a more pragmatic policy in dealing with the Soviets than theoretical analyses, Shultz met with the Soviet ambassador, Anatoly Dobrynin, early in 1983 with a view to resolving Soviet–American differences. The first fruit of their discussions was an agreement to renew arms negotiations in Geneva.

Soviet–American relations were severely strained when on September 1, 1983, the Soviets shot down a South Korean airliner that had strayed into Soviet air space, killing all 269 passengers. Reagan branded the shootdown a "crime against humanity" and an "act of barbarism," but he limited his official response to demanding a Soviet apology and compensation to the victims. Moreover, in that same month he concluded the biggest grain deal in history with the Soviet government. Early in the following year he expressed publicly his desire for a more conciliatory Soviet policy, saying that the United States was "in its strongest position in years to establish a constructive and realistic working relationship with the Soviet Union." Further, after objecting to European trade with the Soviet bloc and attempting to block the construction of a pipeline to bring Soviet natural gas to Europe, he reversed his position on the gas pipeline and encouraged European sales of high-tech equipment to the Soviet bloc.

❑ *Reagan, Nuclear Arms and the Strategic Defense Initiative (SDI)*

Reagan's policies also contradicted his rhetoric condemning a nuclear freeze. His letter to Brezhnev expressing his desire for a nuclear-free world was not intended as a mere diplomatic ploy. In a speech to the Japanese parliament, he let his audience know that he was fully aware of the catastrophic consequences of a nuclear war. "A nuclear war can never be won and must never be fought . . . for it would certainly mean the end of civilization as we know it." In his memoirs, Reagan tells us that he wanted to go far beyond a nuclear freeze. "My dream," he says, "became a world free of nuclear weapons." He goes on to say: "Since I knew it would be a long and difficult task to rid the world of nuclear weapons, I had this second dream: the creation of a defense against nuclear missiles, so we could change from a policy of assured destruction to one of assured survival."

In March 1983 he set forth a program he believed would fulfill this dream. He called upon America's scientists to turn their great talents to creating a weapons system to destroy enemy missiles before they reached American soil or the soil of America's allies, a defense system that would render the enemy's nuclear weapons "impotent and obsolete." This was his Strategic Defense Initiative (SDI), popularly known as Star Wars, which grew into a 17-billion-dollar research-and-development program.

Reagan's nuclear defense program was inspired by admirable intentions, but that program was as illusionary as anything proposed by Jimmy Carter—and far more expensive. As virtually all nuclear scientists have agreed, it was impossible to create an absolutely impenetrable defense system. In the event of a nuclear war, a few nuclear missiles were certain to get through and would thus be enough to ensure the destruction of modern civilization. Further, a nuclear shield would provide no defense against nuclear weapons *not* delivered by long-range missiles or against the incalculable dangers of biological and chemical warfare. Yet no arguments or evidence could convince Reagan of the futility of his SDI initiative, which was one of the few issues that engaged his full attention to the end of his years in the White House.

To the dismay of critics of Reagan's SDI, this program had been revived under President George W. Bush, who seems similarly deaf to all arguments about its futility.

❑ *The Succession of Mikhail Gorbachev*

Leonid Brezhnev had become increasingly senile in the years before his death in November 1982. His successor as party chairman, Yuri Andropov, the chief of the Soviet intelligence organization (KGB), was already ill at the time of his election and died in February 1984. Andropov's successor was the elderly Konstantin Chernenko, who died in March 1985.

After Chernenko's death, however, the succession passed to Mikhail Gorbachev, and with his election as party chairman a new generation at last took over the leadership of the Soviet Union. Even the Soviet old guard had come to realize that radical reforms were necessary to revive a declining Soviet economy and instill new vigor into the party and the Soviet political system. At the time of Gorbachev's election no one, certainly not Gorbachev himself, could foresee that his attempts at reform would result in the collapse of the Soviet empire in Eastern Europe and the disintegration of the Soviet Union itself.

Mikhail Gorbachev was born into a peasant family in the northern foothills of the Caucasus Mountains in March 1931. His hard work and managerial skills on a collective farm earned him an invitation to attend Moscow State University, where he studied law and became a member of the legal faculty. He joined the Communist party in 1952, rose rapidly through the party ranks, and became a protégé of Yuri Andropov. Gorbachev's election as first secretary of the party on March 11, 1985, which surprised many foreign Soviet experts, apparently came as no surprise to Moscow's political insiders.

Highly intelligent and self-confident, with a youthful energy not seen for many years in the Kremlin, Gorbachev was fully aware of his country's social and economic difficulties and the ossification of the Communist party. The Soviet Union, he said, was in danger of becoming an Upper Volta with missiles. In addressing the problems of Soviet society, he called for a fundamental restructuring of the party and of the Soviet political and economic system (*perestroika*), a new honesty or openness (*glasnost*) in dealing with the country's problems, and a shake-up of the entrenched party and state bureaucracies that had presided over the country's economic decline.

Gorbachev led the way in openness with his criticism of previous party leaders. He accused them of indulging in "grandiloquent twaddle" and "meaningless slogans," of making too many "ambitious and unfounded promises and predictions," of tying up attempts at economic reform in red tape for fear that any kind of change would expose their own incompetence. Party leaders, who were supposed to be the champions of the working classes, were living in ostentatious luxury while the majority of the population was plunged in economic misery.

Gorbachev went beyond criticizing Soviet leadership. He attacked the fundamental principles of the existing political and economic system. He argued that the attempt to build up a modern industrial economy by means of a centrally-controlled master plan, conceived and operated by party and government functionaries, had produced nothing but stagnation. Socialism could only work by making room for individual initiative and personal gain, by permitting the operation of a market economy, and by legalizing the flourishing black market capitalism that had grown up within the existing economic system. Gorbachev was no apostate. He continued to believe that a socialist society was the only true guarantor of human welfare and dignity, but he was also convinced that it was in desperate need of revitalization and reform.

As Gorbachev saw it, a major reason for the Soviet economic decline was the government's investment of so large a proportion of the economy in armaments. Soviet social as well as economic recovery would require a drastic cutting of the military budget. Fundamental to this purpose was a reassessment and reorientation of Soviet foreign policy. The Soviet Union must abandon its economically disastrous effort to compete in an arms race with the West. Instead of the futile and potentially suicidal policy of seeking security through a never-ending arms buildup, Soviet policy should be dedicated to seeking security through international agreements and the resolution of crises through peaceful negotiation.

Gorbachev was the first Soviet leader to repudiate publicly the idea of the class struggle. Peaceful coexistence, he said, could no longer be dismissed as an interlude before the inevitable confrontation with capitalism or as a stage on the road to a final Communist victory. Instead, peaceful coexistence must now be viewed as an end in itself, a permanent component of the relationship between the Communist and capitalist worlds. Like Reagan, and indeed like everyone with any sense of reality, Gorbachev had come to recognize that a nuclear war would mean the destruction of human civilization and perhaps of life on earth. "In the present situation," he said, "we are talking . . . about a choice between survival and mutual annihilation." Gorbachev was therefore prepared to go further than any previous Soviet leader in seeking to reduce the danger of a nuclear war and, to the surprise of almost everyone concerned, he found a partner in Ronald Reagan in pursuing that objective.

❑ The Reagan–Gorbachev Relationship

In November 1985, Reagan and Gorbachev met in Geneva to resume Soviet–American arms reduction talks. On the eve of his departure for Geneva, Reagan, in a nationally televised address, described his forthcoming meeting with the Soviet leader as "a historic opportunity to set a steady, more constructive course in the 21st century." Fearful about what the president meant by a "constructive course," Reagan's militantly anti-Soviet secretary of defense, Casper Weinberger, sent him a letter listing previous Soviet treaty violations. Because the Soviets could not be trusted, Weinberger urged the president to reject any Soviet suggestion that the United States continue its practice of observing the terms of the still-unratified SALT II treaty, nor should he give an inch over his Strategic Defense Initiative. On the day after the president's speech, Weinberger leaked this letter to the press, an action the historian Stephen Ambrose has described as "sabotage pure and simple."

As it proved, Reagan did not need Weinberger's prompting. At his Geneva meeting with Gorbachev, he adamantly rejected any compromise over the SDI, the program he believed would render nuclear weapons obsolete. Gorbachev writes in his memoirs that the president's advocacy of SDI struck him as bizarre—was it science fiction or a trick to make the Soviet Union more forthcoming? The SDI, he told Reagan, was a continuation of the arms race into the more dangerous sphere of outer space, but if the Americans remained deaf to commonsense arguments, the Soviets would have no choice but to accept the challenge.

Nothing of substance was achieved in Geneva, but in looking back, Gorbachev believed that something important had happened "in spite of everything. . . . The 'human factor' had quietly come into action. We both sensed that we must maintain contact and try to avoid a break. Somewhere in the back of our minds a glimmer of hope emerged that we could still come to an agreement."

It was Gorbachev who made the next move. Early in 1986 he proposed that the United States and the Soviet Union reduce their nuclear arsenals by one-half and eliminate them altogether by the year 2000. He also dropped the previous Soviet demand that British and French nuclear weapons be included in the count of the Western missiles capable of striking the Soviet Union.

A tragic nuclear disaster propelled Gorbachev into making even more determined efforts to control nuclear weaponry. On April 26, 1986, there was a meltdown of an atomic reactor in Chernobyl in the northern sector of the Ukraine. Some days passed before the Soviet government understood the scale of the disaster, which Gorbachev soon came to recognize as "not just a national catastrophe but one that affected the whole world." In a televised address of May 14 he described what had happened in grim detail, and called the meltdown a warning bell to the peoples of the world. "Chernobyl showed again what an abyss will open if nuclear war befalls mankind." Chernobyl also served as a wake-up call in the Soviet Union. "Chernobyl shed light on many of the sicknesses of our system as a whole," Gorbachev writes in his memoirs. "Everything that had built up over the years converged on this drama: the concealing or hushing up of accidents and other bad news, irresponsibility and carelessness, slip-shod work, wholesale drunkenness. This was one more convincing argument in favour of radical reforms." It was an even move convincing argument for nuclear arms control.

Reagan and Gorbachev met again at Reykjavik in Iceland on October 11 and 12, 1986, a meeting held in response to Gorbachev's appeal for a "preliminary" summit to break the post-Geneva deadlock. At Reykjavik he again put forward his January proposal for a 50 percent across-the-board cut in the American and Soviet strategic arsenals, which was to be a prelude to a complete ban on nuclear weapons by the year 2000. In return Gorbachev asked that Reagan's SDI program be limited to research. On this question, however, Reagan remained adamant, with the result that the Reykjavik meeting, like that of Geneva, ended in disarray and disappointment.

Reagan's more militant advisers were much relieved. They saw that the president had been tempted by Gorbachev's proposal to eliminate all nuclear arsenals, which they believed could only benefit the Soviet Union, for a world free of nuclear weapons would leave the West at the mercy of the Soviets' superior conventional forces.

In June 1987 Reagan paid a visit to Germany, where the coolness of his reception was a sad contrast to the enthusiasm that had greeted Kennedy 26 years earlier. Nevertheless, on June 12 Reagan gave one of his most dramatic foreign policy speeches. At the Brandenburg gate on the western side of the Berlin Wall, he called upon Gorbachev to demonstrate whether all his talk about reform and openness signaled a genuine change in Soviet policy or was merely a propaganda gesture. "There is one sign the Soviets can make that would be unmistakable, that would advance dramatically the cause of freedom and peace. General Secretary Gorbachev, if you seek peace, if you seek prosperity for the Soviet Union and Eastern Europe, if you seek liberalization, come here to the gate! Mr. Gorbachev, open this gate! Mr. Gorbachev, tear down this wall!"

Gorbachev did not open the gate or tear down the wall. He did, however, continue his efforts on behalf of nuclear disarmament. In 1987 and 1988 he concluded treaties with Reagan that provided for the removal of all Soviet and American medium- and short-range nuclear missiles in Europe and joint on-site inspections to verify their removal. Gorbachev called these treaties "the first well-prepared step on our way out of the Cold War, the first harbinger of new times." But, Gorbachev added, "there was still a long way to go. The world was crammed with deadly weapons and the great powers still confronted each other. We had to continue our work."

They did continue their work. The treaties on medium- and short-range missiles were followed by negotiations over a Strategic Arms Reduction Treaty (START) for a reduction of all nuclear arsenals, a treaty finally concluded in July 1991 during the administration of Reagan's successor, George Herbert Walker Bush. Gorbachev tells us in his memoirs that he wanted to do far more: to create a new global security system and to conclude far-reaching treaties on international law, human rights, and the environment. He never had the opportunity to do so, because he was ousted by a coup shortly after the signature of the START treaty and resigned on December 25, 1991.

Reagan maintained to the end his adamant refusal to abandon his Strategic Defense Initiative program. "We are going forward with the research and development to see if this is a workable concept," he told Gorbachev in December 1987, "and if it is, we are going to deploy it." Gorbachev reiterated his objections to the project, arguing that it was not purely defensive because it would open the way for the development of weapons in outer space that could hit targets on earth. In any case, he asked, "What is SDI for? What missiles is it supposed to bring down if we eliminate all nuclear weapons?" "It will be there just in case," Reagan replied, because there was no way to destroy the technology for building missiles or nuclear weapons. "Who am I to tell you what to do?" Gorbachev said. "I think you are wasting your money." There the matter was left.

❑ *Gorbachev's Reduction of Soviet Military and Foreign Commitments*

Meanwhile Gorbachev was seeking to liquidate Soviet commitments in other parts of the world. In April 1988 he accepted an accord mediated by the United Nations providing for the withdrawal of all Soviet forces from Afghanistan by early 1989. (On Soviet intervention in Afghanistan, see pp. 520–521.) "The significance of this unprecedented settlement went far beyond its regional implications," Gorbachev wrote in his memoirs. "It was the first time that the Soviet Union and the United States, together with the conflicting parties, had signed an agreement which paved the way for a political solution of the conflict." The Soviet withdrawal took place on schedule, ending the Soviet equivalent of America's Vietnam experience.

Gorbachev also took decisive measures to relieve the Soviet economy of its immense military burden. In a speech before the UN on December 7, 1987, he announced his government's decision to reduce the Soviet armed forces by half a million men within two years, with corresponding cuts in artillery, tanks, and aircraft. He also announced a Soviet agreement with its Warsaw Pact allies to withdraw and disband six Soviet armored divisions from East Germany, Czechoslovakia, and Hungary by 1991. The remaining forces in Eastern Europe were to be reorganized for defensive purposes only. These military cuts were not to be restricted to Europe. With a view to repairing Soviet relations with China, Gorbachev announced the withdrawal of a "major portion" of Soviet troops from Mongolia.

Gorbachev went further. In January 1989 he announced plans to reduce the Soviet military budget by over 14 percent and cut arms production by almost 20 percent.

In June of that year the Soviet government proposed a colossal 50 percent reduction in military spending. The Soviet leader emphasized the unilateral nature of the Soviet cuts, but at the same time he expressed the hope that the United States and Western Europe would follow the Soviet lead and take similar steps.

The United States did not do so. Henry Kissinger theorized that unilateral steps of such magnitude signaled either extreme self-confidence or exceptional weakness. He eventually concluded that the Soviets' new defensive posture represented the ultimate vindication of George Kennan's containment theory: if the Soviets were held in check long enough, they would be obliged to abandon their dream of world revolution and the Soviet system itself would crumble from within. Supporters of Reagan's massive arms buildup had a different theory. They believed that Reagan had called the Soviets' bluff, that America's economic and military superiority had bankrupted the Soviet Union in its vain efforts to keep up, and that Gorbachev's arms reduction measures represented, in effect, a Soviet surrender and an acknowledgment of defeat in the Cold War.

Both theories neglect the immense personal contribution of Gorbachev in acknowledging the futility of the arms race, his refusal to indulge in political repression or dramatic foreign policy gestures to cover up the deficiencies of the Soviet political and economic system, and his courage in facing up to Soviet problems and seeking a peaceful resolution to international crises.

❑ Reagan and Central America: Nicaragua and El Salvador

In dealing with the Soviet Union and the problem of arms control, Reagan abandoned the simplistic formulas of his campaign rhetoric. In his negotiations with the Soviets he demonstrated unexpected flexibility, a realistic awareness of the need to resolve differences with Moscow and to reduce and eventually eliminate the danger of a nuclear holocaust.

It is therefore surprising that in dealing with the problems of the Western Hemisphere his views remained rigidly simplistic and his policies followed the most extreme prescriptions of Cold War rhetoric. It is still more surprising that the objects of his greatest concern were two tiny poverty-stricken states of Central America, Nicaragua and El Salvador, to which he devoted an attention that seemed incongruous at the time and appears no less so in retrospect. His administration's argument, a domino theory even more ludicrous than the one previously applied to Vietnam, was that if the Communists were not stopped in Central America, they would eventually have to be stopped at the Rio Grande: The United States itself was the last domino.

Reagan was to have great difficulty convincing Congress and the American people that Nicaragua and El Salvador represented mortal threats to American security, and his obsession with these countries would hardly seem to merit extensive treatment in a discussion of great-power diplomacy. That obsession would eventually assume decisive importance, however, because his Central American policies eventually became enmeshed in global politics and came perilously close to toppling the Reagan government.

In 1978 revolutionaries in Nicaragua who called themselves Sandinistas (after an earlier revolutionary, Agostino Sandino) overthrew the oppressive dictatorial regime of Anastasio Somoza, whose family had been the de facto rulers of the country since 1937. Hoping to win the friendship of the Sandinistas, Jimmy Carter recognized their regime on July 24 and subsequently sent economic and medical aid to Nicaragua to help the country recover from the ravages of civil war. But the Sandinistas, with bitter memories of past American intervention in Nicaragua and Washington's longstanding support of the Samoza government, turned instead to Cuba, which over the next few years supplied Nicaragua with hundreds of military and technical advisers, doctors, and teachers.

Only a few days after taking office, Ronald Reagan cut off Carter's aid package to Nicaragua, accusing the Sandinistas of "aiding and abetting violence" in neighboring El Salvador. On December 1, 1981, he signed an order empowering the CIA to provide covert aid to Nicaraguan counterrevolutionaries (Contras), who were attempting to overthrow the Sandinista regime, and he subsequently made repeated appeals to Congress to aid the Contras openly. In April 1983 Reagan told a joint session of Congress that "the national security of all the Americas is at stake in Central America." Dismayed by the paltriness of the aid finally appropriated by Congress, the president appealed directly to the American public. In a nationally televised address of May 9, 1984, he described the Sandinista government as "a Communist reign of terror." Thousands of men who had originally fought with the Sandinistas saw their revolution betrayed and had now taken up arms against them. Reagan called these counterrevolutionaries "freedom fighters," and he would later compare them to America's own founding fathers.

With official American aid severely restricted, Reagan's national security adviser Robert McFarlane concocted a scheme with CIA Director William Casey to use foreign governments as conduits for aid to the Contras and to seek direct financial support from foreign governments as well as from wealthy individuals and organizations. Reagan gave his blessing to this enterprise and subsequently discussed the legality of these-third party contributions with his principal advisers. "If such a story gets out," Reagan quipped, "we'll all be hanging by our thumbs in front of the White House."

The story did get out, as did revelations of continuing CIA support for the Contras, though Reagan himself never paid the penalty of hanging by his thumbs. The Associated Press discovered a manual prepared by the CIA suggesting assassination and kidnapping as techniques to be employed in their struggle with the Sandinistas—this by the agency of a government that was trumpeting its denunciations of international terrorism. These revelations, together with evidence of mounting anti-American sentiment throughout Latin American, provoked Congress into passing the Boland Amendment, signed into law on October 12, 1984, banning the use of any funds "available to the Central Intelligence Agency, the Department of Defense or any other agency or entity involved in intelligence activities" for the purpose of "supporting, directly or indirectly, military or paramilitary operations in Nicaragua by any nation, group, organization or individual." This ban remained in force over the next two years, but it did nothing to stem Reagan's efforts to secure support for the Contras, because, he said, this was "the right thing to do."

Officials in the Reagan administration soon came up with another way to provide funds for the Contras. To secure the release of American hostages kidnapped by terrorists in the Middle East, Reagan had adopted the dubious expedient of selling arms to Iran via Israel, clutching at vague Iranian promises to mediate with the kidnappers. (For Reagan's Middle East policy, see Chapter 37.) These arms, sold at vastly inflated prices to an Iranian government desperate for supplies in its long drawn out war with Iraq, reaped enormous profits which the Reagan administration now began using to finance the Contras. When this procedure became known, it resulted in a media outcry that might well have toppled a less popular president or one less skilled in evasion.

Reagan went beyond fund-raising for the Contras. In May 1985 he imposed an economic embargo on Nicaragua and blocked loans from the World Bank and the Bank for Inter-American Development. In March of the following year he went on national television warning of the consequences if the Communists remained in control of Nicaragua and asking Congress for 100 million dollars in humanitarian and military aid. If America did not stop the Communists in Nicaragua, he said "we will soon be fighting them along the Rio Grande." In June, under heavy presidential pressure, Congress approved Reagan's 100-million-dollar aid package by a margin of twelve votes and rescinded the Boland Amendment.

But neither foreign nor private contributions, neither the profits from Iranian arms sales nor congressional appropriations, proved sufficient to turn the tide in Nicaragua. The Contras, unable to unite behind a single leader or program, failed to gain permanent control over a single major city or town or secure decisive popular support. By the time Reagan left office, the Sandinistas were still in power.

In the end, the Nicaraguans themselves were to oust the Sandinistas, at least temporarily. In trying to introduce what they regarded as salutary reforms, the Marxist-oriented Sandinistas had alienated a substantial segment of the traditionally conservative peasantry. Failing to recognize, or refusing to believe, the hostility they had aroused, the Sandinistas agreed to hold free elections under international supervision in February 1990 — elections which they confidently expected to win. Instead, victory went to a coalition of anti-Sandinista parties led by Violeta Chamorro, the widow of a newspaper magnate murdered by the Samoza regime. With Chamorro's election victory Nicaragua disappeared as a major preoccupation of American foreign policy.

The situation in El Salvador was as complicated as that of Nicaragua, but American policy there was a good deal more straightforward. In El Salvador it was a question of supporting what appeared to be a moderate government, that of José Napoléon Duarte, the centrist leader of El Salvador's Christian Democratic party, against extremists of both the Left and the Right who kept the country in a state of de facto civil war: on the Left, radicals who demanded faster and more sweeping reforms than those initiated by the Duarte regime; on the Right, murderous militias known as Death Squads, which were attempting to restore an authoritarian government.

In the belief that Duarte offered the best hope for establishing democracy in El Salvador, President Carter had extended military and economic aid to his government. Reagan not only continued Carter's policy but sought a large-scale increase in

American aid to enable the Duarte government to suppress the Marxist rebels and prevent El Salvador from going the way of Nicaragua. Congress, however, was slow to respond, put off by reports of the Duarte's inability to control either the Salvadoran death squads or his own troops, who were reported to be committing atrocities of their own. Congress finally approved a 25-million-dollar increase in aid to the Duarte government, which promised to hold national elections in the hope of bringing the civil war to an end.

This hope was not fulfilled. Elections held in March 1982 were boycotted by the radicals, and Duarte was defeated by the extreme right-wing leader, Roberto d'Aubuisson, who was reputed to have been a commander of one of the death squads. These results were reversed two years later. Thanks to a massive infusion of bribes distributed by CIA agents, Duarte returned to power in March 1984 and in May the United States Congress approved a Reagan request for 500 million dollars in military aid to El Salvador. By the end of the decade the United States was sending Duarte some 300 million per year, but even this was not enough to enable him to defeat the rebels. The Salvadoran civil war was still raging when Reagan left office.

❑ *Grenada*

Reagan intervened with more decisive results in another part of the Western hemisphere, the tiny Caribbean island of Grenada, which since March 1979 had been ruled by the Marxist government of Maurice Bishop. Like the Sandinistas in Nicaragua, Bishop turned to Fidel Castro for support and modeled his regime on that of the Cuban dictator. While carrying out improvements in the island's health and education systems, Bishop suppressed dissent, jailed opponents, and failed to keep his promise to hold democratic elections.

In 1983 Cuban workers began the construction of an airstrip in Grenada, allegedly to stimulate the island's tourist industry by providing landing facilities for large aircraft. The Reagan administration, however, suspected that the airstrip was being built to make Grenada another Communist supply base in the Caribbean. On October 13, 1983, Bishop was arrested by the leader of an even more radical faction within his own party, and six days later he was murdered. On the day of his murder, the Organization of Eastern Caribbean States, a group of six small former British colonies, requested American military aid to restore "peace and stability" in Grenada. A more urgent appeal came from Governor General Sir Paul Scoon, the nominal chief of state of Grenada which had remained a member of the British Commonwealth, who asked that his appeal remain secret because he feared for his life. By this time Reagan had already decided on American military intervention to end the anarchy in Grenada and protect the lives of the Americans on the island, including some 800 medical students attending the St. George's School of Medicine

On October 23, in a nationally televised speech, Reagan displayed an aerial photo of the 1,000 foot runway being built by Cuban laborers in Grenada, which when completed could be used by Libya and other foes of the United States to deliver arms and supplies to the Sandinista regime in Nicaragua. On the afternoon of October 24 Reagan informed Congressional leaders of his decision to invade Grenada, and at

6:55 P.M. he signed the formal invasion order. Only then did he inform the British prime minister, Margaret Thatcher. Although usually a warm supporter of Reagan's policies, Mrs. Thatcher bluntly told him she opposed his invasion plan. Reagan, however, had no intention of calling it off, and on the morning of October 25 American forces began landing on the island.

The invasion was a pathetically mismanaged operation. There were mixed signals between the navy and the troops on land, whose only maps of the island were out-of-scale tourist brochures. Nevertheless, within two days the Americans had overcome the unexpectedly stiff resistance of the 800 Cuban soldiers and laborers in Grenada. The Reagan administration claimed to have scored a glorious victory, and Americans on the whole seemed delighted to believe him. After the disaster of Vietnam, they chose to see the Grenadan operation as a vindication of American military prowess. The sentiment of the day was that "we've won one, for once." A new Grenadan government was formed under Governor General Scoon, the Cubans were ordered off the island, the Soviet embassy was closed, and by mid-December the American troops withdrew, their mission accomplished.

Non-Americans were less happy about the Grenadan operation. The British were infuriated that they had not been consulted in advance—the island, after all, was still a member of the British Commonwealth. Latin Americans were alienated yet again by this latest display of unilateral Yankee interventionism, and Washington was obliged to use its veto power to block a UN Security Council resolution condemning the Grenadan invasion.

There was another dimension to the Grenadan operation. The invasion was carried out two days after Washington learned of a terrorist attack on the American marine barracks in Lebanon in which 241 marines had been killed (see p. 525). Opponents of the Reagan administration charged that the entire Grenadan business had been an effort (and a successful one at that) to divert American attention from Reagan's disastrous Middle East policy. There seems little doubt, however, that Reagan was sincerely concerned about the Americans in Grenada, if only because he feared that they might become victims of another hostage crisis. He nevertheless made effective use of Grenada to explain the tragedy in Lebanon, linking Grenada and Lebanon as examples of the perfidy of the Soviets and their surrogates. It was no coincidence, he said in a speech of October 27, that "when the thugs tried to wrest control of Grenada, there were thirty Soviet advisers and hundreds of Cuban military and paramilitary forces on the island."

❑ Libya

Reagan scored what his administration claimed as another foreign policy triumph in a very different part of the world. In April 1986 an American soldier was killed when a bomb exploded in a West Berlin discotheque. Reagan blamed this outrage on the Libyan dictator, Muammar Qadafy, the "mad dog of the Middle East," whom he accused of being a major sponsor of international terrorism. On April 14, in retaliation for the Berlin bombing, he ordered American aircraft based in England to strike at the

Libyan cities of Tripoli and Benghazi in the evident hope of killing Qadafy. The operation killed Qadafy's adopted two year old daughter, wounded two of his sons, and killed scores of civilians. Qadafy himself escaped injury and his regime survived.

The bombing of Libya provoked outrage in the Arab states of the Middle East, but it also aroused alarm in Europe, where Reagan was widely perceived as being trigger-happy, too much inclined to take unilateral action that might jeopardize European interests—in this case their access to Libyan and Middle East Oil. Especially concerned was the French government, which had forbidden American bombers en route to Libya to fly over French air space. Most Americans, on the other hand, appear to have been delighted by the vigorous response of their leader to international terrorism. Following the Libya bombing, Reagan's approval ratings soared to new heights.

❑ *The Bush Succession*

In the presidential elections of November 1988, Reagan's vice-president, George H. W. Bush, basing his campaign largely on domestic issues, soundly defeated the Democratic candidate Michael Dukakis, the governor of Massachusetts.

George Bush was a member of a wealthy New England family. He went to Yale, where he captained the baseball team, and he won decorations as a navy pilot in World War II. After the war he moved to Texas, where he made a fortune in the oil business. Defeated in a run for the Senate after two terms in Congress as a representative from Texas, he was appointed ambassador to the United Nations by Nixon in 1970 and subsequently served as ambassador to China and director of the CIA. In 1980 he fought Reagan for the Republican presidential nomination, condemning Reagan's fiscal proposals as "voodoo economics," but he was happy to accept the offer to run as Reagan's vice president.

Bland, with a somewhat petulant voice, Bush was seen as an indecisive wimp by many of his opponents and supporters alike, an image he tried to erase by assuming what he evidently believed to be the manners and speech of Texas masculinity. After a vice-presidential debate in 1984 with the Democratic candidate Geraldine Ferraro, the first woman to be nominated to that office, he boasted that he had "kicked a little ass around," a remark that somehow did not lose the Republicans the women's vote.

As vice-president, Bush was a loyal supporter of Reagan's foreign and domestic politics, including his voodoo economics, but he had spent his years in that office traveling to many parts of the world, meeting foreign dignitaries, and gaining a first-hand knowledge of international problems. He thus came to the presidency not only with a wealth of administrative and diplomatic experience, but with an unusually broad knowledge of foreign affairs. Practical, without strong ideological preconceptions, he conducted a cautious policy and contributed to the resolution of some of the century's most critical international crises.

❑ *The Bush–Gorbachev Relationship*

Shortly after his inauguration, Bush sent Gorbachev a letter via Henry Kissinger informing him that he needed time to review the major foreign policy issues confronting the United States. But, he assured the Soviet leader, "we are in no way attempting to slow down or reverse the progress that marked the past couple of years." It was not until mid-May, however, that Bush informed the Soviets that his "strategic review" was completed and that he was ready for serious discussion of all the items on the Soviet–American agenda, including disarmament and global cooperation.

When Bush finally met with Gorbachev personally on December 2 and 3, 1989, on shipboard off the Mediterranean island of Malta, the cordial Soviet–American relationship established during the last years of the Reagan administration was continued. Bush still expressed concern about the situation in Nicaragua and El Salvador, which he described as a "giant thorn" in Soviet–American relations, and he asked Gorbachev to persuade Castro to stop supplying arms to antidemocratic forces in those states. Gorbachev assured him that the Soviet Union had no intention of creating bases in Central America, that the Soviets had agreed long since not to supply weapons to Nicaragua, and that the most effective way to clear up misunderstandings with Cuba would be to talk directly to Fidel Castro. Nobody could give him orders.

Gorbachev was obviously not really interested in Central America. He wanted to deal with problems he regarded as fundamental to Soviet–American relations, and he took the initiative in doing so. "First," he said, "the United States should take as a starting point that the Soviet Union will never, under any circumstances, start a war with the United States. . . . Second, we propose to join efforts to ensure mutual security—we are committed to continuing disarmament in all areas." Third, the Soviet Union had adopted a defensive doctrine with regard to its military establishment and was sharply reducing the number of its offensive weapons and equipment. While trying to make clear Soviet intentions, Gorbachev wanted clarification about the position of the United States. Why did the Americans adhere to the "flexible response" military strategy; why had the U.S. navy not yet been included in disarmament negotiations; why was NATO not reducing the contingents of America's NATO allies? To deal with these and a variety of other problems, Gorbachev believed it was essential to continue and develop the Helsinki process. As he was to say later, "We needed a Helsinki Two to agree on common criteria and objectives."

Bush evidently succeeded in reassuring the Soviet leader about American intentions, for Gorbachev expressed genuine satisfaction over the results of their meeting. The Malta Summit had set a precedent, he said. For the first time American and Soviet leaders had agreed on a joint statement that "had brought our relations onto a new plane."

When Gorbachev met with Bush a second time in Washington and Camp David at the end of May and early June 1990, the primary topic of discussion was the problem of German reunification. (See pp. 537–538.) The most important result of these meetings from a global point of view, however, was their decision to step up the pace of disarmament negotiations, their success in laying the basis for a strategic arms reduction treaty, and their signature of agreements providing for closer Soviet–American economic, scientific, and cultural cooperation.

❑ *Bush, Gorbachev, and the Persian Gulf War*

The international crisis set off by Iraq's invasion of Kuwait on August 2, 1990, will be discussed in connection with the overall problems of the Middle East. According to his own account, Gorbachev made vigorous efforts to persuade the Iraqis to withdraw from Kuwait in order to avoid a military confrontation, warning them that in the event of war they would not have the support of the Soviet Union. Of fundamental importance, he believed, was the meeting he had had with Bush in Helsinki on September 9, because at issue was the maintenance and consolidation of the American–Soviet partnership in dealing with the Gulf crisis. Throughout that crisis, he said, the Soviet government had been able "not just to preserve but also to reinforce Soviet–American mutual understanding, trust, and partnership, sustaining them throughout this acute conflict—the first such test since the Cold War's end."

❑ *The Strategic Arms Reduction Treaty (START)*

From July 20 to August 1, 1991, Bush and Gorbachev met for the last time in Moscow and in nearby Novo-Ogarevo, the Soviet equivalent of Camp David, where, with little fanfare, they signed the Strategic Arms Reduction Treaty (START) that had been initiated during the Reagan administration. Bypassing the hard-liners in their respective governments, they broke through nine years of deadlock and worked out the terms of the treaty through personal correspondence. The heart of that treaty was a mutual pledge to reduce their nuclear arsenals by one-half.

"With this treaty," Bush said at the signing ceremony, "we are solidifying the new opportunities being created between our countries, which promise further progress toward a stable peace." Gorbachev spelled out what he hoped to achieve through these "new opportunities." "My main theme," he says in his memoirs, "was the prospect for creating a new common security system through a world policy conducted *jointly* (for the first time in history) and based on new criteria that had already undergone some testing in practice." "New opportunities" also involved such global concerns as natural resources, the environment, and population growth, all of which, though to varying degrees, "were giving rise to the question of the role our two countries should play under the new circumstances and what our relationship should be in the future."

As noted earlier, Gorbachev never had the chance to explore these possibilities. Bush did what he could to support the Soviet leader in the crises that were engulfing him at home, so much so that he was accused of putting all his eggs in one basket in his relations with the Soviet Union. Bush's support was not enough, however. Gorbachev barely survived a coup in August of 1991, but he was no longer able to control the domestic forces he himself has done so much to unleash. He resigned on Christmas Day, 1991. Documents from Soviet archives may reveal a different picture of Gorbachev, but on the evidence now available he stands out as one of the most impressive figures of the twentieth century, whose concern for universal human values is all the more remarkable in that he emerged as a political leader out of the cauldron of Communist party politics, which produced some of history's most inhuman monsters.

❑

THIRTY-SIX

The Middle East:
From the Suez Crisis
to the Camp David Accords

While Willy Brandt undertook the first cautious moves in his *Ostpolitik* and the British applied in vain for membership in the Common Market, the chronic crisis situation in the Middle East once again erupted into open warfare.

Warfare had never actually ceased since the Suez crisis of 1956. It will be recalled that in November of that year, a United Nations force had been sent to the Suez Canal zone to enforce a cease-fire between the Anglo-French-Israeli forces and the Egyptians. (See p. 408.) Elsewhere, however, the Israelis continued to be involved in hostilities with Syria to the north and Jordan to the east, as well as with the Palestinians, who waged a guerrilla-terrorist war from Palestinian enclaves within Israel itself and from bases and refugee camps in neighboring Arab states.

❑ Egyptian Policy after the Suez Crisis

Meanwhile, Egyptian President Gamal Abdel Nasser, fresh from his Suez triumph, was engaged in a political campaign to unite the Arab countries under Egyptian leadership. That campaign began promisingly enough with the formation on February 1, 1958, of a political union between Egypt and Syria, which took the name of the United Arab Republic. Other Arab states were invited to join this union, but none did so because once again the individual Arab governments refused to submerge their special interests on behalf of establishing a pan-Arab state. In July 1958 Lebanon and Jordan appealed to the United States and Britain for help in preserving their independence, ostensibly to prevent a Communist takeover but in fact to defend their governments against pro-Nasser forces.

Nasser not only failed to put together a pan-Arab confederation—even his union with Syria collapsed. In September 1961 the Syrian army overthrew the union government and proclaimed Syria's independence. Two years later an attempt by pro-Nasserites to revive the union was successfully suppressed by the Syrian government.

With his prestige badly tarnished, Nasser sought to revive his fortunes by dramatic confrontations with Israel and the Western powers. In May 1967, citing information (via Soviet sources) that Israel was preparing to attack Syria, he assumed the role of champion of Arab interests by issuing a stern and highly publicized warning to Israel. He followed up this warning with a demand for the withdrawal of the UN peace-keeping force between Egypt and Israel because the existence of that force would prevent Egypt from coming to the aid of Syria.

Nasser appears to have been surprised that the UN secretary general, U Thant, yielded immediately to his demand. In replying to criticism of the UN withdrawal, U Thant pointed out that the UN had no authority to keep troops in an area when a member state requested their removal. As UN troops pulled out, Egyptian troops re-established Egyptian authority over the Sinai Peninsula, including the strategic Sharm al-Sheikh region, which commands the Strait of Tiran at the entrance of the Gulf of Aqaba. Nasser followed up this action by announcing on May 22 the closure of the Tiran Strait to Israeli shipping, thus cutting off Israel's access to the open sea from the Israeli port of Eilat on the Gulf of Aqaba.

❑ *The Six Day War, June 5–10, 1967*

The Israeli response to these provocative Egyptian actions was as swift as it was un-expected. Fearful that Nasser had actually made himself leader of a pan-Arab coalition, the Israelis launched a preemptive strike on June 5 against Egypt and other Arab states they suspected of being in collusion with Egypt. Achieving complete tactical surprise, Israeli aircraft wiped out the air fleets of Egypt, Syria, Jordan, and Iraq in the first hours of the war and rendered their air fields inoperative.

Coordinating ground operations with air strikes, Israeli infantry and tank units drove the Jordanians from the West Bank of the Jordan River and East Jerusalem, which had been annexed by Jordan following the 1948–1949 war. In the south Israeli forces swept through the Gaza Strip and the Sinai Peninsula, reaching the Suez Canal and Sharm El Sheik by June 8. Their subsequent advance in the north was equally swift and successful. On June 9 they drove Syrian forces from the Golan Heights. Al-ready on June 6 the United Nations had passed a resolution calling for a cease-fire, but the Israelis delayed accepting it for four days, presumably to give their troops time to consolidate their gains and carry out their plans to storm the Golan heights. The cease-fire went into effect on June 10.

Nasser, who had appealed to the UN to arrange a cease-fire to save Egyptian troops from further slaughter, could do no more than sink ships in the Suez Canal to block all shipping through this strategic waterway. To explain his humiliating defeat, he charged that American and British planes had participated in the original Israeli aer-ial attack. This was not true, but the Arab states chose to accept this explanation and on June 7 Algeria, Iraq, Sudan, Syria, and Yemen broke off relations with Britain and the United States, and Arab oil producers cut off shipments of oil to those countries.

The cease-fire of June 10 was never fully observed by either side. Air raids and ar-tillery duels over Suez and the Golan Heights took place regularly during the follow-ing years, as did Israeli raids into Jordan and Lebanon to destroy Arab guerrilla bases. On June 27 the Israeli parliament proclaimed that Jerusalem, divided between Jordan and Israel after the 1948–1949 war, would henceforth be permanently united within the state of Israel. At the same time the Israeli government stepped up its efforts to promote the Jewish settlement of Arab Jerusalem. "The object of the settlement," the mayor of Jerusalem stated frankly, "is to ensure that all of Jerusalem remains forever a part of Israel. If this city is to be our capital, then we have to make it an integral part of our country, and we need Jewish inhabitants to do this."

The Israelis issued no similar proclamation about the other territories conquered during the Six Day War, but they kept them under Israeli control and began the construction of fortifications for their defense. Even more ominous, from the Arab point of view, was the Israeli government's encouragement of Jewish settlements in the occupied areas, a policy which seemed to portend Israel's intention to make these territories, as well as Jerusalem, a permanent part of the Jewish state.

❏ *UN Resolution 242*

On November 22, 1967, the UN Security Council passed unanimously Resolution 242, which implicitly recognized Israel's right to exist. The future security of Israel and its neighbors were to be guaranteed by "respect for the . . . sovereignty, territorial and political independence of every state in the area and their right to live in peace within secure and recognized boundaries free from acts or threats of force." Further, Israel and all other Middle East states were to be guaranteed "freedom of navigation through international waterways in the area," including the Suez Canal and the Gulf of Aqaba. Most importantly for the Palestinians, the resolution called for Israel's withdrawal from territories occupied in the recent conflict and a "just settlement" of the refugee problem.

Unfortunately and perhaps inevitably, the terms of Resolution 242 were ambiguous, especially as they concerned the Palestinians. The resolution called for withdrawal from territories, not *the* territories, occupied by Israel, thus leaving open an interpretation that withdrawal from only some of the territories would be sufficient. And what was meant by a "just settlement" of the refugee problem? The resolution spoke of respect for the sovereignty of every state in the area and its right to live in peace, but where did this leave the Palestinians who had no state? By obfuscating the Palestinian issue, Resolution 242, instead of providing a basis for a comprehensive peace in the Middle East, only added to the controversy.

The UN Security Council reaffirmed Resolution 242 in 1969 and again 1973, and it remains central to the UN's effort to resolve the Arab–Israeli controversy. But so far there has been no final agreement over the frontiers between Israel and Syria, which demands the return of the Golan Heights. Nor has there been even a partial resolution of the Palestinian question, which remains at the heart of the controversy.

❏ *The Palestinian Question*

In the wake of the Six Day War, the Palestinian refugees from the Arab–Israeli war of 1948-1949 were joined by some half million refugees from the West Bank and another quarter million from the Gaza Strip. Once again most of these refugees were housed in squalid camps in the territories of their Arab neighbors, but a significant number of Palestinians remained in the territories now occupied by the Israelis. Together with the Palestinians already living in prewar Israel, Palestinians now formed a substantial portion of the population under Israeli rule. Angry and resentful of Israeli authority, they were to be a permanent source of unrest.

An important consequence of this fresh Palestinian diaspora was an effort on the part of Palestinian leaders to form a united political organization to represent Palestinian interests. This was done at a meeting in Cairo in February 1969, where several Palestinian political parties joined together under the banner of the Palestinian Liberation Organization, which elected Yasir Arafat, the leader of one of the more prominent of those parties, as its chairman. The PLO proceeded to establish regional committees among refugee groups and assumed the role of a government in exile. Even after their ostensible union under the PLO, however, the Palestinians, separated as they were among many different countries, remained disorganized and disorderly. Individuals or groups among them continued to act with a good deal of independence, frequently engaging in terrorist activities without regard for the policies of the PLO.

The Palestinians proved to be a disruptive influence not only in Israel but in the lands of their fellow Arabs. In Jordan, where a majority of West Bank Palestinians had taken refuge, they formed so large a percentage of the population as to pose a serious threat to the government of King Hussein. They used Jordan as a base for mounting terrorist attacks on Israel, nor did they disguise their desire to overthrow Hussein in favor of a more militant Palestinian leadership. On September 15, 1970, to put an end to what had become a civil war with the Palestinian guerrillas, Hussein placed his country under martial law and installed a military government with authorization "to restore order and impose the State's authority." The crisis ended in disaster for the Palestinians. The Jordanian army defeated the Palestinian guerrillas, and then swept through their refugee camps to drive the Palestinian militias out of Jordan altogether.

A majority of the Palestinians expelled from Jordan fled to Lebanon, where some 300,000 Palestinian refugees were already encamped. With that the focal point of the Palestinian problem outside Israel itself shifted from Jordan to Lebanon, whose people would soon also become tragic victims of the convulsions in the Middle East.

❑ The Yom Kippur War, October 1973

Nasser died in September 1970 and was succeeded as president of Egypt by Anwar el-Sadat, who shared Nasser's aspirations to unite the Arab world under Egyptian leadership and recover the territories lost to Israel. To build up Egypt's armed forces and secure the means to put pressure on Israel, he continued Nasser's policy of maintaining close relations with Moscow and sought large-scale increases in Soviet military aid.

The Soviets, however, failed to provide it. Deeply concerned about the threat of China (see pp. 444–445), they evidently decided against providing fuel for another bonfire in the Middle East that would lead to further complications with Washington. After almost two years of frustration in dealing with the Soviets, Sadat undertook a major reversal of Egyptian policy. On July 18, 1972, he ordered the Soviet military advisers and technicians to leave Egypt and turned for support to the United States.

Sadat's expulsion of the Soviet advisers took the Soviets and much of the rest of the world by surprise, but he had actually been considering this move for some time. Rather than risk another war with Israel with its superior weaponry supplied by the United States, he had decided that it would be wiser and safer to try to regain the territories lost to Israel through diplomacy. This could only be done through the good offices of Washington, which alone had the means to exercise decisive influence over Israeli policy.

As early as February 1971 Sadat had sounded Washington about securing American support to negotiate a settlement with Israel, and early in the following year he approached Henry Kissinger, Nixon's national security adviser, with a similar request. At this time Kissinger, almost totally preoccupied with the problem of Vietnam, was in no position to undertake a settlement in the Middle East. Moreover, the Nixon administration was determined to avoid even the appearance of exerting pressure on Israel for fear of losing the Jewish vote in the 1972 presidential elections. So it was not until March 1973, following Nixon's landslide victory in the previous November, that Kissinger agreed to see Sadat's national security adviser in Washington. Even then he refused to respond to Sadat's appeal for diplomatic support against Israel. He dismissed as an empty threat the Egyptian leader's warning that, deprived of all hope for a satisfactory peaceful settlement, he would be obliged to take military action. In July 1973 the United States cast the single vote against a UN resolution to implement of Resolution 242. The key to a settlement with Israel might lie in Washington, but Washington did not choose to turn it.

The Israeli government did not make Sadat's position any easier. On October 28, 1972, Golda Meir, Israel's prime minister since March 1969, set forth five conditions for a peace settlement: Israel's permanent retention of the entire city of Jerusalem; total retention of the Golan Heights; retention of the West Bank area, with a minimum Arab population living there; retention of the Gaza Strip; retention of Sharm al-Sheikh at the entrance to the Gulf of Aqaba; and retention of a "broad strip" of territory along the coast of the Sinai Peninsula linking Sharm al-Sheikh to Israel. This left only the barren expanses of the interior of Sinai Peninsula as a region for possible Israeli concessions to Egypt.

For months Sadat had warned the international community that, denied a satisfactory settlement through diplomatic channels, he would be obliged to go to war. But, despite all the obvious evidence of Egyptian military preparations—and perhaps because they *were* so obvious—the American and Israeli governments remained convinced that he was bluffing. Sadat may in fact have intended these preparations as bluff, for he knew that Israel retained a decisive edge in the quality and quantity of its weaponry. With the failure of his bluff, however, he evidently concluded that there was no longer any alternative to war.

His hope now lay in launching a preemptive strike of his own that might shock the Israelis into recognizing that it would be in their own interest to negotiate a satisfactory settlement with the Arabs. In the early morning of October 6, 1973, during the Jewish religious festival of Yom Kippur (and the final days of the Islamic festival of Ramadan), Egyptian forces mounted an invasion across the Suez Canal into the Sinai Peninsula that was coordinated with a Syrian attack on the Golan Heights. The Israelis, who had been as confident as their American friends that Sadat had been bluffing, were taken by surprise as the Arabs had been by the Six Day War. The Egyptians broke through the Israeli defensive line on the Asian side of the Suez Canal, which the Israelis had believed to be impregnable, and the Syrian army, equipped with 800 Soviet tanks, stormed the Golan Heights. The Egyptian offensive, however, was limited in scope from the beginning and appears to have been intended primarily to propel the Israelis into negotiations. For, after their thrust across the canal, Egyptian forces stopped and dug into defensive positions without even attempting to block the passes connecting Israel with the Sinai battlefront. Sadat is presumed to have exercised restraint for fear that the Israelis, who were in possession of nuclear weapons, might be provoked into using them.

On October 10, following the initial success of the Arab offensives, the Soviets began a large-scale airlift to the Egyptian and Syrian armies in the evident hope of regaining their influence in the Arab world. In some panic, Prime Minister Golda Meir appealed directly to Nixon and Kissinger to expedite an American airlift to Israel, warning that if American support did not come soon Israel would use "every means" at its disposal to ensure its survival, a term Kissinger interpreted as a reference to Israel's nuclear capacity. An American airlift began on October 13 and was soon delivering far more than the airlift of the Soviets. Two days later, now equipped with superior American weaponry, the Israelis mounted a counteroffensive on both the Sinai and Syrian fronts. After some of the fiercest tank battles since World War II, the Israelis recaptured the Golan Heights and advanced to within twenty miles of Damascus. In the south they crossed to the African side of the Suez Canal and began the encirclement of Egypt's Third Army, which was dug in on the Asian side and was now threatened with annihilation.

In supporting opposite sides in the Yom Kippur war, the two superpowers once again found themselves on the brink of a dangerous confrontation. That danger was temporarily defused by Kosygin, the Soviet prime minister, who invited Henry Kissinger to collaborate in drafting a cease-fire agreement. Adopted unanimously by the UN Security Council on October 22 as Resolution 338, that agreement called for an immediate cease-fire on all fronts plus the implementation of the ill-fated Resolution 242 of November 1967, which the Israelis had so far ignored.

The Israelis also ignored Resolution 338. Accusing the Egyptians of cease-fire violations, they continued their offensive in the Suez area to complete their cutoff of Egypt's Third Army. Brezhnev denounced Israel for its "brazen" flouting of the UN resolution, and more importantly, he took immediate steps to respond to Sadat's appeal for joint Soviet-American intervention to enforce the cease-fire. On the evening of October 24, he sent Nixon a letter urging the immediate dispatch of American and Soviet troops to Egypt. "I will say it straight, that if you find it impossible to act with us in this matter, we should be faced with the necessity urgently to consider the question of taking appropriate steps unilaterally."

Kissinger chose to regard Brezhnev's letter "as, in effect, an ultimatum." "We were determined to resist by force if necessary the introduction of Soviet troops to the Middle East regardless of the pretext under which they arrived." He concluded that the United States must not only reject the Soviet proposal, but "do so in a manner that shocked the Soviets into abandoning the unilateral move they were threatening."

Fearing that Nixon was too distraught by domestic difficulties (the Watergate affair) to understand the implications of the Soviet proposal for joint intervention, Kissinger took it upon himself to order a worldwide alert of the American armed forces at 3:00 A.M. on October 25—the shock he believed necessary to prevent the Soviets from sending their forces to the Middle East.

Kissinger's fear that Nixon might actually agree to joint Soviet-American intervention derived from a recent experience. While he was in Moscow, Nixon had instructed him to inform Brezhnev that he shared the Soviet leader's belief that the superpowers must now step in to secure a settlement in the Middle East. Kissinger professes to have been aghast on receiving this message, for Nixon was evidently prepared to invite the Soviet Union to exercise a joint condominium over the Middle East. Confident that Nixon had been too preoccupied with Watergate to follow up on this instruction, Kissinger decided simply to ignore it.

It was Kissinger who now applied the requisite pressure on the Israelis to agree to another UN cease-fire resolution of October 25 (Security Council Resolution 340), but not before giving the Israelis time to advance well beyond the lines occupied at the time of the UN's first cease-fire resolution of October 22. Later in the day of October 25 the Security Council voted 14–0 to establish a Middle East Emergency Force to supervise the cease-fire, but that force was not to include troops from any member of the Security Council. This meant that neither Soviet nor American troops would be sent to the Middle East. Kissinger had thus prevented the dispatch of Soviet troops to the region while demonstrating to the Arab states that Washington was their only hope in securing concessions of any kind from Israel.

Israel's agreement to a cease-fire, though still delayed for several days, ended the immediate danger that the Yom Kippur war might escalate into a global conflict. That danger, however, may never have been as great as Kissinger and some of his contemporaries have pictured it. Brezhnev's appeal for joint Soviet-American intervention looks less like an ultimatum than an effort to resolve the crisis. Thereafter the Soviets acted with remarkable restraint. They issued no protests in response to America's provocative global military alert, nor did they adopt a threatening posture during Kissinger's subsequent maneuvers to freeze them out of the Middle East peace process.

❑ *The Arab Oil Weapon*

The American decision to pressure Israel into agreeing to a cease-fire and, somewhat later, to allow food and medical supplies to be sent to Egypt's beleaguered Third Army, was not due entirely to humanitarian concerns or to avoid incurring the wrath of Egypt.

On October 16, as the tide of war turned against the Egyptians and Syrians, the Arab members of the Organization of Petroleum Exporting Countries (OPEC) increased the price of oil from $3.01 to $5.12 a barrel. On the following day they voted to cut oil production by 5 percent, and to continue reducing it by an additional 5 percent a month until Israel withdrew from all occupied Arab territories. On October 19, following Nixon's request to Congress for an additional 2.2 billion dollars to pay for the airlift to Israel, the Arab members of OPEC imposed a total oil embargo on the

United States, which was later extended to the Netherlands, the country most supportive of American policy.

The Arabs kept the pressure on. In December 1973 they boosted the price of oil from $5.12 to $11.65 a barrel, a 128 percent rise on top of the 70 percent increase in October. "It is now obvious," Kissinger admits in his memoirs, "that this decision was one of the pivotal events in the history of this century." The decision was at least pivotal enough to persuade Kissinger to use American influence to pressure Israel into a settlement not only with Egypt but with Syria, where the war with Israel continued well into the following year.

The impact of the Arab use of their oil weapon went far beyond the Middle East. America's European allies as well as Japan, already indignant about Washington' unilateral activity in that region, were dealt a serious economic blow by the Arab boost in oil prices, dependent as they were on foreign oil imports. From the standpoint of the Europeans, American support for Israel, which they saw as the major obstacle to a Middle East peace settlement, not only threatened them with economic ruin but with nuclear destruction. Without consulting or even informing them, Washington had begun its airlift to Israel, which had triggered the increases in the price of Arabian oil. Worse still, Washington had put American military forces on global alert, thereby placing the Europeans in the path of a superpower confrontation in which they were likely to be the first and most grievous victims. The European Community openly proclaimed its policy differences with the United States with a declaration of November 6, 1973, calling for Israel's withdrawal to the cease-fire line of October 22 and its implementation of Resolution 242, which required its withdrawal from territories occupied during the Six Day War of 1967 and a just settlement of the refugee problem.

The Israelis paid no more attention to the European declaration than they had to the various UN resolutions. But on November 11, 1973, they at last agreed to a six-point plan negotiated by Kissinger, which set aside the most meaningful provision of UN Resolution 340, namely, Israel's withdrawal from the occupied territories.

❑ *Kissinger's Shuttle Diplomacy*

Early in January 1974, Kissinger began his so-called shuttle diplomacy for the purpose of arranging final peace treaties, in the first instance between Israel and Egypt, and then between Israel and Syria. His negotiations with Egypt were facilitated by the fact that Sadat remained convinced that the United States was the only power that could secure concessions from Israel. The Israelis for their part saw the advantage of using the Americans to conduct one-on-one negotiations with Egypt, which would drive a wedge between Egypt and the other the Arab countries. A peace treaty with Egypt would allow them to concentrate their forces against Syria, with which they were still at war. Finally, the Israelis had to face the fact that the Arab oil embargo had turned much of the rest of the world against them and that, apart from the United States, they were diplomatically isolated.

In his first negotiations with Israel, Kissinger secured minuscule gains for Egypt in a so-called "disengagement" agreement, which stated specifically that this was not a peace treaty but only a "first step toward a final, just, and durable peace." A final disengagement agreement was not signed until September 1, 1975. It provided for Israel's withdrawal beyond the Sinai's Gidi and Mitla passes and the return of the Sinai oil fields at Abu Rodeis to Egypt. A new UN buffer zone was to be created between the Egyptians and the Israelis, supervised by a civilian American team equipped with the most sensitive modern monitoring devices. In return, the Egyptians agreed to allow nonmilitary Israeli cargoes to pass through the Suez Canal, which had been reopened on November 20, 1974. On October 31, 1975, for the first time in twenty-seven years, a ship carrying an Israeli cargo passed through the canal.

Kissinger's success in arranging this agreement appears to have involved a good deal of outright bribery. American aid to Egypt was dramatically increased, from 8.5 million dollars in 1974 to 250 million in 1975 and to 750 million in 1976 and beyond. Israel was promised annual subsidies of 2.3 billion dollars.

Kissinger's shuttle diplomacy was put to a more severe test in brokering a disengagement agreement between Israel and Syria, which had never agreed to a cease-fire. In continuing their war against Israel, the Syrians had been receiving substantial military aid from the Soviet Union, which clearly hoped that Syria would take the place of Egypt as a fulcrum for Soviet influence in the Middle East. The problem for Syria, however, was that the Israelis still retained control of the Golan Heights and of Syrian territory within twenty miles of Damascus. With a large part of his country occupied and confronted with the irrefutable fact of Israel's military superiority, the Syrian leader, Hafez al-Assad, reluctantly came to the same conclusion as Sadat: he would have to seek American mediation in securing anything approaching a satisfactory settlement with Israel.

Once again Kissinger was happy to oblige, for he now had another opportunity to freeze out the Soviet Union. An Israeli–Syrian disengagement agreement was signed on May 31, 1974, whereby Israel retained the strategic Golan Heights and part of the natural observation tower of Mount Hermon. Syria, however, secured Israel's withdrawal from the greater part of Syrian territory conquered in the Yom Kippur War—some three hundred square miles—and the return of a symbolic strip of territory adjacent to the Golan Heights, lost in the Six Day War. Israel's disengagement treaty with Syria, like that with Egypt, provided for the establishment of a UN buffer zone between the contending parties. This agreement, too, was specifically defined as not being a peace treaty but only a step toward a just and durable peace. Technically, Israel was still at war with both Egypt and Syria.

Kissinger regarded the disengagement agreement with Syria as a major breakthrough. If radical Syria could sign a treaty with Israel, there could no longer be any ideological obstacles to peace talks with any other Arab state.

❑ The Middle East Policy of Jimmy Carter

Kissinger was never able to test whether the agreement with Syria had in fact been a breakthrough, for his attention was soon to be diverted from the Middle East by the domestic crisis in the United States that culminated in the resignation of Nixon on

August 8, 1974, and the collapse of the American-backed governments in Cambodia and Vietnam in the following April. Nixon's successor, Vice-President Gerald Ford, retained Kissinger as secretary of state, but in the elections of November 1976 Ford was defeated by the Democratic candidate Jimmy Carter, who was to adopt a different strategy in the Middle East. He abandoned Kissinger's step-by-step tactics in favor of seeking a comprehensive Middle East peace treaty that would settle the Arab–Israeli problem once and for all.

In a speech of March 16, 1977, Carter outlined three conditions for permanent peace in the Middle East: Arab recognition of Israel's right to exist; the negotiation of agreements by Middle East governments establishing permanent frontiers between their states, to be backed up by international guarantees; and the creation of a "homeland" for the Palestinians. The next day, after presenting his conditions for permanent peace to the United Nations, Carter shook hands with the official observer of the Palestinian Liberation Organization, presumably to demonstrate the sincerity of his concern for the Palestinians.

Carter departed from Kissinger's strategy in another important respect. Whereas Kissinger had endeavored to exclude the Soviet Union from his Middle East negotiations, Carter believed it would be impossible to achieve an overall Middle East peace settlement without Soviet cooperation. In response to a Carter initiative, the Soviet government joined the United States in October 1977 in issuing a call for an international Middle East Conference, whose agenda would include consideration of the Palestinian problem. Unfortunately for Carter's Middle East peace initiative, Yitzhak Rabin, the prime minister and head of Israel's Labour party, who had sought an accomodation with the Palestinians by yielding to some of their territorial demands in return for guarantees of peaceful relations, was defeated in the elections of May 1977. He was succeeded in by Menachim Begin, the leader of the Likud (Unity) party, who had won fame as a Zionist guerrilla fighter in the days of the British mandate. Begin was a zealous advocate of retaining the territories conquered in the Six Day War, and he would have nothing to do with the Carter proposals. Under no circumstances would he negotiate with the Palestinian Liberation Organization, he said, nor would he ever agree to the establishment of a Palestinian state on the West Bank.

Whatever discouragement Carter experienced from the attitude of Begin had meanwhile been offset by his discovery of a kindred spirit in the Arab camp. In April 1977, he tells us in his memoirs, "a shining light burst on the Middle East for me. I had my first meeting with President Anwar Sadat of Egypt, a man who would change history and whom I would come to admire more than any other leader." In November 1977 Sadat astonished the world by proposing to go to Jerusalem to address the Israeli parliament (the Knesset). The Begin government, with only a slim electoral majority, agreed to receive him. There were distinct advantages for Israel of direct negotiations with Egypt, which would exclude the other Arab states and drive a wedge between them. Most importantly, direct negotiations would sidetrack Carter's proposal of an international conference to consider the Palestinian question. For at such a conference the Arab participants would be certain to side with the Palestinians, and Carter, with his call for a Palestinian homeland, seemed prepared to support them as well.

In his speech to the Knesset on November 19, Sadat appealed for peace on the basis of a set of interrelated proposals: the right of all states in the Middle East to live in peace within secure frontiers, the settlement of differences between them without resort to force, and the termination of the state of belligerency between Egypt and Israel. At the same time, however, Sadat set forth conditions which doomed his peace proposals: Israel's withdrawal from all occupied territory, including East Jerusalem, and its acknowledgment of the right of the Palestinians to a state of their own.

Begin responded as he had done to Carter's proposal for an international conference: he would never negotiate with the PLO, nor would he ever cede Judea and Samaria, "which others chose to call the West Bank." As for Jerusalem, "the return of any part of that city to the Arabs was unthinkable."

Carter's hopes for a Middle East peace settlement were dealt a further blow by developments in Lebanon, which was invaded by Israeli forces in March 1978 to knock out the bases of Palestinian terrorists in that country and to prop up the government of Lebanon's Christian president against the Palestinian refugees and the Lebanese Muslims. The Begin government assured Washington that this "retaliatory strike" would be strictly limited in time and scope. But Carter, fearing that the Israeli invasion might escalate into a major international crisis, was determined to end it before it spun out of control. Under pressure from the Carter administration, exercised through the United Nations, Begin agreed to withdraw Israeli forces from Lebanon and allow them to be replaced by a UN peacekeeping force.

❑ *The Camp David Accords, September 1978*

The potentially explosive nature of the Lebanese crisis (which did indeed explode four years later; see pp. 523-525) reinforced Carter's belief in the need for a general Middle East peace settlement. During Begin's subsequent two visits to Washington, however, Carter signally failed to soften the prime minister's position over the Palestinians or the occupied territories. Finally, as he tells us in his memoirs, he decided to go all-out. He invited both Begin and Sadat to join him at the presidential Camp David retreat in the Maryland hills, where they would stay as long as necessary to hammer out an agreement. Unable to risk jeopardizing their relations with the United States and lured by the prospect of additional American military and economic aid, both leaders agreed to accept the president's invitation.

The meeting at Camp David, which took place from September 5 to 17, 1978, produced two documents supplemented by explanatory protocols: a framework for a comprehensive Middle East peace settlement, including a "just settlement" of the refugee problem, and a framework for a bilateral Egypt-Israel peace treaty. Carter hailed the Camp David Accords as a triumph of his personal diplomacy and the high point of his presidency. Begin and Sadat were subsequently awarded the Nobel Peace Prize.

The Camp David framework for an Egypt-Israel treaty actually led to peace, though only after many more months of tortuous negotiation. The framework for comprehensive peace, on the other hand, was a farce. It called for the governments of Egypt, Israel, and Jordan to agree on establishing "an elected self-governing authority" in the West Bank and the Gaza Strip for a transitional period not exceeding five years. During those five years these same three governments were to negotiate an agreement "to determine the final status of the West Bank and Gaza" and recognize "the legitimate rights of the Palestinian people and their just requirements." This agreement would then be submitted for final approval to the elected representatives of the inhabitants of the West Bank and Gaza.

Altogether these provisions were so complicated and their wording so ambiguous as to make the entire document meaningless. No rules were set down as to how the "self-governing authority" was to be elected, and there was no definition of the legitimate rights of the Palestinians or their just requirements. The Israelis certainly behaved as though the document was meaningless. Their troops remained firmly in control of the West Bank and Gaza, and the Israeli government actively encouraged the extension of Jewish settlements in these areas as well as in East Jerusalem and the Golan Heights, where they engaged in large-scale expropriations of Arab land and property. In July 1980 the Israeli parliament declared an undivided Jerusalem to be the permanent capital of Israel. In December 1981 Israel formally annexed the Golan Heights.

The only substantive achievement that came out of the Camp David Accords was a bilateral Egypt–Israel peace treaty, signed by Begin and Sadat in Washington on March 26, 1979. Israel agreed to restore the Sinai Peninsula to Egyptian control in stages extending to 1982. Meanwhile, an international force was to be stationed in the Sinai to ensure the adherence of both parties to the agreement. Israel was to have unlimited shipping rights through the Suez Canal and the Gulf of Aqaba. Both countries agreed to abstain from the use of force in settling disputes and to restore normal diplomatic and economic relations.

Even this agreement was only achieved through substantial American financial inducements. Israel was promised another 3 billion dollars in military aid, a guaranteed oil supply for fifteen years should its other supplies of oil be cut off, and an American guarantee that the present treaty would be observed. Egypt was promised 1.5 billion dollars in American aid.

With this treaty Sadat achieved what no other Arab leader had been able to accomplish: the recovery of territory conquered by Israel. He had done so, however, at the cost of compromising the interests of other Arab countries and the Palestinians, who would henceforth be denied Egyptian support in seeking concessions of their own from Israel. Further, by concluding a treaty with Israel at all, Sadat had acknowledged Israel's right to exist, which in the eyes of the Arabs made him a traitor to the Arab cause. Driving this wedge between Egypt and other Arab states may well have been made a greater contribution to Israel's security than the treaty itself, and the opportunity to do so was undoubtedly a major reason for Begin's acceptance of that treaty.

The Egypt–Israel treaty was not followed, as Carter at least had hoped and expected, by similar treaties between Israel and other Arab states. Quite the opposite happened. Infuriated by what they regarded as Sadat's betrayal of the Arab cause, all the Arab states with the exception of Oman and Sudan recalled their diplomatic missions from Cairo and severed diplomatic and economic relations with Egypt. In October 1981 Sadat was assassinated by an agent of Egyptian Muslim radicals.

THIRTY-SEVEN

❑

The Middle East: From the Islamic Revolution in Iran to the 1991 Gulf War

❑ *Iran, the Shah, and the Islamic Revolution*

In 1979 yet another crisis developed in the Middle East, this time in Iran, a country well outside the orbit of the Camp David Accords.

Since the first years of the twentieth century, when Britain and Russia had divided the territory of what was then called Persia into spheres of influence between them, the great powers have been intervening in the affairs of Iran. They continued to do so throughout World War II, their primary concern now being to keep the Germans out and preserve their own access to Iranian oil. In the years after World War II, however, foreign political and economic intervention in Iran was meeting with increasingly angry and determined resistance on the part of the Iranian people. That resistance took practical form in the spring of 1951 when the Iranian parliament elected a radical nationalist, Mohammad Mossadeq, as prime minister, and at the same time voted to nationalize the Iranian oil industry "throughout its territory and without exception . . . in order to ensure the happiness and prosperity of the Iranian people and to safeguard world peace."

Western oil interests responded by sponsoring a global boycott of Iranian oil, confident that so serious a blow to the Iranian economy would compel the Iranian government to change course and overthrow Mossadeq. To hasten this process the CIA, with lavish expenditures of economic and political favors, attempted to promote a coup against the government. Mossadeq countered by appealing to nationalist anti-Western sentiment and holding a plebiscite, which in August 1953, in the manner of such plebiscites, gave him 99.4 percent of the vote.

The shah of Iran, Mohammad Reza Pahlavi, installed in 1941 under great-power auspices, fled into exile after the August plebiscite, but in that same month the Iranian army, built up by the shah with American military aid, overthrew Mossadeq and restored Pahlavi to the Peacock Throne. The Americans promptly rewarded the new government with a grant of 45 million dollars, and in December the United States and Britain resumed diplomatic relations with Iran, severed after Iran's nationalization of their oil interests.

517

In the negotiations that now took place with Western oil companies, the shah's government took full advantage of the leverage provided by the threat of nationalization. An agreement finally hammered out on August 5, 1954, gave Iran 50 percent of the profits, an immense improvement over the 15 percent previously paid by the Anglo-Iranian Oil Company. Anglo-Iranian was now reorganized as a consortium and renamed British Petroleum, in which a 40 percent interest was retained by the British. Five American companies (Standard Oil of New Jersey, Standard Oil of California, Gulf, Texaco, and Socony-Mobil) claimed another 40 percent (8 percent each), with the balance going to Dutch Shell and French Petroleum. After August 1954, with the shah securely anchored in the Western camp, Iranian oil once again flowed freely to the markets of the world.

This happy state of affairs, for the West and Iran's Westernized elite, continued until the summer of 1978. Meanwhile, the shah ruled in an increasingly autocratic manner, using his army and secret police to suppress opposition and using his oil money to purchase immense quantities of arms from the West. While continuing to build up his army, the shah also tried to carry out a radical Westernization program that was intensely resented by his Muslim subjects, most of them adherents of the conservative Shiite branch of Islam. (See p. 92.) Unnoticed by Western observers, who believed Iran to be an oasis of stability in the Middle East, a cauldron of anger and discontent simmered under the Peacock Throne, fueled by government brutality and the fulminations of Shiite conservative religious leaders, who denounced the shah's Westernization program as a flagrant violation of Islamic laws and traditions.

The shah's government, too, failed to perceive the extent of popular hostility and continued to rely on repression in dealing with opposition forces. On September 9, 1978, a day subsequently known as Black Friday, the army and police killed an estimated 2,000 demonstrators in attempting to restore order. This massacre only intensified popular hostility. Antigovernment demonstrations grew steadily larger and more violent. Seriously alarmed at last, the shah entrusted the prime ministership to Shahpour Bakhtiar, a former associate of Mossadeq and a political leader with solid nationalist credentials, but unrest continued unabated. On January 16, 1979, the shah, his energy and will sapped by the cancer that would soon kill him, fled into exile. He left the government in charge of Bakhtiar, who, under intense public pressure, authorized the return to Iran of the shah's most virulent opponent, the Ayatollah Khomeini, the foremost leader of Iran's Shiite Muslims.

In exile since 1964 in Iraq, Turkey, and most recently in Paris, Khomeini had kept up a steady attack on the shah's Westernization policies through writings and speeches smuggled into Iran, and over the years he had become the country's most revered religious figure. Within days of his return on February 1, 1979, Khomeini, ignoring Bakhtiar altogether, put together a new government composed largely of Islamic fundamentalist clerics. This regime, overwhelmingly endorsed in a staged referendum held at the end of March, proclaimed Iran an Islamic Republic under the leadership of the Ayatollah Khomeini.

The aim of the new rulers was not merely the overthrow of the shah, but the complete transformation of the government and society on the basis of a fundamentalist Shiite interpretation of Islamic law. They undertook a wholesale purge of former political, economic, and cultural leaders, their revolutionary courts tried, convicted, and executed hundreds. They created their own version of the shah's secret police, took control of the media, and crushed all voices of dissent. In short, Iran's new theocratic regime was even more brutal and repressive than the government of the shah, and thousands of Westernized Iranians fled the country.

Delighted by the overthrow of the pro-American shah, the Soviet Union immediately recognized the new Iranian government and proposed closer political and economic ties. This gesture did the Soviets no good, for the Islamic Republic despised the secular Bolshevik regime quite as much as the godless governments of the West. One of its first acts was to cancel plans to build a second pipeline to the Soviet Union and to increase the price of oil sold to Moscow. Not to be outdone by the Soviets, the Americans too sought to curry favor with the Iranian fundamentalist regime, revealing yet again Washington's complete failure to understand what had been happening in Iran or the radical nature of the Iranian revolution.

❏ *The Iranian Hostage Crisis*

Shortly after the shah's flight from Iran, the world learned that he was dying of cancer. Embarrassed by Washington's cold-blooded desertion of the shah, who for so long had been hailed as America's most dependable ally in the Middle East (apart from Israel), American supporters of the shah persuaded President Carter to disregard Iranian protests and permit him to come to New York for medical treatment. This humanitarian gesture was to have disastrous consequences. On November 4, 1979, an Iranian mob stormed the American embassy in Teheran, seizing 69 hostages. Khomeini ordered the release of the women and blacks among them, but the remaining 53 were kept hostage and became the central preoccupation of the Carter administration. They were not released until January 20, 1981, 444 days later, by which time Carter had gone down to defeat in the presidential elections of the previous November.

Carter's immediate reaction to the hostage crisis had been to prohibit the import of Iranian oil and to freeze Iranian assets in the United States as well as those under American control abroad. But, as other countries continued to purchase Iranian oil, the American boycott did nothing more than stoke the fires of anti-American sentiment. American diplomatic efforts to secure the release of the hostages were similarly futile, as was Washington's ignominious capitulation to Iranian demands to expel the shah from the United States. He died on July 17, 1980—in Egypt, an interesting indication of the absence of unity within the Islamic world.

Altogether disastrous was a secret military mission Carter authorized in April 1980 to rescue the hostages. The rescue mission did not remain secret for long. In attempting to carry it out, an American plane collided with a helicopter, killing eight members of the rescue team. To a frustrated American public, this display of incompetence seemed a symbol of the overall futility of the Carter administration.

❑ *The Soviet Invasion of Afghanistan*

Meanwhile, Carter had been obliged to deal with another Middle East crisis. On December 27, 1979, less than two months after the seizure of the American hostages in Iran, the Soviets invaded Afghanistan, thereby posing a renewed threat, as Americans saw it, to Western interests in the Middle East.

Since the British East India Company's takeover of India in the eighteenth century (its authority transferred to the British crown in 1858), the British government had sought to preserve Afghanistan as a neutral buffer state between Russia and British India. Afghanistan had remained neutral in World War II, and after the war the Afghan government tried to steer a course of nonalignment. Over the next quarter century, the Soviet Union and the United States jockeyed for position in Afghanistan, as elsewhere in the Third World. In April 1978 the Soviets appeared to have gained the upper hand in Afghanistan when the first of two Marxist-led revolutions overthrew a nominally neutral Afghan government and established an overtly pro-Soviet regime in Kabul. These Marxist governments, however, faced steadily mounting opposition from assorted bodies of fundamentalist Muslims.

To justify their invasion of Afghanistan in December 1979, the Soviets claimed that Afghanistan's pro-Soviet government had asked for their aid to protect the country from a fundamentalist Muslim revolution supported by China, Pakistan, and the United States.

The Soviets had several interconnected reasons for their invasion. Their most immediate and obvious motive was to ensure the maintenance of a pro-Soviet government in Kabul. The Soviet leader Leonid Brezhnev stated the case succinctly: "To have acted otherwise would have meant . . . looking on passively while the source of a serious threat to the security of the Soviet state developed on our southern border." A far greater threat to Soviet security, however, was the possibility that a successful Islamic revolution in Afghanistan would set off revolutions in the predominantly Muslim states of the Soviet Union. There were approximately 50 million Muslims in the Soviet provinces of central Asia. Among these 50 million were people with a proud historical heritage who only a century ago had fallen under Russian dominion and who, despite four decades of Communist indoctrination, had remained faithful to Islam. Here was combustible material that might shake the foundations of the Soviet state. As is now evident from Soviet documents, it was primarily to forestall Islamic revolutions in the Soviet Union itself that Moscow decided to invade Afghanistan, a decision made all the easier because Soviet leaders were convinced that a takeover of Afghanistan would be a relatively quick and simple operation.

With the Soviet invasion of Afghanistan, President Carter gave up all hope for ending the Cold War and establishing a cooperative relationship with Moscow. He withdrew the still unratified Salt II treaty (see p. 488) from the Senate, ordered an embargo on shipments of grain and technology to the Soviet Union, endorsed a new program of draft registration, asked for an increase in defense spending, and called upon America's allies to join the United States in boycotting the Olympic Games, scheduled to be held in Moscow. "The Soviet invasion of Afghanistan is the greatest threat to world peace since the Second World War," Carter told Congress on January 8, 1980. "It's a sharp escalation in the aggressive history of the Soviet Union." In his State of the Union address of January 23, he set forth a Carter Doctrine: "Any attempt by any outside force to gain control of the Persian Gulf will be regarded as an assault on the vital interests of the United States of America, and such assault will be repelled by the use of any means necessary, including military force."

Carter's extreme reaction to news of the Soviet invasion was an example of how his sense of moral outrage influenced his policy. But it also revealed his profound ignorance of the overall situation in the Middle East, an ignorance unfortunately shared by his senior advisers. A cursory study of the map would have shown that Afghanistan, a land dissected by mountain ranges and steep valleys, with few and for the most part poor roads, was hardly an avenue for extending control over the Persian Gulf. And the difficulty of controlling Afghanistan itself would have been obvious from the history of that country, with its multitude of feuding and fiercely independent tribes that had never yielded to the authority of a central government.

As neighbors of Afghanistan, the Soviets should have known more about that country, but their policies revealed an ignorance quite as great as that of the Americans. Their invasion of Afghanistan became what Vietnam had been for the United States. The operation proved extremely costly, the Soviet army met with determined resistance from Afghanistan's warlike tribes, and the army never established effective control over more than a small segment of the country. The Afghan leaders they installed were eager to accept Soviet support but balked at Soviet control. Corrupt, inept, and engaged in domestic feuds and power struggles, they proved incapable of rallying popular support, and they were seen by a large proportion of the conservative and xenophobic Afghan population as puppets of the godless Bolsheviks.

After years of inconclusive fighting, Mikhail Gorbachev, who had come to power in Moscow in March 1985, concluded that his country could no longer sustain the moral and economic drain of the Afghan war and decided on the gradual withdrawal of Soviet forces. To ensure that other powers would not take advantage of the situation to install an anti-Soviet government in Kabul, he called for a renewal of Middle East negotiations in Geneva, which produced yet another set of Geneva Accords. In treaties signed on April 14, 1988, the Soviet government promised to remove half of its forces from Afghanistan by August and to complete the Soviet withdrawal by February 2 of the following year; the United States and the Soviet Union promised not to continue the war in Afghanistan through surrogates; and Afghanistan and Pakistan pledged to refrain from any kind of intervention in each other's affairs.

The Soviets kept their promise to withdraw from Afghanistan by February 2, but Afghanistan itself remained torn by civil strife. In April 1992 a coalition government of Islamic ultra-conservatives was installed in Kabul—Shiite conservatives at that—which attempted to transform Afghanistan into an Islamic republic on the model of Iran. Civil war continued, but by the end of the century one of the most extreme of Islamic fundamentalist sects, the Taliban, took over the government in Kabul and proceeded to impose their conception of Islamic law on the country.

❑ *The Iran–Iraq War*

In dealing with the problems of the Middle East, Moscow as well as Washington failed to give adequate consideration to the many-layered schisms that divided the Islamic world, the traditional hostilities among the peoples of that region, and the personal rivalries and ambitions of their leaders. The differences within the Islamic world were soon to be dramatically exposed by Saddam Hussein, the dictator of Islamic Iraq, who in September 1980 went to war against Islamic Iran.

Islamic though they both might be, the differences between the Iraqis and Iranians had always been readily apparent. The Iranians were Persians, the Iraqis were Arabs. The Iranians were mostly Shiite Muslims, but although roughly half of the Iraqis were also Shiites, Iraqi Sunnis dominated the political and economic life of the country. Whereas the Iranians had remained independent of the Ottoman empire, the Iraqis had been part of that empire for centuries and had only achieved independence after World War I. Both Iran and Iraq shared with Turkey a large Kurdish minority.

A prime objective of Saddam Hussein's invasion of Iran was to gain control of the region surrounding the Shatt-el-Arab waterway, which the Allies had made the frontier between Iraq and Iran after World War I. The Shatt al-Arab begins at the confluence of the Tigris and Euphrates rivers, some 250 miles south of Baghdad, and flows another 75 miles into the Persian Gulf. Its importance lies in the fact that it constitutes the prime access route to major ports and oil refineries of the Persian Gulf.

The domestic turmoil in Iran following the Islamic revolution had encouraged Saddam to believe that his invasion would meet with little resistance. The shah had spent a large part of his country's oil revenue to build up a large and modern army, but his fundamentalist successors, in their zeal for Islamic religious purity and rejection of Western values, had carried out a sweeping purge of the army's American-trained officer corps and virtually destroyed its air force. Confident that Iran was ripe for plucking, Saddam Hussein launched his invasion on September 5, 1980. But Saddam had underestimated the resilience of the Iranian people, and instead of scoring a quick victory, he found himself bogged down in a long and ultimately inconclusive war.

For a time, the Americans and Israelis found themselves on opposite sides of the Iran–Iraq conflict. America's hostility to Iran had been kept alive after the hostage crisis by Muslim terrorism in the Middle East, which Washington believed to be instigated by Iran's fundamentalist government. The United States appealed to other industrialized states to stop arms sales to Iran and support negotiations to end a war that threatened their Middle East oil supplies. The Reagan administration openly acknowledged that it was "tilting" toward Iraq, and in November 1984, after a break of seventeen years, the United States resumed diplomatic relations with that country.

The Israelis, on the other hand, were tilting toward Iran, a non-Arab state which had not taken part in the Arab wars against Israel, whereas Iraq had joined the Arab coalition whose avowed purpose had been the destruction of the Jewish state. The government of the shah had been a major purchaser of Israeli weaponry and Israel continued to sell arms to Iran's revolutionary government, motivated in part by fear that a cutoff of arms shipments would imperil the lives of the 80,000 Jews living in Iran. On June 7, 1981, informed by Israeli intelligence that Iraq was on the verge of developing nuclear weapons, the Israelis had taken the drastic step of bombing an Iraqi nuclear facility near Baghdad. At the time of the hostage crisis, they had halted their arms sales to Iran at the request of the Carter administration, but they resumed their arms shipments in the summer of 1984 when Iran seemed on the verge of defeat. Defense Minister Yitzhak Rabin candidly admitted that Israel did not want a settlement of the Iran–Iraq conflict, which was so effectively weakening a dangerous enemy.

❑ *The Tragedy of Lebanon*

The Israelis had every reason to keep the Iran–Iraq conflict on the boil, for with Iraq temporarily checked, they had a freer hand in dealing with dangers closer to home. Foremost among these was the Palestinian threat, which since the 1970s seemed to emanate most ominously from neighboring Lebanon, a country with a large Christian population and ruled by a government dominated by Lebanese Christians.

In the course of the Arab–Israeli wars, as we have seen, large numbers of Palestinians had fled to Lebanon and Jordan. They had subsequently become a powerful political force in both countries. Palestinians were expelled from Jordan in the autumn of 1970 because of the threat they posed to the Jordanian government. A majority of these refugees had fled to Lebanon, which was to become the principal base of Palestinian militants for launching terrorist attacks against Israel and Israeli targets abroad. On September 5, 1972, they shocked the world by their abduction and murder of eleven members of the Israeli squad at the Munich Olympic Games.

The number of Palestinian refugees in Lebanon was swollen yet again by the Yom Kippur War of October 1973. With a steadily growing army of their own and in alliance with the militias of various factions of Lebanese Muslims, the Palestinians were soon powerful enough to challenge the authority of the Lebanese Christian leadership. Sporadic fighting began in the autumn of 1973 and rapidly developed into a full-scale civil war that became increasingly savage over the years. A UN peacekeeping force, sent in to help the government restore order, was not strong enough to be effective. The war soon took on international dimensions, as both Syria and Israel sent troops into the country. Mortal enemies though they might be, Syria and Israel intervened for the same purpose: to curb the power of the Palestine Liberation Organization in Lebanon, which threatened the interests of both countries. The size and strength of the army the Syrians sent into Lebanon suggests that they had more far-reaching purposes in view, namely, the takeover of Lebanon itself, which they had always regarded as an integral part of Syria and had never recognized as an independent state.

On June 6, 1982, frustrated by stepped-up PLO terrorism and justifiably fearful that the 40,000 Syrian troops in Lebanon were a prelude to a Syrian takeover, Israel launched a large-scale invasion of Lebanon with the announced objective of eliminating Palestinian bases once and for all, dislodging the Syrians, and restoring a Lebanese Christian government capable of keeping the country's Palestinian refugee population under control. The Israelis quickly overran the UN peacekeepers and surged toward Beirut, which they declared to be a "powerful political and intellectual center of Palestinian nationalism."

The Israelis met greater resistance in their campaign against the Syrians, but here too they won a quick victory. With the destruction of Syrian surface-to-air missiles and the Syrian air force, they achieved complete air superiority, while on land they defeated a larger Syrian army equipped with the most modern Soviet tanks. On June 11, after five days of intense fighting, the Syrians agreed to a cease-fire which left Syria in control northeastern Lebanon.

The American government, now under the leadership of Ronald Reagan, voted with Israel against a UN resolution calling for Israel's immediate withdrawal from Lebanon. A Reagan emissary subsequently helped the Israelis achieve one of their major objectives, the ouster of the Palestinian militiamen from Beirut, by persuading them to leave the city under the supervision of a multinational force made up of American, French, and Italian soldiers. By mid-September some 8,000 Palestinian fighters had left Beirut, which was promptly occupied by the Israelis. The Palestinians found refuge in Tunisia, Algeria, and other radical centers of the Muslim world.

Reagan followed up the evacuation of the Palestinian militiamen with a peace initiative designed to complete the work of the Camp David Accords negotiated under President Carter. In a nationally televised speech of September 1, 1982, he called upon Israel to grant self-government to the Palestinians in the West Bank and the Gaza Strip. In addition, he called for an immediate freeze on Jewish settlements in the West Bank, which he believed to be a major obstacle to the peace process. Menachim Begin, the Israeli prime minister, not content with rejecting the Reagan proposals, announced the formation of new Jewish settlements on the West Bank, and in the ensuing months the Israeli government mounted an extensive advertising campaign to speed up the creation and enlargement of these settlements.

Reagan's peace plan was doomed in any case by subsequent events. On September 15 assassins murdered the Lebanese Christian leader, Bashir Gemayel, who had been elected president of Lebanon in the previous August. To avenge what they assumed to be an act of Islamic terrorism, Christian militiamen struck at the Palestinian civilian refugee camps outside Beirut, massacring some 1,200 Palestinians, a slaughter that went on for two days while Israeli troops stood by and did nothing to stop these grim reprisals.

Horrified by this bloodbath, Reagan announced on September 20 the formation of a new multinational force "to bring the nightmare in Lebanon to an end." This force was assigned two tasks: the restoration of strong central government and the removal of all foreign troops from Lebanon. Reagan estimated that these objectives could be achieved within 60 days and that American troops could then be withdrawn. In fact they were to remain in Lebanon for another 18 months, and their mission was to end in tragic failure.

In calling for the removal of foreign troops, Reagan's primary concern was the ouster of the Syrians, who were regarded in Washington as surrogates of the Soviet Union. America's intervention in Lebanon, however, only served to propel the Syrians into closer relations with Moscow. In December 1982 they concluded a new military assistance pact with the Soviets, which was to provide them with the most technically advanced Soviet weapons, plus 8,000 Soviet technicians and military advisers to train Syrian troops in their use.

The American government had failed to understand the depth and complexity of the crisis in Lebanon. The multinational force sent to Lebanon proved to be woefully inadequate to achieve the objectives of establishing a strong central government or removing foreign troops. Syrian and Israeli forces remained in in the country, the various Christian and Muslim political factions all maintained their own militias, and the Lebanese government, without popular support, proved incapable of restoring order. The multinational army was not only inadequate. It also proved to be exceptionally vulnerable. On October 23, 1983, a Shiite fanatic drove a truck loaded with TNT into the American camp at the Beirut airport killing 241 American marines. On that same day a bomb killed 58 French paratroopers.

President Reagan declared that America would never give in to terrorists. It was "central to our credibility on a global scale" to keep the marines in Lebanon, where they would remain until the Lebanese government was in full control of the situation. But even as he made these bold pronouncements, Reagan ordered the "redeployment" of the marines to naval vessels off the Lebanese coast. By the end of February 1984 all the marines had left Lebanon. A month later the Sixth Fleet sailed away from Lebanese waters. The French and Italian contingents of the multinational army had been withdrawn long since. The civil war in Lebanon continued.

The bombing of American marines in Beirut had shocked and angered American public opinion, but events in Lebanon were overshadowed almost immediately afterwards by Reagan's wildly popular invasion of the tiny Caribbean island of Grenada, allegedly to forestall the use of that island as a Soviet air base. (See pp. 500–501.) In the presidential elections of 1984, in which Reagan was triumphantly reelected, the fiasco of American policy in Lebanon played no role at all.

❑ Arms for Hostages

Throughout the Lebanese crisis, the Iran–Iraq war had continued with mounting ferocity, and in the fourth year of that war the United States became involved in one of the most bizarre episodes in its history.

On March 16, 1984, Muslim terrorists kidnapped William Buckley, the CIA chief in Beirut. Two more Americans were seized in 1984 and four more in 1985, including the director of Catholic Relief Services and the head of the American hospital in Beirut. Washington suspected that terrorist activity in Lebanon, including the bombing of American marines in October 1983, had been carried out with the support of Iran, which the Reagan administration had placed on its list of sponsors of international terrorism. Reagan defiantly proclaimed that this hostage taking would do the terrorists no good. The United States, he said, would "make no concessions . . . make no deals" to secure their release.

Making concessions and deals is exactly what the United States did do, however. Operating in great secrecy and while still calling on other nations to continue their arms embargo of Iran, the Reagan government began selling arms to Iran as a means of enlisting Iran's aid to secure the release of the hostages in Lebanon. This program appears to have been initiated by Reagan's national security adviser, Robert McFarlane, with the support and approval of CIA Director William Casey. In May 1985 a McFarlane emissary met with Prime Minister Shimon Peres and other Israeli officials to arrange Israel's cooperation in these arms sales.

Thus began the clandestine arms-for-hostages program whereby the United States was to sell Iran large quantities of weapons, chiefly through Israel, in the expectation that Iran would arrange the release of the American hostages. In presenting the case for this operation to the president in August 1985, McFarlane argued that the arms deal went well beyond the hostages issue and would serve important national interests. It would enable the United States to counter Soviet influence in Iran, diffuse the hostility of Iranian hard-liners, strengthen the hand of Iranian moderates, and lead to better overall relations between Iran and the United States. The secrecy of the arms deal would avoid international repercussions, for by transhipping the arms through Israel, the American government could deny that it was violating the international arms embargo.

Reagan's diary entries indicate that he accepted these explanations. Although his own concern appears to have centered on the hostages, he approved the arms deal with the understanding that the "transaction was to be solely between Israel and the Iranian moderates and would not involve our country." Reagan did not raise the question as to who these Iranian moderates might be, or, if they existed at all, how they could operate independently of their government dominated by extremists. In January 1986 Reagan signed a top-secret authorization of direct American arms sales to Iran on the grounds that this transaction did indeed serve American national interests.

The arms-for-hostages operation was as futile as it was dishonest. Even if it secured the release of hostages, the terrorists could always seize more—which they did. By the end of 1985 only one hostage had been released, and the hostage the Americans wanted most, CIA agent William Buckley, was later found to have been tortured to death. In July 1986 the terrorists released one more hostage, only to replace him in September and October with three more. In November they released a third hostage, but once again they promptly seized three more. By that time it should have been obvious that arms for hostages had become an incentive to seize hostages rather than release them.

At approximately the same time that McFarlane had presented the arms-for-hostages case to President Reagan in August 1985, McFarlane made a member of his National Security Council staff, a lieutenant colonel of the marines named Oliver North, his principal liaison with key figures involved in the operation. A man of great energy and ingenuity, North worked out a precise schedule of weapons deliveries in return for the release of hostages. Unfortunately for North, the Iranians and their agents failed to observe his schedule, for the few hostages who were released were quickly replaced by even more hostages. The bad faith was by no means one-sided. North took considerable pride in how badly he was cheating the Iranians. He boasted that he had lied every time he met them, and that he had instructed his deputy to use a 3.7 multiplier in calculating the price of weapons being purchased, a surcharge that appears to have soared as high as 600 percent.

❑ *The Nicaragua Factor*

The Reagan administration used the profits from arms sales to Iran for purposes even more bizarre than the arms-for-hostages operation, namely, to support the counter-revolutionaries (Contras) who had risen in revolt against the Sandinista regime in Nicaragua. (On the Reagan government's involvement in Central America, see pp. 497–500.) Convinced that the Sandinistas were surrogates of the Soviet Union, President Reagan became an enthusiastic champion of the Contras. In October 1984, however, the American Congress, alarmed by reports of Contra terrorism and the hostility Reagan's policies were arousing in Latin America, ordered a ban on all American support for the Contras.

Barred from supporting the Contras openly, Reagan resorted to raising funds from foreign governments and wealthy individuals to keep them supplied with arms. Oliver North became a key player in this operation, and he was later to express considerable pride in having helped implement a new fund-raising stratagem by using profits from the Iran arms sales (he called them "residuals") as a source of revenue for the Contras. For, by promoting arms sales to Iran and diverting the risiduals to the Contras, he was helping to stem the tide of Soviet influence in both Iran and Nicaragua.

On November 3, 1986, an article in a Lebanese journal broke the news of the arms-for-hostages operation, a story taken up by the American press two days later. In a press conference of November 6, Reagan refused to comment on whether the American government had been involved in an arms-for-hostages deal. At the same time he bitterly criticized the journalists for taking up the Middle East story "that to us has no foundation," because in doing so they had gravely damaged his government's efforts "to get our hostages freed."

A week later, no longer able to deny that his government had sanctioned arms shipments to Iran, Reagan defended his policy with the argument that Iran represented a strategic bulwark against the Soviet Union, and he compared his approach to Iran with Nixon's secret visit to China. He insisted that only defensive weapons had been sold to Iran, that no third country had been involved, and that "no U.S. law had been or will be violated." He indignantly denied that there had been any other deal. "Our government has a firm policy not to capitulate to terrorist demands." That policy remained in force, he said, "in spite of wildly speculative and false stories about arms for hostages and alleged ransom payments. We did not—repeat, did not—trade weapons or anything else for hostages, nor will we."

Unable to stem the flood of criticism with denials, which were hardly rendered more convincing by their confused and conflicting nature, Reagan ordered his attorney general, Edwin Meese, to initiate an investigation. On November 21 Admiral John Poindexter, who had succeeded McFarlane as Reagan's national security adviser, warned Oliver North that Meese would be sending investigators to examine documents in his office. Justifiably alarmed, North proceeded to hold what he himself called a "shredding party." Besides destroying evidence, North undertook the alteration or falsification of key documents relating to his covert Iran-Contra operations. On November 25 Reagan found it expedient to dismiss both Poindexter and North. Privately he praised North as "an American hero," but he disclaimed all personal responsibility for what had taken place, finally resorting to saying, in response to pressing questions, "I don't remember."

A congressional investigation committee formed in the spring of 1987 established conclusively that the arms-for-hostages operation had taken place, as had the diversion of profits from arms sales to the Contras. The verdict of the committee was that these policies represented "confusion and disarray of the highest levels of government, evasive dishonesty, and inordinate secrecy, deception and disdain for the law," and that President Reagan himself had abdicated his "moral and legal responsibility to take care that the laws be faithfully executed."

These charges were far graver than those that had forced Nixon to resign, but no serious move was made to impeach Ronald Reagan, who retained his astonishing popularity. At the congressional hearings, Oliver North wrapped himself in a mantle of piety and patriotism. Though the revelations of his illegal and irresponsible conduct were shattering, he emerged in the eyes of large sectors of American public opinion as the hero that Reagan had proclaimed him to be.

❑ *The Iran–Iraq Armistice*

In the Middle East, thanks to American and Israeli arms sales to both sides, the Iran–Iraq war dragged on. In the summer of 1987 Saddam Hussein agreed to accept a UN resolution calling for a cease-fire. But it was not until July 18, 1988, after a succession of Iranian military setbacks, that the Ayatollah Khomeini agreed "to drink the bitter poison" of an armistice. A cease-fire went into effect two days later. It was not followed by a peace treaty.

A major reason for Saddam Hussein's agreement to a cease-fire was his alarm over his Kurdish minority population, which had taken advantage of his government's involvement in the war with Iran to revive its demands for an independent Kurdish state. Even as the cease-fire was under negotiation, Saddam moved against the Kurds. According to the Human Rights Watch, his army slaughtered as many as 50,000 to 100,000 Kurds (Kurdish estimates ran as high as 182,000), while some 5,000 Kurds fled to Turkey, another 17,000 to Iran.

In August 1990 Iraq announced it was withdrawing from all areas in Iran it had occupied in the recent war, and Iran formally announced an end to hostilities with Iraq.

❑ *Iraq's Invasion of Kuwait, August 2, 1990*

Thanks to the loyal support of his army, Saddam Hussein managed to survive the humiliating failure of his attempt to conquer Iran. The maintenance of a large army, however, plus the need to repair the economic ravages of the Iran war, imposed an immense strain on his country's resources. To replenish those resources he now undertook what appeared to be a far easier conquest than Iran, namely, the tiny but immensely oil-rich neighboring state of Kuwait, which the Iraqis had always claimed to be part of Iraq.

This claim was based on the fact that under Ottoman rule Kuwait had been part of the province of Basra, one of the three Ottoman provinces that were joined together by the British to form their mandate of Iraq after World War I. Already in 1899, however, to block possible German or Russian attempts to establish a base on the Persian Gulf, the British had secured a promise from the sheikh of Kuwait not to cede any part of his domain to foreign powers without Britain's consent. At the outbreak of World War I the British went a step further, declaring Kuwait to be an independent state under British protection.

With the decline of British strength in the Middle East after World War II, Saddam Hussein had good reason to believe that Britain no longer represented a serious obstacle to an Iraqi takeover of Kuwait. He played a cautious game, however, and before making any move against Kuwait he undertook to repair or strengthen his country's relations with its neighbors. He concluded an agreement with Turkey to cooperate in suppressing the Kurds, he arranged a mutually profitable oil-exporting agreement with Syria, and in March 1989 he concluded a nonaggression pact with Saudi Arabia.

On July 25, 1990, Saddam sounded the American ambassador to Baghdad, April Glaspie, about how the United States might react to an Iraqi attempt to "rectify" its frontier with Kuwait. According to an Iraqi transcript of their conversation (which the State Department later certified as being 80 percent correct, whatever that might mean), Ambassador Glaspie told Saddam: "I know you need funds. We understand that and . . . that you should have the opportunity to rebuild your country. But we have no opinion in the Arab–Arab conflicts, like your border disagreement with Kuwait."

From this conversation, Saddam could not help but draw the conclusion that he had been given a green light by the Bush administration in Washington, which might indeed have tolerated a mere frontier rectification. But Saddam soon revealed that he had far grander ambitions. On August 2, 1990, a week after his talk with the American ambassador, he launched a full-scale invasion of Kuwait, occupying the entire country and proclaiming its formal annexation to Iraq.

Saddam Hussein's seizure of Kuwait posed a serious threat to the economy of the United States and all other countries dependent on Middle East oil, which were now confronted with the question of where Saddam would stop. Would Saudi Arabia, that other great depository of Middle East oil, be next? With a large proportion of the world's oil reserves under his control, Saddam would be in a position to blackmail the entire industrialized world. And with oil money to lubricate his military machine, he might have the means to extend Iraqi control over the greater part of the Middle East.

With its vital economic interests threatened, the industrialized world for once reacted swiftly and decisively. Only four days after the Iraq invasion of Kuwait, the UN Security Council voted unanimously to impose a worldwide trade embargo on Iraq. Three weeks later it approved the use of military measures to enforce that embargo. In response to an appeal for protection from Saudi Arabia, the United States dispatched substantial naval forces to the Persian Gulf and began a massive airlift of troops to the Middle East, an operation given the code name of Operation Desert Shield. At the same time twelve of the twenty-one members of the Arab League, including Egypt and Syria, voted to send troops to aid in the defense of Saudi Arabia.

Arguing on the basis of past experience that economic sanctions would not be enough to expel Iraq from Kuwait, President Bush persuaded the Security Council to pass a resolution on November 29 authorizing the use of military force if Iraq had not left Kuwait by January 15, 1991. By the time of that deadline, a half million American troops had been sent to the Gulf area, where they had been joined by token contingents from Britain and France and three Arab states—Egypt, Syria, and Saudi Arabia. Bush calculated that this overwhelming show of force would persuade Saddam to back down. Saddam, however, evidently hoped that this latest display of Western imperialism would rally the Arab peoples to his side and inspire uprisings against the Arab governments which had joined the American-led coalition. Far from backing down, Saddam became steadily more defiant, predicting that if war came there would be no end to the columns of enemy dead. When the January 15 deadline arrived, his troops were still in Kuwait.

❑ *The Persian Gulf War*

By refusing to withdraw from Kuwait, Saddam left Bush no alternative but to go to war. Operation Desert Shield became Operation Desert Storm, which was waged during the first six weeks by allied aircraft alone. Realizing that his own air force was no match for that of the allies, Saddam sent his planes to Iran to avoid their destruction (in Iran, hostility to the West evidently still eclipsed hostility to Iraq.) Therefore, when allied aircraft attacked Iraqi targets, they were exposed only to antiaircraft fire from the ground.

Saddam resorted to missile attacks against Israel, which had remained neutral, in the evident hope of provoking Israel into joining the allied coalition and therewith transforming the conflict into an Arabian holy war against the Jews. But the Israelis, rigorously held in check by the United States, were not lured into this trap. On February 22 President Bush set another deadline for Iraq's withdrawal from Kuwait, demanding that Iraqi troops begin their pullout by noon of the following day.

Saddam's refusal set the stage for the next stage of the war: an all-out ground offensive to drive the Iraqis out of Kuwait. In preparing their offensive, the allies appear to have vastly overestimated the strength of the Iraqi army. Saddam withdrew his crack troops—the vaunted Republican Guard—into the interior of Iraq, safeguarding them, as he had his aircraft, from immediate destruction and leaving the troops of his regular army to bear the brunt of the allied attack. Within four days the Iraqi forces were driven from Kuwait and the allies began an invasion of Iraq, meeting with remarkably weak and inept resistance as they did so. On February 27 Bush announced that Kuwait had been liberated and ordered a cease-fire, which the Iraqi government hastened to accept.

Bush's precipitate-order of a cease-fire, leaving Saddam Hussein in power and his Republican Guard intact, was bitterly criticized at the time and has been the subject of intense debate ever since. Yet the president had compelling reasons for restraint. The objective of the war as defined by the UN, namely, the liberation of Kuwait, had been achieved. A drive to Baghdad and an allied occupation of Iraq, the only certain way to topple Saddam, might have been difficult and costly. Moreover, the launching of an offensive not authorized by the UN would not necessarily have been supported by other members of the allied coalition, in particular its Arab members.

Bush also had to take into account the political configuration of the postwar world. An invasion of Iraq and destruction of the Iraqi army would have left Iran the dominant power in this part of the Middle East, so that the Americans and their allies would have been obliged to take the place of Iraq in countering Iranian influence. The situation within Iraq itself had to be considered. During the war, Bush had encouraged the Kurds and Shiite Muslims in Iraq to rise up against the Sunni-dominated Iraqi government. They had done so, but the prime objective of the Kurds—the establishment of an independent Kurdish state—threatened the security of America's ally Turkey, with its own large Kurdish population. The Iraqi Shiites represented an even greater danger. If they overthrew Iraq's Sunni government, they might be tempted to unite with their co-religionists in Iran, thereby contributing significantly to the prestige and power of Iran's fanatically anti-American Shiite government. By ordering a cease-fire that left Saddam in power and the crack troops of his army intact, Bush preserved Iraq as a counterweight to Iran.

In doing so he also sold out both the Kurds and Shiites, for Saddam used the cease-fire to crush both rebellions. Using the troops of his Republican Guard equipped with helicopter gunships, heavy artillery, and poison gas, he launched a campaign of merciless ferocity against Iraq's Kurdish and Shiite populations, indulging in persecution and mass murder on so gross a scale that the victorious allies were obliged to create safe zones in northern and southeastern Iraq where these people could find sanctuary. Seeking vengeance with a savage vindictiveness, Saddam opened the Kuwait oil pipelines and torched Kuwait oil wells, creating a mammoth oil spill in the Persian Gulf and setting off fires that would not be successfully capped for another year.

In the United States, a majority of Americans were filled with patriotic pride over their quick and decisive military victory. Bush's popularity soared to 87 percent, the highest ever attained by an American president since the use of polls to measure public opinion. The massive sums previously spent by the American government on weapons development seemed to have been money well invested, for the army announced that its bombers and guided missiles had reached their targets with pinpoint accuracy and successfully destroyed Iraq's capacity to wage war. After the war, however, UN investigators learned that the claims about the performance of American weaponry had been grossly exaggerated. Only three of Iraq's thirty nuclear weapons facilities had been destroyed, a large proportion of Iraq's missiles had escaped destruction, and the Republican Guard had retained its heavy artillery and armor.

As Americans became aware of how little the war had actually accomplished and learned of the crimes against humanity and the environment committed by Saddam Hussein, who remained firmly in power, Bush's popularity plummeted. Not even the liberation of Kuwait could be regarded as an unadulterated triumph, certainly not a triumph for democracy. For the victorious allies had simply restored the old ruling elites to power who resumed their authoritarian rule and excluded political opponents from participation in their government.

There is no way to measure whether Bush was right in leaving Saddam in power and preventing the disintegration of Iraq. But the disillusionment following the initial euphoria over the Gulf War appears to have had a critical impact on the presidential elections of November 1992, when Bush went down to defeat at the hands of the Democratic candidate, Bill Clinton.

THIRTY-EIGHT

The Disintegration of the Soviet Empire

Between 1988 and 1991 the world witnessed the most extraordinary revolution in modern history: the breakup of a major empire that had not been defeated in war or overthrown by violent revolution; that possessed one of the world's most powerful armies, which had remained loyal to the government; that was the standard bearer of a political ideology with global appeal that extended the range of its authority and influence.

A major factor in that breakup, or at least a major reason the breakup took place without massive bloodshed, was Gorbachev's renunciation of the use of force in undertaking his radical restructuring of the Communist party and the Soviet political and economic system. He thought he was safe in criticizing the party, relaxing censorship, and calling for greater popular participation in politics because he had inherited a system that seemed inherently stable and a party he believed to be sufficiently well established to survive criticism and radical reform. What he forgot was that the authority of the Communist party and the Soviet state had, from their inception, been imposed and maintained by force. With the threat or use of force removed, there would be nothing to contain the resentments and frustrations, the rivalries and ambitions, and the popular passions that had seethed beneath the surface of Communist societies but had been kept in check by the Red Army and the secret police.

One of most powerful and disruptive of those passions was the spirit of nationalism among the peoples of Eastern Europe and the many nationalities that made up the Soviet empire. Gorbachev had been willing to concede the nationalities a large measure of autonomy, convinced that nationalities nourished under socialism could not help but remain convinced, as he was, of the superiority of a socialist system—a reformed and restructured socialism, to be sure—over all other forms of human social organization. In believing in the inherent loyalty of the nationalities to socialism, he failed to appreciate to what extent the nationalities associated socialism with Russian domination and control and that, for them, reform included their total emancipation from the Russian-Soviet empire.

As several of his predecessors had done, Gorbachev sought to appease the nationalities by reaffirming the principle that there were many roads to socialism. But he abandoned the Brezhnev Doctrine whereby Moscow reserved the right to intervene

532

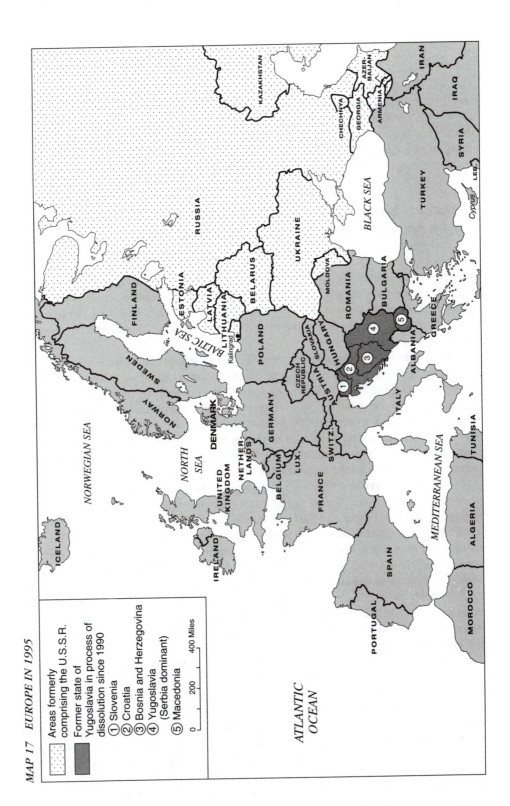

MAP 17 *EUROPE IN 1995*

Areas formerly
comprising the U.S.S.R.

Former state of
Yugoslavia in process of
dissolution since 1990

① Slovenia
② Croatia
③ Bosnia and Herzegovina
④ Yugoslavia
   (Serbia dominant)
⑤ Macedonia

0   200   400 Miles

in a socialist country if the Soviet government believed that the socialist system there were threatened. Immediately after coming to power in March 1985, he met with Warsaw Pact leaders informing them of his desire for a relationship with their countries on the basis of the principle of equality and respect for each country's sovereignty and independence.

To his surprise and dismay, they took him at his word.

❏ *Poland, Solidarity, and the Formation of a Non-Communist Government*

The first of the East European nationalities to take advantage of Gorbachev's abandonment of the use of force to maintain a Communist regime was the Poles, who had engaged in periodic antigovernment agitation since the country came under Communist leadership. In Poland, moreover, there was a long tradition of anti-Russian hostility, which had developed over the centuries when much of Poland had been under tsarist rule.

The revolution that finally won Poland's independence from Soviet/Russian control began in August 1980, when some 16,000 workers went on strike at the Lenin shipyards in Gdansk. This strike quickly spread to enterprises throughout the country, their activity coordinated by a shipyard strike committee led by an electrician named Lech Walesa. Confronted by a total breakdown of the Polish economy, the Polish Communist government gave in to the strike committee's demand to permit the formation of trade unions independent of the Polish Communist party. These independent unions now joined together to form a movement they called Solidarity.

Over the next sixteen months approximately 12 million out of a total workforce of 16 million joined the Walesa-led Solidarity Union, which soon became powerful enough to challenge state and party authority. The Soviet government, still under the leadership of Leonid Brezhnev and still determined to enforce the Brezhnev Doctrine, denounced a Solidarity mass meeting in September 1981 as an "anti-socialist and anti-Soviet orgy." The Soviets did not intervene directly. Instead, they massed their troops along the Polish frontier and transferred the leadership of the Polish Communist party to the Polish premier and defense minister, General Wojciech Jaruzelski, who did what was expected of him. On December 13 he proclaimed a "state of war" in Poland, placed the country under martial law, arrested the leaders of Solidarity, and banned the Solidarity Union.

Jaruzelski lifted martial law in July 1983, but toward the end of the decade his government was faced with renewed waves of strikes and demonstrations, many of them instigated and led by the Solidarity movement, which had flourished underground. Instead of clamping down, as in the days of Brezhnev, the Soviet government, now under the leadership of Gorbachev, urged negotiations with Solidarity and its leader Lech Walesa. These produced an agreement of April 5, 1989, whereby the government once again legalized Solidarity and promised parliamentary elections in which nongovernment candidates were to be allowed to contest 35 percent of the 460 seats in the lower house of the Polish parliament (Sejm) and all the seats in a newly created upper house, the Senate.

In the elections held in June, despite the short time it had to prepare and organize, Solidarity won all the contested seats in the Sejm and 99 of the 100 seats in the Senate. In August, with Solidarity members joined by Communist apostates, the new Polish parliament elected a Solidarity leader to the office of prime minister who formed the first non-Communist government in the former East Bloc. In December 1990 Lech Walesa was elected president of Poland.

❑ *The End of Communist Rule in Hungary*

The winds of change were blowing hard throughout Eastern Europe. In May 1988 János Kádár, who had been installed as leader of the Hungarian Communist party after Soviet tanks suppressed the 1956 revolution, resigned, allegedly for reasons of old age. Although he had come to office under Soviet auspices, Kádár had taken a relatively independent line and had initiated an economic reform program which attracted the admiration of Gorbachev. His resignation nevertheless opened the way to further and more rapid change. Symbolic of that change was the official rehabilitation on June 16, 1989, of Imre Nagy, the leader of the 1956 revolution, who had been hanged by the Soviets for treason.

More substantive changes had already begun. In February 1989 the Central Committee of the Hungarian Communist party agreed to the legalization of non-Communist political parties. In October the Hungarian parliament, although still controlled by Communists, ratified a new constitution, the product of negotiations with opposition leaders, which provided for free parliamentary elections in March of 1990. Following the constitution's ratification, the red star on top of the parliament building in Budapest was removed, and the Hungarian People's Republic became simply the Hungarian Republic, which was described in the constitution's preamble as "an independent democratic state based on the rule of law, in which the values of bourgeois democracy and democratic socialism are equally recognized."

The elections held in March and April 1990 resulted in an overwhelming victory for a populist-nationalist coalition. The Hungarian Socialist Worker's party (the Communists), now called simply the Hungarian Socialist party, won only 8 percent of the vote.

❑ *The Hungarian Blow to Communist East Germany*

In May 1989, before the promulgation of the new Hungarian constitution, the Hungarian Communist government had taken a step that was to have dramatic international repercussions. The barbed wire barrier on the Austrian frontier was cut in an official ceremony, opening the way to free travel between Hungary and Austria. The immediate result was that thousands of East Germans poured into Hungary, an East Bloc country to which they were allowed to travel. From Hungary they crossed over into Austria and thence to West Germany, a mass exodus not seen since the construction of the Berlin Wall.

In response to complaints from the East German government, Hungary began enforcing exit permission requirements, a measure that left thousands of East Germans stranded in Hungary. The Hungarians resolved this problem through a deal with the West German government. In return for 1 billion marks in West German credits, the Hungarians agreed to relax their exit controls, but to avoid the wrath of the East German government they suggested that a decent interval elapse before the credits promised by the West Germans were handed over. On September 11, 1989, the East Germans were once again given unrestricted freedom to cross the Hungarian frontier into Austria. By November an estimated 200,000 East Germans had migrated to the West.

❑ Crisis in East Germany and the Opening of the Berlin Wall

Hungary's opening of its frontier with Austria and the resulting mass exodus of East Germans had a catastrophic impact on the East German economy, which had long been in serious decline. In many areas public services and economic production simply came to a halt for lack of personnel. As the economy disintegrated, the people who remained in East Germany engaged in mass demonstrations against their Communist regime. Gorbachev was able to observe the situation at first hand, for on October 7, 1989, at the pressing invitation of the East German government, he participated in ceremonies commemorating the 40th anniversary of the establishment of German Democratic Republic. Gorbachev's presence, however, proved to be a serious embarrassment for the East German leaders, for they were virtually ignored, whereas Gorbachev was applauded by immense crowds chanting "Perestroika! Gorbachev! Help us!" "The country reminded me of an overheated boiler with the lid tightly closed," Gorbachev wrote in his memoirs. "The danger was there for everyone to see."

On the occasion of Gorbachev's visit, East German security forces tried to break up popular demonstrations in East Germany's major cities, but as the demonstrations grew in size and intensity, they found it impossible to keep the crowds under control. On October 18, after a good deal of Soviet prodding, the East German Communist party ousted its leader, Erich Honecker, who had become a symbol of Communist repression. This gesture, however, did nothing to quell popular unrest.

There followed some of the most dramatic moments in modern German history. Mass demonstrations throughout East Germany culminated on the night of November 9-10 as huge crowds gathered at the Berlin Wall demanding that it be dismantled. Faced with the alternative of a massacre or yielding, the East German authorities opened the checkpoints to the West. As Gorbachev described the event: "The wall fell, or, rather, it was transformed into a monument to the Cold War, which had become a thing of the past. Thank God, the new East German leadership had the courage and enough common sense to refrain from trying to quench the popular unrest in blood." Gorbachev took some pride in his own contribution to this restraint. He had left the East German leaders in no doubt "that Soviet troops would not leave their barracks under any circumstances."

With the opening of the wall, the mass exodus of East Germans to West Germany took on truly alarming proportions, a population drain that brought East Germany to the verge of social chaos. Hans Modrow, who had taken over the leadership of the East German government after the breaching of the Berlin Wall, confessed to Gorbachev that he saw no way to preserve the East German regime. He had yielded to popular demands for free elections, and there could no longer be any doubt that these elections would result in a vote favoring German reunification under a West German government.

Gorbachev could not help but agree. He himself, however, now faced a question of decisive importance for the Soviet Union: how was German unification to be implemented without once again imperiling the peace of Europe and Soviet security? In the weeks that followed the breaching of the Berlin Wall, that question became the prime subject of negotiation between the Soviet Union, the Germans, and the Soviets' wartime allies.

❏ *The Reunification of Germany*

Although Gorbachev believed that his summit meeting with President Bush in Malta in December 1989 "had drawn the curtain on the Cold War," he was acutely aware that there were still difficult problems to be resolved, Germany foremost among them. As he recorded in his memoirs, "Germany was to become a crucial test of the progress we had achieved in our relations with the United States, and with the nations of Western Europe, including Germany herself." Hans Modrow, in acknowledging the inevitability of German reunification, had warned Gorbachev that if the Communist leadership did not take the initiative immediately, "we won't be able to influence developments in any way."

Gorbachev had already come to the same conclusion: an immediate initiative was needed to safeguard Soviet interests and to prevent Germany from once again becoming a menace to the peace of Europe. For that purpose he now proposed that the international aspects of German reunification be negotiated by a group of six: the four victorious Allied powers and the two Germanies. In that way, the Allies as well as the East Germans could impose conditions on the West German government that would ensure international control over a unified Germany and minimize that country's threat to the international order.

Gorbachev's proposal for negotiations between the two Germanies and the four Allied powers (later known as the 2 plus 4 formula) was the central topic of his talks in Moscow from February 8 to 10, 1990, with James Baker, the American secretary of state. They agreed that German unification was inevitable, and that they would have to base their policy on this fact. They also agreed that the "internal" aspect of unification could be left to the Germans themselves. Gorbachev, however, insisted that "the four victorious powers should be involved in the negotiating process, being responsible for the preservation of peace and stability in Europe and focusing on the international aspect of unification."

Gorbachev's primary concern was the future military-political status of a united Germany. Baker tried to convince him of the desirability of keeping Germany within NATO, which gave the United States and the West leverage over Germany's domestic as well as foreign policy. A neutral Germany, on the other hand, could again become a generator of instability in Europe. While agreeing about the need for some kind of controlling mechanism, Gorbachev thought this should be provided by a new structure within a pan-European framework, not by an America-dominated NATO. In subsequent talks with President Bush in Washington and Camp David from May 30 to June 3, 1990, Gorbachev finally accepted the American argument about the desirability of allowing a united Germany to be a member of NATO to ensure that Germany remained under the control and supervision of the Western allies—a remarkable achievement of the Bush-Baker diplomacy.

In mid-July 1990 the German chancellor Helmut Kohl and his foreign minister, Hans-Dietrich Genscher, met with Gorbachev in Moscow and a retreat in the Caucasus, where they concluded a final agreement over the future status of Germany on the basis of Gorbachev's earlier agreement with the United States. A united Germany was conceded the right to remain in NATO and Soviet troops were to be withdrawn from East Germany. In return, Germany was to agree to the entire package of political and military guarantees demanded by the Soviet Union, which were to be embodied in a final 2 plus 4 treaty between the two Germanies and the four victorious Allies. The path to Soviet agreement was greased by promises of German economic aid: 12 billion marks in subsidies, plus a further 5.7 billion to cover the costs of the withdrawal of Soviet troops.

Elections to the East German parliament on March 18, 1990, had resulted in a landslide victory for the Alliance for Germany, backed by Helmut Kohl's Christian Democratic party and its pro-unification allies. The East German Communists obtained less than 17 percent of the vote; their Left-wing allies, a bare 8 percent. On August 23 the new East German parliament voted to join the Federal Republic of Germany in accordance with Article 23 of the West German Basic Law. Eight days later the East and West German governments signed the German unification treaty.

The final 2 plus 4 treaty on German reunification was signed in Moscow on September 12, 1990. A united Germany was to have "full sovereignty over its internal and external affairs." The Germans for their part reaffirmed the previous guarantees of the East and West German governments recognizing existing international frontiers, limiting the size of the German army, and renouncing atomic, biological, and chemical weaponry. Soviet troops were to be withdrawn from East Germany within four years, the cost of their relocation to be paid by Germany. Separate German-Soviet treaties, replete with assurances of mutual friendship, provided for comprehensive cooperation in the fields of economic, industrial, scientific, and technological development. A separate German-Polish treaty guaranteed the German frontier with Poland.

On October 3, 1990, the Germans celebrated the Day of German Unity with fireworks and champagne. Very few foresaw at that time how costly and painful the actual process of reunification would be.

❑ *Czechoslovakia's Velvet Revolution*

The Czechs were to boast later that the overthrow of Communist rule had taken ten years in Poland, ten months in Hungary, ten weeks in East Germany, but only ten days in Czechoslovakia.

In fact, revolution had been simmering in Czechoslovakia since the suppression of the Prague Spring in 1968, but as elsewhere in Eastern Europe, it was Gorbachev's renunciation of the use of force that made the Czech revolution possible. During an official visit he paid to Czechoslovakia in April 1987, Czech Communist leaders assured him that the Soviet government had been right in suppressing the Prague Spring, for in doing so the Soviet Union had saved socialism, repelled imperialism, and thereby averted a world war; they continued to count on Soviet support to suppress popular unrest. "They simply could not believe," Gorbachev wrote later, "that we truly had no intention of interfering in the affairs of other countries."

The Czechoslovak public made it very clear that they did not agree with their Communist leaders' assessment of the Prague Spring. In August 1988 large-scale demonstrations took place throughout the country to mark the 20th anniversary of its suppression. The Communist leadership tried to take a firm line. Following a mass demonstration in January 1989, to commemorate a student who had set himself on fire to protest the Warsaw Pact's intervention, they arrested the internationally famous playwright Vaclav Havel, who had become a leading spokesman of the protest movement. Havel's sentence to nine months in jail provoked new rounds of demonstrations, which were met by a government crackdown and warnings that demonstrations would no longer be tolerated.

The demonstration that is credited with igniting the final stage of the Czech revolution took place on November 11, 1989, when some 500 students, waving Czech flags and calling for freedom of speech and assembly, marched to Prague's Wenceslas Square to commemorate the death of a student killed by the Nazis. The government responded by sending in riot police, whose bloody suppression of the demonstration set off new rounds of protests, culminating on November 24 when an estimated half-million people assembled on Wenceslas Square demanding an end to Communist rule. At this rally. Alexander Dubček, the leader of the Prague Spring movement who had been deposed and ousted from the party following the Soviet-led intervention, spoke in public for the first time in twenty-one years. There followed a general strike that paralyzed the country's economy. With both the political and economic situation out of control, the Communist government resigned. Early in December a government was formed dominated by non-Communists. On December 28 Dubček was elected leader of the Federal Parliament; the next day Vaclav Havel was elected president of Czechoslovakia. The Velvet Revolution, so-called because it had been achieved with relatively little violence and bloodshed, had triumphed.

On May 21, 1990, Dubček paid a courtesy call on Gorbachev in Moscow, where he had been brought in disgrace twenty-one years earlier. As Gorbachev described the scene, Dubček walked toward him "with his arms opened slightly in friendly greeting. We met warmly, and Dubček's eyes were wet."

❏ *The Secession of Slovakia*

Elections held in Slovakia in June 1992 revealed yet again the potent role of nationalism in the East European revolutions, for they resulted in victory for Slovak nationalist candidates demanding freedom from the Czech-dominated Czechoslovak union. On June 21 Czech and Slovak leaders meeting in Prague agreed to end the Czechoslovak federation, and on July 17 Slovakia declared its independence. The final break took place on December 31, 1992, when Czechoslovakia was divided into two separate states, the Czech Republic, and the Republic of Slovakia.

❏ *Bulgaria*

On November 10, 1989, the day after the opening of the Berlin Wall, the 78-year-old Todor Zhivkov, the leader of the Bulgarian Communist party since 1954, resigned his posts as party leader and president. His successor, Foreign Minister Petar Mladenov, was confronted by popular demonstrations similar to those that had overturned Communist party rule elsewhere in Eastern Europe. Following the example of his Communist counterparts in Hungary and Czechoslovakia, he yielded to popular demands for free elections. Held on June 10, 1990, these elections resulted in a solid victory for the Bulgarian Communist (now renamed the Socialist) party—the only Communist victory in free elections in Eastern Europe.

Now, however, it was a Communist regime that was obliged to cope with a country's economic travails without support from Moscow—soaring inflation, strikes, a 25 percent unemployment rate, and a new rash of popular demonstrations. Elections held in October 1991 brought a non-Communist coalition to power, and with that, Communist rule in Bulgaria, too, came to an end, at least temporarily.

❏ *Romania*

The only violent revolution in the Soviet satellite states of Eastern Europe took place in Romania, ruled with an iron hand since 1965 by Nicolae Ceauşescu, a Communist leader who had long since fallen out of favor in Moscow by taking an independent line, especially in foreign policy. He had refused to integrate the Romanian economy with the Soviet-controlled Comecon, he had not joined in the Warsaw Pact's suppression of Czechoslovakia's Prague Spring, and he had sent a Romanian team to the Olympic Games in Los Angeles, which had been boycotted by the Soviet Union and its more loyal allies.

For a time the Americans cheered Ceauşescu's anti-Soviet stance, but they could not ignore that his government was among the most repressive and corrupt in Eastern Europe. It was also the most incompetent. While milking the economy to amass personal wealth, Ceauşescu had inaugurated a crash industrialization program that devastated the country's once-flourishing agricultural economy and reduced a large part of the population to outright starvation. Contributing to the ruin of the economy was the dictator's megalomaniac building project to destroy the towns and villages of old Romania and replace them with extravagant modern building developments.

Not at all reluctant to use Stalinist tactics of mass arrests, torture, and executions to maintain his government, Ceauşescu had succeeded in preventing the development of an organized opposition, but over the years hatred for his regime had built up into volcanic fury. That fury exploded in December 1989 when his security forces tried to arrest a Hungarian Protestant minister who had protested Ceauşescu's treatment of Romania's Hungarian minority population. Rebellion in Transylvania, where the majority of Romania's Hungarians lived, quickly spread to the rest of the country. Ceauşescu placed Romania under martial law, but now even his army had turned against him. Ceauşescu and his wife attempted to leave the country by helicopter, but they were captured and brought back to Bucharest. On Christmas Day, 1989, they were put on trial by a military court, condemned to death for crimes of genocide, and executed by firing squad that same day.

❏ An Uncertain Future

By the early 1990s Soviet rule over Eastern Europe had come to an end, as had the rule of Soviet-controlled Communist parties in the former Soviet satellite states. In June 1990 Moscow agreed to transform the Warsaw Pact into "a treaty of sovereign states with equal rights, formed on a democratic basis," but this was no longer enough for the new governments of Eastern Europe. In January 1991 the foreign ministers of Poland, Hungary, and Czechoslovakia issued a joint statement demanding the phasing out of the Warsaw Pact altogether by March 1992, a position subsequently adopted by Bulgaria and Romania. The final breakup of the Warsaw Pact took place well before that date. The military structure was dissolved on March 31, 1991, the political structure on July 1. The Soviet Council for Mutual Economic Assistance (Comecon), set up by Stalin in 1949 to include all the members of the East Bloc as a Communist Common Market, was dissolved in June 1991.

The peoples of Eastern Europe were to find that emancipation from Soviet control and the establishment of independent non-Communist governments did not provide automatic solutions to their manifold political and economic problems. All of them, including East Germany (which was bailed out at the cost of billions of marks by West Germany) were teetering on the brink of economic disaster, the legacy of almost a half-century of Communist rule and misconceived Communist economic policies. Burdened by immense foreign debts, their technologically backward industries unable to compete in the markets of the world, their agriculture crippled by collectivization and the lack of production incentives, the countries of Eastern Europe were hardly ideal settings for the establishment of democratic governments and a free market economy. The leaders of the new non-Communist governments were for the most part inexperienced, but even the most accomplished administrators would have found it impossible to provide their countries with a quick economic fix.

With the removal of centralized controls and government subsidies for food and housing, the peoples of Eastern Europe were confronted with soaring inflation, mass unemployment, and serious shortages of food and consumer goods. Small wonder that disillusionment soon set in, and with it nostalgia for the social security formerly provided by their Communist regimes.

In the first totally free parliamentary elections held in Poland in October 1991, only 40 percent of an apathetic electorate went to the polls, and of the thirty parties that had put forward candidates, none received more than 12 percent of the vote, while a satirically conceived Beer Lovers party received 3.3 percent. In Poland's parliamentary elections in September 1993, a reconstituted Communist party won a majority of the seats in the Sejm, and in November two years later Lech Walesa was defeated in his bid for reelection by a former Communist, now calling himself a Socialist. In the Hungarian parliamentary elections of May 1994, former Communists (now Socialists) won a landslide victory. The Slovaks, too, turned to a former Communist for leadership, and in Bulgaria and Romania the governments, while purporting to be democracies, employed authoritarian methods to deal with their own seemingly intractable economic problems.

Disillusionment with a free market economy and the return to various forms of government control did not mean that the states of Eastern Europe were reverting to the economic model once provided by the Soviet Union. Instead, as some of their new authoritarian leaders acknowledged, they were looking to the tigers of East Asia, whose spectacular economic success (at the time of the Soviet empire's breakup) had been fueled in part by government support and intervention. Nor did the electorate's turn to former Communists (or whatever they now chose to call themselves) portend a desire to return to the political and economic security once provided by the Soviet Union. Quite the contrary—since the 1990s all the states of Eastern Europe have sought closer political as well as economic ties with the European Community and the United States, and all of them are seeking security not in a revived Warsaw Pact but in the American-dominated NATO alliance.

❑ *The Disintegration of the Soviet Union*

The reasons for the breakup of the Soviet Union were in many ways similar to those that contributed to the breakup of the Soviet empire in Eastern Europe. In the Soviet Union itself, however, the personality and policies of Gorbachev played an even greater role. For it was here that Gorbachev sounded his calls for political and economic reconstruction and for greater freedom of public discourse and criticism. It was here that he initiated changes in the Communist party and the Soviet government that were designed to advance his reform program but that ultimately weakened the authority of both institutions. In the end, however, the decisive factor in the Soviet Union as in Eastern Europe was Gorbachev's reluctance to use force when faced with the prospect of massive bloodshed and civil war.

In relaxing party and government controls and promoting political and economic freedom, Gorbachev had hoped to revitalize the economy and generate renewed popular support for the Soviet government. His policies achieved neither purpose. Instead, again as in Eastern Europe, the most striking result of the new freedoms was the radicalization of national self-consciousness among the peoples of the Soviet Union. That state, it is important to recall, was made up of a conglomerate of nationalities conquered by the Russian tsars over the centuries and incorporated into the immense Russian empire. Many of these nationalities had their own languages and religions as well as their own political and cultural heritage. Despite years of Russian/Bolshevik indoctrination, many of them had retained a pronounced sense of national identity, which had been reinforced by Soviet oppression and by the forced relocation of numerous ethnic groups to other parts of the Soviet empire.

As is evident from the nature of his policies, Gorbachev was unaware of the strength and tenacity of these national loyalties. He has been described as suffering from ethnic blindness, insensitive to the revolutionary nature or the strength of the emotional appeal of nationalist sentiment. As observed earlier, he found it impossible to imagine how the nationalities could be so unrealistic, so blind to their own self-interest, as to opt for independence from the security and economic common market provided by the Soviet Union. Even after two years in office as general secretary of the Communist party, he could write with smug complacency that "the USSR represents a truly unique example [of preventing ethnic strife] in the history of human civilization. . . . Our entire experience shows that nationalist attitudes can be effectively countered by consistent internationalism." This complacency may explain in part Gorbachev's failure to deal earlier and more decisively with the ethnic passions his reforms had unleashed.

By the end of his first year in office as general secretary of the Communist party, Gorbachev had succeeded in establishing his authority over the party's Central Committee, but he had no illusions that his control of the party would ensure the party's support for his reform program. If the party were to become a vehicle of reform, as be hoped to make it, the party itself—ossified and riddled with corruption—had to be reformed and its role reduced. The revitalization of the political and economic life of the nation required the creation of more democratic government institutions.

For this purpose Gorbachev initiated the formation of a new parliamentary organization, a Congress of People's Deputies, whose members were to be elected by secret ballot, and voters were to be given a choice of candidates representing differing views within the Communist party. The elections to this new parliament, held on March 26, 1989, resulted in the defeat of large numbers of old-guard Communists and brought in a sizeable body of reform deputies, as Gorbachev had hoped. At its first session, the new Congress elected from its membership a Supreme Soviet to act as a permanent steering committee, which in turn elected Gorbachev as its chairman.

As subsequent events were to show, even more important than the elections to this new parliament for the Soviet Union were similar elections to parliaments in the individual Soviet republics and other provincial entities. These regional parliaments were to become the platforms for the expression of grievances and aspirations of the Soviet Union's multitude of ethnic and religious minorities.

Gorbachev followed up his creation of a more democratic parliament with a radical—indeed revolutionary—challenge to the authority of the Communist party itself. At a plenary session of the party's Central Committee in early February of 1990, he proposed that the party formally abandon its monopoly on political power, a change that would force the party to reform itself in order to compete effectively in the political arena. This proposal was duly endorsed a month later at a meeting of the newly formed Congress of People's Deputies, thus opening the way to the establishment of a multiparty political system.

Gorbachev subsequently secured the approval of the Supreme Soviet and the Congress of People's Deputies to give the USSR a presidential system of government, the president to be elected by the Congress of People's Deputies to a five-year term. In the vote for the presidency, which took place on March 14, 1990, Gorbachev ran unopposed after two other nominees withdrew their names, but that election also revealed an ominous undercurrent of opposition as 495 delegates voted against him and 313 others cast invalid ballots or abstained.

Gorbachev nevertheless appeared to have strengthened his position. With his election to a five-year term as president, he was assured a fixed period in office to campaign for his reform program free from the threat of ouster by an adverse vote in any state or party congress. In July 1990, the Congress of the Soviet Communist party reelected him as its general secretary; in September the USSR Supreme Soviet granted him emergency powers to implement reforms to revive the floundering Soviet economy; and in December the USSR Congress of People's Deputies approved constitutional amendments that would give the president even more authority.

In fact, however, Gorbachev's reforms of the party and state had opened the way to the dissolution of the Soviet Union. Here it is essential to bear in mind the decisive role of the Communist party in the government of the Soviet Union. The various Soviet constitutions had provided for elections to soviets (councils, parliaments) from local and regional levels to the All-Union Congress of Soviets, and they had also given the individual soviet republics the right to secede from the Soviet Union. But, certainly by Stalin's time, the soviets had become little more than window dressing, described by Stalin himself as mere transmission belts for the will of the Communist party. For it was the Communist party, rigidly centralized and dominated by the party leadership in Moscow, which controlled all offices of the Soviet state and maintained an iron discipline over all state and party organizations. This discipline was exercised through the party bureaucracy and ultimately by the secret police, which ruthlessly suppressed all deviation, or suspected deviation, from the line laid down by the party leadership. Even the periodic Communist party congresses, where all the party's regional organizations were represented, did little more than endorse the policy decisions of the Moscow leadership.

By relinquishing the Moscow party's monopoly on political power and his relaxation of party discipline, Gorbachev had destroyed the Soviet Union's machinery of control. Freed from the control of the Moscow leadership, the regional soviets, often in partnership with the regional Communist parties, pursued policies in line with their own interests and aspirations, providing leadership as well as a new legitimacy to the popular protests that were already taking place in many parts of the Soviet Union. The pursuit of independent policies quickly developed into outright revolution, a demand for sovereignty and political independence on the part of individual soviet and regional republics.

❑ *The Role of Boris Yeltsin*

The most surprising of those revolutions, and the one that dealt the mortal blow to Soviet authority, took place in Russia itself, the nucleus of the tsarist empire that became the Soviet Union—the soviet republic which might have been expected to be that union's principal defender. A historian hesitates to ascribe so momentous an event as Russia's destruction of the Soviet Union to a sordid political rivalry, yet it is difficult to escape the conclusion that Boris Yeltsin's power struggle with Gorbachev was a major factor in this extraordinary development.

It was Gorbachev himself who had first promoted Yeltsin to high office. Recognizing Yeltsin's energy and political talent, he had hoped to enlist him on his side by arranging his appointment as head of the Moscow Communist party and as a candidate member of the party's Politburo. Instead of supporting Gorbachev, however, Yeltsin had devoted much of his energy to criticizing the scope and pace of Gorbachev's reforms, and to get rid of this troublesome gadfly, Gorbachev had engineered his dismissal from both posts.

In the March 1989 elections to the Congress of People's Deputies, which Gorbachev had hoped to make a vehicle for his reform program, Yeltsin won 89 percent of the vote in his Moscow constituency. In May he secured a seat in the Supreme Soviet, from which Gorbachev had sought to exclude him. And in July he was elected chairman of a group of some 300 reformist members of the Congress of People's Deputies, the very group Gorbachev had hoped would fall into line behind his own leadership.

While reviving his political fortunes in the Gorbachev-led Congress of People's Deputies, Yeltsin established a second and far more stable power base in Russia, the largest and most powerful of the Soviet republics. On May 29, 1990, he was elected chairman of the Supreme Soviet of the Russian Republic (officially the Russian Soviet Federated Socialist Republic, or RSFSR). A bare ten days after Yeltsin was elected its chairman, the Russian Supreme Soviet voted to declare the Russian Republic a sovereign state whose laws should take precedence over those of the USSR.

By engineering Russia's declaration of sovereignty, Yeltsin made his power base independent of the Gorbachev-led Soviet government, but at the same time he dealt a catastrophic blow to that government's authority. Gorbachev had warned the Russian parliament of the consequences of Yeltsin's maneuver. "Under the banner of restoring Russia's sovereignty," he said, "[Yeltsin] is calling for the collapse of the [Soviet] Union." And indeed, the declaration of sovereignty by the most important of the Soviet republics led to a stampede by other republics to do the same.

Yeltsin followed up this blow to the Soviet government with a blow to the authority of the Communist party. On July 12, 1990, at the 20th Soviet party Congress that had reelected Gorbachev as general secretary, Yeltsin delivered a flamboyant speech announcing his resignation from the party. He thereby made himself independent of the Gorbachev-led Communist party, but at the cost of undermining further the organization which had been the cement holding the Soviet Union together.

❑ *The Disintegrating Forces of Ethnic Nationalism and Religion*

Unlike the revolution of the Russian Soviet Republic, which appears to have been the product of a political power struggle, the most potent revolutionary force in the other Soviet republics, as in Eastern Europe, was ethnic nationalism, although here too the ambitions and rivalries of individual leaders played a critical role. The Russia Soviet Republic itself, however, was soon confronted with ethnic nationalist revolutions, for the Russian republic, like the Soviet Union, was home to a multitude of ethnic and religious minorities.

The revolutions which most closely resembled the uprisings in Eastern Europe were those that took place in the Baltic states of Estonia, Latvia, and Lithuania, whose brief independence between the two world wars had been snuffed out in 1940 following the signature of the Hitler–Stalin pact. On August 23, 1989, the fiftieth anniversary of that pact, an estimated 2 million people (out of a total population of 5 million) linked arms to form a human chain 400 miles long to protest their incorporation into the Soviet Union. Moscow sent forth ominous warnings, denouncing "nationalist extremist groups" that were taking advantage of democracy and glasnost to delude the public and whipping up nationalist hysteria. These warnings were ignored and may even have contributed to nationalist momentum. On December 20, 1989, the Lithuanian Communist party voted overwhelmingly to break with the Communist party of the Soviet Union. This rejection of the authority of the Soviet party was followed by demands for the restoration of Lithuania's independence, the repeal of the Hitler-Stalin pact, the removal of the Soviet "occupation" army, and compensation for the thousands of victims of Soviet genocide and population transfers.

Gorbachev was appalled, still unable to believe that the quest for independence from the Soviet Union was a genuine popular mass movement. On January 10, 1990, he went to Lithuania personally to urge the Lithuanians to reconsider the demand for secession "foisted on them by the separatist movement." His warnings about the political and economic perils of leaving the Soviet Union went unheeded. As he described the situation in his memoirs, he found himself confronted by people "obsessed with a fanatical determination to act in accordance with what had become their creed." In a free and open election held in Lithuania on February 24, 1990 (the kind of election Gorbachev himself had encouraged), nationalists soundly defeated hardline Communist candidates, and on March 11 the newly elected Lithuanian parliament voted 126–0, with six abstentions, for the reestablishment of Lithuanian independence. At the same time, the Lithuanian Supreme Soviet declared Soviet laws to be null and void on the territory of the Lithuanian Republic, and Lithuanians began to persecute ethnic Russians.

Although Gorbachev had renounced the use of force to suppress the revolutions in Eastern Europe, he was prepared to use force to deal with what he regarded as threats to law and order in the Soviet Union itself. On March 25, 1990, he sent Soviet tanks into the Lithuanian capital of Vilnius, and on April 19 the Soviet government imposed a partial economic boycott on the country. The Lithuanians gave in, or appeared to do so. They agreed to suspend their declaration of independence pending

MAP 18   THE RUSSIAN FEDERATION IN 2000

Former Soviet States
Boundary of former U.S.S.R.

500 miles
250
0

Kamchatka

SEA OF OKHOTSK

Sakhalin

Okhotsk

Khabarovsk

Vladivostok

JAPAN

NORTH KOREA

SOUTH KOREA

CHINA

OUTER MONGOLIA

Lena R.

Lake Baikal

RUSSIAN FEDERATION

Yenisey R.

ARCTIC OCEAN

Ob R.

Novosibirsk

Yekaterinburg

Astana

KAZAKHSTAN

Alma Ata

Bishkek

KYRGYZSTAN

TAJIKISTAN

Dushanbe

Tashkent

UZBEKISTAN

ARAL SEA

TURKMENISTAN

Ashgabat

AFGHANISTAN

IRAN

Volga R.

Moscow

FINLAND

Tallinn

EST.

LATVIA

Riga

LITH.

Vilnius

Kalingrad

POLAND

BALTIC SEA

SWEDEN

Minsk

BELARUS

Kiev

UKRAINE

Chisinau

Donetsk

MOLDAVIA

BLACK SEA

TURKEY

GEORGIA

Tbilisi

Erivan

ARMENIA

IRAQ

CHECHNYA

Grozny

CASPIAN SEA

Baku

AZERBAIJAN

Inset:

Baku

Sumgait

AZERBAIJAN

Gyandzha (Kirovabad)

Agdam

NAGORNO-KARABAKH

Stepanakert

Kafan

CASPIAN SEA

IRAN

ARMENIA

Tbilisi

Erivan

NAKHICHEVAN (Azerbaijan)

547

negotiations with the Soviet government. After nine months of futile negotiation, however, Gorbachev lost patience. He instructed the Lithuanian Supreme Soviet to restore immediately the constitutions of the USSR and the Lithuanian Soviet Socialist Republic and to rescind its unconstitutional declarations. Before the Lithuanians had time to reply, Soviet troops began the takeover of government buildings in Vilnius, actions which led to bloody confrontations with the local population.

In response to international protests, Gorbachev declared that his policy toward Lithuania had been intended to prevent civil war, and in his memoirs he maintains that the violence had been the work of Soviet hardliners who were trying to force his hand. Gorbachev's claim rings true, for faced with the prospect of a major bloodbath, he acted quickly to end the violence and subsequently observed remarkable restraint. In May 1990 the Supreme Soviets of both Estonia and Latvia issued declarations of independence, but by this time major disruptions were taking place in other parts of the Soviet Union, which on June 8, 1990, as noted earlier, was shattered by the declaration of independence of the Soviet Republic of Russia.

The point has already been made frequently that the drive for sovereignty and independence in Eastern Europe and the Baltic states, which had been independent before World War II, was fueled in large part by nationalist sentiment and resentment of Russian/Soviet control. Elsewhere in the Soviet Union, however, the disintegration was propelled not only by hostility to Russia but by the virulent hatreds between ethnic and religious minorities within the various Soviet republics.

A case in point was the conflict between the Christian Armenians and the Shiite Muslims who formed a large part of the population of the Soviet republic of Azerbaijan. Both Armenians and Shiites had a proud cultural heritage, both had their own language, and both aspired to independence in national states that would include the large number of Armenians and Shiites living in Turkey and Iran. The immediate object of their dispute in Azerbaijan was the tiny enclave of Nagorno-Karabakh, which, though its population was predominantly Armenian, had been assigned to the jurisdiction of Azerbaijan because it lay entirely within Azeri-populated territory. On February 28, 1988, the regional Soviet of Nagorno-Karabakh voted for union with Armenia, a vote endorsed by the Communist party of Armenia but declared illegal by the Communist party of Azerbaijan—a split between Communist parties along ethnic lines that set off the bloodiest ethnic clashes yet seen in the Soviet Union in peacetime and caused the flight of some half-million refugees to escape pogroms carried out by their Armenian or Azeri neighbors.

Similar ethnic revolt and civil strife had erupted throughout the Soviet border provinces. The Soviet Republic of Georgia, while demanding autonomy for itself, was suppressing similar demands by its own ethnic minorities and threatened to go to war with the Soviet Union if Moscow attempted to intervene. There were ethnic riots in Tajikistan and Uzbekistan, where the Uzbeks indulged in pogroms of their Turkish-speaking Shiite Muslim population, while in Kazakstan the Kazaks carried out pogroms of the Chechens and other ethnic minorities under their jurisdiction.

In the Soviet Republic of Moldavia, the Romanians, who constituted a majority of the population, clashed with their Ukrainian and Russian minorities. In August 1989 the Moldavian Supreme Soviet made Romanian the state language, replaced the Cyrillic alphabet imposed by the Russians with the Latin alphabet, and replaced the Soviet flag with the national flag of Romania. These symbolic gestures were followed up in June of the following year by a Moldavian declaration of independence. Alarmed by the prospect of persecution by the Romanians or their incorporation into the state of Romania itself, the Ukrainians and Russians living on the eastern side of the Dniester River proclaimed the establishment of a sovereign state of their own, the Dniester Soviet Republic, and seceded from Moldavia.

With the Russian declaration of independence in June 1990, the dam broke. Moldavia and Uzbekistan declared their independence, as did Armenia, Belorussia, Ukraine, and the other Central Asian republics. At the same time, religious and ethnic minorities within the individual Soviet republics, for example, the Georgian Abkhasians and South Ossetians, declared their independence from Georgia, and shortly afterward the Chechens and Volga Tatars voted for independence from Russia.

❑ Gorbachev's Rescue Efforts and the August 1991 Coup

Gorbachev made vigorous efforts to stop the nationalist hemorrhage. Still convinced that nationalist rebellion was the work of local demagogues and that a majority of the Soviet people favored the preservation of the Soviet Union, he arranged to hold an all-Union referendum to gauge the true sentiment of public opinion. This referendum, conducted on March 17, 1991, posed the question: "Do you consider necessary the preservation of the USSR and a renewed federation of equal sovereign republics, in which the rights and freedoms of an individual of any nationality will be guaranteed?" Gorbachev interpreted the results of this referendum as a victory because a strong majority in Russia, Belorussia, and the Central Asian republics had voted yes. But six republics did not participate at all (the Baltic states, Georgia, Armenia, and Moldavia), and the vote in the Ukraine was perilously close.

In dealing with the referendum question, Yeltsin once again succeeded in outmaneuvering Gorbachev. He had originally opposed holding the referendum in Russia, but finally agreed provided that Russia could hold a simultaneous referendum asking whether Russians favored establishing the office of president of Russia, to be elected by direct popular vote. The approval of this proposition by the Russian voters opened the way to greater power for Yeltsin, who was elected to the Russian presidency on June 12, 1991, the first popularly elected Russian head of state. (Gorbachev had been elected president of the USSR by the Congress of People's Deputies, not by direct popular vote.)

In the April preceding Yeltsin's election as president of Russia, Gorbachev, encouraged by fact that 76 percent of the voters in the March 17 referendum had favored the preservation of the Soviet Union, met with leaders of nine of the Soviet republics, including Yeltsin, to hammer out a treaty that would ensure their adherence to the Soviet confederation. (Missing were the leaders of the six republics that had not participated in the March referendum.) After three months of negotiation they reached agreement on a 9 plus 1 formula for a restructured federal union. The Soviet government was to be decentralized, and the individual republics were to be given almost complete autonomy at the local level. The central government would still be left a powerful role, however, for it would continue to deal with matters of common concern, including foreign affairs, finance, and the military. Final agreement on the union treaty was reached on July 23, 1991, and on August 4 an exhausted Gorbachev left for a holiday in the Crimea, confident that the 9 plus 1 treaty would be signed sixteen days later in Moscow.

At this point Soviet hardliners, including the Soviet vice-president, the prime minister, defense and interior ministers, and the head of the KGB, initiated a coup to topple Gorbachev, who in their view was leading their country to political and economic ruin. On August 18 they placed Gorbachev under house arrest and announced that, in view of "Gorbachev's inability to fulfill the duties of the office of president of the USSR," the vice-president was assuming the duties of president, as of August 19, 1991.

The objective of the coup was to stop the disintegration of the Soviet Union, restore the authority of the Communist party, impose martial law on the Baltic states, and put an end to all agitation on the part of the individual Soviet republics for independence. The leaders of the coup evidently did not expect resistance. To maintain secrecy they had not organized broader support (their failure to ensure the support of the army was probably their worst mistake), nor did they take the elementary precaution of arresting political or military leaders who might have been expected to oppose them.

Foremost among these opponents was Boris Yeltsin, who saw his own interests threatened by a restoration of the authority of the Soviet Communist party and government of the USSR. Making effective use of his immense popularity in Moscow, he rallied popular support for the government and called upon the army to put an end to the conspirators' illegal usurpation of power. Within three days the coup collapsed without a shot being fired. Gorbachev returned to Moscow, but with his own power and prestige sorely diminished.

The coup which had been designed to preserve the Communist party and the USSR hastened their destruction. The first victim was the Communist party. Although the party as such had not initiated the coup, Yeltsin took advantage of the ensuing confusion to denounce the party as "one of the principal villains" and "an unlawful apparatus that took over the Soviet state." He went on to suspend its activities throughout the Russian republic and take over its property and archives, including the files of the secret police. Gorbachev continued to express the hope that the party could be transformed into an instrument of reform, "the living instrument of perestroika," but here again he was outmaneuvered by Yeltsin. Confronted by massive antiparty demonstrations, he found himself obliged to resign as general secretary on August 24 in order to retain what was left of his own plummeting authority. On August 29 the Supreme Soviet of the USSR formally suspended the party's activities throughout the entire Soviet Union until its role in the plot had been clarified.

But the coup also dealt a final blow to the Soviet Union. It had prevented the ratification of the federal union treaty and, as Gorbachev later described it, it had dislodged a rock that started a landslide. Between August 24 and September 9, the Baltic states and eight other Soviet republics issued renewed and final declarations of independence. Armenia followed on September 21, Ukraine on December 5. In some cases these declarations were a response to popular pressure, but in others they were the work of local leaders seeking to insulate themselves from any attempt on the part of the Moscow leadership to undermine their powerful—and lucrative—state or party positions.

On December 8, 1991, the presidents and prime ministers of Russia, Ukraine, and Belorussia (which now called itself Belorus) met at a hunting lodge near the Belorus capital of Minsk. Here they agreed to dissolve the USSR and establish in its place a new federal union, to be called the Commonwealth of Independent States (CIS). Later that month, at Alma Ata, the capital of Kazakstan, eight more republics agreed to join the CIS, which now included all former Soviet republics except the Baltic states, Moldavia (now called Moldova), and Georgia. On December 25 Gorbachev, who three months earlier had resigned as general secretary of the Soviet Communist party, resigned as president of a Soviet Union that had ceased to exist. The hammer and sickle flag came down over the Kremlin, to be replaced by the red, white, and blue flag of imperial Russia.

□ *The Commonwealth of Independent States (CIS)*

The members of the CIS had committed themselves to "recognize and respect one another's territorial integrity and the inviolability of borders within the Commonwealth"—an important provision, because Russian nationalists were already talking of the need to revise borders to include areas with a large Russian population in the republic of Russia. Even more important for the neighbors of the former Soviet Union was a CIS commitment "to preserve and maintain under united command a common military-strategic space, including unified command over nuclear weapons." But the new union had no enforcement mechanism, no authority to collect taxes, no president or prime minister or even a general secretary. The Soviet Union had disintegrated into a cockpit of squabbling independent states, the common economic infrastructure was destroyed, and ethnic strife continued with merciless ferocity in many areas. Despite their commitment to a unified command, each of the former Soviet republics has maintained its own armed forces. And despite the lip-service some of the Soviet successor states paid to democratic ideals, the democracies established in some of them remain fragile at best, while others remain as cruel and authoritarian as the Communist regimes they have supplanted.

◻

THIRTY-NINE

The Disintegration of Yugoslavia

The breakup of the Soviet empire and the end of the Cold War did not inaugurate a New World Order of peace and international understanding, as many Americans had hoped and expected. Regional wars and genocidal conflicts continued in many parts of Africa and Asia, while in Europe the breakup of the Soviet empire was followed almost immediately by the disintegration of Yugoslavia, the federation of South Slavs established after World War I, in which Serbia, the largest and most powerful member of that federation, played a dominant role comparable to that of Russia in the Soviet Union.

As discussed in chapter 6, Yugoslavia had never been a harmonious federation. Serbian domination was intensely resented from the beginning by the Croats and other national minorities within the new country. And, although Yugoslavia was indeed a union of South Slavs, there were profound religious and cultural differences between them stemming from their long history of separation under different types of government. The depth and ferocity of those differences was tragically revealed during World War II, when, even while under German and Italian occupation, the Serbs and Croats waged a war of horrifying brutality between themselves.

A united Yugoslavia was reestablished after World War II by the Communist leader, Josip Broz Tito, who had carried on the most effective resistance against the Germans and Italians under the banner of Communism while appealing, with apparent success, to a common Yugoslav nationalism. Solidly entrenched as head of the Yugoslav government after the war, Tito, a native of Croatia, sought to heal ethnic rivalries by abandoning Serbian claims to domination and conceding an equal status and a large measure of regional autonomy to the major nationalities within the Yugoslav federation. In addition to the six, nominally autonomous, republics that made up Yugoslavia—Slovenia, Croatia, Serbia, Montenegro, Bosnia-Herzegovina, and Macedonia—Tito created two autonomous provinces within the republic of Serbia: Kosovo, to conciliate the Albanians, who made up 90 percent of the population of that province, and Vojvodina, the home of a large Hungarian minority.

During Tito's lifetime, his prestige and popularity held the Yugoslav union together, but after his death in 1980 individual political leaders and ethnic organizations, inspired by ambition and ethnic fervor, once again sounded the trumpet of re-

MAP 19   THE DISINTEGRATION OF YUGOSLAVIA

gional nationalism. Prominent among the leaders exploiting this nationalism was Franco Tudjman of Croatia and the Serbian Communist party leader Slobodan Milosevich, who employed a particularly virulent xenophobic rhetoric to consolidate his political authority.

In March 1989, in a calculated appeal to Serbian nationalist sentiment Milosevich stripped Kosovo and Vojvodina of the autonomous status granted them by Tito and restored them to centralized Serbian control. For patriotic Serbs, Kosovo was akin to hallowed ground, for it was at the Battle of Kosovo in June of 1389 that the Ottoman Turks had defeated a Serbian-led coalition, a defeat that inaugurated the centuries-long subjugation of Serbian Christians to the Muslim Turks. The anniversary of that battle had remained a Serbian national day of mourning to keep alive memories of Serbian heroism and hatred for their Muslim oppressors memories that nourished Serbian hatred of the Kosovo Albanians, most of them Muslims, who now constituted a majority of the population of Kosovo.

The fate of Kosovo and Vojvodina aroused understandable alarm in Yugoslavia's autonomous republics, where a resurgence of nationalist sentiment had reawakened resentment of the Serbs. Elections held in Slovenia and Croatia in April and May of 1990 resulted in decisive victories for nationalist candidates, and in June of the following year Slovenia and Croatia issued formal declarations of independence.

❑ The Serbo–Croatian War and Ethnic Cleansing

Anticipating just such a development, leaders of the large Serbian minority in Croatia had already taken steps to protect their community. In October 1990 the Serbian National Council in Croatia proclaimed the Serbian-dominated area of Croatia to be a Serbian Autonomous Region. In June of the following year, after the Croatian and Slovenian declarations of independence, Milosevich sent the Serb-dominated Yugoslav army into Croatia in support of the Croatian Serbs, while calling upon Serbs throughout Yugoslavia to join in the creation of a Greater Serbia. By the end of the year 1991, one-third of Croatia was in Serbian hands.

In their war with Croatia, the Serbs inaugurated a program they themselves were to call "ethnic cleansing," a campaign of rape and mass murder, the expulsion of the Croatian population from the territory conquered by the Serbs, and the destruction of all evidence of the Croatian presence to ensure that this land should be ethnically and culturally Serbian.

Milosevich had also sent the Yugoslav army into Slovenia, but there were relatively few ethnic Serbs in that country and after a brief ten-day conflict the Yugoslav forces withdrew from Slovenia to join in the war in Croatia.

❑ The Response of the European Community

Unlike the regional conflicts elsewhere in the world, the Yugoslav situation was a matter of immediate concern to other states of Europe because of the danger of foreign intervention in the Yugoslav imbroglio. Since the late nineteenth century, Russia had looked upon Serbia, a land of fellow Slavs who used the same Cyrillic alphabet, as a Russian protege. Both Greece and Bulgaria coveted Yugoslav Macedonia. And any threat to the Muslim populations of Macedonia and Kosovo was likely to provoke the intervention of Turkey, the archenemy of Greece.

In November 1991, after concluding that there was no way to preserve the Yugoslav federation, an Arbitration Committee of the European Community invited the individual Yugoslav republics to apply for recognition of their independence, naming December 23 as the deadline for such applications. By the time of that deadline, the EC had received applications from Slovenia, Croatia, Macedonia, and Bosnia-Herzegovina. On the basis of the ethnic criteria they had established for evaluating applications for recognition, the Arbitration Committee decided that they were met in full by Slovenia and Macedonia (although one-third of the population of Macedonia was Albanian), but that Croatia and Bosnia-Herzegovina would have to provide guarantees recognizing the special status of their large Serbian populations—this at a time when the Serbs had already occupied one-third of Croatia and were making no effort to disguise their campaign of ethnic cleansing.

On December 23, the date of the EC recognition deadline, the government of the newly united Germany, acting with what many foreign observers regarded as unseemly haste, announced its intention to recognize the independence of both Slovenia and Croatia. In defense of this policy, the Germans argued that the Serbs were representing their war against Croatia as a domestic conflict in which (as stipulated in the Helsinki Accords) neither the United Nations nor the European Community had any right to intervene, diplomatically or otherwise; intervention would only be possible if the Serbian action could be seen as aggression against a sovereign state. Hence the need to accord sovereignty to Croatia. The German argument was evidently convincing, for at their Maastricht meeting in January 1992 all twelve members of the European Community agreed in principle to recognize the independence of Croatia as well as Slovenia.

By that time, however, there no longer seemed to be any need for European intervention, for on January 1 the former American secretary of state, Cyrus Vance, acting on behalf of the United Nations, had negotiated a cease-fire agreement in Croatia. That agreement was overwhelmingly favorable to the Serbs, for it not only left them in control of all the Croatian territory they had conquered but provided that UN forces be stationed in Croatia to monitor the cease-fire, thereby making the UN a guarantor of the Serbian takeover. As it proved, the Vance cease-fire was to be only a temporary respite in the Serbo-Croatian conflict.

❑ *The Case of Macedonia*

In November 1991 the Yugoslav Republic of Macedonia had also issued a declaration of independence. The Macedonian request for recognition was turned down by the EC, not because of belated awareness of Macedonia's large Muslim-Albanian population but because of the opposition of the Greeks. They maintained that the only legitimate Macedonia, the homeland of Alexander the Great, was Greek Macedonia and that no other country had a right to bear that name, although the Yugoslav republic had long since done so. The Greeks objected further to Yugoslav Macedonia's decision to incorporate in their national flag the sixteen-pointed Vergina Star because this symbol of the ancient Macedonian empire implied a claim to rule over all of Macedonia (Greek and Bulgarian as well as Yugoslav Macedonia.)

The Macedonian situation posed particularly dangerous threats to international peace and the NATO alliance. A Serbian invasion to suppress the Macedonian independence movement might lead to complications with both Greece and Turkey, both members of NATO. And any threat to Macedonia's Muslim-Albanian population was likely to provoke the intervention not only of Turkey but also of the state of Albania.

In November 1993 the European Community (now the European Union) recognized the independence of Macedonia under the awkward name of the Former Yugoslav Republic of Macedonia, which the Greeks were persuaded to accept. Still suspicious of Yugoslav Macedonia's intentions, however, the Greeks imposed an economic blockade on that country. Because of the threat the Macedonian situation posed to the NATO alliance, the United States took the unprecedented step of sending 550 American soldiers to join a 1,000-man NATO peacekeeping mission in Macedonia.

In September 1995 Cyrus Vance persuaded the Yugoslav Macedonians to abandon their use of the Vergina Star, and with that the Greeks lifted their economic embargo. But the peacekeepers remained, and in 1997 the Macedonian government appealed to NATO to extend their mission because they played an important stabilizing role. Just how important would be seen in the course of the Kosovo crisis. (See p. 560.)

❑ *The Agony of Bosnia-Herzegovina*

Bosnia-Herzegovina poses a particularly complex problem in a complex region. The population consists largely of South Slavs who are divided primarily along religious, not ethnic, lines. Approximately 44 percent are Muslims, 31 percent are Serbian Eastern Orthodox Christians, and 17 percent are Croatian Roman Catholics. But, with the exception of a small number of Jews and Gypsies, they are all ethnic Slavs. During the Middle Ages, the provinces had been a territorial and administrative entity without particular political significance, and under their medieval rulers, the Roman Catholic, Eastern Orthodox, and Bosnian churches—all representing different versions of Christianity—were all tolerated and coexisted in relative harmony. With the conquest of the provinces by the Ottoman Turks in the late fifteenth century, Islam was added to the existing religious mix, but the Ottoman government continued the tradition of religious toleration.

During the centuries of Ottoman rule, large numbers of South Slavs converted to Islam, whether out of opportunism or genuine conviction, for the Ottomans did not impose their religion on subject populations. A great deal of intermarriage took place among members of different religious groups, and under Ottoman rule their relatively peaceful coexistence continued. The theory, widely circulated in the West, that the provinces had for centuries been seething cauldrons of ethnic and religious hatred was an unfortunate misconception, because it contributed to the belief that any foreign intervention in that region, whether to maintain or restore peace, would be futile.

By the late nineteenth century, however, the nationalist-ethnic-religious hatreds that had fomented conflict elsewhere in Europe had also reared their divisive heads in Bosnia, which had been incorporated into the Austro-Hungarian empire in 1909. That annexation had aroused the fury of the Serbs, who aspired to make Bosnia part of a Greater Serbia. It was to protest Austrian rule that on June 28, 1914, the anniversary of the Battle of Kosovo, a Bosnian Serb nationalist assassinated the heir to the Austrian crown, the incident that lit the fuse setting off World War I. Bosnian-Serb nationalism was kindled afresh in the 1980s by Slobodan Milosevich, with his call for the union of all Serbs in a Greater Serbia.

In January 1992, in response to the application for the recognition of Bosnian independence by a Bosnian parliament dominated by Bosnian Muslims and Croatians, the European Community called for an all-Bosnian referendum to take into account the interests of Bosnia's large Serbian community. Before such a referendum could be held, however, the Bosnian Serbs held a referendum of their own to create an autonomous Serbian state in Bosnia in the manner of the Serbs in Croatia. The Bosnian Serbs subsequently boycotted what was to have been an all-Bosnian referendum. Held on February 28 and March 1, 1992, that referendum resulted in a 99 percent vote for independence. The Bosnian parliament promptly issued a declaration of independence, and on March 6 and 7 Bosnia's independence was recognized by the European Community and the United States. On May 22 Bosnia, Croatia, and Slovenia, were made members of the United Nations.

Foreign recognition and membership in the UN did not save Bosnia from civil war. On March 27 the Bosnian Serbs issued their own declaration of independence and proclaimed the establishment of the Serbian Republic of Bosnia-Herzegovina. In April, with the support of the Serb-dominated Yugoslav army, they proceeded to lay siege to the Bosnian capital of Sarajevo and to conquer as much territory as possible on behalf of a Greater Serbia.

In the early stages of the civil war in Bosnia, the Croatian and Bosnian governments joined forces in fighting the Serbs, but their cooperation was sporadic at best and broke down completely in the spring of 1993. Franjo Tudjman, the fervently nationalistic leader of the Croatian government, evidently decided that Croatia's interests would be better served by following the Serbian example and conquering as much Bosnian territory as possible on behalf of the state of Croatia.

The Croats soon demonstrated that they could match the Serbs in the loathsome practice of ethnic cleansing. Despite the fact the the majority of Bosnia's Muslims came from the same South Slavic stock, the Croats and Serbs persecuted them with merciless ferocity, driving them from their homes, murdering the male population of military age, and engaging in the deliberate and systematic rape of Muslim women to plant their seed in the infidels and pollute their heritage. The Bosnian Muslims responded with horrifying brutalities of their own. By the autumn of 1993 an estimated 2.5 million Bosnians out of a total population of 4.3 million had become refugees, fleeing from the Bosnian, Croatian, or Serbian armies.

Meanwhile, the European Community and the United States stood by, warned by their Balkan experts and military establishments that intervention in the mountainous terrain of Bosnia would be costly and futile, for there could be no solution to the ethnic conflict. To impose peace on this faction-riven land, a large army of occupation would be required that would have to remain in the country indefinitely. A UN peacekeeping mission was sent a mission to Bosnia, but being denied a combat role, its work was largely confined to providing humanitarian aid, and the peacekeepers themselves were constantly in danger of being taken hostage by rival factions. Unwilling to commit an effective peacekeeping force in Bosnia, yet fearful that the conflict in Bosnia would spill over into neighboring countries, European and American diplomats put forth various proposals to partition the country, all of which were rejected by one or another of the warring parties because these proposals were not backed up by credible threats of intervention.

On February 2, 1994, a Serbian mortar exploded amid a Sunday crowd in Sarajevo's open market, killing 68 and wounding over 200. This incident, only one of a long succession of such outrages, finally broke through the crust of foreign apathy and propelled America's Clinton administration to take action in Bosnia. With the approval of the UN, Washington issued an ultimatum in the name of the NATO alliance demanding the withdrawal of Bosnian Serb artillery beyond a 20-kilometer radius of Sarajevo and establishing a no-fly zone over the city. Threatened with massive air strikes in the event of noncompliance, the Bosnian Serbs lifted their siege of Sarajevo and agreed to a cease-fire. The foreign intervention on this occasion has been described as a turning point in the Bosnian war, but the cease-fire failed to hold and the war would soon be resumed with unabated ferocity.

A genuine turning point was the success of an American-led negotiating team in brokering a treaty between the Croatians and the Bosnian Muslims, an agreement achieved through lavish promises of political and economic support. In the so-called Washington Accords of March 18, 1994, the two parties agreed to make peace, enter into a loose political federation, and merge their forces into a single army. With that, the Americans had secured the essential supplement to NATO air power—ground troops that the Europeans and Americans had been unwilling to provide.

In June 1994, European and American negotiators scored another significant diplomatic success in persuading Milosovich to end his support of the Bosnian Serbs. Milosovich had long been infuriated by the Bosnian Serbs' defiance of the orders of Belgrade, and he was facing rising discontent at home resulting from the economic embargo the powers had imposed on Serbia in response to Milosovich's Greater Serbia policies. Taking advantage of this combination of circumstances, Western diplomats secured the Serbian leader's promise to close the Serbian border with Bosnia. In return, Milosovich was promised a partial lifting of the economic embargo—and probably a good deal more that was not made public. More important for Milosovich personally was the political fallout from this agreement. He could claim, correctly, that Serbia itself had never entered the war on the side of the Bosnian Serbs, whom he accused of being solely responsible for the war crimes committed in that conflict. He could then argue that the Bosnian Serbs had forfeited every right to speak for Serbia, and that the Western powers must henceforth look to Milosovich as the sole legitimate representative of Serbian interests.

The Bosnian Serbs played into Milosovich's hands. Upon learning of the Croatian-Bosnian partnership, they denounced the cease-fire agreement of the previous February, resumed their military offensive, and once again laid siege to Sarajevo. They also resumed their ethnic cleansing, taking United Nations peacekeepers hostage and arousing such international indignation that the NATO powers were virtually compelled to intervene—and, subsequently, to deal exclusively with Milosovic in negotiations involving the Bosnian Serbs.

The Bosnian-Serb atrocity that finally provoked intervention took place at Srebrenica, one of several towns the United Nations had designated as "safe areas" for Bosnia's Muslim population, their "safety" provided by token UN peacekeeping forces. On July 6, 1995, the Bosnian Serbs attacked Srebrenica, the largest of these safe areas, its population swollen by Muslim refugees. After taking the small force of Dutch peacekeepers hostage, the Bosnian Serbs proceeded to carry out the biggest single mass murder in Europe since World War II. Paralyzed by Serbian threats to kill their soldiers, the Dutch government refused to allow NATO air strikes or any kind of intervention until all their men were out of Bosnia.

But now the credibility of the United Nations and the NATO alliance itself were at stake, and, once the Dutch soldiers were evacuated, the NATO countries prepared to take action. Whatever hesitation they may have had was quashed by Richard Holbrooke, the forceful American assistant secretary of state. A long-time advocate of intervention, Holbrooke called for NATO air strikes—not just pinpricks but a massive and sustained bombing campaign. That campaign achieved its purpose, for on September 27, 1995, the Bosnian Serbs once again agreed to a cease-fire.

For the Americans, this demonstration of the effectiveness of airpower was a welcome contrast to their experience in Vietnam, where bombing had signally failed to score a victory. Bombing alone, however, had not brought the Bosnian Serbs to the conference table. For the bombing campaign had been supported by a large Bosnian-Croatian army of ground troops, the fruit of the Bosnian-Croatian alliance forged by the Washington Accords of March 18, 1994.

❑ *The Croatian Card*

The Serbian-Croatian war, set off by the Croatian declaration of independence in June 1991, had ended with a cease-fire of January 1, 1992, which had left one-third of Croatia in the hands of the Croatian Serbs and provided that the cease-fire itself should be monitored by a force of UN peacekeepers. (See p. 555.)

Since concluding that cease-fire, the president of Croatia, Franjo Tudjman, with the encouragement of Washington, had built up a powerful Croatian army, equipped in part with American weaponry and trained by retired American officers. In January 1995, again with American encouragement, Tudjman arranged for the removal of the UN peacekeepers, thereby clearing the way for the reconquest of the Croatian territory taken over by the Croatian Serbs.

The first stage in that reconquest, a Croatian victory over the Serbs in western Slavonia in May 1995, was followed on August 4 by a lightning strike against Krajina, the principal stronghold of the Serbian separatists. In a campaign of just two days the Croatians succeeded in gaining control of the entire Krajina region, where they indulged in ethnic cleansing of their own to clear the area of its Serbian population. The bulk of the Croatian army then moved into Bosnia, where it joined the Croatian-Muslim forces fighting the Bosnian Serbs. By mid-September, aided by NATO air strikes, they had reduced the territory controlled by the Bosnian Serbs from 70 percent to 50 percent. This was the situation that persuaded the Bosnian Serbs to agree to the cease-fire of September 27.

❏ *The Dayton Accords, December 14, 1995*

In October 1995 the Clinton administration issued an ultimatum to all of Yugoslavia's warring parties demanding that their leaders meet to negotiate a final settlement. This meeting took place in an aircraft hangar near Dayton, Ohio, where American mediators, led by Richard Holbrooke, forced them to hammer out a peace agreement. Signed in Paris on December 14, the Dayton Accords divided Bosnia into two largely autonomous regions: a Muslim-Croat Federation controlling 51 percent of the territory, including Sarajevo and its suburbs; and a Serb Republic controlling 49 percent. The accords stipulated further that 60,000 NATO troops, 20,000 of them American, would be deployed in Bosnia to enforce the peace. These troops, sent to Bosnia early in the following year, succeeded in separating the belligerents and establishing a precarious peace that has endured into the year 2001. The implementation of the civil provisions of the Dayton Accords was assigned to a joint civilian commission that was to supervise economic reconstruction and the restoration of law and order, promote human rights, and prepare for political elections.

❏ *The Kosovo Crisis*

The travails of the former Yugoslavia were far from over. Trouble had long been brewing in the province of Kosovo, which had been part of the Ottoman empire until conquered by the Serbs in the Balkan Wars of 1912–1913. Although the Serbs might view Kosovo as hallowed ground (see p. 553), the population of that province was 90 percent Albanian (approximately one-third of all Albanians lived in Kosovo), most of these Albanians were Muslims, and the politically conscious among them bitterly resented their subjection to Serbian rule.

As noted earlier, Tito had attempted to reconcile the Albanian Kosovars to their membership in the Yugoslav federation by granting the province a quasi-autonomous status within the Republic of Serbia. But after Tito's death, his successors had stirred up the fires of nationalism in all the Yugoslav republics to bolster their claims to leadership and generate popular support. In March 1989 Slobodan Milosovich had stripped Kosovo of its autonomous status and made it once again an organic part of Serbia. The Kosovar Albanians responded with mass demonstrations and a general strike, and in July 1990, following the example of Croatia and Slovenia, they issued a declaration of independence and proclaimed the establishment of the Republic of Kosovo. Infuriated by this challenge to their authority over the sacred soil of Kosovo, the Serbs crushed the Albanian separatists with such merciless ferocity that Kosovo remained relatively quiescent during the subsequent Serbian wars in Croatia and Bosnia.

In 1997 Albanian guerrillas who called themselves the Kosovo Liberation Army once again confronted the Serbs with the specter of a Kosovar separatist movement. Frustrated by their defeats in Croatia and the Dayton Accords, the Serbs, still under the leadership of Milosevich, reacted with even greater severity than in 1990. In yet another campaign of ethnic cleansing, they subjected the Kosovar Albanians to mass executions, rape, and torture, while at the same time laying waste their crops and live-stock and destroying their towns and villages.

The Western powers were deterred from intervention in this case by the fact that Kosovo was legally a province of Serbia, and they were prohibited by treaty from in-terfering in the domestic affairs of sovereign states. Richard Holbrooke had neverthe-less called for intervention, and on October 12, 1998, he appeared to have scored an-other diplomatic triumph. Using a combination of threats and promises, he pressured Milosevich into an agreement to end the war in Kosovo. It was soon evident, how-ever, that Milosovich had no intention of honoring this agreement. Unimpressed by the threat of airpower alone and fully aware of the reluctance of the Americans and Europeans to risk their troops in combat, he allowed the Serbian campaign in Kosovo to continue.

Another four months went by before Washington secured the agreement of its NATO allies to back up its threats with action and to launch air strikes on the Serbian capital itself. From March to June 1999, at first somewhat tentatively, then with in-creasing ferocity and effectiveness, NATO aircraft carried out bombing raids against Belgrade. Although the bombing was supposed to be restricted to military and indus-trial targets, an American bomb struck the Chinese embassy in Belgrade, setting off an ugly dispute with China. Nor did the bombing of Belgrade put a quick end to the war in Kosovo. With no NATO ground troops to deter them, the Serbian forces in Kosovo actually stepped up their persecution of the Kosovar Albanians, driving what was left of the Albanian population as refugees into Albania and Macedonia.

After eleven weeks of bombing, however, Milosovich's resistance finally crum-bled. On June 3, 1999, he agreed to withdraw Serbian troops from Kosovo and to their replacement by a five-nation peacekeeping force. The military historian John Keegan has called this Serbian capitulation a turning point in military history, for "it proved that a war can be won by airpower alone." But the was not won by airpower alone. Milosovich had counted on Russian arms shipments and diplomatic intervention on Serbia's behalf; he believed that war would exacerbate differences among the NATO allies; and he was confident that Serbia's neighbors could be tempted to breach the international economic blockade. None of these expectations was realized. American diplomats, ably seconded by the British government of Tony Blair, held the NATO al-liance together, they preserved the international blockade, they reminded the Rus-sians of their dependence on Western economic aid, and in the end they secured their NATO allies' agreement to the use of ground troops, a threat that may have been de-cisive in securing Serbia's surrender.

Following the withdrawal of Serbian forces from Kosovo, Albanian refugees were able to return to the ruins left behind by the Serbs, and the Kosovar Serbs became the refugees. Fearful that the peacekeepers installed in Kosovo would be unable to pro-tect them from the vengeance of the Albanians, they fled in droves to Serbia.

The status of Kosovo itself remains in abeyance. The Serbs insist that Kosovo should remain part of Serbia; the Kosovar Albanians demand complete independence or union with Albania.

❑ *The Repercussion in Macedonia*

Meanwhile, the massive influx of Albanian refugees in Macedonia threatened to set off a crisis in that country, where Albanians already constituted one-third of the population. Complaining of discrimination and unfair treatment by Macedonia's Slav-dominated government, Macedonian Albanians put forward demands for greater autonomy or outright independence, setting off ugly confrontations between the Albanians, backed by the Albanian Liberation Army, and the Macedonian army and police.

Fortunately, the NATO peacekeeping force, installed in Macedonia at the time of the earlier crisis with Greece (see p. 556), was still in place, and so far a civil war has been prevented. The situation in Macedonia, as in most other parts of the former Yugoslavia, remains tense, but on the basis of the Yugoslav experience, a strong case can be made for the effectiveness of UN and NATO intervention in keeping crisis situations localized and contributing to their resolution.

Conclusion

In the years after the American defeat in Vietnam, successive American administrations pursued a foreign policy drawing on what were perceived to be the "lessons" of Vietnam: the United States should intervene militarily in crises abroad only when its vital interests were at stake, and should do so then with overpowering force to ensure victory. Such intervention would also require an "exit strategy" to avoid the danger of becoming bogged down in a Vietnam-like quagmire. In line with this policy, Washington has virtually ignored genocidal wars being waged in Africa and Asia. The wisdom of this policy nevertheless seemed confirmed when the United States intervened in Somalia to relieve famine and put an end to anarchy in that country, only to have a murderous mob kill American soldiers and drag one of them through the streets.

Washington intervened decisively in the Middle East when Iraq's takeover of oil-rich Kuwait threatened American oil interests, and the belated intervention in Yugoslavia was undertaken to prevent the escalation of the civil war in that country into a major international conflict as much as for humanitarian reasons. The Middle East remains a major concern, but after the Iraq war the United States has refrained from military intervention in that region.

America's most conspicuous foreign policy initiative was its campaign to break down international economic barriers to promote the expansion of global trade and commerce. This was done on behalf of American business interests and America's association with multinational corporations that were playing an increasingly influential role in the global economy. But this policy was also driven by a belief that the expansion of trade would benefit all the peoples involved and that, to use a favored cliché, a rising tide of global prosperity would lift all boats. More important still was the calculation that a steadily increasing contact with the institutions and values of the Western world would encourage the "developing" countries to emulate the Western example and adopt democratic systems of government.

As was soon evident on every hand, however, the global market economy did not necessarily make for greater global prosperity or lead to a widespread adoption of democratic institutions. On the contrary, the poorest of the developing countries, sucked into the mainstream of global economic competition and without a sound political or economic infrastructure, were unable to compete and remained victims of exploitation by stronger powers. Further, the effort to provide those societies with showcase democratic institutions often had the effect of destroying whatever social cohesion they may have had. There was the additional problem that in many parts of the world, the Middle East in particular, Western values and the whole process of "modernization" are regarded as a threat to indigenous cultures. In this hostile environment, Westernization, instead of contributing to international understanding, has produced a cultural backlash that has given birth to authoritarian theocracies dedicated to the overthrow of a secular American-dominated world order.

The bombing of the World Trade Center and the Pentagon on September 11, 2001, revealed the intensity of this cultural backlash and, as noted in the preface to this volume, led to an about-face in the conduct of American foreign policy. After pursuing a quasi-unilateral policy that ignored the interests of much of the rest of the world, the administration of George W. Bush has taken the lead in putting together an international coalition dedicated to the destruction of terrorism and has gone to war in Afghanistan. That war has succeeded in overthrowing the Taliban theocracy that was accused of harboring terrorists. But even if the terrorists held responsible for the catastrophe of September 11 are captured or killed, and even if terrorist networks are destroyed in other parts of the world, terrorism will continue in one form or another. For throughout history terrorism has been used as a weapon of protest by the weak, the oppressed, and the paranoid. And, to a far greater extent, it has been used for purposes of repression and control by authoritarian governments, including governments Washington has sought as allies in its war against terrorism.

Terrorism, moreover, is only one of the multitude of problems that confront the world's leaders as they enter the new millennium. There are trouble spots in almost every part of the world where crisis situations already exist or where fresh crises may erupt at any time. Nor should the crises of the moment obscure such long-range problems as the depletion of the ozone layer, the pollution of the atmosphere and the environment, the exhaustion of the world's natural resources, and the population explosion, to name only a few.

Instead of a New World Order we are obliged to deal with the same Old World Disorder, rendered even more disorderly by the shattering of the European and Ottoman empires that had imposed some measure of control over a large part of the world. Further, the existence of weapons of mass destruction—and of fanatics willing to use them—have made this disorder more dangerous than ever before.

Americans are understandably dismayed that, despite their country's victory in the Cold War, its vast expenditure on weaponry, and its overwhelming military and economic power, the United States remains vulnerable to attack from "rogue" states as well as terrorists. But such threats can never be eliminated, certainly not by the crude bludgeon of military might which can inspire a deadly backlash. In this connection we should bear in mind the paradox that one party's terrorists are another party's freedom fighters, and vice-versa.

It is even more important to recall that America's victory in the Cold War was not achieved through a hot war but through confidence in America's political and economic institutions, and that American diplomacy has been most effective when it took into account the interests of other states, whether rogues or rivals, as well as the fears and prejudices of their leaders. To take those interests into account, however, it is necessary to understand them, an understanding not only essential for the conduct of foreign policy but, in a democracy, for the development of a well-informed public opinion. And it is here that the study of diplomatic history comes into play.

Bibliography

Students of modern diplomacy are literally overwhelmed by the available evidence—multivolume document publications, diaries, memoirs, scholarly monographs based on unpublished sources, and, most copious of all, unpublished documents in government and private archives.

Thanks to the Allies' capture of German and Japanese government records after World War II, we have had unlimited access to the archives of both powers—the catalogs alone of the captured German documents amount to hundreds of volumes. The war crimes trials at Nuremberg and Tokyo produced a new wave of document publications, which were supplemented by a multivolume publication of captured German diplomatic documents by a team of American, British, and French scholars. The documents covering the Nazi era are published in translation, *Documents on German Foreign Policy,* in many volumes; the German originals are published in *Akten zur deutschen auswärtigen Politik;* which also cover the Weimar era.

The publication of German documents was followed by multivolume publications of the diplomatic records of other governments. Kenneth Bourne and Donald Watt, eds., *British Documents on Foreign Affairs; Documents on British Foreign Policy, 1919–1939; Documents diplomatiques français; I documenti diplomatici italiani; Papers Relating to the Foreign Relations of the United States.* Jane Degras has edited several collections of documents on Soviet foreign policy.

Many governments have opened their archives to scholars, though usually with chronological and departmental restrictions. Unlike the German and Japanese archives, to which we had unrestricted access, we will never know whether other governments have removed or destroyed particularly sensitive archival records. With the end of the Cold War and the breakup of the Soviet Union, researchers now have spotty access to the archives of the Soviet Union and their satellite states in Eastern Europe. Documents dealing with selected topics are being published in English by the Cold War International History Project at the Woodrow Wilson Center in Washington, which has produced important revelations.

J. A. S. Grenville, ed., *The Major International Treaties, 1914–1945: A History and Guide with Texts* (1988), is a valuable work of reference. A second volume, edited in collaboration with Bernard Wasserstein, includes treaties concluded after 1945.

In addition to government archives, many private and semiprivate document collections have been opened to scholars. Christopher M. Kimmich's valuable guide to German diplomatic documents, *German Foreign Policy, 1918–1945: A Guide to Research and Research Materials,* has been followed by similar guides edited by Sidney Aster for Britain, Robert J. Young for France, Alan Cassels for Italy, and Robert H. Johnston for the Soviet Union, all of which are periodically revised. Richard D. Burns has edited a guide to American foreign policy; Sadao Asada for Japan; Ann Schultz for the Middle East; Richard Kozicki for South Asia. Up-to-date information about access to government and private archives, the publication or microfilming of document collections, articles, and reviews of the most recent scholarly works covering every aspect of the field of international affairs are available in several scholarly journals, notably *Foreign Affairs, Diplomatic History, International Affairs* (the journal of the Royal Institute of International Affairs), and *The International History Review*. Byron Dexter, ed., *The Foreign Affairs 50-Year Bibliography. New Evaluations of Significant Books on International Relations, 1920-1970*, provides brief critiques of works published before 1970. A third edition of the American Historical Association's *Guide to Historical Literature* (1995), edited by Mary Beth Norton and Pamela Gerardi, contains useful annotated listings of works on the histories of individual countries and international relations. There is a superb bibliography on all aspects of modern history in R. R. Palmer and Joel Colton, *A History of the Modern World*, periodically brought up to date. Jerald A. Combs, *The History of American Foreign Policy* (1997), includes a valuable bibliographical discussion of controversial issues.

Even a partial listing of the published works dealing with the period covered in this volume would require a volume in itself. I have restricted myself here to a sampling of books in English.

On the fundamental problem of economics in international politics: Klaus Knorr, *The Power of Nations: The Political Economy of International Relations* (1975); Robert Gilpin, *The Political Economy of International Relations* (1987); Joan Spiro, *The Politics of International Relations* (1990).

James Joll, *The Origins of the First World War* (1984), is a brief and penetrating analysis. On the controversial problem of responsibility, J. W. Langdon, *July 1914: The Long Debate, 1918-1990* (1991), and Gregor Schöllgen, *Escape into War? The Foreign Policy of Imperial Germany* (1990).

World War I: among the many excellent general histories, John Keegan, *The First World War* (1999), and Holger Herwig, *The First World War: Germany and Austria, 1914-18* (1997), embody recent scholarship. Paul Kennedy, ed., *The War Plans of the Great Powers, 1880-1914* (1979), explains a major reason for the rapid escalation of the 1914 crisis. The horror of life in the trenches is conveyed in Erich Maria Remarque's novel *All Quiet on the Western Front* (1929).

Z. A. B. Zeman, *The Gentlemen Negotiators: a Diplomatic History of World War I* (1971), and David Stevenson, *The First World War and International Politics* (1988), explore the enormously important subject of wartime diplomacy. On the lack of political or military coordination among the Central Powers, Holger Herwig, *The First World War* (cited above); Gerard E. Silberstein, *The Troubled Alliance: German-Austrian Relations, 1914-1917* (1970); Ulrich Trumpener, *Germany and the Ottoman Empire, 1914-1918* (1968); Frank G. Weber, *Eagles on the Crescent: Germany, Austria, and the Diplomacy of the Turkish Alliance, 1914-1918* (1970); William A. Renzi, *In the Shadow of the Sword; Italy's Neutrality and Entrance into the Great War, 1914-1915* (1987).

Barry Hunt and Adrian Preston, eds., *War Aims and Strategic Policy in the Great War, 1914-1918* (1977); Victor Rothwell, *British War Aims and Peace Diplomacy, 1914-1918* (1971); David French, *British Strategy and War Aims, 1914-1916* (1986); David Stevenson, *French War Aims Against Germany, 1914-1919* (1982); Fritz Fischer, *Germany's Aims in the First World War* (1967), a damning indictment of German policy based on a vast accumulation of evidence that deserved more critical analysis. Gerhard Ritter has challenged the Fischer thesis in *Bethmann Hollweg as War Chancellor, 1914-1917* (1972), the third volume of his multivolume work on the problem of German militarism, *The Sword and the Scepter*. David

Fromkin, *A Peace to End all Peace: Creating the Modern Middle East, 1914-1922* (1989), on the wartime and postwar diplomacy that made for problems that are still very much with us.

The Russian Revolution: The two volume history by William H. Chamberlin, *The Russian Revolution, 1917-1923* (1935), remains one of the best and includes copious citations from the available documents. We are fortunate to have a wealth of literature in English on the revolution, the Soviet Union, Soviet foreign policy, and Soviet leaders. I have relied heavily on the works of Adam Ulam, Richard Pipes, Robert Conquest, Robert C. Tucker, and George Kennan. Recent studies of Lenin, Robert Service, *Lenin: A Biography* (2000), based on newly released official records, and Dmitri Volkavonov, *Lenin: Life and Legacy* (1994), by a Soviet military officer with access to Soviet archives, confirm the most critical Western views. Hélène Carrère d'Encausse, *The Great Challenge: Nationalities and the Bolshevik State, 1917-1930* (1991, translation of 1987 French publication), deals with a problem that proved to be a fatal weakness. In a book published in 1939, John W. Wheeler-Bennett reminded us of the harsh terms of the Central Powers' peace treaty with Russia, *The Forgotten Peace: Brest-Litovsk, March 1918.* Arthur Koestler's *Darkness at Noon,* is a fictional reconstruction of Stalin's purge trials; the works of Alexsandr Solzhenitsyn provide terrifying insights into the Soviet slave labor camps.

American intervention: Ross Gregory, *The Origins of American Intervention in the First World War* (1971); Ernest May, *The World War and American Isolation, 1914-1917* (1959); Robert Ferrell, *Woodrow Wilson and World War I, 1917-1921* (1985).

The problems of peacemaking: Manfred F. Boemke et al., *The Treaty of Versailles: A Reassessment after 75 Years* (1998), based on new archival materials, offering divergent perspectives, but essentially a return to familiar controversies; A. Sharp, *The Versailles Settlement: Peacemaking in Paris* (1991); H. Elcock, *Portrait of a Decision. The Council of Four and the Treaty of Versailles* (1972); M. L. Dockrill and J. D. Goold, *Peace without Promise: Britain and the Peace Conferences, 1919-1923* (1981); A. Walworth, *Wilson and his Peacemakers: American Diplomacy at the Paris Peace Conference, 1919* (1987), sympathetic to Wilson; Klaus Schwabe, *Woodrow Wilson, Revolutionary Germany, and Peacemaking, 1918-1919; Missionary Diplomacy and the Realities of Power* (1985), a trenchant analysis of this crucial problem; Thomas Knock, *To End all Wars: Woodrow Wilson and the Quest for a New World Order* (1992). For Clemenceau, the biographies of David R. Watson and Jean-Baptiste Duroselle; for Lloyd George, the biographies of Bentley Gilbert and J. Grigg; for Wilson, the authoritative works of Arthur Link, biographer and editor of the Wilson Papers. Harold Nicolson, *Peacemaking, 1919* (1933), a lively memoir by a disillusioned member of the British delegation. J. M. Keynes, *The Economic Consequences of the Peace* (1920), the most influential postwar critique of reparations, which still makes for fascinating reading. A response by Etienne Mantoux did not appear until after World War II, *The Carthaginian Peace—Or the Economic Consequences of Mr. Keynes* (1946). Philip Burnett, *Reparations at the Paris Peace Conference,* 2 vols. (1940), a collection of documents on this critical subject, with a valuable commentary.

The Middle East: J. C. Hurewitz, ed., *The Middle East and North Africa in World Politics: A Documentary Record,* vol. 2, *British-French Supremacy, 1914-1945* (1979), a valuable collection. George Lenczowski, *The Middle East in World Affairs* (1980); William Cleveland, *A History of the Middle East* (1994); Ritchie Ovendale, *The Middle East since 1914* (1992), with an excellent bibliography; Malcolm E. Yapp, *The Near East since the First World War* (1991); Bernard Lewis, *The Emergence of Modern Turkey* (1968); Andrew Mango, *Atatürk: The Biography of the Founder of Modern Turkey* (1999); Paul Mansfield, *The Ottoman Empire and its Successors* (1973); Elie Kedourie, *England and the Middle East: The Destruction of the Ottoman Empire* (1956); Elizabeth Monroe, *Britain's Moment in the Middle East, 1914-1971* (1981); D. A. Farnie, *East and West of Suez: The Suez Canal in History, 1854-1956* (1969).

The Palestinian Question: Leonard Stein, *The Balfour Declaration* (1961), well-documented and authoritative; R. Sanders, *The High Walls of Jerusalem: A History of the Balfour Declaration and the Birth of the British Mandate* (1984); Tom Segev, *One Palestine, Complete: Jews and Arabs under the British Mandate* (2000), impressive documentation from British and Zionist sources, argues that state of Israel was achieved with substantial British support; Aaron David Miller, *The Arab States and the Palestine Question: Between Ideology and Self-Interest* (1986); Isaiah Friedman, *The Question of Palestine, 1914-1918: British, Jewish, and Arab Relations* (1973), a defense of British policy; the same author's *Germany, Turkey, and Zionism, 1897-1918* (1977), which emphasizes the importance of the German role; Benny Morris, *Righteous Victims: A History of the Zionist-Arab Conflict, 1881-1991* (1999), a "revionist" critique of Israeli policy.

On the crucial question of oil: Daniel Yergin, *The Prize: The Epic Quest for Oil, Money, and Power* (1990); Fiona Venn, *Oil Diplomacy in the Twentieth Century* (1986); Benjamin Schwadran, *The Middle East, Oil and the Great Powers* (1973); Peter R. Odell, *Oil and World Power* (1986).

On the Soviet Union, see the works of the historians cited above, in particular Adam Ulam, *Expansion and Coexistence: The History of Soviet Foreign Policy, 1917-1973* (1974), and *The Rivals: America and Russia since World War II* (1971); Teddy Uldricks, *Diplomacy and Ideology: the Origins of Soviet Foreign Relations, 1917-1930* (1979); John Bradley, *Allied Intervention in Russia: A Study of Allied Diplomatic and Military Plans in Russia, 1917-1920* (1968); John M. Thompson, *Russia, Bolshevism, and the Versailles Peace* (1966); Xenia Eudin and H. H. Fisher, eds., *Soviet Russia and the West, 1920-1927: A Documentary Survey* (1957); the same editors' *Soviet Russia and the East, 1920-1927* (1957); George B. Ginsburg and Alvin Z. Rubinstein, *Soviet Foreign Policy toward Western Europe* (1978); John Erickson, *The Soviet High Command: A Military and Political History, 1918-1941* (1962); D. Volkogonov, *Stalin: Triumph and Tragedy* (1992), by a Soviet intelligence officer with a unique access to sources; Allen Weinstein and Alexander Vassiliev, *The Haunted Wood: Soviet Espionage in America; the Stalin Era* (1999), the fascinating but depressing saga of Soviet espionage and the treason of American officials; Obert L. Benson and Michael Warner, eds., *Venona: Soviet Espionage and the American Response, 1939-1957* (1996), American interceptions of Soviet intelligence; Stéphane Courtois, Nicolas Werth et al., *The Black Book of Communism: Crimes, Terror, Repression* (1999), a documentary and statistical summary of the Communist record.

For East Asia, we are once again exceptionally well served by historians writing in English. Among the many outstanding works, the overall survey by John K. Fairbank, E. O. Reischauer, and A. M. Craig, *East Asia: Tradition and Transformation* (1989); James B. Crowley, ed., *Modern East Asia. Essays in Interpretation* (1970), an important collection; Marius B. Jansen, *Japan and China: From War to Peace, 1894-1972* (1975); Akira Iriye, *After Imperialism: The Search for a New Order in the Far East, 1921-1931* (1965); Akira Iriye and Warren Cohen, eds., *American, Chinese, and Japanese Perspectives on Wartime Asia, 1931-1949* (1990).

John K. Fairbank, Albert Feuerwerker, Denis Twitchett, eds., *The Cambridge History of China*, vols. 12-13, *Republican China, 1912-1949,* with chapters by specialists on domestic and foreign policy; John K. Fairbank, *China: A New History* (1992); the works of Jonathan Spence, in particular *The Search for Modern China* (1990); Lloyd Eastman, *The Abortive Revolution: China under Nationalist Rule, 1927-1937* (1990), and *Seeds of Destruction: Nationalist China in War and Revolution, 1937-1949* (1984).

Peter Duus, ed., *The Cambridge History of Japan*, vol. 6, *The Twentieth Century* (1989), authoritative essays by specialists; Marius B. Jansen, *The Making of Modern Japan* (2000); Richard Storry, *A History of Modern Japan* (1960); James. L. McClain, *Japan: A Modern History* (2001), an excellent recent survey. Herbert Bix, *Hirohito and the Making of Modern Japan,* argues that the emperor, far from being a mere figurehead, played a decisive role in the formulation of Japanese policy. James W. Morley, ed., *Japan's Foreign Policy, 1868-1941: A Research Guide* (1974); the same author's *The Japanese Thrust into Siberia, 1918* (1957); and Morley's invaluable series: *Japan Erupts: The London Conference and the Manchurian Incident, 1928-1932* (1984), *Deterrent Diplomacy: Japan, Germany, and the USSR, 1935-1940* (1976), *The China Quagmire: Japan's Expansion on the Asian Continent, 1933-1941* (1983), and *The Fateful Choice: Japan's Advance in Southeast Asia, 1939-1941* (1980). James B. Crowley, *Japan's Quest for Autonomy: National Security and Foreign Policy 1930-1938* (1966); Ian Nish, *Japan's Foreign Policy, 1869-1942* (1978), includes documents in translation; Yale C. Maxon, *Control of Japanese Foreign Policy: A Study of Civil-Military Rivalry, 1930-1945* (1957); William G. Beasley, *Japanese Imperialism, 1894-1945* (1987); Ramon Myers and Mark Peattie, eds., *The Japanese Colonial Empire, 1895-1945* (1984), with a valuable bibliographical essay; Peter Duus, Ramon Myers, Mark Peattie, eds., *The Japanese Informal Empire in China, 1895-1937* (1989); Duus and Peattie, eds., *The Japanese Wartime Empire, 1931-1945* (1996); F. C. Jones, *Japan's New Oder in Asia: Its Rise and Fall* (1954); Sadako Ogata, *Defiance in Manchuria: The Making of Japanese Foreign Policy, 1931-1932* (1984); Ian Nish, *Japan's Struggle with Internationalism: Japan, China, and the League of Nations, 1931-1933* (1993); Takehiko Yoshihashi, *Conspiracy at Mukden: The Rise of the Japanese Military* (1980).

The Western Powers and Asia: Christopher Thorne, *The Limits of Foreign Policy: The West, the League, and the Far Eastern Crisis of 1931-1932* (1964), an excellent analysis; Ian Nish, *Alliance in Decline: A Study in Anglo-Japanese Relations, 1908-1923* (1972); William R. Louis, *British Strategy in the Far East, 1919-1939* (1971); Ann Trotter, *Britain and East Asia, 1933-1937* (1975); Bradford A. Lee, *Britain and the Sino-Japanese War, 1937-1939: A Study in the Dilemmas of British Decline* (1973); Frank Ikle, *German-Japanese Relations, 1936-1940* (1956); John P. Fox, *Germany and the Far Eastern Crisis, 1931-1938: A Study in Diplomacy and Ideology* (1982); Joseph Grew, *Ten Years in Japan* (1944), by the American ambassador, and *Turbulent Era: A Diplomatic Record of Forty Years, 1904-1945*, 2 vols. (1952); Dorothy Borg, *The United States and the Far Eastern Crisis of 1933-1938; From the Manchurian Incident through the Initial Stages of the Undeclared Sino-Japanese War* (1964).

Western Europe between the Wars: Raymond Sontag, *A Broken World, 1919-1939* (1971); Hans W. Gatzke, ed., *European Diplomacy between the Two Wars, 1919-1939*, a valuable collection of essays; Sally Marks, *The Illusion of Peace: International Relations in Europe, 1918-1933* (1976), an excellent brief overview; Arnold Wolfers, *Britain and France between two Wars: Conflicting Strategies of Peace since Versailles* (1940), stands up well.

David Reynolds, *Britannia Overruled: British Policy and World Power in the Twentieth Century* (1991); Paul Kennedy, *The Realities behind Diplomacy: Background Influences on British External Policy, 1865-1980* (1981), stresses the link betweeen domestic and foreign policy; W. M. Medlicott, *British Foreign Policy since Versailles, 1919-1963* (1968), an authoritative survey; Martin Gilbert, *Britain and Germany between the Wars* (1964); Robert P. Shay, *British Rearmament in the Thirties: Politics and Profits* (1977); Maurice Cowling, *The Impact of Hitler: British Politics and British Policy, 1933-1940* (1975); Keith Feiling, *The Life of Neville Chamberlain* (1946), draws on Chamberlain's personal papers, while David Dilks, *Neville Chamberlain* (1984) incorporates evidence made available more recently.

Jacques Neré, *The Foreign Policy of France from 1914 to 1945* (1975); Piotr S. Wandycz, *France and her Eastern Allies, 1919-1925* (1962), and *The Twilight of French Eastern Alliances, 1926-1936: French-Czechoslovak-Polish Relations from Locarno to the Remilitarization of the Rhineland* (1988); Walter A. McDougall, *France's Rhineland Diplomacy, 1914-1924: The Last Bid for a Balance of Power in Europe* (1978); Stephen Schuker, *The End of French Predominance in Europe: The Financial Crisis of 1924 and the Adoption of the*

Dawes Plan (1976), a valuable study; Haim Shamir, *Economic Crisis and French Foreign Policy, 1930-1936* (1989); Robert J. Young, *In Command of France: French Foreign Policy and Military Planning, 1933-1940* (1978); Eugenia Kiesling, *Arming against Hitler: France and the Limits of Military Planning* (1996), deals with French self-deception, from strategy to training and equipment; William E. Scott, *Alliance Against Hitler: The Origins of the Franco-Soviet Pact* (1962); G. Warner, *Pierre Laval and the Eclipse of France, 1931-1945* (1968) deals judiciously with this controversial figure.

John W. Wheeler-Bennett, *The Pipe Dream of Peace: the Collapse of Disarmament* (1935); B. Kent, *The Spoils of War: the Politics, Economics, and Diplomacy of Reparations* (1989); Marc Trachtenberg, *Reparations in World Politics: France and European Economic Diplomacy, 1916-1923* (1980); Jon Jacobson, *Locarno Diplomacy: Germany and the West, 1925-1929* (1972); Edward W. Bennett, *Germany and the Diplomacy of the Financial Crisis, 1931* (1962); the same author's *German Rearmament and the West, 1932-1933* (1979); Aurel Schubert, *The Credit-Anstalt Crisis of 1931* (1991); David E. Kaiser, *Economic Diplomacy and the Origins of the Second World War: Germany, Britain, France, and Eastern Europe, 1930-1939* (1980); Stephen Schuker, "France and the Remilitarization of the Rhineland, 1936," in *French Historical Studies,* 1986, a persuasive interpretation of this critical subject that differs from my own. On the complex problem of appeasement, Keith Middlemas, Ritchie Ovendale, Callum MacDonald, Gaines Post, Jr., and Arnold Offner provide valuable analyses, as do the essays collected by Wolfgang Mommsen and Lothar Kettenacker, eds., *The Fascist Challenge and the Policy of Appeasement* (1983).

The impact of the Great Depression: Charles P. Kindleberger, *The World in Depression, 1929-1939* (1986); W. Laqueur and G. L. Mosse, eds, *The Great Depression* (1970); Thomas C. Cochran, *The Great Depression and World War II. 1929-1945;* Karl Brunner, ed., *The Great Depression Revisited* (1981); Jonathan Haslam, *Soviet Foreign Policy, 1930-1933: The Impact of the Depression* (1983).

Italy, Mussolini, and the Ethiopian War: Christopher Seton-Watson, *Italy from Liberalism to Fascism, 1870-1925* (1967); Alan Cassels, *Fascist Italy* (1985), and *Mussolini's Early Diplomacy* (1970); Ivone Kirkpatrick, *Mussolini: A Study in Power* (1964); Denis Mack Smith, *Mussolini* (1982) and *Mussolini's Roman Empire* (1976), both uncompromisingly critical; Esmonde M. Robertson, *Mussolini as Empire-Builder: Europe and Africa, 1932-1936* (1978); Edwin P. Hoyt, *Mussolini's Empire. The Rise and Fall of the Fascist Vision* (1995); Goerge W. Baer, *The Coming of the Italian-Ethiopian War* (1967), and *Test Case: Italy, Ethiopia, and the League of Nations* (1976); Mario Toscano, *The Origins of the Pact of Steel* (1967). Particularly interesting are the diaries and diplomatic papers of Galeazzo Ciano, Mussolini's son-in-law and foreign minister, 1936-1943 (various editions).

Germany and the Weimar Republic: Richard Bessel, *Germany after the First World War* (1993); Marshall M. Lee and W. Michalka, *German Foreign Policy, 1917-1933: Continuity or Break?* (1987); Gaines Post, *The Civil-Military Fabric of Weimar Foreign Policy* (1973); Henry A. Turner, *Stresemann and the Politics of the Weimar Republic*(1979); Hans Gatzke, *Stresemann and the Rearmanent of Germany* (1954); H. L. Dyck, *Weimar Germany and Soviet Russia, 1926-1933* (1956); R. H. Haigh, *German-Soviet Relations in the Weimar Era: Friendship from Necessity* (1985).

Works on Nazi Germany continue to pour from the press in profusion. On the Weimar prelude: A. J. Nicholls, *Weimar and the Rise of Hitler* (1991), and Martin Broszat, *Hitler and the Collapse of Weimar Germany* (1987). Ian Kershaw, *The Nazi Dictatorship: Problems and Perspectives of Interpretations* (1989), and P. Ayçoberry, *The Nazi Question: An Essay on the Interpretaion of National Socialism, 1922-1975* (1981), provide excellent introductions to this complex and controversial subject. Karl Dietrich Bracher, *The German Dictatorship: The Origins, Structure, and Effects of National Socialism* (1970); Ian Kershaw has written an authoritative two-volume biography of Hitler, but see the eminently readable older work of Alan Bullock, *Hitler: A Study in Tyranny* (1952), as well as Bullock's *Hitler and Stalin: Parallel Lives* (1992). The biography by Joachim Fest, *Hitler* (1975), is excellent, but even more interesting is his *The Face of the Third Reich: Portraits of the Nazi Leadership* (1977).

On Nazi foreign policy: Klaus Hildebrand, *The Foreign Policy of the Third Reich* (1974), and the massively detailed and authoritative two-volume work of Gerhard L. Weinberg, *The Foreign Policy of Hitler's Germany,* vol. I, *Diplomatic Revolution in Europe, 1933-1936* (1970), and vol. II, *Starting World War II, 1937-1939* (1980). Norman Rich, *Hitler's War Aims, Ideology, the Nazi State, and the Course of Expansion* (1973), seeks to integrate ideology, politics, and diplomacy. Vol. II, *The Establishment of the New Order* (1974), a survey of Nazi occupation policies, the implementation of Hitler's ideology. Hitler's own book, *Mein Kampf,* is enormously revealing, its importance recognized in Eberhard Jäckel, *Hitler's Worldview: A Blueprint for Power* (1981), though the use of the word *blueprint* is unfortunate.

There is an immense literature on the Nazi racial war: A pioneering study and still one of the best works on this tragic subject is Raul Hilberg, *The Destruction of the European Jews,* 3 vols. (1983), much revised and expanded over the years; Israel Gutman, *Encyclopedia of the Holocaust,* 4 vols., (1990); Martin Gilbert, ed., *Atlas of the Holocaust* (1993). Lucy S. Dawidowicz, *The Holocaust and the Historians* (1981), and Michael R. Marrus, *The Holocaust in History* (1987), are fascinating studies in historiography; Charles S. Maier, *The Unmasterable Past: History, Holocaust, and German National Identity* (1988), deals with the controversy over the uniqueness of the German Holocaust, as does Peter Novick, *The Holocaust in American Life* (1999), who contends that the uniqueness concept trivializes human rights violations elsewhere; there are general studies by Lucy Dawidowicz, Martin Gilbert, Yehuda Bauer, and Leni Yahil, to name only a few; on the failure of the Allies to do more for the Jews, see Walter Laqueur, *The Terrible Secret: An Investigation into the Suppression of Information about Hitler's 'Final Solution'* (1980); Monty Noam Penkower, *The Jews were Expendable: Free World Diplomacy and the Holocaust* (1983); Bernard Wasserstein, *Britain and the Jews of Europe, 1939-1945* (1979).

The Spanish Civil War: Hugh Thomas, *The Spanish Civil War* (1977); Gabriel Jackson, *The Spanish Republic and the Civil War, 1931-1939* (1965); Raymond Carr, *The Civil War in Spain, 1936-1939* (1986), all excellent general works; on the war's international dimensions, Dante A. Puzzo, *Spain and the Great Powers, 1936-1941* (1962); Michael Alpert, *A New International History of the Spanish Civil War* (1994); Robert Whealey, "Foreign Intervention in the Spanish Civil War," in Raymond Carr, ed. *The Republic and the Civil War in Spain* (1971); John F. Coverdale, *Italian Intervention in the Spanish Civil War* (1975); Robert Whealey, *Hitler and Spain: The Nazi Role in the Spanish Civil War* (1989); Burnett Bolloton, *The Spanish Civil War: Revolution and Counterrvolution* (1991), emphasising the Communist role; David T. Cattell, *Communism and the Spanish Civil War* (1965); the same author's *Soviet Diplomacy and the Spanish Civil War* (1957); Ronald Radosh, Mary R. Habeck, Grigory Sevostyanov, eds., *Spain Betrayed: The Soviet Union in the Spanish Civil War* (2001), documents Soviet betrayal of the Spanish republic and the idealists who fought for it, based on Soviet archives; Jill Edwards, *The British Government and the Spanish Civil War, 1936-1939* (1979); Douglas Little, *Malevolent Neutrality: The United States, Great Britain, and the Origins of the Spanish Civil War* (1985); F. J. Taylor, *The United States and the Spanish Civil War* (1956); A. Guttmann, *The Wound in the Heart: America and the Spanish Civil War* (1962); R. P. Traina, *American Diplomacy and the Spanish Civil War* (1968). George Orwell, *Homage to Catalonia* (1938), a penetrating study by a disillusioned participant in the conflict; on Franco, there are biographies by Paul Preston, Sheelagh Ellwood, and Stanley Payne.

U.S. foreign policy: There are excellent surveys by Robert Ferrell and Jerald Combs, whose text includes a set of bibliographical essays; Jean-Baptiste Duroselle, *From Wilson to Roosevelt:*

Foreign Policy of the United States, 1913-1945 (1963), from a French perspective; Lloyd C. Gardner, *A Covenant with Power: America and World Order from Wilson to Reagan* (1984); Arnold Offner, *The Origins of the Second World War: American Foreign Policy and World Politics, 1917-1941* (1975); Robert Ferrell, *American Diplomacy in the Great Depression: Hoover-Stimson Foreign Policy, 1929-1933* (1957), and *Peace in Their Time: The Origins of the Kellogg-Briand Pact* (1969); Arnold A. Offner, *American Appseasement: United States Foreign Policy and Germany, 1932-1938* (1969); Callum A. MacDonald, *The United States, Britain, and Appeasement, 1936-1939* (1980); Robert Dallek, *Franklin D. Roosevelt and American Foreign Policy, 1933-1945* (1979); Stephen E. Ambrose, *Rise to Globalism: American Foreign Policy since 1938* (1985).

The origins of World War II in Asia: You-Li Sun, *China and the Origins of the Pacific War, 1931-1941* (1993); Akira Iriye, *The Origins of the Second World War in Asia and the Pacific* (1987); Leonid Kutakov, *Japanese Foreign Policy on the Eve of the Pacific War: A Soviet View* (1972); Michael A. Barnhart, *Japan Prepares for Total War* (1988); Robert Butow, *Tojo and the Coming of the War* (1961); Nobutaka Ike, ed., *Japan's Decision for War; Records of the 1941 Policy Conferences (1967)*, an invaluable source; Jonathon Utley, *Going to War with Japan, 1937-1941* (1985); Goerge M. Waller, ed., *Pearl Harbor: Roosevelt and the Coming of the War* (1985); Dorothy Borg and Shumpei Okamoto, eds., *Pearl Harbor as History: Japanese-American Relations, 1931-1941* (1973); Gordon W. Prange, *At Dawn We Slept: The Untold Story of Pearl Harbor* (1981); Robert Love, ed., *Pearl Harbor Revisited* (1994).

The Origins of World War II in Europe: Christopher Thorne, *The Approach of War, 1938-1939* (1968), still one of the best; Pierre Renouvin, *World War II and its Origins: International Relations, 1929-1945* (1969), by the distinguished French historian; E. M. Robertson, ed., *The Origins of the Second World War: Historical Interpretations* (1970), a valuable collection, primarily by British historians; Anthony Adamthwaite, *The Making of the Second World War* (1993); P. M. H. Bell, *The Origins of the Second World War in Europe* (1986); Donald Watt, *How War Came: The Immediate Origins of the Second World War, 1938-1939* (1989), massively detailed and authoritative. The war memoirs of Winston Churchill and Charles de Gaulle dominate the large memoir literature. There is a multivolume biography of Churchill by Martin Gilbert and of de Gaulle by Jean Lacouture.

World War II: John Keegan, *The Second World War* (1989); Peter Calvocoressi, Guy Wint, and John Pritchard, *Total War: Causes and Courses of the Second World War* (frequently revised); Gerhard L. Weinberg, *A World at Arms: A Global History of World War II* (1994), which correlates developments in the European and Asian theaters; John Erickson, *Stalin's War with Germany* (1975), outstanding military history; Saul Friedländer, *Prelude to Downfall: Hitler and the United States, 1939-1941* (1967); A. Iriye, *Power and Culture: The Japanese-American War, 1941-1945* (1981); Christopher Thorne, *The Far Eastern War: States and Societies, 1941-1945* (1988); Saburo Ienaga, *The Pacific War, 1931-1945: A Critical Perspective on Japan's Role in World War II* (1979), by a distinguished Japanese scholar; Tang Tsou, *America's Failure in China, 1941-1945* (1963); Gordon Prange, *Miracle at Midway* (1982), the decisive Pacific naval battle; Robert Butow, *Japan's Decision to Surrender* (1954); Richard B. Frank, *Downfall: The End of the Imperial Japanese Empire*.

Martin J. Sherwin, *A World Destroyed: The Atomic Bomb and the Grand Alliance* (1975); Gregg Herken, *The Winnng Weapon: The Atomic Bomb in the Cold War, 1945-1950* (1980); Richard Rhodes, *The Making of the Atomic Bomb* (1986); Michael Mandelbaum, *The Nuclear Revolution: International Politics before and after Hiroshima* (1981). Gar Alperowitz, *Atomic Diplomacy: Hiroshima and Potsdam* (1985), and Barton J. Bernstein, *The Atomic Bomb: The Critical Issues* (1975), argue that primary purpose of using bomb was to intimidate the Soviet Union; J. Samuel Walker, *Prompt and Utter Destruction: Truman and the Use of Atomic Bombs against Japan* (1997), balanced analysis with excellent bibliographical essay.

On code-breaking and intelligence operations: P. Calvacoressi, *Top Secret Ultra* (1980); F. W. Winterbotham, *The Ultra Secret* (1974); Ronald Lewin, *Ultra Goes to War* (1978); the same author's *The American Magic: Codes, Ciphers, and the Defeat of Japan* (1982); John X. Masterman, *The Double-cross System in the War of 1939 to 1945* (1972); Walter Laqueur, *A World of Secrets: The Uses and Limits of Intelligence* (1985); F. H. Hinsley, *British Intelligence in the Second World War*, 3 vols. (1979–1988); Richard Langhorne, ed. *Diplomacy and Intelligence during the Second World War* (1985).

Wartime diplomacy: F. P. King, *The New Internationalism: Allied Policy and the European Peace, 1939-1945* (1973); J. Menzel, *Hitler and Japan: The Hollow Alliance* (1966); Christopher Thorne, *Allies of a Kind: The United States, Britain, and the War against Japan, 1941-1945* (1979); S. M. Miner, *Between Churchill and Stalin: The Soviet Union, Great Britain and the Origins of the Grand Alliance* (1989); Herbert Feis, *Churchill, Roosevelt, Stalin: The War They Waged and the Peace They Sought* (1967); the same author's *Between War and Peace: The Potsdam Conference* (1960); William H. McNeill, *America, Britain, and Russia: Their Co-operation and Conflict, 1941-1946* (1953); Lloyd C. Gardner, *Spheres of Influence: The Great Powers Partition of Europe, from Munich to Yalta* (1993); E. L. Woodward, *British Foreign Policy in the Second World War*, 5 vols. (1962-1967); Vojtech Mastny, *Russia's Road to the Cold War: Diplomacy, Warfare, and the Politics of Communism, 1941-1945* (1979); G. C. Herring, *Aid to Russia, 1941-1946: Strategy, Diplomacy, and the Origins of the Cold War* (1973); Gaddis Smith, *American Diplomacy during the Second World War, 1941-1945* (1985), the best brief survey, critical of Roosevelt; Robert A. Divine, *The Reluctant Belligerent: America's Entry into World War II* (1965); the same author's *Roosevelt and World War II* (1969); Warren F. Kimball, *The Juggler: Franklin Roosevelt as Wartime Statesman* (1991); Lloyd C. Gardner, *Architects of Illusion: Men and Ideas in American Foreign Policy, 1941-1949* (1970), critical of U.S. policies.

General studies, post–World War II, Cold War: Louis Halle, *The Cold War as History* (1967), a superb overview; J. L. Black, *Origins, Evolution, and Nature of the Cold War: An Annotated Bibliography* (1985); John W. Young, *The Longman Companion to Cold War and Détente, 1941-1991* (1993); Hugh Thomas, *The Beginnings of the Cold War, 1945-1946* (1987); John W. Wheeler-Bennett and Anthony Nicholls, *The Semblance of Peace: The Political Settlement after the Second World War* (1972); Marc Trachtenberg, *The Making of the European Settlement, 1945-1963* (1999); Peter Calvocoressi, *World Politics since 1945* (periodically revised); Alan Milward, *The Reconstruction of Western Europe, 1945-1951* (1987); Cyril Black et al., *Rebirth: A History of Europe since World War II* (1992); Alfred Grosser, *The Western Alliance: European-American Relations since 1945* (1980); R. Levering, *The Cold War, 1945-1987* (1988); John W. Young, *Cold War Europe, 1945-1989: A Political History* (1991); Charles S. Maier, ed., *The Cold War in Europe: Era of a Divided Continent* (1991); Lloyd Gardner, Arthur Schlesinger, and Hans Morgenthau, *The Origins of the Cold War* (1970); David Reynolds, ed., *The Origins of the Cold War in Europe: International Perspectives* (1994); Martin Walker, *The Cold War and the Making of the Modern World* (1993); Michael J. Hogan, ed., *The End of the Cold War: Its Meaning and Implications* (1992), an excellent collection of essays representing a variety of opinions

American foreign policy, Cold War, relations with the Soviet Union: There is a profusion of memoir literature by America's postwar presidents, secretaries of state, and other major or lesser lights in the American government offering insights into their personalities as well as policies. There is an additional profusion of studies of American political leaders; to name only a few: Forrest Pogue and Robert Ferrell on Marshall; David McCullough on Truman, uncritical but eminently readable; Gaddis Smith and David McClellan on Dean Acheson; Fred Greenstein, H. W. Brands, and Robert Divine on Eisenhower; Richard Immerman, ed., on John Foster Dulles; Richard Reeves, James Giglio, Thomas Paterson, Herbert Parmet on Kennedy; Philip Geyelin,

Robert Dallek, and Robert Divine on Johnson; Garry Wills, Lloyd Gardner, Stephen Ambrose, Robert Litwak, Franz Schurman on Nixon; Seymour Hersch, Walter Isaacson, Marvin Kalb, and above all Kissinger himself on Kissinger; Gaddis Smith and Burton Kaufman on Carter; Lou Cannon on Reagan.

Among the many excellent monographs on American foreign policy: Raymond Aron, *The Imperial Republic: The United States and the World, 1945-1973* (1974), by the brilliant French political theorist; Gordon H. Chang, *Friends and Enemies: The United States, China, and the Soviet Union, 1949-1972* (1990); Daniel Yergin, *The Shattered Peace: The Origins of the Cold War and the National Security State* (1977); John Gimbel, *The Origins of the Marshall Plan* (1976); Michael Hogan, *The Marshall Plan: America, Britain, and the Reconstruction of Western Europe, 1947-1952* (1987); Stanley Hoffmann and Charles Maier, eds., *The Marshall Plan: A Retrospective* (1984); Stanley Hoffmann, *Dead Ends: American Foreign Policy in the New Cold War* (1993); Thomas G. Paterson, *Soviet-American Confrontation: Postwar Reconstruction and the Origins of the Cold War;* Walter Lafeber, *America, Russia, and the Cold War, 1945-1984* (1985); Melvyn P. Leffler, *A Preponderance of Power: National Security, the Truman Administration, and the Cold War* (1992); Michael Hogan, *A Cross of Iron: Harry S. Truman and the Origins of the National Security State* (1998); S. Brown, *The Faces of Power: United States Foreign Policy from Truman to Clinton* (1994); Michael Beschloss, *The Crisis Years: Kennedy and Khrushchev, 1960-1963* (1992); Lawrence Freedman, *Kennedy's Wars: Berlin, Cuba, Laos, and Vietnam* (2000); Raymond Garthoff, *Détente and Confrontation: American-Soviet Relations from Nixon to Reagan* (1994); the same author's *The Great Transition: American-Soviet Relations and the End of the Cold War* (1994); Michael Beschloss and Strobe Talbott, *At the Highest Levels: The Inside Story of the End of the Cold War* (1993); six valuable studies by the prolific John Lewis Gaddis: *The United States and the Origins of the Cold War, 1941-1947* (1972), *Strategies of Containment: A Critical Appraisal of Postwar American National Security Policy* (1982), *Russia and the United States: An Interpretive History* (1990), *The United States and the End of the Cold War: Implications, Reconsiderations, Provocations* (1992), *The Long Peace: Inquiries into the History of the Cold War* (1987), and *We Now Know: Rethinking Cold War History* (1997), rethought, despite pretentious title.

Soviet policy after World War II: Melvyn P. Leffler, "Inside Enemy Archives: The Cold War Reopened," *Foreign Affairs,* July–August 1996, valuable review article. The memoir literature is especially valuable because it provides insight into Soviet leaders who were shrouded in mists of myth and prejudice: Albert Resis, ed., *Molotov Remembers: Inside Kremlin Politics: Conversations with Felix Chuev* (1993), the revealing views of an unreconstructed Bolshevik; Milovan Djilas, *Conversations with Stalin* (1962), a fascinating record by a disillusioned Yugoslav; Valentin Berezhkov, *At Stalin's Side: His Interpreter's Memoirs, from the October Revolution to the Fall of the Dictator's Empire* (1994); Andrei Gromyko, *Memoirs* (1989). Particularly fascinating are the memoirs of Khrushchev, written or dictated after his fall from power, seemingly without benefit of official documents, which are refreshingly frank and bear up well in the light of the available documentary evidence. His son Sergei tells the fascinating history of these memoirs in *Khrushchev on Khrushchev: An Inside Account of the Man and his Era* (1990); Sergei Khrushchev, *Nikita Khrushchev and the Creation of a Superpower* (2000), more than filial piety; Vladislav Zubok and Constantine Plekhanov, *Inside the Kremlin's Cold War: From Stalin to Khrushchev* (1996), the world as it looked to Soviet leaders based on Soviet archives and memoirs; confirms Western fears that Stalin and his successors were indeed aggressive imperialists; John Keep, *Last of the Empires; A History of the Soviet Union, 1945-1991* (1995), a balanced and intelligent survey; Joseph Nogee and R. H. Donaldson, *Soviet Foreign Policy since World War II* (1981); Alvin Z. Rubinstein, *Soviet Foreign Policy since World War II: Imperial and Global* (1992); Marshall Shulman, *Stalin's Foreign Policy Reappraised* (1962);

William Taubman, *Stalin's American Policy: From Entente to Détente to Cold War* (1982); David Holloway, *Stalin and the Bomb: The Soviet Union and Atomic Energy, 1939–1956* (1995); Edward Radinsky, *Stalin: The First In-Depth Biography Based on Explosive New Documents from Russia's Secret Archives* (1996), adds to the already voluminous record of Stalinist tyranny and the extent of his mass slaughter, but the only "explosive" evidence concerns Stalin's buildup for a war against Hitler, which Hitler forestalled by his own invasion of the Soviet Union; Harry Hanak, *Soviet Foreign Policy since the Death of Stalin* (1972); William Zimmerman, *Soviet Perspectives on International Relations, 1956–1967* (1969); Donald Zagoria, ed., *Soviet Policy in East Asia* (1982); John Gittings, ed. *Survey of the Sino–Soviet Dispute* (1968); George Ginsburg and Carl F. Pinkele, *The Sino–Soviet Territorial Dispute, 1949–1964* (1978); Tai Sung An, *The Sino–Soviet Territorial Dispute* (1973); Donald Zagoria, *The Sino–Soviet Conflict, 1956–1961* (1964); Rajendra Kumar Jain, *The USSR and Japan, 1945–1980* (1981).

Postwar Europe: John W. Young, *Britain, France, and the Unity of Europe, 1945–1951* (1984); K. O. Morgan, *The People's Peace: British History 1945–1990* (1991); on Britain's decline as a major power, the works of M. W. Kirby, Robert Blake, C. Burnett, and B. Porter; Herbert Tint, *French Foreign Policy since the Second World War* (1972); John W. Young, *France, the Cold War, and the Western Alliance, 1944–1949* (1990); Wladyslaw Kulski, *De Gaulle and the World: The Foreign Policy of the Fifth French Republic* (1966); Alistair Horne, *A Savage War of Peace: Algeria, 1954–1962* (1978); William B. Bader, *Austria Between East and West, 1945–1955* (1966), on Austria's neutralization in 1955; Timothy Garton Ash, *In Europe's Name: Germany and the Divided Continent* (1993); Michael Balfour, *Western Germany: A Contemporary History* (1982); Henry A. Turner, *Germany from Partition to Reunification* (1992); Paul Ginsborg, *A History of Contemporary Italy: Society and Politics, 1943–1988* (1990); Joseph Rothschild, *Return to Diversity: A Political History of East Central Europe since World War II* (1989); G. Schöpflin, *Politics in Eastern Europe, 1945–1992* (1993); Dennison Rusinow, *The Yugoslav Experiment, 1948–1974* (1977).

East Asia: Donald F. Lach and Edmund S. Wehrle, *International Politics in East Asia since World War II* (1975); Akira Iriye, *The Cold War in Asia: A Historical Introduction* (1974); Steven Hugh Lee, *Outposts of Empire: Korea, Vietnam, and the Origins of the Cold War in Asia, 1945–1954* (1995); R. MacFarquhar and John K. Fairbank, *The Cambridge History of China*, vol. 15/1, *The People's Republic; The Emergence of Revolutionary China, 1949–1965* (1987); vol. 15/2, *The People's Republic; Revolutions within the Chinese Revolution, 1966–1982* (1992); Michael H. Hunt, *The Genesis of Chinese Communist Foreign Policy* (1996); Thomas W. Robinson and David Shambaugh, eds., *Chinese Foreign Policy: Theory and Practice* (1994); Maurice Meisner, *Mao's China and After: A History of the People's Republic* (1986); Dick Wilson, ed., *Mao Tse-tung in the Scales of History: A Preliminary Assessment* (1977); Stuart R. Schram, *Mao Zedong: A Preliminary Reassessment* (1983); the same author's *The Political Thought of Mao Tse-tung* (1969); Zhisui Li, *The Private Life of Chairman Mao* (1994), the horrifying revelations of the chairman's private physician. More recently, Jonathan Spence, *Mao Zedong* (1999), and Philip Short, *Mao: A Life* (2000); Chen Jian, *Mao's China and the Cold War* (2001), contends that Mao, driven by ideology, made consistent efforts to foment revolution in Asia and that there never was a "last chance" for the U.S. to establish normal relations with his regime; offers new insights into China's role in the Korean and Vietnamese wars.

The Cambridge History of Japan, cited earlier, and the works of E. O. Reischauer, a former American ambassador to Japan and acute student of Japanese history and society; P. Bailey, *Japan since 1945* (1993); Michael Schaller, *The American Occupation of Japan: The Origins of the Cold War in Asia* (1985); Robert Scalapino, ed., *The Foreign Policy of Modern Japan* (1977), records views of American and Japanese scholars.

The turmoil in the Middle East: Bernard Lewis, *The Shaping of the Modern Middle East* (1993) and the same author's *What Went Wrong? Western Impact and Middle Eastern Response* (2002); A. Roshwald, *Estranged Bedfellows: Britain and France in the Middle East during World War II* (1990); W. R. Louis, *The British Empire in the Middle East, 1945-1951* (1984); Howard M. Sachar, *Europe Leaves the Middle East, 1936-1954* (1976); Favaz A. Gerges, *The Superpowers and the Middle East: Regional and International Politics, 1955-1967* (1994); L. Carl Brown, ed., *Diplomacy in the Middle East: The International Relations of Regional and Outside Powers* (2001); Burton Kaufman, *The Arab Middle East and the United States; Inter-Arab Rivalry and Superpower Diplomacy* (1996); Bruce R. Kuniholm, *The Origins of the Cold War in the Near East: Great Power Conflict and Diplomacy in Iran, Turkey, and Greece* (1980), and *The Persian Gulf and United States Policy: A Guide to Issues and References* (1984); H. W. Brands, *Into the Labyrinth: The United States and the Middle East, 1945-1993* (1994); S. P. Tillman, *The United States and the Middle East* (1982); Stephen Spiegel, *The Other Arab-Israeli Conflict: America's Middle East Policy, from Truman to Reagan* (1985); James A. Bill, *The Eagle and the Lion: The Tragedy of American-Iranian Relations* (1988); Galia Golan, *Soviet Politics in the Middle East from World War Two to Gorbachev* (1990).

Israel: H. M. Sachar, *A History of Israel,* 2 vols. (1987); Yossi Beilin, *Israel: a Concise Political History* (1994); Fred Khouri, *The Arab-Israeli Dilemma* (1985), based on Arab as well as Zionist sources; M. J. Cohen, *The Origins and Evolution of the Arab-Zionist Conflict* (1987); the same author's *Truman and Israel* (1990); Ritchie Ovendale, *The Origins of the Arab-Israeli Wars* (1992); Donald Neff, *Fallen Pillars: U.S. Policy towards Palestine and Israel since 1945* (1995), reveals intensity of debate in government and public arena; Edward Said, *The Question of Palestine* (1979), presents the Palestinian case; B. Kimmerling and J. S. Migdal, *Palestinians: The Making of a People* (1992); Ann Lesch, *Arab Politics in Palestine, 1917-1939: The Frustration of a Nationalist Movement* (1979); Benny Morris, *Israel's Border Wars, 1949-1956: Arab Infiltration, Israeli Retaliation, and the Countdown to the Suez War* (1993), solidly based on Israeli archives, an important revisionist critique of Israeli policy; Avi Schlaim, *The Iron Wall: Israel and the Arab World since 1948* (1999), akin to Morris, with emphasis on competition and disagreement among Israeli leaders; Uri Bialer, *Between East and West: Israel's Foreign Policy Orientation, 1948-1956* (1984); Sydney Bailey, *Four Arab-Israeli Wars and the Peace Process* (1990); William B. Quandt, *Decade of Decisions: American Policy toward the Arab-Israeli Conflict, 1967-1976* (1977); *Camp David: Peacemaking and Politics in the Middle East* (1986); *The Middle East: Ten Years after Camp David* (1988).

W. R. Louis and Roger Owen, eds., *Suez 1956: the Crisis and Its Consequences* (1989); Hugh Thomas, *The Suez Affair* (1966); Diane Kunz, *The Economic Diplomacy of the Suez Crisis* (1991).

Korea: William Stueck, *The Road to Confrontation: American Policy toward China and Korea, 1947-1950* (1981); the same author's *The Korean War: An International History* (1995); Burton Kaufman, *The Korean War: Challenges in Crisis, Credibility, and Command* (1986); Peter Lowe, *The Origins of the Korean War* (1986); Bruce Cumings, *The Origins of the Korean War,* vol. 1, *Liberation and the Emergence of Separate Regimes, 1945-1947,* and vol. 2, *The Roaring of the Cataract, 1947-1950* (1981, 1990), bitterly critical of the U.S.; Sergei Goncharov, John Lewis, and Xue Litai, *Uncertain Partners: Stalin, Mao, and the Korean War* (1993); Chen Jian, *China's Road to the Korean War: The Making of the Sino-American Confrontation* (1994); Katheryn Weathersby, *Soviet Aims in Korea and the Origins of the Korean War, 1945-1950* (1993), and her translations of Chinese and Soviet documents in the *Cold War International History Project Bulletin* (Fall 1993, Spring 1995).

The Cuban Missile Crisis: Hugh Thomas, *The Cuban Revolution* (1971); M. Merez-Stable, *The Cuban Revolution: Origins, Course, Legacy* (1993); Tad Szulc, *Fidel: A Critical Portrait* (1986); Robert Quirk, *Fidel Castro* (1993); Graham T. Alison and Philip Zelikow, *Essence of Decision: Explaining the Cuban Missile Crisis* (1999, updates 1972 publication); Jorge Dominquez, *To Make a World Safe for Revolution: Cuba's Foreign Policy* (1989); Lawrence Chang and Peter Kornbluh, eds., *The Cuban Missile Crisis, 1962: A National Security Documents Reader* (1992); Robert A. Divine, ed., *The Cuban Missile Crisis* (1990); James A. Nathan, ed., *The Cuban Missile Crisis Revisited* (1992). Especially interesting are the records of conferences with the major participants in the crisis, edited by James G. Blight, Bruce J. Allyn, David A. Welch, and David Lewis.

Southeast Asia and Vietnam: Nicholas Tarling, ed., *The Cambridge History of Southeast Asia*, 2 vols. (1992); Stanley Karnow, *Vietnam: A History* (1991); William J. Duiker, *The Rise of Nationalism in Vietnam, 1900-1941* (1976), *The Communist Road to Power in Vietnam* (1981), and *United States Containment Policy and the Conflict in Indochina* (1994); M. B. Young, *The Vietnam Wars, 1945-1990* (1991); Anthony Short, *The Origins of the Vietnam War* (1989); George Herring, *America's Longest War: The United States and Vietnam, 1950-1975* (1986); Guenther Lewy, *America in Vietnam* (1978), a defense of American policy; Marvin E. Gettleman et al., *Vietnam and America: A Documented History* (1995); George Kahin, *Intervention: How America became involved in Vietnam* (1986); David Kaiser, *American Tragedy: Kennedy, Johnson, and the Origins of the Vietnam War;* William J. Duiker and Lloyd C. Gardner, *Pay any Price: Lyndon Johnson and the Wars for Vietnam* (1995); Larry Berman, *No Peace, No Honor: Nixon, Kissinger, and Betrayed Vietnam* (2001), bitterly critical; Ilya Gaiduk, *The Soviet Union and the Vietnam War* (1996); King C. Chen, *Vietnam and China, 1938-1954* (1969); the same author's *China's War with Vietnam, 1979* (1982); Qiang Zhai, *China and the Vietnam Wars, 1950-1975* (2000), based on declassified Chinese sources, records substantial Chinese support during wars against France and the U.S.; Charles McGregor, *The Sino-Vietnamese Relationship and the Soviet Union* (1988); William Shawcross, *Sideshow: Kissinger, Nixon, and the Destruction of Cambodia* (1987), another bitter critique; David P. Chandler, *The Tragedy of Cambodian History: Politics, War, and Revolution since 1945* (1992); the same author's *Brother Number One: Pol Pot* (1992); Ben Kiernan, *How Pol Pot Came to Power: A History of Communism in Kampuchea* (1985); Arnold Isaacs, *Without Honor: Defeat in Vietnam and Cambodia* (1983); Robert Divine, "Vietnam Reconsidered," *Diplomatic History,* Winter 1988, a valuable bibliographical essay.

The end of European imperialism: R. F. Holland, *European Decolonization, 1918-1981: An Introductory Survey* (1985); M. F. Chamberlain, *Decolonization: The Fall of the European Empires* (1985); J. D. Hargreaves, *Decolonization in Africa* (1988); Prosser Gifford and William Roger Louis, eds., *The Transfer of Power in Africa: Decolonization, 1940-1960* (1982); the same editors' *Decolonization and African Independence: The Transfers of Power, 1960-1980* (1988); J. Darwin, *Britain and Decolonization: The Retreat from Empire in the Postwar World* (1990); William Roger Louis, *Imperialism at Bay: The United States and the Decolonization of the British Empire, 1941-1945* (1978).

India and Pakistan: Stanley Wolpert, *Roots of Confrontation in South Asia: Afghanistan, Pakistan, India, and the Superpowers* (1982); the same author's *A New History of India* (1993); Percival Spear, *The Oxford History of Modern India* (1979); Anita Singh, *The Origins of the Partition of India, 1936-1947* (1987); H. V. Hodson, *The Great Divide: Britain-India-Pakistan* (1985); on Gandhi, the impressive series of volumes by Judith M. Brown and the biographies of S. Wolpert and A. Copley; R. N. Iyer, *The Moral and Political Thought of Mahatma Gandhi* (1973); Francis G. Hutchins, *India's Revolution: Gandhi and the Quit India Movement* (1973); Sarvepalli Gopal, *Jawaharlal Nehru: A Biography*, 3 vols., (1976-1984); A

Jalal, *The Sole Spokesman: Jinnah, the Muslim League, and the Demand for Pakistan* (1985); S. Wolpert, *Jinnah of Pakistan* (1984); the voluminous writings of Gandhi and Nehru, in particular their autobiographies; John W. Graver, *Protracted Contest: Sino-Indian Rivalry in the Twentieth Century* (2001), on a critical problem that is still very much with us.

The breakup of the Soviet Empire: the memoirs and writings of Gorbachev, Yeltsin, and Anatoly Dobrynin, Moscow's long-time ambassador to the United States; Anatoly Chernyaev, *My Six Years with Gorbachev* (2000), the diaries and commentary of a senior aide, providing insights into Kremlin politics; Andrei S. Grachev, *Final Days; The Inside Story of the Collapse of the Soviet Union* (1995), by another Gorbachev aide; and Jack F. Matlock, *Autopsy of an Empire: The American Ambassador's Account of the Collapse of the Soviet Union* (1995), a trenchant analysis by an ambassador fluent in Russian and thoroughly familiar with Russian history; the many works of the British historian-journalist Timothy Garton Ash, who writes as an eye-witness on the basis of a solid historical background; Charles Gati, *The Bloc that Failed: Soviet-East European Relations in Transition* (1990); Hélène Carrère d'Encausse, *The End of the Soviet Empire: The Triumph of the Nations* (1993); Ronald Suny, *The Revenge of the Past: Nationalism, Revolution, and the Collapse of the Soviet Union* (1993); Archie Brown, *The Gorbachev Factor* (1996); Karen Dawisha and Bruce Parrott, *Russia and the New States of Eurasia: The Politics of Upheaval* (1994); Gale Stokes, *The Walls Came Tumbling Down: The Collapse of Communism in Eastern Europe* (1993); B. Wheaton and Z. Kavan, *The Velvet Revolution* (1992), of Czechoslovakia; Charles S. Maier, *The Crisis of Communism and the End of East Germany* (1997); Konrad Jarausch, *The Rush to German Unity* (1993); P. H. Merkl, *German Unification in the European Context* (1993); A Lieven, *The Baltic Revolution: Estonia, Latvia, Lithuania and the Path to Independence* (1993).

The breakup of Yugoslavia: Ivo Banac, *The National Question in Yugoslavia: Origins. History, Politics* (1984); John R. Lampe, *Yugoslavia as History: Twice There Was a Country* (1996); Christopher Bennett, *Yugoslavia's Bloody Collapse; Causes, Course, and Consequences* (1995); Robert Kaplan, *Balkan Ghots; A Journey Through History* (1994), influential in promoting the belief that the area had long been a cockpit of irreconcilable tribal hatreds, a view countered by Robert J. Donia and John V. Fine, *Bosnia and Herzegovina: A Tradition Betrayed* (1994), which emphasizes the tradition of diversity and toleration; B. Magus, *The Destruction of Yugoslavia: Tracking the Break-Up, 1980-1992* (1993); Carole Rogel, *The Breakup of Yugoslavia and the War in Bosnia* (1998), brief survey with valuable annotated bibliography; Noel Malcom, *Bosnia: A Short History* (1995), an acute analysis of the complexities; Loring M. Danforth, *The Macedonian Conflict; Ethnic Nationalism in a Transnational World* (1995); Richard Holbrooke, *To End a War* (1998), valuable memoir by a principal American negotiator.

Terrorism in world politics: Theodore von Laue, *The World Revolution of Westernization: The Twentieth Century in Global Perspective* (1987), a prescient analysis, fundamental for understanding the genesis of the contemporary problem; Scott L. Bills, *Empire and the Cold War: The Roots of U.S.-Third World Antagonism, 1945-1947* (1990). There was a copious literature on terrorism before September 11, 2001: J. B. Bell, *On Revolt: Strategies of National Liberation* (1976); Walter Laqueur, *The Age of Terrorism* (1987); R. Rubinstein, *Alchemists of Revolution: Terrorism in the Modern World* (1987); Paul R. Pillar, *Terrorism and US Foreign Policy*. Also see the more recent warnings by Philip Heymann, Bruce Hoffman, Jessica Stern, and collected essays edited by Barry Rubin, Brad Roberts, and Richard Falkenrath.

Afghanistan, Osama bin Laden, and the Taliban: Mark Urban, *War in Afghanistan* (1990), the Soviet experience; Henry Bradsher, *Afghanistan and the Soviet Union* (1985); Simon Reeve, *The New Jackals: Ramzi Yousef, Osama Bin Laden, and the Future of Terrorism;* Ahmed Rashid, *Taliban: Militant Islam, Oil, and Fundamentalism in Central Asia* (2000).

Index

Nixon, Richard. Vice-president of the U.S., 1953–1961; president, 1969–Aug. 1974: biog.: 434–35; India: 386; foreign policy: 435, 474; arms control: 436–37; Cuba: 418–19; China: 434–36, 448–50, 452–53, 475, 527; Vietnam: Cambodia, Laos, 434, 436, 473–80, 509; Soviet Union: 475; Panama: 487; Middle East: 509–11, 513; resignation: 435, 439, 452, 479, 513, 528

Nomohan: 234

Nomura Kichisaburo. Japanese admiral; foreign minister, Sept. 1939–Jan. 1940; ambassador to Washington, Feb.–Dec. 1941: 238, 245

Norodom Sihanouk. See Sihanouk, Norodom.

North, Lt. Col. Oliver. Member of McFarlane's national security council staff: 526–28

North Atlantic Treaty Organization (NATO), formed Apr. 4, 1949: 329–30, 332, 352, 397, 403, 411, 423, 464, 503, 538, 542, 555–56, 558–62

Northern Bukovina: 226, 229

North Manchurian Railway: 127

Norway: 217–19, 261, 280, 316, 328–29

Novotny, Antonin. First secretary, Czechoslovak Communist party, 1953–1968; president, Nov. 1957–Mar. 1968: 432

Nuclear Non-Proliferation Treaty, 436–37

Nuclear Test Ban Treaty, 427–29, 445

Oder-Neisse line: 284, 287–89, 297–98, 331, 437

Oil: World War I: 10, 12, 96; Romania: 12, 29, 224, 226–27, 229, 231, 272; Middle East: 61, 95–98, 511–12, 517–19, 528–29, 531; Netherlands E. Indies: 235–38

Oil companies: 95–98, 518

Okinawa: 339

Olympic games: Berlin, 1936: 181; Munich, murder of Israeli athletes, Sept. 5, 1972: 523; Moscow, 1980, boycotted by U.S.: 520; Los Angeles: 540

Open Door notes, China, 1899: 99, 101

Oppenheimer, Robert. American physicist: 301

Organization of Petroleum Exporting Countries (OPEC): 511–12

Orlando, Vittorio. Itlian prime minister, Oct. 29, 1917–June 19, 1919: 42, 44

Ostpolitik: 431–32, 437

Ottoman empire: World War I and Armenian massacres: 6–7, 10–12; Allies' secret treaties over: 12–15; peace settlements: 28, 30, 34, 61–62, 82; abolition of Sultanate: 87. See also Turkey

Outer Mongolia. See Mongolia, Outer

Pakistan: 372, 377–79, 381–83, 385–86, 447, 449–50, 464

Pakistan, East. See Bangladesh.

Palacký, František. Czech historian and patriot: 75, 78

Palestine: A new political entity: 15, 91; Balfour Declaration: 15–17, 93; British mandate: 90–91, 93–95, 390–91, 393. See also Israel, Zionists

Palestine Liberation Organization: 508, 514–15, 523

Palestinian Arabs: 92–95, 390, 394, 505, 507–8, 514–16, 523–24

Panama Canal Treaties, July 9, 1977: 486–87

Panay incident, Dec. 12, 1937: 141

Panmunjom: 369, 442

Papacy. See Vatican

Pathet Lao. Left-leaning Laotian nationalist movement: 484

Patterson, Robert. American secretary of war, Sept. 1945: 317

Pauker, Anna. Romanian foreign minister, Nov. 5, 1947–May 29, 1952: 325

Pavelich, Ante. Leader of Croatian Ustashe party; head of German/Italian puppet government, Apr. 1941–1945: 228

Peace ballot, British, 1935: 179

Pearl Harbor: 134, 242–44, 246–49, 252–54, 256, 258–60, 298–99

Peiping. See Peking.

Peking (Beijing): 109–10, 113, 117–18, 126, 132, 137, 139, 351–53

Pendergast, Tom. Head of Kansas City political machine: 293

Peng Teh-huai, Marshal. Chinese defense minister, 1954–Sept. 1959: 443

Peres, Shimon. Leader, Israeli Labour party; prime minister/foreign/finance minster, coalition government, Sept. 1984–90: 526

Perestroika. Restructuring (of Soviet government): 536, 550

Persia. See Iran.

Persian Gulf: 10, 12, 95–96, 281, 521–22, 529, 531

Persian Gulf War, Jan.–Feb. 1991: 531–32

Pescadores Islands: 278, 339

Pétain, Marshal Henri-Philippe. Head of French Vichy government, June 16, 1940–1944: 220–22, 271

Petsamo nickel mines: 217, 219, 280, 284, 316

Philippine Islands: 243, 246–47, 254, 281, 299, 338, 340, 464

Pichon, Stéphen. French foreign minister, 1916: 77

Picot, François Georges-. French consul-general in Beirut: 14–15

Ploesti oil fields. See Oil, Romanian

Pnom Penh: 482, 484

Poincaré, Raymond. French president, 1913–1920; prime minister and foreign minister,